Treaties with American Indians

Treaties with American Indians

An Encyclopedia of Rights, Conflicts, and Sovereignty

VOLUME II

Donald L. Fixico

EDITOR

A B C ⬤ C L I O

Santa Barbara, California • Denver, Colorado • Oxford, England

Copyright 2008 by ABC-CLIO, Inc.

Library of Congress Cataloging-in-Publication Data
Treaties with American Indians: an encyclopedia of rights, conflicts, and sovereignty / Donald L. Fixico, editor.
  p. cm.
  Includes bibliographical references and index.
  ISBN 978-1-57607-880-8 (hard copy: alk. paper)—ISBN 978-1-57607-881-5 (ebook)
1. Indians of North America—Legal status, laws, etc.—United States—Encyclopedias.
2. Indians of North America—United States—Treaties—Encyclopedias.   3. Indians
of North America—Government relations.   I. Fixico, Donald Lee, 1951–
  KF8203.6.R74 2008
  342.7308'72—dc22

                    2007027797

12 11 10 09 08   1 2 3 4 5 6 7 8

Senior Production Editor: Vicki Moran
Editorial Assistant: Sara Springer
Production Manager: Don Schmidt
Media Editor: Caroline Price
Media Resources Coordinator: Ellen Brenna Dougherty
Media Resources Manager: Caroline Price
File Manager: Paula Gerard

ABC-CLIO, Inc
130 Cremona Drive, P.O. Box 1911
Santa Barbara, California 93116-1911

This book is also available on the World Wide Web as an ebook. Visit www.abc-clio.com for details.

This book is printed on acid-free paper. ∞

Manufactured in the United States of America

This important study of Indian treaties is dedicated to the people of my tribes, who have suffered, endured, and now prosper again:

To the Shawnee,
To the Sac and Fox,
To the Seminole, and
To the Muscogee Creek

—Donald L. Fixico

Contents

Volume II

Important Treaty Sites

Primary Source Documents

Introduction

PEACE AND FRIENDSHIP is the most commonly used phrase in the language of Indian treaties. The intent of the United States as a young country was to persuade Indian communities to deal only with the United States. Many things were unsettled following the American Revolution, and the tribes found themselves in the middle of it. In the early years of U.S.-Indian relations, the tribes also had common interest with the British, the French, and the Dutch.

Indian agents and other government officials in the United States negotiated more than four hundred treaties and agreements with American Indians; treaty talks occurred for more than one hundred years. Interestingly, Indian and white leaders met at various sites that often had been the meeting places for previous trading and council meetings. Negotiating in Native languages and English through interpreters was difficult, although some Native people spoke some of the white man's tongue. Beginning in 1778 with the Delaware, when the United States negotiated its first successful treaty with an Indian tribe and ratified it, a historic precedent was set, one that has made Native Americans a unique minority in their own country. For the record, Indian tribes in what is now the United States also made treaties with the British, the French, the Confederate States during the Civil War, and with other Indian tribes.

In Canada, the federal government negotiated seventeen treaties with the First Nations peoples, starting in 1871 and ending in the twentieth century. These consist of thirteen numbered treaties plus the four Robinson and Williams treaties.

The mid-nineteenth century represented the zenith of treaty making; during the next twenty years, the practice sharply declined. A rider attached to a congressional appropriations act in 1871 ended the Indian treaty-making business in the United States, although agreements were negotiated until 1917. The Act of 1871 did not end the recognition of Indian treaties, however; it merely halted the treaty-making process.

U.S.-Indian treaties often included more than one tribe, and some tribes signed many treaties.

There are 374 ratified treaties and 16 agreements. The first treaty was concluded in 1778; the last one, during the late nineteenth century. The shortest treaty is with the Kickapoo in 1820. The treaty is 16 lines long, with 8 Kickapoo leaders and 6 American officials who signed, involving $2,000 to be paid for Kickapoo removal. The longest treaty is the Treaty with the New York Indians of 1838 at Buffalo Creek in New York; that treaty is 15 pages long. The Potawatomi signed the most treaties of any tribe, a total of 26. The biggest gathering was the council held at Medicine Lodge, Kansas, during October 1867, at which 500 soldiers met with more than 15,000 Plains Indians gathered from the Cheyenne, Arapaho, Apache, Kiowa, and Comanche. The largest number of treaties were signed in 1825 and 1836, 20 each year; 19 treaties were signed in 1855, 18 in 1865, and 17 in 1832.

In regard to categories, 229 treaties involve ceded lands; 205 are about payments and annuities; 202 include the phrase *peace and friendship*; 115 are about boundaries; 99 address reservations; 70 include civilization and agriculture; 59 are about roads and free passages; 52 address the sovereignty or the authority of the United States or tribes; 49 include allotment and guaranteed lands; 47 contain gifts, goods, or presents; 38 contain provisions on education; 34 contain provisions on hunting, fishing, and gathering rights; 28 authorize forts and military posts; 25 include trade; 12 address railroads; several include agents for the tribes; and a few treaties deal with one or more of the following: stolen horses, returning prisoners, slavery, returning criminals, intruders, scalping, alcohol, missions, and mail routes.

Treaties between Indian tribes and the United States are binding agreements. For Native peoples, each step of the negotiation was important, not just the resulting words on a piece of paper. Indian agents, military officials, and officials of the Indian Office met with Native leaders to begin negotiations, which usually began with a council held at a previously agreed-upon site. To Native people, the chosen site was important, and the talk itself was just as significant as the resulting treaty or agreement. The site itself, such as the one near Medicine Lodge in southwestern Kansas and Prairie du Chien in western Wisconsin, set the tone of the council. Medicine Lodge has made a lasting impression and is re-enacted every five years.

The first meeting, or council, between Indian and white leaders likely made or broke the tone of the talks. The council was a fundamental concept among the Indian nations, and tribal protocols varied from tribe to tribe. Unsure of how to approach the various tribes, federal officials depended upon local whites, guides, and traders to introduce them to the tribes in their areas. Familiar with the ways of the Indian tribe, these individuals advised officials how to approach Native leaders.

In learning the protocol for dealing with tribes, federal officials experienced difficulty in meeting with more than one tribe at the same time. They made the mistake of trying to get enemy tribes to meet at the same council. Even tribes who met only sometimes, such as the Plains Indians, who gathered annually during the summer to hold the Sun Dance, had a mutual understanding of the importance of the arrival at camp, as exemplified by the Medicine Lodge Council in 1867. Dressed in their finest ceremonial garb, a tribe also sometimes wanted to be the last to arrive so that other tribal groups would acknowledge that an important group had arrived.

Protocol is involved in any type of summit, council, or important discussion involving conflicting interests, especially if there are deep differences between cultures. In the general situation of treaty talks, white officials learned a lot about the importance of kinship relations in forming an agreement, especially if it resulted in an alliance between the two sides. Early treaties—those concluded before the mid-nineteenth century—were often peace treaties, for the United States wanted tribes to acknowledge their relationship with the new nation and abrogate relations with the British and the French. Bringing about peace following a battle or other conflict created balance between two opposites, and this tranquil state of existence fostered mutual respect between the two parties and a need for ceremonial acknowledgement. Thus, smoking the pipe was germane to solidifying the new relationship of nonconflict.

The language barrier between the two sides caused great skills in diplomacy to be exercised. During the height of contact between Indians and whites in the seventeenth and eighteenth centuries, more than 250 indigenous languages were spoken. The role of interpreters, both Indian and white, became crucial to treaty negotiations. The varying protocols among tribes for holding councils compelled American officials to learn about tribal leaders before talks of a serious nature began. Cultural differences added to language barriers as problems arose, often intensifying the clashing views of Indians and whites over land. One perceived land and what it meant economically, and the other understood the earth philosophically and celebrated it with ceremonies. The same commodity became homeland for both sides, and ensuing treaties named who owned the land. A new culture of treaty making emerged from the older Indian way of holding council and talking.

Gift giving played a crucial role in the early contact and negotiations between Indian and white leaders. Federal officials typically brought gifts of inexpensive items such as mirrors, metalwork, and beads to get the Indians into a peaceful frame of mind that would lead to the discussion of bigger issues, such as land cessions. As mentioned, at least forty-seven treaties contained provisions for giving gifts and presents. Officials understood the importance of generosity and sharing among Native peoples and used this against them, hence the "Great White Father" in Washington held a position of respect and generosity.

The cultural difference between Indians and whites proved to be enormous. In addition to the language barriers, both sides operated from different mind-sets; each held different ideas about what was important for the negotiations and what the negotiations meant. Native leaders and federal officials had a challenging situation to overcome before they could begin successful discussions. It is said that, on one occasion Osceola, the noted leader of the Seminole in Florida, disagreeing with tribal leaders who signed the Treaty of Fort Gibson in 1833, stabbed his knife through the two pieces of paper on the table. This was his angry response to all treaties, letting others know that his mind was set on going to war. It is likely that this did happen since there is a hole in the original treaty kept in a vault at the National Archives in Washington.

"Touching the pen" became a common occurrence during Indian treaty making. Native leaders were unable to write their names because they did not know the English language, and therefore white officials asked Native leaders to "make their

mark"—which was of little importance to American Indians, who believed that the spoken word was superior to any words on a piece of paper, which might be blown away by the wind or destroyed; the spoken word would always be remembered. Several treaty councils witnessed impressive oratory articulated by tribal leaders. This was not the white way. The majority of Indian treaties verify the marks made by the tribal leaders. In other situations, the leaders refused to hold the white man's writing instrument, and the federal officials asked the Native leaders to touch the pen after the names were written by the official in charge.

The most important concern for Native peoples in treaty negotiations was their sovereignty. Sovereignty is an important issue of concern resulting from the U.S.-Indian and Canada-First Nations agreements. The signing of a treaty creates binding responsibilities between both sides and includes the respectful recognition of each for the other. Theoretically, the relationship between the two sides is one of a sovereign forming an agreement with another sovereign—that is, government-to-government in a lateral relationship of similar status. The status is one of international law and based on each party to the treaty having faith in the agreement and recognizing each other as being sovereign.

Trust is a meaningful legal responsibility between two nations and their people, and treaties established this reciprocal relationship. Both sides of a treaty agreement must abide by the provisions and must continue to fulfill the responsibilities outlined in the document. That trust responsibility continues into this century, in the hands of the assistant secretary of the Department of the Interior, who supervises the Bureau of Indian Affairs for all tribes in the United States.

Treaties were a systematic procedure for dealing with Indian tribes. By examining the history of these agreements, some assessment can be made about them in stages or phases. For example, treaty negotiations, talks, or councils were the first step in this system of agreements. During these important gatherings, significant Indian individuals were recognized and acknowledged so the representatives of the United States would know who they were dealing with. In some cases, such as the Prairie du Chien meeting, "making chiefs" occurred; this happened more than once when government officials persuaded certain individuals to sign for their tribes as leaders. The federal government operated on the political philosophy that a head of state represented

a nation, thus an Indian nation must have one significant leader or chief. This was not the case with many tribes, such as the Muscogee Creek, the Ojibwa, and others, who had leaders for each town or village and settlements scattered over a vast region of the country.

Discussion of the treaty's provisions was another critical phase of Indian treaty making. Both sides met with an agenda of needs, according to their thinking, and they lobbied to obtain agreement from the other side. Some acute Native leaders saw that education was an important part of the future of their people and wanted educational assistance in the form of teachers. Common provisions included goods and annuities over a number of years and perhaps blacksmiths. Most of all, large sums of money were paid to the tribes for their lands.

The next phase consisted of the results of treaties—some of which caused important changes, such as the exchange of enormous tracts of land for perpetual gifts, or changes in fishing or hunting rights on ceded lands. The treaties led to a new era in Indian-white relations and actually marked the decline of the strength of Indian nations. This decline became evident as tribes such as the Potawatomi, Delaware, Chippewa, and others signed several treaties with the United States. After 1800, the federal government almost always had the leverage in treaty talks.

Strategies of treaty-making involve several motives, all of which resulted in the decline of the Indian nations. These strategies involved introducing the idea of one nation, one leader; setting boundaries; manipulating leadership; making chiefs; courting treaty signers; and giving gifts to influence tribes and their leaders. Such actions almost always were directed toward Indian men, not toward women (although, in many tribes, women held the authority to select their leaders).

Peace was the main objective in the early U.S. treaties until about 1850. The federal government found it much easier to make peace with the Indian nations than to fight them, which proved costly, especially as great effort was needed just to find them. The United States signed 374 treaties but fought more than 1,600 wars, battles, and skirmishes against Indian tribes. The Navajo Treaty of 1849 and the Fort Laramie Treaty of 1851 were negotiated with peaceful objectives in mind rather than more land cessions. The Fort Laramie agreement involved multiple groups of the Northern Plains, Sioux, Gros Ventre, Mandan, Arikara, Assinaboine, Blackfeet, Crow,

Cheyenne, and Arapaho. Boundaries were set to keep them apart, with additional provisions for roads and military posts included as part of the treaty.

The establishment of boundaries for tribes was another goal for government officials as they treated with Indian leaders. Many tribes hunted over vast territories; government officials were able to contain tribes within certain areas, and they reminded leaders of the boundaries established in the agreements. Officials introduced Native peoples to the idea of land ownership and individual ownership. In 1858, the Sisseton and Wahpeton Sioux signed a treaty in Washington, D.C., agreeing to new reservation boundaries. This led to the surveying of the tribal land for division into individual eighty-acre allotments. In this way, tribal lands were reduced in size.

At times, the United States undermined and manipulated leadership to get the lands it wanted. The importance of kinship played a vital role in treaty making between Indians and the United States. Federal officials learned of the importance of kinship and symbolic bonds in tribal communities and used this knowledge to develop a tribal dependence on the "Great White Father" in Washington. When the leaders of tribes refused to negotiate, federal officials sought out other Indians who were more easily persuaded to sign treaty documents.

Land acquisition was the principal reason for treaties and was pursued to such an extreme extent that, by the end of the nineteenth century, American Indians held less than 2 percent of the land that they had once possessed totally. The unleashed white settler became an uncontrollable force to consume Indian lands. Such was the settlers' greed that federal officials were forced to deal with tribes, which resulted in many Indian removal treaties or war. A domino effect occurred as eastern tribes moved onto lands of interior groups, who moved onto lands of western tribes, and so forth.

Expansion of the United States was another goal of government officials. During the Civil War, federal officials negotiated, and the government ratified, eighteen treaties that called for expanding the territory held by the Union. During the three years between March 1862 and March 1865, federal officials concluded treaties with the Kansa, Ottawa, Chippewa, Nez Percé, Shoshone, Ute, Klamath, Modoc, Omaha, Winnebago, and Ponca Nations. These agreements included land cessions and fur-

ther diminished the territories of the tribes. Indian lands were further reduced by the systematic creation of "permanent" reservations.

Control of tribal movements was the final strategy and result of the treaties. With treaties in place and with military power greater than that of the tribes, the United States could enforce control over the weakened Indian nations. Once the leaders were undermined and control exerted over them, Indian superintendents controlled the Indians and conditions on the almost two hundred reservations throughout Indian country.

Land was the central issue of U.S.-Indian treaties. As more settlers arrived from England and other countries, the need for more Indian land placed considerable pressure on the Indian tribes. A domino effect began to occur as eastern seaboard tribes of the Atlantic coast retreated inland, thereby encroaching on the hunting domains and farming areas of tribes nearby to the west. The expansion of white settlement across the Appalachian Mountains caused the newly formed United States to treat with the inland tribes. British agents and traders worked among the Indian nations to gain their allegiance and convince them to reject the proposed talks of federal officials.

At the same time, other European interests in the form of French, Scots, and Irish traders proved successful in obtaining acceptance among tribes. These trading activities made it more difficult for the United States as more Americans pushed into the Ohio Valley and the back country of the Southeast.

The most obvious kind of treaty called for tribes to surrender their lands. In less than thirty years, from 1801 to 1829, federal officials made thirty-one treaties with the Chickasaw, Choctaw, Muscogee Creek, Cherokee, and Florida tribes. These cession treaties extinguished Indian title to all of the area east of the Mississippi River from the Ohio River to the Gulf of Mexico.

Officially, treaties had to be ratified by the U.S. Congress and signed by the president of the United States. Congressional ratification was most active during the 1800s, as federal officials met with Native leaders at an increasing rate. Treaty making fell into a pattern: More and more treaties were negotiated with eastern tribes, who were thus forced to keep moving westward; the Delaware, for example, were forced to remove at least nine times.

Unratified treaties were agreements not confirmed by the U.S. Congress. Naturally, many agreements were submitted to Congress; most submissions were ratified, and some had their provisions amended. It is estimated that between forty-seven and eighty-seven treaties were unratified. Most Native leaders did not understand the ratification process and believed that all the agreements they made were official.

Organization of the Encyclopedia

This encyclopedia is intended as a comprehensive reference tool for anyone interested in American Indian treaties with the United States. In these three volumes, the larger number of U.S.-Indian treaties, their lengths and complexity, and the complexity of Canada-Indian treaties are described. The volumes are organized in sections. The first volume consists of major essays that explain various perspectives on Indian treaties, and regional treaties. In the second volume, entries are included that describe each treaty; short entries address treaty sites and terms; and there are primary source documents of many treaties. The third volume contains a historical chronology, brief biographies of noted individuals involved in the treaties, and a section on treaty-related issues.

Acknowledgments

This three-volume project has been the work of many people. I have often felt like an academic Sisyphus, facing the enormous task of rolling the big boulder up the mountain. More than three hundred people have helped, supported, and written entries or essays for this encyclopedia. I am grateful for the help of the following individuals, who assisted with this project in the early years at the Center for Indigenous Nations Studies at the University of Kansas: research assistants Viv Ibbett, Melissa Fisher Isaacs, David Querner, and Elyse Towey. I appreciate the support given my work by Chancellor Robert Hemenway, Provost David Shulenburger, former Associate Dean Carl Strikwerda, and former Dean Kim Wilcox at the University of Kansas.

I would like to express appreciation to the following individuals at Arizona State University, who have been helpful in the completion of this project over the last two years: President Michael Crow; Executive Vice President and Provost Elizabeth Capaldi; former Provost Milton Glick; Vice President David Young, Divisional Dean Debra Losse; former Chairperson Noel Stowe of the History Department; and Chairperson Mark von Hagen. I am grateful for the support from the ASU Foundation, which sponsors my Distinguished Professorship of History, and for ASU as a leading university that supports scholarship in American Indian history. I especially want to thank Clara Keyt as a research and editorial assistant. I thank my research assistants during the final phase: Matt Garrett, Cody Marshall, and Kristin Youngbull; they have helped to track down a lot of information as well as doing other chores. With their help, after I moved to Arizona, the boulder was pushed the rest of the way to the top of the mountain in the sun with a smile.

Appreciation is also expressed to all the contributors who wrote entries and the noted scholars who wrote the essays for the encyclopedia. Nor would this project have been possible without the patience, effort, and tremendous understanding of my good friend and editor, Steven Danver. Thank you to Caroline Price for the tremendous illustrations; and to April Wells-Hayes for the thorough copyedit of the manuscript. I wish all editors were like Vicki Moran who guided this project smoothly through all its production stages. I am especially grateful to my wife, Professor April Summitt, whose words of support encouraged me to complete this project. I am also grateful to my son, Keytha Fixico, who has patiently waited for me so that we could go to a movie and do other son-and-dad stuff. Always, I am grateful for the support of my parents, John and Virginia Fixico; and I want to acknowledge my four tribes—the Shawnee, Sac and Fox, Seminole, and Muscogee Creek—to whom this three-volume encyclopedia is dedicated.

Donald L. Fixico
Arizona State University

Treaties with American Indians

U.S. and Canadian Indian Treaties

Treaty of Albany with the Five Nations

July 31, 1684

To stop Iroquois incursions along the western frontier of the British colonies and to forge a stronger alliance against the French, Francis, Lord Howard of Effingham, who was then the governor of Virginia, and Colonel Thomas Dongan, who was the governor of New York, went to Albany to meet with the sachems and warriors of the Five Nations.

On July 31 at the Albany courthouse, the Mohawk, Oneida, Onondaga, and Cayuga (the Seneca had not arrived yet) agreed that the Five Nations would no longer attack the Indians living along the frontiers of Virginia and Maryland. In return, they requested the Duke of York's coat of

Thomas Dongan, governor of New York from 1682 to 1688, helped negotiate the Treaty of Albany with the Five Nations. (Hulton Archive/Getty Images)

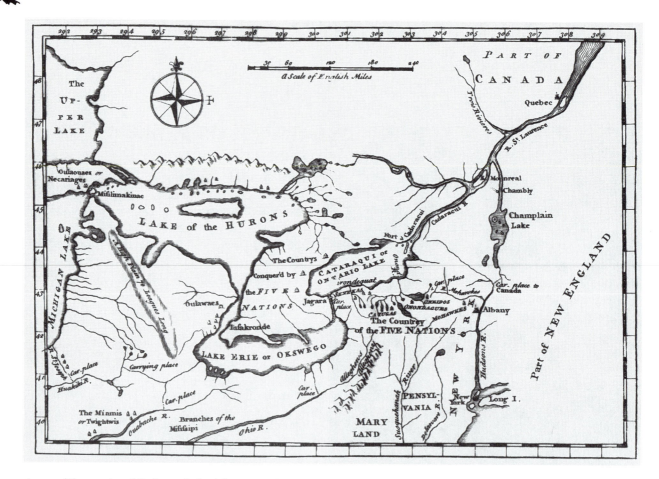

A map of the country of the Iroquois Confederacy, or Five Nations, c. 1650. The Iroquois Confederacy was a good example of intertribal alliance, consisting of the Mohawks, Oneidas, Onondagas, Cayugas, Senecas, and later the Tuscaroras. The area covered by the alliance is present-day New York, as well as part of Canada and Lakes Huron, Michigan, Superior, Erie, and Ontario. (Hulton Archive/Getty Images)

arms to place in their villages as a symbolic deterrent against French aggression. Governor Dongan responded favorably to this request and asked the Five Nations to "make no Covenant and Agreement with the French or any other Nation without my knowledge and Approbation. And that they say the same to the Sennekas" (Wraxall 1915, 10). The Mohawks thereafter offered a tract of land along the Mohawk River to Dongan and his descendants, and another tract of land for Christian use.

On August 2, the colonial officials and leaders of the Five Nations met again at the courthouse. The Onondaga and Cayuga addressed Governor Dongan, telling him that they had treated the English well when they (the English) had first arrived in the colonies. They said, "[now] that you are grown Numerous and we decreased, you must Protect us from the French, which if you dont we shall loose our Hunting and Bevers: The French want all the Bevers and are Angry that we bring any to the

English." They then proceeded to lay claim to lands along the Susquehanna River, which they had won "by the Sword" and which they had recently refused to sell to William Penn, the proprietor of Pennsylvania. As a token of this agreement, they offered "Two white Buckskins" to be sent to Charles II, so "that He may write and put a great Red Seal thereto, that we put under the Protection of the Great Duke of York, the Susquahanna River above the Wasaghta or Falls together with the rest of our Lands and no one else" (Wraxall 1915, 11–12).

On August 5, the Seneca arrived and addressed Governor Howard about the peace: "We are informed, that the Mohawks, Oneidas, Onondagas, and Cayugas, have buried the axe already; now we that live remotest off, are come to do the same." Disavowing their complicity in the Indian raids along the colonial borders and confirming the conditions of the present treaty, they pledged to remain outside Maryland and Virginia: "We understand, that because of the Mischief that been done to the People and Castles of Virginia and Maryland, we must not come near the Heads of your Rivers, nor near your Plantations, but keep at the Foot of the Mountains. . . . We . . . shall wholly stay away from Virginia" (Colden 1904, 49–50).

With the conclusion of the treaty, the Iroquois became a buffer between French and English interests in North America. Although the Iroquois successfully maintained a neutral position for much of the colonial period, they continued to send small expeditions southward, attacking Indian interests along the Virginia and Maryland borders as well as French interests to the west and north. In response to these incursions, Virginia sent a delegation to Albany in September 1685; among the members was Colonel William Byrd, who accused the Iroquois of breaking their promises under the Albany treaty of 1684. In response, the Iroquois said that the parties that had been out when the peace was concluded in 1684 were responsible for the raiding

expeditions. The Mohawk and Seneca also blamed the Onondaga, Cayuga, and Oneida for the incursions. For much of the colonial period, the issue of Iroquois incursions continued to trouble the British as well as the French in Canada, the effect of an active foreign policy on the part of the Iroquois by which they sought to bring tributary tribes into their Covenant Chain while at the same time playing off the French and English against each other.

Michael A. Sletcher

See also Sovereignty; Treaty; Trust Land; Trust Responsibility.
References and Further Reading
Colden, Cadwallader. 1904. *The History of the Five Indian Nations of Canada Which are Dependent on the Province of New York, and are a Barrier Between the English and the French in that Part of the World.* New York: A. S. Barnes.
Snow, Dean R. 1994. *The Iroquois.* Cambridge, MA: Basil Blackwell.

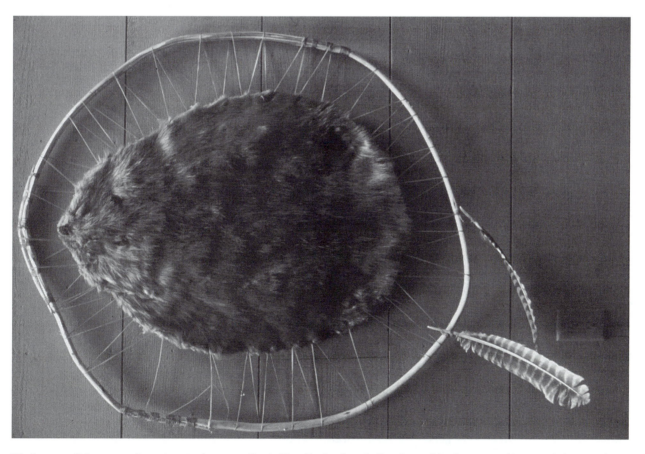

The beaver pelt became an important trade commodity in New England, as Indian demand for firearms and iron goods increased during the seventeenth century. The Beaver Wars were a continuing series of conflicts between the tribes of the Iroquois Confederacy and other tribes of New England over the control of the beaver pelt supply. (North Wind Picture Archives)

Wraxall, Peter. 1915. *An Abridgement of the Indian Affairs, Contained in Four Folio Volumes, Transacted in the Colony of New York, from the Year 1678 to the Year 1751.* Vol. 21, *Harvard Historical Studies.* Cambridge, MA: Harvard University Press.

Treaty of Montreal

August 7, 1701

Also known as the Great Peace or the Great Peace of Montreal of 1701, the Treaty of Montreal ended the Beaver Wars. This ended a century of conflict between New France and its Native allies on one side and the Five Nations Iroquois on the other. From July 23 to August 7, more than thirteen hundred Native delegates representing forty nations from Acadia to the Mississippi, from James Bay to the Missouri, met in Montreal to discuss the planting of a tree of peace. Under the terms of the treaty, all sides promised to stop killing one another, the Five Nations promised to remain neutral in all future conflicts between France and Britain, the various Great Lakes nations allowed Iroquois hunters into the region, France promised to mediate between all nations to prevent future conflicts, and the Iroquois agreed to allow France's Native allies access to Albany.

The treaty involved representatives from the Odawa (Ottawa), Wyandot (Huron-Petun), Sauk, Fox, Menominee, Winnebago, Potawatomi, Ojibwa, Miami, Cree, Abenaki, Mascouten, Onondaga, Oneida, Cayuga, and Seneca Nations. Although the Mohawk did not sign the treaty, they agreed to abide by its terms. Although the French suggested the inclusion of the Dakota, the Great Lakes nations refused. The Huron of the Lorette, located near Quebec City, and the Montagnais, both key allies of the French, did not send representatives to sign the treaty. Although intermittent violence continued, usually sporadic killings of Iroquois hunters in the Great Lakes, the peace held. Yet, the Great Peace failed to end all warfare in the interior. The conflict with the Dakota continued, and in 1712 the entire region was engulfed in the Fox Wars.

All sides wanted peace, for a variety of reasons. The French sought to reinforce their position and restore the lucrative fur trade in North America by bringing peace to the *pays d'en haut.* Additionally, in 1701 Louis XIV announced that French policy in America would be predicated on containment of the English along the Atlantic seaboard. Depriving New York of Iroquois support in future conflicts gave the central French colony a buffer and would allow its Native allies unhindered access to English colonial settlements. After a series of defeats at the hands of the Great Lakes nations as well as the French, since the 1690s the Iroquois had realized that a permanent peace was needed before the fate of the Huron befell them, too. The motives of the allies of the French are less clear. It appears that many wanted access to the Albany market, to recover people captured by the Iroquois (the Iroquois also wanted prisoners returned), and to live and hunt in safety. The Iroquois' failure to bring captives to the conference nearly scuttled the treaty. Wyandot and French diplomacy garnered a promise from the Iroquois to release captives, thereby preventing renewed warfare.

As the conference got under way, an epidemic struck the delegates. Many people fell sick before they even reached the conference, and some turned back. The epidemic almost proved the undoing of the conference. First, Natives knew that Europeans were connected to these new epidemics; they often accused the newcomers of using witchcraft to destroy their nations. Second, a Huron chief and key proponent of peace, Kondiaronk (the Rat), died of the sickness. The French held a funeral and gave gifts to wipe the tears away from his people metaphorically and to show that no one was to blame for the death. The Seneca dignitaries used the opportunity to present themselves as most saddened by Kondiaronk's death by singing his triumphs and their condolences. It is likely that Kondiaronk, even in death, helped bring the delegates together for peace.

The treaty of 1701 had an important impact on French-Indian relations. It struck at the core of the French alliance system, strengthening and weakening it at the same time. Although the French became the mediators in all disputes and the nominal heads of the alliance, New France's dependence on Natives was reinforced. The general tranquility in the East allowed the movement of people back into the partially abandoned Great Lakes-Ohio Valley area. This movement placed many French allies within reach of the thirteen colonies. The Iroquois also encouraged French allies to trade at Albany, which allowed the development of contacts with the English. Moreover, many French allies were drawn to Albany by cheaper, more plentiful, and better-quality trade items. Refugees from the East, such as the Delaware, brought information about the English. As the French alliance system had been founded largely on trade and protection from the Iroquois, these events gave the British potential access to the French allies and vice versa, and thereby posed a threat to the French alliance system. The treaty also recognized Native nationhood.

Karl S. Hele

References and Further Reading

Brandão, J. A., and William A. Starna. 1996. "The Treaties of 1701: A Triumph of Iroquois Diplomacy." *Ethnohistory* 43(2): 209 244.

Havard, Gilles. 2001a. *The Great Peace of Montreal of 1701*. Translated by Phyllis Aronoff and Howard Scott. Montreal: McGill-Queen's University Press.

Havard, Gilles. 2001b. *Montreal, 1701: Planting the Tree of Peace*. Montreal: Recherches amérindiennes au Québec and McCord Museum of Canadian History.

Matusky, Julia G. 2001. "The Great Peace of Montreal, 1701." *Beaver* 81(3): 8 12.

Richter, Daniel K. 1992. *The Ordeal of the Longhouse: The Peoples of the Iroquois League in the Era of European Colonization*. Chapel Hill: University of North Carolina Press for the Institute of Early American History and Culture.

British-Labrador Inuit Peace Treaty

April 8, 1765

Arguably the only historic treaty with Canadian Inuit, this 1765 peace and friendship accord marked a turning point in the troubled relationship of Inuit and Europeans in Labrador. A cornerstone of British colonial policy, the pact brought the Natives under the King's protection. It also fostered an alliance with Moravian missionaries, who helped secure British interests by settling among the Inuit, converting them to Christianity, and courting their trade.

Labrador passed from French to British hands by the 1763 Treaty of Paris and was soon annexed to the colony of Newfoundland. With its new possession came a history of Inuit-white conflict. Hostilities were largely confined to southern Labrador, where Basque and French whalers and fishers had frequented the Strait of Belle Isle for centuries. Inuit voyaged here from their customary territory in the north to harvest its resources and trade with the newcomers. Tensions plagued their contacts; Native looting of shore stations sparked a cycle of retaliation and a climate of fear that resisted remedy for generations. On appointing Sir Hugh Palliser military governor of Newfoundland in 1764, the Crown instructed him to end the bloodletting lest it threaten metropolitan investment in the hard-won Labrador fisheries. Preferring diplomacy to a costlier military solution, Palliser laid the groundwork of lasting peace by making the Inuit a solemn promise of the King's friendship and protection and promising them liberty to trade safely with British merchants. Two documents, his "Proclamation to Bring About Friendly Intercourse with Esquimaux Indians" (July 1, 1764) and "Order for Establishing Communication and Trade with the Esquimaux Savages on the Coast of Labrador" (April 8, 1765), embody key elements of the accord (Great Britain 1927, 930 931, 1297–1298).

Palliser enlisted Inuktitut-speaking Moravian missionaries, veterans of the church's Greenland mission, as go-betweens in peacemaking. Jens Haven initiated the process in 1764 among a small, late-summer gathering of Inuit on Quirpon Island, declaring the King's goodwill, distributing gifts, and encouraging the Inuit to accept the British as partners (Lysaght 1971, 189). Having opened the door to rapprochement, Haven proposed and received British support for a Moravian mission deep inside Inuit country to the north. Combined with a trade outlet, Palliser advised his superiors, such a post would "keep the rest of the Coast open & free for our Adventurers" (Great Britain 1927, 935). So resolved, the governor visited Labrador in summer 1765 to conclude his accord.

With missionaries Christian Drachard and John Hill as intermediaries, Palliser met with more than three hundred Inuit at Pitts Harbour, Chateau Bay, on August 21. The governor looked on as the Moravians distributed gifts and pledged the King's lasting friendship in return for an end to hostilities and acceptance of missionaries in their midst. The proceedings ended when Palliser asked the people if they were prepared to live in peace with the British. Speaking for his compatriots, the shaman Segulliak "gave him his hand, called him Capt[ain] Chateau, Struck him on the Breast & kissed him saying we will remain your good friends" (Lysaght 1971, 200–201). In a homeward dispatch, Palliser assured the lords of the admiralty that peace was at hand. Moreover, judging by the quantities of baleen and furs the

Moravians ascend the Delaware River in the 1700s. Originally from Bohemia, a number of Moravian Brethren left Germany during the eighteenth century to do missionary work in America and Great Britain. The British-Labrador Inuit Peace Treaty helped foster an alliance with Moravarian missionaries. (MPI/Getty Images)

Inuit had supplied to licensed English merchants at Chateau Bay, so, too, was a lucrative trade partnership (Great Britain 1927, 946).

Four years passed before the Moravians came to terms with the Crown on land grants for their mission, and it was another two years before they founded Nain, their first station, in 1771. Interethnic violence continued to flare in the interim, much of it due to the illegal presence on shore of whalers from the American colonies. Palliser stationed a small garrison at Pitts Harbour in 1766 to shore up his still-fragile pact, a step that did more to suppress Inuit reprisals than the "Crimes and Enormities" of the "Lawless Crews from the Plantations" that fanned the flames of revenge (Great Britain 1927, 1006). Despite these troubles, British officials considered Palliser's accord unbroken, as did the Inuit who met the governor on his last official visit to Labrador the next year (Whiteley 1969, 158). Once Nain was established, however, the sit-uation materially improved the mission's trade arm and the spread of independent merchants well north of the strait, gradually stemming the southward flow of traffic and, with it, the bloodshed that marked the contact period. By the mid-1780s, the full effect of Palliser's diplomacy had been realized.

Barnett Richling

See also Aboriginal Title; Canada; Inuit; Sovereignty; Treaty.

References and Further Reading

Great Britain. Privy Council. 1927. In *The Matter of the Boundary Between the Dominion of Canada and the Colony of Newfoundland in the Labrador Peninsula . . .* 12 vols. London: W. Clowes and Sons.

Lysaght, A. M., ed. 1971. *Joseph Banks in Newfoundland and Labrador, 1766: His Diary, Manuscripts and Collections.* Berkeley: University of California Press.

Whiteley, William. 1964. "The Establishment of the Moravian Mission in Labrador and British Policy, 1763–1783." *The Canadian Historical Review* 45(1): 29–50.

Whiteley, William. 1969. "Governor Hugh Palliser and the Newfoundland and Labrador Fishery, 1764–1768." *The Canadian Historical Review* 50(2): 141–163.

Treaty Conference with the Six Nations at Fort Stanwix

November 1768

The treaty conference with the Six Nations—the Cayuga, Mohawk, Oneida, Onondaga, Seneca, and Tuscarora tribes—held at Fort Stanwix, New York, from October to November 1768 opened a large area of the trans-Appalachian West to white settlement, from southwestern New York to Kentucky. The Treaty of Fort Stanwix in 1768 was the British government's attempt to quell illegal encroachment of Native American lands closed to white settlement by the Royal Proclamation of 1763 and to slow burgeoning colonial land speculation fueled by a period of frontier peace. Negotiated by William Johnson—the royal government's superintendent of Indian affairs for the Northern Department (the region above the Ohio River)—the treaty was to formalize the northern boundary between Native American territories and the British colonies' western fringe.

Britain's first step in developing a western policy for its American colonies, the boundary line established by the Proclamation of 1763, was a stimulus for the Treaty of Fort Stanwix. The line was strictly geographic, a hurried response to the crisis of Pontiac's Rebellion, and followed the Appalachian Mountains from New York to Georgia. Frontier settlers, land speculators, and government agents protested the proclamation's boundary and restrictive provisions. Settlers viewed the boundary as an affront to westward expansion: in western Pennsylvania, Virginia, and North Carolina the line straddled the frontier, restricting settlement growth. The line also failed to incorporate some existing white settlements, now proclaimed illegal. Land speculators were displeased by the provision forbidding private land purchases from Native Americans. Government agents were concerned

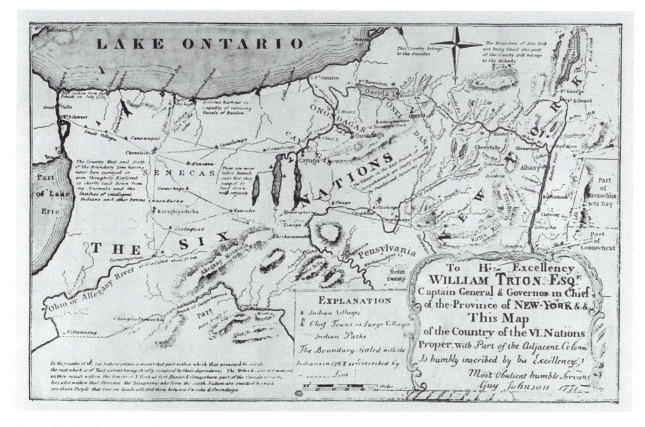

A map showing the territory of the six nations of the Iroquois Confederacy in 1771. The Iroquois were a dominant Native American military power in North America during the eighteenth century. (North Wind Picture Archives)

Pontiac's men release captives taken during Pontiac's War of 1763, an outgrowth of the French and Indian War. (Library of Congress)

that the provision opening trade to all who obtained licenses would result in the same unscrupulous practices that had angered Native Americans and helped precipitate Pontiac's Rebellion. The Plan of 1764—proposed by government agents to avert another uprising by confining licensed trade to established posts—failed, as Native Americans refused to trade at distant locales and as free-ranging, unlicensed traders and French voyageurs undermined licensed traders restricted to posts.

Factions dissatisfied with the Proclamation of 1763 and the Plan of 1764, especially influential land companies, pressured the royal government to revise its western policy. In 1767, the British government directed Johnson and John Stuart, superintendent of Indian affairs for the Southern Department (the region below the Ohio River), to negotiate with Native American tribes to shift the boundary line of 1763 farther west. Johnson, who was assigned the

northern line that was to run from the Great Kanawha River in present-day West Virginia through Pennsylvania to the village of Owege in southern New York, was to treat with the Six Nations. Stuart, who was assigned the southern line through Virginia, the Carolinas, and Georgia, was to treat with the Cherokee.

Johnson convened the Fort Stanwix conference in autumn 1768 to settle the northern boundary line. The conference, largest of the colonial period, began on October 22, as more than three thousand Native Americans, colonial delegates, and land speculators arrived at the fort. Prominent colonial attendees included William Franklin, governor of New Jersey and son of Benjamin Franklin; Frederick Smith, chief justice of New Jersey; Richard Peters and James Tilghman, commissioners from Pennsylvania; and Thomas Walker, commissioner from Virginia. Besides the Six Nations, other northern tribes were present who had been displaced from their homelands by white settlement: the Conoy, Delaware, Minisink, Nanticoke, Shawnee, Tutelo, and others.

The Treaty of Fort Stanwix was finalized on November 5, 1768. Franklin, Smith, Peters, and Tilghman signed for the colonies of New Jersey and Pennsylvania; Chiefs Tegaya (Cayuga), Teyanhasire (Mohawk), Conaquieso (Oneida), Chenughiata (Onondaga), Gostrax (Seneca), and Sesquaressura (Tuscarora) signed for the Six Nations. The boundary line minted by the treaty (different from that sought by the British government) began near Fort Stanwix and ran southwest into Pennsylvania to include the forks of the Susquehanna River, then along the Allegheny and Ohio rivers to the mouth of the Tennessee River. This vast tract of land was ceded for £10,460 British sterling.

Not all lands ceded by the Six Nations in the Treaty of Fort Stanwix were in their control, particularly the Tennessee River region of Kentucky—the historic hunting ground of the Cherokee and Shawnee. The Six Nations may have ceded these lands as proof of their shadowy ownership or as a gesture of goodwill toward the British. Johnson accepted this cession, which violated orders to stop the line at the Great Kanawha River, thus throwing in turmoil the southern boundary line established by Stuart in the 1768 Treaty of Hard Labor with the Cherokee. The northern boundary line, instead of joining with the southern line, ended more than three hundred miles to the west. The British Board of Trade, preoccupied with homeland issues, let the

William Franklin, governor of New Jersey, 1763–1766, and Benjamin Franklin's son, was a delegate to the Treaty Conference with the Six Nations in 1768. (Courtesy of Rutgers University Libraries, Special Collections and Archives).

northern line stand, bolstering land speculators and settlers while infuriating the Cherokee and Shawnee.

Charles E. Williams

See also Albany Conferences of 1754 and 1775; Royal Proclamation of 1763; Treaty; Treaty of Albany with the Five Nations–July 31, 1684.

References and Further Reading

Billington, Ray A. 1944. "The Fort Stanwix Treaty of 1768." *New York History*, 25: 182–194.

Billington, Ray A. 1974. *Westward Expansion: A History of the American Frontier*, 4th ed. New York: Macmillan.

Hamilton, M. W. 1957. *The Papers of Sir William Johnson*. Albany: State University of New York.

Marshall, Peter. 1967. "Sir William Johnson and the Treaty of Fort Stanwix, 1768." *Journal of American Studies*, 1: 149–179.

Merk, Frederick. 1978. *History of the Westward Movement*. New York: Alfred A. Knopf.

Merrell, James H. 1999. *Into the American Woods: Negotiators on the Pennsylvania Frontier*. New York: W. W. Norton.

Robinson, W. Stitt. 1987. *Early American Indian Documents: Treaties and Laws, 1607–1789*. Vol. 5, *Virginia Treaties, 1723–1775*. Frederick, MD: University Publications of America.

Treaty with the Delaware
September 17, 1778

Among the first treaties entered into with a foreign power by the American government was the treaty of 1778 with the Lenni Lenape, or Delaware Nation. This treaty is significant because it came at a time when the United States had placed an important emphasis upon forging treaty alliances; it was the American government's first ratified treaty with a North American indigenous nation, and many were to follow. The treaty is particularly interesting in light of its language and because the United States, which was at war with England and was operating under its own Articles of Confederation, embraced a strategy that sought either to draw the Delaware Nation into an alliance or to ensure that the Delaware would remain neutral.

The first two articles of the treaty proclaim all offenses to be mutually forgiven and require the contracting parties to assist each other if engaged in a "just and necessary" war with any other nation or nations. Article 3, after announcing that the United States was engaged in a just and necessary war, requested that the Delaware provide their most expert warriors to join the American army against a "common enemy."

The first article states that offenses are mutually forgiven. Reference to a "common enemy" in Article 2 is interesting because the Delaware were conquered and made a political dependent of the Iroquois, who claimed they could order the Delaware to go to war and to give up land at their discretion. The United States, realizing that the strength of the Iroquois and the Delaware, when combined with British forces, could create disadvantageous conditions, reasoned that a successful alliance with the Delaware could enhance its position in its war for independence. Throughout negotiations, the Delaware were treated by agents of the American government as a people capable of making the politically independent and sound decisions required of such a treaty. The fact that the Delaware had been made a political dependent of the Six Nations, who were still loosely allied with the British, raises the possibility that the common

Period drawing of Delaware Indians. Delaware was the name given by the British to members of the Algonquian Indian confederation who lived in the Delaware River Valley. The Delaware signed the first ratified treaty with the newly formed United States of America. (North Wind Picture Archives)

enemy referred to in the treaty was most likely presented to the Delaware as the Iroquois, not the British. Thus, the treaty can be viewed from the perspective of a contract between two distinct cultures allied for the purpose of breaking free from the subjugation of another's rule.

In Articles 4 and 6, it is apparent that the language has been carefully worded to negate any impression that America was exerting dominion over the Delaware. Rather, the treaty favors an image of two distinct nations entering into an activity that acknowledges each other's political competence and character as sovereign entities. For example, Article 4 expresses that the execution of justice over infractions by "citizens" of either party should be adjudicated in accordance with the laws and customs of both contracting parties:

> Whereas the enemies of the United States have endeavored, by every artifice in their power . . . that it is the design of the States . . . to extirpate the Indians and take possession of *their* country:

To obviate such false suggestion, the United States do engage to guarantee to the . . . nation of Delawares, and their heirs, all territorial rights in the fullest and most ample manner, as hath been bounded by former treatise . . . it is further agreed on between the contracting parties should it for the future be found conducive for the mutual interest of both parties to invite any other tribes who have been friends to the interest of the United States, to join the present confederation, and to form a state whereof the Delaware nation shall be the head, and have representation in Congress. (Kappler 1904)

The same idea was also emphasized in a letter from Secretary of War Henry Knox to the president, stressing that the independent nations and Indian tribes should be considered foreign nations and not the subjects of any particular state. Knox also stated, ". . .[A]ll treaties with Indian nations, however equal and just they may be in their principles, will not only be nugatory but humiliating to the sovereign, unless they shall be guaranteed . . ." (American State Papers 1962).

By including an offer to form an "Indian state" replete with congressional representation, the tenor of this treaty can be viewed to adhere to America's espoused philosophy in the division of sovereign powers. On the basis of this offer, the language of the treaty acknowledges the sovereign status of the Delaware and a confidence in the ability of other Indian nations to function as sovereign entities.

S. Neyooxet Greymorning

See also Sovereignty; Treaty; Trust Doctrine; Trust Land.

References and Further Reading

Abel, Annie H. 1908. "Proposals for an Indian State, 1778–1878," *American Historical Association*, Annual Report for the Year 1907: 87–104.

American State Papers. 1962. *Papers, Indian Affairs, Documents, Legislation and Executive of the Congress of the United States*, vol. 4. Washington, DC: Gales and Seaton.

Barsh, Russel, and James Henderson. 1980. *The Road, Indian Tribes and Political Liberty*. Berkeley: University of California Press.

Israel, Fred L., ed. 1967. *Major Peace Treaties of Modern History: 1648–1967*, 4 vols., New York: Chelsea House/McGraw-Hill.

Kappler, Charles J., ed. 1904. *Indian Affairs: Laws and Treaties*, vol. 2, *Treaties*. Washington, DC: Government Printing Office.

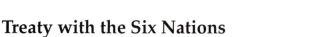

Treaty with the Six Nations

October 22, 1784

This treaty was completed at Fort Stanwix to facilitate an exchange of prisoners, to determine boundaries, and to organize the delivery of goods to the Six Nations. Oliver Wolcott, Richard Butler, and Arthur Lee signed on behalf of the United States. Twelve leaders, representing the Mohawk, Onondaga, Seneca, Oneida, Cayuga, and Tuscarora, signed on behalf of the Six Nations.

Treaty with the Wyandot, Etc.

January 21, 1785

Also known as the Treaty of Fort McIntosh, this treaty was entered into by thirteen representatives of the Wyandot, Delaware, Chippewa, and Ottawa Nations with the United States. The purpose was to smooth relations fractured by the war, to identify territorial boundaries, and to dictate that certain Indian crimes against Americans be tried in the American justice system.

Treaty with the Cherokee

November 28, 1785

Better known as the Treaty of Hopewell, this treaty was concluded between the Cherokee peoples and the United States. It reflected a generally accepted pattern of treaty making between America and American Indian tribes that was commonly practiced throughout the late 1780s. After the American Revolution, the newly constituted federal government decided to use a peaceful treaty process to order its relations with Native Americans rather than subduing them outright through conquest. The thirteen articles that constitute the treaty were entered into by four American commissioners and thirty-seven Cherokee "head-men and warriors" on the banks of the Keowee River on November 28, 1785.

Specifically, the Treaty of Hopewell provided for post-hostility prisoner exchange, collective placement of the Cherokees under the protection of the United States, determination of boundaries, prohibition of settlement by American citizens on Indian lands, extradition of non-Indian criminals to the United States and their punishment by the United States, prohibition of retaliation by either side, supremacy of the federal government (over the states) to regulate trade with the Cherokees and special regulation of that trade, notice to the United States by the Cherokees of designs against it which they may discover, allowance of an Indian deputy to Congress, and perpetual peace and friendship.

In legal theory, the inherent sovereignty of the Cherokee to manage internal Indian relations among themselves was preserved and protected from outside interference—either by the federal government or by the governments of the states wherein they resided. American federal jurisdiction was triggered only when the actions and/or rights of American citizens were implicated and in relation to trade.

The Hopewell treaty, like all treaties concluded by Congress as that body existed in its unicameral form under the Articles of Confederation prior to adoption of the Constitution, reflected the broad federal policy of separation that was based upon George Washington's suggestion of 1783:

> As the Country is large enough to contain us all; and as we are disposed to be kind to them and to partake of their Trade, we will . . . draw a veil over what is past and establish a boundary line between them and us beyond which we will endeavor to restrain our People from Hunting or Settling, and within which they shall not come, but for the purposes of Trading, Treating, or other business unexceptionable in its nature. (Washington 1783)

However, within five years white settlement had increased dramatically on the lands set aside for the Cherokee in the treaty, despite a proclamation by Congress on September 1, 1788, forbidding such activity and directing those citizens who had settled with their families on Cherokee hunting grounds to depart immediately.

By 1790, under the new American constitutional system of government, President Washington was obliged to ask Congress its pleasure regarding the issue:

> Notwithstanding the [Hopewell] treaty and proclamation upward of 500 families have settled on the Cherokee lands exclusively of those settled between the fork of French Broad and Holstein rivers, mentioned in the said treaty. [Thus] I shall conceive myself bound to

exert the powers entrusted to me by the Constitution in order to carry into faithful execution the treaty of Hopewell, unless it shall be thought proper to attempt to arrange a new boundary with the Cherokees, embracing the settlements, and compensating the Cherokees for the cessions they shall make on the occasion. (Washington 1790)

Congress directed the president to renegotiate with the Cherokee, resulting in the July 2, 1791, Treaty of Holston, which reiterated the general terms of the Treaty of Hopewell but reduced the breadth of Indian lands. This was followed by a succession of treaties gradually reducing both Cherokee lands and sovereignty until their final removal from the Georgia, Tennessee, and Arkansas area to west of the Mississippi River along the Trail of Tears in 1838.

Michael J. Kelly

See also Indian Removal; Trail of Tears; Treaty with the Cherokee July 2, 1791; *Worcester v. Georgia,* 1832.

References and Further Reading

Kappler, Charles J., ed. and comp. 1975. *Indian Treaties, 1778–1883.* New York: Interland.

Wardell, Morris L. 1938. *A Political History of the Cherokee Nation 1838–1907.* Norman: University of Oklahoma Press.

Washington, George. 1990. "Letter to James Duane (Sept. 7, 1783)." In *Documents of United States Indian Policy,* ed. Francis Paul Prucha, 2nd ed., 1– 2. Lincoln: University of Nebraska Press.

Treaty with the Choctaw

January 3, 1786

Designed to restore peace between the Choctaw and the United States, this treaty was signed at Hopewell. It was also designed to regulate trade and to maintain friendly relations between the two nations. Benjamin Hawkins, Joseph Martin, and Andrew Pickens; representing the United States, signed the document. Approximately thirty Choctaw leaders signed the treaty as well.

Treaty with the Chickasaw

January 10, 1786

This treaty was intended to restore peaceful relations between the Chickasaw Nation and the United

States. Concluded at Hopewell, this treaty was signed by Joseph Martin, Benjamin Hawkins, and Andrew Pickens, commissioners of the United States. Piomingo, Mingatushka, and Latopia signed as respected leaders of the Chickasaw Nation.

Treaty with the Shawnee

January 31, 1786

This treaty allots land to the Shawnee people and prohibits Americans from settling on that land. The primary purpose of this treaty was to end hostilities and promote peaceful relations between the Shawnee Nation and the United States. The commissioners plenipotentiary signing for the United States were G. Clark, Richard Butler, and Samuel H. Parsons. Aweecony, Kakawipilpathy, Malunthy, Musquaconocah, Meanymsecah, Waupaucowela, Nihipeewa, and Nihinessicoe, warriors and chiefs, signed on behalf of the Shawnee Nation. The treaty was concluded on the Ohio River at the mouth of the Miami River.

Treaty with the Wyandot, Etc.

January 9, 1789

Signed at Fort Harmar by the governor of the territory, Arthur St. Clair, this treaty redefines certain territorial boundaries (reservations) and seeks further regulation of trade. It is also an attempt to maintain a relative balance of friendship between the respective nations. The treaty was signed by twenty-eight leaders and warriors of the Sauk, Ottawa, Delaware, Chippewa, Potawatomi, and Wyandot.

Treaty with the Six Nations

January 9, 1789

This treaty was signed at Fort Harmar by Governor Arthur St. Clair for the purpose of settling boundaries, regulating trade, and promoting good relations between the tribes and the United States. The Mohawks were not involved in the settlement of this treaty. However, twenty-four leaders and warriors of the five other confederated nations signed.

Portrait of Red Jacket (c. 1758–1830), late-eighteenth- and early-nineteenth-century Seneca leader. (Library of Congress)

American nation would be gravely threatened; thus, Washington was especially anxious to affirm Haudenosaunee friendship.

General Israel Chapin called for a treaty meeting to be held in September 1794 in Canandaigua ("The Chosen Spot") in the heart of Seneca territory, where Sullivan and Denonville had burned numerous villages in recent memory. An estimated sixteen hundred Haudenosaunee were in attendance. Red Jacket opened negotiations with the following statement: "Brothers, we, the Sachems of the Six Nations will now tell our minds. The business of this treaty is to brighten the Chain of Friendship between us and the fifteen fires. We told you the other day it was but a small piece that was the occasion of the remaining trust in the Chain of Friendship." This allusion to trust refers to the plans to build two four-mile-wide roads between Fort Schlosser and Buffalo Creek and between Cayuga Creek and Buffalo Creek. The two sides were able to reach a settlement in which the first road was built but not the second. The tribes were

also able to negotiate for lands that had been ceded in the Treaty of Fort Stanwix and to confirm the rest of their landholdings in the face of impending white expansion. The United States and the tribes affirmed peace and international friendship in the treaty, and both parties signed it on November 11, 1794.

Despite violations of the treaty, including the building of the Kinzua Dam in 1964, which flooded more than nine thousand acres of Seneca land in Pennsylvania and New York, this treaty has never been broken; the Haudenosaunee still receive trade cloth from the U.S. government as agreed in 1794, symbolizing the treaty's continued recognition by the United States. Because this treaty so directly recognizes the sovereignty and right to self-determination of the Six Nations, the tribes have used this treaty on several occasions to advocate for Iroquois rights. Each year, on November 11, delegates from each of the Six Nations and the state (and sometimes federal) government gather to acknowledge the pledge of goodwill set forth in this document.

Penelope M. Kelsey

See also Fort Pitt, Pennsylvania; Sovereignty; Treaty; Treaty with the Delaware–September 17, 1778.

References and Further Reading

Jemison, G. Peter, and Anna Schein, eds. 2000. *The Canandaigua Treaty, 1794: 200 Years of Treaty Relations between the Iroquois Confederacy and the United States.* Santa Fe, NM: Clear Light.

McConnell, Michael. 1992. *A Country Between: The Upper Ohio Valley and Its Peoples, 1724–1774.* Lincoln: University of Nebraska Press.

Starkey, Armstrong. 1998. *European and Native American Warfare, 1675–1815.* Norman: University of Oklahoma Press.

Steele, Ian K. 1994. *Warpaths: Invasions of North America.* New York and Oxford, UK: Oxford University Press.

Tebbel, John, and Keith Jennison. 2003. *The American Indian Wars.* Edison, NJ: Castle Books. Originally published 1960 by Harper and Brothers, New York.

Utley, Robert M., and Wilcomb E. Washburn. 1977. *Indian Wars.* Houghton Mifflin.

Treaty with the Oneida, Etc.
December 2, 1794

This treaty was intended to apply to the Oneida and to the Tuscorora and Stockbridge Indians living on Oneida land. The purpose of the treaty was to fulfill previous material obligations to these peoples based on their assistance during the war with England. Timothy Pickering signed for the United States, and eleven chiefs signed the treaty.

Treaty with the Wyandot, Etc.
August 3, 1795

This treaty was established to facilitate peace between the Wyandot, Shawnee, Ottawa, Chippewa, Potawatomi, Miami, Eel River, Wea, Kickapoo, Piankashaw, and Kaskaskia tribes and the United States. The treaty was concluded at Greenville, Ohio, headquarters of the U.S. Army troops under Major General Anthony Wayne. The treaty provisions included land cessions by the tribes and by the United States. It stipulated that annuities be provided by the United States to the tribes, opened trade, and negated previous treaties between these tribes and the United States. It was signed by General Anthony Wayne on behalf of the United States and by ten Wyandot, seventeen Delaware, nine Shawnee, seven Ottawa, eleven Chippewa, twenty-four Potawatomi, five Miami and Eel River, three Wea, and three Kickapoo and Kaskaskia.

Treaty with the Seven Nations of Canada
May 31, 1796

Concluded in New York City, Commissioner Abraham Ogden held the meeting for the cession of lands to New York State. Chiefs Ohnaweio (Goodstream) and Teharagwanegen (Thomas Williams) of the Caghnawaga, Atiatoharognwan (Col. Lewis Cook) of the St. Regis Indians, and William Gray represented the Seven Nations. This treaty also created a reservation for the village of St. Regis.

Treaty with the Creeks
June 29, 1796

Concluded at Colerain in New York, this treaty was intended to establish a lasting peace between the Creek Nation and the United States. It provided for the establishment of military posts and the release of prisoners and established a fixed boundary with the Choctaw and Chickasaw. The treaty was signed by Benjamin Hawkins, George Clymer, and Andrew Pickens on behalf of the United States and by 122 Creeks.

Treaty with the Mohawk
March 29, 1797

This treaty, concluded in Albany, is a land cession by the Mohawks to the State of New York for $1,000. The treaty was signed by Commissioner Isaac Smith on behalf of the United States. The document was signed by five others, including Joseph Brandt.

Agreement with the Seneca
September 15, 1797

This is a contract between the Seneca Nation and one Robert Morris for the sale of land. As part of this contract, certain lands were reserved for the use of the Seneca people. This agreement was sanctioned by the U.S. government. The document was signed by Robert Morris and fifty-two Seneca leaders and warriors, including Handsome Lake, Young King, Red Jacket, and Corn Planter.

Treaty with the Cherokee
October 2, 1798

Initially organized on Holston River in July 1791 and in Philadelphia in 1794, this treaty was intended to renew previous peace contracted between the United States and the Cherokee Nation. It arranged for the cession of some Cherokee lands and required that the Kentucky Road remain open, and Cherokee people retained the right to hunt on the lands ceded. George Walton and Lieutenant Colonel Thomas Butler were appointed commissioners for the treaty process. The treaty was concluded near Tellico, within Cherokee boundaries, and signed by thirty-nine members of the Cherokee Nation.

Treaty with the Chickasaw
October 24, 1801

Signed at Chickasaw Bluffs, this is a treaty between the United States and the Chickasaw Nation. In the treaty, the Chickasaw allowed the building of a road, and the United States pledged protection to the

Chickasaw people. Brigadier General James Wilkinson, Benjamin Hawkins, and Andrew Pickens signed as commissioners on behalf of the United States. The document was signed by twenty-one others, including William McGillivray, George Colbert, and Samuel Mitchell, the Chickasaw agent.

Treaty with the Choctaw
December 17, 1801

This was a contract for peace and friendship between the Choctaw Nation and the United States. It was also an agreement to make a roadway through Choctaw lands. The treaty was signed at Fort Adams by General James Wilkinson, Benjamin Hawkins, and Andrew Pickens on behalf of the United States. It was also signed by sixteen members of the Iroquois Confederacy and the Choctaw Nation.

Treaty with the Creeks
June 16, 1802

Signed near Fort Wilkinson, this treaty was a Creeks land cession. It also allowed for the construction of garrisons on Creeks land. The document was signed by General James Wilkinson, Agent Benjamin Hawkins, and Andrew Pickens for the United States and by forty-five leaders and warriors of the Creek Nations.

Treaty with the Seneca
June 30, 1802

In this agreement, the Seneca ceded lands and redefined boundaries. The treaty meeting took place at Buffalo Creek, Ontario County, New York. The treaty was signed by Corn Planter, Young King, Red Jacket, and sixteen other Seneca leaders and warriors. It was also signed by nine members of the City of Amsterdam and by Agent Joseph Ellicott.

Treaty with the Seneca
June 30, 1802

Signed by Oliver Phelps, Isaac Bronson, and Horatio Jones on one part and by Corn Planter, Young King, Red Jacket, and nine other Seneca men on the other, this treaty documents the cession of Little Beard's Reservation in full. This treaty assembly convened at Buffalo Creek, New York.

Treaty with the Choctaw
October 17, 1802

Signed on the Tombigbee River at Fort Confederation, this treaty marks a land cession by the Choctaw to the United States. General James Wilkinson signed for the United States. Ten Choctaw leaders and warriors signed for the Choctaw Nation.

Treaty with the Delaware, Etc.
June 7, 1803

This treaty was entered into the by the Delaware, Shawnee, Potawatomi, Miami, Eel River, Wea, Kickapoo, Piankashaw, and Kaskaskia Nations and by the United States. It was signed on Miami Lake at Fort Wayne by William Henry Harrison on behalf of the United States and by Little Turtle of the Miami Nation and fourteen other representatives of the concerned tribes. Both the tribes and the United States relinquished tracts of land, which included the post at St. Vincennes and the salt springs on the Saline Creek. The tribes ceded the salt springs upon an agreement that the United States would deliver salt to them each year. The treaty provided for the United States to build houses of entertainment along two main roads for the purpose of entertaining travelers.

Treaty with the Eel River, Etc.
August 7, 1803

This treaty was between the United States and the Eel River, Wyandot, Piankashaw, Kaskaskia, and Kickapoo tribes. It was signed at Fort Wayne by William Henry Harrison and ten tribal representatives. The treaty ceded to the United States three tracts of land between Vincennes and Kaskaskia and one between Vincennes and Clarksville, to be used for building houses of entertainment for travelers.

Treaty with the Kaskasia
August 13, 1803

This treaty was signed by William Henry Harrison and six Kaskaskia leaders and warriors at Vincennes in Indiana Territory. Treaty settlements included the cession of Kaskaskia lands, increased annuities, money to build a church, a new house for the chief, and enclosed fields for the tribe. The treaty indicated that the Kaskaskia retained hunting privileges on the ceded lands.

Treaty with the Choctaw
August 31, 1803
This treaty determined territorial boundaries after a cession by the Choctaw Nation. The treaty was concluded at Hoe-Buckin-too-pa and signed by General James Wilkinson, Mingo Pooscoos, and Alatala Hooma.

Treaty with the Delaware
August 18, 1804
This treaty provides for an increased annuity, clarifies Delaware rights to certain lands, requires the return of stolen horses, and holds the United States responsible for persuading the Piankashaw to recognize Delaware title. This document was signed at Vincennes by William Henry Harrison and five Delaware leaders.

Treaty with the Piankeshaw
August 27, 1804
This treaty, signed at Vincennes, related to Piankeshaw land cession. The Piankeshaw agreed to cede certain lands and retained the right to sell further portions of their land. A ten-year annuity to the tribe was agreed upon. The treaty was signed by William Henry Harrison on behalf of the United States and by five Piankeshaw leaders.

Treaty with the Cherokee
October 24, 1804
This treaty was made between the United States and the Cherokee Nation regarding a land cession and annuity arrangements. It was concluded on Cherokee land in the garrison at Tellico. Daniel Smith and Return J. Meigs signed for the United States; Tolluntuskie, Broom, J. McLamore, Quotequeskee, Path Killer, Tagustiskee, Tulio, Sour Much, Keatechee, and James Vann signed for the Cherokee.

Treaty with the Sauk and Fox
November 3, 1804
A treaty between the United States and the Sauk and Fox, this document was concluded at St. Louis in the Louisiana District. It concerned land cessions, new boundaries, trade regulations, Sauk and Fox hunting rights on ceded lands, the foundation of a military post, and a trading house. Another aim of the treaty was to secure peaceful terms between the United States and the Sauk and Fox. William Henry Harrison signed on behalf of the United States. Layauvois, Pashepaho, Hahshequarhiqua, Quashquame, and Outchequaka signed as leaders of the Sauk and Fox.

Treaty with the Wyandot, Etc.
July 4, 1805
This treaty was between the Wyandot, Chippewa, Munsee and Delaware, Shawnee, Ottawa, and Potawatomi Indians and the United States. It involves Indian land cession and annuities to be provided by the United States, and established tribal rights to use ceded lands for the procurement of game. Charles Jouett signed as a commissioner of the United States. The document was signed by two Potawatomi, seven Wyandot, four Shawnee, nine Ottawa, four Munsee and Delaware, and six Chippewa leaders and warriors.

Treaty with the Chickasaw
July 23, 1805
Concluded on Chickasaw land, this treaty provided for the cession of Chickasaw lands. It arranged for the appointment of a commissioner to determine boundaries and forbade American settlement on remaining Chickasaw lands. It was signed by Silas Dinsmoor and James Robertson on behalf of the United States and by George Colbert, William McGillivray, and eight other Chickasaw leaders and warriors.

Treaty with the Delaware, Etc.
August 21, 1805

This was a treaty between the United States and the Delaware, Potawatomi, Miami, Eel River, and Wea Nations. The treaty provides for Delaware and Miami land cessions. It also requires a permanent increase in the annuity received by the Miami Nation.

Concluded at Grouseland, Indiana Territory, this treaty was signed for the United States by Governor William Henry Harrison. Nineteen men of the tribes involved signed, including Little Turtle and William Anderson.

Treaty with the Sioux
September 23, 1805

This treaty was ratified in April 1808 but never put forth by the president beyond the Senate. The treaty documented a meeting between the United States and the Sioux Nation. It established a land cession of nine square miles at the mouth of the St. Croix River and also a tract along the Mississippi between St. Peters River and the falls at St. Anthony. This land cession was valued at $2,000. The Sioux retained hunting rights and so forth on the ceded land. The document was signed by Zebulon M. Pike for the United States and Le Petit Carbeau and Way Aga Enogee.

Treaty with the Cherokee
October 25, 1805

Concluded at Tellico, this treaty was between the United States and the Cherokee Nation. With this treaty, the Cherokee ceded lands in return for payment from the United States. New boundaries were therefore determined, and specific roads were opened to travel for U.S. citizens. Return J. Meigs and Daniel Smith signed on behalf of the United States. More than thirty Cherokee representatives signed the treaty.

Treaty with the Cherokee
October 27, 1805

This treaty was signed at Tellico by Return J. Meigs and Daniel Smith, representatives of the United States. It was also signed by Black Fox and fourteen other Cherokee men. The treaty included a land cession and the use of a road for transporting mail.

Treaty with the Creeks
November 14, 1805

Concluded at Washington, this was a treaty between the Creek Nations and the United States. It involved a land cession, the establishment of new boundaries and a military post, the opening of a road to the United States, and organization of annuity payments to the Creek Nations. It was signed by Henry Dearborn, the secretary of war, and Oche Haujo, William McIntosh, Tuckenehau Chapco, Tuckenehau, Enehau Thlucco, and Chekopeheke Emanthau.

Treaty with the Choctaw
November 16, 1805

This treaty marked a land cession and the establishment of a reservation, stipulating new boundaries. It was concluded at Mount Dexter, Pooshapukanuk, on Choctaw land. It was signed by James Robertson and Silas Dinsmoor for the United States and by twenty-three Choctaw men.

Treaty with the Piankashaw
December 30, 1805

This treaty is a land cession made in return for annuities as compensation. The Piankashaw maintain hunting and similar rights on the ceded land. Concluded at Vincennes, Indiana Territory, the treaty was signed by Governor William Henry Harrison and Wabakinklelia (Gros Bled), Pauquia (Montour) and Macatiwaaluna (Chien Noir) of the Piankashaw.

Treaty with the Cherokee
January 7, 1806

Concluded at Washington, this treaty was another Cherokee land cession in return for payment. As part of the treaty negotiations, the United States was to inform and insist upon recognition of the new boundaries by the Chickasaw Nation. The treaty was signed by Henry Dearborn on behalf of the United States and by seventeen Cherokee men.

Treaty with the Ottawa, Etc.
November 17, 1807

This treaty included land cessions, new boundaries, and annuity arrangements, and it preserved the tribes' rights to hunt and carry on other activities on the ceded lands. It also created reservations. Concluded in Detroit, the treaty was signed by Governor William Hull, seventeen Chippewa leaders, five Ottawa leaders, five Potawatomi leaders, and three Wyandot leaders.

Treaty with the Osage
November 10, 1808

This treaty allowed for the building of a fort, specified goods to be furnished, established new boundaries and protection of hunting grounds, and required the Osage to refrain from supplying arms to tribes in conflict with the United States. Concluded at Fort Clark in Louisiana Territory, this treaty was signed by Peter Chouteau, agent to the Osage, Captain E. B. Clemson, Lieutenant L. Lorimer, and Reazen Lewis on behalf of the United States. It was signed in November by 111 Osage men. The following August, it was signed in St. Louis by fifteen more Osage leaders.

Treaty with the Chippewa, Etc.
November 25, 1808

Concluded at Brownstown, Michigan Territory, this treaty was between the United States and the Chippewa, Ottawa, Potawatomi, Wyandot, and Shawnee Nations. The treaty was a land cession obtained for the purpose of building a road. The tribes retained hunting and fishing rights on the ceded land. The treaty was signed by Governor William Hull on behalf of the United States and by four Chippewa, two Ottawa, three Potawatomi, four Wyandot, and two Shawnee.

Treaty with the Delaware, Etc.
September 30, 1809

This treaty was made between the United States and the Delaware, Potawatomi, Miami, and Eel River Miami Indians. It was a land cession and arrange-

ment for annuities. It required the approval of the Wea Indians and was designed to implement measures against trespassing. The treaty also required the agreement of the Kickapoo Indians, who had close relations with these tribes. Concluded at Fort Wayne, the treaty was signed by Governor William Henry Harrison on behalf of the United States. It was also signed by five Delaware, ten Potawatomi, five Miami (including Little Turtle), and three Eel River leaders.

Supplemental Treaty with the Miami, Etc.
September 30, 1809

Concluded separately from the treaty with the Delaware, etc., this treaty was also concluded at Fort Wayne. It provided for additional compensation for the Miami and Eel River Indians, as they relinquished a majority of the lands ceded in the treaty with the Delaware, etc. This supplemental treaty was signed by Governor William Henry Harrison and by Little Turtle and eight other Eel River and Miami leaders.

Treaty with the Wea
October 26, 1809

This treaty was the result of a meeting at Vincennes, Indiana Territory. Signed by William Henry Harrison for the United States and by nine leaders of the Wea, this treaty was an agreement by the Wea to comply with the treaty signed at Fort Wayne with the Delaware, Miami, Eel River, and Potawatomi Nations.

Treaty with the Kickapoo
December 9, 1809

This treaty was between the United States and the Kickapoo Nation. As a part of the treaty, the Kickapoo ceded lands to the United States in return for annuity payments and agreed to a portion of the September 30, 1809, treaty at Fort Wayne. It was signed by Governor William Henry Harrison and five Kickapoo leaders.

Treaty with the Wyandot, Etc.
July 22, 1814

This was a treaty of peace between the United States and the Wyandot, Delaware, Shawnee, Seneca, and

Miami Nations. It stipulated boundaries and pledged alliance against Great Britain in the War of 1812. Concluded at Greenville, Ohio, it was signed by William Henry Harrison and Lewis Cass for the United States and by Crane (Tarhe) and twelve other Wyandot, sixteen Delaware, Corn Stalk and thirteen other Shawnee, five Ottawa, and thirteen Seneca.

Treaty with the Creeks
August 9, 1814

Concluded at Fort Jackson, Alabama, this treaty was designed to reestablish friendly relations with the Creek Nations. It was designed to chastise the Creeks, who had opposed the United States and aided the British during the war. It established military posts, effected a land cession, and required a break in relations between the Creek Nations and the Spanish and British. It also called for the Creeks to give up those (prophets, etc.) who had advocated fighting the United States. The treaty was signed by Major General Andrew Jackson on behalf of the United States and by thirty-six Creeks representatives.

Treaty with the Potawatomi
July 18, 1815

This treaty was designed to reestablish friendship and peace. It was concluded at Portage des Sioux between the United States and the Potawatomi Nation. William Clark, Ninian Edwards, and Auguste Chouteau signed for the United States. Six Potawatomi leaders signed as well.

Treaty with the Piankashaw
July 18, 1815

Concluded at Portage des Sioux, this treaty is between the United States and the Piankashaw Nation. It was designed to reestablish peace and friendship and to reconfirm previous treaties. It was signed by William Clark, Ninian Edwards, and Auguste Chouteau on behalf of the United States. La-ma-noan (the Axe), La-mee-pris-jeau (Sea Wolf), Mon-sai-raa (Rusty), Wa-pan-gia (Swan), and Na-maing-sa (the Fish) signed on behalf of the Piankashaw.

Treaty with the Teton
July 19, 1815

This treaty reestablished peace between the Teton and the United States. It was concluded at Portage des Sioux. William Clark, Ninian Edwards, and Auguste Chouteau signed for the United States. Nine Teton leaders also signed the treaty.

Treaty with the Sioux of the Lakes
July 19, 1815

Signed by William Clark, Ninian Edwards, and Auguste Chouteau, this is another treaty to reestablish peace. Concluded at Portage des Sioux, this treaty with the Sioux of the Lakes was signed by Tatangamania (Walking Buffalo), Haisanwee (Horn), Aampahaa (Speaker), Narcesagata (the Hard Stone), and Haibohaa (Branching Horn).

Treaty with the Sioux of St. Peter's River
July 19, 1815

This was one of a series of treaties concluded at Portage des Sioux at this time. Signed by William Clark, Ninian Edwards, and Auguste Chouteau, it was designed to reestablish peace. Enigmanee (Flies as He Walks), Wasoukapaha (Falling Hail), Champisaba (Black War Club), Manpinsaba (Black Cloud), Tatarnaza (Iron Wind), and Nankanandee signed on behalf of the Sioux.

Treaty with the Yankton Sioux
July 19, 1815

One of a series concluded at Portage des Sioux by William Clark, Ninian Edwards, and Auguste Chouteau, this treaty was designed to reestablish peace and friendship between the Yankton and the United States. Eleven Yankton leaders signed the treaty.

Treaty with the Makah
July 20, 1815

One of a series of treaties signed at Portage des Sioux under William Clark, Ninian Edwards, and Auguste

Chouteau, this treaty was intended to reestablish peace and friendship with the Makah. The treaty was signed by seven Makah leaders.

Treaty with the Kickapoo
September 2, 1815

This was a treaty to reestablish peace and friendship between the United States and the Kickapoo Nation and to reaffirm former treaties. It was concluded at Portage des Sioux and signed by ten Kickapoo representatives and by William Clark and two other U. S. representatives.

Treaty with the Wyandot, Etc.
September 8, 1815

This treaty was between the Wyandot, Delaware, Seneca, Shawnee, Miami, Chippewa, Ottawa, and Potawatomi Nations and the United States. The treaty was concluded at Spring Wells, Ohio, and was intended to reestablish peaceful relations. It pardoned these tribes for their alliance with Great Britain during the war. William Henry Harrison, Duncan McArthur, and John Graham signed as representatives of the United States. Seven Wyandot, eight Shawnee, eleven Ottawa, one Winnebago, ten Chippewa, seven Delaware, four Seneca, twenty-five Potawatomi, and eighteen Miami leaders signed the treaty.

Treaty with the Osage
September 12, 1815

This was a treaty of peace concluded at Portage des Sioux. It was signed by William Clark, Ninian Edwards, and Auguste Chouteau for the United States and by twenty-four men of the Osage.

Treaty with the Sauk
September 13, 1815

This was a treaty of peace between the Sauk Nation on the Missouri River and the United States and was concluded at Portage des Sioux. During the war, this group of Sauk had left the rest of the Sauk Nation to avoid fighting the United States. The treaty guaranteed this portion of the Sauk Nation the privileges granted by the Treaty of St. Louis of 1804. It also provided for annuities. It required that the Sauk on the Missouri River remain separate from those who fought against the United States. The treaty was signed by William Clark, Ninian Edwards, and Auguste Chouteau for the United States and by twelve leaders of the Missouri River Sauk Indians.

Treaty with the Fox
September 14, 1815

This was a treaty reestablishing peace between the United States and the Fox Indians. It required the Fox to return prisoners taken during hostilities and to agree to the Treaty of St. Louis of 1804. It was concluded at Portage des Sioux and signed by William Clark, Ninian Edwards, and Auguste Chouteau. Twenty-two leaders of the Fox Nation signed the treaty.

Treaty with the Iowa
September 16, 1815

Concluded at Portage des Sioux, this treaty was intended to reestablish peace and friendship between the Iowa and the United States. The U.S. representatives signing the treaty were William

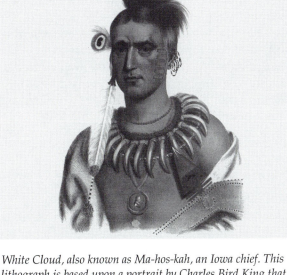

White Cloud, also known as Ma-hos-kah, an Iowa chief. This lithograph is based upon a portrait by Charles Bird King that was commissioned by Thomas McKenney, the superintendent of Indian affairs. The painting is c. 1820, some years after the treaty with the Iowa was forged September 16, 1815. (Library of Congress)

Clark, Ninian Edwards, and Auguste Chouteau. Sixteen Iowa representatives signed the treaty.

Treaty with the Kansa

October 28, 1815

This treaty was intended to reestablish peace between the United States and the Kansa Indians. Concluded at St. Louis, the treaty was signed by Ninian Edwards and Auguste Chouteau on behalf of the United States and by eighteen leaders of the Kansas Nation.

Treaty with the Cherokee

March 22, 1816

This treaty marked a land cession by the Cherokee to South Carolina and stipulated that South Carolina pay $5,000 for the cession. The treaty was concluded in Washington; George Graham represented the United States. The treaty was also signed by Colonel John Lowry, Major John Walker, Major Ridge, Richard Taylor, John Ross, and Cheucunsene.

Treaty with the Cherokee

March 22, 1816

This treaty determined the boundaries of the land cession and granted the United States the right to build in the Cherokee Nation. It also stipulates that the Cherokee were to be granted indemnity in relation to U.S. operations on Cherokee land. Concluded at Washington, this treaty was signed by George Graham, Colonel John Lowry, Major John Walker, Major Ridge, Richard Taylor, John Ross, and Cheucunsene.

Treaty with the Sauk

May 13, 1816

Concluded at St. Louis, this treaty was intended to reestablish peace between the United States and the Rock River Sauk, who fought the United States during the war with Great Britain. It also reaffirmed the 1804 Treaty of St. Louis. The treaty was signed by William Clark, Ninian Edwards, and Auguste Chouteau on behalf of the United States. Twenty-two Rock River Sauk also signed the treaty.

Treaty with the Sioux

June 1, 1816

This was a treaty to reestablish peace and friendship between the United States and eight bands of Sioux. It was concluded at St. Louis and signed on behalf of the United States by William Clark, Ninian Edwards, and Auguste Chouteau. It was also signed by forty Sioux representatives.

Treaty with the Winnebago

June 3, 1816

Concluded at St. Louis, this treaty was intended to reestablish peaceful relations between the United States and the Winnebago of Ouisconsin River. It required the tribe to return prisoners taken during hostilities and reaffirmed former treaties made with the United States. It also called for the continued separation of the Winnebago on Ouisconsin River from the rest of their nation. This treaty was signed on behalf of the United States by William Clark, Ninian Edwards, and Auguste Chouteau. Eleven leaders of the Ouisconsin River Winnebago signed the treaty.

Treaty with the Wea and Kickapoo

June 4, 1816

Concluded at Fort Harrison, Indiana Territory, this treaty of peace also reaffirmed the land cession of December 1809. Benjamin Parke signed for the United States, nine men signed for the Wea tribe (including two Miami men), and eleven leaders signed for the Kickapoo Nation.

Treaty with the Ottawa, Etc.

August 24, 1816

This treaty was between the United States and the Ottawa, Chippewa, and Potawatomi tribes along the Milwaukee Rivers and the southwestern parts of Lake Michigan. It addressed concerns regarding a dispute over the land cession of the Sauk and Fox in 1804. It was signed at St. Louis by William Clark, Ninian Edwards, and Auguste Chouteau for the United States and by twenty-seven representatives of the tribes.

Treaty with the Cherokee
September 14, 1816

This document was both a treaty of peace and a land cession by the Cherokee. It set up boundaries and arranged for a meeting between the Cherokee, Generals Andrew Jackson and David Meriwether, and Jesse Franklin at a council at Turkey's Town on the Coosa River later the same month. The treaty was signed for the United States by Andrew Jackson, David Meriwether, and Jesse Franklin. Toochalar, Oohulookee, Wososey, Gousa, Spring Frog, Oowatata, John Beuge, John Bawldridge, Sallocooke Fields, George Guess, Bark, Campbell, Spirit, Young Wolf, and Oolitiskee signed on behalf of the Cherokee.

Treaty with the Chickasaw
September 20, 1816

This treaty renewed friendship, ceded lands to the United States, and reserved certain lands for use of the Chickasaw. It also obligated the United States to give gifts to the Chickasaw and ended the licensing of merchants to the Chickasaw Nation. Andrew Jackson, David Meriwether, and Jesse Franklin signed for the United States, and twenty-three representatives signed on behalf of the Chickasaw Nation at the Chickasaw council house.

Treaty with the Choctaw
October 24, 1816

This treaty was a land cession by the Choctaw to the United States. It was concluded at the Choctaw trading house and signed by thirteen representatives of the Choctaw Nation and by John Coffee, John Rhea, and John M'Kee representing the United States.

Treaty with the Menominee
March 30, 1817

Concluded at St. Louis, this was a treaty to renew peace and friendship. William Clark, Ninian Edwards, and Auguste Chouteau signed for the United States. Ten leaders of the Menominee also signed.

Treaty with the Oto
June 24, 1817

This treaty was designed to reestablish peaceful relations after the war with England. The treaty was signed by William Clark and Auguste Chouteau on behalf of the United States and by twelve Oto and five Missouri.

Treaty with the Ponca
June 25, 1817

The purpose of this treaty was to reestablish friendly relations between the United States and the Ponca after the War of 1812. The treaty was signed by Auguste Chouteau and William Clark on behalf of the United States and by eight representatives of the Ponca Nation.

Treaty with the Cherokee
July 8, 1817

This treaty arranged for the cession of certain lands in exchange for others and also for an additional cession of land. Under the treaty arrangements, a census would be taken of the Cherokee Nation, and lands would be set aside for the heads of Cherokee families. The treaty was signed by Andrew Jackson, Joseph McMinn (governor of Tennessee), and David Meriwether on behalf of the United States and by forty-six Cherokee representatives.

Treaty with the Wyandot, Etc.
September 29, 1817

This treaty entailed the cession of lands by the Wyandot, Potawatomi, Ottawa, and Chippewa Nations and grants to be distributed by the United States to the Wyandot, Seneca, Shawnee, and Ottawa as well as specified individuals. It provided for the division of lands and dealt with issues of hunting, building, taxes, and education. The treaty was concluded at the Rapids of the Miami of Lake Erie. It was signed by Lewis Cass and Duncan Arthur on behalf of the United States and by numerous representatives of the Wyandot, Seneca, Shawnee, Delaware, Potawatomi, Ottawa, and Chippewa Nations.

Agreement with the Piankeshaw

January 3, 1818

This was an agreement between Governor Thomas Posey, superintendent of Indian affairs, and Chekommia (Big River), principal chief of the Piankeshaw tribe. The treaty was concluded at Vincennes.

Treaty with the Creeks

January 22, 1818

Concluded on the Flint River at the Creek agency, this treaty arranged the cession of lands in return for payment from the United States and set boundaries. David Brydie Mitchell, agent to the Creeks, signed for the United States. Eighteen representatives of the Creek Nations signed the treaty.

Treaty with the Grand Pawnee

June 18, 1818

This treaty of peace and friendship was concluded at St. Louis. William Clark and Auguste Chouteau signed as representatives of the United States. Sixteen representatives of the Grand Pawnee signed as well.

Treaty with the Noisy Pawnee

June 19, 1818

This was a treaty of peace concluded at St. Louis. It was signed by William Clark and Auguste Chouteau, representatives of the United States, and by nine representatives of the Pawnee.

Treaty with the Pawnee Republic

June 20, 1818

This treaty officially established peace and friendship between the Pawnee Republic and the United States. It was signed at St. Louis by William Clark and Auguste Chouteau on behalf of the United States. It was also signed by Petaheick (Good Chief), Rarnleshare (Chief Man), Shernakitare (First in the War Party), Sheterahiate (Partisan Discoverer), Tearekatacaush (the Brave), Pa (the Elk), and Tetaw-

iouche (Wearer of Shoes), representatives of the Pawnee Republic.

Treaty with the Pawnee Marhar

June 22, 1818

This treaty establishes peaceful relations with the United States. It was concluded at St. Louis and signed by William Clark and Auguste Chouteau on behalf of the United States. It was also signed by twelve Pawnee representatives.

Treaty with the Quapaw

August 24, 1818

This treaty arranged for the cession of Quapaw lands and the organization of a reservation. It also stipulated the distribution of annuities to the tribe. William Clark and Auguste Chouteau signed for the United States, and thirteen leaders signed for the Quapaw. The treaty was concluded at St. Louis.

Treaty with the Wyandot, Etc.

September 17, 1818

This treaty set forth stipulations for the Wyandot Reservation and provided for an additional reservation for the Shawnee, Seneca, and Wyandot. Concluded at the rapids of the Miami of Lake Erie, the treaty was signed by Lewis Cass and Duncan McArthur on behalf of the United States and by numerous representatives of the Ottawa, Shawnee, Wyandot, and Seneca tribes.

Treaty with the Wyandot

September 20, 1818

Concluded at St. Mary's, Ohio, this treaty arranged for a land cession by the Wyandot Nation. It also set forth restrictions on the use of the reservation lands of the Wyandot south of the Huron River. The treaty was signed by Lewis Cass on behalf of the United States and by Ronesass (Honas), Haunsiaugh (Boyer), Ronaess (Racer), Ronioness (Joseph), Scoutash, Dunquod (Half King), Aronne (Cherokee Boy), and Taruntne (Between the Logs).

Treaty with the Peoria, Etc.
September 25, 1818
Concluded at Edwardsville, Illinois, this treaty was a cession of land to the United States by the Peoria, Kaskaskia, Cahokia, and Tamarois tribes. The treaty also obligated the United States to leave 640 acres to the Peoria and to pay them for the cessions. It was signed by Ninian Edwards and Auguste Chouteau on behalf of the United States and by representatives of each tribe.

Treaty with the Osage
September 25, 1818
This treaty was an Osage lands cession. Concluded at St. Louis, it was signed by Governor William Clark for the United States and by forty-five Osage representatives.

Treaty with the Potawatomi
October 2, 1818
Concluded at St. Mary's, Ohio, this treaty was a cession of land to the United States by the Potawatomi; it also arranged for annuities and grants. As a part of this treaty, the United States bought the Kickapoo claim. Jonathan Jennings, Lewis Cass, and Benjamin Parke signed on behalf of the United States, and thirty-five representatives signed for the Potawatomi.

Treaty with the Wea
October 2, 1818
This treaty was a land cession by the Wea to the United States and gained their approval of the 1809 Kickapoo cession. Concluded at St. Mary's, Ohio, the treaty was signed by Jonathan Jennings, Lewis Cass, and Benjamin Parke on behalf of the United States and by seven Wea representatives and two Kickapoo leaders.

Treaty with the Delaware
October 3, 1818
With this treaty, the Delaware ceded all their lands in Indiana in exchange for lands set aside for them by the United States west of the Mississippi River. The treaty also arranged for annuities and individual land grants for the Delaware. Jonathan Jennings, Lewis Cass, and Benjamin Parke signed on behalf of the United States. Nineteen representatives of the Delaware Nation also signed.

Treaty with the Miami
October 6, 1818
Concluded at St. Mary's, Ohio, this treaty included land cession by the Miami, a portion of which was to be used for reservations, and required the Miami to recognize the Kickapoo cession. It also arranged for various grants. It was signed by Jonathan Jennings, Lewis Cass, and Benjamin Parke on behalf of the United States and by sixteen Miami representatives.

Treaty with the Chickasaw
October 19, 1818
This treaty was intended to end disputes over boundaries and to establish peaceful relations. It included a Chickasaw land cession and arrangements for reservations and individual grants. It was signed at the treaty ground east of Old Town by twenty-one representatives of the Chickasaw Nation and by Isaac Shelby and Andrew Jackson on behalf of the United States.

Treaty with the Cherokee
February 27, 1819
This treaty arranged for the further cession of lands by the Cherokee. It arranged for land grants, reservations, new boundaries, and annuities and prohibited intrusion onto remaining Cherokee lands. The treaty was signed at Washington by John C. Calhoun, secretary of war, and by twelve Cherokee representatives, including John Ross.

Treaty with the Kickapoo
July 30, 1819
This treaty arranged for the cession of Kickapoo lands to the United States, new boundaries, and annuities. The Kickapoo were to relinquish former lands in return for $3,000 in merchandise and a

land grant in Missouri. The United States was to furnish boats and other materials for the successful removal of the Kickapoo to the new lands. Concluded at Edwardsville, Illinois, the treaty was signed by Auguste Chouteau and Benjamin Stephenson on behalf of the United States and by twenty-three representatives of the Kickapoo Nation.

Treaty with the Kickapoo
August 30, 1819

This treaty arranged for the Kickapoo cession of all lands on the Wabash River and in other areas, set new boundaries, and required the Kickapoo to relinquish a third of the payment by the United States agreed upon in the treaty the previous month. Concluded at Fort Harrison, the treaty was signed by Benjamin Parke on behalf of the United States and by Tecumcena, Kaahna, Macacanaw, La Ferine, Macatewaket, Pelecheah, Kechemaquaw, and Pacakinqua of the Kickapoo.

Treaty with the Chippewa
September 24, 1819

This treaty arranged for a cession of Chippewa lands to the United States and arranged for new boundaries, payments, reservation, and the retention of hunting and other rights on ceded lands. Concluded at Saginaw, Michigan Territory, the treaty was signed by Lewis Cass on behalf of the United States and by more than one hundred Chippewa representatives.

Treaty with the Chippewa
June 16, 1820

This treaty arranged for further cession of Chippewa lands but granted the retention of fishing rights at the falls of St. Mary's. Concluded at Sault Ste. Marie, Michigan Territory, the treaty was signed by Lewis Cass on behalf of the United States and by fifteen representatives of the Chippewa Nation.

Okee-makee-quid, a Chippewa chief, as depicted in 1826 by Charles Bird King. (Getty Images)

Treaty with the Ottawa and Chippewa
July 6, 1820

This treaty marked the cession of St. Martin Island by the tribes and arranged for a payment in goods. Concluded at L'Arbre Croche and Michilimackinac, Michigan Territory, the treaty was signed by Lewis Cass on behalf of the United States and by twenty Chippewa and Ottawa leaders.

Treaty with the Kickapoo
July 19, 1820

This treaty was designed to alter the 1819 Kickapoo treaty at Edwardsville, Illinois. It was concluded at St. Louis and signed by Auguste Chouteau and Benjamin Stephenson on behalf of the United States and by twenty-eight Kickapoo representatives.

Treaty with the Wea

August 11, 1820

This was a land cession by the Wea tribe, to be paid for with $5,000 in goods and money. The treaty also arranged for an annuity to be paid to the Kaskaskia Nation. Benjamin Parke signed on behalf of the United States, along with sixteen tribal representatives. The treaty was concluded at St. Mary's, Ohio.

Treaty with the Kickapoo of the Vermilion

September 5, 1820

This treaty arranged for annuity payments to the Kickapoo tribe. Concluded at Vincennes, the treaty was signed by Benjamin Parke on behalf of the United States and by Wagohaw, Tecumsena, Pelecheah, Kechemaqua, Nasa Reah, Katewah, and Paca Rinqua on behalf of the Kickapoo.

Treaty with the Choctaw

October 18, 1820

This treaty arranged a land cession by the Choctaw, who were being removed to lands set aside for them by the United States west of the Mississippi River. It stipulated payments, new boundaries, and the boundaries east of the Mississippi.

It was also designed as a treaty of peace. Concluded at the treaty grounds of the Choctaw Nation, near Doak's Stand on the Natchez Road, the treaty was signed by Major General Andrew Jackson and General Thomas Hinds on behalf of the United States and by numerous representatives of the Choctaw Nation.

Treaty with the Creeks

January 8, 1821

This treaty arranged for a Creeks land cession and for the reservation of certain lands. It stipulated a payment plan and also required the United States to pay the debts Georgia claimed against the Creeks. Concluded at the Indian Spring, Creek Nation, this treaty was signed by David Meriwether and Daniel M. Forney for the United States and by more than twenty Creeks representatives.

Treaty with the Creeks

January 8, 1821

This treaty was designed to help settle the Creeks debt claimed by the state of Georgia. Concluded at the Indian Springs, Creek Nation, the treaty was signed by J. McIntosh, David Adams, Daniel Newman, and William McIntosh for the United States and by Tustunnuggee Hopoie and Efau Emauthlau for the Creeks.

Treaty with the Ottawa, Etc.

August 29, 1821

This treaty arranged for a further cession of lands from the Ottawa, Chippewa, and Potawatomi tribes. It also stipulated grants and reservations, allowed the United States to build a road, and maintained the rights of the tribes to hunt on the ceded lands. Concluded in Chicago, Illinois, the treaty was signed by Lewis Cass and Solomon Sibley for the United States and by numerous representatives of the Ottawa, Chippewa, and Potawatomi tribes.

Treaty with the Osage

August 21, 1822

Concluded at the U.S. Factory on the M. De Cigue Augt. (Fort Clark on the Missouri), this document releases the United States from payments promised in the November 1808 treaty with the Osage in return for $2,329 in merchandise from the factory. The treaty was signed by Richard Graham on behalf of the United States and by twenty-two Osage representatives.

Treaty with the Sauk and Fox

September 3, 1822

This treaty abrogated the ninth article of the treaty of November 1804. It released the United States from its agreement to open a factory for the tribes and to keep out traders who took advantage of the tribes. The treaty also required the United States to pay the Sauk and Fox $1,000 in merchandise from the factory. The agreement was signed at Fort Armstrong by Thomas Forsyth for the United States and by Pushee Paho,

Quash Quammee, Nesowakee, Keeocuck, Wapulla, Themue, Mucathaanamickee, and Nolo.

Treaty with the Florida Tribes of Indians

September 18, 1823

This treaty arranged for the cession by the tribes of the Florida Territory, except for a district to be set aside for their residence and use. Under this treaty, the tribes were not allowed to aid fugitive slaves. They were to be allotted certain foods by the United States for one year and were placed under the supervision of an Indian agent. Concluded along Moultrie Creek, Florida Territory, the treaty was signed by William P. Duval, James Gadsden, and Bernard Segui on behalf of the United States and by thirty-two representatives of the Florida tribes.

Agreement with the Seneca

September 3, 1823

This treaty arranged for the cession of the Gordeau Reservation in Livingston and Genesee Counties. Concluded at Moscow, Livingston County, New York, this treaty was signed by John Greig and Henry B. Gibson for the United States and by nineteen representatives of the Seneca Nation.

Treaty with the Sauk and Fox

August 4, 1824

This treaty arranged for the cession of all Sauk and Fox lands within the borders of the state of Missouri. A small portion of this land was to be set aside for the use of mixed-blood Sauk and Fox. Concluded at Washington, the treaty was signed by William Clark for the United States and by six Sauk and four Fox representatives.

Treaty with the Iowa

August 4, 1824

This treaty arranged for the cession of lands within Missouri State borders and for the payment of annu-ities. Concluded at Washington, the treaty was signed by William Clark for the United States and by Ma-hos-kah (White Cloud) and Mah-ne-hah-nah (Great Walker) of the Iowa tribe.

Treaty with the Quapaw

November 15, 1824

This treaty arranged for the cession of Quapaw lands in the Arkansas Territory and restricted the Quapaw to living within the bounds of the Caddo tribe. The treaty required the United States to pay the head chiefs $2,000 and the tribe $4,000 in goods. Under this treaty, the Quapaw retained the right to hunt on ceded lands. Concluded at Harrington's, Arkansas Territory, the document was signed by Robert Crittenden for the United States and by fifteen representatives of the Quapaw Nation.

Treaty with the Choctaw

January 20, 1825

This treaty arranged the cession of Choctaw lands, the payment of annuities, payment for the Pensacola campaign, and provisions for those Choctaw choosing not to leave. Concluded at Washington, the treaty was signed by John C. Calhoun, U.S. secretary of war. Mooshulatubbee, Robert Cole, Daniel McCurtain, Talking Warrior, Red Fort, Nittuckachee, David Folsom, and J. L. McDonald signed as representatives of the Choctaw Nation.

Treaty with the Creeks

February 12, 1825

Under the terms of this treaty, the Creeks ceded all land within the state of Georgia, land north and west of the Chatauhoochie River, and the reservations located at Indian Springs on the Ocmulgee River. In return, the Creeks were to receive land between the Arkansas and Canadian rivers equal to the number of acres ceded. The treaty was concluded at Indian Springs, Georgia. The signatories were Duncan G. Campbell, James Meriwether (both U. S. commissioners), William McIntosh (head chief of the Cowetau), and more than fifty other chiefs and headmen.

Treaty with the Osage
June 2, 1825

Under the terms of this treaty, the Osage ceded all their land within the states of Missouri, Kansas, and Arkansas and in the Indian Territory, except for a fifty-mile-wide tract of land in southern Kansas running from Fort Scott to Dodge. Concluded in St. Louis, the treaty was signed by William Clark, superintendent of Indian affairs, for the United States and by Chief Claremont, Chief White Hair, and fifty-eight other representatives of the Osage.

Treaty with the Kansa
June 3, 1825

Under the terms of this treaty, the Kansa ceded all remaining lands in Missouri, Kansas, and present-day Nebraska. In return, the Kansa would retain a tract of land thirty miles wide running from Topeka to Goodland. Concluded in St. Louis, the treaty was signed by William Clark for the United States and by twelve representatives of the Kansa.

Treaty with the Ponca
June 9, 1825

This treaty explained the U.S. government's authority, protection, and power to regulate the trade of the Ponca and forbade the distribution of guns to tribes hostile to the United States. The treaty was concluded in Poncar Village at the mouth of White Paint Creek. The signatories were Henry Atkinson and Benjamin O'Fallon for the United States and nineteen chiefs and headmen of the Ponca Nation.

Treaty with the Teton, Etc., Sioux
June 22, 1825

This treaty explained the U.S. government's authority, protection, and power to regulate trade and for-bade the distribution of guns to tribes hostile to the United States. Concluded at Fort Look-out, South Dakota, the treaty was signed by Henry Atkinson and Benjamin O'Fallon on behalf of the United States and by twenty-eight representatives of the Teton, Yankton, and Yanktonai.

Agreement with the Creeks
June 29, 1825

This was an agreement made with the Creek Nations at the council house in Broken Arrow. The agreement, signed in council by eleven Muscogee, dealt with issues of debt payment and the opposition to Creek laws by U.S. citizens. The agreement was not ratified.

Treaty with the Sioune and Oglala Tribes
July 5, 1825

This treaty set forth stipulations for the regulation of trade by the United States and forbade the Sioune and Oglala to furnish guns to tribes hostile to the United States. The treaty was concluded at the mouth of the Teton River. Henry Atkinson and Benjamin O'Fallon signed for the United States, and six Sioune chiefs, three Sioune warriors, four Oglala chiefs, and four Oglala warriors signed for their people.

Treaty with the Cheyenne Tribe
July 6, 1825

This treaty set forth stipulations for the regulation of trade by the United States and forbade the Cheyenne to furnish guns to tribes hostile to the United States. Concluded at the mouth of the Teton River, the treaty was signed by Henry Atkinson and Benjamin O'Fallon on behalf of the United States. It was also signed by Chiefs Sho-e-mow-e-to-chaw-ca-we-wah-ca-to-we (the Wolf with the High Back), We-che-gla-la (Little Moon), Ta-ton-ca-pa (Buffalo Head), and J-a-pu (the One Who Walks against the Others), and nine Cheyenne warriors.

Treaty with the Hunkapapa Band of the Sioux Tribe

July 16, 1825

This treaty arranged for the regulation of trade by the United States and forbade the Sioux to furnish guns to tribes hostile to the United States. The treaty was concluded at Auricara Village and signed by Benjamin O'Fallon and Henry Atkinson for the United States. It was also signed by Mato-che-gal-lah (Little White Bear), Cha-sa-wa-ne-che (the One that Has No Name), Tah-hah-nee-o-tah (the Womb), Mah-to-wee-tah (White Bear's Face), Pah-sal-sa (Auricara), and Ha-hah-kus-ka (White Elk) on behalf of the Hunkapapa Sioux.

Treaty with the Arikara Tribe

July 18, 1825

This treaty arranged for the regulation of trade by the United States and forbade the Arikara to furnish guns to tribes hostile to the United States. Concluded at the Arikara village, this treaty was signed by Brigadier General Henry Atkinson and Benjamin O'Fallon, U.S. agent of Indian affairs. It was also signed by six Arikara chiefs and fourteen warriors.

Treaty with the Belantse-Etoa or Minitaree Tribe

July 30, 1825

Concluded at the Lower Mandan village, this treaty arranged for the regulation of trade by the United States and forbade the Minitaree tribe to furnish guns and other items to tribes hostile to the United States. The treaty was signed by Henry Atkinson and Benjamin O'Fallon for the United States and by nine Minitaree chiefs and sixteen warriors.

Treaty with the Mandan Tribe

July 30, 1825

This treaty arranged for the regulation of trade by the United States and forbade the Mandan tribe to furnish guns and other items to tribes hostile to the United States. Concluded at the Mandan village, the treaty was signed by Henry Atkinson and Benjamin

O'Fallon for the United States and by seven Mandan chiefs, six warriors of the First Village, and six warriors of the Second Village.

Treaty with the Crow Tribe

August 4, 1825

This treaty arranged for the regulation of trade by the United States and forbade the Crow tribe to furnish guns and other items to tribes hostile to the United States. Concluded at the Mandan village, the treaty was signed by Henry Atkinson and Benjamin O'Fallon for the United States and by sixteen chiefs of the Crow Nation.

Treaty with the Great and Little Osage

August 10, 1825

This treaty was designed to promote peaceful relations between the Osage, who resided along the intended course of a trade route to the Mexican Republic, and those who would travel the road, in return for payment of $500. Concluded at Council Grove, the treaty was signed by Benjamin H. Reeves, George C. Sibley, and Tomas Mather on behalf of the United States and by sixteen Osage representatives.

Treaty with the Kansa

August 16, 1825

This treaty was designed to promote peaceful relations between the Kansa, who resided near the intended course of a trade route to the Mexican Republic, and those who would travel the road, in return for payment of $500. Concluded along the Sora Kansas Creek 238 miles southwest of Fort Osage, this treaty was signed by Benjamin H. Reeves, George C. Sibley, and Thomas Mather for the United States and by sixteen Kansa leaders.

Treaty with the Sioux, Etc.

August 19, 1825

The actual title of this agreement is the Treaty with the Sioux and Chippewa, Sacs and Fox, Menominie,

Ioway, Sioux, Winnebago, and a portion of the Ottawa, Chippewa, Potawattomie Tribes (1825), also known as the Great Council at Prairie du Chien.

In 1825, federal negotiators invited representatives of nearly a dozen different Indian nations of the Great Lakes to Prairie du Chien in present-day southwestern Wisconsin for what was described as a peace and friendship treaty. More than a thousand Native Americans attended the sixteen-day gathering. U.S. officials were anxious to end intertribal conflict, especially between the Ojibwe and the Dakota, which was seen as an impediment to white settlement and trade. Indian agents insisted that chiefs and headmen establish boundaries between each tribe. The demarcation of borders paved the way for future land cession treaties.

The fur trade and other activities had created considerable enmity between the tribes in the Great Lakes. Along the Mississippi River, diplomacy between the Dakota and the Ojibwe had given way to continual attacks and reprisals. In the Fever River valley in present-day southeastern Wisconsin, the Ho-Chunk, Sac, and Fox Indians were at odds with more than ten thousand miners who had illegally invaded their territory. The Menominee were nervous about the arrival, several years earlier, of three New York tribes: the Oneida, the Mohican Nation Stockbridge-Munsee bands, and the Brothertown, who were trying to buy Menominee land. Representatives of the Great Lakes tribes viewed the council at Prairie du Chien as an opportunity to settle some of these disputes.

At the council, General William Clark and Governor Lewis Cass insisted that the tribes declare their boundaries, an exercise that confused some of the Native leaders. Carimine, the Ho-Chunk chief, expressed the sentiments of many tribal leaders at the gathering. Members of the Anishinabe Confederacy—Ojibwe, Potawatomi, and Odawa—were also reluctant to declare their borders. Chambly, an Odawa chief, told the gathering, "I never yet heard from my ancestors that any one had an exclusive right to the soil." Eventually, with the exception of the Menominee, who were underrepresented at the conference, most of the tribes declared their territories and negotiated boundaries.

Federal negotiators complained about the "dispersed condition" of tribes like the Ojibwe and the lack of principal chiefs with whom they could bargain. Each Ojibwe band had several clan leaders and headmen who "governed" by consent rather than ruled by authority. The decentralized nature of the tribes represented at the treaty negotiations was evident in the number of signatures on the document. A total of forty-one Ojibwe, twenty-six Sioux, and twenty-nine Sac and Fox chiefs and headmen signed the treaty.

Although at the time tribal leaders did not understand the implications of declaring boundaries, within a few years they began to realize what it meant. The U.S. government began to approach Indian nations individually and negotiate land cessions.

In 1830, President Andrew Jackson signed the Indian Removal Act, by which government officials began moving tribes located in the eastern portion of the United States to lands west of the Mississippi River. Officials first removed the Sac and Fox, then the Ho-Chunk, then the Potawatomi. Removal orders against the Ojibwe and Menominee were signed but never carried out. The "peace and friendship treaty" at Prairie du Chien had laid the groundwork for the disenfranchisement of thousands of indigenous people from their lands in the Great Lakes region.

Patricia A. Loew

See also Plenary Power; Sovereignty; Treaty; Treaty with the Chippewa–December 20, 1837; Treaty with the Chippewa–October 4, 1842; Trust Doctrine; Trust Lands.

References and Further Reading

Bureau of Indian Affairs. 1960. "Minutes of the 1825 Treaty at Prairie du Chien, August, 1825." *Documents Relating to the Negotiation of Ratified and Unratified Treaties with Various Tribes of Indians, 1801–1869,* in Record Group 75, Records of the Bureau of Indian Affairs, microfilm P97–2750, reel 1. Washington, DC: National Archives.

Loew, Patty. 2001. *Indian Nations of Wisconsin: Histories of Endurance and Renewal.* Madison, WI: Wisconsin Historical Society Press.

Proclamation, "Treaty with the Sioux and Chippewa, Sacs and Fox, Menominie, Ioway, Sioux, Winnebago, and a portion of the Ottawa, Chippewa, Potawattomie, Tribes (1825)," 7 *Stat.* 272 (Feb. 6, 1826).

Treaty with the Otoe and Missouri Tribes

September 26, 1825

Concluded at Fort Atkinson, Council Bluffs, this treaty was designed to regulate trade and perpetuate friendship between the Otoe and Missouri and the United States. It also put into place a negotiated justice system as it related to stolen property and personal conflicts. Under the trade regulations, the Otoe and Missouri were forbidden to trade weapons to tribes hostile to the United States. The treaty was signed by Major Benjamin O'Fallon, Indian agent, and Brigadier General Henry Atkinson on behalf of the United States. It was also signed by eighteen Otoe and Missouri representatives.

Treaty with the Pawnee Tribe

September 30, 1825

Concluded at Fort Atkinson, Council Bluffs, this treaty was designed to regulate trade and perpetuate friendship between the Pawnee and the United States. It also put into place a negotiated justice system as it related to stolen property and personal conflicts. Under the trade regulations, the Pawnee were forbidden to trade weapons to tribes hostile to the United States. The treaty was signed by Major Benjamin O'Fallon, Indian agent, and Brigadier General Henry Atkinson on behalf of the United States. It was also signed by twenty-five Pawnee chiefs, headmen, and warriors.

Treaty with the Makah Tribe

October 6, 1825

Concluded at Fort Atkinson, Council Bluffs, this treaty was designed to regulate trade and perpetuate friendship between the Makah and the United States. Under the trade regulations, the Makah were forbidden to trade weapons to tribes hostile to the United States. The treaty also put into place a negotiated justice system as it related to stolen property and other conflicts. The treaty was signed by Major Benjamin O'Fallon, Indian agent, and Brigadier General Henry Atkinson on behalf of the United States. Fourteen Makah delegates also signed the treaty.

Treaty with the Shawnee

November 7, 1825

This treaty was designed as a renewal of friendship and a Shawnee land cession. Concluded at St. Louis, the treaty recorded the cession of lands near Cape Girardeau, Missouri, taken over by citizens of the United States, in exchange for lands west of the Mississippi River purchased from the Osage for the Missouri and Ohio Shawnee. The United States agreed to pay the tribe $14,000 for the losses related to removal, $5,000 of which was to be paid in provisions upon arrival at the new lands. The treaty was signed by William Clark for the United States and by twelve Shawnee delegates.

Treaty with the Creeks

January 24, 1826

This treaty nullified the Treaty of Indian Springs of February 12, 1825, which the majority of Creeks declared had been signed by individuals lacking authority to enter into treaty negotiations. Concluded at Washington, this new treaty arranged for the cession of Creek lands in Georgia along the Chatahoochie River and a tract along the boundary between Creek and Cherokee lands in Georgia, for $30,000. The Creek Nations agreed to send five representatives to inspect lands west of the Mississippi to find desirable lands to which to remove that were not possessed by the Choctaw or Cherokee or within the states or territories. The Creeks would then have two years to relocate, and the United States agreed to be responsible for expenses incurred and to provide one year's subsistence. Secretary of War James Barbour represented the United States; thirteen representatives of the Creek Nations signed the treaty proper and the supplementary article.

Treaty with the Chippewa

August 5, 1826

The parties to this treaty agreed to the treaty of August 1825 at Prairie du Chien between the Sioux and Chippewa. The treaty arranged for a meeting at Green Bay the following year and allocated land specifically for the use of individuals of mixed Chippewa and white descent, called for a $2,000 yearly annuity to the Chippewa, and appropriated

$1,000 to build a school and support an education program for the youth. The treaty was concluded at Fond du Lac of Lake Superior, Michigan Territory; it was signed by Lewis Cass and Thomas L. McKenney for the United States and by four St. Marys, eleven River St. Croix, five La Pointe, six Lac De Flambeau, twelve Ontonagon, nine Vermilion Lake, four Snake River, six Sandy Lake, ten Fond du Lac, seventeen River de Corbeau, one Rainy Lake, and one Ottawa.

Treaty with the Potawatomi
October 16, 1826

This treaty involved the cession of Potawatomi lands, arranged a twenty-two-year annuity agreement of $2,000 to be paid in silver, with an additional $2,000 to be paid annually toward education for an indeterminate period of time. The treaty also arranged for a mill on the Tippecanoe River, and an annuity of 160 bushels of salt to be delivered by the Indian agent at Fort Wayne. The treaty also includes provisions relating to grants and hunting rights. Concluded in Indiana near the mouth of the Mississinewa on the Wabash River, this treaty was signed by more than sixty Potawatomi leaders and by Lewis Cass, John Tipton, and James Brown Ray on behalf of the United States.

Treaty with the Miami
October 23, 1826

Concluded on the Wabash River near the mouth of the Mississinewa in Indiana, this treaty organized the cession of Miami lands in the state of Indiana north and west of the Miami and Wabash rivers, as well as the land ceded in the October 6, 1818, treaty with the Miami. Reservations were made of certain portions of the ceded lands. The treaty also arranged for the construction of a canal or road through these lands, payment in goods, and annuities; it preserved hunting rights on the ceded lands and provided $2,000 annually for an undetermined period of time to be used for education and the support of the unwell and the unfortunate. The treaty was signed by thirty-seven Miami chiefs and warriors and by Lewis Cass, James Brown Ray, and John Tipton for the United States.

Treaty with the Chippewa, Etc.
August 11, 1827

Concluded on the Fox River at the Butte des Morts, Michigan Territory, this treaty settled the southern boundary of the Chippewa, which the treaty at Prairie du Chien in August 1825 had not determined. It also referred the territorial disputes between the Menominee, the Winnebago, and other New York tribes to the discretion of the president. Under the treaty, the tribes recognized the boundary established between U.S., French, and British jurisdictions. The treaty also arranged for the distribution of goods and an educational appropriation for the tribes. It also asserted that the United States maintained the right to punish certain Winnebago for previous offenses and to act to prevent further offenses. The treaty was signed by Lewis Cass and Thomas L. McKenney for the United States, by sixteen Chippewa representatives, and by more than twenty Menominee representatives.

Treaty with the Potawatomi
September 19, 1827

This treaty organized a further cession of land by the Potawatomi tribe to consolidate the various bands in Michigan Territory in an area removed from the white population. This treaty was concluded at St. Joseph, Michigan Territory, and signed by Lewis Cass for the United States and by nineteen Potawatomi delegates.

Treaty with the Creeks
November 15, 1827

This treaty arranged for the cession of all Creek lands not previously ceded within the state of Georgia. Under this agreement, the United States was obligated to pay the Creek Nations $27,491. It also arranged for a $15,000 payment, with $5,000 to be reserved for the education and support of the children at the Choctaw Academy in Kentucky; $1,000 to be appropriated for the support of the Withington station; $1,000 toward Asbury station; $2,000 for the construction of four horse mills; $1,000 for the purchase of carts and wheels; and $5,000 in blankets and other goods. Concluded at the Creek agency, the treaty was signed by Thomas L. McKenney and John

Cromwell for the United States and by Little Prince and five other Creeks representatives.

Treaty with the Miami
February 11, 1828

This treaty was a cession of land at a village on Sugartree Creek in Indiana previously reserved in treaty to the tribe. In exchange for relinquishing these lands without destroying any improvements already on the lands, the United States was obligated to provide $2,000 in goods, with the promise of $8,000 in goods the succeeding summer. The United States also promised further provisions, including a provision for education, based on terms of ratification. Concluded in Indiana on the Wabash River at the Wyandot village, this treaty was signed by seventeen chiefs and warriors of the Miami of Eel River and Thorntown and by John Tipton, commissioner for the United States.

Treaty with the Western Cherokee
May 6, 1828

Concluded at Washington, this treaty determined the western boundary of Arkansas and required the Cherokee to cede all lands within the boundaries of Arkansas. The United States, in turn, promised seven million acres to the Cherokee west of the determined line and also promised to prevent the trespass of whites on that land. Under this treaty, the Cherokee were to be compensated for the value of improvements left behind on their land and for the cost of removal, which was to occur within fourteen months of the conclusion of the treaty. Thomas Graves, George Maw, George Guess, Thomas Marvis, and John Rogers signed the ratified treaty as chiefs of the Cherokee west of the Mississippi. The initial treaty was signed by John Barbour for the United States and by eight Cherokee leaders.

Treaty with the Winnebago, Etc.
August 25, 1828

This treaty was between the United States and the Sac, Fox, Winnebago, Potawatomi, Ottawa, and Chippewa Nations. It established a provisional boundary between the United States and tribal lands. It also established a system for the United States to deal with white trespassers, miners in par-

The arrival by boat of Lewis Cass and Colonel McKenney at Butte des Morts, Wisconsin, 1827. Cass and McKenney signed the 1827 Treaty with the Chippewa at this site. (Library of Congress)

ticular, on the Indian side of the provisional boundary and required the United States to compensate the tribes for white intrusions. Under the treaty, the United States was allowed to build two ferries over the Rock River and promised to distribute $20,000 in goods among the tribes at a future treaty meeting. Concluded at Greenbay, Michigan Territory, this treaty was signed by more than thirty Winnebago on behalf of the tribes and by Lewis Cass and Pierre Menard for the United States.

Treaty with the Potawatomi

September 20, 1828

This treaty involved the cession of Potawatomi lands and arranged for individual land grants. It also arranged for a permanent annuity of $2,000; a twenty-year annuity of $1,000; $30,000 in goods; and $5,000 in currency to be paid to the tribe in 1829. An additional $7,500 was to be allocated for building, for the support of laborers, and for the purchase of animals and farming equipment. The treaty was concluded at the missionary establishments on the St. Joseph River in the Michigan Territory. It was signed by sixty-nine Potawatomi representatives and by Lewis Cass and Pierre Menard for the United States.

Treaty with the Chippewa, Etc.

July 29, 1829

This treaty was concluded at Prairie du Chien, Michigan Territory. It was an agreement between the United States and the Chippewa, Potawatomi, and Ottawa Nations for land cessions to the United States. In return, the United States agreed to deliver $12,000 worth of goods in October of the same year and permanently to pay the tribes $16,000 annually in currency along with fifty barrels of salt. Certain portions of the cessions were to be reserved for particular bands. The treaty arranged for individual land grants, reserved hunting rights for the tribes, and assumed responsibility for payment of claims against the tribes. The treaty was signed by U.S. delegates John McNiel, Pierre Menard, and Caleb Atwater. Thirty-five tribal representatives also signed.

Treaty with the Winnebago

August 1, 1829

This treaty arranged a Winnebago land cession and the compensation to be provided for that cession by the United States. It also provided for the establishment of three blacksmith shops, for the United States to pay claims against the tribe, and for individual land grants. It was signed by forty-four Winnebago leaders and by John McNiel, Pierre Menard, and Caleb Atwater for the United States.

Treaty with the Delaware

August 3, 1829

Concluded at Little Sandusky, Ohio, this treaty organized a Delaware land cession. Payment of $3,000 was to be made to the Delaware for the cession, $2,000 of which would be paid immediately and $1,000 in the form of provisions for the Delaware's removal west of the Mississippi. The treaty was signed by Captain Pipe, William Matacur, Captain Wolf, Eli Pipe, Solomon Journeycake, Joseph Armstrong, and George Williams for the Delaware and by John McElvain for the United States.

Treaty with the Delaware

September 24, 1829

This treaty was supplemental to the Ohio treaty of October 1818. This treaty stipulated that the United States was responsible for providing lands west of the Mississippi for the Delaware Nation's permanent residence, as well as for furnishing provisions to aid in removal. It required of the United States an additional permanent $1,000 annuity for lands ceded in Missouri and stipulated that certain portions of the ceded land would be sold and the proceeds applied to the education of Delaware children. The treaty was signed by George Vashon, Indian agent, and by principal chief William Anderson and eleven other Delaware representatives at Council Camp on the James Fork of the White River in Missouri.

Treaty with the Sauk and Fox, Etc.

July 15, 1830

This treaty outlined the cession of lands by the Omaha; the confederated Sauk and Fox; the Missouri, Otoe, and Iowa tribes; and the Medawah-Kanton, Wahpeton, Wahpacoota, and Sisseton bands of Sioux. It outlined the purposes for which lands would be used, arranged for annuities and other payment, organized reservation lands, and determined new boundary lines. It was signed by fourteen Sauk, more than forty Fox, nine Wahpacoota, two Sisseton, thirteen Omaha, ten Iowa, fourteen Otoe, five Missouri, and six Missouri Sauk at Prairie du Chien, Michigan Territory. The Yankton and Santee bands of Sioux officially agreed to the treaty on October 13, 1830, at St. Louis by the signing of twenty-three representatives. William Clark, superintendent of Indian affairs, and Colonel Willoughby Morgan signed on behalf of the United States.

Treaty with the Chickasaw

August 31, 1830

Under this treaty, the Chickasaw ceded all lands east of the Mississippi and agreed to remove to lands west of the Mississippi—approximately half one year and the other half the following year. In return, the United States agreed to pay a twenty-year annuity of $15,000 to the tribe, to compensate for the expense of removal, and to aid in subsistence for the first year. The treaty also allotted a ten-year stipend of $2,000 for the hire of Christian teachers and stipulated that the Chickasaw Nation would send twenty "Chickasaw boys of promise, from time to time" over twenty years, to be educated in the United States under the direction of the secretary of war. Concluded at Franklin, Tennessee, this treaty was signed by General John Coffee and Secretary of War John H. Eaton for the United States and by twenty Chickasaw representatives.

Treaty with the Choctaw

September 27, 1830

Also known as the Treaty of Dancing Rabbit Creek, this treaty, signed on September 27, 1830, was the first removal treaty negotiated after the passage of the Indian Removal Act of 1830. By the terms of the treaty, the Choctaw Nation signed away all its land holdings east of the Mississippi River for land in Indian Territory. In exchange for their land, the Choctaw received a twenty-year annuity of $20,000 as well as other monetary allowances to build schools, churches, and a tribal council house in Indian Territory.

The federal government had begun pressuring the Choctaw to relocate in 1820, when General Andrew Jackson was commissioned to meet with three Choctaw district chiefs and other lesser Choctaw officials at Doak's Stand to discuss removal. All three chiefs opposed removal, but Jackson presented to them a bill, proposed by a Mississippi representative to Congress, that would prevent the Choctaw from using or settling on land west of the Mississippi. Although this sounds contrary to government policy, the federal officials thought that, as long as the Choctaw had free access to their western hunting grounds, they would never cede their Mississippi land. They reasoned that, if the Choctaw believed that the United States already owned the western land, the Indians might be willing to cede part of their eastern land in order to keep their western hunting grounds. The treaty did not require any Choctaw to leave their homes; those wishing to stay on the ceded land would receive a one-square-mile tract of land, to include their improvements.

The Choctaw's new territory had not yet been surveyed when the Treaty of Doak's Stand was ratified. When the land was surveyed, it was discovered that white settlements already existed on the land. The federal government believed it would be almost impossible to remove the white settlers, so government officials requested that a Choctaw delegation come to Washington in the fall of 1824 to negotiate a new boundary line for the Choctaw's western land.

After the treaty of 1825 was negotiated, the United States expected the Choctaw to leave for their new land in Indian Territory. However, the majority of the Choctaw did not move. Consequently, the federal government and the state of Mississippi increased pressure on the Choctaw to remove. In 1829, the Mississippi legislature took strong action against the Choctaw people and extended Mississippi state laws over the Indians. In January 1830, the Choctaw became citizens of Mississippi; their tribal government was abolished, and any Indian exercising the office of chief or headman became subject to fines and imprisonment. The federal government passed the Indian Removal Act and informed the Choctaw Nation that they would not be protected from hostile Mississippi State laws.

After Mississippi extended its laws over the Choctaw, the Indians were constantly harassed by white settlers. To obtain relief, the Choctaw leadership requested a meeting with federal officials at the Dancing Rabbit Creek campgrounds. The negotiations dragged on for about two weeks. When the negotiations began to fail, the government purchased the signatures of the leaders with valuable land grants, lifelong salaries, and other presents. In the end, the government secured the leadership's cooperation by playing to the Choctaw leadership's lust for money and power.

As soon as the Treaty of Dancing Rabbit Creek was signed, the Choctaw people let it be known that they were outraged by the actions of their chiefs. Different factions elected different chiefs, and anarchy prevailed in the Choctaw Nation. However, little could be done. A few Choctaw left immediately for Indian Territory in order to claim the best land, but most waited to be moved by the U.S. government in one of three planned moves in 1831, 1832, or 1833. Removal proved to be an extremely difficult experience for the Choctaw. Out of 14,000 tribal members and 512 slaves who left Mississippi during these years, at least 2,500 died during the travel west. More died after reaching Indian Territory due to inadequate food supplies and severe weather.

Around 6,000 Choctaw decided to take advantage of Article 14 of the treaty, which provided an opportunity for the Choctaw to remain in Mississippi; any head of household could apply for and receive U.S. citizenship, along with 640 acres of land. These people did not fare well, either. The Choctaw agency refused to let most of the Indians register for land allotments, and the paperwork for most of the remaining people who did register was lost. In the end, only sixty-nine heads of household were officially registered. The vast majority of the Choctaw remaining in Mississippi became squatters living in isolated areas on poor farmland. They lost all access to schools and public services and survived as best they could by gathering nuts and wild berries and by growing corn, pumpkins, and potatoes. Some worked for white farmers picking cotton, hoeing the fields, and doing other menial tasks. Many of these people eventually went to Indian Territory during the 1840s.

Joyce Ann Kievit

See also Dancing Rabbit Creek, Mississippi; Doak's Stand, Mississippi; Doaksville, Oklahoma; LeFlore, Greenwood; Treaty with the Choctaw–October 18, 1820.

References and Further Reading

Baird, W. David. 1973. *The Choctaw People*. Phoenix, AZ: Indian Tribal Series.

Debo, Angie. 1967. *The Rise and Fall of the Choctaw Republic*. Norman: University of Oklahoma Press.

Kidwell, Clara Sue. 1995. *Choctaws and Missionaries in Mississippi, 1818–1918*. Norman: University of Oklahoma Press.

McKee, Jesse O., and Jon A. Schlenker. 1980. *The Choctaws: Cultural Evolution of a Native American Tribe*. Jackson: University Press of Mississippi.

Treaty with the Menominee
February 8, 1831

This treaty settled the boundaries of Menominee lands, as they were disputed by other New York tribes, in part by requiring the Menominee to cede certain portions of these lands. The United States agreed to compensate them with $20,000 to be paid over four years, $1,500 annually for education the first year, and $2,000 for the following ten years. Certain privileges, including hunting and fishing rights, were reserved to the tribe, and arrangements were made for reservation lands and structural improvements, including a gristmill and a sawmill. Concluded at the city of Washington, this treaty was signed by John H. Eaton, secretary of war, and Samuel C. Stambaugh, the Indian agent at Green Bay, for the United States and by twelve Menominee leaders.

Treaty with the Menominee
February 17, 1831

This treaty was supplemental to the treaty of February 8, 1831. It amended the first and sixth articles of the previous treaties, which related to the settlement or removal of New York Indians on Menominee lands. The changes gave increased discretionary power over the issue to the president of the United States. Concluded at Washington, the treaty was signed by John H. Eaton and Samuel C. Stambaugh for the United States and by twelve chiefs and warriors of the Menominee.

Treaty with the Seneca

February 28, 1831

This treaty organized the cession of Ohio lands and the removal of the Seneca to lands west of the Mississippi. It also obligated the United States to implement certain compensatory measures, including a $6,000 advancement, annuities, land grants, supplies, and defrayment of costs incurred through removal. Concluded at Washington, the treaty was signed by Comstick, Small Cloud Spicer, Seneca Steel, Hard Hickory, and Captain Good Hunter of the Seneca and by Commissioner James B. Gardener for the United States.

Treaty with the Seneca, Etc.

July 20, 1831

Concluded at Pleasant Plains near Lewiston, Logan County, Ohio, this treaty arranged for Seneca and Shawnee land cessions and for the removal of these people to land west of the Mississippi. Under this treaty, the United States would provide $6,000 for improvements on the ceded lands, a sawmill and a blacksmith shop on the new lands, and goods and provisions to sustain the tribes for the first year after removal. The treaty was signed by James B. Gardner and Indian agent John McElvain on behalf of the United States and by thirteen chiefs and warriors of the mixed band of Shawnee and Seneca.

Treaty with the Shawnee

August 8, 1831

This treaty arranged for the cession of Shawnee lands in Ohio and for removal of the Wapaghkonnetta and Hog Creek Shawnee west of the Mississippi. Under this agreement, the United States agreed to supply goods and provisions for the first year after removal; to defray the costs of the move; to build a sawmill, a gristmill, and a blacksmith shop on the new land; to pay compensation of $13,000 for land sales; and to continue to pay annuities promised in former treaties. The treaty was signed at Wapaghkonnetta, Allen County, Ohio, by twenty-one Shawnee chiefs, headmen, and warriors and by James B. Gardiner and John McElvain for the United States.

Treaty with the Ottawa

August 30, 1831

This treaty arranged the cession of Ottawa lands in Ohio, negating the reservation of lands promised the tribe in the treaty of November 17, 1807, and the treaty of September 29, 1817, in exchange for lands west of the Mississippi. This treaty specifically affected the bands residing on the Little Auglaize River at Oquanoxie's Village and along Blanchard's Fork of the Great Auglaize River. Under this treaty, the United States was obligated to defray the cost of removal, to supply one year's provisions upon arrival of the Ottawa in the West, to pay $2,000 in advance for improvements on ceded Ohio lands, to pay a portion of the annuities promised the Ottawa Nation in former treaties, and to distribute goods. It also stipulated that certain lands would be temporarily reserved for certain individuals and organized individual land grants. Concluded at Miami Bay Lake Erie, the document was signed by James B. Gardiner for the United States and by more than twenty Ottawa headmen and warriors.

Treaty with the Wyandot

January 19, 1832

Concluded at McCutcheonsville, Crawford County, Ohio, this treaty arranged the cession of sixteen thousand acres of Wyandot land in Ohio. Under this treaty, the Wyandot of Big Spring were expected to choose between moving to Canada, to the Huron River in Michigan, or to any other Indian lands where they were welcome. This treaty called for a subagent to be appointed to this band and for the United States to pay for improvements. The treaty was signed by Roe-nu-nas, Bear-skin, Shi-a-wa (John Solomon), John McLean, Matthew Grey Eyes, Isaac Driver, John D. Brown, and Alex Clark for the Wyandot and by John B. Gardiner for the United States.

Treaty with the Creeks

March 24, 1832

This treaty arranged for the cession of all remaining Creek lands east of the Mississippi in exchange for five years of $12,000 annuities followed by fifteen years of $10,000 annuities, $100,000 with which to pay debt claims against the tribe, and $16,000 for the expenses of the delegation to Washington and for claims brought against them. The United States was also to pay for the cost of removal to the new lands. Concluded at Washington, the treaty was signed by Lewis Cass for the United States and by Opothleholo, Tuchebatcheehadgo, Efiematla, Tuchebatche Micco, Tomack Micco, William McGilvery, and Benjamin Marshall for the Creek Nations.

Treaty with the Seminole
May 9, 1832

Concluded at Payne's Landing on the Ocklewaha River, this treaty arranged for the cession of Seminole lands in Florida and for removal to Creek lands west of the Mississippi, which might be extended proportionate to their number. The United States agreed to pay the Seminole tribe $15,400 in compensation, $400 of which would be divided between the two treaty interpreters. The treaty also obligated the United States to increase present annuity arrangements made in the treaty at Camp Moultrie by $3,000 a year for fifteen years, to defray the costs of the move, and to supply subsistence for up to one year after arrival. The treaty was signed by James Gadsden for the United States and by fifteen Seminole chiefs and headmen.

Treaty with the Winnebago
September 15, 1832

Concluded at Fort Armstrong, Rock Island, Illinois, this treaty organized the cession of Winnebago lands in exchange for lands west of the Mississippi. The United States agreed to pay $10,000 in currency annually for twenty-seven years, to establish and maintain educational facilities for the tribe, to pay $2,500 annually in agricultural support, to supply 1,500 pounds of tobacco annually to the Rock River band, to provide funding for two physicians, to relocate the blacksmith shop, and to provide limited rations. The treaty required the bands to deliver up offenders to U.S. authorities for punishment and to relinquish all hunting, planting, fishing, and other privileges on the ceded lands. The treaty was signed by Winfield Scott and John Reynolds for the United States and by more than thirty Winnebago chiefs, warriors, and headmen.

Treaty with the Sauk and Fox
September 21, 1832

Concluded at Fort Armstrong, Rock Island, Illinois, this treaty organized the cession of Sauk and Fox lands and arranged for removal of the confederated tribes to reservation lands near the Mississippi River and spanning the Iowa River. The United States was obligated to pay a thirty-year annuity of $20,000, to provide a blacksmith shop and a gunsmith shop for thirty years, to provide a yearly allowance of tobacco and salt for thirty years, to pay $40,000 of debt owed two traders by the Sauk and Fox, and to release Sauk and Fox prisoners, with the exception of certain leaders who would be kept as hostages to ensure the compliance of recently hostile bands. The treaty also required the hostile bands to be absorbed by the neutral bands. General Winfield Scott and John Reynolds signed on behalf of the United States; nine Sauk and twenty-four Fox also signed.

Treaty with the Appalachicola Band
October 11, 1832

This treaty called for the relinquishment of the reservation set aside for the Appalachicola in the Fort Moultrie treaty in Florida in September 1823, in exchange for land west of the Mississippi. It obligated the United States to cover the expense of removal, to pay $3,000 in currency and $10,000 when complete removal was under way, and to distribute the $5,000 annuities promised in the former treaty. The treaty was signed at Tallahassee, Florida Territory, by John Blunt, O Saa-Hajo (Davy), and Co-ha-thlock-co (Cockrane) for the Appalachicola band and by James Gadsden for the United States.

Treaty with the Potawatomi
October 20, 1832

Concluded at Camp Tippecanoe, Indiana, this treaty arranged for the cession of Potawatomi lands and allowed for individual reservations. In return, the United States agreed to pay the Potawatomi $15,000 annually for twenty years, with additional lifetime annuities going to certain individuals; to pay claims against the tribe; to pay $45,000 in merchandise immediately upon signing the treaty and an additional $30,000 the following year; and to pay for horses taken from the tribe during the recent war. The treaty guaranteed the Potawatomi the right to hunt and fish on the ceded lands. It was signed by Jonathan Jennings, John W. Davis, and Marks Crume as commissioners for the United States and by more than sixty Potawatomi.

Treaty with the Chickasaw
October 20, 1832

This treaty arranged for the cession of Chickasaw lands east of the Mississippi in exchange for land west of the Mississippi. Under this treaty, the United States was obligated to pay arranged annuities and other compensation and to settle boundary lines with the Choctaw. The treaty also forbade the occupation of Chickasaw lands before their sale. Concluded at the Council House on Pontitock Creek in the Chickasaw Nation, the treaty was signed by John Coffee for the United States and by sixty-five representatives of the Chickasaw Nation.

Treaty with the Chickasaw
October 22, 1832

This agreement was supplementary to the treaty of October 20, 1832, and specified that lands reserved to Chickasaw families were not to be sold or leased by them to anyone. Instead, sale agreements would be determined by chiefs and the president. The treaty also arranged for a mail route to cross Chickasaw lands. Concluded at Pontitock Creek, the treaty was signed by John Coffee for the United States and by more than seventy Chickasaw representatives.

Treaty with the Kickapoo
October 24, 1832

Under this treaty, the Kickapoo relinquished the lands reserved for them by the 1822 Treaty of Edwardsville and all other lands in the state of Missouri, in exchange for land southwest of the Mississippi River. The United States also agreed to pay $18,000, $12,000 of which would be given to the superintendent of Indian affairs to be applied to the tribe's debts, and any balance remaining would be returned to the tribe. The United States was also to pay a $5,000 annuity in currency or goods for nine-

teen years, to begin the second year after ratification, with additional sums to be paid for other services and establishments. Concluded at Castor Hill, St. Louis County, Missouri, the treaty was signed by William Clark, Frank J. Allen, and Nathan Kouns for the United States and by nineteen Kickapoo representatives.

Treaty with the Potawatomi
October 26, 1832

The treaty was a cession of Potawatomi lands in the state of Indiana, with limited reservations for certain bands, in exchange for annuities and payments in goods. The United States agreed to pay for debts against the tribe and to construct a sawmill on the reserved lands. Concluded on the Tippecanoe River in Indiana, this treaty was signed by Marks Crume, Jonathan Jennings, and John W. Davis for the United States and by more than forty Potawatomi chiefs, headmen, and warriors.

Treaty with the Shawnee, Etc.
October 26, 1832

Concluded at Castor Hill, St. Louis County, Missouri, this treaty organized the cession of Shawnee and Delaware lands in Missouri. In return, the United States agreed to pay the Delaware for improvements to the land, maintenance of a mill, support for education, purchase of cattle and other stock, to pay Delaware debts, and to help compensate for costs incurred during removal. The treaty required the Shawnee to remove all bands in the Arkansas Territory to the Kansa River. The United States would compensate the tribes in currency and goods, to be applied toward removal expenses. The treaty was signed by William Clark, Frank J. Allen, and Nathan Kouns for the United States and by ten representatives of the Shawnee and Delaware.

Treaty with the Potawatomi
October 26, 1832

This treaty made limited reservations for certain bands from the cession. The United States was obligated to pay the tribe a twenty-year annuity of $20,000; to deliver $100,000 in goods upon the conclusion of the treaty; to pay an additional $30,000 in goods the following year, to be delivered by the Indian agent; and to pay the debts of the Potawatomi. Concluded on the Tippecanoe River in Indiana, the treaty was signed by Marks Crume, Jonathan Jennings, and John W. Davis for the United States and by more than forty Potawatomi chiefs, headmen, and warriors.

Treaty with the Kaskaskia, Etc.
October 27, 1832

Concluded at Castor Hill, St. Louis County, Missouri, this treaty was arranged between the Peoria and Kaskaskia tribes and the Michigamia, Cahokia, and Tamarois bands, formerly of the Illinois Nation. The treaty arranged for the uniting of the Kaskaskia and Peoria through the cession of lands occupied by the Kaskaskia under the August 13, 1803, treaty at Vincennes in Illinois and Missouri, for their removal from those lands to those possessed by the Peoria west of Missouri, and for some addition to these lands. The Kaskaskia were required to give up former annuity agreements. The treaty was signed by William Clark, Frank J. Allen, and Nathan Kouns for the United States and by five Peoria and four Kaskaskia.

Treaty with the Menominee
October 27, 1832

This treaty was a follow-up to the February 1831 treaties, which stipulated that the Menominee would relinquish some of their lands for the use of the Munsee, Brothertown, and Stockbridge Indians of New York. It determined the new boundaries and reservations. The treaty was signed at the agency house at Green Bay by George B. Porter for the United States and by eighteen Menominee representatives.

Treaty with the Piankashaw and Wea
October 29, 1832

This treaty organized the cession of remaining Piankashaw and Wea lands in Missouri and Illinois in exchange for a tract of land near the Peoria west of Missouri. The United States agreed to pay the Piankashaw in livestock and merchandise annually for five years for losses incurred during removal, up to a $500 value; it also agreed to pay $750 for agricul-

tural assistance and $200 in merchandise upon conclusion of the treaty. The Wea received a $500 value in livestock and other goods, and $200 in cash and merchandise upon signing. The Wea of Indiana would be assisted in joining this group. Concluded at Castor Hill, St. Louis County, Missouri, the treaty was signed by William Clark, Frank J. Allen, and Nathan Kouns on behalf of the United States and by three Wea and two Piankashaw.

Treaty with the Seneca and Shawnee
December 29, 1832

Concluded at the Seneca agency on the Cowskin River, this treaty organized the cession of Seneca and Shawnee land granted in the July 1831 treaty, in exchange for different lands west of the Mississippi that would better accommodate the recent union of the two tribes. The United States agreed to build immediately a gristmill, a sawmill, and a blacksmith shop and to pay $1,000, to be divided between the Seneca of Sandusky and the Seneca and Shawnee from Lewiston. The treaty was signed by Henry J. Ellsworth and John F. Schermerhorn for the United States and by fourteen Seneca chiefs and twelve chiefs of the Seneca and Shawnee mixed band.

Treaty with the Western Cherokee
February 14, 1833

This treaty took place after councils held between the Cherokee and the Creek Nations regarding overlapping lands outlined in treaties; it stipulated the new boundary agreed on between the two nations. It also obligated the United States to correct the situation by recognizing this new boundary and by reserving additional lands to the tribes to equal the intended space documented in previous treaties. The United States also agreed to provide materials to build and support four blacksmith shops, one wagon-maker's shop, and one wheelwright shop, and to erect eight patent railway corn mills. Concluded at Fort Gibson on the Arkansas River, the treaty was signed by Montfort Stokes, Henry L. Ellsworth, and John F. Schermerhorn for the United States and by John Jolly, Black Coat, Walter Weller, and principal chiefs John Rogers and Glass for the Western Cherokee.

Treaty with the Creeks
February 14, 1833

This treaty supports the same objects as the treaty made the same day with the Western Cherokee. This treaty also covered the Seminole, who wished to rejoin the Creeks, noting that the Seminole would live on land reserved for the Creek Nations but located in a separated area. This treaty also obligated the United States to build and support certain shops and mills and to fund education. The treaty was concluded at Fort Gibson; it was signed by Montfort Stokes, Henry L. Ellsworth, and John F. Schermerhorn for the United States and by nine Creek chiefs.

Treaty with the Ottawa
February 18, 1833

Under this treaty, the Ottawa ceded two reservations and any other land located in the vicinity of the Miami River or Miami Bay of Lake Erie. The treaty outlined reservations to be made for individuals or small groups and obligated the United States to pay $29,440 to the tribe for payment of claims against them. Concluded at Maumee, Ohio, the treaty was signed by George B. Porter for the United States and by twenty-one Ottawa chiefs and headmen.

Treaty with the Seminole
March 28, 1833

This treaty related to the treaty with the Creek in February 1833 and the 1832 treaty at Payne's Landing. Under this treaty, the Seminole were allotted their portion of the lands then occupied by the Creek Nation, and the appointment of Major Phagen was requested to organize and aid in Seminole relocation west of the Mississippi. Concluded at Fort Gibson, the treaty was signed by Montfort Stokes, Henry L. Ellsworth, and John F. Schermerhorn for the United States and by John Hick, Holata Emartta, Jumper, Coe Hadgo, Charley Emartta, Ya-ha-hadge, and Ne-ha-tho-clo for the Seminole.

Treaty with the Quapaw
May 13, 1833

This treaty recognized the difficulties encountered by the Quapaw due to the location in which the United States placed them according to the November 15, 1824, treaty. With this treaty, the Quapaw ceded the lands on the Bayou Treache of the Red River (Caddo land) in exchange for different land west of Missouri. The United States agreed to pay for relocation and debts; to supply the Quapaw with a year of provisions, livestock, and other merchandise, including farming and agricultural tools; and to pay $1,000 dollars annually for educational purposes and a twenty-year annuity of $2,000. The treaty was signed by John F. Schermerhorn for the United States and by eleven Quapaw.

Treaty with the Appalachicola Band
June 18, 1833

This treaty called for the cession of lands set aside for the band in the September 1823 treaty at Camp Moultrie, in exchange for small individual or group reservations. It also stipulated that, once the Seminole were removed, the protection of the United States would cease, and the Appalachicola would be subject to the laws of Florida Territory if they chose to remain. The United States was still obligated to pay to those remaining in Florida Territory the $5,000 annuity promised under the Camp Moultrie treaty. Concluded at Pope's, Fayette County, Florida Territory, this treaty was signed by James Gadsden for the United States and by nine Appalachicola.

Treaty with the Otoe and Missouri
September 21, 1833

Concluded at the Otoe village on the Platte River, this treaty organized a land cession and outlined the conditions of the cession. The United States was obligated to continue the $2,500 annuity promised in the Treaty of Prairie du Chien, to continue the $500 annuity for agricultural supplies, to pay a five-year annuity of $500 for education, to construct a corn-grinding mill, to provide five years of agricultural assistance, to provide $1,000 in livestock, and to pay $400 in goods and merchandise at the conclusion of the treaty signing. The treaty was signed by Henry L. Ellsworth for the United States and by twenty-six Otoe and Missouri representatives.

Treaty with the Chippewa, Etc.
September 26, 1833

Also called the Treaty of Chicago, this treaty was negotiated in September 1833 in Chicago, Illinois, and it arranged for the cession of lands in northeastern Illinois, southeastern Wisconsin, and southern Michigan. It also provided for the removal of the United Band of Ottawa, Chippewa, and Potawatomi Indians from the region. As a result of both the rapid expansion in settlement in the western Great Lakes region and the military might displayed by federal and local governments in the Black Hawk War a year earlier, representatives of the United Band and other Potawatomi groups agreed to meet with U.S. commissioners. At the end of the negotiations, the Indians had ceded approximately five million acres, and most had agreed to relocate to new homes west of the Mississippi River.

Fleeing bands of Sauk and Fox caught and attacked by American troops, leading to the Battle of Bad Axe August 1, 1832, at the mouth of the Mississippi River, the final conflict of the Black Hawk War. This war, in which the federal and local governments displayed their military might, was one of the factors leading up to the historic 1833 Treaty of Chicago. (North Wind Picture Archives)

The opening of the Erie Canal in 1825 after eight years of construction. The Erie Canal was the longest canal of its time, running throughout the New York wilderness and linking Lake Erie to the Hudson River. (Library of Congress)

By the early 1830s, the advancement of American settlement and the opening of the Erie Canal had tremendously increased the scale of American migration into the western Great Lakes region. The non-Indian population of Illinois alone had tripled in the period from statehood in 1818 to 1830. Although initial settlement had focused on the lead-mining region in the northwestern part of the state, the scope had begun to change. This encroachment, combined with the passage of the Indian Removal Act in 1830, increased the pressure on resident Indian groups to move to lands west of the Mississippi. In the fall of 1833, three government-designated treaty commissioners met in Chicago with the representatives of some of the largest Native landholders remaining in the region. More than eight thousand Indians and Americans gathered by the shores of Lake Michigan to participate in the negotiations, which lasted for more than two weeks.

The treaty can be separated into two parts. The first and largest portion of the treaty addressed the negotiations made with the representatives of the United Band of Ottawa, Chippewa, and Potawatomi Indians. In this section, the United Band ceded claims to all of its lands in northeastern Illinois and southeastern Wisconsin, which consisted of approximately five million acres. In return, the United States granted an equal amount of land located just north of the state of Missouri, to which the Indians were required to remove within three years from the date of ratification of the treaty. Additional articles provided money for education, agriculture, debt payments, and expenses related to the future removal. The second part of the treaty encompassed several supplementary agreements and addressed separate negotiations with the Potawatomi residents of southern Michigan. These bands and their main spokesman, Pokagun, represented the strongest opposition to removal among the participating Indian groups. As a result of this resistance to relocation, the treaty commissioners negotiated a separate accord with these Indians. Although the primary supplement did arrange for the cession of all their lands in southern Michigan, an addendum allowed for some of these Michigan Potawatomis to move onto lands in northern Michigan, as opposed to lands west of the Mississippi.

Assessment of this treaty's impact must take into account a number of issues. In the first place, the treaty arranged the removal of a significant population of Indians from the western Great Lakes region and opened up five million acres to American settlers. But the treaty's influence went beyond this cession of Native-owned lands. Significantly, the treaty and its addenda illustrated some of the ways in which populations of Indian peoples avoided removal. In particular, Pokagun's stance against the land cession led to the treaty addendum that provided an exemption for his band in southern Michigan. This community of Potawatomi maintained a presence in the region long after the United Band had moved to the Council Bluffs area in Iowa Territory. Finally, the negotiations in 1833 illustrated the growing influence of individuals of mixed descent within the United Band in particular. Two of the men designated as chiefs who signed the treaty, Billy Caldwell and Alexander Robinson, were not men born into the United Band. Caldwell, or Saukenuk, came from a Mohawk-Irish lineage; Robinson, or Cheecheebinquay, from an Ottawa-British one. Both men received lifetime annuities through the treaty as well as $5,000 each to pay debts incurred through trading with the United Bands.

John P. Bowes

See also Caldwell, Billy; Indian Removal; Indian Removal Act, 1830; Pokagun.

References and Further Reading
Clifton, James A. 1977. *The Prairie People: Continuity and Change in Potawatomi Indian Culture 1665–1965*. Lawrence: Regents Press of Kansas.
Edmunds, R. David. 1978. *The Potawatomis, Keepers of the Fire*. Norman: University of Oklahoma Press.
Tanner, Helen Hornbeck. 1987. Ed. *Atlas of Great Lakes Indian History*. Norman: University of Oklahoma Press.

Treaty with the Pawnee
October 9, 1833
This treaty arranged for the cession by confederated bands of Pawnee of all land south of the Platte River, with the retention of hunting rights upon said land. The United States was obligated to pay the Pawnee a twelve-year annuity of $4,600 in goods, an additional five-year annuity of $500 for agricultural supplies, and a ten-year annuity of $1,000 for education, and to supply and support a blacksmith shop and four corn-grinding mills. The four bands would also receive $1,000 in goods and merchandise upon signing the treaty. Concluded at the Grand Pawnee village on the Platte River, this treaty was signed by Henry L. Ellsworth for the United States and by four Grand Pawnee, four Pawnee Republican, four Tappaye Pawnee, and four Pawnee Loup representatives.

Treaty with the Chickasaw
May 24, 1834
This treaty was designed to maintain peaceful relations, to aid the Chickasaw in removal, to protect Chickasaw lands, to distribute grants and reservations, to determine boundaries, and to regulate land sales. It also included supplementary articles regarding individuals, ceded reservation land, stolen money, and educational provisions. Concluded at Washington, the treaty was signed by Commissioner John H. Eaton for the United States and by George Colbert and Isaac Albertson for the Chickasaw.

Treaty with the Miami
October 23, 1834
This treaty arranged the cession of lands reserved to the Miami in Indiana for previous cessions. In return, the United States agreed to pay the Miami $200,000, to issue individual patents and land grants, to substitute a miller for the blacksmith promised in a previous treaty, and to compensate the tribe for horses stolen by whites. Concluded at the forks of the Wabash River in Indiana, the treaty was signed by William Marshall for the United States and by thirty-one Miami chiefs and warriors.

Treaty with the Potawatomi
December 10, 1834
The tribe ceded six sections of land temporarily reserved to them in the October 1832 treaty at Tippecanoe. The United States agreed to pay $400 in goods and a two-year annuity of $1,000. Concluded on the Tippecanoe River in Indiana, the treaty was signed by William Marshall for the United States and by Muck Rose, Paw-tisse, Sis-see-yaw, Wau-pish-shaw, and Koo-tah-waun-nay for the Potawatomi.

Treaty with the Potawatomi
December 16, 1834

Because the cessions made in the previous treaty included mills, the United States agreed to compensate for the losses by paying $700 in currency and putting $900 toward the tribe's debts. Concluded at the Potawatomi mills in Indiana, this treaty was signed by twenty-five Potawatomi chiefs, headmen, and warriors and by U.S. Commissioner William Marshall.

Treaty with the Potawatomi
December 17, 1834

This treaty arranged for the removal of the tribe west of the Mississippi at the cost of the United States. The United States agreed to pay $680 in goods to the chief and headmen at the signing of the treaty, as well as $600 in currency for the 1835 annuity. Concluded at the Indian agency, Logansport, Indiana, this treaty was signed by Commissioner William Marshall for the United States and by Chief Mo-ta and seventeen Potawatomi headmen.

Treaty with the Potawatomi
December 24, 1834

Concluded on Lake Max-ee-nie-kue-kee in Indiana, this treaty arranged for further cession of Potawatomi lands reserved in the 1832 treaty at Tippecanoe. In return, the United States paid $400 in goods at the conclusion of the treaty. The treaty was signed by William Marshall for the United States and by Com-o-za, Ah-ke-pah-am-sa, Nee-so-aw-quet, and Paw-pee for the Potawatomi.

Agreement with the Cherokee
March 14, 1835

Concluded at Washington, this treaty is a provisional set of arrangements to be presented to and potentially approved by the Cherokee east of the Mississippi, including a proposal for the United States to pay $4,500,000 for the cession of all Cherokee lands east of the Mississippi. This agreement was not ratified.

Treaty with the Caddo
July 1, 1835

This treaty arranged a land cession and required removal at the expense of the Caddo Nation. The United States agreed to pay the Caddo $30,000 in goods and horses at the conclusion of the treaty and a five-year annuity of $10,000 in currency. Concluded at the agency house in the Caddo Nation, Louisiana, this treaty was signed by Jehiel Brooks for the United States and twenty-five Caddo chiefs, headmen, and warriors.

Treaty with the Comanche, Etc.
August 4, 1835

This treaty was between the Comanche, Wichita, and tribes or bands associated with them, and the Cherokee, Muscogee (Creek), Choctaw, Osage, Seneca, and Quapaw. The treaty was designed to establish peace between these contending tribes and to arrange safe passage of U.S. citizens through their lands while traveling to or from Mexico. It also arranged for a negotiated justice system. The treaty was signed by Montfort Stokes and Brigadier General M. Arbuckle for the United States and by nineteen Comanche, fifteen Wichita, two Cherokee, more than forty Muscogee, thirty-one Choctaw, thirty-seven Osage, eighteen Seneca, and twenty-two Quapaw.

Treaty with the Cherokee
December 29, 1835

Also called the Treaty of New Echota, this was a removal agreement between the federal government and a minority faction of the Cherokee Nation signed on December 29, 1835, in the town of New Echota, Georgia. According to the terms of the treaty, the Cherokee Nation exchanged all their land east of Mississippi for a large tract of land in Indian Territory and $5 million.

In 1830, Congress passed the Indian Removal Act, which provided funds for the president to conduct land-exchange treaties with Indians living east of the Mississippi. Initially, federal negotiators tried to coerce principal chief John Ross and members of the Cherokee National Council to remove to the West. When federal negotiators were unable to convince the elected Cherokee leadership to sign a removal treaty, President Andrew Jackson sent

John Ridge (1827–1867), one of the Cherokees who supported removal in the negotiation of the Treaty of New Echota. (Library of Congress)

General William Carroll and Reverend John Schermerhorn to draw up a treaty with a few prominent Cherokees who favored removal. Members of this faction, later called the Treaty Party, included Major Ridge, John Ridge, Stand Watie, and Elias Boudinot.

Major Ridge was a former acting chief of the Cherokee Nation and a wealthy, slave-owning planter. He was familiar with the laws of the Nation and knew he was in violation of the Blood Law, which made the sale or cession of Cherokee land a crime punishable by death. However, he and other members of the faction were greatly disturbed by the constant harassment they and other Indians received from white settlers. In 1829 and 1830, the Georgia legislature passed a series of laws that outlawed the Cherokee government and authorized a survey of Cherokee land and a lottery to distribute the land to the white residents of Georgia. The legislature also passed the Indian Code, which prohibited Cherokees from testifying in court against white persons, mining gold on their own land, speaking against removal, and meeting in council.

After several trips to Washington to talk to federal officials and a survey of the countryside, Ridge believed that it was in the best interest of the Cherokee Nation as a whole to relocate in the West. He thought that further resistance to federal removal demands would be futile, that the Chero-

kee should get the best terms possible from the government and depart before there was more bloodshed.

Immediately after signing the document and receiving their payment from the government, the members of the Treaty Party moved west. They selected the best land in the new Cherokee Nation and made alliances with the three thousand "Old Settler" Cherokees, who had left the main body of the Cherokee Nation in the late eighteenth and early nineteenth centuries for various reasons. While the Treaty Party adjusted to their homes in the West, principal chief John Ross, members of the Cherokee National Council, and the vast majority of the Cherokees living in the East repudiated the treaty and refused to move.

They vigorously protested the treaty and made their cause known to the American people. Regardless of the protests, the Senate ratified the treaty by one vote in May 1836. Undaunted, the Cherokee Nation continued to lobby against the treaty and to postpone the removal process. In April 1838, approximately 15,600 of the 16,000 members of the Cherokee Nation signed and presented a petition to Congress requesting that the treaty be voided. Congress ignored the petition.

In May 1838, federal officials became frustrated with the Cherokee resistance. President Martin Van Buren ordered General Winfield Scott and seven

Major Ridge (1771–1839) was a former acting chief of the Cherokee Nation and a wealthy, slave-owning planter. (Library of Congress)

lots to select the assassins. Early in the morning of June 22, the assassins left the campgrounds in search of Major Ridge, John Ridge, Elias Boudinot, and Stand Watie. Both of the Ridges and Boudinot were executed; fortunately, Stand Watie was able to escape. The executions intensified the preexisting tribal divisions and caused an intermittent civil war to rage through the Cherokee Nation for the next forty years.

Joyce Ann Kievit

See also Boudinot, Elias; Indian Removal; Indian Removal Act, 1830; New Echota, Georgia; Ridge, John Rollin; Ridge, Major; Ross, John; Trail of Tears; Watie, Stand.

References and Further Reading

Agnew, Brad. 1980. *Fort Gibson, Terminal on the Trail of Tears*. Norman: University of Oklahoma Press.

Dale, Edward Everett, and Gaston Litton. 1969. *Cherokee Cavaliers: Forty Years of Cherokee History as Told in the Correspondence of the Ridge-Watie-Boudinot Family*. Norman: University of Oklahoma Press.

Foreman, Grant. 1953. *Indian Removal: The Emigration of the Five Civilized Tribes of Indians*. Norman: University of Oklahoma Press.

Moulton, Gary E., ed. 1985. *The Papers of Chief John Ross*. 2 vols. Norman: University of Oklahoma Press.

Stand Watie (1806–1871), a member of the Treaty Party faction during the development of the Treaty of New Echota. (National Archives and Records Administration)

thousand soldiers to round up all Cherokees living in Georgia, Alabama, and Tennessee, and place them into camps to prepare for removal. To discourage the people from running away and returning to their homes, Scott had all Cherokee property burned and all crops destroyed. The forced march to the West began during the summer of 1838 and continued through the harsh winter of 1839. Of 16,543 Cherokees and 1,592 slaves removed, one quarter of the people died. The Cherokee call their trek west *Nunna daul Tsuny*—"the trail where they cried."

Once the majority of the Cherokee arrived in the West, the three distinct groups of Cherokee people— the Old Settlers, the Treaty Party, and the Ross Party—were expected to merge into one single nation. Unfortunately, the transition was not easy. Many of the new arrivals were furious with the members of the Treaty Party and wanted to avenge the loss of their relatives and the loss of their homeland. However, Chief John Ross would not authorize the execution of the Treaty Party members.

On the night of June 21, 150 to 200 people gathered at Takatoka Camp Ground to discuss recent events. Angry about removal and holding the Treaty Party responsible for their losses, they decided that now was the right time to enforce the Blood Law on the signers of the Treaty of New Echota. They drew

Treaty with the Potawatomi
March 26, 1836

This treaty arranged the cession of four sections of land reserved to the Potawatomi by the October 1832 treaty at Tippecanoe. The United States agreed to pay an additional $2,560 in currency with the next annuity payment. Concluded at a camp in Turkey Creek Prairie, Indiana, the treaty was signed by Abel C. Pepper for the United States and by Mes-quaw-buck, Mess-Sett, Muck Rose, Waw-baw-que-ke-aw, Naush-waw-pi-tant, and Che-qua-sau-quah for the Potawatomi.

Treaty with the Ottawa, Etc.
March 28, 1836

This treaty arranged for the cession of lands by the Chippewa and Ottawa, reserving for common use by the two tribes certain tracts for five years and lands reserved specifically for the Chippewa north of the straits of the Michilimackinac for five years. The treaty also obligated the United States to pay the

Ottawa and Chippewa a twenty-year annuity of $30,000 in specie, with other sums to be paid to five individual groups and $1,000 to be invested in stock by the Treasury Department. Additional sums to be paid by the United States were to be applied to missions, debts, education, agricultural endeavors, tools, medicines, and payment of chiefs. The United States also agreed to help compensate for the move to other reservations and to provide monies for additional provisions. Mixed-blood people were to be paid an additional sum of money instead of given reservation land. Concluded at Washington, D.C., the treaty was signed by Henry R. Schoolcraft and John Hulbert for the United States and by thirty-nine Ottawa and Chippewa chiefs and delegates.

Treaty with the Potawatomi
March 29, 1836
This treaty organized the cession of the four tracts of Potawatomi lands reserved to them in a prior treaty and required the Potawatomi to remove west of the Mississippi within two years. The United States was to pay $2,560 in specie at the first annuity payment. Concluded at Tippecanoe River in Indiana, this treaty was signed by Abel C. Pepper for the United States and by Wau-ke-wau, Waw-was-mo-queh, Te-shaw-gen, Mes-quaw, Pah-Siss, and She-aw-ke-pee for the Potawatomi.

Treaty with the Potawatomi
April 11, 1836
The treaty arranged for the cession of the thirty-six sections of land reserved to the Potawatomi by the October 26, 1832, treaty at Tippecanoe and removal of the Potawatomi west of the Mississippi within two years. The United States agreed to pay $2,000 in specie to the tribes for their cession and removal. Concluded at a camp on Tippecanoe River in Indiana, this treaty was signed by Abel C. Pepper for the United States and by sixteen Potawatomi representatives.

Treaty with the Potawatomi
April 22, 1836
This treaty arranged the cession of ten sections of land reserved for the Potawatomi by the second arti-cle of the treaty at Tippecanoe made October 26, 1832. The United States agreed to pay the tribe $6,400 at the first annuity payment after the treaty was ratified. The treaty required the Potawatomi on said lands to relocate west of the Mississippi within two years. Concluded at the Indian agency in Indiana, this treaty was signed by Abel C. Pepper for the United States and by thirteen Potawatomi chiefs and headmen.

Treaty with the Potawatomi
April 22, 1836
This treaty arranged the cession of three sections of Potawatomi land, reserved for them by the second article of the treaty at Tippecanoe made October 26, 1832, and required them to relocate west of the Mississippi within two years. The United States agreed to pay $1,920 at the first annuity payment after the ratification of the treaty. The treaty was signed by Abel C. Pepper for the United States and by Quash-quaw, Me-cos-ta, Nas-waw-kee, Wem-se-ko, and Ah-quash-she for the Potawatomi.

Treaty with the Wyandot
April 23, 1836
This treaty organized a cession of land to the United States by the Wyandot. It arranged for the United States to defray the costs to the Wyandot and made arrangements for roads, schools, and the manner of financial compensation. It allowed the owners of certain reservations to receive payment for the sale of their lands. The treaty was signed by John A. Bryan for the United States and by William Walker, John Barnett, and Peacock, leaders of the Wyandot in Ohio.

Treaty with the Chippewa
May 9, 1836
This treaty arranged the cession by the Swan Creek and Black River Chippewa bands of lands reserved to them in the November 1807 treaty at Detroit, in exchange for certain payments by the United States in monies and in land west of the Mississippi. Concluded at Washington, D.C., this treaty was signed by Henry R. Schoolcraft for the United States and by Esh-ton-o-quot (Clear Sky), Nay-gee-zhig (Driving

Clouds), May-zin (Checkered), and Kee-way-gee-zhig (Returning Sky) for the Chippewa.

Treaty with the Potawatomi
August 5, 1836

This treaty arranged the cession of two sections of land reserved for the Potawatomi by the second article of the treaty at Tippecanoe made October 26, 1832, in exchange for payment of $14,080 after treaty ratification. The tribe also agreed to relocate to land west of the Mississippi within two years. Concluded at a camp near Yellow River, Indiana, this treaty was signed by Abel C. Pepper for the United States and by thirteen Potawatomi headmen and thirteen chiefs of the Wabash Potawatomi.

Treaty with the Menominee
September 3, 1836

This treaty arranged the cession of Menominee land and required the United States to pay a twenty-year annuity of $20,000 and to supply various amounts of specified goods annually for twenty years. The United States also agreed to pay debts of the Menominee and $80,000 to be distributed among the mixed-blood people of the tribe. The tribe also agreed to release the United States from certain obligations contained in the 1831 and 1832 treaties. Concluded on the Fox River at Cedar Point on Green Bay in Wisconsin Territory, this treaty was signed by Governor Henry Dodge for the United States and by twenty-four chiefs and headmen of the Menominee.

Treaty with the Sioux
September 10, 1836

This treaty arranged the cession of certain Sioux lands, to be dealt with according to the July 15, 1830, treaty at Prairie du Chien. The United States provided $400 worth of goods at the conclusion of the treaty. The treaty was signed by Colonel Zachary Taylor, acting Indian agent for the United States, and by Sau-tabe-say, Wau-kaun-hendee-oatah, Nau-tay-sah-pah, Mauk-pee-au-cat-paun, and Hoo-yah (the Eagle) for the Sioux of Wa-ha-shaw.

Treaty with the Iowa, Etc.
September 17, 1836

The treaty arranged the cession of lands between the state of Missouri and the Missouri River. The United States paid the tribes $7,500 as a gift for their cooperation. The Missouri band of Sauk and Fox was granted a small tract of land south of the Missouri River, to be split with the Iowa tribe. The United States agreed to help construct housing, aid the tribes in establishing farms, and so forth. Concluded at Fort Leavenworth, the treaty was signed by William Clark for the United States and by twelve Iowa and fifteen Sauk and Fox chiefs, counselors, and warriors.

Treaty with the Potawatomi
September 20, 1836

Under this treaty, the Potawatomi ceded ten sections of land reserved for them by the second article of the treaty at Tippecanoe, October 27, 1832. The United States agreed to pay them $8,000 for this cession and required the relocation of the tribe west of the Mississippi. Concluded at Chippewanaung, Indiana, this treaty was signed by U.S. Commissioner Abel C. Pepper and by We-we-sah (To-I sa's Brother), Me-

Fort Leavenworth, Kansas, c. 1867. The fort was the scene of various treaty agreements, including a key treaty with the Iowa in 1836. Named after Colonel Henry Leavenworth, Fort Leavenworth is the oldest U.S. fort west of the Mississippi River. (Library of Congress)

mot-way, Che-quaw-ka-ko, Min-tom-in, Shaw-gwok-skuk, and Mee-kiss (Kaw's Widow).

Treaty with the Potawatomi
September 22, 1836

Under this treaty, the Potawatomi ceded four sections of land reserved for them by the second article of the treaty at Tippecanoe, October 27, 1832. The United States agreed to pay $3,200 for the cession and required the relocation of this band west of the Mississippi within two years. The treaty arranged for the appointment of a commissioner to pay the debts of this Potawatomi band. Concluded at Chippewanaung, Indiana, the treaty was signed by Abel C. Pepper for the United States and by Chief Mo-sack, Nawb-bwitt, Skin-cheesh, Spo-tee, Naw-squi-base, and Mose-so of the Potawatomi.

Treaty with the Potawatomi
September 23, 1836

This treaty required the cession of all remaining Potawatomi lands in Indiana, reserving sections for the use of particular bands. The United States agreed to pay $1.25 per acre, or $33,600 in specie in 1837, and required the Potawatomi to relocate west of the Mississippi within two years. The treaty arranged for the appointment of a commissioner to pay the debts of this Potawatomi band. Concluded at Chippewanaung, Indiana, this treaty was signed by Abel C. Pepper for the United States and by nineteen chiefs, headmen, and warriors of the Wabash Potawatomi.

Treaty with the Sauk and Fox Tribe
September 27, 1836

This treaty organized the cession of Sauk and Fox lands between the state of Missouri and the Missouri River. The treaty was signed by Henry Dodge, superintendent for Indian affairs, and by twenty-three Sauk and Fox representatives.

Treaty with the Sauk and Fox
September 28, 1836

Under this treaty, the Sauk and Fox ceded all four hundred sections of land reserved to them in the second article of the September 21, 1832, treaty. The United States agreed to pay $30,000 in specie for ten years and $48,458 toward Sauk and Fox debts. The United States also agreed to deliver two hundred horses in June 1837. Provisions were also made for the mixed-blood Sauk and Fox. Concluded at the treaty ground on the bank of the Mississippi in Debuque County, Wisconsin Territory, opposite Rock Island, this treaty was signed by Commissioner Henry Dodge and twenty chiefs, warriors, and headmen of the confederated tribes.

Treaty with the Otoe, Etc.
October 15, 1836

Under this treaty, tribes ceded to the United States the lands lying between the state of Missouri and the Missouri River and south of a line running due west from the northwest corner of the state to the Missouri River. The United States presented the representatives with $4,520 in merchandise and agreed to furnish the Otoe and Missouri tribes with five hundred bushels of corn and to break up one hundred acres of Omaha land and fence it. Concluded at Bellevue, Upper Missouri, this treaty was signed by John Dougherty, Indian agent, and Joshua Pilcher for the United States and by thirteen Otoe, seven Missouri, fifteen Omaha, and twelve Yankton and Santee.

Treaty with the Sioux
November 30, 1836

The treaty organized the cession of the lands lying between the state of Missouri and the Missouri River. The United States presented the signatories with $550 in goods. Concluded at St. Peters, the treaty was signed by Lawrence Taliaferro, Indian agent, for the United States and by four Sisseton, four Wahpaakootah, and nine Upper Medawakanton leaders.

A Chippewa man with a rifle. The Treaty of 1837 was the treaty that guaranteed Chippewa fishing, hunting, and gathering rights in the Voigt Decision in 1983. (Library of Congress)

the treaty of 1837 with the Ojibwe was unique because it contained no removal clause. With the Ojibwe able to hunt, fish, and gather on the lands they ceded to the United States in the treaty of 1837 (and in subsequent treaties in 1842 and 1854), they had legal footing to challenge the U.S. government, in the late 1900s, to retain the right to hunt and fish that had been increasingly disputed throughout the late nineteenth and twentieth centuries.

The primary circumstance that led to the treaty of 1837 was the interest of the United States in the bounty of timber resources located in northern Wisconsin. The Ojibwe, who had established a reliance on, and had sunk into debt to, traders who had provided them with guns, blankets, and other necessary equipment during the fur trading era, were willing to negotiate with the United States to alleviate their economic difficulties. Commissioner Henry Dodge, the Wisconsin territorial governor acting on behalf of the United States, called together more than a thousand Ojibwe from various locations in Wisconsin, Minnesota, and Michigan to negotiate the sale of the timber-rich lands. The three major groups represented were the Ojibwe of the Mississippi, the Ojibwe of Lake Superior, and the Pillager Ojibwe. Dodge stressed

Treaty with the Chippewa

January 14, 1837

The treaty of 1837 with the Ojibwe (or Chippewa) was between the United States and three groups of the Ojibwe across Minnesota, Wisconsin, and Michigan. After extensive negotiations between the parties near present-day Minneapolis and St. Paul, the United States agreed to provide the Ojibwe with cash annuities, blankets, rifles, cooking utensils, and other provisions in exchange for the cession of the timber-rich lands in northern Wisconsin and eastern Minnesota. Of more value to the Ojibwe was the agreement of the United States to refrain from seeking to remove the Native Americans from the lands they ceded and to provide payments to traders to whom the Ojibwe were heavily in debt. In an era in which the United States was actively engaged in removing the Native Americans from the eastern portion of the country,

Wa-em-Boesh-Kaa, a Chippewa chief. (Library of Congress)

to these groups that the United States desired the land in northern Wisconsin specifically for its timber resources. As the forests were a renewable resource, the Ojibwe agreed to cede the land under the important stipulation that they could continue to hunt, fish, and gather on it, provided they did so peacefully and did not interfere with logging operations. In exchange for the land, Dodge was authorized to pay $9,500 in currency, $19,000 in goods, $3,000 to support three blacksmiths, $1,000 for agricultural pursuits, $2,000 in provisions, $500 for tobacco, and money to settle debts between the Ojibwe and their traders.

The land the United States acquired from the treaty of 1837 was for logging operations and not initially intended for white settlement; thus, there was no massive influx of settlers who sought to displace the Ojibwe in the years following the treaty. It was not until the reservation system was created in 1854 that the Ojibwe way of life became radically altered; even then, they retained the right to hunt and fish on the land they ceded. The treaty of 1837 set in motion the tradition of a nonremoval policy by the United States that appeared again in the 1842 and 1854 treaties with the Ojibwe. The Ojibwe have not forgotten this important aspect of the treaties, and in the late 1900s many groups asserted in court the right to hunt and fish on ceded land, for the growing inclination of the United States in the late nineteenth and twentieth centuries was to restrict those rights. The lasting impact of these cases has yet to be determined.

Troy Henderson

See also Sovereignty; Treaty with the Chippewa–October 4, 1842; Treaty with the Chippewa–September 30, 1854; Trust Doctrine; Trust Lands.

References and Further Reading

Danziger, Edmund Jefferson, Jr. 1978. *The Chippewas of Lake Superior.* Norman: University of Oklahoma Press.

McClurken, James M., ed. 2000. *Fish in the Lakes, Wild Rice, and Game in Abundance: Testimony on Behalf of Mille Lacs Ojibwe Hunting and Fishing Rights.* East Lansing: Michigan State University Press.

Satz, Ronald. 1991. *Chippewa Treaty Rights: The Reserve Rights of Wisconsin's Chippewa Indians in Historical Perspective.* Madison: Wisconsin Academy of Sciences, Arts and Letters.

Treaty with the Choctaw and Chickasaw

January 17, 1837

This treaty organized the Chickasaw district of the Choctaw Nation and required the Chickasaw to pay the Choctaw for the rights and privileges discussed in the treaty. Concluded on Choctaw lands near Fort Towson at Doaksville, this treaty was signed by William Armstrong, acting superintendent for the Western Territory, and Henry R. Carter, conductor of the Chickasaw Delegation, for the United States; by John McLish, Pitman Colbert, James Brown, and James Perry for the Chickasaw; and by twelve commissioners and seven captains of the Choctaw.

Treaty with the Potawatomi

February 11, 1837

Under this treaty, the signatory chiefs and headmen agreed to the Indiana land cessions organized by the August 5, September 23, October 26, and October 23, 1832, treaties. This treaty also dealt with the payment issues relating to the cessions. The tribe was expected to relocate to a tract of land on the Osage River southwest of the Missouri River. Concluded at Washington, the treaty was signed by Commissioner John T. Douglass for the United States and by various Potawatomi leaders.

Treaty with the Kiowa, Etc.

May 26, 1837

This treaty was designed as a treaty of peace and friendship. It includes stipulations regarding hunting, payment for stolen property, payment for injuries to U.S. traders, hunting boundaries, and arrangements for a limited negotiated justice system. It also required peaceful relations with Mexico. It was signed by Commissioners Montfort Stokes and A. P. Chouteau for the United States and by ten Kiowa, three Ka-ta-ka, four Ta-wa-ka-ro, ten Muscogee, and twenty Osage chiefs, headmen, and representatives.

Treaty with the Chippewa

July 29, 1837

This treaty arranged the cession of Chippewa lands, set new boundaries, required the United

States to make payments for twenty years and to pay the claims against the tribe, stipulated a separate payment for the mixed-blood Chippewa, and reserved hunting rights for the Chippewa. Concluded at St. Peters, Wisconsin Territory, the treaty was signed by Governor Henry Dodge and by numerous chiefs, headmen, and warriors of the Chippewa.

Treaty with the Sioux

September 29, 1837

This treaty required the Medawakanton Sioux to cede all lands east of the Mississippi, including the islands in the Mississippi River. The United States agreed to pay various amounts through investments and annuities, to pay for the debts of these Sioux, and to provide supplies necessary for agricultural and other endeavors. This treaty was concluded at Washington and signed by Joel R. Poinsett for the United States and by twenty-one chiefs and warriors of the Medawakanton Sioux.

Treaty with the Sauk and Fox

October 21, 1837

This treaty organized a land cession to the United States, called for aid in the form of buildings, goods, horses and gifts, investments, and payment of tribal debts, and required the Sauk and Fox to relocate from all lands except those in Kee-o-kuck's Village, who would relocate in two years. Concluded at Washington, the treaty was signed by Carey A. Harris for the United States and by Kee-o-kuck (the Watchful Fox) and twenty-two other Sauk and Fox representatives.

Treaty with the Yankton Sioux

October 21, 1837

Under this treaty, the Yankton ceded lands described in the second article of the treaty of July 15, 1830. The United States agreed to pay $4,000 for this cession. Concluded at Washington, this treaty was signed by Carey A. Harris for the United States and by nine Yankton chiefs and delegates.

Treaty with the Sauk and Fox

October 21, 1837

This treaty organized the cession of lands between the Missouri and Mississippi rivers and the rights to hunt, and other purposes, granted the Sauk and Fox on the land ceded in the first article of the treaty of July 15, 1830. They also ceded all claims under the treaties of November 3, 1804, August 4, 1824, July 15, 1830, and September 17, 1836. The treaty also stipulated the manner in which the United States should make payments to the Sauk and Fox. Concluded at Washington, the treaty was signed by Carey A. Harris for the United States and by Po-ko-mah (the Plum), Nes-mo-ea (the Wolf), Au-ni-mo-ni (the Sun Fish) of the Sauk, and Sa-ka-pa (son of Quash-qua-mi) and A-ka-ke (the Crow) of the Fox, chiefs and delegates of the Sauk and Fox of Missouri.

Treaty with the Winnebago

November 1, 1837

The treaty organized the cession of all lands east of the Mississippi and required the Winnebago to relinquish the right to occupy and hunt on certain lands set aside for their use west of the Mississippi. The tribe was to relocate within eight months. The United States agreed to pay $200,000 toward debtors' claims, goods, provisions, individual payments, construction, and agriculture. Concluded at Washington, this treaty was signed by Carey A. Harris for the United States and by twenty Winnebago chiefs and delegates.

Treaty with the Iowa

November 23, 1837

This treaty arranged the cession of lands discussed in the July 15, 1830, treaty. It required the United States to pay $2,500 in horses, goods, and presents upon conclusion of the treaty. Concluded at St. Louis, this treaty was signed by Joshua Pilcher, Indian agent, for the United States and by Ne-o-mon-ni, Non-che-ning-ga, Wat-che-mon-ne, and Tah-ro-hon for the Iowa tribe.

Treaty with the Chippewa
December 20, 1837
This treaty organized the payment for lands ceded in the January 1837 treaty and required the United States to reserve land on the headwaters of the Osage River. It also noted that the sixth article in the January treaty did not entitle the Chippewa to land west of Lake Superior. The treaty also set forth guidelines for payments to the tribe to be made by the United States. Concluded at Flint River in Michigan, the treaty was signed by Commissioner Henry R. Schoolcraft for the United States and by ten chiefs and headmen of the Chippewa.

Treaty with the New York Indians
January 15, 1838
This treaty called for land cessions, removal, and the reservation of other lands for the signatory tribes and stipulated methods of payment to them. Concluded at Buffalo Creek, New York, this treaty was signed by Commissioner Ransom H. Gillet for the United States and by numerous chiefs, headmen, and warriors of the Seneca, Tuscarora, St. Regis, Onondaga, Cayuga, and Oneida of New York, Green Bay, and the Seneca Reservation.

Treaty with the Chippewa
January 23, 1838
This treaty dealt with the sale of the lands ceded by the Chippewa under the January 14, 1837, treaty. Concluded at Saginaw, Michigan, the treaty was signed by Commissioner Henry R. Schoolcraft on behalf of the United States and by Ogima Keegido, Mo-cuck-koosh, Oe-quee-wee-sance, Saw-wur-bon, Show-show-o-nu-bee-see, and Ar-ber-too-quet for the Chippewa.

Treaty with the Oneida
February 3, 1838
Under this treaty, the First Christian and Orchard Oneidas ceded lands reserved to them by the February 1831 treaty with the Menominee. Certain portions of the lands were reserved to the Oneida. The treaty also outlined the methods of payment for these cessions. Concluded at Washington, the treaty was signed by Carey A. Harris for the United States and by Henry Powles, John Denny (John Sundown), Adam Swamp, Daniel Bread, and Jacob Cornelius for the Oneida.

Treaty with the Iowa
October 19, 1838
This treaty outlined the cession to the United States of all lands between the Mississippi and Missouri rivers and between the Sauk and Fox and the Sioux, reserving for the Iowa two hundred acres. It also sets forth the methods of payment to be employed by the United States for the cession and obligates the United States to build ten homes at locations chosen by the tribe. Concluded at the Great Nemowhaw subagency, this treaty was signed by John Doughtery, agent of Indian affairs, and by thirteen chiefs and headmen of the Iowa Nation.

Treaty with the Miami
November 6, 1838
This treaty called for the cession of certain reservation lands, with some portions of the land to be kept in reserve. It also required the United States to assign new lands west of the Mississippi and outlined the means of compensation to be employed by the United States for the Miami. Concluded in Indiana at the forks of the Wabash River, the treaty was signed by Commissioner Abel C. Pepper for the United States and twenty-three Miami representatives.

Treaty with the Creeks
November 23, 1838
This treaty arranged for the dropping of Creeks "claims for property and improvements abandoned or lost, in consequence of their emigration west of the Mississippi" in exchange for $50,000 in stock animals and the proceeds of a $350,000 investment to be made by the United States on behalf of the Creeks for twenty-five years, after which the investment would be appropriated to the tribe. Further financial provisions were made for the McIntosh party of Creek emigrants, for the relocation, and in "consideration of the suffering condition of about 2,500 of Creek nations who were removed to this country as hostiles." Concluded at Fort Gibson, the treaty was signed by

Captain William Armstrong and Brevet Brigadier General M. Arbuckle for the United States and by twenty-seven Creeks delegates.

Treaty with the Osage
January 11, 1839

Under this treaty, the Osage ceded all claims to lands lying within the boundaries of other tribes or reserved to them under the treaties of November 10, 1808, and June 2, 1825 (except that described in the sixth article). The treaty outlines the means of compensation to be paid to the Osage by the United States. Concluded at Fort Gibson, the treaty was signed by Brigadier General M. Arbuckle for the United States and by more than seventy Osage chiefs, headmen, and warriors.

Treaty with the Chippewa
February 7, 1839

This treaty arranged the sale of lands ceded in Michigan in the January 14, 1837, treaty. Concluded at Lower Saganaw, Michigan, this treaty was signed by John Hulbert, acting superintendent of Indian affairs, for the United States and by Ogima Kegido, Waubredoaince, Muckuk Kosh, Osaw Wauban, Sheegunageezhig, Penayseewabee, Caw-ga-ke-she-sa, and Shawun Epenaysee of the Chippewa.

Treaty with the Stockbridge and Munsee
September 3, 1839

This treaty arranged the cession of the eastern half of the lands reserved to the Stockbridge and Munsee by the October 7, 1832, treaty with the Menominee. It also outlined the compensation to be paid by the United States. Concluded at Stockbridge, Wisconsin Territory, this treaty was signed by Commissioner Albert Gallup for the United States and by thirty-five representatives of the Stockbridge and Munsee.

Treaty with the Miami
November 28, 1840

This treaty called for lands to be ceded to the United States, for commissioners to investigate claims, and for payments to be made to John B. Richardville and executor of Francis Godfroy. It stipulated that payments were to be made to the family of Francis Godfroy in lieu of labor, that the United States was to convey certain land to Me-shing-go-me-zia, and that the Miami people were to move to the land stipulated in the treaty. It further stipulated what was to be done if the payment of debts was too great, and gave sections of land to John B. Richardville and Francis Lafountain. The treaty was signed by Samuel Milroy and Allen Hamilton for the United States and by twenty leaders of the Miami.

Treaty with the Wyandot
March 17, 1842

This treaty called for a cession of lands to the United States, gave a grant from the United States to the Wyandot, and provided for an annuity. It also stipulated that a school was to be built, that the value of improvements was to be paid to the Wyandot, and that debts would be paid in full. It further provided for a blacksmith, a subagent, and an interpreter and required the mission and buildings to remain. It set forth who could share the annuity, what was done with land formerly owned by Horonu, and required the Wyandot to move to their new reservation; and it allowed for a grant and payment to certain persons, including Catherine Walker. The treaty was signed by John Johnston for the United States and by seven leaders of the Wyandot.

Treaty with the Seneca
May 20, 1842

This treaty set forth indentures between Ogden and Fellows and the Seneca Indians. Under its terms, the United States agreed to the said indentures and that Seneca who moved from the state of New York were entitled to the benefits thereof. The treaty was signed by Ambrose Spencer and thirty-two leaders of the Seneca.

Treaty with the Chippewa
October 4, 1842

The treaty of 1842 with the Ojibwe (or Chippewa) took place at La Pointe, Wisconsin, between the United States and twenty-three distinct bands of the Ojibwe, which represented two major groups called the Ojibwe of Lake Superior and the Ojibwe of the Mississippi. Like the 1837 treaty with the Ojibwe, the 1842 treaty involved the cession of lands to the United States in exchange for annuity payments, provisions, an agricultural fund, and, most important for the Ojibwe, the right to hunt, fish, and gather on the land they ceded. The land ceded in the treaty of 1842 included the western portion of the Upper Peninsula of Michigan and the last of the Ojibwe lands in northern Wisconsin. Although the U.S. government had a growing inclination to displace the Ojibwe from their homelands in the 1840s and early 1850s, the 1842 treaty continued the unique tradition of nonremoval established by the United States and the Ojibwe in the treaty of 1837.

Pressured by the profitability of the mineral deposits on the southern shore of Lake Superior, the United States commissioned Robert Stuart, former chief factor of the American Fur Company, to acquire the land that contained the valuable resources. Stuart was given instructions by the commissioner of Indian affairs to attempt to include a stipulation in the treaty that would remove the Lake Superior Ojibwe westward to lands held by the Ojibwe of the Mississippi, to form a common territory for both groups. This act of combining Native American groups into political entities that did not naturally was characteristic of U.S. policy of that time. The Ojibwe of Lake Superior and the Ojibwe of the Mississippi balked at the idea of being categorized together as well as at the notion of removal.

Recognizing the Ojibwes' concern over the removal clause, Stuart did not force the issue, and the content of the treaty of 1842 was very similar to the treaty of 1837. The Ojibwe retained the right to hunt, fish, and gather on the land they ceded to the United States, but Stuart made it clear that future removal was a possibility. The discretion to remove the Ojibwe at a future date was given to the president of the United States. In exchange for the land in the western Upper Peninsula of Michigan and a portion of northern Wisconsin, the Ojibwe were given annual payments of $12,500 in currency, $10,500 in goods, $2,000 to support two blacksmiths, $1,000 to support two farmers, $1,200 to support two carpenters, $2,000 to support schools, $2,000 for tobacco, and money to settle debts with traders to whom the Ojibwe were in debt.

By supporting schools, carpenters, farmers, and blacksmiths, the United States was clearly attempting to inject elements of white society into the Ojibwe culture. Like the missionaries who had established themselves among the Ojibwe, the United States embarked on "civilizing" the Ojibwe by encouraging the Native Americans to adopt a lifestyle similar to that of white society. Paradoxically, the policy of the United States was also to threaten the removal of the Ojibwe, which did nothing to help incorporate them into "civilized" society. After the treaty of 1842 was signed, confusion over which Ojibwe would receive the annuity payments, as well as a growing threat by the United States to remove the Ojibwe, led to another treaty negotiation in 1854.

Troy Henderson

See also Treaty with the Chippewa–January 14, 1837; Treaty with the Chippewa–September 30, 1854.
References and Further Reading
Cleland, Charles E. 1992. *Rites of Conquest: The History and Culture of Michigan's Native Americans.* Ann Arbor: University of Michigan Press.
Danziger, Edmund Jefferson, Jr. 1978. *The Chippewas of Lake Superior.* Norman: University of Oklahoma Press.
McClurken, James M., ed. 2000. *Fish in the Lakes, Wild Rice, and Game in Abundance: Testimony on Behalf of Mille Lacs Ojibwe Hunting and Fishing Rights.* East Lansing: Michigan State University Press.

Treaty with the Sauk and Fox
October 11, 1842

This treaty arranged for lands to be ceded to the United States and stipulated that the United States would pay for these ceded lands. It further required land to be assigned for permanent residence, blacksmith and gunsmith shops to be maintained, and the boundary to be run and marked. Further, the treaty called for the tribes to move and gave provisions for these moves. It stated that each principal chief was to receive $500 annually and that $30,000 was to be retained at each annual payment. It explained how each payment was to be expended, set forth the application of any portion of annuities, and set aside certain funds for agricultural purposes. The treaty also stipulated that the area where Chief Wa-pel-lo was buried, which amounted to 640 acres, was to be given to Mrs. Eliza M. Street. The treaty was signed by John Chambers for the United States and by forty-five leaders of the Sauk and Fox tribes.

Agreement with the Delaware and Wyandot

December 14, 1843

This agreement stated that the Wyandot Nation should take no better right or interest in and to said lands than was then vested in the Delaware Nation. The agreement was signed by nine Delaware chiefs and six Wyandot chiefs in the presence of John Chambers, the U.S. commissioner for Indian affairs.

Treaty with the Creeks and Seminole

January 4, 1845

This treaty permitted the Seminole tribe to settle in any part of Creek country, rendered the Seminole subject to the Creek council, and stipulated no distinction between them except in pecuniary affairs; and it required Seminole tribe members who had not moved to Creek country to do so immediately. The treaty further required certain contested cases concerning the right of property to be subject to the decision of the president. It allowed for a twenty-year annuity of $3,000 for education for the Creeks, set forth the uses of the education fund and annuities, and stipulated the rations to be issued to the Seminole tribe members who moved to Creek country. It also set forth sums from previous treaties and allowed $1,000 for agricultural implements. The treaty was signed by William Armstrong, P. M. Butler, James Logan, and Thomas L. Judge for the United States and by forty-one leaders of the Creeks and twenty-two leaders of the Seminole.

Treaty with the Kansa Tribe

January 14, 1846

This treaty arranged for lands to be ceded to the United States and for the United States to pay for these ceded lands. The treaty provided funds for education and agriculture and for a sum to be paid to the Methodist Episcopal Church, set provisions and boundaries, and established May 1, 1847, as the date by which the Kansa were to be moved from the ceded lands. It granted to the president of the United States the power to decide whether or not a sufficiency of timber remained on Kansas lands, asked for additional cession by the Kansas, stipulated that a subagent would reside among them, and provided for a smith and support for same. The treaty was signed by Thomas H. Harvey and Richard W. Cummins for the United States and by nineteen leaders of the Kansa tribe.

Treaty with the Comanche, Aionai, Anadarko, Caddo, Etc.

May 15, 1846

This treaty involved trade regulations, the release of black and white prisoners in Texas, and a limited negotiated justice system. It also stipulated that anyone bringing liquor to the tribe would be punished by law. Blacksmiths, schoolteachers, and preachers of the gospel were to be sent among the tribes to reside among them. The treaty was signed at Council Springs in Robinson County, Texas, near the Brazos River by Commissioners P. M. Butler and M. G. Lewis for the United States and by sixty-one chiefs, counselors, and warriors of the Comanche, I-on-i, Ana-da-ca, Caddo, Lepan, Long-wha, Keechy, Tah-wa-carro, Wichita, and Wacoe tribes.

Treaty with the Potawatomi Nation

June 5 and 17, 1846

The Chippewa, Ottawa, and Potawatomi, the Potawatomi of the Prairie, the Potawatomi of the Wabash, and the Potawatomi of Indiana, subsequent to the year 1828, entered into separate and distinct treaties with the United States by which they were separated and located in different countries. After this treaty, they were to be recognized as the Potawatomi Nation. The main concerns of the treaty were peace, cession, title to former grants and reservations, and payments and provisions for their annual improvement fund and school fund. The treaty also stipulated the means by which the United States would compensate the tribe. The treaty was signed at the agency on the Missouri River near Council Bluffs and at Potawatomi

Creek near the Osage River, south and west of the state of Missouri, by T. P. Andrews, Thomas H. Harvey, and G. C. Matlock, commissioners for the United States, and by numerous chiefs and delegates of the Potawatomi bands.

Treaty with the Cherokee
August 6, 1846

This treaty was intended to unite the Cherokee Nation with a patent to be issued. It established a judicial system and outlined the means by which the United States would compensate the tribes. Provisions were also made for the heirs of Major Ridge, John Ridge, and Elias Boudinot. It was also guaranteed that no rights or claims under the treaty of 1835 or its supplement would be taken away from the Cherokee who were residing in the states east of the Mississippi River. The treaty was signed in Washington, D.C., by three commissioners—Edmund Burke, William Armstrong, and Albion K. Parris—for the United States and by John Ross, principal chief of the Cherokee Nation. David Vann, William S. Coody, Richard Taylor, T. H. Walker, Clement V. McNair, Stephen Foreman, John Drew, and Richard Fields signed as delegates of the Cherokee Nation; George W. Adair, John A. Bell, Stand Watie, Joseph M. Lynch, John Huss, and Brice Martin signed as a delegation of the portion of the Cherokee tribe recognized as the Treaty Party. John Brown, Captain Dutch, John L. McCoy, Richard Drew, and Ellis Phillips represented the Western Cherokees, or Old Settlers.

Treaty with the Winnebago
October 13, 1846

This treaty was designed to promote peace and to arrange the cession of lands to the United States. It also outlined the means by which the United States agreed to compensate the tribe, and it gave the Winnebago one year to relocate to lands assigned them west of the Mississippi. Concluded at Washington, the treaty was signed by Commissioners Albion K. Parris, John J. Abert, and T. P. Andrews of the United States and by twenty-four chiefs, headmen, and delegates of the Winnebago.

Treaty with the Chippewa of the Mississippi and Lake Superior
August 2, 1847

This treaty was designed to promote peaceful relations and to arrange land cessions and determine boundaries. It also stipulated the means by which the United States agreed to compensate the tribe. Concluded at the Fond du Lac of Lake Superior, this treaty was signed by Isaac A. Verplank and Henry M. Rice for the United States and by forty Chippewa chiefs, headmen, and warriors.

Treaty with the Pillager Band of Chippewa Indians
August 21, 1847

This treaty was designed to promote peaceful relations and to arrange the cession of Chippewa lands to the United States. Under its terms, the ceded lands were to be held as Indian lands until the president chose to allocate them otherwise. The treaty also stipulated the means by which the United States would compensate the tribe. Concluded at Leech Lake, the treaty was signed by Isaac A. Verplank, Henry M. Rice, and interpreter George Bonja for the United States and by nine chiefs, headmen, and warriors of the Chippewa.

Treaty with the Pawnee–Grand, Loups, Republicans, Etc.
August 6, 1848

This treaty arranged a Pawnee land cession, outlined the means by which the United States would compensate the Pawnee, and arranged for the arbitration of disputes with whites or other tribes. It also allowed the United States to use the timber along the Wood River. Concluded at Fort Childs on the south side of the Nebraska or Great Platte River, the treaty was signed by Lieutenant Colonel Ludwell E. Powell for the United States and by principal chief Chef Malaigne and twelve other Pawnee representatives.

Treaty with the Menominee
October 18, 1848

Concluded at Lake Pow-aw-hay-kon-nay, Wisconsin, this treaty outlined the cession of Menominee lands and arranged for removal to "tract of land ceded to the said United States by the Chippewa Indians of the Mississippi and Lake Superior, in the treaty of August 2, 1847, and the Pillager band of Chippewa Indians, in the treaty of August 21, 1847." It allowed the Menominee two years to relocate. The treaty also outlined U.S. responsibilities to the tribe and the means by which the tribe would be compensated. W. Medill, commissioner, signed on the part of the United States, and thirty-seven Indians signed representing the Menominee tribe of Wisconsin.

Treaty with the Stockbridge Tribe
November 24, 1848

This treaty outlined the cession of rights guaranteed the tribe under certain previous treaties and the means by which the United States would compensate the tribe. Under this treaty, the Stockbridge were allowed one year to relocate to lands set apart for them or to lands west of the Mississippi. Concluded at Stockbridge, Wisconsin, the treaty was signed by Morgan L. Martin and Albert G. Ellis for the United States and by Augustin E. Quinney (a sachem), Zeba T. Peters, Peter D. Littleman, Abram Pye, and twenty-three counselors for the Stockbridge.

Treaty with the Navajo
September 9, 1849

This treaty was designed to bring about peaceful relations; it called for Navajo recognition of U.S. authority and for the Navajo to release captives and return stolen property, and it allowed the establishment of military posts. It required the tribe to give up individuals suspected in a murder and to allow free passage of U.S. citizens through their lands, and it required the United States to provide gifts. Concluded at Cheille Valley, the treaty was signed by Indian Agent James S. Calhoun and Brevet Lieutenant Colonel John M. Washington for the United States and by Mariano Martinez, head chief, Chapitone, second chief, and five others for the Navajo.

Treaty with the Utah
December 30, 1849

This treaty was intended to bring about peaceful relations. It forbade the Utah to associate with other tribes hostile to the United States and required them to return captives and stolen goods. It also required the Utah to accept boundaries stipulated by the United States, to allow the establishment of military posts and agencies, and to take up agricultural lifestyles. It also outlined the means of compensation to be employed by the United States. Concluded at Abiquiu, New Mexico, the treaty was signed by Indian Agent and Commissioner James S. Calhoun for the United States and by principal chief Quixiachigiate and more than twenty-five other Utah representatives.

Treaty with the Wyandot
April 1, 1850

Under this treaty, the United States agreed to pay the Wyandot, for relinquishing claim to certain lands, $100,000 to be invested in government stocks for 5 percent per annum and $85,000 to be paid to the Wyandot or on their drafts. The expenses of negotiating this treaty were to be paid by the United States. The treaty was signed in Washington by Ardavan S. Loughery, commissioner for the United States, and by the head chief and deputies of the Wyandot tribe.

Robinson Superior Treaty (First Robinson Treaty)
September 7, 1850

The Robinson treaties of 1850, negotiated between the Ojibwe of the Upper Great Lakes and the Crown, were essentially land cession treaties whereby the Ojibwe people of northern Ontario granted the Canadian government the right to grant mining companies and others access to certain areas from the shorelines of Lake Huron and Lake Superior "to the height of land." The Native people reserved some areas for their exclusive use and also retained the right hunt in fish in the ceded territories.

Because two treaties were negotiated on behalf of the Crown by the same person, William Benjamin Robinson, and in the same place, Sault Ste. Marie, the fact that there are two separate treaties is often overlooked. The first treaty to be signed is usually designated the Robinson Superior Treaty, signed on September 7, 1850. This treaty covered lands along the north shore of Lake Superior from Batchewanenng [sic] Bay in the east (northeast of the Sault) to the outlet of the Pigeon River at the far western end of the lake, forming the U.S.-Canada border near what is now Grand Portage, Minnesota. The land cession included all lands and waters "to the height of land," in reference to the land which was still under the control of the Hudson's Bay Company (that is, all lands that drained into either James Bay or Hudson Bay).

The second of the two treaties is referred to as the Robinson Huron Treaty, and it was signed on September 9, 1850. Of course, the Crown negotiators were the same, but the assembled "chiefs and principal men" decided that the two groups would be better served by negotiating separate treaties, although the language of the two treaties is virtually identical—both groups agreed to relinquish control over much of the land in exchange for an immediate sum of £2,000 British, a "perpetual annuity" of £500 for the Superior Ojibwes, and £600 for the Huron tribes.

The Superior tribes sent nine chiefs to the negotiation and retained control of three areas set aside as reserves. The Huron tribes had thirty-eight men sign the treaty, creating seventeen reserves for their bands. As the language of the two treaties is virtually identical, it seems obvious that the two groups conducted extensive discussions between themselves before they agreed to sit down with Mr. Robinson to work on the details of the respective treaties.

It should be noted that, in both treaties, the Crown agreed "to allow the said Chiefs and their Tribes the full and free privilege to hunt over the Territory now ceded by them, and to fish in the waters thereof, as they have heretofore been in the habit of doing; saving and excepting such portions of the said Territory as may from time to time be sold or leased to individuals or companies of individuals, and occupied by them with the consent of the Provincial Government." This language is quite similar to the language of the Treaty of Washington of 1836 signed by the Ottawa and Chippewa of northern Michigan, which says, "The Indians stipulate for the right of hunting on the lands ceded, with the other usual privileges of occupancy, until the land is required for settlement."

That the U.S. and Canadian treaties from this general area are quite similar should come as no surprise, as both sets of treaties were negotiated on behalf of the same peoples, who, although perhaps living on one side of the border or the other (or on both sides over time), nonetheless considered themselves Anishnaabeg first and Americans or Canadians second, if at all. Most notable among these cross-border connections is that of Shawano, the Sault area chief who signed both the U.S. treaty of 1836 and the Robinson Huron Treaty of 1850. Another notable chief who signed the Robinson Huron Treaty was Shinguakouce, who also signed the treaty of 1820 with Michigan, which was the first land cession treaty of the Upper Great Lakes area (he signed the 1820 treaty with his French pseudonym, Augustin Bart). The treaty of 1820 also recognizes a "perpetual right of fishing at the falls of St. Mary's" as well as access to the fisheries, as long as such access does not interfere with military or civilian settlements.

Phil Bellfy

See also Sault Ste. Marie, Michigan and Ontario.
References and Further Reading
Danziger, Edmund J., Jr. 1979. *The Chippewas of Lake Superior.* Norman: University of Oklahoma Press.
Morrison, James. 1996. *The Robinson Treaties of 1850: A Case Study.* Ottawa: Royal Commission on Aboriginal Peoples.
Quimby, George Irving. 1960. *Indian Life in the Upper Great Lakes: 11,000 B.C. to A.D. 1800.* Chicago and London: University of Chicago Press.

Robinson Huron Treaty (Second Robinson Treaty)

September 9, 1850

Nearly identical to the Robinson Superior Treaty, this treaty ceded the lands along the north shore of Lake Superior from Batchewanenng [sic] Bay in the east (northeast of the Sault), to the outlet of the Pigeon River at the far western end of the lake. In return for the ceded lands, the Huron Ojibwes were given an immediate payment of £2,000 British and a "perpetual annuity" payment of £600. The tribe also received reserved areas for their use only in the ceded territory and was allowed to continue to hunt and fish in the territory. This agreement was negotiated by William Benjamin Robinson and the Huron Ojibwe and signed by thirty-eight Huron tribe members.

Treaty with the Sioux–Sisseton and Wahpeton Bands

July 23, 1851

This treaty recognized the peaceful status of the bands and stipulated that liquor laws were to remain in force. The United States agreed to pay the sum of $1,665,000. Concluded at Traverse des Sioux in the Territory of Minnesota, the treaty was signed by Luke Lea, commissioner of Indian affairs, and Alexander Ramsey, governor and ex-officio superintendent of Indian affairs, for the United States and by thirty-five representatives from the Sisseton and Wahpeton.

Treaty with the Sioux–Mdewakanton and Wahpakoota Bands

August 5, 1851

This treaty acknowledged peace and confirmed existing liquor laws. In exchange for cession and relinquishment of lands, the United States agreed to pay the sum of $1,410,000. Concluded at Mendota in the Territory of Minnesota, the treaty was signed by Commissioner Luke Lea and Governor Alexander Ramsey and by eight chiefs and fifty-seven other Sioux.

Treaty of Fort Laramie with the Sioux, Etc.

September 17, 1851

The first Treaty of Fort Laramie, signed at Fort Laramie in southeastern Wyoming on September 17, 1851, established formal relations between the U.S. government and the Northern Plains American Indian nations. The purpose of the treaty was to ensure the safety of the increasing number of overland travelers crossing the plains. The encroaching European American population was competing with American Indians for available resources, and the number of reprisals conducted by both sides was mounting at that time.

The treaty was signed on behalf of the United States by D. D. Mitchell, superintendent of Indian affairs, and Thomas Fitzpatrick, Indian agent. Both commissioners were appointed and authorized for this special occasion by the president. The present

Mandan of the upper Missouri River were among those tribes represented during negotiations leading to the Treaty of Fort Laramie in 1851. (Library of Congress)

American Indian leaders represented nations residing south of the Missouri River, east of the Rocky Mountains, and north of Texas, namely the Sioux (referring to Lakota, Dakota, and Nakota), Cheyenne, Arapahoe, Crow, Assiniboine, Mandan, and Arikara.

The treaty contains eight articles, which bound the Indian nations to make peace with one another, to recognize the right of the United States to establish roads and posts within their respective territories, and to make restitution for any wrongs committed by their people against the citizens of the United States. The Indian nations were further supposed to acknowledge the prescribed boundaries of their respective territories and to select head chiefs, through whom all national business would be conducted. The United States bound itself to protect the Indians against U.S. citizens and to deliver certain annuities. If any Indian nation violated a single provision of the treaty, the annuities could be withheld.

The Senate ratified the first Treaty of Fort Laramie on May 24, 1852; however, an amendment changing the annuities from fifty to ten years, with an additional five years at the discretion of the president, was subject to acceptance by the Indian nations. Assent of all the nations was procured; the last were the Crow, who assented on September 18, 1854. The treaty was never published as ratified in the *U.S. Statutes at Large;* consequently, there has been some discussion concerning its validity. The Department of the Interior inadvertently failed to certify the ratification of the treaty by the Indian nations to the State Department; therefore, the treaty was not promulgated by the president of the United States. However, in subsequent agreements and by decisions of the court of claims (*Moore v. the United States* and *Roy v. the United States*), the treaty was recognized as in force.

Due to the lack of good interpreters, the terms of the treaty were not fully explained to most of the Indian leaders present at the council grounds. The ten thousand Indians gathered at their camps near Fort Laramie paid more attention to the fact that many nations that had previously fought each other were engaging in diverse ways of peacemaking there, and that celebrations, dancing, hand games, and various kinds of races were continuing for several days.

The Lakota, dominating the treaty negotiations on the Indian side, had significant influence on the demarcation of the territorial boundaries. Although most of the Indian nations retained their usual territory, the Northern Cheyenne were not given title to their land, which adjoined the Lakota land. Instead, they were assigned a territory, together with the Southern Cheyenne and Arapaho, between the North Fork of the Platte River and the Arkansas River in the south. This treaty gave the Lakota rights to the Black Hills and other land that was inhabited by the Northern Cheyenne, thus provoking the dispute over the Black Hills between these nations.

Drawing the boundaries of territories assigned to the Indian nations made it possible for the United States to negotiate with specific nations to secure land cessions from them. In the long run, the treaty contributed to the ultimate loss of almost all Indian land involved, which was eventually opened up for settlement by European Americans. Temporary peace, secured by the Treaty of Fort Laramie of 1851, enabled many settlers to cross the plains and populate what are today the states of Oregon and California. The fact that, in an effort to secure better control over the Indian nations, they were made responsible for any crimes committed within their territories led to many accusations, although not always correct ones. A treaty originally written to assure peace and to serve as a cost-effective alternative to war fueled disputes, leading ultimately to the Indian Wars and the subsequent decimation of Indian populations.

Antonie Dvorakova

See also Fort Laramie, Wyoming.
References and Further Reading
Berthrong, Donald J. 1963. *The Southern Cheyennes.* Norman: University of Oklahoma Press.
Kappler, Charles Joseph, ed. 1972. *Indian Treaties, 1778–1883.* New York: Interland.
Stands In Timber, John, and Margot Liberty. 1998. *Cheyenne Memories.* 2nd ed. New Haven, CT, and London: Yale University Press.

Treaty with the Chickasaw
June 22, 1852

This treaty established that an Indian agent would reside among the Chickasaw, who were to be settled in Tennessee, and provided burial ground forever. Payment for the reservation was not to exceed $1.25 per acre and was to be decided by the secretary of the interior. The Chickasaw requested that the whole sum of their national funds remain in trust. For negotiating this treaty, $1,500 was to be paid directly to the Chickasaw Nation. Concluded at Washington, the treaty was signed by Commissioner Kenton Harper for the United States; Commissioners Colonel Edmund Pickens, Benjamin S. Love, and Sampson Folsom were chosen by the Chickasaw tribe of Indians to sign for them.

Treaty with the Apache
July 1, 1852

This treaty set forth a negotiated justice system, stipulated that attacks in the territory of Mexico were to cease, forbade the taking of captives, and required the surrender of all captives previously taken. Military posts, agencies, trading houses, and territorial boundaries were established. Concluded at Santa Fe, New Mexico, the treaty was signed by Colonel E. V. Sumner, U.S. commander in the Ninth Department, and John Greiner, Indian agent, for the United States and by seven Apache chiefs.

Treaty with the Comanche, Kiowa, and Apache

July 27, 1853

This treaty acknowledged peace among the Comanche, Kiowa, and Apache tribes inhabiting the territory south of the Arkansas River and between the United States and the tribes, allowed the United States to build roads and military posts, and called for restitution for any damage or injury made by the tribe. It stipulated that attacks in the territory of Mexico were to cease, forbade the taking of captives, and required the surrender of all captives previously taken. The United States agreed to pay the tribes $18,000 per year. Annuities would be withheld for noncompliance with the treaty or paid in goods, at the discretion of the president. Concluded at Fort Atkinson in the Indian Territory, the treaty was signed by Indian agent Thomas Fitzpatrick for the United States and by nine chiefs and seven headmen of the Comanche, Kiowa, and Apache tribes.

Agreement with the Rogue River Tribes

September 8, 1853

This was a treaty of peace, which called for a cession of hostilities and the return of all the property taken from the whites, in battle or otherwise, to either General Joseph Lane or the Indian agent. It established a negotiated justice system and, in return for payment in goods, required the surrender of firearms belonging to the tribe. Under the treaty, tribal land sales would defray the cost of property destroyed by the tribe during the war, not to exceed $15,000. An agent would reside near the tribe and enforce the terms of the agreement. The treaty was signed by Joseph Lane, commander of the forces of Oregon Territory, for the United States; and by Joe, principal chief of the Rogue River tribe; Sam, subordinate chief; and Jim, subordinate chief, on the part of the tribes under their jurisdiction.

Treaty with the Rogue River Tribe

September 10, 1853

The treaty concerns land cession, temporary occupancy of the land until a permanent home could be provided, buildings to be erected, protection of travelers, and restitution of stolen property. Under the treaty, the United States had the right to establish farms as payment of the annuities at the president's discretion. Concluded at Table Rock near the Rogue River in the Territory of Oregon, the treaty was signed by Joel Palmer, superintendent of Indian affairs, and Samuel H. Culver, Indian agent, for the United States and by three chiefs and other headmen of the bands of the Rogue River tribe of Indians.

Treaty with the Umpqua–Cow Creek Band

September 19, 1853

This treaty required the Cow Creek tribe to give up all claim to their lands but allowed temporary occupation of part of the land until permanent homes could be selected. Annuities were to be paid in monies and in goods. Houses were to be erected, travelers protected, and a negotiated justice system put in place. Concluded at Cow Creek, Umpqua Valley, in the Territory of Oregon, the treaty was signed by Joel Palmer, superintendent of Indian affairs, and by three Cow Creek chiefs.

Treaty with the Otoe and Missouri

March 15, 1854

This treaty concerned land cession and new boundaries. Annuities were to be paid in monies and goods. The United States was to establish a gristmill and a sawmill, to provide a blacksmith, and to employ an experienced farmer to instruct the tribe in agriculture. The tribe agreed to peace and requested that no liquor be brought into their territory. Roads, highways, and railways were to be built through the reservation, with just compensation. The United States paid Lewis Barnard the sum of $300 for service to the tribes. Concluded in the city of Washington, the treaty was signed by Commissioner George W. Manypenny for the United States and by seven chiefs of the Otoe and Missouri tribes.

Treaty with the Omaha

March 16, 1854

This treaty concerns cession of lands to the United States, removal of the Omaha to lands reserved for them, protection from hostile tribes, establishment of a gristmill and a sawmill, provision of a blacksmith, construction of roads and railways, a grant to the Presbyterian Church, and relinquishment of former claims. Annuities were to be paid to the tribe in monies and goods. Lewis Sounsosee was paid $1,000 for services to the tribe. Concluded at the city of Washington, the treaty was signed by Commissioner George W. Manypenny for the United States and by seven chiefs of the Omaha tribe.

Treaty with the Delaware
May 6, 1854

This treaty concerns the cession of land, establishment of a reservation, construction of roads, provisions made for Christian tribal members, and a negotiated justice system. The introduction of liquor was to be suppressed. Annuities were to be paid in monies or invested, and the value of the school on the reservation was to remain at the previous rate of interest. Concluded at the city of Washington, the treaty was signed by Commissioner George W. Manypenny for the United States and by nine delegates of the Delaware tribe.

Treaty with the Shawnee
May 10, 1854

This treaty concerns land cession, new boundaries and payments for the cession of land, land grants, and the building of roads and railways. A negotiated justice system was established, and Congress was given authority to create laws to further carry out the treaty. The Shawnee agreed to suppress the use of liquor. The treaty was signed in Washington by Commissioner George W. Manypenny for the United States and by eight delegates representing the Shawnee.

Treaty with the Menominee
May 12, 1854

Under the terms of this treaty, the United States transferred to the Menominee all the tract of land ceded by the Chippewa Indians of the Mississippi and Lake Superior. The Menominee agreed to cede, sell, and relinquish to the United States all the lands assigned to them under the treaty of October 18, 1848. The United States agreed to cede the tract of country lying upon the Wolf River in Wisconsin. The treaty also explained payment arrangements. Concluded at the Falls of Wolf River, Wisconsin, the treaty was signed by Francis Huebschmann, superintendent of Indian affairs, for the United States and by twenty-one chiefs, headmen, and warriors of the Menominee tribe.

Treaty with the Iowa
May 17, 1854

This treaty concerns land cession, with the exception of a "small strip of land on the south side of the Missouri River . . ." described in the second article of a treaty concluded with the Iowa and the Missouri band of Sac and Fox on September 17, 1836. The Iowa immediately were to pursue agriculture, to allow the building of roads and railways, to suppress liquor, to release all claims from former treaties, and to give Congress authority to create new laws to promote the interests, peace, and happiness of the Iowa people. Additionally, the treaty discussed proceeds from the sale of lands, disposition of ceded lands, division of land, and land grants; stipulated that private debts could not to be paid out of general funds; and allowed a part of the funds set aside by the treaty of October 19, 1838, to be spent and the remainder to be held in trust. Concluded in the city of Washington, the treaty was signed by Commissioner George W. Manypenny for the United States and by four delegates of the Iowa tribe.

Treaty with the Sauk and Fox of Missouri
May 18, 1854

Under this treaty, the Sauk and Fox of Missouri ceded to the United States all their right, title, and interest in and to the country assigned to them by the treaty concluded on September 17, 1836. The treaty detailed payment for the cession of lands and the disposition of the reservation. Provisions were made respecting the funds invested under treaty of October 21, 1837. Other concerns of the treaty were the retention of the present farm and mill, a grant to the Board of Foreign Missions, the building of roads and railways, the suppression of liquor, and the authority given to Congress to create new laws. The tribe released the United States from all claims or demands from previous treaties and stipulated that private debts were not to be charged on the general fund. Concluded at the city of Washington, the treaty was signed by Commissioner George W. Manypenny for the United States and by five delegates of the Sauk and Fox of Missouri.

Treaty with the Kickapoo
May 18, 1854

The main concerns of this treaty were the cession of land, the reservation of land for a permanent home, payment for cession and improvements, a land grant for Peter Cadue (interpreter), and the building of roads. The treaty recognized the Kickapoos' desire that liquor not be brought into the territory and their promise of peace with U.S. citizens and among themselves. Private debts were not to be paid from general funds, and Congress could create new laws concerning the management of the treaty. Concluded at the city of Washington, the treaty was signed by Commissioner George W. Manypenny for the United States and by five delegates of the Kickapoo tribe.

Treaty with the Kaskaskia, Peoria, Etc.
May 30, 1854

The main concerns of the treaty were unification of the Kaskaskia, Peoria, Piankeshaw, and Wea tribes; cession and reservation; tribe conduct; and building of roads. The treaty stipulated that ceded lands were to be surveyed, and it provided for the selection of lots, the sale of land, the proceeds from land sale, and a land grant to the American Indian Mission Association. It further provided for persons omitted in the schedule, and settlements by others were not permitted until after tribe selections. The tribes were to relinquish all annuities and claims under former treaties, and payment was determined for those releases. Concluded at the city of Washington, the treaty was signed by Commissioner George W. Manypenny for the United States and by five delegates representing the united tribes of Kaskaskia and Peoria, Piankeshaw, and Wea.

Treaty with the Miami
June 5, 1854

This treaty concerned cession of lands, reservation for homes and schools, building of roads, repair of the mill and schoolhouse, disposition of ceded lands, sale of reservation, and payment for cession. The remaining annuity installments, under the treaty of November 28, 1840, were to be divided and paid. The blacksmith and the miller were to continue to serve the tribe. Other payments for release of claims to previous treaties were decided upon, and private debts were not to be paid from the general fund. Further, the conduct of the tribe was discussed, and Congress was authorized to create new laws to manage the treaty. Concluded at the city of Washington, the treaty was signed by Commissioner George W. Manypenny for the United States and by five delegates representing the Miami tribe and five Miami tribe members who were residents of the state of Indiana.

Treaty with the Creeks
June 13, 1854

This is a supplementary article to the treaty with the Creek tribes made and concluded at Fort Gibson on November 23, 1838. It annulled the third and fourth articles of that treaty, and funds were to be divided. It was signed by W. H. Garrett, U.S. agent for the Creeks, and by four delegates representing the Creek tribes.

Treaty with the Chippewa
September 30, 1854

Negotiations for the treaty of 1854 with the Ojibwe (or Chippewa) took place at La Pointe, Wisconsin, between the United States and two groups of the Ojibwe: the Ojibwe Lake Superior and the Ojibwe of the Mississippi. In the 1854 treaty, the Ojibwe ceded their lands in northeastern Minnesota to the United States in exchange for annuity payments over twenty years and the creation of a patchwork of reservations within the land ceded by the Ojibwe in the treaties of 1837, 1842, and 1854. In something of a compromise between the U.S. government, which had unsuccessfully attempted to remove the Ojibwe from their lands in the late 1840s and early 1850s, and the Ojibwe, who had strongly asserted their desire to remain on their homelands, the 1854 treaty created a reservation system, and the Ojibwe retained their rights to hunt, fish, and gather on all of the lands they ceded. Yet, because of the growing presence of white settlers in the late 1800s and 1900s on the land the Ojibwe had once occupied, the opportunity for the Ojibwe to continue to live in a traditional lifestyle dwindled after 1854.

The principal issue that led to the treaty of 1854 with the Ojibwe centered on removal. In 1850, President Zachary Taylor issued an order that revoked the privileges of the Ojibwe under the treaties of 1837 and 1842 and called for the removal of the Ojibwe to the lands they had not yet ceded. This decision sparked numerous petitions from missionaries, American citizens, and Ojibwe leaders who stood staunchly against the removal of the Ojibwe. In 1852, Ojibwe leaders Pishake, Kisketuhug, and Oshaga traveled from La Pointe to Washington to argue their case to President Fillmore. Eventually, the United States relented, and Commissioner of Indian Affairs George Manypenny sent agents David Herriman and Henry Gilbert to La Pointe in 1854 to negotiate a treaty with the Ojibwe that would purchase for the United States the mineral-rich district in northeastern Minnesota and set up reservations for the Ojibwe on the land they ceded. The Ojibwe, who preferred the creation of reservations to removal, agreed to meet at La Pointe for treaty negotiations.

More than four thousand Ojibwe meet at La Pointe in 1854 to take part in or witness the treaty negotiations. Instead of combining the Ojibwe of the Mississippi and the Ojibwe of Lake Superior into a single entity to represent the Ojibwe, as previous treaty negotiators had done, Henry Gilbert recognized the resentment between the two groups and separated them during the negotiations. Treaty negotiations concluded with the Ojibwe of Lake Superior receiving two-thirds of the annuity benefits and the Ojibwe of the Mississippi receiving the remaining one-third. The Ojibwe ceded the land in northeastern Minnesota for twenty-year annuities in the form of money, cattle, cooking utensils, building materials, funds for education, money for the settlement of debts with traders, and various other funds and supplies designed to assist assimilation into white society. Of more importance, the 1854 treaty also set up a group of small reservations for the Ojibwe dispersed across the lands they ceded in northeastern Minnesota, northern Wisconsin, and the Upper Peninsula of Michigan. Reservations were established for the following Ojibwe bands in 1854:

Millard Fillmore was vice president when he succeeded to the presidency upon the death of Zachary Taylor in July 1850. Taylor had ordered removal of the Chippewa (Ojibwe) to unceded lands prior to his death. Chippewa leaders then petitioned Fillmore to rescind that order, setting the stage for an 1854 treaty. (Library of Congress)

L'Anse and Vieux De Sert, La Pointe, Lac De Flambeau, Lac Court Orielles, Fond du Lac, Grand Portage, and Ontonagon.

The Ojibwe retained their rights to hunt and fish on the lands they ceded under the treaties of 1837, 1842, and 1854, yet the growing presence of white settlers throughout the late 1800s and 1900s led to the depletion of resources and the impracticability of maintaining a traditional lifestyle. Thus, the treaty of 1854 and the creation of the reservation system was a watershed in Ojibwe history that significantly altered the Ojibwe lifestyle.

Troy Henderson

See also Treaty with the Chippewa–January 14, 1837; Treaty with the Chippewa–October 4, 1842.
References and Further Reading
Cleland, Charles E. 1992. *Rites of Conquest: The History and Culture of Michigan's Native Americans*. Ann Arbor: The University of Michigan Press.

Danziger, Edmund Jefferson, Jr. 1978. *The Chippewas of Lake Superior.* Norman: University of Oklahoma Press.

McClurken, James M., ed. 2000. *Fish in the Lakes, Wild Rice, and Game in Abundance: Testimony on Behalf of Mille Lacs Ojibwe Hunting and Fishing Rights.* East Lansing: Michigan State University Press.

Treaty with the Choctaw and Chickasaw

November 4, 1854

This was an agreement by the Choctaw and Chickasaw tribes concerning the second article of a treaty on January 17, 1837, settling district boundary disputes between the Chickasaw and Choctaw. It was signed by five Choctaw and five Chickasaw in the presence of William K. McKean and Douglas H. Cooper, U.S. Indian agent.

Treaty with the Rogue River Tribe

November 15, 1854

This was an agreement between Joel Palmer, superintendent of Indian affairs, and twelve chiefs and headmen of the Rogue River tribe. The treaty allowed other tribes to settle on the Table Rock Reserve and provided for the payment of annuities, for the building of roads, and for possible removal from the reserve. It also specified arrangements in the event the treaty was not ratified or no tribes were removed to the reserve.

Treaty with the Chasta, Etc.

November 18, 1854

This treaty's main concerns were cession, removal to Table Rock Reserve, payments, provision in case of removal from the reserve, stipulations for all tribes on the reserve, survey and allotment of said reserve, annuities not to be taken for debt, and the conduct of the tribes. Concluded at the council ground opposite the mouth of Applegate Creek on the Rogue River in the Territory of Oregon, the treaty was signed for the United States by Joel Palmer, superintendent of Indian affairs, and by seven chiefs and headmen of the Quil-si-eton and Na-hel-ta bands of the Chasta tribe, the Cow-nan-ti-co, Sa-cher-i-ton, and Na-al-ye bands of Scotons, and the Grave Creek band of Umpqua.

Treaty with the Umpqua and Kalapuya

November 29, 1854

The main concerns of this treaty were cession, residence on the reservation, removal from said reserve if expedient, removal from ceded lands, payments for cession and expense of removal, survey and allotment of reserve, blacksmith shop, power of future states over restrictions limited, conduct of the tribes, building of roads, annuities not to be taken for debt, and some annuity payments made in goods. Concluded at Calapooia Creek, Douglas County, Oregon Territory, the treaty was signed for the United States by Joel Palmer, superintendent of Indian affairs, and by ten chiefs and heads of the confederated bands of the Umpqua tribe and of the Calapooia residing in Umpqua Valley.

Treaty with the Confederated Otoe and Missouri

December 9, 1854

This treaty was to be taken and considered as a supplement to the treaty made on March 15, 1854, to clarify reservation boundaries. It was signed at Nebraska City, Nebraska, by George Hepner, Indian agent, for the United States and by two chiefs and two headmen of the confederate tribes of the Otoe and Missouri tribes.

Treaty with the Nisqually, Puyallup, Etc.

December 26, 1854

This treaty's main concerns were cession, reservation for the signatory tribes and removal thereto, building of roads, rights to fish, payments for cession and expenses of removal, conduct of tribes, intemperance, schools and shops, and slaves to be freed. No foreign trade was allowed, and no foreign tribal members were allowed to reside on the reservation without consent of the agent. Concluded on the She-nah-nam, or Medicine Creek, in the Territory of Washington, the treaty was signed by Isaac I. Stevens, governor and superintendent of Indian affairs of the said territory, and sixty-two chiefs, headmen, and delegates of the Nisqually, Puyallup, Steilacoom, Squawskin, S'Homamish, Stehchass, T' Peek-sin, Squi-aitl, and Sa-heh-wamish tribes and bands occupying the lands lying around the head of Puget Sound and the adjacent inlets.

Treaty with the Kalapuya, Etc.
January 22, 1855

This treaty's main concerns were cession, temporary reservation, protection from other hostile tribes, removal to a home, payments, provision if any refused to sign the treaty, provision if any claim to territory north of the Columbia River was established; provision of a physician, a schoolteacher, a blacksmith, and a superintendent of farming operations; survey and allotment of reservation, conduct of tribes, intemperance, and building of roads. Concluded at Dayton, Oregon Territory, the treaty was signed for the United States by Joel Palmer, superintendent of Indian affairs, and seventeen chiefs of the confederated bands of Indians residing in the Willamette Valley.

Treaty with the Dwamish, Suquamish, Etc.
January 22, 1855

This treaty was between the United States and the Dwámish, Suquámish, Sk-táhlmish, Sam-áhmish, Smalh-kamish, Skope-áhmish, St-káh-mish, Snoquál-moo, Skai-wha-mish, N' Quentl-má-mish, Sk-táh-le-jum, Stoluck-whá-mish, Sha-ho-mish, Skágit, Kik-i-állus, Swin-á-mish, Squin-áh-mish, Sah-ku-méhu, Noo-whá-ha, Nook-wa-cháh-mish, Mee-sée-qua-quilch, Cho-bah-áh-bish, and other allied and subordinate tribes and bands. The treaty concerns were cession, boundaries, reservation, schools, tribes to be settled on the reservation within one year, rights and privileges, and payment of annuities. Under the treaty, tribe members could be removed to reservation,

$15,000 was appropriated for expenses of removal, settlement and lots could be assigned to individuals, and whites were not allowed to reside on the reservation without permission. Tribes were to preserve friendly relations, to pay for depredations, to be peaceful, to free all slaves, and to surrender tribal offenders. Further, the tribes were not allowed foreign trade. The United States was to establish a school, to provide instructors, and to furnish mechanics, shops, and physicians. Concluded at Múcklte-óh, or Point Elliott, in the Territory of Washington, the treaty was signed for the United States by Isaac I. Stevens, governor and superintendent of Indian affairs, and by numerous chiefs, headmen, and delegates of the tribes.

Treaty with the S'Klallam
January 26, 1855

This treaty's concerns were cession, boundaries, reservation, whites not to reside on said reserve, privileges of the tribes, payments for cession and removal, tribes to be removed to other reservations, and survey and allotment of land. Concluded at Hahdskus, or Point No Point, Suquamish Head, in the Territory of Washington, the treaty was signed for the United States by Isaac I. Stevens, governor and superintendent of Indian affairs, and by fifty-six chiefs and delegates of the different villages of the S'Klallams occupying certain lands on the Straits of Fuca and Hood's Canal in the Territory of Washington.

Treaty with the Wyandot
January 31, 1855

Under the terms of this treaty, the Wyandot became U.S. citizens, with some exceptions. Other treaty concerns were cession, partition of said lands among the Wyandot, patents, payments, and appraisal of the improvements. The Wyandot released claims under previous treaties and received payments in lieu thereof. Grantees under former treaty of March 17, 1842, were permitted to locate elsewhere. Concluded at the city of Washington, this treaty was signed by Commissioner George W. Manypenny for the United States and by the following chiefs and delegates of the Wyandot tribe of Indians: Tan-roo-mee, Matthew Mudeator, John Hicks, Silas Armstrong, George J. Clark, and Joel Walker.

Treaty with the Makah
January 31, 1855

The main concerns of the treaty were the surrender of lands, boundaries, reservations, building of roads, rights and privileges, provisions, payments, and appropriation for removal and for clearing and fencing land. The tribes were to be settled on the reservation within a year; whites were not to reside on said reserve; other friendly tribes were allowed to reside on the reservation; tribes could be removed from the reservation and/or consolidated; annuities were not to be used to pay individual debts and would be withheld from those who drank liquor. Tribes were to be peaceful, to pay for depredations, to free all slaves, and to surrender tribal offenders. Foreign trade was not allowed, and foreign tribes were not to reside on the reserve. The United States was to establish a school, to provide instructors, and to furnish mechanics, shops, and a physician. Concluded at Neah Bay in the Territory of Washington, the treaty was signed for the United States by Isaac I. Stevens, governor and superintendent of Indian affairs, and by Tse-kauwtl, head chief of the Makah tribe, and forty-one delegates of several villages of the Makah tribe occupying the country around Cape Classett or Cape Flattery.

Treaty with the Chippewa
February 22, 1855

This treaty's main concerns were cession, reservations for permanent homes, boundaries, survey and allotment of reservations, payments in monies and goods, preemption rights, land grants to mixed-blood persons, establishment of a judicial system, building of roads, and conduct of the tribe. Concluded at the city of Washington, this treaty was signed by Commissioner George W. Manypenny for the United States, by three chiefs and delegates representing the Mississippi bands of Chippewa, and by thirteen chiefs and delegates representing the Pillager and Lake Winnibigoshish bands of Chippewa.

Treaty with the Winnebago
February 27, 1855

The main concerns of this treaty were cession of land granted pursuant to a treaty of October 13, 1846; sale of lands; payment for cession and sale of lands; provision for a permanent home; survey and allotment of a permanent home; and payments under former treaties. Annuities were to be withheld from the ill-behaved. This treaty was in lieu of the agreement of August 6, 1853, which was never ratified. The United States was to pay the cost of the trip to Washington. Concluded at the city of Washington, this treaty was signed by Commissioner George W. Manypenny for the United States and by ten chiefs and delegates from the Winnebago tribe.

Treaty with the Wallawalla, Cayuse, Etc.
June 9, 1855

This treaty was between the United States and the Wallawalla, Cayuse, and Umatilla tribes and bands occupying lands partly in Washington Territory and partly in Oregon Territory. The main concerns of the treaty were cession of lands, boundaries, reservation, rights and privileges, provisions, allowance for improvements, payments, land allotments, and patents; whites were not to reside (with exception) on the reserve; tribes were to settle within one year. The United States was to build sawmills, schools, mechanics' shops, and a trading post and was to employ mechanics and teachers. The United States also agreed to build dwelling houses and other things for head chiefs. Ten thousand dollars was expended to open a wagon road from Powder River, and a right-of-way was reserved for roads through the reservation. Tribes were to be peaceful, to pay for depredations, and to submit to regulations. Annuities were to be withheld from those who drank liquor. Concluded at Camp Stevens in the Walla Walla valley, the treaty was signed for the United States by Isaac I. Stevens, governor and superintendent of Indian affairs for the Territory of Washington, and Joel Palmer, superintendent of Indian affairs for the Oregon Territory; thirty-six chiefs, headmen, and delegates signed on behalf of the tribes.

Treaty with the Yakama
June 9, 1855

This treaty was between the United States and the Yakama, Palouse, Pisquouse, Wenatshapam, Klikatat,

Klinquit, Kow-was-say-ee, Li-ay-was, Skin-pah, Wish-ham, Shyik, Ochechote, Kah milt-pah, and Se-ap-cat, confederated tribes and bands. The main concerns of the treaty were the cession of lands, boundaries, reservation, privileges, improvements, payments, building of roads, survey and allotment. Whites were not to reside (with exception) on the reserve. The United States was to establish schools and to build a sawmill, a flour mill, mechanics' shops, and a hospital. The United States also agreed to pay the head chief, Kamaiakun, a salary. Tribes were to be peaceful, to pay for depredations, to refrain from making war except in self-defense, and to surrender offenders. Annuities were to be withheld from those who drank liquor. The Wenatshapam fishery was reserved for the benefit of the tribe. Concluded at Camp Stevens in the Walla Walla valley, the treaty was signed for the United States by Isaac I. Stevens, governor and superintendent of Indian affairs for the Territory of Washington, and for the tribes and bands by fourteen chiefs, headmen, and delegates.

Treaty with the Nez Percé
June 11, 1855

This treaty was between the United States and the Nez Percé, occupying lands lying partly in Oregon and partly in Washington Territories between the Cascade and Bitterroot Mountains. The main concerns of the treaty were cession of lands, boundaries, reservation, improvements, building of roads, privileges, payments, survey, and allotment; whites were not to reside on the reservation without permission. The United States was to establish schools and to build a sawmill, mechanics' shops, and a hospital. The United States also agreed to pay the head chief a salary and to build him a home, and other benefits. Tribes were to be peaceful, to pay for depredations, to refrain from making war except in self-defense, and to surrender offenders. Annuities were to be withheld from those who drank liquor. The tribe granted William Craig the land he then occupied. The treaty was concluded at Camp Stevens in the Walla Walla valley and signed for the United States by Isaac I. Stevens, governor and superintendent of Indian affairs for the Territory of Washington, and Joel Palmer, superintendent of Indian affairs for Oregon Territory, and for the Nez Percé by Aleiya, or

Lawyer, head chief of the Nez Percé, and fifty-six other delegates.

Treaty with the Choctaw and Chickasaw
June 22, 1855

The main concerns of this treaty were the boundaries of the Choctaw and Chickasaw country, lands guaranteed to them, provision of sales and reversion of said lands, cession of land by the Choctaw, lease by the Choctaw and Chickasaw for the use of other tribes, and payments. Districts were established for each tribe, although either tribe could settle within the limits of the other. Extradition of criminals between the districts was required, as well as extradition of criminals to the United States or particular states. The current laws and government were to remain in force until altered. The tribes could be self-governed as long as they were lawful. There was to be amnesty between the tribes, and the United States was to protect tribal members from hostiles and whites not

Peter Pitchlynn (1806–1881) was a Choctaw leader and diplomat who helped negotiate the removal of the Choctaw to Oklahoma, and served as the Choctaw tribal delegate in Washington, D.C. (Library of Congress)

subject to their jurisdiction and laws. Military posts, post roads, agencies, and a right-of-way for railroads and telegraphs were to be established. Some questions concerning previous treaties and payments were to be submitted to the Senate for decision. This treaty was to supersede all former treaties with the Choctaw and all inconsistent treaties with the Chickasaw or between said tribes. The United States was to pay the commissioners. The treaty was concluded in Washington and signed for the United States by Commissioner George W. Manypenny; by Peter P. Pitchlynn, Israel Folsom, Samuel Garland, and Dixon W. Lewis, on the part of the Choctaw; and by Edmund Pickens and Sampson Folsom on the part of the Chickasaw.

Treaty with the Tribes of Middle Oregon
June 25, 1855

The main concerns of this treaty were cession, boundaries, reservation, rights and privileges, provision in case any band did not accede to the treaty, allowance for improvements, payments, stipulations on annuities, patents, and building of roads; whites were not to reside on the reservation without permission. Fifty thousand dollars additional was to be expending for buildings. The United States was to erect sawmills, a schoolhouse, and other buildings and to furnish farmers, mechanics, and a physician. Dwelling houses and a salary were to be given to head chiefs, but any successor to a head chief would take same. Tribes were to be peaceful, to pay for depredations, and to refrain from making war except in self-defense. This treaty was concluded at Wasco, near The Dalles on the Columbia River in Oregon Territory, and was signed by Joel Palmer, superintendent of Indian affairs, for the United States and by fourteen chiefs and numerous headmen of the confederated tribes and bands of Indians residing in Middle Oregon.

Treaty with the Quinaielt, Etc.
July 1, 1855

This treaty was between the United States and the different tribes and bands of the Qui-nai-elt and Quil-leh-ute. Its main concerns were the surrender of lands, boundaries, reservation within the Territory of Washington, and appropriations for removal and for clearing and fencing lands. Whites were not to reside on the reservation without permission; further, tribal members could be removed from the reservation. Additional points were the building of roads, rights and privileges, and annuities. The United States was to establish an agricultural and industrial school and to employ a blacksmith, a carpenter, a farmer, and a physician. Tribes were to be peaceful, to pay for depredations, to refrain from making war except in self-defense, to free all slaves, and to surrender offenders. No foreign trade was allowed, and no foreign tribes were to reside on the reservation. This treaty was signed for the United States by Isaac I. Stevens, governor and superintendent of Indian affairs for the Territory of Washington, and for the Qui-nai-elt and Quil-leh-ute by thirty-one chiefs, headmen, and delegates.

Treaty with the Flatheads, Etc.
July 16, 1855

This treaty was between the United States and the confederated tribes of the Flathead, Kootenai, and Upper Pend d'Oreilles. The main treaty concerns were cession of land, boundaries, reservation, survey and allotment, guarantee against certain claims of the Hudson Bay Company, allowances for improvements, building of roads, rights and privileges, and payments; whites were not to reside on the reservation without permission. The United States was to establish schools, mechanics' shops, and a hospital. The head chiefs of the tribes were to receive a salary. Tribes were to be peaceful, to pay for depredations, to refrain from making war except in self-defense, and to surrender offenders. Annuities were to be withheld from those who drank liquor in excess. Concluded at Hell Gate in the Bitterroot Valley, the treaty was signed for the United States by Isaac I. Stevens, governor and superintendent of Indian affairs for the Territory of Washington, and for the tribes by eighteen chiefs, headmen, and delegates.

Treaty with the Ottawa and Chippewa
July 31, 1855

The main concern of this treaty was the withdrawal of unsold lands, specified use for bands, individual land grants to tribal members, and a promise that a list of entitlement would be prepared by the Indian agent by class. Possession was to be taken at once;

sale within ten years was forbidden, but there were restrictions on the sale of said lands. A provision was made in case of death. Grants were possible for churches and schools. Additional concerns were payments, appropriations for blacksmith shops, release of liabilities under former treaties, continued employment for interpreters, dissolution of tribal organization in most respects, and the detailing of how future treaties would be negotiated. Concluded at the city of Detroit, Michigan, the treaty was signed by Commissioners George W. Manypenny and Henry C. Gilbert for the United States and by the Ottawa and Chippewa delegates of Michigan, parties to the treaty of March 28, 1836.

Treaty with the Chippewa of Sault Ste. Marie

August 2, 1855

This treaty dealt with three main concerns: the surrender of fishing rights, payments to the tribe, and a land grant to Chief Oshawwawno. Concluded at Detroit, Michigan, the treaty was signed by Commissioners George W. Manypenny and Henry C. Gilbert for the United States and by twelve chiefs and headmen of the Chippewa of Sault Ste. Marie.

Treaty with the Chippewa of Saginaw, Etc.

August 2, 1855

The main concerns of this treaty were the lands to be withdrawn from sale, land grants to individual tribal members, and payments in full of previous claims. Other concerns were cession, release of liability, surrender of annuities, and land entries. An interpreter was to be provided, and the tribal organization was to be dissolved. The treaty was signed in Detroit, Michigan, by Commissioners George W. Manypenny and Henry C. Gilbert for the United States and by the Chippewa of Saginaw, parties to the treaty of January 14, 1837, and that portion of the band of Chippewa Indians of Swan Creek and Black River, parties to the treaty of May 9, 1836, and now remaining in the State of Michigan.

Treaty with the Blackfeet

October 17, 1855

This treaty was between the United States and the Blackfoot, the Flathead, the Kootenai, and the Nez Percé tribes, who occupied, for the purposes of hunting, the territory on the Upper Missouri and Yellowstone Rivers. The main concerns of the treaty were

Blackfoot on horseback, chasing buffalo near Three Buttes, Montana. Artwork by John M. Stanley c. 1853–1855. (National Archives and Records Administration)

provisions of peace, protection against depredations, and recognition of the Blackfoot territory as common hunting ground. Settlement by the tribes was not permitted on the hunting ground; however, citizens could pass through and live in the Indian Territory. Rules for entering and leaving the hunting ground were established. All tribes were to remain in their respective territories except when hunting. The Blackfoot Nation was designated a certain territory and would receive annual payments. Other concerns were protection against depredations, building of roads, telegraph lines, and military posts. Annuities would be withheld in case of violation of the treaty and would not be taken for individual debt. The tribes requested that liquor be excluded from their country. The treaty was signed at the council ground on the Upper Missouri, near the mouth of the Judith River, in the Territory of Nebraska by Commissioners A. Cumming and Isaac I. Stevens for the United States and by numerous chiefs, headmen, and delegates of the Blackfoot, Flathead, Kootenai, and Nez Percé.

Treaty with the Molala

December 21, 1855

The main concerns of this treaty were cession, boundaries, removal to reservation, and payments. Rights and privileges of former treaties were to be secured, and provision made for the establishment of a flourmill and a sawmill, a blacksmith and tin shop, and a manual-labor school; a carpenter, a joiner, and an additional farmer were to be employed. Expense of removal was to be borne by the United States, and rations were to be furnished to the tribe. An appropriation was made to extinguish title, and so on, of white settlers to lands in Grand Round Valley. It was not stated where the treaty was signed. This treaty was signed by Joel Palmer, superintendent of Indian affairs, for the United States and by four chiefs and headmen of the Molala or Molel tribe.

Treaty with the Stockbridge and Munsee

February 5, 1856

This was an amendment to the treaty with the Menominee of February 28, 1831. It made many provisions and stipulations regarding payments, claims, cessions, placement of dislocated tribes, education,

grounds for a cemetery, construction of roads, alcohol, and inconsistent treaties. The treaty was signed at Stockbridge, Wisconsin, by Commissioner Francis Huebschmann for the United States and by William Mohawk and Joshua Wilson, delegates of the Stockbridge and Munsee tribes, and such of the Munsee who were included in the treaty of September 3, 1839, and were yet residing in the state of New York.

Treaty with the Menominee

February 11, 1856

This treaty was an amendment to the treaty entered into at Stockbridge, Wisconsin, on February 5, 1856. The main concerns of the treaty were cession, payment for said cession, authorization of Congress to create new laws, suppression of use of liquor, annuities, and rights-of-way for roads. This treaty was signed at Keshena, Wisconsin, by Commissioner Francis Huebschmann for the United States and by twenty-seven Menominee.

Treaty with the Creeks, Etc.

August 7, 1856

The main concerns of this treaty were the cession by the Creeks to the Seminole, boundaries, and a guarantee of countries to the Seminole and the Creeks. No state or territory was to pass laws for the tribes, and said countries were not to be included in any state or territory without the tribes' consent. The Creeks released all title to other lands and all claims against the United States, with some exceptions. The Seminole also released claims. Payments to the Creeks and the Seminole were decided. The United States was to remove the Seminole, who would emigrate, and to give the Seminole certain supplies. The western Seminole were to send a delegation to Florida. A tract of land was set apart for the Florida Seminole. Other concerns were the rights of the Creeks and the Seminole in each other's countries, extradition of criminals between said countries, extradition of criminals to the United States or to the states, and the establishment of a justice system. Additional concerns were building of railroads, telegraphs, posts, and agencies, and the regulations respecting same. Traders were to pay for the use of land and timber. Protection of the tribes was secured, and amnesty was declared. This treaty superseded former treaties. Concluded at the city of Washington, the treaty was signed by George W. Manypenny for the United States and by six commissioners on the part of the Creeks and four commissioners on the part of the Seminole.

Treaty with the Pawnee
September 24, 1857

The main concerns of the treaty were lands ceded; reservation; payments; establishment of manual labor schools; supply of tools, farming utensils, and stock; establishment of a mill; and dwellings for interpreter; protection of the Pawnee in their new homes; and the requirement to keep children in school. Additionally, the United States was to furnish six laborers; $2,000 was to be paid to Samuel Allis, and payment in monies or goods was to be made to guides for services rendered to the United States. Tribes were to be peaceful, to pay for depredations, to refrain from making war except in self-defense, and to surrender offenders. Concluded at Table Creek, Nebraska Territory, the treaty was signed by Commissioner James W. Denver for the United States and by sixteen chiefs and headmen of the four confederate bands of the Pawnee.

Treaty with the Seneca–Tonawanda Band
November 5, 1857

This treaty concerns former treaties with the Six Nations of New York on January 15, 1838, and with the Seneca Nation on May 20, 1842. Certain claims under former treaties were relinquished, and unimproved lands were surrendered. Payment was determined, and the Tonawanda were told they could purchase reservation land, that the deed was to be held in trust by the secretary of the interior, and that they were allowed to appoint attorneys. Part of the purchase money was to be invested in stocks. Improvement money was to be apportioned. Concluded on the Tonawanda Reservation in the county of Genesee, New York, the treaty was signed by Commissioner Charles E. Mix for the United States and by Jabez Ground, Jesse Spring, Isaac Shanks, George Sky, and Ely S. Parker, delegates to the Tonawanda band of Seneca, and by forty-five chiefs and headmen of the said tribes.

Treaty with the Ponca
March 12, 1858

The concerns of the treaty were cession of lands; reservation; boundaries; release of claims; U.S. stipulations; protection of the Ponca; provisions; payments and annuities; and appropriations for building homes, a sawmill, a gristmill, and a mechanic's shop and for furnishing apprentices. Children were to be kept in a school maintained by the United States. Scrip of 160 acres each was given to those who chose to leave the tribe and reside among the whites and to Francis Roy, interpreter. The United States was to maintain military posts, roads, and the like. The Ponca were to maintain peace, to pay for depredations, to refrain from making war except in self-defense, and to surrender offenders. Annuities were not to be taken for individual debts and were to be withheld from those who drank liquor. Concluded in the city of Washington, the treaty was signed by Commissioner Charles E. Mix for the United States and, on the part of the Ponca tribe, by Wa-gah-sah-pi, or Whip; Gish-tah-wah-gu, or Strong Walker; Mitchell P. Cera, or Wash-kom-moni; A-shno-ni-kah-gah-hi, or Lone Chief; Shu-kah-bi, or Heavy Clouds; Tah-tungah-nushi, or Standing Buffalo.

Treaty with the Yankton Sioux
April 19, 1858

The main concerns of the treaty were relinquishment of lands; boundaries of ceded land; islands in the Missouri River; the building of roads; settlement of the tribe in one year; protection; the payment of annuities; the purchase of stock; the building of schools, mills, mechanic shops, and houses; and the maintenance of military posts and the like. A portion of the annuities were allowed to be paid for debts. Land grants were given to Charles F. Picotte, Zephyr Rencontre, Paul Dorian, and others. No trade was allowed unless licensed. The Yankton were to preserve peace and to surrender offenders. Annuities were not subject to individual debt and were to be withheld for intemperance. The Yankton were to be given an Indian agent. Concluded in the city of Washington, the treaty was signed by Commissioner Charles E. Mix for the United States and by sixteen chiefs and delegates of the Yankton tribe of Sioux or Dakota.

Treaty with the Sioux
June 19, 1858

This treaty was between the United States and the Mendawakanton and Wahpahoota bands of the Dakota or Sioux tribe. Its main point was that eighty acres of reservation land were to be allotted to each head of a family, and the residue was to be held in common. Further survey and allotments were made. Some lands were made exempt from taxes. Additional concerns were provisions and amendments of the treaty of August 5, 1851. Bands were to be peaceful, to pay for depredations, to refrain from engaging in hostilities except in self-defense, and to surrender offenders. Annuities were to be withheld from those who drank liquor. The secretary of the interior was to have discretion over the manner and object of annual expenditures, and the Senate was to decide whether $10,000 was to be paid to A. J. Campbell, son of then-deceased Scott Campbell. Concluded in the city of Washington, the treaty was signed by Commissioner Charles E. Mix for the United States and by seventeen chiefs and headmen of the Mendawakanton and Wahpahoota bands.

Treaty with the Sioux
June 19, 1858

This treaty was between the United States and the Sisseton and Wahpeton bands of the Dakota or Sioux tribe. Its main point was that eighty acres of reservation land were to be allotted to each head of a family, and the residue was to be held in common. Further survey and allotments were made. Some lands were made exempt from taxes. Additional concerns were provisions and amendments of the treaty of July 23, 1851. The United States was to maintain military posts, roads, and the like. Bands were to be peaceful, to pay for depredations, to refrain from engaging in hostilities except in self-defense, and to surrender offenders. Annuities were to be withheld from those who drank liquor. Members of the bands were allowed to dissolve tribal connections. The secretary of the interior was to have discretion over the manner and object of annual expenditures. Rights of the tribes and allowances were determined. Settlers who settled in good faith on reservation land would have the right of preemption. Concluded at the city of Washington, the treaty was signed by Commissioner Charles E. Mix for the United States and by eight chiefs and headmen of the Sisseton and Wahpeton bands.

Treaty with the Winnebago
April 15, 1859

Under the terms of this treaty, the eastern portion of the reservation, to be known as the Winnebago Reservation, was to be set apart and assigned in severalty to members of the tribe. Whites were not to reside on the reserve. The division of lands was to be under the direction of the secretary of the interior, with certificates issued to the commissioner of Indian affairs. Certain lands could be sold as dictated, and the debts of the tribe were to be paid out of the proceeds of the sale. Provisions were made in case the proceeds were insufficient to pay debts. All members of the tribe were to be notified of this agreement, and the expenses were to be paid from tribal funds. Concluded in the city of Washington, the treaty was signed by Commissioner Charles E. Mix for the United States and by twelve chiefs and delegates representing the Winnebago tribe.

Treaty with the Chippewa, Etc.
July 16, 1859

This treaty was between the United States and the Swan Creek and Black River Chippewa and the Munsee or Christian tribe. Its intent was to manifest tribal liberality, to encourage agricultural pursuits, and to remove all erroneous impressions respecting the nonfulfillment of stipulations of former treaties. Provisions were made for the sale of the reservation held by the Christian tribe and for a suitable and permanent home as directed by Congress on June 8, 1858. Whites were not permitted to settle on the reserve. Appropriations were made for stock, agricultural implements, a schoolhouse, a church building, a blacksmith shop, and the like. The tribes relinquished all claims and granted rights-of-way for roads and highways. Concluded at the Sac and Fox agency, the treaty was signed by Commissioner David Crawford for the United States and by eight delegates representing the tribes.

Treaty with the Sac and Fox
October 1, 1859

This treaty was between the United States and the Sac and Fox of the Mississippi. Under its terms, part of the present reservation was to be set apart and boundaries defined; the new reserve would be known as the reservation of the Sac and Fox of the Mississippi. Eighty acres were set apart for each member of the tribe, along with a tract of land to support a school. Whites were not to reside on the land without permission. All members of the tribe were to share in the benefits. Certificates were to be issued to the commissioner of Indian affairs for division of lands. Rights-of-way for roads, highways, and railroads were allowed. Certain lands could be sold as dictated, and the debts of the tribe were to be paid out of the proceeds of the sale. Provisions were made in case the proceeds were insufficient to pay debts. Provisions of former treaties could be changed by Congress. Provisions were made for Thomas Connelly. Concluded at the Sac and Fox agency in the Territory of Kansas, the treaty was signed by Commissioner Alfred B. Greenwood for the United States and by nine chiefs and delegates representing the tribes.

Treaty with the Kansa Tribe

October 5, 1859

The main concerns of the treaty were assignment of portions of the reservation, boundaries, certificates to be issued, rules and regulations, schools and agency, and naming the Kansas Reservation. Certain assignments were given to the children of Julia Pappan and others. Whites were not allowed to reside on the reserve. Certain lands were allowed to be sold, and the debts of the tribe were to be paid out of the proceeds from the sale. Provisions were made in case the proceeds were insufficient to pay debts. Provisions of treaties could be changed by the president with assent of Congress. The right-of-way for roads was given. Concluded at the Kansas agency in the Territory of Kansas, the treaty was signed by Commissioner Alfred B. Greenwood for the United States and by twenty-seven chiefs and headmen representing the Kansa tribe.

Treaty with the Delaware

May 30, 1860

This treaty dealt with the distribution and allocation of land and allowed eighty acres per tribe member. The treaty stipulated what was to be done in the case of abandonment of land and also set the price per acre at $1.25; it also specified what the United States was to pay for certain depredations. Concluded at

Sarcoxieville on the Delaware Reservation, the treaty was signed by Commissioner Thomas B. Sykes for the United States and by John Conner, Sar-cox-ie, Ne-con-he-con, Rock-a-to-wha, and James Conner, chiefs of the Delaware tribe.

Treaty with the Arapaho and Cheyenne

February 18, 1861

This treaty covered the cession to the United States of lands not owned by the Arapaho and Cheyenne and set boundaries, locations, and stipulations. The treaty also stipulated the disposition of lands, the name of the reservation, and the protection of persons and property. Concluded at Fort Wise, the treaty was signed by Commissioners Albert G. Boone and F. B. Culver for the United States and by the following chiefs and delegates representing the confederated tribes of Arapahoe and Cheyenne Indians of the Upper Arkansas River: Little Raven, Storm, Shave-Head, and Big-Mouth (on the part of

Cheyennes and Kiowas—Southern Plains Delegation in the White House Conservatory on March 27, 1863. The white woman standing at the far right, top row, is often identified as Mary Todd Lincoln. The Indians in the front row are, left to right: War Bonnet, Standing in the Water, Lean Bear of the Cheyennes, and Yellow Wolf of the Kiowas. Lean Bear was a key representative in the 1861 treaty with the Arapaho and Cheyenne. Yellow Wolf is wearing the Thomas Jefferson peace medal. The identities of the Indians in the second row are unknown. (Library of Congress)

the Arapaho), and Black Kettle, White Antelope, Lean Bear, Little Wolf, and Left Hand, or Namos.

Treaty with the Sauk and Fox, Etc.

March 6, 1861

This treaty was between the United States and the Sac and Fox of Missouri and the Iowa. The treaty called for the cession of the reservation in Missouri to the United States and also set boundaries and improvements. Further, it stated that the Iowa must cede land to the United States for the use of the Sac and Fox and that Joseph Tesson and certain chiefs would be allowed to select certain quarter sections of land. It also arranged a grant for education, stipulated that no persons could abide on the reservation without a permit, and stated that a toll bridge was to be built over the Great Nemaha River. The treaty was signed by Daniel Vanderslice, Indian agent, for the United States; by Pe-ta-ok-a-ma, Ne-sour-quoit, Moless, and Se-se-ah-kee, delegates of the Sac and Fox of Missouri; and by No-heart, Nag-ga-rash, Mah-hee, To-hee, Tah-ra-kee, Thur-o-mony, and White Horse, delegates of the Iowa tribe.

Treaty with the Delaware

July 2, 1861

This treaty set forth certain lands pledged by the railroad company to secure its bonds. It included a list of lands, set forth the authority of the agent of the road to make conveyance, and stipulated the form of bond. It also stated that the company was entitled to patent and to execute bonds and mortgage. Concluded at Leavenworth City, Kansas, the treaty was signed by Commissioner William P. Dole for the United States and by head chief John Conner and four other representatives of the Delaware tribe.

Treaty with the Potawatomi

November 15, 1861

This treaty dealt with the disposition of the Kansas Reservation and arranged for a census of the tribe; it also set forth assignments of land, certificates to issue, exemption from levy, and pay-

ments to be made. The treaty authorized the president to cause lands to be granted in fee to certain male adults, allowed for the Leavenworth, Pawnee, and Western Railroad to purchase certain land, and set the price and terms of purchase. It also allowed for a reservation of land for the Baptist Mission, for annual interest of the improvement fund, and for former claims to hold good. The treaty was signed by Commissioner William W. Ross for the United States and by seventy-five chiefs, braves, and headmen of the Potawatomi Nation.

Treaty with the Kansa

March 13, 1862

This treaty is an amendment to a treaty made in 1859. It authorized the secretary of the interior to ascertain the value of the improvements made by persons who settled on the diminished reserve of the Kansa, and it granted a half-section of land to Thomas S. Huffaker. Concluded in the state of Kansas at the Kansas Indian agency, the treaty was signed by Commissioners Alfred B. Greenwood and H. W. Farnsworth for the United States and by twenty-seven representatives of the Kansa tribe.

Treaty with the Ottawa of Blanchard's Fork and Roche de Boeuf

June 24, 1862

This treaty allowed certain Ottawa Indians to become citizens of the United States within five years of the treaty date. It also sectioned land to compensate chiefs, stated that heads of families would receive either 160 or 80 acres of land, set forth annuities and debts, and set apart land for a school. The treaty also stated there would be no tax, and it also specified how the school land was to be managed and what was to be taught in the school. The treaty was signed by Commissioner William P. Dole for the United States; by Pem-ach-wung, chief; and by John T. Jones, William Hurr, and James Wind, chief and councilmen of the Ottawa Indians of the united bands of Blanchard's Fork and Roche de Boeuf.

Treaty with the Chippewa of the Mississippi and the Pillager and Lake Winnibigoshish Bands

March 11, 1863

This treaty arranged for the cession of certain reservations to the United States and set the boundaries and annuities thereof. It allowed for the reservation to be cleared in lots and gave houses to the chiefs, and the United States agreed to furnish oxen and tools. It also stated who was to be recognized as chief, who was to receive said annuities, and set the salary of female teachers. Concluded in Washington, D.C., the treaty was signed for the United States by William P. Dole, commissioner of Indian affairs, and Clark W. Thompson, superintendent of Indian affairs of the Northern Superintendency; and by Henry M. Rice of Minnesota for and on behalf of the Chippewa of the Mississippi and the Pillager and Lake Winnibigoshish bands of Chippewa Indians in Minnesota.

Treaty with the Nez Percé

June 9, 1863

This treaty arranged for the cession of lands to the United States and set the reservation boundaries. It also required the tribe to settle on the reservation within a year, allowed portions of land to be sold to loyal whites, allowed for certificates of sale, and specified that the lots were to be exempt from levy, taxes, and the like. The treaty also asked the tribe to elect subordinate chiefs, gave the tribe money for two churches, schools, a hospital, blacksmith's tools, houses, mills, and so forth. The treaty was signed for the United States by C. H. Hale, superintendent of Indian affairs, and Charles Hutchins and S. D. Howe, U.S. Indian agents for the Territory of Washington; and for the Indians by fifty chiefs of the Nez Percé Nation.

Treaty with the Kickapoo

June 28, 1863

This treaty dealt with the division of land, arranged for an accurate census of the reservation to be taken, and set for the conditions of land sale. It allowed heads of families to be allottees and to become citizens of the United States, stated when contracts were to be null, provided for those members who wished

Chief Joseph (c. 1840–1904) was a courageous leader of considerable diplomatic skill who came to be regarded as the spokesman for the united bands of Nez Percé. His legend was sealed by his famous declaration upon surrendering in 1877 that "from where the sun now stands, I will fight no more forever." (Library of Congress)

to hold their lands in common, and stipulated that the Atchison and Pike's Peak Railroad could purchase certain lands. Concluded at the Indian agency on the Kickapoo Reservation in Kansas, the treaty was signed by Commissioner Charles B. Keith for the United States and by eight chiefs of the Kickapoo Nation.

Treaty with the Eastern Shoshone

July 2, 1863

This treaty reestablished friendly relations and perpetual peace between the United States and the Eastern Shoshone. Further, the treat set forth routes of travel, settlements and posts, and telegraph and stage lines, permitted the railway to come through the land, set the boundaries of the Shoshone land, and provided an annuity for loss of game. Concluded at Fort Bridger, Utah Territory, the treaty was signed by James Duane Doty and Luther Mann, Jr., for the United States and by eleven chiefs of the Shoshone Nation.

Treaty with the Shoshone–Northwestern Bands

July 30, 1863

This was a treaty of peace and friendship, stating that the Shoshone Nation understood and agreed with the Treaty of Fort Bridger (Treaty with the Eastern Shoshone–July 2, 1863); it also increased annuities and set the boundaries of the Shoshone country. Concluded at Box Elder, Utah Territory, the treaty was signed by Brigadier General P. Edward Connor, commanding the military district of Utah, and James Duane Doty for the United States, and by nine chiefs of the Shoshone Nation.

Treaty with the Western Shoshone

October 1, 1863

This treaty established peace and asked the Western bands of Shoshone to cease depredations. It also set forth routes of travel, settlements and posts, and telegraph and stage lines, permitted the railway to come through the land, and set the boundaries of the Shoshone land, as well as allowing for explorations, mines, and use of timber. The treaty was signed by James W. Nye and James Duane Doty for the United States and by twelve leaders of the Shoshone Nation.

Treaty with the Chippewa–Red Lake and Pembina Bands

October 1, 1863

This treaty established perpetual peace between the United States and the Red Lake and Pembina bands and requested the cession of land to the United States. It also set boundaries, set payments for lands ceded, granted amnesty for past offenses, and appropriated compensation for former depreda-

tions. This treaty also stipulated how claims were to be audited, allowed for a road to be built from Leach Lake to Red Lake, and prohibited spirituous liquors. It also granted 160 acres to certain members of the Red Lake and Pembina bands as well as a reservation of 640 acres each for Chiefs Moose Dung and Red Bear. The treaty was signed by Alexander Ramsey and Ashley C. Morrill for the United States and by fifteen chiefs and leaders of the Chippewa Nation.

Treaty with Utah– Tabeguache Band

October 7, 1863

This treaty set forth the boundaries of land, admitted the authority of the United States, asked for the cession of lands, and permitted military posts to be established on unceded lands. It permitted the mining of lands and their settlement by the Mohuache band of Utah with no molestation, and arranged protection for certain persons, redress of injuries, and delivery of offenders. The treaty also stipulated that stolen property would go to a government agent, that no munitions of war were to be given to bands not in amity with the United States, and that the band would receive five American stallions to improve their breeding of horses. Concluded at the Tabeguache agency at Conejos, Colorado Territory, the treaty was signed by J. Evans, M. Steck, Simeon Whiteley, and Lafayette Head for the United States and by ten leaders of the Tabeguache band.

Treaty with the Shoshone-Goship

October 12, 1863

This treaty established peace and requested the Shoshone-Goship band to cease depredations. It established routes of travel, settlements and posts, and telegraph and stage lines, granted right-of-way for the railway, set the boundaries of the Shoshone-Goship land, and allowed for explorations, mines, and use of timber. Concluded at Tuilla Valley, Utah Territory, the treaty was signed by P. Edw. Connor and James Duane Doty for the United States and by four leaders of the Shoshone-Goship band.

Treaty with the Chippewa–Red Lake and Pembina Bands

April 12, 1864

This treaty stated the bands' assent to the amendment of the treaty of October 2, 1863, and that the U.S. government would pay each band a sum in lieu of annuity by the former treaty. The treaty also set forth the annual expenditures of the U.S. government for blankets, provisions, and the like, and stipulated that the United States would furnish one blacksmith, one physician, one miller, and one farmer, as well as iron, steel, and a sawmill. Concluded at Old Crossing of Red Lake River in the state of Minnesota, the treaty was signed by Clark W. Thompson and Ashley C. Morrill for the United States and by sixteen leaders of the Red Lake and Pembina bands.

Treaty with the Chippewa, Mississippi, Pillager, and Lake Winnibigoshish Bands

May 7, 1864

This treaty called for the cession of various lakes and other reservations to the United States; it also set boundaries, specified reservations, set payments, and allowed for houses for the chiefs. The treaty also stated that the United States would furnish oxen, plows, agricultural implements, carpenters, blacksmiths, laborers, and physicians, and that a sawmill, roads, and bridges were to be erected for common use by the bands. Chiefs with bands of fewer than fifty were not to be recognized; gratuities were stated and salaries set for female teachers. Concluded at Washington, D.C., the treaty was signed by William P. Dole, commissioner of Indian affairs, and Clark W. Thompson for the United States, and by the Chippewa chief Hole-in-the-Day and Mis-qua-dace.

Treaty with the Klamath, Etc.

October 14, 1864

This treaty required the Klamath to move to and live on the reservation, called for cession of lands to the United States, set boundaries, and stated that white persons were not to remain on the reservation. The treaty also called for a right-of-way for railroads; set payments to be made by the United States, along with additional payments and their use; provided for the building of mills, shops, a schoolhouse, and a hospital; and arranged the provision of tools, books, stationery, farmers, mechanics, and teachers. This treaty stated that the reservation could be surveyed, was not to be alienated or subject to levy, and that restrictions could be removed. It also established peace and friendship, stipulated that tribe members who drank liquor would not benefit from the treaty, and permitted other tribes to be located on the reservation. The treaty was signed by J. W. Perit Huntington, superintendent of Indian affairs in Oregon, and William Logan for the United States and by twenty-six leaders of the Klamath.

Treaty with the Chippewa of Saginaw, Swan Creek, and Black River

October 18, 1864

This treaty requested certain lands to be released to the United States and specified the amount of land each type of person (chiefs, headmen, etc.) was to receive. The treaty permitted William Smith and others to select lands and receive patents therefore; it further required the agent to make a list of lands selected and by whom, and to separate that list into "competents" and "those not so competent." The treaty provided for a manual labor school, a farm, buildings, an annual appropriation, and control of the school and farm, stipulating also that, if the school and farm were abandoned, the rights under the treaty would be lost; that the land and buildings could be sold; and that the missionary society was to use the schoolhouse already present. It also said that the mill and land at Isabella City could be sold, that James Nicholson could select eighty acres, and that the eighth article of the former treaty was not affected. Concluded at the Isabella Indian Reservation in the state of Michigan, the treaty was signed by H. J. Alvord and D. C. Leach for the United States and by thirty leaders of the Chippewa bands.

Treaty with the Omaha

March 6, 1865

The main concerns of this treaty were cession, boundaries, provisions, payments, and division of land among tribe members, with certificates to be issued for tracts assigned. Articles of a treaty of

March 16, 1854, were extended. Payment was to be made for damages to the reservation for use and destruction of timber by the Winnebago tribe. The name of the reserve was to be Omaha, and whites were not allowed to enter or reside on the reserve without permission. If the location of the Winnebago affected their peace, the Omaha could repurchase the land. Concluded at Washington, D.C., the treaty was signed by Commissioners Clark W. Thompson and Robert W. Furnas for the United States and by the Omaha tribe chiefs E-sta-mah-za (Joseph La Flesche), Gra-ta-mah-zhe (Standing Hawk), Ga-he-ga-zhinga (Little Chief), Tah-wah-gah-ha (Village Maker), Wah-no-ke-ga (Noise), Sha-da-na-ge (Yellow Smoke), Wastch-com-ma-nu (Hard Walker), Pad-a-ga-he (Fire Chief), Ta-su (White Cow), and Ma-ha-nin-ga (No Knife).

Treaty with the Winnebago
March 8, 1865
The main concerns of this treaty were cession, reservation, boundaries, and expense of removal. The United States was to erect mills, to section and fence land, and furnish seed, tools, and the like. The United States further agreed to build an agency building, a schoolhouse, a warehouse, and buildings suitable for the physician, interpreter, miller, engineer, carpenter, and blacksmith, and a house for each chief. Concluded at Washington, D.C., the treaty was signed by Commissioners William P. Dole, C. W. Thompson, and A. D. Balcombe and by the Winnebago chiefs Little Hill, Little Decoria, Whirling Thunder, Young Prophet, Good Thunder, and White Breast.

Treaty with the Ponca
March 10, 1865
This was a supplementary article to the treaty of March 12, 1858, and its main concerns were cession, boundaries, and land ceded back to the Ponca by the United States. The tribe was to satisfy or pay the claims, if any, of any settlers for improvements on the lands ceded by the United States; further, the United States was to indemnify the tribe for spoliation committed against them. Concluded in the city of Washington, the treaty was signed by Commissioner William P. Dole for the United States and by

White Eagle, chief of the Ponca tribe, c. 1860. (Getty Images)

Wah-gah-sap-pi (Iron Whip), Gist-tah-wah-gu (Strong Walker), Wash-com-mo-ni (Mitchell P. Cerre), Ash-nan-e-kah-gah-he (Lone Chief), and Tah-ton-ga-nuz-zhe (Standing Buffalo), delegates of the Ponca tribe.

Treaty with the Snake
August 12, 1865
The main concerns of the treaty were peace, the release of slaves, prohibition of the sale of firearms, establishment of a justice system, land cession, boundaries, and reservation. The United States agreed to pay for fencing, breakup, and cultivation of land and to supply seed, tools, and stock. Further, the tribe was given a physician, mechanics, farmers, teachers, and an interpreter and had the use of the mills and schoolhouses. The tribe wanted to prevent

the use of liquor among themselves by the withholding of annuities in the case of disobedience. Concluded at Sprague River Valley, the treaty was signed by J. W. Perit Huntington, superintendent of Indian affairs in Oregon, for the United States and by eleven chiefs and headmen of the Woll-pah-pe band of the Snake tribe.

Agreement with the Cherokee and Other Tribes in the Indian Territory
September 13, 1865

This agreement was never ratified. Its main concerns were to place the tribes under the protection and jurisdiction of the United States. In return, the United States promised to reestablish peace and friendship and to provide protection, and declared its willingness to enter into treaties to settle all questions resulting from former treaties. The agreement was signed most probably at Fort Smith by five commissioners for the United States and by numerous chiefs and delegates of the Creek, Cowskin Seneca, Seneca and Shawnee, Cherokee, and Seminole tribes.

Treaty with the Osage
September 29, 1865

The main concerns of this treaty were land sales, surveys, boundaries, payments in monies and goods, cession, funds in trust, individual land grants, annual salary for chiefs, land grant for purposes of education, and patents. Further, tribes were to be peaceful, to commit no depredations, and to refrain from making war. A right-of-way for highways and railroads was granted. The Osage were allowed to unite with other tribes and to receive a portion of annuities. If tribes removed from Kansas, their diminished reservation was to be sold and 50 percent of the proceeds used by the United States to purchase lands suitable for homes for the tribe. Concluded at the Canville trading post, Osage Nation, Kansas, the treaty was signed by Commissioner D. N. Cooley and Elijah Sells, superintendent of Indian affairs, for the United States and by eight chiefs of the Great and Little Osage tribes.

Treaty with the Sioux–Miniconjou Band
October 10, 1865

The main concerns of this treaty were submission to the laws of the United States, peace, settlement of differences between tribes by arbitration, tribal withdrawal from overland routes, payments, and protection of the tribal members. Subsequent amendment to the treaty was to be binding. Concluded at Fort Sully in the Territory of Dakota, the treaty was signed for the United States by Newton Edmunds, governor and ex-superintendent of Indian affairs for the Dakota Territory; Edward B. Taylor, superintendent of Indian affairs for the Northern Superintendency; and four commissioners; and for the Indians by fourteen chiefs and headmen of the Miniconjou band of the Dakota or Sioux.

Treaty with the Sioux–Lower Brulé Band
October 14, 1865

The main concerns of this treaty were peace, arbitration, withdrawal of the tribes from overland routes, payments, building of roads, and establishment of schools. The United States was to engage a blacksmith and a farmer for the tribe's benefit, but all stock, agricultural equipment, and other implements were to remain U.S. property. The reservation boundaries were laid out, and the reserve was to be known as the Lower Brulé. Whites were not to enter or reside on the reserve, and individual tribesmen locating on lands were to be protected. Two Kettle bands could be located adjoining the Brulé. Concluded at Fort Sully, Dakota, the treaty was signed by Newton Edmunds, governor and ex-superintendent of Indian affairs for the Dakota Territory; Edward B. Taylor, superintendent of Indian affairs for the Northern Superintendency; and four commissioners, for the United States; and by fifteen chiefs and headmen of the Lower Brulé band of Dakota or Sioux.

Treaty with the Cheyenne and Arapaho
October 14, 1865

The main concerns of the treaty were peace, arbitration, surrender of tribal members committing depredations, reservation, boundaries, payments and annuities, patents, land grants, and building of roads and military posts. Whites were not allowed to settle on the reserve, except for officers, agents, and employees of the government, and the tribes were not required to settle thereon until the United States extinguished all claims of title from other tribes. However, the tribes were not to encamp within ten miles of any main road and were to refrain from depredations. A census was to be taken each year, and these tribes were to urge other portions of the tribe not then present to join in this treaty. Concluded at the camp on the Little Arkansas River in Kansas, the treaty was signed by Commissioners John B. Sanborn, William S. Harney, Thomas Murphy, Kit Carson, William W. Bent, Jesse H. Leavenworth, and James Steele for the United States and by six Cheyenne and seven Arapaho chiefs and headmen.

Treaty with the Apache, Cheyenne, and Arapaho
October 17, 1865
This treaty unites the Apache tribe, heretofore confederated with the Kiowa and Comanche tribes, with the Cheyenne and Arapaho bound under the provisions of the treaty of October 14, 1865, at the council grounds on the Little Arkansas River, Kansas. It was signed by Commissioners John B. Sanborn, William S. Harney, Thomas Murphy, Kit Carson, William W. Bent, Jesse H. Leavenworth, and James Steele for the United States and by six Apache, six Cheyenne, and seven Arapaho chiefs and headmen.

Treaty with the Comanche and Kiowa
October 18, 1865
The main concerns of this treaty were peace, arbitration, refrainment from depredations, surrender of tribal members committing crimes, reservation, boundaries, rights-of-way for roads and military posts, and payment of annuities. No whites were to settle on the reserve without permission. The tribe was to remove thereto and not leave without written permission; when absent from the reservation, tribe members were not to encamp within ten miles of any road or military post. Claims to other lands were

relinquished, and other portions of the tribes were urged to join in this treaty. The treaty was signed by Commissioners John B. Sanborn, William S. Harney, Thomas Murphy, Kit Carson, William W. Bent, Jesse H. Leavenworth, and James Steele for the United States, and by twenty-two chiefs and headmen of several bands of the Comanche and Kiowa tribes.

Treaty with the Sioux– Two-Kettle Band
October 19, 1865
The main concerns of this treaty were the authority and jurisdiction of the United States, peace, arbitration, withdrawal from overland routes, protection, and payments for agricultural developments and implements. The United States was to engage a farmer, a blacksmith, and teachers. The United States was to make payment and receive indemnity for killing Ish-tah-chah-ne-aha (Puffing Eyes), a friendly chief of the Two-Kettle band of Dakota or Sioux. All amendments to the treaty were deemed binding. Concluded at Fort Sully in Dakota, the treaty was signed for the United States by Commissioners Newton Edmunds, governor and ex-superintendent of Indian affairs for the Dakota Territory; Edward B. Taylor, superintendent of Indian affairs for the Northern Superintendency; Major General S. R. Curtis; Brigadier General H. H. Sibley, Henry W. Reed, and Orrin Guernsey; and for the Natives by twenty-two chiefs and headmen of the Two-Kettles band of Dakota or Sioux.

Treaty with the Blackfeet Sioux
October 19, 1865
The main concerns of this treaty were the authority and jurisdiction of the United States, peace, arbitration, withdrawal from overland routes, and payments. All amendments to the treaty were deemed binding. Concluded at Fort Sully, Dakota, the treaty was signed for the United States by Commissioners Newton Edmunds, governor and ex-superintendent of Indian affairs for the Dakota Territory; Edward B. Taylor, superintendent of Indian affairs for the Northern Superintendency; Major General S. R. Curtis, Brigadier General H. H. Sibley, Henry W. Reed, and Orrin Guernsey, and by two chiefs, Wah-hah-chunk-i-ah-pee (The One That Is Used as a Shield)

and Wah-mun-dee-wak-kon-o (The War Eagle in the Air), and twelve braves of the Blackfeet band of Dakota or Sioux.

Treaty with the Sioux– Sans Arcs Band

October 20, 1865

The main concerns of this treaty were the authority and jurisdiction of the United States, peace, arbitration, withdrawal from overland routes, protection, and payments for agricultural development and implements. A farmer, a blacksmith, and teachers were to be employed. All amendments to the treaty were deemed binding. Concluded at Fort Sully, Dakota, the treaty was signed for the United States by Commissioners Newton Edmunds, governor and ex-superintendent of Indian affairs for the Dakota Territory; Edward B. Taylor, superintendent of Indian affairs for the Northern Superintendency; Major General S. R. Curtis; Brigadier General H. H. Sibley; Henry W. Reed; and Orrin Guernsey; and for the Indians by the three chiefs Wah-mun-dee-o-pee-doo-tah (The War Eagle with the Red Tail), Cha-tau-'hne (Yellow Hawk), and Shon-kah-we-to-ko (The Fool Dog) and six chief soldiers of the Sans Arcs band of Dakota or Sioux.

A Hunkapapa Sioux leader, Gall (c. 1840–1894) came into prominence at the Battle of the Little Bighorn, where he opened the fight by leading warriors against the charge of Major Marcus Reno's battalion down the valley of the Little Bighorn. (National Archives)

Treaty with the Sioux–Hunkpapa Band

October 20, 1865

The main concerns of this treaty were the authority and jurisdiction of the United States, peace, arbitration, withdrawal from overland routes, protection, and payments for agricultural development and implements. A farmer, a blacksmith, and teachers were to be employed. All amendments to the treaty were deemed binding. Concluded at Fort Sully, Dakota, the treaty was signed for the United States by Commissioners Newton Edmunds, governor and ex-superintendent of Indian affairs for the Dakota Territory; Edward B. Taylor, superintendent of Indian affairs for the Northern Superintendency; Major General S. R. Curtis; Brigadier General H. H. Sibley; Henry W. Reed; and Orrin Guernsey; and for the Indians by six chiefs and four chief soldiers of the Onkpahpah band of Dakota or Sioux.

Treaty with the Sioux–Yanktonai Band

October 20, 1865

The main concerns of this treaty were the authority and jurisdiction of the United States, peace, arbitration, withdrawal from overland routes, protection, and payments for agricultural development and implements. A farmer, a blacksmith, and teachers were to be employed. All amendments to the treaty were deemed binding. Concluded at Fort Sully, Dakota, the treaty was signed for the United States by Commissioners Newton Edmunds, governor and ex-superintendent of Indian affairs for the Dakota Territory; Edward B. Taylor, superintendent of Indian affairs for the Northern Superintendency;

Major General S. R. Curtis; Brigadier General H. H. Sibley; Henry W. Reed; and Orrin Guernsey; and for the Indians by eight chiefs and seven chief soldiers of the Yanktonai band of Dakota or Sioux.

Treaty with the Sioux–Upper Yanktonai Band

October 28, 1865

The main concerns of this treaty were the authority and jurisdiction of the United States, peace, arbitration, withdrawal from overland routes, protection, and payments for agricultural development and implements. A farmer, a blacksmith, and teachers were to be employed. All amendments to the treaty were deemed binding. Concluded at Fort Sully, Dakota, the treaty was signed for the United States by Commissioners Newton Edmunds, governor and ex-superintendent of Indian affairs for Dakota Territory; Edward B. Taylor, superintendent of Indian affairs for the Northern Superintendency; Major General S. R. Curtis; Brigadier General H. H. Sibley; Henry W. Reed; and Orrin Guernsey; and for the Indians by three chiefs and eleven chief soldiers of the Upper Yanktonai band of Dakota or Sioux Indians.

Treaty with the Sioux–Oglala Band

October 28, 1865

The main concerns of this treaty were the authority and jurisdiction of the United States, peace, arbitration, withdrawal from overland routes, protection, and payments for agricultural development and implements. A farmer, a blacksmith, and teachers were to be employed. All amendments to the treaty were deemed binding. Concluded at Fort Sully, Dakota, the treaty was signed for the United States by Commissioners Newton Edmunds, governor and ex-superintendent of Indian affairs for the Dakota Territory; Edward B. Taylor, superintendent of Indian affairs for the Northern Superintendency; Major General S. R. Curtis; Brigadier General H. H. Sibley; Henry W. Reed; and Orrin Guernsey, and for the Indians by Chief Long Bull (Tan-tan-ka-has-ka) and three headmen of the Oglala band of Dakota or Sioux.

Treaty with the Middle Oregon Tribes

November 15, 1865

This is an amendment to the treaty of June 25, 1855. Certain rights granted by the former treaty were relinquished; the tribes were to remain on the reservation unless given a written permit to go outside the boundaries; and an allotment of land was to be given to each head of the family. The United States was to pay for teams, agricultural implements, seeds, and the like. Annuities would be withheld from tribal members who broke the treaty, and tribe members would be punished for using or possessing liquor. Concluded at the Warm Springs agency, Oregon, the treaty was signed by J. W. Perit Huntington, superintendent of Indian affairs for Oregon, for the United States and by twenty-one chiefs and headmen of the confederated tribes and bands of Middle Oregon.

Reconstruction Treaties with the Cherokee, Choctaw, Chickasaw, Creeks, and Seminole

April 28–July 19, 1866

These agreements were signed with the Seminole, Choctaw, Chickasaw, Creek, and Cherokee Nations between February and August 1866. All five Indian groups had signed treaties of alliance with the Confederacy in 1861; as a result, the federal government declared that the tribes had lost all rights to annuities and land promised in former treaties.

The negotiations with the five nations began in September 1865 with a twelve-day meeting at Fort Smith, Arkansas. During the conference, the federal government stated the seven basic stipulations required in each treaty. First, each nation had to enter into a treaty of peace and friendship with the United States, with other Indian nations, and between tribal factions. Second, they were to assist the federal government in pacifying the western Indians. Third, slavery had to be abolished, all slaves were to be unconditionally emancipated, and the freed slaves had to be incorporated into the tribes or other suitable provisions made for former slaves. Fourth, involuntary servitude could be tolerated only as punishment for a crime. Fifth, each nation holding land in Indian Territory had to set aside land for the settlement of Kansas Indians. Sixth, all tribes of Indian Territory were expected to prepare for the eventual consolidation of all Indians under one government. Finally, no white persons, except those connected with the military or assigned as Indian agents and employees of the government and of internal improvement agencies, were to be permitted to reside in Indian Territory unless they had been formally incorporated into the tribe. The Indians would have some ability to negotiate how much land each nation forfeited, the size of rights-of-way for railroads, and the status of former slaves.

The Seminole delegation was the first to arrive in Washington. The inexperienced and impoverished representatives were war weary and just wanted to go home; consequently, they put up little resistance to the demands of federal negotiators. They agreed to all the demands of the Fort Smith meeting, ceding their entire homeland for fifteen cents an acre, and they agreed to purchase two hundred thousand acres from the Creek Nation at fifty cents an acre. Their treaty established rights-of-way for railroads, abolished slavery, and stated that all Seminoles, freedmen, and adopted white people would have equal rights within the nation.

The harsh treaty with the Seminole was followed a few weeks later by a far more benevolent treaty with the Choctaw and Chickasaw Nations. The two nations hired an attorney and worked closely together. Overall, the Choctaw, the Chickasaw, and their attorneys proved to be very able negotiators, and the Choctaw and Chickasaw did not incur any liability or forfeiture of land as a result of their alignment with the Confederacy. They were not forced to grant citizenship to their former slaves. If the two nations did not pass legislation providing for the civil rights of their former slaves, the United States would use $300,000 of Choctaw and Chickasaw money to relocate the people of African descent elsewhere. Rights-of-way were established for railroads, and the Choctaw and Chickasaw made provisions to purchase stock in the company that built through their nation. The Indians were to pay for the stock by selling to the railroad sections of land six miles wide on each side of the track.

The Creek Nation's negotiations in many ways mirrored the Seminole negotiations. The delegates did not resist federal demands, and they accepted all the Fort Smith demands. They ceded the west half of the Creek domain, estimated to contain 3,250,560 acres; they adopted their freedmen, established rights-of-way for the railroads, and accepted provi-

sions for the eventual consolidation of all Indians under one government.

The most contentious negations were with the Cherokee, who sent both Southern and Union representatives; federal officials played the two factions against each other. After months of bitter debate, federal negotiators dismissed the Loyal Cherokee delegation and concluded a treaty with the minority Southern representatives. This treaty was never recognized, and a few weeks later, the Loyal delegation was invited back. In the end, the Cherokee agreed to most of the Fort Smith provisions. Former slaves were granted citizenship and were to have equal rights with other Cherokee citizens. The nation was also forced to sell the Neutral Lands, but they refused to sell the Cherokee Strip. Fortunately, on the issue of land cession, the Loyal faction negotiated better terms than the other four nations did. The land was to be appraised by two disinterested parties and then to be sold to the highest bidder, and he Cherokee Nation was guaranteed at least $1.25 per acre.

The unique sovereign status of the five nations allowed Indian commissioners to make demands of the slave-owning Indians that were not made of former Confederate states. No former Confederate state was required to give up territory as war reparations, yet all five nations were required to cede or lease land so the federal government could concentrate all unwanted indigenous people in Indian Territory. Furthermore, although Southern slaveowners simply had to free their slaves, the Indians were required to give their freedmen land and, in some cases, tribal membership and a share of tribal funds. In effect, three nations lost the right to determine their own tribal membership. In the end, once the negotiations were over, the Indians knew that they were the real losers of the Civil War.

Joyce Ann Kievit

References and Further Reading
Abel, Annie Heloise. 1925. *The American Indian under Reconstruction*. Cleveland: Arthur H. Clark. Reprint, St. Clair Shores, MI: Scholarly Press, 1972.
Foreman, Grant. 1934. *The Five Civilized Tribes: Cherokee, Chickasaw, Choctaw, Creek, Seminole*. Norman. University of Oklahoma Press.
Foreman, Grant. 1932. *Indian Removal: The Emigration of the Five Civilized Tribes of Indians*. Norman. University of Oklahoma Press.
Kappler, Charles J., ed. 1971. *Indian Affairs: Laws and Treaties*, vol. 2. New York: AMS Press.

Treaty with the Seminole

March 21, 1866

The main concerns of this treaty were peace, military occupation and protection, amnesty, prohibition of slavery, rights of those of African descent, cession of lands, boundaries, land grants, payments by the United States, rights-of-way for railroads, and construction of agency buildings. A council was organized and pay determined. No session of the council was allowed to exceed thirty days in any one year, and a special session could be called by the superintendent or the secretary of the interior. This treaty constituted full settlement of all claims; obligations from the treaty of August 1, 1861, were reaffirmed, and it was determined that any treaty provisions inconsistent with the articles of the current treaty would be annulled. Concluded at Washington, D.C., the treaty was signed by Commissioner D. N. Cooley, Superintendent of Indian Affairs Elijah Sells, and Ely S. Parker for the United States and by the Seminole chiefs John Chup-co (Long John), Cho-cote-harjo, Fos-har-jo, and John F. Brown.

Treaty with the Potawatomi

March 29, 1866

Amendments were desired by the Potawatomi Indians to their treaty concluded at the Potawatomi agency on November 15, 1861. Provisions of the third article of the former treaty were extended to all adult persons of the tribe. This treaty was signed by Commissioner Dennis N. Cooley and a business committee acting on behalf of said tribe.

Treaty with the Chippewa– Bois Fort Band

April 7, 1866

The main concerns of this treaty were peace, cession, boundaries, reservation, payments, land grants, and annuities. The United States agreed to build a blacksmith shop, a schoolhouse, houses for the chiefs, and other buildings. Obligations from the treaty of September 30, 1854, were reaffirmed, and it was determined that any treaty provisions inconsistent with the articles of the current treaty would be abrogated. Concluded at Washington, D.C., the treaty was signed by Commissioner of Indian Affairs D. N. Cooley and Special Commissioner E. E. L. Taylor for the United States and by nine chiefs, headmen, and warriors of the Bois Fort band of Chippewa.

Treaty with the Choctaw and Chickasaw

April 28, 1866

The main concerns of this treaty were peace, cessation of slavery and involuntary servitude, cession, rights of blacks and freedmen, amnesty for past offenses, rights-of-way for railroads, laws governing companies, patents, payments, investments, land grants, mode of land selection, rights of citizens by adoption or intermarriage, and the survey and division of lands with maps to exhibit actual occupancies. A justice system was organized, and the building of military posts and Indian agencies was allowed. Post offices and a postal service were to be established. A council was organized and pay determined. No session of the council was allowed to exceed thirty days in any one year, and a special session could be called by the superintendent or the secretary of the interior. Missionaries were not to be interfered with and were given certain rights. No more that ten thousand Kansas tribe members would be received into these districts, and no white persons were to enter the territory without special permission. Former rights and immunities of tribe members were to remain in force. Concluded at the city of Washington, the treaty was signed by Special Commissioners Dennis N. Cooley, Elijah Sells, and E. S. Parker for the United States; by Alfred Wade, Allen Wright, James Riley, and John Page, commissioners, on the part of the Choctaw; and by Winchester Colbert, Edmund Pickens, Holmes Colbert, Colbert Carter, and Robert H. Love, commissioners, on the part of the Chickasaw.

Treaty with the Creeks

June 14, 1866

This was a treaty of cession and indemnity, establishing military occupation and protection by the United States and amnesty. Slavery was prohibited, and the rights of people of African descent were outlined. Payment was to be made for the cession of lands and for losses of loyal refugee members and freedmen who had enlisted in the Federal army. Right-of-way was granted for a railroad. Land grants were made for missionary and educational purposes. The Seminole were allowed to sell or convey land to the United States, and the boundary dividing the Creek country was to be surveyed. Agency buildings were to be erected. A council was organized and powers and pay determined. No session of the council was allowed to exceed thirty days in any one year, and a special session could be called by the superintendent or the secretary of the interior. This treaty constituted full settlement of all claims and reaffirmed obligations from the treaty of July 10, 1861; further, any treaty provisions inconsistent with the articles of the current treaty would be annulled. Concluded at the city of Washington, the treaty was signed for the United States by Dennis N. Cooley, commissioner of Indian affairs; Elija Sells, superintendent of Indian affairs for the Southern Superintendency; and Colonel Ely S. Parker, special commissioner; and by the Creek Nations of Indians, represented by Ok-tars-sars-harjov (Sands), Cow-e-to-me-co, and Che-chu-chee, delegates at large, and D. N. McIntosh and James Smith, special delegates of the Southern Creek.

Treaty with the Delaware
July 4, 1866

The main concerns of this treaty were payment for reservation land previously sold, and authorization to sell the remaining part as well as to reserve for sale the lands of those members who elected to become citizens. Improvements were to be appraised and each member paid accordingly. Provisions were made to set apart land for allotment to children born after the treaty. The United States was to sell certain lands to the Delaware and to survey and define boundaries. Proceeds from the sales were to be paid to tribe members. Peaceable possession was guaranteed. Procedures for citizenship were defined, a registry was to be made of those electing to become citizens, and a patent was to be granted to those who became citizens. A settlement of all claims for depredations was made. The Delaware were not to move until new homes were provided. The treaty was signed by Superintendent Thomas Murphy, Indian Agent John G. Pratt, and Special Commissioner W. H. Watson for the United

States, and by three chiefs and four councilors of the Delaware tribe.

Treaty with the Cherokee
July 19, 1866

Under the terms of this treaty, the treaty of October 7, 1861, was declared void, amnesty was given, confiscation laws were repealed, and rights were restored to former owners. Slavery was prohibited, although emancipated slaves were not to be paid. Cherokee, freed slaves, and free blacks could elect to reside in the Canadian district southwest of the Arkansas River, and a justice system was outlined. The United States guaranteed protection and was allowed to build military posts and to settle other civilized tribes in the Cherokee country. However, those wishing to preserve the tribal organization were allowed to have land set aside for them. The tribe was given the right of representation in the national council. No trade licenses were to be issued without the express permission of the Cherokee. The Cherokee were allowed to sell farm products. A council was organized and powers and pay determined. No session of the council was allowed to exceed thirty days in any one year, and a special session could be called by the superintendent or the secretary of the interior. Land grants were allowed for missionary and educational purposes. This treaty reaffirmed all previous treaties, and any treaty provisions inconsistent with the current treaty would be annulled. Concluded at the city of Washington, this treaty was signed by Dennis N. Cooley, commissioner of Indian affairs, and Elijah Sells, superintendent of Indian affairs for the Southern Superintendency for the United States, and by six delegates of the Cherokee Nation. Principal chief John Ross of the Cherokee was too unwell to join in these negotiations.

Agreement at Fort Berthold
July 27, 1866

The main concern of this treaty was peace with the white people and among the Arikara, Gros Ventres, and Mandan. A supplement to the treaty states that the Gros Ventre and Mandan tribes became parties to the treaty. Concluded at Fort Berthold in the Territory of Dakota, the treaty was signed for the

Arikara night medicine men, c. 1908. The Arikara participated in several treaty negotiations, including the Agreement at Fort Berthold July 27, 1866. (Library of Congress)

United States by Newton Edmunds, governor and ex-superintendent of Indian affairs, Major General S. R. Curtis, Orrin Guernsey, and Henry W. Reed; and by twenty-four chiefs and headmen of the Arikara tribe.

Treaty with the Sauk and Fox
February 18, 1867

This treaty dealt mainly with cession, reservation, survey, construction of buildings, land grants, patents, and payments. The United States was to establish a manual labor school, to build schools, and to supply a physician, medicine, tobacco, and salt. Claims against the tribe and claims against the United States were to be paid. Absent members of the tribe were to be notified of the treaty. The treaty was signed for the United States by Lewis V. Bogy, commissioner of Indian affairs; William H. Watson, special commissioner; Thomas Murphy, superinten-

dent of Indian affairs for Kansas; and Henry W. Martin, U.S. Indian agent; and by Keokuk, Che-kus-kuk, Uc-quaw-ho-ko, Mut-tut-tah, and Man-ah-to-wah, chiefs of the tribes of Sac and Fox of the Mississippi.

Treaty with the Sioux–Sisseton and Wahpeton Bands
February 19, 1867

The main concerns of the treaty were peace; cession of rights to construct wagon roads, railroads, mail stations, and telegraph lines; boundaries; reservation; patents; and appropriations to enable the tribes to return to an agricultural life. Payments were to be made in monies, except for the erection of houses and articles to facilitate agriculture. No one was authorized to trade for furs or pelts within the reserve. Members of the bands were the only ones allowed to reside on the reserve without special permission. Chiefs and headmen were allowed to set up a judicial system under the direction of the agent. Concluded at Washington, D.C., the treaty was signed by Lewis V. Bogy, commissioner of Indian affairs, and Commissioner William H. Watson for the United States and by numerous chiefs and headmen of the Sisseton and Wahpeton bands of the Dakota or Sioux.

Treaty with the Seneca, Mixed Seneca and Shawnee, Quapaw, Etc.

February 23, 1867

The main concerns of the treaty were cession by all the signatory tribes, payments, education and schools, aid in agriculture, investigation of claims, citizenship, and removal to permanent homes. The United States agreed to pay for a blacksmith and all necessary iron, steel, and tools in exchange for the tribes' relinquishment of all claims of damage and loss during the late war. Concluded at Washington, D.C., the treaty was signed for the United States by Lewis V. Bogy, commissioner of Indian affairs; as W. H. Watson, special commissioner; Thomas Murphy, superintendent of Indian affairs; and George C. Snow and G. A. Colton, U.S. Indian agents. The treaty was signed for the Seneca by George Spicer and John Mush; for the Mixed Seneca and Shawnee by John Whitetree, John Young, and Lewis Davis; for the Quapaw by S. G. Vallier and Ka-zhe-cah; for the Confederated Peoria, Kaskaskia, Wea, and Piankeshaw by Baptiste Peoria, John Mitchell, and Edward Black; for the Miami by Thomas Metosenyah and Thomas Richardville; for the Ottawa of Blanchard's Fork and Roche de Boeuf by John White and J. T. Jones; and for certain Wyandot by Tauromee (John Hat) and John Karaho.

Treaty with the Potawatomi

February 27, 1867

The parties to this treaty agreed that a commission would select a reservation that would not be included in any state. The Prairie band had no interest in the reservation but would receive a share in the proceeds. A registry was to be made listing the tribe members who desired to remove and those who decided to remain. Money from the sale would be retained until the party was ready to remove to a new reservation.

The third article of the treaty of November 15, 1861, was reaffirmed, and amounts due the Potawatomi were to be ascertained. Land was set aside for schools. Certain persons were allowed to purchase unallotted lands. The treaty was signed at Washington, D.C. Lewis V. Bogy, commissioner of Indian affairs; W. H. Watson, special commissioner; Thomas Murphy, superintendent of Indian affairs for Kansas; and Luther R. Palmer, Indian agent, signed for the United States. Eight chiefs, braves, and headmen signed for the Potawatomi tribe.

Treaty with the Chippewa of the Mississippi

March 19, 1867

The main concerns of this treaty were cession, reservation, boundaries, survey, Hole-in-the-Day and his heirs, land for farming, payments for lands ceded, schools, mills, houses, stock, agriculture, land grants, and provisions. A physician was also to be supplied. Further, all tribe members having ten acres under cultivation were entitled to receive a certificate for forty acres. The land was made exempt from taxation and was not to be alienated. A justice system was established. The treaty was signed at Washington, D.C., by Special Commissioner Lewis V. Bogy, William H. Watson, and U.S. Agent Joel B. Bassett for the United States; and by the Chippewa of the Mississippi, represented by Que-we-zance (Hole-in-the-Day), Qui-we-shen-shish, Wau-bon-a-quot, Min-e-do-wob, Mijaw-ke-ke-shik, Shob-osk-kunk, Ka-gway-dosh, Me-no-ke-shick, Way-namee, and O-gub-ay-gwan-ay-aush.

Treaty with the Kiowa and Comanche

October 21, 1867

The main concerns of this treaty were to stop the war, to ensure that no captives were taken, and to keep the peace. Offenders against the Indians were to be arrested, and wrongdoers against the whites were to be punished. Further concerns were permanent reservation, survey, boundaries, and restriction of residence to certain persons. Children were to attend school; the United States agreed to provide schoolhouses and teachers, seeds and agricultural implements, instructions in farming, and a blacksmith.

After ten years, the United States could withdraw the physician, farmer, blacksmiths, carpenter, engineer, and miller by paying an additional $10,000 per year to the tribe. The right to occupy territory outside the reservation was surrendered, but the right to hunt was reserved. The United States was allowed to build railroads, wagon roads, and military posts. No treaty for cession of reservation, which is held in common, was to be considered valid unless permitted by three-fourths of the male tribe members occupying the reserve. This treaty was signed at the Council Camp on Medicine Lodge Creek, seventy miles south of Fort Larned, Kansas, by Nathaniel G. Taylor, William S. Harney, C. C. Augur, Alfred Terry, John B. Sanborn, Samuel F. Tappan, and J. B. Henderson for the United States, and by the confederated tribes of the Kiowa and Comanche, represented by their chiefs and headmen.

Treaty with the Kiowa, Comanche, and Apache
October 21, 1867

Under this treaty, the Apache agreed to keep peace and to incorporate with the Kiowa and Comanche. The Apache were to observe the stipulations and to participate in the same advantages and annuities of the former treaty. The treaty was signed at the Council Camp on Medicine Lodge Creek, seventy miles south of Fort Larned, Kansas, by Nathaniel G. Taylor, William S. Harney, C. C. Augur, Alfred Terry, John B. Sanborn, Samuel F. Tappan, and J. B. Henderson for the United States and by numerous chiefs and headmen of the Kiowa, Comanche, and Apache tribe.

Treaty with the Cheyenne and Arapaho
October 28, 1867

The Treaty of Medicine Lodge was negotiated with the largest American Indian nations of the southern plains—the Cheyenne, Arapaho, Comanche, Kiowa, and Kiowa-Apache—in October 1867. This treaty represented the last effort of the United States to solve its conflict with these nations in a diplomatic way. Extensive European American intrusion into the central and southern plains had culminated during the Colorado gold rush of 1859; the resulting in uneasiness was expressed in reprisals on both sides during the 1860s. After the massacre of a whole Cheyenne village on Sand Creek in 1864 and the

Ten Bears led the Comanches on the way to the Great Treaty Council on Medicine Lodge Creek, Monday, October 16, 1867. (Library of Congress)

The Great Treaty Council on Medicine Lodge Creek in southern Kansas lasted several days, and involved the Cheyenne, Arapaho, Comanche, Kiowa, and Apache. (National Archives)

burning of another one at Pawnee Fork in 1867, Cheyenne war parties retaliated with raids. The treaty aimed not only at securing peace but also at confining the American Indians to reservations, where they would be assimilated. The treaty thus marked the beginning of the reservation period.

Indian agent Colonel Jesse Leavenworth met with the pertinent Indian chiefs to negotiate a place for the signing of the treaty. The site of Medicine Lodge Creek in Southern Kansas, seventy miles west-southwest of Wichita, was chosen as a compromise, allowing easy transportation of gifts from Fort Larned. The Indian nations were hesitant to go farther north, where they risked attack or exposure to the outbreak of cholera along the Arkansas River.

The members of the U.S. Peace Commission were Generals Alfred Terry, William Harney, John Sanborn, and Christopher Augur; Senator John B. Henderson; Commissioner N. G. Taylor; and Colonel Samuel Tappan. A number of newspaper correspondents were present. One of them, H. M. Stanley, reported that there were 150 lodges of the Kiowa, with their representatives Sitting Bear (Satank) and White Bear (Satanta); 100 lodges of the Comanche, with Ten Bears and Silver Brooch; 171 lodges of the Arapaho, with Little Raven and Yellow Bear; 85 lodges of the Kiowa-Apache, with Poor Bear; and 250 lodges of the peaceful fraction of the Cheyenne, with Black Kettle and Little Robe. The chiefs of the militant Cheyenne band Dog Soldiers, such as Tall Bull and Bull Bear, did not agree with the treaty at first. The Cheyenne came and signed only after they finished their ceremonies of Sacred Arrows Renewal, when Black Kettle persuaded them to do so.

The negotiations were conducted in three sessions; the result of each was a treaty between the Peace Commission and the Indian nations represented at each session. The Kiowa and Comanche signed on October 21, the Kiowa-Apache on the same day, and the Cheyenne and Arapaho on October 28, 1867. Because the terms of the treaties were nearly identical, and the three documents were a result of a single peace effort, the treaty is usually referred to as one single treaty.

The peace agreement guaranteed the right of European Americans to travel over emigrant roads through the southern and central plains, the safety of the railroads and their construction, and cession of the American Indian land. The Comanche, Kiowa, and Kiowa-Apache were assigned a reservation in southwestern Indian Territory between the Red River and the Washita River. The Cheyenne and Arapaho were granted a reservation in northeastern Indian Territory between the Arkansas River and the Cimarron River. All these nations were expected to adopt the European American pattern of civilization on their reservations. The Medicine Lodge treaty provided for the compulsory education of children between ages six and sixteen, a resident Indian agent, a physician, a farmer, and other permanent agency personnel. Any head of a family could select 320 acres of land within the reservation for private farming, whereas single adults would receive eight acres. Compensating for previous treaty agreements, the U.S. government bound itself to deliver clothing and to provide funds for the benefit of the Indian nations for a period of thirty years.

The treaty was successful in setting an example for a new period in the plains conflict, but it did not stop the frontier wars. Detainment of promised provisions, the activities of liquor peddlers, continuing intertribal warfare, and the impending breakdown of the buffalo economy—related to European American encroachment—created a dismal situation that led to more killing on both sides. Eventually, nearly two years after concluding the treaty, all the Indian nations settled down on their reservations. The treaty was a clear declaration of the further intentions of the United States. Up to this time, the Indian nations had been just pushed aside from the settlement areas of the European Americans and allowed to live in their own ways. Now they would be forced to assimilate.

Antonie Dvorakova

Black Kettle (1803/07–1868), chief of the southern Cheyenne in Colorado, sought peace with the white men who encroached on Cheyenne land on the Great Plains in the mid-nineteenth century. Although he signed numerous treaties, more than half his people died in the Sand Creek Massacre in November 1864. Four years later, Black Kettle and hundreds of Native Americans died in an attack led by General George Custer on their village along the Washita River in western Oklahoma. (Oklahoma Historical Society)

See also Assimilation; Black Kettle; Satanta; Sitting Bear (Setangya or Satank); Treaty.

References and Further Reading

Berthrong, Donald, J. 1963. *The Southern Cheyennes.* Norman: University of Oklahoma Press.

Grinnell, George Bird. 1956. *The Fighting Cheyennes.* Norman: University of Oklahoma Press.

Jones, Douglas C. 1966. *The Treaty of Medicine Lodge: The Story of the Great Council as Told by Eyewitnesses.* Norman: University of Oklahoma Press.

Kappler, Charles Joseph, ed. 1972. *Indian Treaties, 1778–1883.* New York: Interland.

Treaty with the Ute

March 2, 1868

This treaty reaffirmed all provisions of the October 17, 1863, treaty that were not inconsistent with this treaty. Its main concerns were reservation boundaries, release of claims to all other lands, appropriations, buildings, and education. The United States agreed to supply schools, teachers, seeds, agricultural implements, a farmer for instruction, a blacksmith, goods, and stock. A right-of-way was granted for railways and highways. Only authorized persons would be permitted to pass on, settle upon, or reside on the reserve, and two agencies were to be established on the reserve. Decisions regarding depredation were to be made by the commissioner of Indian affairs; tribes and whites alike were to be subject to the laws of the United States. Other concerns were the selection of lands for cultivation; the tracts of land were to be recorded in the *Ute Land-Book.* The president was authorized to order a survey of the reserve at any time, to protect improvements of the individual tribal members. The United States was allowed to pass laws concerning alienation and descent of property and government issues on the reservation. If the treaty was broken in any manner, the chief was to forfeit his position and all rights to any benefits of the treaty. Any individual tribe member who remained at peace and abided by the terms of the treaty would be entitled to benefits of the treaty. Concluded at Washington, D.C., this treaty was signed for the United States by Nathaniel G. Taylor, commissioner of Indian affairs; Alexander C. Hunt, governor of Colorado Territory and former superintendent of Indian affairs; and Kit Carson, Ten representatives of the Tabaguache, Muache, Capote, Weeminuche, Yampa, Grand River, and Uintah bands signed for the Utes.

Treaty with the Cherokee

April 27, 1868

This was a supplemental article to a treaty concluded at the city of Washington on July 19, 1866. This was a contract signed by James Harlan, secretary of the interior, with the American Emigrant Company for the sale of "Cherokee neutral lands" in the Kansas, and a contract with James F. Joy of Detroit, Michigan, for the sale of aforesaid lands. A previous contract dated October 9, 1867, between

Orville H. Browning for the United States and James F. Joy, Detroit, was cancelled. The modifications of the contract were listed and assigned to Joy.

Treaty with the Sioux, Etc., and Arapaho

April 29, 1868

Under the terms of this treaty, war was to cease, peace was to be kept, and offenders against the tribe or against whites were to be arrested and punished. Damages were to be decided by the commissioner of Indian affairs. Other concerns of the treaty were reservation boundaries, persons allowed to enter or reside thereon, land selection, additional land for farming, surveys, patents and citizenship, and certificates issued and recorded in the *Sioux Land-Book*. Additionally, right-of-way was granted for the building of roads, railroads, and military posts. The United States was to supply an agent's residence and office, a schoolhouse, teachers, seeds, agricultural implements, farming instruction, a second blacksmith, a physician, and a farmer. Delivery of goods in lieu of money or other annuities was allowed. An annual census was to be taken each year, and appropriations were to continue for thirty years. An army officer was to attest to all delivery of goods. The reservation was to be a permanent home of the tribes, and no treaty for cession of reservation land would be valid unless three-fourths of all adult males of the tribe agreed. The United States agreed that the country north of the North Platte River and east of the summits of the Bighorn Mountains would be unceded Indian territory and agreed that no white person or persons would be allowed to settle upon or occupy any portion of that land without permission of the tribes. This treaty released the United States from obligations made in previous treaties to furnish money, goods, or land. The treaty was signed by Commissioners William T. Sherman, William S. Harney, Alfred H. Terry, C. C. Augur, J. B. Henderson, Nathaniel G. Taylor, John B. Sanborn, and Samuel F. Tappan for the United States; by twenty-five chiefs and headmen of the Brule, Oglala, Miniconjou, Yanktonai, Hunkpapa, Blackfeet, Cuthead, Two-Kettle, Sans Arcs, and Santee bands of the Sioux Nation; and by twenty-six representatives of the Arapaho Nation.

Treaty with the Crow

May 7, 1868

Under this treaty, peace was to be kept, offenders against the tribe or whites were to be arrested and punished, and rules for ascertaining damages were noted. Other concerns of the treaty were reservation boundaries, an agent to reside on the reserve (duties outlined), persons not allowed to reside thereon, land selection, surveys, certificates issued and recorded in the *Crow Land-Book*. Children aged six to sixteen were required to attend school. Further, the United States was to supply schoolhouses, teachers, seeds, agricultural implements, farming instruction, and a physician. Each family was to receive a cow and a pair of oxen. Delivery of goods in lieu of money or other annuities was allowed. An annual census was to be taken. An army officer was to attest to all delivery of goods. The reservation was to be a permanent home of the tribes, and no treaty for cession of reservation land would be valid unless a majority of all adult males of the tribe agreed. This treaty was concluded at Fort Laramie, Dakota Territory, and signed for the United States by Commissioners W. T. Sherman, William S. Harney, Alfred H. Terry, C. C. Augur, John B. Sanborn., S. F. Tappan, and Ashton S. H. White, and by eleven chiefs and headmen representing the Crow.

Treaty with the Northern Cheyenne and Northern Arapaho

May 10, 1868

Under the terms of this treaty, peace was to be kept, offenders among the whites were to be arrested and punished, and tribal wrongdoers were to be given up to U.S. authorities. Damages were to be decided by the commissioner of Indian affairs. The main concerns of the treaty were reservation, surrender of territory outside the reservation area, retention of hunting rights, and selection of a reservation. The heads of families and persons over the age of eighteen who desired to commence farming were allowed to select lands. Certificates of selection were to be recorded in the *Northern Cheyenne and Arapaho Land-Book*. Children aged six to sixteen were required to attend school. Additionally, the United States was to supply schoolhouses, teachers, seeds, agricultural implements, farming instruction, and a physician. Each family was to receive a cow and a pair of oxen. An annual census was to be taken and appropriations made in money for ten years. An army officer was to attest to all delivery of all goods. The reservation was to be a permanent home of the tribes, and no treaty for cession of reservation land would be valid unless a majority of all adult males of the tribe agreed. This treaty was signed at Fort Laramie, Dakota Territory, by Commissioners W. T. Sherman, William S. Harney, Alfred H. Terry, C. C. Augur, John B. Sanborn, and S. F. Tappan for the United States, and by thirteen chiefs and headmen of the Northern Cheyenne and Northern Arapaho tribes.

Treaty with the Navajo

June 1, 1868

On June 1, 1868, after four years in an American internment camp, Navajo leaders, including Barboncito and Manuelito, signed what would be the last treaty with the United States. The treaty is a symbol of the Navajo Nation's sovereign status, although, like other indigenous nations, it is still dependent upon the United States. Importantly, the treaty allowed the *Diné* ("the People") to return to their beloved homeland after four years in an internment camp at Fort Sumner, New Mexico. Navajos commemorated the signing of the 1868 treaty in 1968 and 1999.

The colonial Southwest was a place where indigenous peoples successively encountered three different foreign cultures: the Spaniards, the Mexicans, and finally the Americans, each of which sought to impose their ways of life on the indigenous peoples. Pueblo peoples like the Santo Domingo, the Acoma, and the San Juan, among others, appeared to accept imposed values and policies of the colonizers; however, they practiced their own way of life, including their religion, in secret. The Diné, who were different from their Pueblo neighbors in lifeways, openly thwarted colonial expansion, including that of the Americans, beginning in 1846.

One of the most enduring legacies that shaped southwestern cultures was the slave trade, which intensified with the Spanish and then peaked in the 1860s under American rule. Slave traders targeted Navajo women and children; as a result, cycles of peace and conflict characterized Navajo relationships with colonizers. By the 1860s, Navajos could no longer resist American westward expansion and were subjected to an all-out war, in which they were

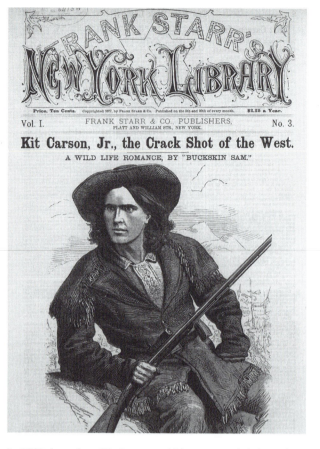

In 1863, legendary Kit Carson and his men traveled through Navajo country destroying cornfields, slaughtering livestock, burning hogans, and cutting down peach orchards. (Library of Congress)

defeated. In 1864, more than ten thousand Navajos were sent to an internment camp near Fort Sumner, New Mexico.

Following the U.S. federal policy of forcing indigenous peoples to relocate to reservations and exterminating them if they resisted, General James Carleton conceived an assimilation plan for Navajos. Navajos would be removed to an internment camp at Bosque Redondo, near Fort Sumner in northeastern New Mexico. There, they would become farmers, would live in villages, and would be instructed in Christianity and other American practices. To force the Navajos' surrender, Carleton enlisted the Indian fighter Kit Carson, who literally scorched *Dinétah*. In 1863, Carson and his men traveled through Navajo country destroying cornfields, slaughtering livestock, burning hogans, and cutting down peach orchards. By 1864, Navajos were rendered destitute, and they turned themselves in at the American forts. Thousands of Navajos made the journey, the Long Walk, to Carleton's prison.

General James Carleton, First California Infantry, c. 1860–1870. (Library of Congress)

Navajos suffered immensely on the Long Walk, for slave raiders waited to steal unsuspecting women and children, and soldiers shot the elderly and pregnant women who could not keep up with the rest. As they crossed the Rio Grande River, many were swept away by the rapids and drowned. The journey ended at the prison camp, where they endured starvation, poverty, sickness, and cold for four long years. Manuelito remained free until 1866 when, ill and starving, he and his band turned themselves in and also made the journey to the prison. The Diné were unsuccessful at farming because of the poor soil and water. Outside the fort's perimeters, Comanches and New Mexicans waited to steal women and children for the slave trade.

Finally, in 1868, the United States admitted that the assimilation plan was a failure. They were also no longer willing to pay the cost of keeping the Diné at the internment camp. At first, it seemed a possibility that the Navajos could be sent to Indian Territory, where many other indigenous peoples had been sent. Barboncito, a respected peace chief, spoke on behalf of his people: "I hope to God you will not ask me to go to any other country than my own." Eventually, Navajo leaders persuaded the military officers to allow them to return to their homeland.

On June 1, 1868, Navajo leaders signed a treaty with the United States. Navajo leaders agreed to peace between their people and the Americans. Most important to the Navajos was that they would return to their homeland. Other stipulations included the restoration of property seized in times of conflict, trade provisions, and 160-acre land allotments for Navajo families. Navajo leaders promised not to obstruct the building of a railroad that would slice through their best pasturing lands. They promised that their children would go to American schools.

The United States promised to keep the peace as well. They also promised annuities as compensation for lands taken and agreed to provide sheep, goats, and horses so that Navajos could reestablish their pastoral economy. The treaty of 1868 is the last one the Navajos signed with the U.S. government, although a number of executive orders increased the

Manuelito was one of the most accomplished Navajo war leaders and was recognized as head chief of the Navajo from 1870 to 1884. (National Archives)

A Navajo silversmith with examples of his work and tools, c. 1880. The Navajo are a Southern Athapascan tribe of the American southwest and came to be feared as raiders. Many Navajo were imprisoned at the Bosque Redondo following the Navajo War of 1863–1864, but were allowed to return to their homeland following a treaty in 1868. (National Archives)

size of the Navajo Reservation up to the early twentieth century.

On June 18, the People formed a column that stretched at least ten miles long. They were going home. The old people wept in relief. Back home in Dinétah, Navajo families returned to their former homes and reestablished their lives. Their prayers to the Holy People had been answered. The Diné prospered. Their livestock increased. They continued to follow the teachings of their ancestors. They have not forgotten the Long Walk and the prison camp at Bosque Redondo. They also remember the courage and bravery of their leaders during those dark times. Today, the Navajo Nation government continues to remind the U.S. government of the treaty of 1868 and its agreement to recognize and uphold Navajo sovereignty.

Jennifer Nez Denetdale

See also Barboncito; Fort Sumner, New Mexico; Long Walk; Manuelito.

References and Further Reading
Bighorse, Tiana. 1990. *Bighorse the Warrior.* Ed. Noel Bennet. Tucson: University of Arizona Press.
Iverson, Peter. 2002. *Diné: A History of the Navajos.* Albuquerque: University of New Mexico Press.
Roessel, Ruth. 1973. *Navajo Stories of the Long Walk Period.* Tsaile, AZ: Navajo Community College Press.
Tapahonso, Luci. 1993. *Sáanii Dahataal: The Women Are Singing.* Tucson: University of Arizona Press.

Treaty with the Eastern Band Shoshone and Bannock

July 3, 1868

This agreement's official title is "Treaty between the United States of America and the Eastern Band of Shoshones and the Bannack Tribe of Indians." Concluded on July 3, 1868, at Fort Bridger, Wyoming (then Utah Territory), and proclaimed on February 24, 1869, this treaty remains the basis for the sovereign relations between the United States and both the Eastern Shoshone Tribe of the Wind River Reservation (Wyoming) and the Shoshone-Bannock Tribes of the Fort Hall Reservation (Idaho). The treaty declared continued peaceful relations between the parties, established the Wind River Reservation, provided for a Bannock Reservation in Idaho, provided for extensive off-reservation resource rights, allowed individual Indians to take up tracts of land in severalty, and included assistance for agricultural development and education.

The various bands of Shoshones and Bannocks had maintained generally peaceful relations with the United States during the overland migration and had been parties to previous treaties both ratified and unratified. Washakie, the principal headman of the Eastern Shoshones, was renowned for his friendship with the United States as well as his influence among his own people. He was a signatory of the ratified Fort Bridger treaty of 1863. The most influential Bannock leader, Taghee, had approved the Soda Springs treaty of October 1863 (part of the same series of treaties negotiated by James Duane Doty), but a legal technicality prevented its ratification. The treaties in 1863 included no land cessions, nor did they designate reservations.

The Fort Bridger treaty of 1868 was the final treaty negotiated by the Great Peace Commission of 1867–1868. Conceived of as an all-encompassing solution to the "Indian problem" in the American

Fort Bridger, Utah Territory (Wyoming), 1858. (Corbis)

A wood engraving of a group of Bannock published in Harper's Weekly. *(Library of Congress)*

West, the peace commission negotiated treaties with the tribes of the northern and southern plains and the Navajos as well as the Shoshones and Bannocks. The commission consisted of four civilians and four generals, including General William T. Sherman and Commissioner of Indian Affairs Nathaniel G. Taylor. General Christopher C. Augur was the sole member of the commission present at Fort Bridger. Washakie

ated by executive order in June 1867. Instead, Article II provided that, at a future date, the president might set apart the reservation which was to include "reasonable portions of the 'Port neuf' [Fort Hall] and 'Kansas [sic] Prairie' countries." The clerk's obvious misspelling of *Kamas* gave later interlopers a specious claim to that area. The federal government never fulfilled its promise to reserve a portion of the Great Camas Prairie. A subsequent executive order designated the Fort Hall Reservation as the Bannock Reservation under the terms of the Fort Bridger treaty. The original dimensions of the reservation were reduced by agreements in 1880, 1881, 1887, and 1900.

The off-reservation provisions of the Fort Bridger treaty are especially noteworthy. Article 4 of the treaty reserved to the Shoshones and Bannocks "the right to hunt on the unoccupied lands of the United States so long as game my be found thereon, and so long as peace subsists among the whites and Indians on the borders of the hunting districts."

Gregory E. Smoak

References and Further Reading
Augur, C. C. 1868. C. C. Augur to President of the Indian Peace Commission, Omaha, Nebraska, 4 October 1868. *Bureau of Indian Affairs, Irregular Sized Papers*. Washington, DC: Record Group 75, U.S. National Archives.
Deloria, Vine, Jr., and Raymond J. DeMallie. 1975. "Introduction," in *Proceedings of the Great Peace Commission of 1867–1869*. Washington, DC: The Institute for the Development of Indian Law.
Prucha, Francis Paul. 1994. *American Indian Treaties: The History of a Political Anomaly*. Berkeley: University of California Press.
St. Germain, Jill. 2001. *Indian Treaty Making Policy in the United States and Canada, 1867–1877*. Lincoln: University of Nebraska Press.

Washakie, Shoshone chief, c. 1798–1900. (National Archives and Records Administration)

spoke for the Eastern Shoshones, while Taghee represented the Bannocks (in fact, his followers were a mixed band of Shoshones and Bannocks).

Article II of the treaty established the boundaries of the Wind River Reservation and provided for the creation of a "Bannack Reservation." Washakie claimed "all the country lying between the meridian of Salt Lake City and the line of the North Platte River to the mouth of the Sweetwater," and wanted "the valley of the Wind River and lands on its tributaries as far east as the Popo-agie" for his reservation. The original dimensions of the Wind River Reservation were reduced by agreements in 1872 and 1898.

General Augur sought to consolidate all the bands on a single reservation, but Taghee refused and demanded a separate reservation that would include the Fort Hall area and the Great Camas Prairie of south central Idaho. Augur relented, but as he was "not sufficiently acquainted" with Idaho's geography, he did not specify the reservation's exact boundaries. Augur was also apparently unaware that the Fort Hall Reservation had already been cre-

Treaty with the Nez Percé
August 13, 1868

This is an amendment to the treaty concluded at the council ground in the valley of the Lapwai, in the Territory of Washington, on June 9, 1863. The main concerns of the treaty were reservation, allotments, and timber to be protected. Further, it was agreed that misappropriated funds would be ascertained and reimbursed to the tribe. The treaty was signed by Commissioner Nathaniel G. Taylor for the United States and by Lawyer, Timothy, and Jason, chiefs of the Nez Percé tribe.

Canadian Indian Treaties 1 and 2

August 1871

Treaties 1 and 2 are also known as, respectively, the Stone Fort Treaty and the Manitoba Post Treaty. Treaty 1 was signed on August 3, 1871, at Lower Fort Garry, a Hudson's Bay Company post (constructed of stone), and Treaty 2 was concluded on August 21, 1871, at the Manitoba House post. Treaty negotiations were conducted with the Saulteaux (Ojibwa), the Swampy Cree, and others; upon conclusion, the treaty encompassed parts of present-day central and southern Manitoba. The earliest of the so-called numbered or western treaties, these agreements provided the foundation for a treaty relationship between the Canadian government and various Cree and Ojibwa nations in western Canada, and played a vital role in the process of securing Canadian sovereignty in the region northwest of the 49th parallel.

By confederation in 1867, more than 120 treaties and land surrenders had been concluded with indigenous peoples in British North America, part of the colonial government's obligations under the Royal Proclamation (1763) to exercise oversight of "Indians and lands reserved for Indians." Practically, the government also negotiated treaties in order to extinguish aboriginal title and set aside reserves to meet the needs of both assimilation and expanding European settlement. Hard on the heels of confederation (and, in fact, earlier), when the new federal government in Ottawa, Ontario, looked to expand Canadian sovereignty into the northwest, its intentions and worldview remained the basis for the removal of "any obstruction" to settlement and development. Treaties 1 and 2 represented both continuity with the past and a transition into a new period.

Neither colonial nor federal governments, however, acted unilaterally in the treaty process. Canada had neither the resources nor the inclination to simply impose its will on aboriginal peoples. Nor was it the only party to initiate the treaty process. Indians also played an important role, pre- and post-confederation, in calling for treaty negotiations as a way of securing protection of

Upper Fort Garry, Manitoba, in the early 1870s. (Library and Archives Canada)

lands and livelihood in the face of expanding white settlement. This was no less true in the case of the earliest numbered treaties. In Manitoba, aboriginal anticipation of the need for a treaty to address collective concerns about settler encroachment, trespass, and cultural dissolution found expression in the convening of grand councils, petitions to the government, and the denial of access to resources for settlers and surveyors until a treaty was negotiated.

Armed with their respective objectives, in the summer of 1871 government and indigenous delegates met at Lower Fort Garry and launched into negotiations. Treaty 1 talks stretched from July 27 to August 3. Ojibwa and Cree spokesmen began negotiations by claiming reserve lands amounting to some 60 percent of Manitoba; the government-appointed treaty commissioners offered 160 acres per family of five, an annuity, and threats of inevitable settler stampede (a formula adopted for all the western treaties). After considerable debate, several deadlocks, and threats from both government and indigenous negotiators to end talks, negotiations nevertheless ended with the signing of Treaty 1 on Thursday, August 3, 1871. Based on the apparent success of Treaty 1, Treaty 2 negotiations (for which there is comparatively little documentation) took only one day and ended on August 21. The terms of Treaties 1 and 2 were identical and included a gift of $3, an annuity of $15 (prorated) for each family of five, schools, and 160 acres of land for each family of five, this last item reluctantly accepted by aboriginal delegates. However, as the Indians pointed out, the treaties were incomplete.

Conspicuous by their absence were treaty provisions for hunting and fishing rights, as well as for agricultural implements, livestock, and clothing, provisions verbally promised by government negotiators but omitted from the written treaty. Dubbed the "outside promises" by the government, these provisions explain the break in the deadlock over the land question, as the treaty commission reassured the Indians of continued access to hunting and fishing and aid in the transition to a farm economy. Although initially unmoved, in 1875 the federal government eventually responded to indigenous protests and the evidence of its own treaty commissioners and revised Treaties 1 and 2 to include the other provisions. Government officials considered the matter resolved.

Treaties 1 and 2 established the precedent and experience for all subsequent treaties in western

Canada. Yet a number of promises were not granted, and government practices in fulfilling treaty obligations, especially in the context of expanding settlement and development, became a source of tension and conflict.

Jason M. Yaremko

See also Canadian Indian Treaties; Robinson Huron Treaty (Second Robinson Treaty)–September 9, 1850; Robinson Superior Treaty (First Robinson Treaty)–September 7, 1850.

References and Further Reading

Asch, Michael. 1984. *Home and Native Land: Aboriginal Rights and the Canadian Constitution.* Toronto: Methuen.

Dickason, Olive Patricia. 1992. *Canada's First Nations: A History of Founding Peoples from Earliest Times.* Norman: University of Oklahoma Press.

Morris, Alexander. 1880. *The Treaties of Canada.* Toronto: Belfords, Clarke.

Ray, Arthur J., Jim Miller, and Frank Tough. 2000. *Bounty and Benevolence: A History of Saskatchewan Treaties.* London: McGill-Queen's University Press.

Agreement with the Sisseton and Wahpeton Bands of Sioux Indians
September 20, 1872

This treaty amended the treaty of February 19, 1867, which was made at Washington, D.C., with the Sisseton and Wahpeton bands of the Dakota or Sioux. Sections 3 through 9 were stricken out of the previously mentioned treaty by amended agreement. The treaty was signed by Commissioners Moses N. Adams, William H. Forbes, and James Smith, Jr., for the United States and by fifty-eight chiefs and soldiers of the Sisseton and Wahpeton bands of the Dakota or Sioux.

Amended Agreement with Certain Sioux Indians
March 2, 1873

This is an amendment to a previous treaty of September 20, 1872, with the Sisseton and Wahpeton Bands of Dakota or Sioux. Sections 3 through 9 were stricken out of the previously mentioned treaty by amended agreement. This treaty was signed by Commissioners Moses N. Adams, James Smith, Jr., and William H. Forbes for the United States and by thirty-one chiefs and headmen of the said bands.

Canadian Indian Treaty 3

October 3, 1873

Treaty 3, or the Northwest Angle Treaty, was signed on October 3, 1873, after several years of protracted and difficult negotiations between the Dominion of Canada and the Lake of the Woods Saulteaux. For Canada, this treaty secured the completion of the Dawson Route, begun in 1868 and designed to link the settlement at Lake of the Woods to Fort Garry. Gaining access to Saulteaux territory would also facilitate a transcontinental railway—a crucial step in maintaining British Columbia's membership in confederation (1871). Canada was a new country, and its success, especially in the face of American expansionism, also depended on colonization, which in turn required friendly relations with area First Nations. These factors made it necessary to enter into diplomatic discussions and, to a great degree, gave these First Nations enhanced negotiating power in dealing with dominion representatives.

The Saulteaux succeeded both in appreciating the value of the lands at stake and in using the rhetoric of the moment. Negotiations began in July 1871 but broke off several times, primarily because the First Nations preferred to treat only for a right-of-way through their territory rather than for an all-out surrender. Talks finally resumed on September 24, 1873, at the North West Angle, Lake of the Woods. Alexander Morris, the lieutenant governor of Manitoba and the Northwest Territories; J. A. N. Provencher, Indian affairs commissioner; and S. J. Dawson, member of parliament for Algoma, represented the dominion. These commissioners met a group of eight hundred Saulteaux, whose chiefs spoke on behalf of an estimated population of fourteen thousand.

After much discussion, the Saulteaux, led by Chief Mawedopenais from Fort Frances, accepted the following terms: a gratuity of $12, plus an annuity of $5 for each member, and a land base of one square mile (640 acres/259 hectares) per family of five or in that proportion. Chiefs would receive an annuity of $25 with an annual payment of $15 for each of their head men, plus a new set of clothes every three years, a commemorative medal, and a flag. The commissioners agreed to offer an annual stipend of $1,500 for agricultural implements and seed, and ammunition and fishing supplies. Natives could also continue to hunt and fish on unsettled lands. At the request of the negotiating chiefs, the commissioners promised that the signatories would be exempt from fighting in commonwealth wars and that schools would be provided for their children. On their part, the Saulteaux transferred more than 55,000 square miles (142,450 square kilometers), situated mostly in the northwestern portion of Ontario and encompassing the watershed of Lake Superior to the northwest angle of the Lake of the Woods, and from the American border north to the height of land where the waters flow to Hudson Bay.

Following the negotiations, the conference broke off for an hour to allow the final terms to be written into the treaty document, and resumed once the document was completed. It was read out in Ojibwa by James McKay, then signed by the commissioners and twenty-four chiefs and headmen. The following day, the Indians were paid by representatives from the Department of Public Works, and the gathering dispersed. Subsequent adhesions to the treaty were signed at Shebadowan on October 13, 1873, at Lac Seul on June 9, 1874, and by the Métis of Rainy River and Rainy Lake on September 12, 1875.

Treaty 3 became the format for future treaties, setting up conditions and promises that—at least in theory—created a living agreement between Canada's First Nations and the Crown. Some scholars attribute to the keen negotiating skills of the Saulteaux and their fortuitous location along the coveted Dawson Route the responsibility for raising the treaty terms and setting a more salubrious precedent for those First Nations signing subsequent numbered treaties in the western provinces of Canada. Treaty 3 was also the first treaty to recognize Métis rights and to provide ongoing funding for the support of education, agriculture, and hunting and fishing.

Laurie Leclair

See also Canadian Indian Treaties 1 and 2–August 1871; Constitution Act (Canada), 1867; Métis; Sovereignty; Trust Doctrine; Trust Land.

References and Further Reading

Daugherty, W. E. 1986. *Treaty Research Report: Treaty Three (1873).* Ottawa: Treaties and Historical Research Centre, Indian and Northern Affairs Canada.

Dickason, Olive Patricia. 1992. *Canada's First Nations: A History of Founding Peoples from Earliest Times.* Norman: University of Oklahoma Press.

Morris, Alexander. 1991. *The Treaties of Canada with the Indians of Manitoba and the North-West Territories including The Negotiations on which they were based* (First Printing 1880), reprint by Fifth House Publishers, Saskatoon, SK. See Chapter 5, "Treaty Number Three or the Northwest Angle Treaty," pp. 44–76, pp. 320–329.

Canadian Indian Treaty 4

September 15, 1874

Treaty 4, or the Qu'Appelle Treaty, represented the fourth of the so-called numbered or western treaties negotiated in western Canada. Treaty 4 was negotiated in September 1874 by the government of Canada and the Cree, Saulteaux (Ojibwa), and Nakota or Assiniboine Indians toward the extinguishment of aboriginal title and establishment of reserve lands in the southern and central regions of the present-day province of Saskatchewan. After a tense and difficult negotiation process that began near the Qu'Appelle lakes on September 8 and ended on September 15, the federal government succeeded in gaining a surrender of some seventy-five thousand square miles of territory.

The Qu'Appelle Treaty was the product of the Canadian government's need, after confederation in 1867, to secure territory ranging from northwestern Ontario to the Pacific Ocean for settlement, development, and the assertion of national sovereignty, a process that began with the 1870 transfer of those lands from the Hudson's Bay Company and the first numbered treaties. Treaty 4 represented another step in that direction. Aboriginal peoples of the Northwest were also deeply interested in negotiating a treaty in order to ensure economic and cultural security in the face of an uncertain future, and they had conveyed such concerns to the lieutenant governor of Manitoba and the Northwest Territories several years earlier. Negotiations in Manitoba and Ontario in 1871 and 1873 set the precedents for the remaining western treaties.

These precedents came into play at the negotiations for Treaty 4. Held near the Qu'Appelle lakes in southern Saskatchewan, the negotiations are notable for their relative brevity because, though government treaty commissioners and Native negotiators met for nearly a week, the actual time dedicated to negotiating treaty terms amounted to barely one day. The first five days were spent amid tense disagreement between the Cree and Saulteaux, and then between the Saulteaux and the treaty commission, over the status of the Hudson's Bay Company and the land in question. Saulteaux negotiators argued

An Assiniboine camp in Lac de Marons, Manitoba, 1874. (Library and Archives Canada)

Cree in Alberta, Canada, c. 1870–1910. (Library and Archives Canada)

that the company did not have the right to dispose of land that belonged to the Cree and Saulteaux. They argued, further, that the company should be restricted in its trading activities, while spokesmen for the Cree added that Indians' debts should be forgiven as a fair exchange for the profits gained when the company transferred the land to Canada. The overriding concern, however, was entitlement to the land covered by the treaty.

By September 15, the sixth day of talks, through a combination of counterarguments and broad promises the commission was finally able to address treaty terms. There remained, however, very little discussion or debate: aboriginal negotiators were prepared to accept terms similar to those agreed to by the Ojibwa at the Lake of the Woods under the Northwest Angle Treaty, or Treaty 3 (1873). The terms were explained by the treaty commission, and in return for the relinquishment of their title to the land ceded, the Indians were to receive reserves based on one square mile for each family of five (prorated) and located by them, annuity payments,

schools, equipment and livestock upon taking up farming, and promises of continued access to hunting and fishing. Over the following year, a number of other Cree, Ojibwa, and Assiniboine groups not in attendance joined Treaty 4 under the same terms.

Notably, in the latter stages of treaty talks, aboriginal negotiators twice asked that the Métis, their mixed-blood kin, also be given due consideration. Shortly after negotiations, these Métis petitioned the treaty commissioners, formally requesting recognition of their land holdings as well as hunting and fishing rights. In both instances, the government gave only vague reassurances.

According to the text of Treaty 4, Indian nations had consented to absolute surrender of their lands in exchange for reserves and other provisions. Based on the records of the negotiations for Treaty 4, however, and not unlike the other numbered treaties, there was a notable contrast between the government's and the Indians' presentations of the land question. Aside from vague reassurances, government negotiators said very little about the land and showed little patience for the specific concerns and questions of the Indians. Not surprisingly, the interpretations of the government and the First Nation elders continue to show a marked contrast in their understanding of Treaty 4.

Jason M. Yaremko

See also Canadian Indian Treaties; Northern Plains.
References and Further Reading
Carter, Sarah. 1991. *Lost Harvests: Prairie Indian Reserve Farmers and Government Policy.* Montreal and Kingston: McGill-Queen's University Press.
Morris, Alexander. 1880. *The Treaties of Canada.* Toronto: Belfords, Clarke. Ray, Arthur J., Jim Miller, and Frank Tough. 2000. *Bounty and Benevolence: A History of Saskatchewan Treaties.* London: McGill-Queen's University Press.

Canadian Indian Treaty 5

September 24, 1875

Another one of the so-called numbered or western treaties, Treaty 5, or the Winnipeg Treaty, encompassed lands in the present-day province of Manitoba, north of Treaty 2 territory, surrounding Lake Winnipeg and eventually extending north to the sixtieth parallel. Negotiations for Treaty 5 took place between the Canadian government and nations of the Saulteaux (Ojibwa) and Swampy Cree in the autumn of 1875; the treaty was concluded September 24, 1875. Although signed in 1875, adhesions to Treaty 5 incorporating more northerly aboriginal groups were conducted in 1876, 1908, 1909, and 1910. In 1910, some 133,400 square miles of land had been ceded.

Like the earlier treaties, aboriginal peoples in central and northern Manitoba petitioned the government for a treaty to ensure the protection of their traditional economy and culture, and to facilitate their adaptation to economic development spreading from eastern Canada. More immediate aboriginal concerns included the increasing intrusions of commercial trapping, the expanding presence of commercial interests such as lumber companies, and the problem of employment as boatmen and couriers lost to steamboats and faster water transport. Initially, from the perspective of a government preoccupied with the agricultural development of the southern regions of western Canada, the Lake Winnipeg region held limited agricultural potential; the need for a new treaty appeared premature and unnecessary. Unlike the

earlier numbered treaties negotiated earlier in western Canada, therefore, Treaty 5 did not entail large tracts of fertile lands coveted for settlement and therefore was not central to federal plans for agricultural development.

By 1875, the government's earlier reluctance to negotiate a new treaty gave way to reconsideration of the long-term potential of the region for (limited) settlement (particularly around the southern shores of Lake Winnipeg), transportation, and resource exploitation. In September of that year, a treaty commission set off for Lake Winnipeg and points north to negotiate with the Saulteaux and Swampy Cree. The commissioners had their orders: negotiations were to be kept short, and the Indians in this region were to be dealt with less generously than the peoples of the plains. Negotiations at Berens River and Norway House were in fact fairly brief (one day each), and any difficult questions posed by aboriginal negotiators were quickly surmounted with a combination of counterarguments and vague reassurances. By September 24, Treaty 5 had been signed, and adhesions (documents that bind the signatories to existing treaties) were obtained from outstanding groups over the next year.

The government, having argued in effect that it was doing the Indians a favor in negotiating for lands that were deemed not as valuable as the fertile belt to the south, granted terms that were less favorable than those under Treaties 3 and 4. The provisions of Treaty 5 characteristically included annuity payments, reserves of 160 acres per family of five, schools, farming equipment and livestock, hunting and fishing equipment (twine), and promises of the continued right to pursue hunting and fishing, subject to the needs of certain lands for government or private use (a qualifier that affected reserves also).

After several decades, as Manitoba's boundaries extended north to the 60th parallel and government interests in resource exploitation heightened in pace with a growing economy, it became necessary to extinguish aboriginal title to lands in that region. Treaty 5 was therefore extended north of Lake Winnipeg. From 1908 to 1910, adhesions were secured, incorporating the remaining Cree and Chipewyan or Dene peoples into Treaty 5 under the same terms.

Treaty 5 stands out rather uniquely as one in the anticipation and initiation of which aboriginal groups played a most substantial role. At the same time, the brevity of negotiations is characteristic of a process in which considerably less attention was paid to the needs of indigenous signatories than to ensuring control of the land for future economic development. As a result, a number of problems emerged that were based in fundamentally different understandings of the treaty terms as explained during negotiations. Although aboriginal peoples expected some measure of aid in times of dislocation, when those sources of dislocation arrived—railway surveys and construction, lumber companies, mining—they were struck by government inaction, in stark contrast to the generosity conveyed at treaty negotiations.

Jason M. Yaremko

See also Canadian Indian Treaties; Indian Treaty Making: A Native View.

References and Further Reading

Asch, Michael. 1984. *Home and Native Land: Aboriginal Rights and the Canadian Constitution.* Toronto: Methuen.

Dickason, Olive Patricia. 1992. *Canada's First Nations: A History of Founding Peoples from Earliest Times.* Norman: University of Oklahoma Press.

Morris, Alexander. 1880. *The Treaties of Canada.* Toronto: Belfords, Clarke. Tough, Frank. 1996. *"As Their Natural Resources Fail": Native Peoples and the Economic History of Northern Manitoba.* Vancouver: University of British Columbia Press.

Canadian Indian Treaty 6
August 28, September 9, 1876

Of the eleven numbered or western treaties, Treaty 6, negotiated and signed in the summer of 1876 at Forts Carlton and Pitt in the present-day provinces of Saskatchewan and Alberta, was one of a group of agreements negotiated between the government of Canada and aboriginal peoples of the northwestern plains. Treaty 6 was also one more in a series of treaties brought about largely through indigenous initiative, in this case predominantly by the majority inhabitants of the Saskatchewan River country, the Cree. Negotiations for Treaty 6 passed through several stages of talks: at Fort Carlton from August 18 to

North West Mounted Police constable with Plains Indian, Alberta, Canada, c. 1874–1890. (Library and Archives Canada)

23, then from August 24 to 28, and at Fort Pitt from September 7 to 9. By the end of the process, the government of Canada had succeeded in extinguishing aboriginal title to some 120,000 square miles of land in central Alberta and Saskatchewan.

By the early 1870s, the Canadian government had planned to extend its sovereignty across the prairie region to the western coast through a very gradual treaty process, but only as its need for more territory (for settlement, resources, and so on) arose. Yet Cree perceptions of their own conditions and needs also informed and influenced government decisions about treaty making in western Canada. After the signing of the first two numbered treaties in 1871, a variety of observers, from Hudson's Bay Company officials to government surveyors, conveyed the dissatisfaction of the Plains Cree and other indigenous groups with the slow pace of treaty making. Cree leaders based their calls for a treaty on the need to protect their lands and culture, both threatened by worsening conditions that included diminishing buffalo numbers and game generally, and increasing intrusions by settlers, hunters, whiskey traders, and surveyors. As well, the decision had been made to adapt to change by taking up farming, for which aid was needed. Though still hesitant, the government, moved by concerns of Indian unrest, finally agreed to negotiate a treaty after receiving reports in the summer of 1875 of Cree interference with the Geological Survey. A treaty commission was struck, and negotiations began the following summer at Fort Carlton.

The main gathering took place at Fort Carlton. Although dominated by the Plains Cree, talks here also included members of the Swampy Cree, Plains Ojibwa, Saulteaux (Ojibwa), and some Assiniboine and Chipewyan (Dene). The opening ceremonies and speeches conveyed the traditional expressions of mutual trust and friendship. Treaty terms resembled those of the first five treaties: cash gratuity and annuity payments, lands to be set aside as reserves (in this case, 640 acres per family of five), agricultural implements and instruction, schools, and hunting guarantees, as well as additional livestock and supplies for each chief. Cree and Ojibwa negotiators raised all the same concerns that neighbors and kin had in Treaty 4 talks. Treaty 6 negotiations proved turbulent, as treaty commissioners vied with Cree and Ojibwa negotiators, who in turn struggled with government negotiators—and interpreters—and dissent among members of their own followings. Some influential dissenters among the Cree and Ojibwa

rejected the government's parceling out of land. In council, however, the positions of the chiefs eventually prevailed. When the treaty was signed on August 23, 1876, treaty terms included government promises of aid in times of famine.

The successful completion of negotiations at Carlton facilitated the signing of Treaty 6 by other Cree and Ojibwa groups in the talks that followed. On August 28, several Cree chiefs, late arrivals to Fort Carlton, accepted the terms of the treaty. In September, at Fort Pitt, the second, more westerly site for Treaty 6 negotiations, the same terms were also accepted by the Cree and other groups of Indians.

As with the earlier treaties, the conclusion of Treaty 6 raised more questions than it resolved. One overriding issue was (and remains) interpretation. Problems appeared at several levels: competent interpreters for treaty negotiations; verbal assurances versus treaty text; and the aboriginal interpretation of such European concepts as land surrender. It is not even clear that land surrender was discussed at Treaty 6 negotiations. Although pursued by some Cree leaders, the government proved more generous with assurances than with details. In the years after 1876, as settlement advanced along with disease, and famine and hardships for plains peoples intensified, discrepancies between government promises and aboriginal understanding became stark.

Jason M. Yaremko

See also Canadian Indian Treaties; Northern Plains.
References and Further Reading
Asch, Michael. 1984. *Home and Native Land: Aboriginal Rights and the Canadian Constitution*. Toronto: Methuen.
Cardinal, Harold. 1977. *The Rebirth of Canada's Indians*. Edmonton, AB: Hurtig.
Dickason, Olive Patricia. 1992. *Canada's First Nations: A History of Founding Peoples from Earliest Times*. Norman: University of Oklahoma Press.
Morris, Alexander. 1880. *The Treaties of Canada*. Toronto: Belfords, Clarke.
Taylor, John Leonard. 1999. "Two Views on the Meaning of Treaties Six and Seven." In *The Spirit of Alberta Indian Treaties*, ed. Richard Price. Edmonton: University of Alberta Press.

Canadian Indian Treaty 7
September 22, December 4, 1877

Treaty 7 was the last of the numbered treaties negotiated by the Canadian government in the 1870s. Also known as the Blackfoot Treaty because the Blackfoot

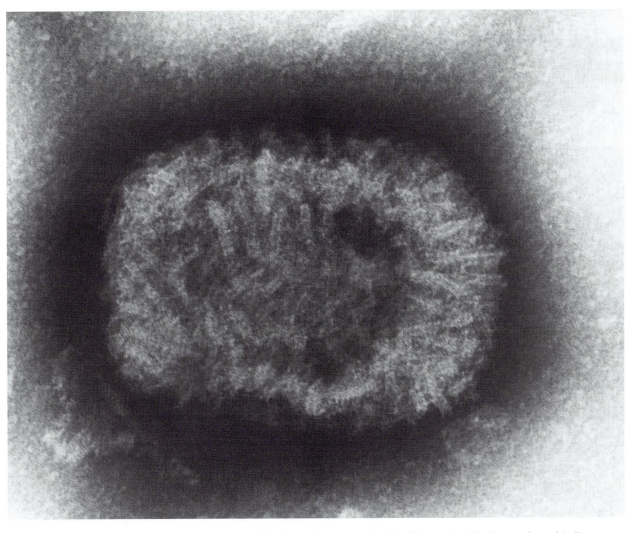

A smallpox (variola) virus particle, or a single "virion" is depicted. Because of a lack of immunity, this disease plagued Indian peoples in Canada and the United States. In a few instances, smallpox-infected blankets were traded to Indians. (Centers for Disease Control and Prevention)

dominated the region ceded, it encompassed some fifty thousand square miles of land near the Rocky Mountains in the southern region of the present province of Alberta, territory inhabited by the Blackfoot Nation—Siksika (Blackfoot), Blood, Peigan—as well as the Sarcee (Tsuu T'ina), Assiniboine, and Stoney. Treaty negotiations were conducted at Blackfoot Crossing along the Bow River in 1877 and ran from September 19 to September 22. Negotiations ended that day, and Treaty 7 was signed by the government and aboriginal leaders.

    The government's motivation for negotiating Treaty 7 rested largely on the need to complete the extension of its sovereignty westward. Specifically, this meant the acquisition of land that would enable Ottawa to run a transcontinental railway to the west

coast, a major condition for the entry of British Columbia into confederation. A rail line would also encourage large-scale immigration into the west. The Blackfoot, meanwhile, favored a treaty precisely because of the rising numbers of settlers and traders penetrating the region they inhabited. By the early 1870s, circumstances for the Blackfoot and their neighbors had changed considerably. The Blackfoot were already weakened and reduced in number by a deadly combination of smallpox and whiskey (a prominent item in the buffalo robe trade); conditions had worsened by 1876, when famine threatened as some five thousand Sioux, refugees from the United States, arrived on the southern edge of their territory. In 1874, the North West Mounted Police were sent in to restore some semblance of order in the region.

Although the Blackfoot resented the intruding settlers and traders who followed in the wake of the Mounted Police, they also saw the Mounties as allies who had cleared out the whiskey traders, restored peace, and treated the Blackfoot fairly. Aboriginal relations with the police were also, therefore, a factor influencing the Blackfoot and other nations toward a treaty in 1877. In the spring of that year, the Blackfoot delegated two missionaries to convey a memorial to the government on behalf of the Blackfoot and their neighbors. The following July, a treaty commission was formed and instructed to proceed to Blackfoot Crossing to negotiate a treaty with the Indians there. One of the treaty commissioners was also a commissioner of the Mounted Police.

After some delay, treaty negotiations began on September 19. Talks proceeded along lines similar to those of earlier treaties, with introductory speeches and government explanations of treaty terms, the latter of which included gratuity and annuity payments, reserves of land of 640 acres per family of five, farming implements and livestock, ammunition for hunting, schools, laws to protect buffalo, and additional supplies for chiefs and councils. Although relatively short, the negotiations were not without incident. Problems occurred with interpreters, one of whom had a weak grasp of English, whereas others proved inadequate to the task of fully explaining such treaty terms as *reserves* and *land surrenders*. Initial indigenous responses to the government's terms ranged from ambivalence and opposition to weak approval. An agreement was reached two days later and has been attributed to a combination of government misinformation, misunderstanding, and the overriding influence of the Blackfoot chief, Crowfoot. Crowfoot, trusted by the other chiefs as one loyal to his people while also enjoying the confidence of the government, was in turn influenced by his good relations with the Mounted Police. When he decided to accept the treaty, the assent of the other chiefs followed. On Saturday, September 22, Treaty 7 was signed, supplies and payments distributed, and reserves then located by the various chiefs. Another signing took place on December 4 to accommodate Blackfeet officials who were not present at the September signing.

Indians on horseback at Blackfoot Reserve, Alberta, Canada. (Library and Archives Canada)

Although initially satisfied with the immediate results of the treaty, the Blackfoot and other tribes soon encountered problems attributed to the terms and administration of Treaty 7. By 1880, as settler populations increased, buffalo numbers rapidly declined, and starvation threatened. The following decade found the Blackfoot and other Treaty 7 tribes wondering about the government's sincerity in fulfilling its obligations, especially as railway construction intruded upon some reserves, and disputes arose over the inadequate size of others. The land question remains a fundamental source of conflict, one based in problems of interpretation and conflicting cultural conceptions.

Jason M. Yaremko

See also Canadian Indian Treaties; Northern Plains.
References and Further Reading
Asch, Michael. 1984. *Home and Native Land: Aboriginal Rights and the Canadian Constitution.* Toronto: Methuen.
Cardinal, Harold. 1977. *The Rebirth of Canada's Indians.* Edmonton, AB: Hurtig.
Dempsey, Hugh. 1989. *Crowfoot: Chief of the Blackfeet.* Norman: University of Oklahoma Press.
Dickason, Olive Patricia. 1992. *Canada's First Nations: A History of Founding Peoples from Earliest Times.* Norman: University of Oklahoma Press.
Treaty 7 Elders and Tribal Council, et al. 1997. *The True Spirit and Original Intent of Treaty 7.* Montreal: McGill-Queen's Press.

Agreement with the Crow
May 14, 1880

This treaty was signed in Washington but never ratified. However, six chiefs of the Crow tribe promised to try to obtain the consent of the adult male members of the tribe to cede all that part of the Crow Reservation in the Territory of Montana on condition. Further, the United States reaffirmed all existing provisions of the treaty of May 7, 1868, and was to give the tribe added annuities and sums.

Agreement with the Sioux of Various Tribes
October 17, 1882, to January 3, 1883

This agreement was made pursuant to an item in the sundry civil act of Congress, approved August 7, 1882, by Commissioners Newton Edmunds, Peter C.

Shannon, and James H. Teller and by twenty chiefs and headmen of the various bands of the Sioux. The main concerns of the treaty were cession of the Great Sioux Reservation, allotments, cattle and oxen to be furnished, education, and land grants for schools. Separate reservations were to be created for those at the Pine Ridge agency, the Rosebud agency, the Rock agency Indians, the Cheyenne River agency, and the Lower Brulés. Further, the United States was to furnish to each reservation a physician, a carpenter, a miller, an engineer, a farmer, and a blacksmith for a period of ten years.

Agreement with the Columbia and Colville
July 7, 1883

Under the terms of this agreement, the Colville Indians were to forfeit rights to the Columbia Reservation and to remove to the Colville Reservation. The agreement was signed by H. M. Teller, secretary of the interior, and H. Price, commissioner of Indian affairs, for the United States; by Chief Moses and Sasr-sarp-kin of the Columbia Reservation; and by Tonaskat of the Colville Reservation.

Canadian Indian Treaty 8
June 21, 1899

One of the last of the eleven numbered or western treaties, Treaty 8 was a product of the mutual con-

Klondike gold rush (1899–1900) burro pack train at Dyea Point. Treaty 8 was a product of the mutual concern of indigenous peoples and the Canadian government over the advance of prospectors and settlers into northwestern Canada in the 1890s. (Library of Congress)

Athapascan mother and children. (Library of Congress)

eralty (individual plots), based on 160 acres per person. Treaty provisions also included annuity payments, schools, farming implements, livestock, and hunting and fishing supplies.

The principle concern of the Cree and Dene was how Treaty 8 would affect their use of the land. For the Cree at Lesser Slave Lake, the first negotiation site, as for virtually all the northern nations affected, the land question was conceived somewhat differently, and reserves were not a part of that conception. The Cree at Lesser Slave Lake, for example, refused to sign the treaty until their demands were met. These included guarantees that the traditional economy of the Cree would be protected and that they would be able to continue to hunt and fish as they always had. The commission's acquiescence to Cree demands enabled treaty proceedings at Lesser Slave Lake to be concluded in three days, and after some additional discussion, designated Cree leaders signed on June 21. The treaty commissioners believed that the treaty signing at Lesser Slave Lake was of paramount importance because it would determine the success of the trip thereafter. Although this proved to be largely the case, it is not clear how well the terms of the treaty were explained during negotiations nor how much was understood by the Cree— with the possible exception of the promises concerning hunting and fishing freedom. The commission, however, considered the first treaty signing a good precedent.

The Cree and Chipewyan who assembled for treaty negotiations at Fort Chipewyan represented the largest gathering of the summer of 1899. Like the Cree of Lesser Slave Lake, the Chipewyan and Cree at Fort Chipewyan also insisted on guarantees to unencumbered hunting, trapping, and fishing before they would sign. The swiftness of the proceedings at Fort Chipewyan suggests that these were granted, as does the report of the commissioners: at Fort Chipewyan and every point thereafter, fears of the curtailment of hunting and fishing rights received assurances that the treaty would not result in any such interference. The treaty was signed on July 13.

Not all Treaty 8 talks went so smoothly. Negotiations at Fond du Lac (along the boundary between present-day Saskatchewan and the Northwest Territories), where the government's principle concern was the development of mining projects in the region between Fond du Lac and the Great

cern of indigenous peoples and the Canadian government over the advance of prospectors and settlers into northwestern Canada in the 1890s. This penetration culminated in the Klondike gold rush in 1897–1898; the government moved to extend the treaty process to the Lake Athabasca, Great Slave Lake, and Peace River regions (present-day northern Saskatchewan, Alberta, southern Northwest Territories, and northeastern British Columbia). Treaty negotiations were conducted at several sites in the summer of 1899 (adhesions were secured the following year) and included more than 2,700 people from two major cultural groups: Athapaskan, or Dene, and Cree peoples, along with some 1,700 Métis or mixed-blood kin.

The main objectives of the treaty commissioners were essentially to obtain the relinquishment of aboriginal title to the government of Canada and to gain the acquiescence of the northern Métis in the surrender. With regard to the primary goal of surrender of title, the commission was instructed to offer reserve lands in common (bands) or in sev-

Murchison's Rapids in the North Thompson River, British Columbia, 1871. (Library and Archives Canada)

Slave Lake, proved volatile. Notably, only after the intervention of a local missionary did the Fond du Lac Dene sign the treaty on July 27. By the end of the summer, Treaty 8 negotiations were concluded; adhesions were completed in the summer of 1900.

The haste with which Treaty 8 negotiations were conducted, and the nature and interpretation of Treaty 8 provisions, most of which were taken directly from earlier prairie treaties and demonstrated little appreciation of subarctic aboriginal cultures, generated more conflict in later years. By the early twentieth century, as the numbers of commercial trappers, game laws, and developers penetrated the northern territories, Treaty 8 appeared to provide little protection for signatory nations. The aboriginal concern with the protection of tradi-

tional economies remained a bone of contention long after the negotiation of Treaty 8.

Jason M. Yaremko

See also Canadian Indian Treaties; Métis.

References and Further Reading

Asch, Michael. 1984. *Home and Native Land: Aboriginal Rights and the Canadian Constitution.* Toronto: Methuen.

Dickason, Olive Patricia. 1992. *Canada's First Nations: A History of Founding Peoples from Earliest Times.* Norman: University of Oklahoma Press.

Fumoleau, Rene. 1973. *As Long as This Land Shall Last: A History of Treaty 8 and 11.* Toronto: McClelland and Stewart.

Price, Richard T., ed. 1999. *The Spirit of the Alberta Indian Treaties,* 3rd ed. Edmonton: University of Alberta Press.

Canadian Indian Treaty 9 (James Bay Treaty)

November 6, 1905, October 5, 1906

Treaty 9, or the James Bay Treaty, was another in the series of agreements known as the numbered treaties that were made with the indigenous peoples of Canada. Not unlike several of the western treaties, Treaty 9 was made with northern aboriginal cultures, in this case, Ojibwa and Cree nations in present-day northern Ontario. It was, in fact, the first treaty negotiated with the Amerindians of the Hudson-James Bay drainage area. In common with the other northern treaties, Treaty 9 came about in part because of indigenous concerns about looming white invasions and the concomitant petitions for a treaty (both of which began in the early 1880s), but also because the Canadian government eventually responded to increasing aboriginal calls for a treaty only when motivated to do so by the needs of mining development and railway construction in the early twentieth century. Signed in 1905 and 1906, Treaty 9 encompassed all unceded lands from the height of land to the Albany River. All remaining territory north of the Albany River and along the southern coast of Hudson's Bay and east of James Bay was

later incorporated into Treaty 9 by adhesions taken in 1929 and 1930.

Treaty 9 negotiations are notable for a couple of reasons. Because the treaty included lands within a constituted province of Canada and therefore involved two jurisdictions, negotiations had to take place at two levels: first, between the federal and provincial governments, and then between the treaty commission (consisting of federal and provincial representatives) and the Cree and Ojibwa Nations. Based on the historical evidence, some scholars argue that negotiations between the two levels of governments were more substantive than those between the treaty commission and indigenous peoples. This is borne out in part by the extensive nature of federal-provincial negotiations, which stretched over a number of years amid considerable struggle over jurisdictions and treaty negotiations with the Ojibwa and Cree Nations that arguably involved little or no significant negotiations. Throughout the summers of 1905 and 1906, treaty commissioners met with northern nations at a number of sites. Among these were Osnaburgh, Forts Hope and Albany, Moose Factory, Fort Abitibi, Mattawagamingue, New Brunswick House, and Long Lake. As was characteristic of some of the other

James Bay Treaty commissioners paddle the Pic River en route to Long Lake, 1906. (Library and Archives Canada)

The town of Moose Factory, Ontario, c. 1870. (Library and Archives Canada)

treaties, negotiations were brief; indigenous concerns about restrictions against hunting and fishing were answered by government officials with reassurances to the contrary (ironically, at about the same time that provincial police and game wardens were confiscating furs obtained out of season from Native hunters in other parts of the province).

By the end of August 1906, Treaty 9 negotiations had ended, and the treaty was signed; notably, a number of chiefs signed in syllabic characters. Adhesions were completed years later. Perhaps more clearly in the negotiations than in the text of the treaty, Treaty 9 nonetheless promised the continued (though not unfettered) right to pursue hunting, trapping, and fishing; reserves of one square mile for each family of five; cash payments; and education, in return for the extinguishment of the signatory nations' aboriginal title, their good conduct, and observance of the King's law. The absence of agricultural provisions in the treaty was due to lack of arable land and to government anticipation that indigenous northern peoples would remain hunters and trappers in the future.

Although, early on, the indigenous peoples of northern Ontario conveyed their gratitude to the government for including them in the treaty and providing them with schools, problems arose on several fronts. A number of concerns were increasingly voiced about the declining value of treaty annuities, problems with reserves, the nonrecognition or exclusion of particular aboriginal communities from the treaty, and the impact of provincial game laws. In the case of reserves, confusion spread regarding their purpose, locations, and entitlement. In some cases, the reserve problem would persist until the 1970s, and problems that involved indigenous hunting and fishing rights would endure even longer. Some of the evidence suggests that these problems lingered in part because, not unlike other treaties, the provincial and federal Canadian governments had determined the terms of Treaty 9 well before negotiations with the indigenous nations, and these terms were not offered but effectively dictated. Other evidence suggests that promises communicated orally during negotiations were inadequately explained and/or simply never implemented by the government.

Jason M. Yaremko

See also Canadian Indian Treaties; Canadian Indian Treaty 3–October 3, 1873; Robinson Huron Treaty (Second Robinson Treaty)–September 9, 1850; Robinson Superior Treaty (First Robinson Treaty)–September 7, 1850.

References and Further Reading

Asch, Michael. 1984. *Home and Native Land: Aboriginal Rights and the Canadian Constitution.* Toronto: Methuen.

Cardinal, Harold. 1977. *The Rebirth of Canada's Indians.* Edmonton, AB: Hurtig.

Dickason, Olive Patricia. 1992. *Canada's First Nations: A History of Founding Peoples from Earliest Times.* Norman: University of Oklahoma Press.

Morrison, James. 1986. *Treaty Research Report: Treaty No. 9.* Ottawa: Treaties and Historical Research Centre. Indian and Northern Affairs Canada.

Rogers, Edward, and Donald B. Smith, eds. 1994. *Aboriginal Ontario.* Toronto: Ontario Historical Studies Series.

Canadian Indian Treaty 10

September 19, 1906, August 19, 1907

Treaty 10 both resembled and differed from the earlier numbered treaties made in western Canada. It resembled the treaties signed with the indigenous peoples of the Canadian plains, which exhorted the Indians to surrender aboriginal title to lands they occupied, in exchange for promises of education, agricultural aid, the provision of reserves (one square mile per family of five) or individual plots (160 acres), cash payments, and continued access to hunting, trapping, and fishing. Like Treaty 8, however, this treaty was distinct in its attention to northern territories occupied by the Cree and Chipewyan or Dene nations, and those parts of the subarctic prairies not ceded (though this was originally intended) under Treaty 8, including northern Saskatchewan and part of east-central Alberta. Like Treaty 8, Indian and Métis calls for protection against the eventual onslaught of white intrusion involving development and settlement were ignored by the federal government in Ottawa until the formation of the province of Saskatchewan in 1905, when potential Indian interference with future resource access, exploitation, transportation, and economic development became a palpable concern. The following year, a commission was struck to negotiate a new treaty in the north. Unable to complete the task in time, this commission was followed by another one in 1907. The principal negotiation sites were Ile á la Crosse in 1906 and Lac du Brochet in 1907.

Like earlier treaties, the treaty parties were aided in their efforts by missionaries. Some treaty commission members involved in Treaty 8 negotiations were instructed to use this document as a template for the negotiation and final agreement for Treaty 10. Negotiations began in the summer of 1906. The treaty commission's essential tasks included the extinguishment of aboriginal title and acquiescence of the northern Métis in the cession. This involved the settlement of outstanding Métis claims through the offer of inclusion in the treaty (as Indians) or provision of a one-time grant, called scrip. As noted, treaty terms resembled those of earlier western treaties, with the exception of farming provisions, which remained vague. This was due in large part to the government's expectation that northern hunters and trappers would maintain their traditional way of life into the foreseeable future.

The fundamental concerns of the Cree and Dene peoples of northern Saskatchewan mirrored those of indigenous concerns in Treaties 8 and 9 and all previous treaty negotiations: the security of traditional livelihoods, the land question, education, and health care. Of these, land loomed largest. Although Indian bands made some requests specific to their regional and local needs (concerning, for example, annuities, farming, and medical aid), northern Cree and Dene peoples all shared the same concerns about the continued freedom to fish, hunt, and trap, and indigenous negotiators voiced their demands for continued access to traditional resources and ways of life. The same fears about maintaining livelihoods without access to resources that were raised in earlier northern treaty negotiations surfaced repeatedly. Cree and Dene negotiators at Ile á la Crosse and Lac du Brochet pressed the government for assurances that their hunting and fishing rights would be protected. In turn, treaty commissioners reassured indigenous leaders that their ways of life would be maintained and not infringed upon, while minimizing the impact of game laws and white encroachment. Of the latter issue one commissioner appears to have made no mention at all.

The directness of indigenous negotiators' questioning and concerns, a product, in part, of the familiarity with the terms of earlier treaties, contrasted with the vague guarantees of the treaty commissions. One chief even enquired as to whether the treaty could be amended at a later date. This, like other points raised, was rejected by the government.

Negotiations, though intense, were relatively brief, ranging from one to three days, suggesting that the vague but repeated guarantees of the government (along with occasional reminders of the inevitability of white penetration and settlement) overcame the initial fears and resistance of northern Indian nations. Negotiations ended with the signing of Treaty 10 at Ile á la Crosse on September 19, 1906, and at Lac du Brochet on August 22, 1907.

The paucity of documentation for Treaty 10 negotiations leaves a number of questions unanswered, especially with respect to the extent to which government negotiators elaborated on treaty terms and how well they were understood by the Cree and Dene peoples who became bound by them. In the clash between the needs and interests of the federal (and provincial) government and those of the northern nations, the legacy of industrial development and indigenous underdevelopment suggests the triumph of government expediency.

Jason M. Yaremko

See also Canadian Indian Treaties; Canadian Indian Treaty 8–June 21, 1899; Métis.

References and Further Reading

Asch, Michael. 1984. *Home and Native Land: Aboriginal Rights and the Canadian Constitution.* Toronto: Methuen.
Cardinal, Harold. 1977. *The Rebirth of Canada's Indians.* Edmonton, AB: Hurtig.
Dickason, Olive Patricia. 1992. *Canada's First Nations: A History of Founding Peoples from Earliest Times.* Norman: University of Oklahoma Press.
Ray, Arthur, Jim Miller, and Frank J. Tough. 2000. *Bounty and Benevolence: A History of Saskatchewan Treaties.* London: McGill-Queen's University Press.

Canadian Indian Treaty 11
June 27 to August 30, 1921

In Canada, numerous treaties have been made between the Crown and indigenous peoples. Generally, these are pacts in which First Nations peoples exchange specific interests and title to land for recognized rights and benefits from the Crown. Although the Crown generally interprets the agreements as contractual ones, First Nations peoples understand treaties as solemn agreements forming the basis for evolving relationships between themselves and recently established, nonindigenous governments. Treating with indigenous peoples became an established diplomatic practice of European governments seeking to consolidate their power in North America from the sixteenth to the

A camp scene of the Imperial Oil Co. expedition to the Fort Norman oil fields, Northwest Territory, 1921. (Library and Archives Canada)

The arrival of the first boat after winter, Fort Providence, Northwest Territory, 1929. (Library and Archives Canada)

nineteenth centuries. After Canadian confederation in 1867 and the dominion government's assumption of responsibilities for relations with indigenous peoples, the primary purpose of treaty making became to secure the surrender of indigenous peoples' rights and interests to lands and resources in order to clear the way for settlement and resource extraction. The numbered treaties were those treaties negotiated by the new dominion government between 1870 and 1922. Treaty 11 was the last such treaty, signed in 1921 and 1922 by Dene along the Mackenzie valley, including the Dogrib, Sahtu, Gwich'in, and Deh Cho Dene peoples. The treaty was motivated by the discovery of significant oil reserves at Norman Wells, near the community of present day Tulita in the Sahtu region of the Northwest Territories.

Canada sent Commissioner Conroy along with Anglican Bishop Breynat to treat with the Dene; in addition, Conroy was head of the associated Halfbreed Commission, charged with taking applications for Halfbreed Scrip. The treaty was signed between June 27 and August 30, 1921, by Dene in the commu-

nities of Fort Providence, Fort Simpson, Fort Wrigley, Fort Norman (Tulita), Fort Good Hope, Fort McPherson, Fort Rae, and Arctic Red River (Tsiigehtchic) with a further adhesion by Deh Cho Dene at Fort Liard the following year. In 1973, plans for development on Dene lands without Dene consent prompted Dene chiefs collectively to register a caveat on their lands as a way to ensure participation in decisions around development, which eventually went to court. In the *Caveat* case, also known as the *Paulette* case, Justice William Morrow of the Northwest Territories Court heard testimony from many Dene elders regarding the issue of whether Dene had agreed to extinguish their rights and surrender their lands during treaty negotiations. The memories and oral traditions of the elders revealed the Dene understanding of the treaty as one of peace and friendship, which did not include surrender of rights or lands. Although Justice Morrow's 1973 ruling in favor of the Dene was later overturned, he had heard evidence sufficient to prompt the Canadian government to negotiate land and resource rights with Dene signatories of Treaty 11.

The treaty was drawn up in Ottawa, and strict instructions were given to Commissioner Conroy that he was not to deviate from the written text of the treaty, perhaps in the wake of reports that oral promises beyond the bounds of the text of Treaty 8 had been made with the Dene's Chipewayan and Cree neighbors to the south twenty years earlier. The treaty instructed that it should be signed by chiefs and headmen chosen by the Indians to do so on their behalf. Its key provision was that, by signing, the Dene "cede, release, surrender, and yield up to the Government of the Dominion of Canada . . . forever, all their rights, titles, and privileges to the lands included within the following limits. . . ." It then described the bounds of the more than 370,000 square miles of Dene territory constituting the Mackenzie valley area of the Northwest Territories. By signing, they also agreed to abide by Canada's laws and to keep relations of peace and goodwill with Canada. In return, the Dene could continue to hunt, fish, and trap in the territory surrendered, and reserves were to be set aside for their exclusive use. A cash annuity of five dollars would also be provided to each treaty Indian in perpetuity. Notably, there was no provision that this amount might be adjusted in accordance with inflation through time. Onetime gifts of tools, money, and clothing were made at the time of signing, and specific equipment, such as net twine and ammunition for hunters and trappers, was to be provided annually. In addition, the treaty promised assistance for those Dene wishing to pursue agriculture—a highly dubious benefit, given that the Arctic climate is highly unsuitable for agricultural pursuits. The most significant provision is perhaps the promise of the salaries of teachers to be paid by Canada, which, as a result of legal principles established since the 1970s requiring treaties to be interpreted liberally, is currently understood as significant educational benefits for treaty Indians.

Stephanie Irlbacher-Fox

See also Aboriginal Title; Canadian Indian Treaties; Reserved Rights Doctrine; Right of Conquest.

References and Further Reading

Daugherty, W. E. 1986. *Treaty Research Report: Treaty Three*. Ottawa: Treaties and Historical Research Centre, Indian and Northern Affairs Canada.

Dickason, Olive Patricia. 1992. *Canada's First Nations: A History of Founding Peoples from Earliest Times*. Norman: University of Oklahoma Press.

Fumoleau, Rene. 1973. *As Long as This Land Shall Last: A History of Treaty 8 and Treaty 11, 1870–1939*. Toronto: McClelland and Stewart.

Morris, Alexander. 1991. *The Treaties of Canada with the Indians of Manitoba and the North-West Territories including The Negotiations on which they were based* (First Printing 1880), reprint by Fifth House Publishers, Saskatoon, SK. See Chapter 5, "Treaty Number Three or the Northwest Angle Treaty," pp. 44–76, pp. 320–329.

Williams Treaties with the Chippewa and the Mississauga
October to November 1923

The Mississauga and Chippewa treaties of 1923 are commonly referred as the Williams Treaties. The Williams Treaties are unique, for they involve two treaties covering the same area. Signatories to the Williams Treaties are the Mississauga of Scugog Lake, Mississauga of Alderville, Mississauga of Hiawatha, and Mississauga of Curve Lake; and the Chippewa of Georgina Island, Chippewa of Christian Island, and Chippewa of Rama.

Of historical significance, the Mississauga and Chippewa had surrendered most of their lands by 1818, 1819, and 1822. These former eighteenth-century treaties represent most of the Mississauga and Chippewa territory below the 45th parallel. The largest portion of Mississauga and Chippewa hunting territory was north of the 45th parallel and had remained not covered by a treaty until 1923.

The Williams Treaties are made up of two documents, a treaty and an attached memorandum of agreement. The memorandum of agreement was negotiated between the Province of Ontario and the Dominion of Canada in April 1923. The memorandum of agreement outlined the federal and provincial shared understanding that the Mississauga and Chippewa lay claim to 10,719 square miles or 6,400,000 acres north of the 45th parallel.

The memorandum of agreement had seven clauses that contained the appointment, financing, and powers of the treaty commission. Clauses one to three dealt with the appointment, selection, and commission question of validity. Clauses four and five outlined the commission's expenses, to be covered by the federal government, and treaty payment by province. Clause six dealt with the issue of reserve lands; the province agreed to provide lands for reserves. Lastly, clause seven is the extinction clause: all lands and monies were to be held and administered for the Mississauga and Chippewa

Native Americans of the Ojibwa tribe (also known as Chippewa) paddle a hand-made canoe c. 1913. The lightweight construction and shallow draft of the canoe made it an ideal craft for navigating the lakes and small rivers of North America. (Library of Congress)

until they are extinct, at which time the lands and monies will be returned to their rightful owner—according to the memorandum of agreement, the province of Ontario.

It is significant that Section 91.24 of the Constitution Act of 1867 had given the federal government legislative control over Indian lands; further, Section 109 stated that "all lands," once surrendered, belonged to the province in which they were located. The federal government had the responsibility to enter into treaties with Indians but could not establish a reserve once a treaty had been signed. In effect, then, the province must loan some of its land to the federal government to create a reserve in the event a treaty is negotiated.

Unlike former Mississauga and Chippewa treaties, the Williams Treaties extinguished not only land rights but also the Native rights to hunt and fish on ceded lands. The treaty has three lands clauses: Clause one describes 17,600 square miles, mostly above the 45th parallel. The second clause includes land below the 45th parallel, describing 2,500 square miles. A third clause, commonly referred to as the "basket clause," surrenders "all other lands . . . to which they ever had, now have, or now claim to have as theirs. . . ." A further clause explains that the treaty is subject to the attached memorandum of agreement.

The final version of the Williams Treaties described lands north and south of the 45th parallel. The treaty terms extinguished rights to hunting and fishing to 20,100 square miles. However, the Mississauga and Chippewa had hired lawyers to protect their hunting and fishing rights, and the memorandum of agreement authorized only a treaty for 10,719 square miles. The terms described in the Williams Treaties were confirmed by the Supreme Court of Canada in May 1994, despite obvious contradictions.

Daniel Edward Shaule

See also Canadian Indian Treaties.

References and Further Reading

Daniels, Richard. 1980. *A History of Native Claims Processes in Canada 1867–1979*. Prepared for the Research Branch, Department of Indian and Northern Affairs, February.

Johnson, Ian. 1985. *1923 Historical Narrative of the Williams Treaties*. Ottawa: Department of Indian Affairs Historical Centre. Also available from any Williams Treaties of 1923 First Nations.

Johnson, Leo. 1973. *History of the County of Ontario 1615–1875*. Whitby, ON: Corporation of the County of Ontario, Chapter 2.

Surtees, Robert. 1986. *The Williams Treaties*. Treaty and Historical Research Report. Ottawa: Department of Indian Affairs.

James Bay and Northern Quebec Agreement

November 11, 1975

The James Bay and Northern Quebec Agreement (JBNQA) was signed on November 11, 1975, by the government of Quebec, the Grand Council of the Cree (Quebec), the Northern Quebec Inuit Association, the James Bay Energy Corporation, the James Bay Development Corporation, the Quebec Hydro-Electric Commission (Hydro-Quebec), and the government of Canada. It came into effect in 1977. It is often referred to as the first "modern treaty" in Canada under the federal government's 1973 extinguishment policy, whereby existing aboriginal title to ancestral lands is extinguished in return for specified rights and interests in treaties between aboriginal peoples and the provincial and federal governments of Canada. The territory covered by the agreement represents 69 percent of the province of Quebec, extending from the 48th parallel to the 62nd parallel north. The 55th parallel demarcates the territory between the Cree in the south and the Inuit in the north.

The JBNQA is the first comprehensive land claims settlement negotiated while development of the hydroelectric project, La Grande, was taking place on Cree lands. The Cree had initially sought and won an injunction from the Quebec Superior Court to stop the project. However, the Quebec

George Manuel (from left), president of the National Indian Brotherhood; Aurilien Gill, third vice president of the Association of Indians, and Chief Max Louis, second vice president of the Association of Indians, speak in November 1974 at a news conference discussing the agreement between the James Bay Cree and the Quebec government. The agreement was finalized in 1975 and was the first treaty in the modern Canadian treaty period. (Bettmann/Corbis)

Court of Appeal overturned the decision. It held that, although the La Grande project would affect Cree interests and rights in land, these could be remedied or compensated. Faced with continuation of the project, the Cree decided to negotiate a settlement to secure certain rights and limit future plans for hydroelectric projects.

Under the JBNQA, both the provincial and federal governments have obligations toward the Cree; the province has jurisdiction over land-related Cree rights, and the federal government has a general fiduciary duty to protect aboriginal rights and interests. The JBNQA does not recognize the right of self-government for the Cree or Inuit, but it does allow them greater control over their lives and affairs. They have rights to land use and access and to the establishment of political organs with powers over education, social services, health, business, and land management. Rights to land are divided into three land categories: Category I lands are for the exclusive use and benefit of Cree and Inuit; Category II lands allow Cree and Inuit the exclusive right to hunt, fish, and trap; and Category III lands are for general public access, but Cree and Inuit retain harvesting rights.

Among the political organs established to administer the territory are the Cree Regional Authority and the Kativik Regional Government. A number of other institutions were established giving Cree and Inuit decision-making powers over education, social services, health, justice, and public security. In relation to preserving aboriginal languages, the JBNQA strengthens formal instruction in Cree and Inuktitut through the establishment of the Cree and Kativik school boards. The provincial and federal governments have obligations to finance building the territory's infrastructure and political organs.

One key feature of the JBNQA is the surrender and extinguishment clause (Article 2.1), under which all Cree and Inuit claims, rights, titles, and interests in land are surrendered and extinguished in exchange for specified rights, privileges, and benefits in the JBNQA (Article 2.2). Surrender and extinguishment clauses have since been used in other comprehensive land claims settlements, with some criticism from aboriginal communities, who point to the historical nature of their claims and rights to land. They argue that, by requiring rights to be defined in agreements, the historical connection between aboriginal peoples and the land is diminished, as well as the historical relations between aboriginal and nonaboriginal peoples that forms the basis of aboriginal rights today. From the provincial and federal governments' point of view, surrender and extinguishment clauses guarantee legal certainty of rights and duties for aboriginal communities as well as the state and, overall, agreements with these clauses represent an enlightened policy of negotiation rather than litigation of aboriginal rights.

In early 2002, the government of Quebec reached a new agreement, La Paix des Braves (Peace of the Braves), with the Cree Indians. This agreement represents a new phase in Cree-Quebec relations by emphasizing economic development, governmental access to lands for development purposes, and Cree participation and benefit from development activities. The JBNQA continues to bind both parties subject to the amendments agreed in La Paix des Braves. This means that the government of Quebec continues to fund Cree health, education, income, and security programs, public security, the work of the Hunting, Fishing and Trapping Coordinating Committee, and environmental committees. La Paix des Braves establishes what a "nation-to-nation relationship" between the Cree and the Province of Quebec, allowing greater negotiating power for the Cree to discuss directly with governmental departments matters that affect their communities. Principles of consent and consultation are means by which this improved political status is realized.

Özlem Ülgen

See also Aboriginal Title; Inuit; Modern Treaties/Comprehensive Land Claim Agreements (Canada).

References and Further Reading

Diamond, Billy. 1990. "Villages of the Damned: The James Bay Agreement Leaves a Trail of Broken Promises." *Artic Circle* (Nov/Dec): 24–34.

James Bay and Northern Quebec Agreement and Complementary Agreements. 1991. Quebec: Les Publications du Quebec.

La Paix des Braves. 2002.

Moss, Wendy. 1985. "The Implementation of the James Bay and Northern Quebec Agreement." In *Aboriginal Peoples and the Law,* edited by B. Morse, 684–696. Ottawa: Carleton University Press.

Royal Commission on Aboriginal Peoples. 1995. *Treaty-Making in the Spirit of Co-existence: An Alternative to Extinguishment.* Ottawa: Canada Communication Group.

Northeastern Quebec Agreement

January 31, 1978

The Northeastern Quebec Act (NQA) was signed on January 31, 1978, by the government of Quebec, the Naskapi Indians (Quebec), the Grand Council of the Cree (Quebec), the Northern Quebec Inuit Association, the James Bay Energy Corporation, the James Bay Development Corporation, the Quebec Hydro-Electric Commission (Hydro-Quebec), and the government of Canada. The Naskapi Indians, who inhabit the northeastern part of Quebec, were one of four aboriginal groups who chose not to sign the James Bay and Northern Quebec Agreement (JBNQA) in 1975 and so were excluded from its provisions. After negotiations between the provincial and federal governments, the Naskapi finally ratified the NQA, which amends the JBNQA to the extent that it incorporates provisions relating to the Naskapi Indians.

The NQA is a comprehensive land claims settlement based on the JBNQA provisions on land rights and on the establishment of political organs with powers over education, social services, health, business, and land management. Under Article 2.1 of the NQA, all Naskapi claims, rights, titles, and interests in land are surrendered and extinguished in exchange for specified rights, privileges, and benefits specified under the NQA. Specified rights in land fall into two categories. Category 1A-N lands are set aside for the exclusive use and benefit of the Naskapi under the administration, management, and control of the federal government (Article 5.1.2). The Province of Quebec retains full ownership of these lands, including the mineral and subsurface resources. Category 1B-N lands are owned exclusively by a Naskapi private landholding corporation established under Quebec laws (Article 5.1.3). These lands can be sold or ceded only to Quebec.

The lands owned by Naskapi constitute a municipality, following the governmental and administrative structure throughout the province of Quebec. Under Article 8.2, the municipality is represented in the Kativik Regional Government, established pursuant to the JBNQA. Lands not owned by Naskapi but set aside for their exclusive use and benefit are governed by a band council (Article 7.1.2).

The federal and provincial governments funded development of the area, and under the NQA the Naskapi Development Corporation was established to administer compensation funds paid by Canada, Quebec, and Hydro-Quebec. Under Article 16.1.1, both the federal and provincial governments paid $6 million in monetary compensation for the surrender and extinguishment of Naskapi existing claims, rights, titles, and interests in Quebec.

On lands designated for the exclusive use and occupation by Naskapi, the laws of general application relating to health and social services apply (Article 10.2). A Naskapi Health and Social Services Consultative Committee ("Consultative Committee") is established to represent Naskapi interests at the Schefferville Hospital Centre, the Community Health Department, and the Social Services Centre (Article 10.3). The Province of Quebec undertakes to consult the Consultative Committee before modifying any program relating to health and social services offered to the Naskapi, and to submit a yearly report about the health and social conditions of the Naskapi community (Article 10.5). The Consultative Committee has the opportunity to make suggestions and recommendations concerning the hiring of health and social services personnel in the Naskapi communities (Article 10.19). Quebec also undertakes to progressively encourage the training of Naskapi health and social services personnel (Article 10.20).

In relation to education, a Naskapi school is established on Category 1A-N lands (lands for exclusive use and occupation), and the Naskapi language is taught; one objective is to use French as a teaching language so that pupils graduating from the school will be capable of continuing further studies in French in school, college, or university (Article 11.19). The Naskapi school's primary objective is kindergarten and elementary education. Where necessary, provision will be made for special courses to Naskapi adults, along with special remedial programs for Naskapi children who have not completed their secondary education (Article 11.14).

In relation to policing, special Naskapi constables are appointed, with duties and functions in Category 1A-N lands (Article 13.1.1.). All future developments (including mining operations, energy production, forestry and agriculture, community and municipal services—such as major sewage and water works—and transportation) on land occupied by the Naskapi are subject to an environmental and social impact assessment (Article 14.1.2.2). The Naskapi do not have the power to stop or prevent

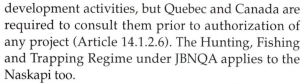

development activities, but Quebec and Canada are required to consult them prior to authorization of any project (Article 14.1.2.6). The Hunting, Fishing and Trapping Regime under JBNQA applies to the Naskapi too.

Özlem Ülgen

See also Aboriginal Title; Inuit; James Bay and Northern Quebec Agreement–November 11, 1975; Modern Treaties/Comprehensive Land Claim Agreements (Canada).

References and Further Reading

Diamond, Billy. 1990. "Villages of the Damned: The James Bay Agreement Leaves a Trail of Broken Promises." *Artic Circle* (Nov/Dec): 24–34.

The Northeastern Quebec Agreement. 1984. Ottawa: Department of Indian and Northern Affairs Canada.

Peters, E. 1989. "Federal and Provincial Responsibilities for the Cree, Naskapi and Inuit Under the James Bay and Northern Quebec, and Northeastern Quebec Agreements." In *Aboriginal Peoples and Government Responsibility–Exploring Federal and Provincial Roles*, ed. D. Hawkes. Ottawa: Carleton University Press.

Royal Commission Report on Aboriginal Peoples. 1995. *Treaty-Making in the Spirit of Co-existence: An Alternative to Extinguishment*. Ottawa: Canada Communication Group.

Inuvialuit Final Agreements

June 1984

In the early 1970s, the Inuvialuit were faced with oil and gas development in the MacKenzie Delta and Beaufort Sea areas. They decided to pursue a land claim settlement with the Canadian government to acquire control over resource development. Beginning in 1976, the Inuvialuit aggressively lobbied federal officials for negotiations, and eight years later the Inuvialuit Agreements were signed in June 1984. The overall settlement provided the Inuvialuit with surface ownership rights to nearly 91,000 square kilometers of land as well as limited subsurface rights to an additional 13,000 square kilometers. A financial component of $152 million was included, as were onetime payments of $10 million to an economic enhancement fund and $7.5 million to a social development fund. The remaining $45 million in financial compensation was paid to the Inuvialuit in annual installments until 1997. The Inuvialuit considered the final settlement a success, and with it

they gained a previously unknown level of influence within government channels.

The Inuvialuit originally signed on as member communities to the Inuit land claim brought forward in the mid-1970s. Reacting to the steady infiltration of non-Native people from the south and the imposition of Canadian social programs, the Inuit and Inuvialuit formed the Inuit Tapirisat Corporation (ITC). The ITC was created to fight for aboriginal rights, to work with government officials to limit large-scale development such as oil exploration and small-scale and local development such as northern tourism. The ITC was also concerned with developing the mechanisms needed to permit Inuit participation in policy formulation, and with the creation of programs and research for dealing with rights to territory and resources, all the while seeking protection and maintenance of traditional land use and harvesting practices.

As research was conducted, interest in the claim heightened following the Supreme Court of Canada *Calder* decision of 1973, which recognized preexisting aboriginal rights and confirmed the existence of a separate system of aboriginal rights. In this instance, aboriginal title arises from the long-term use and continuous occupancy of the land by aboriginal peoples prior to the arrival of European and British colonial powers in North America. In response to *Calder*, Canadian officials acknowledged the need to create a more flexible policy concerning the recognition of aboriginal rights. In 1974, the federal government implemented a new comprehensive land claims policy that permitted the claimant group to receive defined rights, compensation, and other benefits in exchange for relinquishing rights related to the title claimed over all or part of the land in question. The federal government provided funding to, among others, the ITC to determine the land areas over which they wanted ownership rights.

The ITC land claim proposed the creation of a new territory and representative government—unprecedented requests at the time. The ITC's goal was to resolve the land claim, which called for the Beaufort Sea and Yukon North Slope areas used by the Inuvialuit to be included in the proposed Nunavut Territory, while simultaneously promoting Inuit political development. The proposal was later withdrawn because of its complexity. Inuit factionalism also resulted, and the Inuvialuit split from the ITC in 1976 to negotiate a separate land claim agreement.

Standing on an ice floe at the edge of the city of Iqaluit, an Inuk harnesses his sled dog. Iqaluit is the capital city of the Nunavut Territory. (AP/Wide World Photos)

In 1977, the Committee of Original Peoples' Entitlement, which represented 4,500 Inuvialuit in six communities living along or near the mouth of the Mackenzie River, submitted its comprehensive claim with the Canadian government. During the next seven years, negotiations occurred between the Inuit, the Métis, the Inuvialuit, and Canadian officials while the Nunavut claim was still under negotiations. The Inuvialuit Final Agreements were signed in 1984. Whether or not the split was a positive move, intense pressure from impending economic development initiatives led the Inuvialuit to settle the first comprehensive land claim settlement in the Northwest Territories with the government of Canada.

That same year, the Inuvialuit Regional Corporation was formed to receive the lands and financial compensation obtained by the Inuvialuit. The corporation was assigned the responsibility for managing the settlement, the objectives according to the 1997 annual report of the Inuvialuit Corporate Group being to "[p]reserve the Inuvialuit culture, identity and values within a changing northern society. Enable Inuvialuit to be equal and meaningful participants in the northern and national economy and society. Protect and preserve the Arctic wildlife, environment and biological productivity."

To date, the Inuvialuit have secured a sizable land base, which they control, and they share in the management of resources on Crown lands throughout the entire region covered by the agreement. Further, the Inuvialuit have experienced the positive impacts that come with the protection of adequate lands, resources, and political power. The settlement has enabled the Inuvialuit to build their own communities and expand their economic interests beyond the region and settlement area.

Yale D. Belanger

See also *Calder v. Attorney-General of British Columbia* (Canada), 1973; Inuit.

References and Further Reading

Anderson, B., B. Kayseas, L. P. Dana, and K. Hindle. 2004. "Indigenous Land Claims and Economic Development: The Canadian Experience." *American Indian Quarterly*, 28(3–4): 634–648.

Frideres, J. 1998. *Native People in Canada: Contemporary Conflicts.* Scarborough, ON: Prentice-Hall.

Inuvialuit Corporate Group. 1997. *Inuvialuit Corporate Group: 1996 Annual Report.* Inuvik, NT: Inuvialuit Corporate Group.

Gwich'in Comprehensive Land Claim Agreement

April 1992

In Canada, indigenous peoples' rights to their traditional lands and resources are clarified through negotiated agreements with Canada. Generally, indigenous peoples are required to negotiate rights in accordance with the Canadian Comprehensive Land Claims Policy (1986). The policy's most significant feature is that indigenous peoples must surrender undefined aboriginal rights and title in exchange for defined rights and ownership of lands and resources. Known as *extinguishment,* wherein indigenous peoples are required to agree to "extinguish" all their aboriginal rights, in recent years this policy has been replaced by a more politically palatable term, *certainty.* Essentially, it is the same concept repackaged in less hostile terminology.

The Gwich'in, or People of the Caribou, were signatories of Treaty 11 in 1921. Beginning in the 1970s and continuing through the 1980s and 1990s, they attempted to negotiate land and resource rights with Canada as a member of the Dene Nation, along with the Tli Cho, Deh Cho, Akaitcho, and Sahtu peoples. Faced with massive resource development pressures in their traditional territories compounded by a lands and resources agreement reached with the Inuvialuit neighbors, the Gwich'in chose to pursue their own agreement following watershed political events within the Dene Nation in 1990. In 1992, the Gwich'in formalized the Comprehensive Land Claim Agreement with Canada.

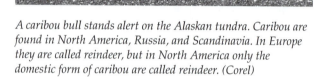

A caribou bull stands alert on the Alaskan tundra. Caribou are found in North America, Russia, and Scandinavia. In Europe they are called reindeer, but in North America only the domestic form of caribou are called reindeer. (Corel)

There are approximately twenty-three hundred Gwich'in beneficiaries, descendants of the original Northern Athapaskan inhabitants. Distinct bands include the Teetl'it Gwich'in of Fort McPherson, the Gwich'ya Gwich'in of Tsiigehtchic, and the Nihtat Gwich'in located in Inuvik, the region's regional centre. The agreement applies to Gwich'in people who have traditionally occupied an area within what is now the northwestern corner of Canada's Northwest Territories. The Gwich'in Settlement Area (GSA) covers fifty-seven thousand square kilometers in the Northwest Territory and a primary use area in the Yukon. The Gwich'in is part of the Gwich'in Nation, which spans Canada's Northwest and Yukon Territories in Canada and Alaska in the United States. The lands of the Gwich'in are rich in flora and fauna and in oil and gas resources. They have been sustained for millennia by the Porcupine caribou herd (named for the Porcupine River, this herd is one of two in the Arctic National Wildlife Refuge), which migrates each year through Gwich'in lands to calve in the Alaska National Wildlife Refuge, which the Gwich'in have mounted an international lobby to protect from development.

The agreement provided the Gwich'in with rights to lands and resources and guaranteed participation of lands, resources, and water in their traditional territories. They received 22,422 square kilometers throughout their traditional territories. Of this, Gwich'in own 6,158 square kilometers of the subsurface, possess mineral rights on 4,299 square kilometers, and own the surface of 1,554 square kilometers of their traditional territories in the Yukon. The land in the Yukon is known as Teetlit Gwich'in land, a traditional use area of Gwich'in now based largely in the community of Fort McPherson.

The Gwich'in also received cash compensation in return for surrendering their claim to much of their traditional territory and ceding it to Canada. The Gwich'in received $75 million (1990 Canadian dollars) over a fifteen-year period. As part of the settlement, Gwich'in is provided a small portion of total resource royalties flowing from development activity in the Mackenzie valley. Within their settlement region, Gwich'in have extensive wildlife harvesting rights, as well as guaranteed participation in decision-making bodies established for the management of wildlife and regulatory bodies for land, water, and the environment. These bodies include the Gwich'in Renewable Resource Board, the Gwich'in Land and Water Board, and the Gwich'in Land Use Planning Board. Each of these is a public decision-making institution with authority in the settlement area. Gwich'in are represented on the Northwest Territory's Mackenzie Valley Environmental Impact Review Board, which has authority to review the environmental impacts of development in the territory and to make recommendations on how projects may proceed. Gwich'in also have the rights of first refusal for some commercial wildlife activities in their settlement area.

Compensation from the land claim has allowed the Gwich'in to invest for the future. A Gwich'in Social and Cultural Institute has been established, which conducts archaeological, oral history, and traditional knowledge research in the GSA. Educational and cultural programs, such as postsecondary scholarships, training programs, and language and culture camps for youth, have also been established.

Although the Gwich'in were required to extinguish their aboriginal rights as part of the agreement, treaty rights not specifically given up, such as education and treaty payments, continue to exist. Rights given up include treaty rights to hunt, fish, and trap in the settlement area and other parts of the Northwest Territory, the Yukon, and Nunavut covered by Treaty 11. Hunting, fishing, and trapping treaty rights in the Mackenzie valley will continue until other resident Dene/Métis groups negotiate agreements. Despite this, the agreement states that nothing in it removes the Gwich'in identity as aboriginal peoples or affects any existing or future constitutional rights for them as aboriginal people.

The agreement recognizes the Gwich'in Tribal Council and community-based Gwich'in organizations as the institutions responsible for implementing the land claim provisions. These political bodies make decisions and administer responsibilities of the agreement within the communities. At the same time, band councils recognized under the Indian Act continue to exercise decision-making authority on local governmental matters specific to the lives of their members. The agreement obligates the federal government to negotiate self-government with the Gwich'in, under which band councils will be replaced by governments recognized through the self-government agreement rather than the Indian Act. Currently, the Gwich'in are negotiating a joint self-government agreement with their Inuvialuit neighbors.

Stephanie Irlbacher Fox

See also Canadian Indian Treaty 11–June 27 to August 30, 1921; Modern Treaties/Comprehensive Land Claim Agreements (Canada); Treaty.

References and Further Reading

Asch, Michael. 1984. *Home and Native Land: Aboriginal Rights and the Canadian Constitution.* Toronto: Methuen.

Cardinal, Harold. 1977. *The Rebirth of Canada's Indians.* Edmonton, AB: Hurtig.

Dickason, Olive Patricia. 1992. *Canada's First Nations: A History of Founding Peoples from Earliest Times.* Norman: University of Oklahoma Press.

Nunavut Land Claims Agreement
May 25, 1993

Events leading to the Nunavut Land Claims Agreement began in the 1970s, when the Inuit started to establish political organizations, such as the Inuit Tapirisat of Canada (ITC), in an attempt to regain the autonomy over their day-to-day lives that had been lost to the federal government. In 1973, the ITC initiated a study of Inuit land use and occupancy in order to demonstrate the extent of Inuit aboriginal title in the Arctic. In 1976, the ITC asked the Canadian government to map out a boundary between the eastern and western regions of the

402   Nunavut Land Claims Agreement – May 25, 1993

Canadian governor general Romeo LeBlanc (center) looks on as the flag of Nunavut is unveiled at the official ceremony to inaugurate Nunavut in Iqaluit, Nunavut, on April 1, 1999. (Tom Hanson/AFP/Getty Images)

Northwest Territories. The ITC proposed the creation of Nunavut out of the eastern region of the Northwest Territories because of Inuit land claims in that area.

Throughout the 1980s, the Inuit, as represented by the Tunngavik Federation of Nunavut (TFN), engaged in land claims negotiations with the government of Canada. The interests of the government of the Northwest Territories were represented at the negotiating table by the government of Canada. In 1990, the parties reached a settlement, which eventually resulted in the Nunavut Land Claims Agreement. In 1992, the Inuit approved the Nunavut Land Claims Agreement, and in 1993 the government of Canada passed the Nunavut Land Claims Agreement Act, which confirmed that the Nunavut Land Claims Agreement is a treaty within the meaning of Section 35 of the Canadian Constitution.

The Nunavut Land Claims Agreement represents the largest indigenous land claim settlement in Canadian history. The objectives of the Nunavut Land Claims Agreement are as follows:

[To] provide for certainty and clarity of rights to ownership and use of lands and resources, and of rights for Inuit to participate in decision making concerning the use, management, and conservation of land, water, and resources, including the offshore; provide Inuit with wildlife harvesting rights and rights to participate in decision making concerning wildlife harvesting; provide Inuit with financial compensation and means of participating in economic opportunities; and encourage self-reliance and the cultural and social well-being of Inuit. (Preamble, Nunavut Land Claims Agreement Act, 1993).

The Nunavut Land Claims Agreement gives the Inuit ownership of more than 350,000 square kilometers (136,000 square miles) of land in the eastern Arctic, of which 36,000 square kilometers (14,000 square miles) includes subsurface mineral rights. It also calls for the creation of several national parks in the settlement area. In return, the Inuit agree to cede, release, and surrender all their aboriginal claims, rights, title, and interests, to lands and waters anywhere within Canada and adjacent offshore areas within the sovereignty or jurisdiction of Canada, and agree not to assert any further legal claims based on these interests. Disputes about any matter concerning the interpretation, application, or implementation of the Nunavut Land Claims Agreement are to be resolved by an arbitration board, by whose decision the parties agree to be bound. A decision of the arbitration board is subject to review by a court.

The Nunavut Land Claims Agreement provides the Inuit with more than $1.148 billion (Canadian dollars) in financial compensation over fourteen years. It guarantees Inuit participation in decision making with respect to lands and resources in the settlement area by mandating Inuit representation on wildlife management, resource management, and environmental boards. It requires the government of Canada to share with the Inuit royalties from resources produced on lands in the settlement area to which the Crown holds legal title.

The Nunavut Land Claims Agreement also commits the parties to work together to increase Inuit participation in government employment to a representative level. A Training Trust Fund of $13 million (Canadian dollars) is established to ensure that the Inuit have the skills necessary to implement the Nunavut Land Claims Agreement. In 1993, Nunavut Tunngavik Incorporated (NTI) was set up as a private corporation to promote Inuit economic, social, and cultural well-being through the implementation of the Nunavut Land Claims Agreement.

Most important, the Nunavut Land Claims Agreement stipulates that the parties work together to found a new territory called Nunavut, with its own public government separate from the government of the Northwest Territories. In this regard, a political accord was reached in October 1992. In April 1999, the Northwest Territories was divided in two, creating Nunavut. *Nunavut* means "our land" in Inuktitut, the Inuit language.

Ritu Gambhir

See also Canadian Indian Treaties; Constitution Act (Canada), 1867; Inuit; Modern Treaties/Comprehensive Land Claims Agreements (Canada); Sovereignty; Treaty; Trust Doctrine; Trust Responsibility.

References and Further Reading
Asch, Michael. 1984. *Home and Native Land: Aboriginal Rights and the Canadian Constitution*. Toronto: Methuen.

Borrows, J. 1997. "Frozen Rights in Canada: Constitutional Interpretation and the Trickster," 22 *American Indian Law Review* 37.

Cardinal, Harold. 1977. *The Rebirth of Canada's Indians*. Edmonton, AB: Hurtig.

Dickason, Olive Patricia. 1992. *Canada's First Nations: A History of Founding Peoples from Earliest Times*. Norman: University of Oklahoma Press.

Nunavut Tunngavik Incorporated. 2004. *A Plain Language Guide to Nunavut Land Claims Agreement*. Nunavut, Canada: Nunavut Tunngavik Incorporated.

Nacho Nyak Dun Final Agreement

May 29, 1993

This is one of four final agreements signed on May 29, 1993, as part of the Yukon land claims settlement process. These agreements were made in accordance with the Umbrella Final Agreement (also signed that day), which allowed each Yukon First Nation to pursue treaty settlements with the governments of Canada and the Yukon Territory. The Nacho Nyak Dun Final Agreement was the first step toward self-government taken by the First Nation of the Nacho Nyak Dun. The agreement was signed by the Nacho Nyak Dun, the government of Canada, and the government of Yukon, to take effect in 1995.

The Nacho Nyak Dun are the northernmost representatives of the Northern Tutchone language and culture. The traditional territory of the Nacho Nyak Dun (also spelled Na-cho Nyak Dun) is located in northeastern Yukon Territory on the border shared with the Northwest Territories. The territory overlaps with that of several other Yukon First Nations: the Tetlit Gwitchin and the Vuntut Gwitchin to the north, the Trondek Hwech'in to the west, and the Selkirk and the Kaska Dena to the south. Similarly to other First Nations in the Yukon, this territory of the Nacho Nyak Dun was included within Canadian borders in 1870, when Rupert's Land and the Northwest Territory were purchased from the Hudson's Bay Company.

Despite the Royal Proclamation of 1763, which directed the negotiation of treaties with aboriginals, no treaties were ever signed between the Nacho Nyak Dun and the governments of Great Britain or Canada. Nor were any attempts made to protect the rights of the Nacho Nyak Dun when gold was discovered on the Stewart River in 1883. The town of Mayo was established in 1903, and the settlement of

Lansing soon followed. The Department of Indian Affairs began providing assistance to the Nacho Nyak Dun in the 1920s, but it was not until the 1950s that the Mayo Indian band was organized. In the 1980s, the Mayo Indians renamed themselves the Nacho Nyak Dun, and the band returned to its traditional forms of government. With the resolution of the Yukon land claims process, the Nacho Nyak Dun were able to pursue self-government.

The final agreement follows the template set by the Umbrella Final Agreement and affirms the rights and benefits of the Nacho Nyak Dun within their own territory. Approximately 1,830 square miles were allocated to the First Nation, with the town of Mayo designated as the administrative center. The agreement also set parameters for a number of issues, including resource use, management of heritage resources, and protection of burial sites. The Yukon and Canadian governments cannot act arbitrarily within Nacho Nyak Dun boundaries. Before any action is taken, the First Nation must be consulted.

Generally, the agreement focuses on cooperation between the Nacho Nyak Dun and the two governments. All parties recognized that some resources, such as water systems and wildlife, could not belong solely to one party. The agreement therefore allowed the establishment of Special Management Areas, such as the McArthur Wildlife Sanctuary and the Peel Watershed, as areas of mutual interest and cooperation. The agreement also addressed the issue of financial compensation, granting the First Nation $14,544,654 in payments over fifteen years.

The Nacho Nyak Dun Final Agreement facilitated the First Nation of Nacho Nyak Dun Self-Government Agreement (also signed May 29, 1993), which, once ratified, transformed the Nacho Nyak Dun from a band under the administration of the Indian Act (1985) to a self-governing First Nation. The population of the First Nation was 434 people in 1997.

Elizabeth Sneyd

See also Royal Proclamation of 1763; Sovereignty; Treaty; Trust Doctrine; Trust Responsibility.

References and Further Reading

Asch, Michael. 1984. *Home and Native Land: Aboriginal Rights and the Canadian Constitution.* Toronto: Methuen.

Cardinal, Harold. 1977. *The Rebirth of Canada's Indians.* Edmonton, AB: Hurtig.

Dickason, Olive Patricia. 1992. *Canada's First Nations: A History of Founding Peoples from Earliest Times.* Norman: University of Oklahoma Press.

"First Nation of Nacho Nyak Dun Final Agreement between the Government of Canada, the First Nation of Nacho Nyak Dun and the Government of the Yukon." May 29, 1993. Ottawa: Indian and Northern Affairs Canada, 1993.

"The First Nation of Nacho Nyak Dun Self-Government Agreement among the First Nation of Nacho Nyak Dun and the Government of Canada and the Government of the Yukon," May 29, 1993. Ottawa: Indian and Northern Affairs Canada, 1993.

"Umbrella Final Agreement Between The Government Of Canada, The Council For Yukon Indians And The Government Of The Yukon," May 29, 1993. Ottawa: Indian and Northern Affairs Canada, 1993.

Vuntut Gwitchin Final Agreement
May 29, 1993

This is one of four final agreements signed on May 29, 1993, as part of the Yukon land claims settlement process. These agreements were made in accordance with the Umbrella Final Agreement (also signed that day), which allowed each Yukon First Nation to pursue treaty settlements with the government of Canada and the government of Yukon Territory. The Vuntut Gwitchin Final Agreement was the first step taken by the Vuntut Gwitchin toward self-government. The agreement was signed between the Vuntut Gwitchin people, the government of Canada, and the government of the Yukon, to take effect in 1995.

The Vuntut Gwitchin, also known as Old Crow, inhabit the northernmost part of Yukon Territory. Their traditional lands overlap with the Tetlit Gwitchin and the Nacho Nyak Dun to the southeast and the Trondek Hwech'in to the south. The main settlement, Old Crow, is located at the Crow and Porcupine rivers. It is accessible only by air or water and is the northernmost community in the Yukon Territory. The traditional means of survival is hunting caribou and muskrat.

Despite the Royal Proclamation of 1763, which directed the negotiation of treaties with aboriginals, there were never any treaties signed between the Vuntut Gwitchin and the governments of Great Britain or Canada. Unlike other First Nations, such as the Nacho Nyak Dun, the isolation of the Vuntut

Gwitchin meant that they were relatively untouched by the influx of European Canadians during the gold rush and afterward, with the exception of a smallpox epidemic in 1911. Like other Yukon First Nations, however, the Vuntut Gwitchin were actively involved in the Yukon land claims process from its start in 1973.

The final agreement used the framework laid out in the Umbrella Final Agreement to affirm the rights and benefits of the Vuntut Gwitchin. The agreement allotted approximately 2,990 square miles of territory to the Vuntut Gwitchin. The agreement also granted the First Nation $19,161,859 in payments over fifteen years.

Like other final agreements, the Vuntut Gwitchin Final Agreement addressed a number of important issues, from membership in the First Nation to land use to resource management. The final agreement affirmed that the territorial and Canadian governments had to consult with the First Nation's council prior to any action taken within Vuntut Gwitchin boundaries. There was also, however, an emphasis on cooperation between the different governments, particularly when dealing with nonstatic resources such as wildlife or waterways.

One aspect of the Vuntut Gwitchin Final Agreement sets it apart from the other final agreements: the confirmation of the establishment of Vuntut National Park in the northwest sector of the Vuntut Gwitchin territory. Although identified in the agreement as a Special Management Area along with the Old Crow Flats Area, the proposed park had to be dealt with in a different manner, since national parks are administered by the Canadian government under the National Parks Act. The signatory parties agreed that the park would remain under Canadian control but that any changes to park boundaries would be subject to consultation with the First Nation. Further, a large part of the park's mandate focused on the recognition of the history, culture, and heritage of the Vuntut Gwitchin. As a result of these negotiations, Vuntut National Park was officially created in 1995.

The Vuntut Gwitchin Final Agreement also facilitated the Vuntut Gwitchin Self-Government Agreement (also signed May 29, 1993), which, once ratified, transformed the Vuntut Gwitchin from a band under the administration of the Indian Act (1985) to a self-governing First Nation. The population of the First Nation was 756 in 2004.

Elizabeth Sneyd

See also Constitution Act (Canada), 1867; Constitution Act (Canada), 1982; Indian Act of Canada, 1876; Sovereignty; Treaty; Trust Doctrine; Trust Land.

References and Further Reading

Asch, Michael. 1984. *Home and Native Land: Aboriginal Rights and the Canadian Constitution.* Toronto: Methuen.

Cardinal, Harold. 1977. *The Rebirth of Canada's Indians.* Edmonton, AB: Hurtig.

Dickason, Olive Patricia. 1992. *Canada's First Nations: A History of Founding Peoples from Earliest Times.* Norman: University of Oklahoma Press.

"Umbrella Final Agreement Between The Government Of Canada, The Council For Yukon Indians And The Government Of The Yukon." May 29, 1993. Ottawa: Indian and Northern Affairs Canada, 1993.

"Vuntut Gwitchin First Nation Final Agreement between the Government of Canada, the Vuntut Gwitchin First Nation and the Government of the Yukon." May 29, 1993. Ottawa: Indian and Northern Affairs Canada, 1993.

"Vuntut Gwitchin First Nation Self-Government Agreement among the Vuntut Gwitchin First Nation and the Government of Canada and the Government of the Yukon." May 29, 1993. Ottawa: Indian and Northern Affairs Canada, 1993.

Sahtu Dene and Métis Comprehensive Land Claim Agreement
September 6, 1993

The Sahtu Dene and Métis Comprehensive Land Claim Agreement was signed on September 6, 1993, and represents one of the "modern treaties" negotiated under the Canadian government's Comprehensive Land Claim Policy. It is constitutionally protected under Section 35 of the Constitution Act, 1982 (Agreement, Vol. 1, § 3.1.1).

This agreement concerns five Dene and Métis communities in the Northwest Territories, Canada: Colville Lake, Fort Good Hope, Fort Norman, Deline (Fort Franklin) and Norman Wells (Agreement, Vol. 1, § 2.1.1). The benefits and terms of the agreement affect a settlement area of approximately 108,200 square miles (280,238 square kilometers) (Indian and Northern Affairs Canada). Two categories of lands were created by the agreement: settlement lands and Sahtu municipal lands (Agreement, Vol. 1, § 2.1.1).

The settlement lands constitute approximately 16,000 square miles (41,437 square kilometers) within the settlement area to which the Sahtu Dene and Métis acquired title (Agreement, Vol. 1, § 19.1.2). This includes title to the subsurface resources over a 700-square-mile area (1,813 square kilometers) (Highlights, at p. 1; Agreement, Vol. 1, Ch. 22). Title to the lands is transferred to the Sahtu Dene and Métis collectively, however; the lands are not "reserves" as defined under the Indian Act (R.S.C. 1985, c. I-5; see also Agreement, Vol. 1, § 3.1.8). Hunting and fishing rights as well as exclusive trapping rights for the Sahtu Dene and Métis are preserved over the entire settlement area (and not solely on the lands to which title is held by the Sahtu Dene and Métis (Agreement, Vol. 1, Ch. 13).

The settlement lands are protected so that they may never be lost to the Sahtu Dene and Métis. These lands cannot be sold, mortgaged, or seized under court order (Agreement, Vol.1, § 19.1.7 and § 19.1.8). Unimproved settlement lands are not subject to real property taxes (Agreement, Vol.1, § 11.5). The settlement lands are generally protected from expropriation. However, in the event that any of the lands are ever expropriated, the Canadian government guarantees that it will replace the lands so that the initial size of the settlement lands is never reduced (Agreement, Vol. 1, § 24.1.5).

The Sahtu municipal lands, while also held by the Sahtu Dene and Métis collectively, are afforded a status different from that of the settlement lands (Agreement, Vol. 1, Ch. 23). The municipal lands are like any other privately owned municipal lands and may be sold or mortgaged and cease to be Sahtu lands (Agreement, Vol. 1, § 23.2.1). Sahtu municipal lands that are developed will be subject to real estate taxation (Agreement, Vol. 1, § 23.4.2).

The agreement also provides that the Sahtu Dene and Métis will receive a settlement payment of $75 million over a period of fifteen years (Agreement, Vol. 1, § 8.1.1 and Schedule I to Ch. 8), as well as receiving a portion of the resource royalties received by the Canadian government and stemming from the Mackenzie valley area (Agreement, Vol. 1, Ch. 10). The participation of the Sahtu Dene and Métis in the management, development, and regulation of the settlement area is guaranteed by the terms of the agreement in such fields as renewable resources (Agreement, Vol. 1, Chs. 13–15), environmental impact assessment (Agreement, Vol. 1, Ch. 17), and the regulation of land and water use (Agreement, Vol. 1, Chs. 20 and 25).

Although federal, provincial, and territorial laws continue to apply on Sahtu Dene and Métis lands, the terms of the agreement will be given priority where a conflict of laws arises. Whereas this agreement concerns land, resources, and compensation, the Sahtu Dene and Métis Comprehensive Land Claim Agreement does provide for the future negotiation of a self-government agreement between the Sahtu Dene and Métis and the federal and provincial governments (Agreement, Vol. 1, Ch. 5).

Lysane Cree

See also Canadian Indian Treaty 11–June 27 to August 30, 1921; Constitution Act (Canada), 1867; Constitution Act (Canada), 1982; Modern Treaties/Comprehensive Land Claims Agreements (Canada); August 30, 1921.

References and Further Reading

Asch, Michael. 1984. *Home and Native Land: Aboriginal Rights and the Canadian Constitution*. Toronto: Methuen.

Cardinal, Harold. 1977. *The Rebirth of Canada's Indians*. Edmonton, AB: Hurtig.

Dickason, Olive Patricia. 1992. *Canada's First Nations: A History of Founding Peoples from Earliest Times*. Norman: University of Oklahoma Press.

Morse, Bradford, ed. 1985. *Aboriginal Peoples and the Law: Indian, Métis and Inuit Rights in Canada*. Ottawa: Carleton University Press.

Nisga'a Final Agreement
April 27, 1999

The Nisga'a Final Agreement (NFA) has three parties: the Nisga'a First Nation, the Province of British Columbia, and the government of Canada. The Nisga'a First Nation and the Province of British Columbia signed the NFA on April 27, 1999, and the government of Canada signed on May 4, 1999. For the terms of the NFA to take effect, it must be ratified by Canada; as of this writing, ratification has yet to take place. The NFA is the culmination of Nisga'a land claims, which began in 1887, when the first request for settlement of claims was made to the provincial government and litigated before the Supreme Court of Canada (*Calder v. Attorney-General of British Columbia* [1973] 1 S.C.R. 313). It is the first "modern treaty" between British Columbia and a First Nation and the first comprehensive land claims settlement in Canada to incorporate the constitutionally protected aboriginal right of self-government. It is full and final settlement of all aboriginal rights and aboriginal title of the Nisga'a Nation.

The NFA contains twenty-two chapters dealing with such matters as lands, forest resources, access to lands, roads and rights-of-way, fisheries, wildlife and migratory birds, environmental assessment and protection, the Nisga'a government and constitution, administration of justice, the Indian Act, capital transfer and negotiation, loan repayment, fiscal relations, taxation, cultural artifacts and heritage, local and regional government relations, and dispute resolution.

The NFA designates and recognizes Nisga'a aboriginal title to 2,000 square kilometers of land in British Columbia, as well as control and ownership of all mineral resources on or under Nisga'a land. The Nisga'a own the land in fee simple, which is the largest form of proprietary right in land without restrictions or conditions. It allows for immediate use and enjoyment of the land and the right to sell or dispose of it according to Nisga'a needs and interests. There are no restrictions on the Nisga'a choosing to sell the land to a third party or to allow development activities, subject to Nisga'a governmental approval (Chapter 3, Articles 3, 4, and 19).

The NFA recognizes Nisga'a right of self-government and provides for establishment of a Nisga'a government, which is to be democratically elected and accountable to Nisga'a citizens, with a constitution (Chapter 11, Articles 1 and 9). The Nisga'a have the right to practice their culture and use their own language (Chapter 2, Article 7), and the Constitution of the Nisga'a Nation (2000) stipulates that the official languages of the Nisga'a government are Nisga'a and English. The government must respect and encourage the use of the Nisga'a language and the practice of Nisga'a culture, including honoring the tradition of ancestors, traditional laws, and the wisdom of elders (Constitution, Chapter 1, Articles 2 and 4). The Canadian Charter of Rights and Freedoms applies to the Nisga'a government in respect of all matters within its authority "bearing in mind the free and democratic nature of the Nisga'a Government" (Constitution, Chapter 1 Article 6[2]). The Constitution is the supreme law of the Nisga'a Nation, subject to the Canadian Constitution and the NFA.

The government has primary law-making authority in the following areas: the administration of government, management of lands and assets, Nisga'a citizenship, and Nisga'a language and culture. The government has contingent law-making authority, whereby any Nisga'a law must conform to federal and provincial standards in order to be valid, in the following areas: education, child and family services, adoption, Nisga'a fisheries and wildlife harvesting, and forestry (NFA, Chapter 11). Individuals who reside on Nisga'a lands but are not Nisga'a citizens are consulted about decisions that directly and significantly affect them (NFA, Chapter 11, Article 19).

The NFA recognizes that the jurisdiction and authority of the Nisga'a government will evolve over time (NFA, Chapter 11, Article 4), including the eventual establishment of a Nisga'a court that may apply "traditional Nisga'a methods and values, such as using Nisga'a elders to assist in adjudicating and sentencing, and emphasizing restitution" (NFA, Chapter 12, Article 41[d]).

There is a three-stage dispute resolution mechanism under NFA. The first stage involves collaborative negotiations between parties. The next stage applies to specific disputes and involves mediation, a technical advisory panel, impartial legal advice, and an elders' advisory panel. The final stage involves settlement of the dispute under binding arbitration or judicial proceedings (NFA, Chapter 19).

Özlem Ülgen

See also Aboriginal Title; *Calder v. Attorney-General of British Columbia* (Canada), 1973; Modern Treaties/Comprehensive Land Claim Agreements (Canada).

References and Further Reading

Calder v. Attorney-General of British Columbia. 1973. 1 S.C.R. 313.

Constitution of the Nisga'a Nation. 2000. (May).

McNeil, K. 1998. "Defining Aboriginal Title in the 90's: Has the Supreme Court Finally Got It Right?" Twelfth Annual Roberts Lecture, March 25, York University, Toronto, ON.

McNeil, K. 2001–2002. "Extinguishment of Aboriginal Title in Canada: Treaties, Legislation and Judicial Discretion," 33 *Ottawa Law Review* 301.

Nisga'a Final Agreement. 1999. (April).

Important Treaty Sites

Camp Stevens (Walla Walla), Washington

Camp Stevens in the Walla Walla valley became the grounds for the Walla Walla Council, where treaties were made by Isaac Stevens, first territorial governor of Washington State, and signed with the tribes who owned lands east of the Cascades.

This place in the Walla Walla valley was chosen by Kamaiakan, chief of the Yakimas, who said, "There is the place where in ancient times we held our councils with neighboring tribes, and we will hold it there now" (Stevens 1900, 27; Josephy 1965, 314). Camp Stevens was on the right bank of Mill Creek, which was a tributary of the Walla Walla River, and six miles north of the Whitman Mission. Colonel Kip Lawrence, who kept a daily account of the Walla Walla Council in his journal, wrote, "It was in one of the most beautiful spots of the Walla Walla Valley, well wooded (in a cotton grove) and with plenty of water. Ten miles distant is seen the range of the Blue Mountains, forming the southeast boundary of the Great Plains along the Columbia, whose waters it divides from those of the Lewis River. It stretches away along the horizon until it is lost in the dim distance where the mountain chain unites with the Snake River Mountains" (Relander et al. 1955, 11).

The council lasted from May 21 to June 11. On May 21, 1855, Governor Isaac Stevens and General Joel Palmer (superintendent for the state of Oregon) arrived on the council grounds (Josephy 1965, 315). In the days that followed, the Nez Perce, Cayuse, Umatilla, Palouse, Walla Walla, and Yakima tribes arrived. A total of five thousand tribe members were in attendance (Relander et al. 1955, 12). Governor Stevens began the council proceedings the day after all the tribes had arrived, only to adjourn shortly thereafter due to rain (Josephy 1965, 318). Stevens eagerly reconvened the council on the following day, May 30, 1855.

From May 1 through June 10, Governor Isaac Stevens and General Palmer explained the terms of the treaties, and the chiefs of each tribe spoke their wishes and concerns. The tribes grew uneasy as they began to understand what the terms of the treaty meant for them. On June 11, Governor Stevens explained the treaty to Looking Glass, the Nez Perce war chief, who had arrived late. There would be three reservations: The Nez Perce would have their own reservation; the Cayuse, Walla Walla, and Umatilla would share a reservation; and the Yakima would also share a reservation with the small Columbia River bands. All the tribes signed the treaties, although some were reluctant.

The Nez Perce had ceded about 11,000,000 acres and were granted a reservation of approximately 7,694,270 acres. The government took much of this acreage during the gold rush; the Nez Perce fought this in court and obtained compensation for their lost lands (Ruby and Brown 1986, 146).

Shortly after the treaty was signed, the Cayuse said that they were unhappy with the reservation because it was too small to be shared with the other tribes. If they were to afford land for farming and grazing their stock, they would need a bigger reservation. This unhappiness was ultimately the cause of the Cayuse War (Ruby and Brown 1986, 210).

The Yakima ceded about 10,000,000 acres and were granted less than 1,250,000 acres. Kamaiakan, head chief of the Yakima, instigated the Yakima War of 1855–1856, in which they were defeated. Their treaty was ratified on March 8, 1859 (Ruby and Brown 1986, 274).

Rene Casebeer

See also Boldt Decision (*United States v. Washington*), 1974; Bureau of Indian Affairs (BIA); Medicine Creek, Washington; Treaty with the Nisqually, Puyallup, Etc.–December 26, 1854.
References and Further Reading
Josephy, Alvin M., Jr. 1965. *The Nez Perce Indians and the Opening of the Northwest*. Boston and New York: Houghton Mifflin.
Ruby, Robert H., and John A. Brown. 1972. *The Cayuse Indians: Imperial Tribesman of Old Oregon*. Norman: University of Oklahoma Press.
Ruby, Robert H., and John A. Brown. 1986. *A Guide to the Indian Tribes of the Pacific Northwest*. Norman: University of Oklahoma Press.
Relander, Click, D. E. LeCrone, Frederick A. Davidson, and Richard Delaney. 1955. *Treaty Centennial 1855–1955 The Yakimas*. Yakima, WA: Republic Press.
Stevens, Hazard. 1900. *The Life of Isaac Ingalls Stevens by His Son Hazard Stevens. Vol II*. Cambridge, MA: Houghton Mifflin/Riverside Press.

Canyon de Chelly, Arizona

Tucked away in the northeast corner of Arizona, Canyon de Chelly serves literally and figuratively as the heart of *Diné Bikéyah*—Navajo country. This twenty-seven-mile-long canyon and its tributaries (the largest is Canyon del Muerto) are formed by meandering streams that originate in the Chuska Mountains and cut their way westward through the Defiance Plateau, ultimately emptying into Chinle Wash. At points along the route, vertical red walls of sandstone painted with deposits of manganese and iron oxide tower a thousand feet over the canyon floor. Within this sanctuary, the ancestors of the Pueblo, Hopi, and possibly Navajo Indians built multistoried villages on ledges and in alcoves above steep talus slopes. There they remained until the thirteenth century, when, for reasons not entirely clear, the canyon was almost completely abandoned.

Although occupied intermittently by migrating Indians of various tribes, Canyon de Chelly remained virtually uninhabited for the next four hundred years. By the eighteenth century, however, continued tensions with neighboring Comanche and Ute tribes, as well as with Spanish settlements along the Rio Grande, prompted Navajo expansion westward. Canyon de Chelly promised safety within its steep and winding walls and fertile bottomlands for the cultivation of crops.

By the late eighteenth century, Spanish land grants in Diné Bikéyah brought migrating Hispanic settlers into the area and triggered the renewal of conflict between the two peoples. Navajo raids against the unwanted newcomers and Spanish reprisals escalated until the Spanish determined to establish their authority over the region once and for all. In late 1804, more than three hundred troops commanded by Lieutenant Antonia Narbona left Sonora and headed north with instructions to eliminate Navajo resistance. Bitterly cold weather hindered the operation, but by January 1805, Narbona's men (augmented by Opata Indians and the New Mexico militia) were poised to enter Canyon de Chelly. The confrontation between the two turned especially tragic as Narbona's men discovered a group of Navajo women, children, and elders hiding in a cave six hundred feet above the floor of Canyon del Muerto. Unable to scale quickly the talus slope and bare rock below the alcove, the soldiers instead fired their weapons into the cave; their ricocheting bullets killed more than a hundred of the refugees.

The assault on "Massacre Cave" lasted for two days, until Narbona's men penetrated the hideout and captured thirty-three Navajo survivors.

Narbona's expedition failed to bring an end to hostilities in Diné Bikéyah. As Spanish troops left the outer reaches of New Mexico to confront the growing Mexican independence movement further south, Navajo raiding parties resumed their activities against Hispanic migrants and their livestock with little fear of Spanish military reprisal. Counter-raids by local Mexican militia and their Ute and Apache allies only exacerbated the situation. Little changed for the next forty years, until the United States moved to claim the Southwest.

At the outset of the war with Mexico in 1846, U.S. troops under the command of Colonel Stephen Watts Kearny occupied Santa Fe, New Mexico, on their way to California. In October that year, Kearny sent Colonel Alexander William Doniphan into Diné Bikéyah to inform the Navajo that they now fell under the authority of the United States and must release all captives and restore stolen property. Doniphan met with mixed success but nevertheless concluded the first of seven peace treaties negotiated between the Navajo and the United States between 1846 and 1868.

For many Navajo, however, Doniphan's treaty had no validity. In an effort to bring broader compliance to U.S. demands, the army launched military expeditions into Diné Bikéyah, specifically targeting the stronghold of Canyon de Chelly. In September 1847, a battalion under the command of Major Robert Walker invaded the upper reaches of the canyon but encountered few people with whom to treat. Two years later, Colonel John Macrae Washington made a similar foray—this time with some success. The Washington expedition resulted in a treaty, signed on September 9, 1849, and ratified by the Senate a year later, that gave the government the power to establish military posts, agencies, and trading posts in Navajo country. However, the unfortunate death of seven Navajo men, including a respected elder, at the hands of Washington's men led to continued resistance to the designs of the United States.

Located in the northeast corner of Arizona, Canyon de Chelly is the literal and figurative center of the Navajo culture. (Corel)

Between 1850 and 1860, animosity between the Diné and the United States intensified. The U.S. Senate, unwilling to pay Indians or to set aside land for their use, was loath to ratify further treaties with the Navajo. In 1860, an attack by a thousand Navajo warriors against U.S. troops at Fort Defiance in the southern part of Diné Bikéyah nearly succeeded. Accordingly, the commander of the Department of New Mexico, Colonel Edward Richard Sprigg Canby, became increasingly convinced that the best way to handle the problem was to move the Navajos out of their homeland and onto a reservation. Canby's threatened removal policy resulted in the treaty of 1861, which was signed by forty-nine Navajo leaders, including Manuelito and Barboncito, who had led the attack on Fort Defiance the previous year. Like many of its predecessors, the treaty never passed the Senate.

As the American Civil War engulfed the country, Canby's focus necessarily shifted away from Indian problems and toward the Confederate presence in New Mexico. Following his victory over Confederate forces at Glorieta Pass, Canby was promoted to brigadier general and transferred to Washington, D.C. Command of the Department of New Mexico fell to Brigadier General James Henry Carleton. With the Confederate threat to New Mexico relieved, Carleton returned to the execution of the removal policy articulated by his predecessor. Carleton sought to remove the Navajo (as well as the Mescalero Apache) from Diné Bikéyah and isolated the Indians at Bosque Redondo along the Pecos River.

Realizing that the Navajo would not leave of their own accord, Carlton sent soldiers under the command of Christopher Houston "Kit" Carson into Diné Bikéyah to force its inhabitants to depart. Carson recognized that control of Canyon de Chelly was the key to the operation. A brief but devastating campaign in the snow-blanketed canyon in January 1864 proved successful; thousands of Navajos were forced out of their homes, rounded up, and sent first to Fort Wingate, near present-day Gallup, New Mexico, and then on the "Long Walk" to Fort Sumner at the Bosque Redondo. There, after several years of virtual incarceration, the Navajo signed a treaty on June 1, 1868, allowing them to return to a portion of Diné Bikéyah—3,328,302 acres, including most of Canyon de Chelly. Although it would take years and numerous executive-order additions to expand the Diné land base, Canyon de Chelly, the heart of Diné Bikéyah, was back in Navajo hands to stay.

Alan C. Downs

See also Long Walk; Treaty with the Navajo–June 1, 1868.

References and Further Reading

Grant, Campbell. 1978. *Canyon de Chelly: Its People and Rock Art.* Tucson: University of Arizona Press.

Iverson, Peter. 2002. *Diné: A History of the Navajos.* Albuquerque: University of New Mexico Press.

Simonelli, Jeanne M. 1997. *Crossing between Worlds: The Navajos of Canyon de Chelly.* Santa Fe, NM: SAR Press, School of American Research.

Chicago, Illinois

During the historic period, the wet prairie that stretched beyond the banks of the Chicago River was home to a succession of Algonquian-speaking Indians. At the time of the first French explorers, members of the Illinois Confederacy inhabited the area. Later, the Miami, Sac, Ottawa, Ojibwe, and Potawatomi had villages near the place where the Chicago River entered Lake Michigan.

The treaty history of Chicago began at Greenville in 1795. As part of a careful selection of strategic sites in the Old Northwest, General Anthony Wayne forced the cession of "one piece of land six miles square at the mouth of the Chikago river" (Kappler 1904, 40). On this land, the United States established Fort Dearborn in 1803. In 1812, the Potawatomi, who were the dominant Indian group in the Chicago area, took advantage of the outbreak of war between the United States and Great Britain to attack and massacre the soldiers at Fort Dearborn. Not until 1816 was the U.S. Army able to reestablish its foothold in Chicago. That same year, in St. Louis, the government negotiated a land cession by the Ottawa, the Ojibwe, and the Potawatomi, who lived along the southwestern margins of Lake Michigan. In return for twelve years of annuity payments, the bands surrendered their claim to a vital wedge of land ten miles on either side of the Chicago River. The cession included much of the same territory ceded at Greenville and almost all the land that would become the city of Chicago and many of its suburbs.

Two treaty councils were held in Chicago, in 1821 and in 1833. In 1821, the agents of the United States turned their attention to the Potawatomi and Ottawa who lived along the eastern shore of Lake Michigan. The treaty council was held in Chicago, even though all the lands being ceded were in Michigan. Lewis Cass, governor of the Michigan Territory, obtained the rich croplands between the St. Joseph and Grand rivers from the Potawatomi in return for annuities ($5,000 for twenty years), blacksmith services, and educational assistance (Kappler 1904, 200). In 1829, when Potawatomi lands in northern Illinois were under pressure from the United States, the negotiation was held not in Chicago but in distant Prairie du Chien in the Wisconsin Territory. A very large section of northwestern Illinois was ceded at this council in return for an annuity of $16,000 and fifty barrels of salt, both to be paid "annually, forever" in Chicago (Kappler 1904, 298). At Tippecanoe, Indiana, in 1832, lands that today include Chicago's far southern suburbs, as well as a large tract of land along the Indiana-Illinois border, were ceded for a mere $15,000 annuity to be paid for twenty years (Kappler 1904, 354).

The 1833 treaty negotiation came on the heels of the Black Hawk War, and although the Potawatomi in Illinois had either remained neutral or rendered positive assistance to the United States during the conflict, sentiment was strong within the state to have all Indians removed west of the Mississippi River. In September 1833, more than six thousand Potawatomi came to Chicago. They were resigned to ceding their last large tract in the Old Northwest, a strip of land along Lake Michigan between Milwaukee and Chicago. A horde of whiskey dealers and horse thieves, "rogues of every description," descended upon them (Edmunds 1978, 248). More than $20,000 in goods intended for the Potawatomi was stolen by the "rogues" as well as by the good citizens of Chicago (Edmunds 1978, 249). The lead negotiators for the Potawatomi were Billy Caldwell, an Anglo-Irish Mohawk, and Alexander Robinson, a Scot-Ottawa, both of whom were recognized as Potawatomi chiefs. The seedy negotiations came to an end with the Potawatomi ceding their land lands in Illinois and Wisconsin in return for five million acres of new lands along the Missouri River. Large sums were also set aside to fund educational and technical services to the Potawatomi. Caldwell and Robinson were paid off handsomely with large grants of land and personal annuities. The Senate nearly choked on the hefty $175,000 settlement awarded to traders for unpaid debts and the $100,000 to "sundry individuals, in behalf of whom reservations were asked" (Kappler 1904, 402). The most important result of the treaty was the removal of the Potawatomi from Illinois, which began in September 1835.

A supplementary article to the 1833 Chicago treaty ended the remaining Potawatomi reservations in the Michigan Territory. The article made special provision for the Catholic Potawatomi, who eventually were allowed to remain in Cass County, Michigan, on the private reservation of their chief, Leopold Pokagon. Perhaps as many as a third of the Potawatomi rejected the U.S. removal policy and immigrated to Upper Canada, where they settled, among other places, on Manitoulin and Walpole Islands (Clifton 1977, 300–306).

Theodore J. Karamanski

See also Cass, Lewis; Greenville, Ohio; Pokagun; Treaty with the Chippewa, Etc.–September 26, 1833; Treaty with the Ottawa, Etc.–August 29, 1821; Treaty with the Wyandot, Etc.–August 3, 1795; Wayne, Anthony.

References and Further Reading
Clifton, James A. 1977. *The Prairie People: Continuity and Change in Potawatomi Indian Culture 1665–1965.* Lawrence: Regents Press of Kansas.
Edmunds, R. David. 1978. *The Potawatomis: Keepers of the Fire.* Norman: University of Oklahoma Press.
Kappler, Charles J., ed. 1904. *Indian Treaties, 1778–1883.* Washington, DC: Government Printing Office.

Council Grove, Kansas

Council Grove, Kansas, is one of the state's oldest historic communities, having played a part in an important chapter in American Indian treaty history. The community is located in Morris County in east central Kansas, on the Neosho River (*Neosho* is an Indian word meaning "wet bottoms"). Because of its location on the Santa Fe Trail, Council Grove became an important gathering place for tribes and traders. It was the intention of the U.S. government to foster a safe route along the trail vis-à-vis treaty with Native Americans in the area. The first of these treaties was concluded on August 10, 1825, with the Big and Little Bands of Osage Indians, so that the U.S. government could obtain the right-of-way for a public highway, thus establishing the Santa Fe Trail.

The treaty was signed under an oak tree in a large grove of timber on the eastern side of the Neosho River. George C. Sibley, one of three commissioners sent by President John Quincy Adams, named the area Council Grove for the convocation of treaty signers. The other two commissioners were Benjamin Reeves and Thomas Mathers. For the right-of-way through their territory, the Osage were paid $800. The commission headed west and six days later met with the Kaw or Kanza Indians to negotiate a treaty.

The treaty was signed on August 16, 1825, although not in Council Grove but in McPherson County, Kansas. The treaty was an exact duplicate of the treaty with the Osage. In this treaty, the Kaw Indians gave up their tribal lands of some twenty million acres in northeast Kansas and relocated to a twenty-square-mile reservation near present-day Topeka, Kansas. For the cession of this vast land base, the Kaw were awarded an annuity of $3,500 for twenty years; a quantity of cattle, hogs, and domestic fowl; a blacksmith; and an agricultural instructor. Another treaty with the Kaw in 1846 relocated the tribal members to a twenty-square-mile reservation and encompassed what is now present-day Council Grove. Provisions of this treaty included the sale of their two-million-acre reservation for ten cents an acre; in return, the tribe received an annuity of $8,000 for thirty years; $2,000 for agriculture and education; a gristmill; and 256,000 acres. Manifest Destiny and the desire to open up more lands for expansion led to yet another treaty with the Kaw. A treaty signed in 1859 pushed the reservation slightly south of Council Grove from Kaw lands and gave the tribe only 80,000 of the poorest acres in the area, to be divided into forty-acre plots for each family. The remaining 176,000 of the 256,000 acres were held in trust by the U.S. government, to be sold to the highest bidder. Finally, on May 27, 1872, the starving Kaw (for whom the state of Kansas is named) were relocated to Oklahoma. The Kaw were relocated and their lands diminished so often in such a short time that Kaw Chief Al-le-ga-wa-ho pleaded to Secretary of the Interior Colombus Delano, "Great Father, you Whites treat us Kan-zey like a flock of turkeys, you chase us to one stream, then you chase us to another stream, soon you will chase us over the mountains and into the ocean" ("Collision" 2003, para. 20).

By the Neosho River, a stump portion of the Council Oak still remains, protected by a shelter. Before it was blown over by a storm in 1958, the tree was seventy feet tall, and its trunk was sixteen feet around. In the area are fifteen more state and federal historic properties, including the Council Grove Historic District and the Kaw Methodist Mission.

Kurt T. Mantonya

See also Treaty with the Great and Little Osage–August 10, 1825; Treaty with the Kansa–August 16, 1825; Treaty with the Kansa Tribe–January 14, 1846; Treaty with the Kansa Tribe–October 5, 1859.

References and Further Reading

Brigham, Lalla Maloy. 1921. *The Story of Council Grove on the Santa Fe Trail.* Topeka: Kansas State Historical Society.

"Collision–Lethal Contact." 2003. Kaw Mission State Historic Site. Retrieved June 5, 2007, from http://ww.kshs.org/places/kawmision/lethalkanzareservations.htm.

Rollings, Willard H. 1995. *The Osage: An Ethnohistorical Study of Hegemony on the Prairie-Plains.* Columbia: University of Missouri Press.

U.S. Department of War. 1825. *Indian Treaties, and Laws and Regulations Relating to Indian Affairs: To Which is Added an Appendix Containing the Proceedings of the Old Congress, and Other Important State Papers, in Relation to Indian Affairs.* Washington City: Way and Gideon.

Dalles, The, Oregon

The Dalles, a place name, refers to two geographic features: a narrow channel of the middle Columbia River near the Cascade Mountain divide, and the adjacent land on the south bank in Oregon. The Dalles was part of a series of rapids and falls where the elevation of the Columbia drops toward the Pacific, creating ideal conditions for netting migrating fish. Dividing the western forests from the eastern high desert, this was a spiritual, fishing, and trading center for thousands of years. Several Upper Chinookan and River Sahaptian peoples lived in the area, and others visited seasonally. In 1811, fur trader Alexander Ross described it as "the great emporium or mart of the Columbia." Trade goods arrived from British Columbia, the Pacific Coast, California, and the Great Plains. In the 1830s, The Dalles was a Christian mission, a colonial settlement, and an army fort. It became a regional treaty site in 1855. Native peoples from Yakama, Warm Springs, Umatilla, and Nez Perce continued to use the area after white settlement. Some people avoided removal to the reservations and formed a multiethnic identity as Columbia River Indians, or the River People. Hydroelectric dams flooded many of the fisheries and sacred places, including The Dalles and neighboring Celilo Falls. Legal battles erupted over salmon procurement. However, the Columbia River Indians who live on the river and on the reservations

Treaties opened up the Pacific Northwest to settlement and The Dalles was at the end of the Oregon Trail, bringing settlers to the region. (Library of Congress)

continue to assert their aboriginal rights to the site and its resources.

The relationship between The Dalles and the Columbia River Indians is ancient. Material evidence of Native occupation of the area dates back over eleven thousand years, and oral traditions describe geological events from the distant past. Culturally, the people of The Dalles region, or Wascopam, included Upper Chinookan peoples, with relatives downriver to the Pacific Ocean, and Sahaptians, with relatives upriver to Priest's Rapids and on the Columbia Plateau. Nez Perce and Cayuse from the plateau were often present at The Dalles for extended periods. Robert Boyd hypothesizes that these winter, multiethnic cohabitations grew with European contact as horses increased and plateau Indians accessed the Great Plains after the 1730s. They then brought Great Plains products to trade. Through the mid-nineteenth century, disease killed many people around The Dalles without decreasing resources, allowing diverse Indians to make homes in the area.

At The Dalles, relations between Native peoples and colonials were rarely violent, although Columbia River Indians consistently pressed the newcomers to accommodate their traditional use of the area. Tense moments occurred during Lewis and Clark's return voyage in 1806, and altercations occasionally occurred from 1812 to 1814 and in 1855. More commonly, however, Native peoples assisted colonials in portaging and navigating the dangerous rapids and incorporated the new people and products into the existing trade network. The Treaty of Middle Oregon of 1855 established the legal identities of the Yakama Nation on the north side of the Columbia (Washington) and the Confederated Tribes of Warm Springs and the Umatilla on the south side (Oregon), with three corresponding reservations. The Nez Perce retained some lands in western Idaho.

Branded "renegades" and "vagabonds" by European Americans, many Indians refused to relocate to the new reservations and continued to live near The Dalles, Celilo Falls, and neighboring fishing sites. In the late 1800s, they earned legal rights to the lands that they had refused to abandon. The River People, notably David Sohappy, have been at the heart of Native efforts to retain fishing rights on the middle Columbia River since the 1960s. Although the namesake geological formation is now drowned by

The Dalles Dam, River Indians continue to occupy "in-lieu" fishing sites that the federal government established, small off-reservation communities such as Celilo Village, and the reservations.

Gray H. Whaley

See also Clark, William; Lewis, Meriwether; Sacred Sites; Sohappy, David, Sr.; *Sohappy v. Smith* and *United States v. Oregon* (1969); Treaty with the Tribes of Middle Oregon–June 25, 1855; Trust Land.

References and Further Readings

Boyd, Robert. 1996. *People of The Dalles, the Indians of Wascopam Mission: A Historical Ethnography Based on the Papers of the Methodist Missionaries.* Lincoln: University of Nebraska Press.

Andrew H. Fisher. 2001. "'They Mean To Be Indian Always': The Origins of Columbia River Indian Identity, 1860–1885." *Western Historical Quarterly* 32:4, 468–492.

Ross, Alexander. 1986. *Adventures of the First Settlers on the Oregon or Columbia River, 1810–1813.* Lincoln: University of Nebraska Press.

Dancing Rabbit Creek, Mississippi

Dancing Rabbit Creek in Mississippi was the site of an important council ground. At this site, the Treaty of Dancing Rabbit Creek was signed on September 27, 1830. This agreement involved the United States and a faction of the Choctaw Nation in Mississippi. It is commonly referred to as the Choctaw removal treaty.

After the signing of this treaty, the Choctaw people were forced to move from their ancient homelands in Mississippi to the unexplored area of the American West called the Great American Desert. Most of this area became the state of Oklahoma in 1906. The council ground at Dancing Rabbit Creek lies between two branches of Dancing Rabbit Creek within Noxubee County in what is now the state of Mississippi. A granite monument was placed there in 1928 by the Bernard Romans Chapter of the Daughters of the American Revolution of Columbus, Mississippi.

The Mississippi band of Choctaw Indians resides on a reservation of thirty thousand acres near this site.

Donna L. Akers

See also Indian Removal Act, 1830; Indian Territory; LeFlore, Greenwood; Treaty with the Choctaw–September 27, 1830.

References and Further Reading

Baird, W. David. 1973. *The Choctaw People*. Phoenix, AZ: Indian Tribal Series.

Cushman, H. B. 1999. *History of the Choctaw, Chickasaw, and Natchez Indians.* Norman: University of Oklahoma Press.

Debo, Angie. 1967. *The Rise and Fall of the Choctaw Republic.* Norman: University of Oklahoma Press.

Kidwell, Clara Sue. 1995. *Choctaws and Missionaries in Mississippi, 1818–1918.* Norman: University of Oklahoma Press.

McKee, Jesse O., and Jon A. Schlenker. 1980. *The Choctaws: Cultural Evolution of a Native American Tribe.* Jackson: University Press of Mississippi.

Doak's Stand, Mississippi

Doak's Stand is a tavern and trading post named for its builder, merchant William Doak, an 1810 emigrant to the Choctaw Nation. Doak's tavern was on the Natchez Trace near modern Jackson, Mississippi. On October 18, 1820, Doak's Stand was the site of a treaty of "friendship" and "limits and accommodation" between the United States and the Choctaw Nation. It was the fifth major Choctaw cession treaty; the first was the Treaty of Fort Adams in 1801. Leading the negotiations for the United States at Doak's Stand was Andrew Jackson of Tennessee, considered by many to be the architect of Indian removal. Thomas Jefferson, early in the nineteenth century, was the first to articulate Indian removal. In 1817, President James Monroe declared that U.S. security depended on rapid settlement of the Southwest and that, accordingly, it was in the best interests of Indians to relocate west of new U.S. settlement. In 1825, Monroe set before Congress the first actual proposal to resettle all eastern tribes on tracts in the West, on which the federal government would prohibit white citizens from living. Jackson had become a forceful proponent of removal by the time of his election to the presidency in 1828. The success of the Doak's Stand treaty set an important precedent for this shift in federal Indian policy, which was fully realized in the 1830s.

Negotiations began at Doak's Stand in 1819. The Choctaw were asked to exchange a "small part" of their national territory for "a country beyond the Mississippi River" in order to relocate all those Choctaw who "live by hunting and will not work." This "small part" of the Choctaw Nation actually amounted to nearly five and a half million acres, comprising a significant portion of central and western Mississippi.

Initially, the Choctaw would not concede to the proposed terms of the treaty. Tribal leaders consulted with Christian missionaries in their nation. Cyrus Kingsbury, a prominent Presbyterian missionary, gave the Choctaw his personal approval of the U.S. plan. Under the direction of Pushmataha, the Choctaws signed the Treaty of Doak's Stand in October 1820, ceding about a third of all Choctaw territory. The treaty gave the United States western Mississippi in exchange for lands west of the Mississippi River, from the Cherokee boundary on the Arkansas River, up the same to its fork with the Canadian River in Oklahoma, then south to the Red River and down the same back up to the Arkansas. In all, this area comprised more than thirteen million acres, or most of western Arkansas and southeastern Oklahoma. Further, the United States agreed to provision each adult male Choctaw emigrant with a blanket, a kettle, a rifle, bullet molds, and enough ammunition for hunting and defense for one year; and each warrior's family received enough corn to support them for one year.

The United States had purchased the cession land first from France in the Louisiana Purchase of 1803 and then from the Quapaw tribe in 1818. Yet there were already several thousand U.S. settlers in the Arkansas Territory who objected to having to vacate and abandon their improvements to the Choctaw. To correct this problem, U.S. commissioners met with Choctaw leaders at the Treaty of Washington City, January 20, 1825. In this, the United States asked the Choctaw to cede back the eastern portion of the land given in the Treaty of Doak's Stand. The Choctaw, in need of money and provisions, were easily persuaded to sign the new treaty. The Treaty of Washington fixed the eastern limit of the Choctaw cession at a line running due south from Fort Smith to Red River, thus forming what became and remains the present Arkansas-Oklahoma boundary.

Doak's Stand was the first large-scale effort at removal. The treaty opened former Choctaw lands to settlement by U.S. citizens. Choctaw who remained in their former country could merge into a new "Mississippi" society by claiming private tracts of land, receiving "American" education, and adopting "civilized" habits. Between 1820 and 1830, nearly thirty thousand settlers moved into the lands opened up by the cession. The remaining Choctaws quickly found themselves surrounded and well outnumbered. By then, the Choctaw were ready to accept further cessions, and the bulk of the nation finally agreed to remove across the Mississippi. A century after Doak's Stand, in Mississippi barely a thousand Choctaw remained, a largely landless and marginalized enclave. At the same time, thousands of other Choctaw struggled to maintain their culture in the relatively new state of Oklahoma. The burgeoning power of the United States and the dwindling influence of the Choctaw readily compromised the terms of the Doak's Stand treaty.

C. S. Everett

See also Indian Removal; Jackson, Andrew; Pushmataha; Treaty with the Choctaw–October 18, 1820; Treaty with the Choctaw–January 20, 1825.

References and Further Reading
De Rosier, Arthur H., Jr. 1970. *The Removal of the Choctaw Indians.* Knoxville: University of Tennessee Press.
Kappler, Charles J., ed. 1904. *Indian Affairs: Laws and Treaties,* vol. 2, *Treaties.* Washington: Government Printing Office.
Reeves, Carolyn Keller, ed. 1985. *The Choctaw Before Removal.* Jackson: University Press of Mississippi.

Doaksville, Oklahoma

One of the largest and most important towns in the Choctaw Nation and in Indian Territory during the 1800s, Doaksville flourished between the 1830s until shortly after the Civil War. Located just north of the Red River in southeast Indian Territory, Doaksville was an economic, social, educational, and political center.

Doaksville's beginnings preceded Choctaw removal. Originally a trading outpost established by Josiah and William Doak in 1821, the settlement began growing after nearby Fort Towson's establishment in 1824 to protect settlers from Plains and Texas tribes and to place federal power on the international boundary with Mexico. During the 1830s, Doaksville became a main destination for removed Choctaw and Chickasaw. For the Chickasaw, Doaksville became a refugee camp between 1837 and 1842 until their lands further west could be made safe from marauding Kiowa and Comanche and cleared of intruders; there, they also suffered disease and malnutrition. For the Choctaw, Doaksville became a major center of activity and the largest town in Indian Territory. Its economy grew during the 1830s and 1840s as a trading and agricultural hub. Traders to the Plains tribes often supplied themselves at Doaksville, returning with tallow, hides, and pelts for export; Indian farmers and Indian plantation owners also relied on Doaksville for its cotton gins and gristmills. Imports and exports via the Red River connected the region to the South.

Other facets of Choctaw and Chickasaw life were centered at Doaksville. It became a significant annuity distribution spot; on annuity days the community was a flurry of social, political, and economic activity. Indian education was also at Doaksville. The Choctaw-run Spencer Academy, founded in 1844, made Doaksville the first town in the region to have a boarding school. However, education and missionary activities were more often connected at places like Armstrong Academy, established by the American Indian Mission Association and later directed by the Cumberland Presbyterian Board of Foreign and Domestic Missions as a missionary day school; the campus served later as the Choctaw capital and as a home for orphan boys. Doaksville was also the first town in the Choctaw Nation with a newspaper; established in 1848, the *Choctaw Telegraph* was a bilingual paper printed in Choctaw and English.

Doaksville's greatest legacy was as a political center in intertribal as well as intratribal matters. Two important treaties were signed there. In 1837, the Choctaw and Chickasaw leaders met at Doaksville and forged agreements with each other and the United States for the Chickasaw to acquire land in the Choctaw territory. This Treaty of Doaksville (arranged before Chickasaw removal) allowed the Chickasaw, for the consideration of $530,000, to settle in the central and western portions of the Choctaw lands, to form the Chickasaw District of the Choctaw Nation, and to hold equal rights throughout the Choctaw Nation. A later treaty between the two tribes was signed at Doaksville in 1854, settling any boundary disputes from the treaty of 1837.

Doaksville served as the Choctaw national capital from 1850 until 1863, a time of tumultuous intratribal politics. Disaffected traditionalists gathered at Doaksville in 1858, created a new constitution, and elected rival officials. Friction and the threat of civil war within the tribe often occurred near Doaksville. Eventually, a compromise was struck at the Choctaw Convention of 1860 at Doaksville, where the Doaksville Constitution was crafted and under which the nation operated thereafter.

Doaksville is also where the Civil War began and ended for the Choctaw Nation. In 1861, tribal pro-secessionists gathered at Doaksville and moved the Choctaw from neutrality to Confederate support. The Choctaw National Council declared Choctaw independence, appointed a committee to enter a treaty of alliance with the Confederacy and to negotiate that agreement with Confederate agent Albert Pike, and authorized the creation of Choctaw military forces to hold Indian Territory. Like much of Indian Territory, the Doaksville region suffered devastation from the war. At the war's end, Doaksville again emerged as important for the Choctaw and for Indian Territory. On June 9, 1865, the Civil War officially ended for the Choctaw when Chief Peter Pitchlynn surrendered his Indian troops to federal officials there. The Civil War in Indian Territory actually ended in Doaksville two weeks later, when Brigadier General Stand Watie (Cherokee) came into town and laid down his arms; he was the last Confederate general to do so.

The Civil War ushered in Doaksville's downturn. In 1863, the Choctaw capital was moved to Chahta Tamaha, and thereafter Doaksville began to decline rapidly. After the turn of the century, new railroad lines and new towns supplanted Doaksville's once-great prominence. Today, little remains of this ghost town to reflect its former importance.

S. Matthew DeSpain

See also Indian Territory; Pitchlynn, Peter; Treaty with the Choctaw and Chickasaw–January 17, 1837; Treaty with the Choctaw and Chickasaw–November 4, 1854; Watie, Stand.

References and Further Reading

Baird, W. David. 1973. *The Choctaw People*. Phoenix, AZ: Indian Tribal Series.

Debo, Angie. 1967. *The Rise and Fall of the Choctaw Republic*. Norman: University of Oklahoma Press.

De Rosier, Arthur H., Jr. 1970. *The Removal of the Choctaw Indians*. Knoxville: University of Tennessee Press.

Kidwell, Clara Sue. 1995. *Choctaws and Missionaries in Mississippi, 1818–1918*. Norman: University of Oklahoma Press.

McKee, Jesse O., and Jon A. Schlenker. 1980. *The Choctaws: Cultural Evolution of a Native American Tribe*. Jackson: University Press of Mississippi.

Fort Gibson, Oklahoma

Fort Gibson is located at the confluence of the Verdigris, Arkansas, and Neosho rivers in the easternmost area of the Cherokee Nation. Colonel Matthew Arbuckle and the Seventh Infantry began construction on the fort in 1824. It replaced Fort Smith, Arkansas, as the westernmost outpost in the territory obtained by the Louisiana Purchase. Arbuckle named the fort after Commissary General George Gibson.

In the 1820s and 1830s, the fort served as the major link between the U.S. government and the Plains Indians and as one of a series of forts charged with maintaining order on the frontier. During the 1820s and 1830s, the fort became the staging area for the resettlement of the Choctaw, Chickasaw, Cherokee, Seminole, and Muscogee (Creek) Indians forced from their homes in the southeastern United States. Emigrating Indians stopped by the fort to obtain provisions such as clothing, blankets, food, guns, knives, farming implements, seeds, and other items necessary to establish new homes in Indian Territory.

The major responsibilities of the soldiers stationed at the fort were to maintain peace between the Osage and Cherokee Indians, to provide military protection for survey teams, to remove white settlers from Indian Territory, and to construct roads. Colonel Arbuckle frequently complained that he had too few soldiers under his command to carry out the assigned duties. As a result, the condition of the facility suffered.

Although the fort was the principal fortification in the West, it developed an unhealthy reputation. According to some of the people who helped build the fort, many of the structures rotted before they were finished. During its first eleven years of occupation, 561 privates and nine officers died of disease. In 1845, the fort was relocated onto higher ground a quarter mile from its original site, and the new buildings were constructed of stone. Unfortunately, the new location was no more healthful than the previous setting, and the soldiers still were plagued by disease.

By the 1850s, the people of the Cherokee Nation wanted the fort closed; they argued that they were no longer "uncivilized" and did not need military supervision. Additionally, they charged that the presence of soldiers increased the availability of alcohol to their citizens, and they wanted the brothels surrounding the fort closed. The Cherokees were eager to assume control of the boat landing and the rivers. Apparently the Cherokees argued effectively, for the fort reverted to Cherokee ownership in June 1857.

The fort did not stay under Cherokee control for long. In 1861, the American Civil War began, and Confederate forces quickly took control of the fort. It was of strategic importance to the Confederacy and also served as the headquarters for their Indian Department. The fort stayed under Confederate control until 1863, when Union forces under the command of William A. Phillips forced the Confederates from the stronghold. Phillips temporarily changed the name of the fortification to Fort Blunt in honor of General James G. Blunt, the commander of the District of Kansas, and the Cherokee Nation moved its headquarters into the fort. Confederate forces harassed the fort throughout the remainder of the war, but the Union forces managed to retain control.

When the Civil War ended, the fort served as the major center of aid for refugee Indians and freedmen returning home. By 1871, most of the troops were removed from the area, and the post became a commissary supply post. However, military forces returned about a year later. As railroads were built through Indian Territory, squatters, outlaws, whiskey traders, and other undesirable people began to enter the area.

From 1872 until its final closure, the fort's primary responsibility was to prevent white intrusions onto Indian lands. The fort had a reputation as a dangerous outpost infested with criminals, fortune seekers, and other riffraff. When allotments came for the Indians and on military paydays, gamblers and whiskey traders swarmed the area in an effort to separate Indians and soldiers from their money.

In the summer of 1890, all troops were withdrawn from the area. The fort was reoccupied for short periods of time during the 1890s, but the buildings were uninhabitable by 1897, and the troops camped on the parade grounds. In the late 1890s, the fort was permanently closed. Today, Fort Gibson is a historic site managed by the Oklahoma Historical Society.

Joyce Ann Kievit

See also Indian Removal; Indian Territory; Ross, John.
References and Further Reading
Agnew, Brad. 1980. *Fort Gibson, Terminal on the Trail of Tears*. Norman: University of Oklahoma Press.
Bearss, Edwin C., and Arrell M. Gibson. 1969. *Fort Smith: Little Gibraltar on the Arkansas*. Norman: University of Oklahoma Press.
Foreman, Grant. 1936. *Fort Gibson: A Brief History*. Norman: University of Oklahoma Press.

Fort Harmar, Ohio

Fort Harmar was established in 1785 near the confluence of the Muskingum and Ohio rivers in what is now the state of Ohio. The base occupied territory opposite the original site of Marietta, Ohio, and has since been assimilated into the city. The fort was built under orders of General Josiah Harmar, the commander of the U.S. force in the area, and was the site of some important treaty negotiations with Indians of the region.

Congress dispatched Harmar to the region in 1784 with orders to prevent the contacts between white settlers and Indians from escalating into a full-scale border war. As the War of Independence came to an end, settlers began pouring into the western territories in large numbers. All those concerned in the delicate maneuverings of frontier Indian policy, from Secretary of War Henry Knox down, knew that the country could ill afford a war with the Native Americans. It was in partial fulfillment of this mission that Josiah Harmar ordered the fort constructed. Thus, Fort Harmar has the distinction of being the only base created to stop unlawful settlement. In reality, the post ended up encouraging illegal settlement in that the people living on the frontier came to it when they were threatened by Indians.

The actual construction of the post was overseen by Captains John Doughty and Jonathan Heart and performed by the men under their command. Initially, the structure consisted of a small, pentagonal, star-shaped stockade fort. The primary material used in construction was logs. At each of the five corners, instead of the more commonly used blockhouse, were pentagonal bastions that mounted several cannons each. The artillery was sited so as to sweep the land approaches to the fort.

In all, the fort covered about three-fourths of an acre. The walls were 120 feet long and constructed of large timbers laid horizontally, reaching a height of between twelve and fourteen feet. All in all, the fort presented a formidable appearance.

The enlisted men's barracks were within the walls and were divided into thirty-foot rooms and furnished with fireplaces. The fireplaces were among the only stone furnishings in the fort. The officers' quarters were built into the bastions.

Once it was decided to open up the Northwest Territory to settlement, Fort Harmar was selected as the site of the first large-scale legal settlement under the Northwest Ordinance. The mission of the fort became one of slowing settlement until the land in the vicinity could be surveyed and divided up into lots for sale. Likewise, as settlers began to move into the area in greater numbers, more friction with the Indians developed. The fort then became more like a frontier military post, from which detachments were sent out to guard surveyors as they marked the area and to guard various movements of men and supplies through the territory. The tensions with the Indians and violence perpetrated by men on both sides eventually led the governor of the territory, Arthur St. Clair, to call the aggrieved tribes to a treaty council.

Later, the fort served as a meeting site for the negotiations with the Indians in the area that led to the Treaty of Fort Harmar. This treaty, negotiated in late 1788 and agreed to in 1789, reaffirmed the boundary line set by the previous Treaty of Fort McIntosh. Likewise, it guaranteed the Indians in the vicinity the right to hunt on lands in the ceded areas. The negotiator for the United States at Fort Harmar was Arthur St. Clair. Treaties were negotiated with the Iroquois and the Wyandot.

The fort remained a frontier garrison until 1790. At that point, the men were ordered to move on to Fort Washington in Cincinnati. The troops that were removed from the fort were later used in St. Clair's expedition against the northwestern tribes.

James McIntyre

See also Knox, Henry; St. Clair, Arthur; Treaty with the Wyandot, Etc.–January 21, 1785; Treaty with the Wyandot, Etc.–January 9, 1789.
References and Further Reading
Gaff, Alan D. 2004. *Bayonets in the Wilderness: Anthony Wayne's Legion in the Old Northwest*. Norman: University of Oklahoma Press.
Havinghurst, Walter. 1976. *Ohio: A History*. New York: W. W. Norton.
Knepper, George W. 1989. *Ohio and Its People*. Kent, OH: Kent State University Press.

Roberts, Robert B., ed. 1988. *Encyclopedia of Historic Forts: The Military, Pioneer, and Trading Posts of the United States.* New York: Macmillan.

Sword, Wiley. 1985. *President Washington's Indian War: The Struggle for the Old Northwest 1790–1795.* Norman: University of Oklahoma Press.

Fort Harrison, Indiana

In August 1811, Governor William Henry Harrison received permission from the secretary of war to construct at least one fort along the Wabash River in present-day Indiana. He chose a site known by the old French name *Battelle des Illinois,* where at some point in the distant past there had been a battle between the Illinois and the Iroquois. Located at present-day Terre Haute, Indiana, the fort was built by the Indiana militia above the east bank of the Wabash as a depot for supplies as part of Harrison's campaign against the Prophet. Farther up the river and closer to the eventual battle of Tippecanoe, another blockhouse was constructed.

After the battle, the fort continued to be occupied by troops. Captain Zachary Taylor of the Seventh Infantry Regiment took command of the post in 1812. Following the Indian success at Fort Dearborn to the north (in present-day Chicago) and while laying siege to Fort Wayne (in present-day Indiana), the Potawatomi and Kickapoo made a raid on Fort Harrison. Early on the third day of September 1812, Miami and Wea Indians visited the fort and told the commanding officer that followers of the Prophet would be making war and that he and his army should leave at once. Later in the day, two civilians haying beyond the stockade walls were shot and killed. With half his fifty-five-man garrison sick with fever, Taylor had good reason to be concerned. During the night, one of the blockhouses was set afire despite sentinels on duty. Taylor issued orders for all posts to be manned. Throughout the ensuing days, Taylor waited for an opportunity to send someone to Vincennes for help. In the meantime, he and his garrison were pinned down. On September 13, he sent one of his sergeants and a settler. Their journey succeeded. On September 15, a ranger force of nearly a thousand men arrived under the command of Colonel William Russell.

Following the end of the War of 1812, a treaty was concluded at Fort Harrison in 1816 between the United States, represented by Commissioner John L.

Fort Harrison in 1812. (Library of Congress)

McCullough, and the headmen representing the Wea and Kickapoo. The treaty included a pledge of peace and acknowledgement of the Treaty of Greenville in 1795.

Sally Colford Bennett

See also Battle of Tippecanoe, 1811; Harrison, William Henry; Treaty with the Wea and Kickapoo–June 4, 1816.

References and Further Reading

Edmunds, R. David. 1978. *The Potawatomis, Keepers of the Fire.* Norman: University of Oklahoma Press.

Esarey, Logan. 1922. *Messages and Letters of William Henry Harrison,* vol. 1. Indianapolis: Indiana Historical Commission.

Fort Harrison Centennial Association. 1912. *Fort Harrison on the Banks of the Wabash, 1812–1912.* Terre Haute, IN: Fort Harrison Centennial Association.

Kappler, Charles A., ed. 1904. "Treaty with the Wea and Kickapoo, 1816." *Indian Affairs: Laws and Treaties,* vol. 2, *Treaties.* Washington, DC: Government Printing Office.

Fort Laramie, Wyoming

Fort Laramie, located in eastern Wyoming, served first as a major trading post and after 1849 as a U.S. Army post. The post played a significant role in the region by protecting overland travelers and as a major juncture, first for the fur trade and later for the Plains Indian campaigns. In 1851 and in 1868, important treaties were signed at the fort with northern Plains tribes. The fort was abandoned by the military in 1890 and serves today as a National Historic Site.

Aspiring to take advantage of the lucrative fur trade in the region, William Sublette and Robert Campbell, two experienced traders, established Fort Laramie in 1834. The fort is located on the left bank of the Laramie River about a mile above its junction with the North Platte River. At the time of its establishment, Fort Laramie was the first permanent settlement of white men in the heart of the buffalo country. The name of the fort has changed over time. In 1834, it was named Fort William; and in 1841, when the second fort was built, its name was changed to Fort John. All along, Fort Laramie was the most popular name for the place. After the military took over in 1849, this popular name was retained and made official. The name comes from the nearby river, which was named after French trapper Jacques Laramie.

On June 26, 1849, the U.S. Army purchased the post for $4,000 from the American Fur Company, which had acquired it in 1836. The site was ideal for a military post. It was located on the Platte River line of overland march and was widely influential in the fur trade of the region. In addition, the fort was outside the buffalo ranges of the Plains tribes and therefore did not interfere with their major commissary. As overland travel increased rapidly, the army recognized the growing importance of the region. The need to protect travelers from Indians was a major concern for the military. Following the purchase, the army embarked on a major transformation of the post. At first, old buildings were occupied by the military units, but gradually they were torn down; by 1862 they had been replaced completely with new structures.

The army used the fort mainly to aid overland travelers and to control Indian tribes. For travelers, the fort provided supplies, medical care, communication facilities, and other services. The army also improved the trails. Fort Laramie was in many ways an isolated community in the middle of the plains, but for many travelers it functioned as an important landmark of civilization amid wilderness.

A Native American encampment outside Fort Laramie in Wyoming, the scene of the Grattan Massacre on August 19, 1854. The massacre of Lieutenant John L. Grattan and almost all of his detachment occurred when the Sioux refused to turn over a warrior who had stolen and butchered a stray cow. Grattan's men opened fire, but were overpowered and slaughtered by the Sioux. (Hulton Archive/Getty Images)

General William T. Sherman and Sioux leaders sign the Fort Laramie Treaty at Fort Laramie, Wyoming in 1868. (National Archives)

The fort had a significant role in the Indian wars. Many small skirmishes were fought in the vicinity, but Fort Laramie's main function was as a supply station for the soldiers during the northern Plains Indian campaigns. In 1851 and 1868, two major treaties with the northern Plains tribes were signed at the fort. With these treaties, the Indians surrendered most of their claims to the region. The Sioux and Cheyenne campaigns of 1876 and 1877 saw the last major military confrontations with Native Americans in the region.

With the coming of the railroads and increasing settlement, the role of the fort changed. The Union Pacific railway ran seventy miles to the south, and the Chicago Northwestern ran fifty miles to the north; no longer on the main routes of travel, the fort began to decline in importance. In the late 1870s, ranchers and homesteaders moved into the region. At first, the fort served as a supply center and offered protection for many of these settlers; but in 1890, four years after recommendations were made for its abandonment and one year after the decision was reached, the troops marched away from Fort Laramie for the last time. For nearly fifty years, the fort was allowed to decay. In 1937, Wyoming appropriated funds for the purchase of the former military site and its donation to the federal government. In 1938, the Fort Laramie Historic Site became a unit in the National Park System. The fort has been restored to its 1876 appearance.

Janne Lahti

See also: Annuities; Treaty; Treaty of Fort Laramie with Sioux, Etc.– September 17, 1851.

References and Further Reading

Hafen, Le Roy R., and Francis Marion Young. 1984. *Fort Laramie and the Pageant of the West, 1834–1890.* Lincoln: University of Nebraska Press.

Hedren, Paul L. 1998. *Fort Laramie and the Great Sioux War.* Norman: University of Oklahoma Press.

Nadeau, Remi. 1997. *Fort Laramie and the Sioux.* Santa Barbara, CA: Crest.

Fort Pitt, Pennsylvania

The Fort Pitt stronghold played an important role in early American history. Its location at the intersection of three major rivers (the Allegheny, the Monongahela, and the Ohio) was strategically important for anyone wanting to secure the area. During the mid-eighteenth century, England and France jockeyed for position and claims to land in the New World. During the 1750s, the French tried to gain an edge on the English by denying them access to Ohio country. To accomplish this task, the French captured many English settlements in the area now known as western Pennsylvania. One such captured outpost was that founded by the Englishman William Trent in the late 1740s at the intersection of those most important three rivers.

The French captured this key outpost in 1754 and immediately began to construct Fort Duquesne. The escalating tension between the French, the English, and the Native Americans peaked in 1756 at the start of the French and Indian War. In the winter of 1758, the English army, led by General John Forbes, was accompanied by George Washington, John Armstrong, and the Swiss officer Colonel Henry Bouquet. Washington commanded 1,900 troops from Virginia, and John Armstrong commanded 2,700 men from Pennsylvania. The troops marched across the Juniata River and over the Allegheny foothills on a course to Fort Duquesne. Washington, sent forward to the fort with 2,500 men, was quite surprised to find only 500 French troops at Fort Duquesne. The French, seeing Washington's forces, burned the fort and ran for cover. On November 25, 1758, the English secured Fort Duquesne and renamed it Fort Pitt in honor of the English statesman William Pitt.

Once the English controlled the strategic area of Fort Pitt, they began construction on a new and improved fort. Construction on the fort officially began on the arrival of General Stanwix's chief engineer, Captain Harry Gordon. The crew arrived in August, and work began on September 3, 1759. The crew felled trees and dug coal and limestone from the surrounding hills in the area that is now Mount Washington. A sawmill was built upstream from the fort, and lumber was sent downriver to the fort. Due to a lack of necessary lumber resources in the area, General Stanwix ordered the fort to be a dirt one. It has been described as

. . . a great five-sided ditch, with the earth of the ditch thrown up to form a rampart over twenty feet high and sixty feet wide. On the landward side, the ramparts supported by strong brick retaining walls, with the tips of the bastions further reinforced by cut stone. On the less vulnerable river sides, the walls and bastions were sodded. They were covered with squares of turf laid perpendicularly to the slope of the wall, and secured with long wooden pins. On top of the ramparts, a sodded parapet 18 feet thick was erected for protection of artillery and soldiers firing small arms. Behind this parapet ran a level space 20 feet wide, providing a platform for cannon and the necessary room for recoil after firing. . . . A sentry walking his post on the high, windy ramparts of Fort Pitt, looked down on a kind of walled city inside the great pentagon of earth and masonry. Around the central parade could be housed from 700 to 1,000 men. Two storied barracks, one of brick 190 feet long quartered the wooden ones of weatherboard and shingles, were provided with chimneys that served four rooms and furnished cooking facilities. In the brick barracks there was a closet in each room, building with cut-stone steps. All these long, narrow buildings could be seen grouped symmetrically around the parade, parallel to the curtain walls. But hidden away in the immensely thick ramparts were large storehouses, magazines, and casements. Most provision and all the ammunition was stored underground. Underground was also the guardhouse and dungeons, where prisoners awaited trial in the darkness. (O'Meara 1965)

Fort Pitt was not only an important geographic location for the French and Indian War, it was the first place where a treaty was signed between the United States and the Delaware (Lanape) Indians. The treaty with the Delaware was signed on September 17, 1778, and was composed of six articles. The first article stated that "all offences or acts of hostilities by one, or either of the contracting parties against the other, be mutually forgiven, and buried in the depth of oblivion, never more to be had in remembrance." This historic document was signed by Andrew Lewis, Thomas Lewis, White Eyes, the Pipe, and John Kill Buck at Fort Pitt.

Arthur Holst

See also Albany Conferences of 1754 and 1775; Knox, Henry; Treaty with the Delaware–September 17, 1778.

References and Further Reading
O'Meara, Walter. 1965. *Guns at the Forks.* Pittsburgh: University of Pittsburgh Press.
Prucha, Francis Paul. 1994. *American Indian Treaties: The History of a Political Anomaly.* Berkeley: University of California Press.
Steele, Ian K. 1994. *Warpaths: Invasions of North America.* New York and London: Oxford University Press.
Williams, Robert A., Jr. 1990. *The American Indian in Western Legal Thought: The Discourses of Conquest.* New York and Oxford: Oxford University Press.

Fort Sumner, New Mexico

Fort Sumner, New Mexico, on a parcel of land that covered more than twenty-five square miles, was the site of the largest internment of Native Americans in U.S. history. The Bosque Redondo Reservation was created in 1861 as part of a new policy for the relocation of Navajos and Apaches. The captive Indians were relocated to the reservation in a forced march called the Long Walk. The treaty of 1868 recognized the failure of the reservation experiment for Navajo and Apache peoples and ordered the abandonment of the remote camp.

Beginning in the 1840s, the United States concluded a series of treaties with the Navajo, annexing their land and regulating trade. By 1851, a network of garrisons had been built to defend sheep and cattle ranches from Indian raids. Using the Indian Trade and Intercourse Act of June 1834 as the foundation for the roundup, military orders were given to halt the attacks and capture raiders and other Native Americans living in the area.

General James H. Carleton and Colonel Christopher "Kit" Carson were the architects of this reservation plan. The Fort Sumner area was selected in 1863 in the belief that it would create a buffer between Native American raiding groups. Almost nine thousand Navajo and Apache were relocated to the

Fort Sumner, New Mexico, was near the end of the 300-mile "Long Walk" of the Navajos resulting in their exile from their homelands. In 1868 they were allowed to return home. (Library of Congress)

remote reservation, where an attempt would be made to "reeducate" them to adopt "white ways" and to develop a "model" agricultural station. The first group, of more than five thousand, was held under prisonlike conditions; food and supply distribution problems caused death from starvation and disease. Insect infestations, hailstorms, and flooding destroyed crops for three straight years. By 1865, the raiding parties regained control, and Indians violated laws by leaving the reservation in droves.

Though the federal government spent over $1 million annually to maintain the camp, the plan was an utter failure. After a year of political debate involving the Doolittle Committee, the Office of Indian Affairs, and an Indian Peace Commission, the remaining Navajos were allowed to leave Fort Sumner in June 1868.

A subsequent agreement signed at Fort Sumner created a permanent reservation of almost 3.5 million square miles along the present New Mexico-Arizona border. Unfortunately, key economic centers and the richest farm and grazing lands were wrested from Navajo control by the agreement. Indian groups were given unwritten permission to use off-reservation land in the Fort Sumner area provided it was not occupied by whites. Many Navajos took this opportunity to return to their original homesites. The Bosque Redondo experience was so traumatic for the Navajo nation that their history marks its timeline from the time of the incarceration forward.

Pamela Lee Gray

See also Carson, Kit; Doolittle Committee; Long Walk; Treaty with the Navajo–June 1, 1868.
References and Further Reading
Bailey, Garrick Alan, and Roberta Glenn Bailey. 1998. *A History of the Navajo: The Reservation Years.* Santa Fe, NM: School of American Research Press.
Iverson, Peter. 2002. *Diné: A History of the Navajos.* Albuquerque: University of New Mexico Press.
Iverson, Peter. 1981. *The Navajo Nation.* Albuquerque: University of New Mexico Press.
Johnson, Broderick H., ed. 1970. *Navajo Stories of the Long Walk Period.* Tsaile, AZ: Navajo Community College Press.

Greenville, Ohio

Greenville, Ohio, is located along Greenville Creek and Mud Creek in western Ohio, about twenty miles west of the city of Piqua. Greenville lends its name to two treaties: the first Treaty of Greenville in 1795, following the Frontier Wars of the Old Northwest, and the second in 1814, during the War of 1812.

Founded in 1794 by General Anthony Wayne, the original place name of Fort Green Ville, used as a supply depot, was bestowed by Wayne in honor of his late friend General Nathaniel Greene, a Revolutionary War comrade. Following the American victory in 1795, Wayne ordered all tribes to attend a council and agree to the treaty to put an end to the war and settle "controversies." The U.S. government wished to "restore harmony and friendly intercourse."

On August 3, 1795, an agreement was concluded that established a boundary line between the land belonging to the Indians and the land belonging to the United States. The Indians agreed not to make war on the United States or any of the people on the American or eastern side of the boundary. Though most of this land was in the Territory of Ohio and later would become the state of Ohio, some of it extended into what became the territory of Indiana, leaving that area to come into some dispute in the very first decade of the nineteenth century. The Indians were to allow whites to freely travel through their country along a chain of posts established in another article of the treaty.

The Indians agreed to give up or cede land covering some sixteen different areas, including Fort Wayne, Detroit, Michilimackinac, and Chicago. These sites had become or were about to become U.S. military garrisons for the purpose of policing and preventing whites from settling on land nearby. Other exceptions of land included the sites of Fort Knox, near Vincennes on the Wabash River; Fort Massac, on the Ohio; and Clarksville, also on the Ohio. During the years following the Treaty of Greenville, the U.S. Army came to be known as the Peace Establishment Army because it was to maintain peace on the frontier and in Indian country and to prevent the intrusion of whites onto land belonging exclusively to the Indians. By the Indians' agreement, the U.S. government would relinquish land north of the Ohio River and west of the agreed-upon boundary line. This treaty brought about fifteen years of uneasy peace—uneasy due to the administration of President Thomas Jefferson in 1801.

In February 1803, President Jefferson commissioned Indiana Territory's governor, William Henry Harrison, to treat for the U.S. government.

Harrison was given the power to work out land cession treaties with all tribes in the Old Northwest territory, beginning in April 1803 at Fort Wayne. Jefferson revealed his intentions and interests in a secretive letter that spelled out how the United States was to encourage the leaders of tribes to run up debts to the U.S. government and then use the land cessions as a way to pay off such debt. In addition, the plan was to eventually move all Indians to land west of the Mississippi. At the time, Jefferson was working under the threat of Napoleon's possible reestablishment of the French in the Louisiana Territory. The treaties that followed in 1803, 1805, and particularly in 1809, contributed to increasing tension along the Greenville treaty line and beyond.

As the name of Fort Greene Ville gave way to Greenville, white settlers poured into western Ohio lands. Just before 1804, two Shawnee brothers—Tecumseh, a political leader, and Tenskwatawa, the Prophet—decided to establish a village alongside Greenville that is often referred to as the first Prophetstown. As the brothers spread their political and spiritual gospel, Indians as well as whites felt hostilities brewing. As the brothers' influence increased, so did their village; followers flocked to make Greenville their home. Voicing their concerns about the treaties of Harrison's manufacture and seeing the influx of settlers, the brothers felt exposed to their enemies by living so close to the whites. So in 1808, they moved to Indiana Territory, along the Tippecanoe and Wabash rivers, to establish the second Prophetstown.

As the War of 1812 extended into 1814, the government directed Harrison, now a general, and Lewis Cass, governor of Michigan Territory, to treat once again—this time with the tribes that had followed the Shawnee brothers but now were interested in settling in favor of peace. Meeting at Greenville on July 22, 1814, the United States offered peace and asked the tribes to help the United States end the war with Great Britain and the tribes that remained hostile to the United States. In return for the Indians' cooperation and aid, the United States agreed to keep land boundaries as they had been prior to the outbreak of the war. But this treaty was not the end of land boundary protection. With the war ending the following January, this Treaty of Greenville heralded a more pressing and demanding era of land cession treaties.

Sally Colford Bennett

See also Cass, Lewis; Harrison, William Henry; Tecumseh; Tippecanoe River, Indiana; Treaty with the Wyandot, Etc.–August 3, 1795; Treaty with the Wyandot, Etc.–July 22, 1814; Wabash River, Indiana; Wayne, Anthony.

References and Further Reading

Edmunds, R. David. 1983. *The Shawnee Prophet.* Lincoln: University of Nebraska Press.

Esarey, Logan, ed. 1922. *Governors' Messages and Letters. Messages and Letters of William Henry Harrison.* 2 vols. Indiana Historical Collections VII and IX. Indianapolis: Indiana Historical Commission.

Hornbeck, Helen Tanner, ed. 1987. *Atlas of Great Lakes Indian History.* Norman: University of Oklahoma Press.

Sugden, John. 1997. *Tecumseh, a Life.* New York: Henry Holt.

Medicine Creek, Washington

The Medicine Creek treaty was the first of ten treaties made with the Indians of Puget Sound, the Pacific Coast, and the lower Columbia River. This first treaty got its name from the location at which it was signed, the right bank of Medicine Creek. This creek parallels the Nisqually River and then runs west, emptying into Puget Sound (Hazard 1952, 123; White 1972, 60). The actual signing of the treaty happen on a wooded knoll, where the "Treaty Tree" (a Douglas fir, *Pseudotsuga menziesii*), now just a snag, stands in remembrance (Wilkinson 2000, 11). Today, this historic spot can be found by traveling on southbound Interstate 5 north of Olympia and taking Exit 114, half a mile after the Nisqually River Bridge. A marker in the Nisqually National Wildlife Refuge commemorates the signing of the treaty (Hazard 1952, 126).

At this historic site, on December 24–26, 1854, Isaac Stevens, the first territorial governor of Washington State (Hazard 1952, 125), sat in council with six hundred to seven hundred Nisqually, Squaxon, Puyallup, Steilacoom, Muckelshoot, and other bands of the upper Puget Sound Indians (White 1972, 60). It was here that sixty-two chiefs, delegates, and headmen of the tribes of King, Pierce, Thurston, and Mason counties signed the crucial treaty (Hazard 1952, 126; Stevens 1900, 460). In doing so, they relinquished title to 2.5 million acres (Wilkinson 2000, 12), thus reducing their tribal holdings to a mere 4,700 acres (Carpenter 1994, 391).

In exchange, they were granted reservations and the right to graze their horses, hunt, and fish

(Stevens 1900, 459; White 1972, 61; Wilkinson 2000, 12). The Puget Sound tribes were also to be paid $32,000 for their land in allotments over a twenty-year period (White 1972, 62); in addition, $3,250 was to be spent to equip the reservations with schools, medical facilities, and farm equipment. They were also promised carpenters, teachers, a blacksmith, and a physician (Stevens 1900, 459).

Soon after the treaty was signed, the tribes began to realize that the heavily wooded reservations agreed to in the treaty were not compatible with their way of life (Hazard 1952, 126; White 1972, 65; Wilkinson 2000, 12). Governor Stevens had immediately forwarded the treaty to the U.S. Senate, who ratified it on March 3, 1855, only two months after the signing (Hazard, 1952, 126; Stevens 1900, 462). Leschi, the influential Nisqually chief, refused to move his people onto the reservation and began to fight for a more suitable land base (Wilkinson 2000, 15). In October 1855, after the United States failed to reach a compromise with Leschi, the Indian War of 1855–1857 erupted. The conflict lasted for more than eight months (Wilkinson 2000, 15). Governor Stevens eventually exchanged those reservations for fertile bottom soil suitable for farming (Hazard 1952, 127).

Conflict over hunting and fishing rights also occurred as a result of the treaty. In the court case *United States v. Washington State*, the Puget Sound tribes argued that, according to the Medicine Creek treaty, they were allowed to fish "at all usual and accustomed grounds and stations . . . in common with all citizens of the Territory." In 1974, in what is referred to as the Boldt Decision, the court ruled in favor of the Nisqually, giving them 50 percent of all the harvestable fish (Carpenter 1994, 392; Weatherford 1994, 202).

Rene Casebeer

See also Boldt Decision (*United States v. Washington*), 1974; Hunting, Fishing, and Gathering; Reserved Rights Doctrine; Treaty with the Nisqually, Puyallup, Etc.–December 26, 1854.

References and Further Reading

Carpenter, Cecelia Svinth. 1994. *Native America in the Twentieth Century: An Encyclopedia*. Ed. Mary B. Davis. New York and London: Garland.

Hazard, Joseph T. 1952. *Companion of Adventure: A Biography of Isaac Ingalls Stevens: First Governor of Washington Territory*. Portland, OR: Binfords, Mort.

Stevens, Hazard. 1900. *The Life of Isaac Ingalls Stevens*, vol. 1. Cambridge, MA: Houghton Mifflin/Riverside Press.

Weatherford, Jack. 1994. *Savages and Civilization*. New York: Crown.

White, Richard. 1972. "The Treaty at Medicine Creek: Indian-White Relations on Upper Puget Sound, 1830–1880." Master's thesis, University of Washington.

Wilkinson, Charles. 2000. *Messages from Frank's Landing: A Story of Salmon, Treaties, and the Indian Way*. Seattle, WA: University of Washington Press.

Michilimackinac, Michigan

Originally, the name *Michilimackinac* was applied only to the 2,100-acre island that stands at the junction of Lakes Huron and Michigan. In time, the name was applied to the entire region of the Straits of Mackinac, the waterway separating Michigan's northern peninsula from the Lower Peninsula. Michilimackinac is usually said to take its name from the Ojibwe for "Big Turtle." The Ottawa historian Andrew Blackbird, in his traditional history, claimed that the proper name was *Mishinemackinong* and that it memorialized an earlier Indian people who made the island their home before being destroyed by the Iroquois.

Following the construction of a French fort on the southern shore of the straits in 1715, Michilimackinac became an annual gathering point for the Ojibwe, Ottawa, and French fur traders. In 1761, the English took possession of the fort but failed to form amicable economic and political relations with the Ottawa and Ojibwe. This led to a successful Ottawa and Ojibwe attack on the fort in 1763. With greater tact, the English reestablished their garrison, only to relocate it from the mainland to Mackinac Island in 1779. From that time onward, Mackinac Island became the leading fur trading center in the Great Lakes region.

In 1795, the Ojibwe and Ottawa ceded Michilimackinac to the United States in the Treaty of Greenville. Although the treaty stated that the cession included "[t]he post of Michilimackinac, and all the land on the island," an Ottawa tradition held that the Ojibwe reserved the entire shore of the island as far inland as a stone could be thrown, to provide a camping place when they came to the island for council or trade. Ojibwe aid was critical to the success of the British in capturing and holding Mackinac Island during the War of 1812.

Another small land cession was wrested from the Ojibwe and Ottawa in 1820. Lewis Cass, gover-

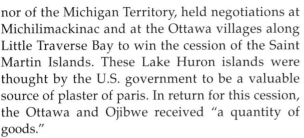

nor of the Michigan Territory, held negotiations at Michilimackinac and at the Ottawa villages along Little Traverse Bay to win the cession of the Saint Martin Islands. These Lake Huron islands were thought by the U.S. government to be a valuable source of plaster of paris. In return for this cession, the Ottawa and Ojibwe received "a quantity of goods."

The most important treaty for the Ottawa and Ojibwe people of the Michilimackinac region was the 1836 Treaty of Washington. Negotiated by Henry Rowe Schoolcraft, the treaty led to the cession of a large arc of northwestern Michigan lands, from the Grand River on the south to the headwaters of the Escanaba River in the Upper Peninsula. The negotiation took place under the shadow of U.S. removal policy. The decline of the fur trade economy and cultural changes triggered by the growth of Christian missions among the Ottawa and Ojibwe also played an important role in shaping the deal negotiated in Washington. For the Ottawa and Ojibwe, the draft treaty secured large reservations in the Michilimackinac area, relief of their fur trade debts, and much valuable aid for expanding their involvement in commercial farming, fishing, and education. The agreement seemed to meet the Ottawa's and Ojibwe's concerns for the future by protecting them from removal and empowering cultural and economic change.

Between July 12 and 16, 1836, a general council of leaders of the Ottawa and Ojibwe bands was held on Mackinac Island. The purpose of the council was to obtain their consent for the treaty as revised by the U.S. Senate. The Senate had made a major revision in the treaty. The large reservations that, according to the draft treaty, were to be held for an unspecified time were altered to be held for a mere five years. In the draft treaty, removal was voluntary, with the region of the Upper Mississippi suggested as the site. The Senate removed all mention of the Upper Mississippi region and instead specified the region "South West of the Missouri River." Instead of protecting the bands from removal, the revised treaty seemed to make that possibility imminent. Schoolcraft, who conducted the council, reported that some of the chiefs "strenuously opposed" giving up the reservations after only five years. In the end, the economic advantages of signing the treaty, together with the right of the Ottawa and Ojibwe to reside upon the ceded lands "until the land is required for settlement," convinced the leaders to agree to the revised treaty.

In 1979, in the federal district court case *United States v. Michigan*, the meaning of the 1836 treaty became once more a matter of controversy. In that case, the Ottawa and Ojibwe successfully asserted that nothing in the 1836 treaty abridged their right to fish when and where they wanted on the Great Lakes, including on the waters of Michilimackinac.

Theodore J. Karamanski

See also Cass, Lewis; Schoolcraft, Henry Rowe; Sovereignty; Treaty; Treaty with the Ottawa and Chippewa–July 6, 1820; Treaty with the Ottawa, Etc.–March 28, 1836; Treaty with the Wyandot, Etc.–August 3, 1795; Trust Doctrine.

References and Further Reading

Danziger, Edmund, Jr. 1979. *The Chippewas of Lake Superior.* Norman: University of Oklahoma Press.

Edmunds, R. David. 1978. *The Potawatomis: Keepers of the Fire.* Norman: University of Oklahoma Press.

Prucha, Francis Paul. 1967. *Lewis Cass and American Indian Policy.* Detroit, MI: Wayne State University Press.

New Echota, Georgia

Today, New Echota is a historic park located in Calhoun, Georgia. Several timber buildings located at the junction of the Coosawatee and Conasauga rivers are the only remaining relics of the capital established by the Cherokee Nation in 1825. The story of New Echota begins with change and the hopes of the Cherokee (*Ani'-Yun' wiya*, "The People") and ends tragically with the death of a group of important leaders and the forced removal of the majority of the nation's citizens to present-day Oklahoma.

The name *New Echota* was derived from Chota, an important historic Cherokee city located in present-day Tennessee. *Chota* describes the center and heart of the Ani'-Yun' wiya.

The Cherokee capital included the print shop of the *Cherokee Phoenix and Indian Advocate,* a bilingual newspaper written and edited by Elias Boudinot (Buck Oowaite) using the Cherokee alphabet invented by Sequoyah in 1821. The printing house was constructed late in 1827. The Vann Tavern, home of missionary Samuel Worcester, one of the major supporters of the Cherokee in Georgia, was also located in the capital. Cherokee surveyors planned the town with a central square and wide main streets. More than fifty people made their homes in the new capital, and many more came to shop, to do business at the government offices, and to attend meetings at the Council House.

The Council House in New Echota, along with the Supreme Court building, was the heart of the new government. New Echota was the capital of the eight districts of the Cherokee Nation, which included Hickory Log, Chickmaugee, Chattoogee, Amoah, Etowah, Tahquohee, Awuohee, and Coosewatee. Each district sent four delegates to the National Council, the lower house; in turn, these members elected twelve individuals to the National Committee, an upper house. The National Committee was responsible for electing the main chief, the assistant chief, and the Cherokee Nation's treasurer. This governmental design changed the traditional Cherokee clan organization and instead used the model of the United States government: an upper and lower legislature, a high court, and an executive branch. The Council House and the Supreme Court building in New Echota were visible symbols of the new Cherokee Nation.

Political treaties changing the course of the nation were debated and signed at the new capital. The Treaty of New Echota of 1835 was instrumental in the downfall and eventual assassination of three important Cherokee leaders. Elias Boudinot, John Ridge, and Major Ridge signed a treaty to sell eastern lands, including the area of New Echota, in exchange for land in present-day Oklahoma. The choice to sign and depart for land in Indian Territory or to stay and fight what seemed to be an unstoppable government from taking Cherokee lands in Georgia was a controversial and detailed decision. Not all Cherokees thought that leaving was the only option. Many of the tribe had left for new lands before the treaty in 1835. The Cherokee Nation presented a challenge, asking the U.S. high court to block the removal of the Cherokee from their lands in Georgia as required by the Cherokee Removal Act of 1830. The Supreme Court of the United States sided with the Cherokee Nation, but U.S. President Andrew Jackson would not recognize the court decision and ordered removal. The group was forcibly taken from the capital in 1838. This forced removal was known as the Trail of Tears.

After the Cherokees were removed or moved away from the capital, the buildings fell into disrepair. The newspaper offices had been burned to the ground in a raid by the Georgia Guard in 1834. The once-proud capital was a ghost town by 1838. Town structures were torn down for wood or simply lifted from their foundations and relocated to other areas. Today, visitors to New Echota can see re-creations of buildings that made up the Cherokee Nation in 1830. In the mid-1950s, Lewis Larsen, Joe Caldwell, and a group of archaeologists began research and restoration work. The Supreme Court and print shop have been reconstructed, and the Vann Tavern has been restored. New Echota is listed on the United States National Register of Historic Places and began operation as a state park in 1962. The buildings are open to the public and host educational events to celebrate Cherokee history and heritage throughout the year.

Pamela Lee Gray

See also Boudinot, Elias; *Cherokee Nation v. Georgia,* 1831; Indian Removal Act, 1830; *Johnson v. M'Intosh,* 1823; Ridge, John Rollin; Ridge, Major; Trail of Tears; Treaty with the Cherokee–December 29, 1835; *Worcester v. Georgia,* 1832.

References and Further Reading

Bays, Brad A. 1998. *Townsite Settlement and Dispossession in the Cherokee Nation, 1866–1907.* New York and London: Garland.

Conley, Robert J. 2005. *The Cherokee Nation: A History.* Albuquerque: University of New Mexico Press.

Finger, John R. 1984. *The Eastern Band of Cherokees: 1819–1900.* Knoxville: University of Tennessee Press.

Prairie du Chien, Wisconsin

Prairie du Chien, Wisconsin, is the site of three treaties among Native nations and the United States, the most significant of which was signed in 1825. In that year, disputes among Native tribes and the resulting impact on white settlement led the United States to convene a peace conference. A thousand representatives from Native tribes met at Prairie du Chien with William Clark, Lewis Cass, Indian agent Thomas Forsyth, and other U.S. negotiators to set boundaries for Native nations.

Situated at the confluence of the Wisconsin and Mississippi rivers, the site where the city of Prairie du Chien now stands had served as neutral ground for meetings among tribes for hundreds of years. French fur traders were established on St. Feriole Island at the confluence soon after the arrival there of Marquette and Jolliet in the late 1600s, and diverse tribes traded there. During the War of 1812, the British secured fleeting control

Bluffs near Prairie du Chien, on the upper Mississippi River, north of the confluence with the Wisconsin River. The British post and settlement of Prarie du Chien had considerable influence over the Indians west of Lake Michigan and Superior. The post was captured by the Americans on June 2, 1814, only to be recaptured by the British less than a month later, remaining under British control until the end of the war. (North Wind Picture Archives)

over the area with the help of local tribes and French traders who were commercially tied to Canadian ports. With the conclusion of that war, the United States regained control over Prairie du Chien and built Fort Crawford, site of the treaty signing in 1825.

By 1825, conflicts among Native groups had become common. Eastern tribes were relocating to new territories; alliances among tribes, the British and U.S. governments, and French fur traders shifted frequently; white settlement increasingly encroached on Native land; and competition for resources was growing. The treaty of 1825 addressed conflicts among tribes that lived in a vast area stretching from New York State to what is now South Dakota. Direct parties to the treaty included "Sioux and Chippewa, Sacs and Fox, Menominie, Ioway, Sioux, Winnebago, and a portion of the Ottawa, Chippewa, and Potawattomie, Tribes."

The tenth article of the treaty asserted the "controlling power" of the United States over the territory in question. Other articles of the treaty stated the boundaries within which each group would live but acknowledged that further negotiation would be necessary to finalize several of the boundaries. Some groups with an interest in lands covered by the treaty—particularly tribes in New York—were not represented or were underrepresented in the negotiations at Prairie du Chien, and separate negotiations were required to secure their consent to provisions of the treaty. Ojibwe bands were spread throughout the area covered by the treaty, and a full year is allocated in the treaty for informing Ojibwe bands of its provisions. The work begun at Prairie du Chien was furthered in treaties at Fond du Lac in 1826 and Butte des Morts in 1827.

While the Prairie du Chien treaty of 1825 was not a land concession treaty, it did serve as a critical step in the acquisition of Indian lands by white settlers and the federal government. Although the fourth article of the 1825 treaty at Prairie du Chien states that "the sole object of this agreement [is] to perpetuate a peace" among Native tribes, historians have debated how central land acquisition was to the intentions of the United States in brokering the treaty. Competing land claims by various tribes made land acquisition problematic, and the concept of strict divisions of territory was not necessarily compatible with traditional relationships to the land among many of the tribes. Regardless of whether the intent of the United States was to "clear the title" to millions of acres through the treaty of 1825, this was decidedly the outcome, and Indian landholdings rapidly diminished after 1825 through purchase by individuals and concessions in subsequent treaties.

The territory of the Dakota people, for instance, as defined in the treaty of 1825, covered part of what are now five states; by 1851, all Dakota people were expected by the federal government to live on a strip of land in Minnesota five miles wide and seventy miles long. Among the many land concession treaties that followed the "peace" treaty of 1825 are two that were signed in Prairie du Chien, by the Ojibwe people in 1829 and by members of a variety of tribes (including Ojibwe and Dakota bands) in 1830.

Martin Case

See also Cass, Lewis; Clark, William; Forsyth, Thomas; Treaty with the Chippewa–August 5, 1826; Treaty with the Chippewa, Etc.–August 11, 1827; Treaty with the Sioux, Etc.–August 19, 1825.

References and Further Reading

Danziger, Edmund J., Jr. 1979. *The Chippewas of Lake Superior.* Norman: University of Oklahoma Press.

Prairie du Chien was a regular trade site between Indians and the French as well as a treaty site between tribes and the United States. (Library of Congress)

Prucha, Francis Paul. 1994. *American Indian Treaties: The History of a Political Anomaly.* Berkeley and Los Angeles: University of California Press.

Satz, Ronald. 1991. "Chippewa Treaty Rights: The Reserved Rights of Wisconsin's Chippewa Indians in Historical Perspective." *Transactions, Wisconsin Academy of Sciences, Arts and Letters* 79(1), 1–251.

Sandy Lake, Minnesota

Sandy Lake in northeastern Minnesota was the intended relocation destination of the Lake Superior Ojibwe and the site of an 1850 Ojibwe tragedy. In violation of terms agreed upon in the 1837 and 1842 Ojibwe land cession treaties, Indian agents moved the 1850 annuity payment location from La Pointe in Wisconsin Territory to Sandy Lake in Minnesota Territory, a distance of nearly three hundred canoe miles away. The change was intended to force the Ojibwe to overwinter in Minnesota, where government officials hoped to permanently relocate them. An estimated four thousand Ojibwe from nineteen bands made the trip. However, agents had not made adequate plans to feed or house them. Winter arrived early, and the payments and supplies were late. Approximately 170 Ojibwe died from dysentery and measles at Sandy Lake. Another 230 died trying to make their way back home. The tragedy increased Ojibwe resistance to relocation and intensified efforts to establish permanent reservations in Wisconsin.

During the treaty negotiations of 1842, federal officials promised the Ojibwe they would not be removed from Wisconsin unless they "misbehaved." Within six years, however, rumors of an impending relocation had reached tribal leaders. Principal Chief Buffalo sent out runners to the Ojibwe villages to see if any of the bands had, in fact, transgressed and broken the terms of the treaty. No such misbehavior was reported. However, on February 6, 1850, at the urging of Minnesota territorial governor Alexander Ramsey, President Zachary Taylor signed the removal order. Territorial officials wanted the patronage jobs that accompanied Indian agencies, along with the annuities that sustained a corrupt system of politicians, businessmen, and traders.

The Ojibwe waited two months for the annuities to arrive at Sandy Lake. Flooding damaged the foodstuffs that the traders—ever-present at annuity gatherings—brought with them. While waiting for their treaty goods, many Ojibwe burned their canoes for firewood and sold their annuities to traders for rancid meat and spoiled supplies. In early December, tribal members received only partial annuities in the form of goods but no cash. Many set out immediately for home, walking because the rivers had frozen over and canoes were useless. Others stayed at Sandy Lake to tend to ill family members. According to oral history accounts, the elders and children died first from sickness and cold. The Ojibwe wrapped scores of bodies in birch bark and placed them on a bank overlooking the frozen lake. When the ground thawed in the spring, they buried many of them at Sandy Lake. Some grieving parents carried the bodies of their children back to their villages for burials. In 1851, when government officials again announced that they would distribute annuity goods at Sandy Lake, most Ojibwe refused to travel there to claim them. The following year, Buffalo traveled to Washington, D.C., and persuaded President Millard Fillmore to rescind the removal order and establish four permanent Ojibwe reservations in Wisconsin.

In 2000, tribal officials and representatives of the Great Lakes Indian Fish and Wildlife Commission erected a memorial at Sandy Lake to commemorate the tragedy. It consists of four hundred stones, one for each of the approximately four hundred Ojibwe who died making the ill-fated journey. The memorial is called *Mikwendaagoziwag*, or "They Will Not Be Forgotten."

Patricia A. Loew

See also Buffalo; Sovereignty; Treaty; Treaty with the Chippewa–July 29, 1837; Treaty with the Chippewa–December 20, 1837; Treaty with the Chippewa–October 4, 1842; Trust Responsibility.

References and Further Reading
Armstrong, Benjamin. 1892. *Early Life Among the Indians.* Ashland, WI: Press of A. W. Bowron.

Chippewa. 1988. "1865 Statement Made by the Indians: A Bilingual Petition." In *Studies in the Interpretation of Canadian Native American Languages and Cultures,* ed. John D. Nichols. London, ON: University of Western Ontario.

Loew, Patty. 2001. *Indian Nations of Wisconsin: Histories of Endurance and Renewal.* Madison, WI: Wisconsin Historical Society Press.

Santa Fe, New Mexico

Situated in the western foothills of the Sangre de Cristo Mountains, Santa Fe has been New Mexico's political hub and capital for nearly four centuries. The city is in close proximity to the nineteen Pueblo villages of the Rio Grande valley and has thus played a key role in relations with the neighboring Indians. The Spanish, Mexican, and American governments may have varied in their respective Indian policies, but they all recognized the utility of Santa Fe's central location.

The Spanish first established La Villa Real de Santa Fe in 1610 on the north bank of the Rio Santa Fe. However, archaeological evidence suggests that the ancestral Pueblo people lived on the site at least a thousand years before the Spanish arrival. The original Pueblo inhabitants moved to other locations, probably because of drought and/or increased raiding by local marauding tribes. The Spanish, nevertheless, saw the site as ideal. Once established, the first Spanish governor of La Provincia de Nuevo Mexico, Pedro de Peralta, immediately set about instituting his Indian policy. Accordingly, the *encomienda* system granted large tracts of land to Spanish settlers, who required the local Pueblos to pay tribute by giving the settlers a portion of their crops. At the same time, Franciscan missionaries sought to convert the Indians, planting churches in each Pueblo village. Tension between the civil and religious arms of Spanish colonialism mounted through the 1600s as each sought to shape the nature and function of the colony. The Pueblos were caught in the middle of this wrangling, with no voice in the policies that affected them and their homeland.

All this changed in 1680. In a carefully planned revolt, eighteen of the nineteen Pueblos rose up and threw off the shackles of Spanish control. It began in Taos Pueblo north of Santa Fe, but soon the entire province was in rebellion. Within days, the capital city was under siege. Governor Antonio Otermín barricaded himself and the city's populace behind Santa Fe's walls. What was once a fortress quickly turned into a prison as the Pueblos cut off the city's food and water supply. Otermín realized that they would have to make a break for it and fight their way to safety. The governor's plan worked. Spanish forces temporarily staved off the Indians and quickly made their way to Isleta Pueblo—the only village not in rebellion—before heading to El Paso. As they headed south, Santa Fe fell to the rebels, signaling defeat for the Spaniards and their colonial policy.

Twelve years later, in 1692, the Spanish returned to New Mexico and once again set up their capital in Santa Fe. This time, however, they recognized Indian land and water rights. Throughout the 1700s, the Spanish government gave legal protection to the Pueblos by parceling out and "granting" tracts of land. When Mexico declared its independence from Spain in 1821, the new regime recognized and respected these land grants. Less than thirty years later, when the Americans signed the Treaty of Guadalupe Hidalgo and took control of New Mexico, they, too, honored the Pueblos' lands as defined by the Spanish the previous century.

Yet relations between the Pueblos and the government in Santa Fe were far from ideal. During the Mexican-American War, Indians from Taos Pueblo assassinated the newly installed American governor. Moreover, through much of the nineteenth century, whites ignored the Pueblos' property titles and settled on their land. The situation was aggravated in 1876 when the Supreme Court ruled in *United States v. Joseph* that federal Indian law did not apply to the Pueblos because the Treaty of Guadalupe Hidalgo granted them citizenship rights. The decision gave the territorial government the power to treat each Pueblo village like any other municipality, leading to further white encroachment. However, in the 1913 case *United States v. Sandoval*, the Supreme Court effectively nullified the earlier verdict, ruling that the Pueblos were indeed wards of the federal government. The decision shifted power from Santa Fe to Washington, D.C.—a decision that has held up to the present.

Bradley Shreve

See also Southern Plains and the Southwest; Treaty of Guadalupe Hidalgo, 1848.
References and Further Reading
Noble, David Grant. 1989. *Santa Fe: History of an Ancient City.* Santa Fe, NM: School of American Research Press.
Sando, Joe S. 1992. *Pueblo Nations: Eight Centuries of Pueblo Indian History.* Santa Fe, NM: Clear Light.
Tobias, Henry J., and Charles E. Woodhouse. *Santa Fe: A Modern History, 1880–1990.* Albuquerque: University of New Mexico Press.

Sault Ste. Marie, Michigan and Ontario

The twin cities of Sault Ste. Marie (pronounced *soo-saint-marie*) are situated at the rapids formed at the outflow of Lake Superior, which fall approximately eighteen feet to the level of Lakes Huron and Michigan. The rapids once constituted North America's greatest inland fishery, a resource that drew indigenous people to this region more than 2,500 years ago as the drainage patterns of the Great Lakes took on their present configuration.

The oral tradition of the Anishnaabeg tells of their original home as being on the eastern coastal region of what is now the United States and Canada, but disease and suffering compelled them to move from this homeland. A spirit being led them west to the area now know as Sault Ste. Marie (French for "the rapids of the St. Mary's River"). When they arrived at this place, many decided to settle, but others chose to continue their migration. Using modern geographic designations, those Anishnaabeg we now call the Chippewa (or the Ojibway), while staying in the Sault area, also moved into the areas surrounding Lake Superior in Michigan, Wisconsin, Minnesota, Manitoba, and Ontario; from the Sault, the Ottawa (or Odawa) moved into the northern Lake Huron area of Ontario, as well as into areas in northern Michigan, especially along the eastern Lake Michigan coast; the third component of the Three Fires People, the Potawatomi, moved farther south into the area of southwestern Michigan, northern Indiana, northeastern Illinois, and southwestern Wisconsin. All of these people consider the Sault their spiritual home; its Anishnaabeg name is Bawating, which some translate as "the gathering place of the People."

The area was first visited by Europeans in the early 1600s, and by 1671 the place had gained such stature that the French, planning a formal ceremony to lay claim to all of North America, staged the Pageant of St. Lusson at the Sault, calling more than a dozen tribes to the area to witness this formal territorial claim. The French also hoped to form alliances with the area's indigenous peoples. Earlier, in 1668, the French had set up a missionary post there, the date of which is used by some to claim that Sault Ste. Marie is the third-oldest European settlement in the United States.

Although the French had established a missionary post in the Sault and had laid formal claim to the area, Sault Ste. Marie essentially remained an indigenous center for the next two centuries, only secondarily becoming an important trading post for furs. The area was too remote to have any direct involvement in the various North American European proxy wars, the American Revolution, or the War of 1812, but warriors from the Sault area were often called upon (by Pontiac, Tecumseh, and others) to defend their Great Lakes homelands, which they did with valor.

The Sault's remote location also kept the area away from the American and British struggle for control of wide swaths of North American territory until 1820, when Michigan territorial governor Lewis Cass accompanied a group of U.S. officials and soldiers to the Sault to extract a land cession from the Anishnaabeg so that the U.S. government could establish a military post at the rapids. Before this time, the Native people of the area had thought not in terms of "American" or "British" but simply "Indian." But, despite some serious early difficulties, representatives of the Native inhabitants on both sides of the putative border did make a cession of land, allowing the United States to establish, for the first time, a presence in the area. (It should be noted that the border through the upper St. Mary's River, with its numerous islands, was not finally established until 1848.)

The first shipping lock was built by the state of Michigan in the Sault in 1853, two years before the Ojibway ceded the land where the locks then stood. This Treaty of Washington of 1855 purportedly also ceded to the U.S. government the Natives' "perpetual" fishing station on the St. Mary's River, retained by them in the treaty of 1820 mentioned previously. To this day, Native people of the area still dispute the cession of this most important tract of land.

Sault Ste. Marie was also the site of other important treaties and councils, notably the British/Canadian Robinson Treaties of 1850. It should be noted that in these Sault area treaties and in many other cases, Native leaders from both sides of the border were involved in negotiating and signing these treaties with both the U.S. and British authorities, and this "cross-border" treaty signing was acknowledged and accepted by all parties.

By the mid-nineteenth century, Native military power and influence began its inexorable decline, and by the late 1800s Sault Ste. Marie was seldom referred to as a place of Native significance but more often as a place of burgeoning industrial development. With the completion of a massive hydroelectric power station on the American side, much of the energy (and water) of the rapids was harnessed. This led to the building of a steel mill and a paper plant on the Canadian side. The construction of new locks on both the U.S. and Canadian sides of the rapids and the building of two more hydroelectric generation plants (one for the locks and one on the Canadian side) reduced the flow of the rapids to a mere trickle and destroyed the tremendous fishery as well.

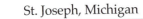

Indians fishing in the rapids, Sault Ste. Marie, Michigan, c. 1900. (Library of Congress)

Sault Ste. Marie, Michigan, has a present population of 16,500 (2000 census), and Sault, Ontario, boasts a population of 74,500 (2001 data). Four tribes have reservations in the area: the Sault Ste. Marie tribe of Chippewa Indians and the Bay Mills Indian Community are on the American side; the Garden River and Batchewana First Nations hold land on the Canadian side of the border.

Phil Bellfy

See also Cass, Lewis; Robinson Huron Treaty (Second Robinson Treaty)–September 9, 1850; Robinson Superior Treaty (First Robinson Treaty)–September 7, 1850; Sovereignty; Treaty; Treaty with the Chippewa–July 29, 1837; Treaty with the Chippewa–December 20, 1837; Treaty with the Chippewa–October 4, 1842; Trust Responsibility.

References and Further Reading
Arbic, Bernard. 2003. *City of the Rapids: Sault Ste. Marie's Heritage.* Allegan Forest, MI: Priscilla Press.
Danziger, Edmund J., Jr. 1979. *The Chippewas of Lake Superior.* Norman: University of Oklahoma Press.
Quimby, George Irving. 1960. *Indian Life in the Upper Great Lakes: 11,000 B.C. to A.D. 1800.* Chicago and London: University of Chicago Press.

St. Joseph, Michigan

Located on the eastern shore of Lake Michigan in the state of Michigan, the community of St. Joseph and the St. Joseph River had a long association with the Potawatomi, the Miami, fur traders, soldiers, and missionaries. The St. Joseph River winds south into Indiana and then back north into Michigan. It is not to be confused with the St. Joseph River, also in southeastern Michigan, that flows south into Indiana, joining the St. Mary's River to form the Maumee. These two rivers form closely in southern Michigan. At this site, two significant treaties were negotiated in the late 1820s that forced the removal of hundreds of Potawatomis.

Although the first decade of the nineteenth century witnessed a flood of treaties with some land cessions led by William Henry Harrison at the direction of President Thomas Jefferson, the years following the end of the War of 1812 revealed a rush to force the removal of the remaining bands of Potawatomi from Michigan, Indiana, and Illinois. The first of the treaties negotiated at St. Joseph was concluded in September 1827. It sought to consolidate the diverse bands of Potawatomi, to remove them far from white settlement, and to distance them from the Detroit Road to Chicago, which swung south along the shores of Lake Michigan, by relocating them to land reserved for them by the U.S. government. Ninety-nine sections of surveyed land formed the reserve south of the St. Joseph River. Nineteen chiefs signed this treaty, which was ratified on February 23, 1829.

The following September, a second treaty was negotiated, known as the Treaty of Carey Mission after a mission at St. Joseph set up by the Baptists. It, too, asked for land cessions. In return, annuities were assigned and trade goods promised. In addition, implements for agriculture and livestock were promised, along with laborers to work for the tribe to get their farming under way. More important, separate land grants were given to people of Indian descent. Many of these grants were assigned to Indian wives of white men or to the half-white, half-Indian children of mixed-race marriages. Some of the grants went to individual chiefs. The location of the mission, which educated the Indian children, became uncertain. The U.S. government made no concrete promises to rebuild or relocate the establishment on the new reserve.

Other treaties negotiated at other locations, particularly at Chicago in 1833, differed from former treaties, which had kept the Potawatomi on reserves, to aim for all-out removal from the Lower Peninsula of Michigan. The Chicago treaty pushed for the destruction of even small reserves. Furthermore, the treaties negotiated in Indiana at places like Tippecanoe insisted on the removal of all Potawatomi to land west of the Mississippi, in particular to Kansas Territory. By 1837, Abel C. Pepper, the U.S. Indian removal agent, sought to remove Potawatomi not only from Illinois and Indiana but also from Michigan—in particular, the St. Joseph Potawatomi. Pokagun and others of the St. Joseph Potawatomi worked to remain on the small reserves that had been assigned to individual members of the tribe. The government could not move them to the west because of the manner in which these lands had been deeded. To this day, descendants of Pokagun and these Potawatomi reside on this land.

The French first arrived on the St. Joseph River about 1679 under the direction of Robert Cavalier LaSalle. They constructed a fort inland along the river to assist in developing trade, first with the Miami, who had settled the area, and, after they moved on, with the Potawatomi. The St. Joseph Potawatomi aligned themselves with Pontiac during his rebellion. They attacked the British and took prisoners. When the British took prisoners from the tribe, the Potawatomi attempted negotiations to get them returned. After long months, the British eventually relented, but not before the St. Joseph Potawatomi distanced themselves from Pontiac. After the end of the French and Indian War, the British built their own fort at the mouth of the river and named it Fort St. Joseph. From here, the British maintained fur trade rights over the St. Joseph band of Potawatomi.

Near the end of the American War of Independence, William Burnett of New Jersey came into the St. Joseph River valley to operate a fur trade establishment. He married Kakima, the sister of Topinbee, a Potawatomi chief, creating a lasting alliance. The Burnett family remained a strong presence in the region well into the nineteenth century.

Sally Colford Bennett

See also Chicago, Illinois; Pokagun; Pontiac; Tippecanoe River, Indiana; Treaty with the Chippewa, Etc.–September 26, 1833; Treaty with the Potawatomi–September 19, 1827; Treaty with the Potawatomi–September 20, 1828.

References and Further Reading

Edmunds, R. David. 1978. *The Potawatomis, Keepers of the Fire*. Norman: University of Oklahoma Press.
Kappler, Charles J., ed. 1904. *Indian Affairs: Laws and Treaties*, vol. 2, *Treaties*. Washington, DC: Government Printing Office.
Tanner, Helen Hornbeck, ed. 1987. *Atlas of Great Lakes Indian History*. Norman: University of Oklahoma Press.

St. Louis, Missouri

Located on the west bank of the Mississippi River just south of the confluence of the Missouri and Illinois rivers, St. Louis was the clashing crossroads of Native American and American culture from the mid-eighteenth century to the mid-nineteenth. As the trading capital of the "westward country," St. Louis saw the negotiation of many treaties, which sometimes led to greater conflicts. Beginning in 1804, treaties between the United States and Native

American tribes of the westward country (now the Midwest) were negotiated in St. Louis.

The first of these treaties was initiated on November 3, 1804, by Indiana territorial governor William Henry Harrison with the Sac (Sauk) and Fox tribes, who resided in present-day northwestern Illinois. Following the Louisiana Purchase of 1803, President Thomas Jefferson and Secretary of War Henry Dearborn sought by treating to end to the warring between the Sac and Fox and the Osage over hunting land. Harrison did not directly summon the Sac and Fox tribal leaders to St. Louis to discuss a treaty as he had in Indiana Territory with the Miami, Shawnee, Delaware, and Potawatomi. Actually, members of the Sac and Fox had come to the city to turn over one warrior of more than three who were responsible for the murder of American settlers. Showing that he was willing to bargain with them, Harrison arrested the single warrior and let the others go without punitive action.

In light of the more favorable situation, Harrison then began to negotiate a treaty with those Sac and Fox present. The agreement stipulated that the Sac and Fox would cease to make war on the Osage; would give up their land on the eastern side of the Mississippi south of the Wisconsin River, east to the Fox River of Illinois, and west and south to the Missouri River; would receive the protection of the United States; and would receive annuities. Although they were allowed to hunt and reside on the land, and the United States assured them that they would be given the full protection of the government against white citizens who sought to "intrude" upon them, the treaty further stipulated that no one could trade in the area with them unless they were licensed by the U.S. government. The government promised to establish a trading factory in the near future, which they did in 1808 with the erection of Fort Madison on the western bank of the Mississippi River, north of the Des Moines River. Five members of the Sac and Fox tribes put their mark to the treaty. It was ratified by Congress on January 25, 1805. When the members of the Sac and Fox returned home and informed their countrymen, the news upset and disturbed the other tribe members. The treaty enraged the warrior Black Hawk, and it continued to infuriate him into the 1830s, as he continued to proclaim that this treaty had stolen their lands.

Other treaties followed with the Osage nation, who had been punished by being banned from trading with St. Louis traders. The new governor of the Louisiana Territory, Meriwether Lewis, sent William Clark, the territorial superintendent of Indian affairs of all tribes but the Osage, along with an army detachment from Cantonment Bellefontaine led by Captain Eli Clemson of the 1st U.S. Infantry, a detachment of mounted militia, and the St. Charles Dragoons to establish a fort and trading factory on the Missouri River near present-day Kansas City.

The northern band of the Osage, who lived by the junction of the Little Osage, Marais des Cygne, and the Marmaton rivers (not to be confused with the southern band, who lived on the Arkansas River), was summoned to meet with Clark, and Clark negotiated a treaty with them. The site of this trading venture had been sighted by the Corps of Discovery members on their trip to the westward country in 1804. Clark and Lewis favored it over a site at the mouth of the Osage River. This site on the Missouri upset the Osage, who now had to permanently move closer to the trading house and garrison rather than have it come to them.

Clark returned to St. Louis with the treaty, but the treaty displeased Governor Lewis. First, Clark had drawn a "buffer zone" boundary line between the United States and the Osage that was literally within sight of the Osage villages, meaning they couldn't venture beyond the outer reaches of their villages. Next, the land cession included *all* their lands in Arkansas and eastern Oklahoma. Other Osage, including the southern or Arkansas band who had not been present during the treaty negotiation at Fort Osage (as the site came to be called, although it was sometimes referred to as Fort Clark), met with Clark and Lewis in St. Louis and voiced their objection to the treaty. Furthermore, they pointed out, the treaty violated Osage political decision making because a majority agreement to it had not been obtained; they therefore declared they had not ceded any territory. Lewis rewrote the treaty to clarify the desires of the United States. He appointed Pierre Chouteau, brother of Auguste, the Indian agent to the southern or Arkansas band of the Osage, and sent him to get the Osage to sign. Upon Chouteau's return with the signed treaty, Lewis discovered that Chouteau and Mongrain, Chouteau's interpreter, had written in two land grants to benefit themselves. Lewis struck these out of the treaty, finding it despicable that white men should profit in land from treaty negotiations; he thereafter held a grave opinion of the Chouteaus. Following Lewis's untimely death, the new governor, Frederick Bates, negotiated additions to open up trade once more

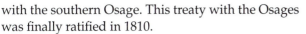

with the southern Osage. This treaty with the Osages was finally ratified in 1810.

The treaties never sat well with the Osage because the trading house/factory was too far from their homes. Although some of them moved to Fort Osage, by the winter of 1809 they had eventually left and returned to their original villages. It divided them into two parties. Those who stayed thought they were making Clark happy. Those who returned were pleasing Chouteau, who had established his own trading house in their villages. The last time a sizable number of the Osage visited at Fort Osage was in April 1812. This distance from their home villages often left them vulnerable to attack from their enemies—the Iowa, Sac and Fox, and Winnebago.

In 1813, William Clark was appointed governor of the newly named Territory of Missouri. In the midst of the War of 1812, his attention was still intensely focused on Indian affairs. Following the end of the war, Clark negotiated more agreements and treaties with diverse tribes in and around St. Louis. In 1818, Secretary of War John C. Calhoun directed Clark to negotiate a treaty to stop the fighting between the Cherokee, Quapaw, and Osage tribes and to acquire millions of acres of land for a pittance of money and goods so that the U.S. government could move Indian tribes residing east of the Mississippi River to the newly acquired lands for resettlement. Both the Osage and the Quapaw signed over large tracts of good lands in Arkansas and Missouri. This would open up those areas for white settlement, much of it on land granted for service in the war of 1812.

Although there were other French villages in the area, St. Louis was founded in late December 1764 by Pierre de LeClede Liguest, who had traveled from New Orleans to establish his own trading site and a village. His fourteen-year-old stepson and employee, Auguste Chouteau, accompanied him. Later, Auguste's brother Pierre joined them. Together they not only built the village and eventually the city of St. Louis but also established a strong foothold in the Indian trade of the Missouri valley. The U.S. government had established a cantonment called Bellefontaine near St. Louis on the Missouri River in 1805. This garrison closed down in 1826 and moved to a new garrison in St. Louis known as Jefferson Barracks, from which military expeditions up the Missouri departed for the West, including some led by General Henry Atkinson.

Sally Colford Bennett

See also Black Hawk; Chouteau, Auguste; Clark, William; Dearborn, Henry; Dodge, Henry; Forsyth, Thomas; Harrison, William Henry; Lewis, Meriwether; Treaty with the Sauk and Fox–November 3, 1804.

References and Further Reading
Carter, Clarence E. 1934–1962. *The Territorial Papers of the United States*, vol. 14, *The Territory of Louisiana-Missouri 1806–1814*. Washington, DC: Government Printing Office.
Esarey, Logan. 1922. *Messages and Letters of William Henry Harrison*, vol. 1. Indianapolis: Indiana Historical Commission.
Foley, William. 1989. *The Genesis of Missouri*. Columbia: University of Missouri Press.
Gregg, Kate L., ed. 1937. *Westward with the Dragoons: The Journal of William Clark on His Expedition to Establish Fort Osage, August 25 to September 22, 1808*. Fulton, MO: Ovid Bell Press.
Hagan, William T. 1958. *The Sac and Fox Indians*. Norman: University of Oklahoma Press.
Jackson, Donald, ed. 1990. *Black Hawk, an Autobiography*. Urbana and Chicago: University of Illinois Press.
Jones, Landon Y. 2004. *William Clark and the Shaping of the West*. New York: Hill and Wang.
Nichols, Roger L. 1992. *Black Hawk and the Warrior's Path*. Arlington Heights, IL: Harlan Davidson.
Rollings, Willard H. 1992. *The Osage: An Ethnohistorical Study of Hegemony on the Prairie-Plains*. Columbia: University of Missouri Press.

Tippecanoe River, Indiana

Meandering through 225 miles of northern Indiana, the Tippecanoe River, which empties into the Wabash River northeast of the city of Lafayette, lends its name to a critical battle in 1811 and a series of treaties of the 1830s between the U.S. government and the Potawatomi of Illinois, Indiana, and Michigan.

This area was once the homeland of the Miami, who gave the river its name, which means "buffalo fish"; but by the mid-eighteenth century, the Potowatomi had moved into the region, making small villages along the river and its streams. In the first decade of the nineteenth century, the Potawatomi, under the leadership of Main Poc, became followers of the Shawnee Prophet, whose village was located in Ohio. The Prophet and his brother, Tecumseh, were anxious to leave the state and find a site more in tune with their ideal of returning to a simpler life that did not depend upon the lifestyle and material possessions of the

Americans. In 1808, Main Poc offered them a section of land along the Wabash River where the Tippecanoe entered it. This village, known as Prophetstown, became an object of controversy. The Americans saw it as a threat to their safety and security as more and more diverse tribes flocked to the Prophet to hear his messages. The various tribes found it a place of strength as the Prophet's brother, Tecumseh, sought to forge all tribes into an alliance against the rising incursion of white settlements, particularly in southern Indiana.

With the direction of President Thomas Jefferson, William Henry Harrison, governor of the Indiana Territory, negotiated treaties at Fort Wayne in 1803, at Vincennes in 1805, and again at Fort Wayne in 1809. With each document, the chiefs signed away land, eventually cutting off the tribes from the Ohio River and placing more and more territory under the control of the U.S. government. The Americans already considered the land theirs; it had been signed over to the French in the eighteenth century by the tribes. From there, the land ownership transferred to Great Britain through the defeat of the French in the Seven Years' War. By the success of the American colonies in the Revolution, the Americans took possession; and the treaty negotiations by Harrison were considered mere formalities to "keep" the peace and make it appear that the land was sold legitimately by the tribes to the Americans.

The tribes, not only those along the Tippecanoe River, sided with Tecumseh and the Prophet in declaring that no one chief had the right to sell any land. The brothers and their followers were particularly upset with the Treaty of Fort Wayne of 1809. This particular treaty contributed more to the alienation from and disdain for the United States on the part of the tribes. Although Tecumseh tried to provoke Harrison to reverse the treaty and promise no more land concessions, his efforts were not successful. Tension within the territory increased. Harrison sought aid from the federal government, which in turn sent the 4th U.S. Regiment of Infantry to Vincennes to shore up the 1st U.S. Regiment at Fort Knox (Vincennes). Militia from Kentucky also came to Harrison's aid. In the fall of 1811, his force advanced up the Wabash toward the Tippecanoe and Prophetstown. The battle began early on the morning of November 7 and resulted in the defeat of the Prophet. The Americans destroyed his village and much of the grain storage. This was not the end of the matter.

The following summer, the War of 1812 broke out. The tribes aligned themselves with the British against the Americans.

At the end of the war, the tribes found themselves in a weak position to negotiate peace with the United States. Hence, the United States came back with treaty after treaty, whittling away at the land long held by the tribes. In the twenty years following the end of the War of 1812, white settlement advanced northward from the Ohio, pushing the tribes into smaller reserves and eventually out of the state entirely.

The tribes along the Tippecanoe were no exception to the removal. The treaties of Tippecanoe were fraught with controversy. The first agreement occurred in 1832, the others in 1834 and 1836. First, full-blood tribe members were given reservations, although in some cases chiefs or headmen obtained land of their own. Mixed-blood individuals were allotted actual land grants, giving them private ownership. Offers came to entice, seduce, and encourage the tribe as a whole to emigrate west of the Mississippi River. Such enticements included offers of goods for the journey and farm implements to assist them upon arrival in the "new" land. Last, the treaties became an avenue to instant riches for men involved in the negotiations. The government created a provision wherein the Potawatomi could pay their debts out of annuities. Suddenly, men who in reality owed absolutely nothing presented vouchers before the actual creditors were able to. Because of this practice, there was not enough money left to pay all the debts.

The U.S. government soon insisted that the Potawatomi move west. Chief Menominee refused. He had written a letter stating that he had not signed away the land or agreed to removal. Nonetheless, in the late summer of 1838, nearly 860 Potawatomi left their villages to assemble near Twin Lakes, Indiana, for the journey west. They were escorted by one hundred soldiers led by General John Tipton; the tribal leaders, including Menominee, rode imprisoned on a wagon for all to see. The journey began with rudeness and coercion on the part of the Americans. In some cases, wagons were not forthcoming, and some members of the tribe had to leave some of their belongings behind. Soldiers aggressively drove the Potawatomi, many of whom were on foot, along the road. The journey lasted about two months as the tribe went from Indiana, passing by the Tippecanoe battlefield one last time en route to Illinois, crossing over to Missouri at Quincy and moving on to Kansas, ending at Potawatomi Creek. Thirty-nine died, many of them children and elderly.

Sally Colford Bennett

See also Battle of Tippecanoe; Harrison, William Henry; Indian Removal; Tecumseh; Treaty with the Delaware, Etc.–September 30, 1809; Vincennes, Indiana.

References and Further Reading

Dowd, Gregory Evans. 1992. *A Spirited Resistance: The North American Indian Struggle for Unity, 1745–1815.* Baltimore and London: Johns Hopkins University Press.

Edmunds, R. David. 1978. *The Potawatomis, Keepers of the Fire.* Norman: University of Oklahoma Press.

Edmunds, R. David. 1983. *The Shawnee Prophet.* Lincoln: University of Nebraska Press.

Kappler, Charles J., ed. 1904. *Indian Affairs: Laws and Treaties,* vol. 2, *Treaties.* Washington, DC: Government Printing Office.

Traverse des Sioux, Minnesota

Traverse des Sioux, Minnesota, is the site of a treaty concluded in 1851 in which Dakota bands ceded millions of acres of land to the U.S. government. In exchange for this land concession, the Dakota people were promised annuity payments in perpetuity and a homeland along the Minnesota River. Delivery of annuity payments, however, became increasingly irregular, leading to widespread misery among the Dakota people and, ultimately, to the Dakota Conflict of 1862.

Traverse des Sioux is a crossing point on the Minnesota River near present-day St. Peter, Minnesota, long used by the Dakota and by French fur traders in their trade routes and as a meeting place. At this site, on July 23, 1851, leaders of the Sisseton and Wahpeton bands of the Dakota ceded twenty-four million acres in what is now Minnesota, Iowa, and South Dakota. A companion treaty was signed at Mendota, Minnesota, a few days later by leaders of the Mdewakanton and Wahpekute bands.

In 1837, Dakota people had ceded all their land east of the Mississippi River to the U.S. government. White settlement had been immediate and intense. By 1851, Little Crow and other Dakota leaders conceded the inevitability of white settlement by exchanging their still-vast land holdings for $300,000 in direct payments and more than $1 million in trust. The trust funds were to be used for yearly annuities payable in gold, food, training, agricultural implements, and other resources. Article 3 of the Treaty of Traverse des Sioux set aside a strip of land seventy miles long and ten miles wide on each side of the Minnesota River for a reservation.

Before all Dakota people had moved to the reservation, however, Article 3 had been stricken out by the U.S. Senate and replaced with a provision for government purchase of the reservation land at ten cents per acre. After skirmishes with white settlers in 1857, the Dakota people were confined to the ten-mile strip of land on the south side of the Minnesota River. The loss of land upon which traditional cultural practices depended, the diversion of monetary payments by unscrupulous traders, and the failure of crops in the late 1850s had the effect of making the Dakota people entirely dependent upon food shipments from the federal government.

With the onset of the Civil War, annuity payments were delayed or skipped, causing universal hardship among the Dakota people. They attacked white settlements in an attempt to gain back the land ceded in 1851. After a military defeat, all lands were taken from Dakota people, and thirty-eight members of the Mdewakanton band were hung at Mankato, about twenty miles from Traverse de Sioux, in the largest mass execution in U.S. history.

Today, the Lower Sioux Agency Indian Reservation (one of four Dakota reservations in Minnesota) is located fifty miles from St. Peter, and an interpretive center at the Traverse des Sioux treaty site is maintained by Nicollet County.

Martin Case

See also Annuities; Sovereignty; Treaty; Treaty with the Sioux–Mdewakanton and Wahpakoota Bands–August 5, 1851; Treaty with the Sioux–Sisseton and Wahpeton Bands–July 23, 1851; Trust; Trust Land.

References and Further Reading

Anderson, Gary Clayton. 1984. *Kinsmen of Another Kind: Dakota-White Relations in the Upper Mississippi Valley, 1650–1862.* Lincoln: University of Nebraska Press.

Hurt, Wesley R. 1974. *Dakota Sioux Indians.* New York: Garland.

Prucha, Francis Paul. 1994. *American Indian Treaties: The History of a Political Anomaly.* Berkeley and Los Angeles: University of California Press.

Vincennes, Indiana

Before the outbreak of the War of 1812, Vincennes, which is located along the east bank of the Wabash River in western Indiana, was the Indiana Territory's capital as well as the site of important council and treaty negotiations with the regional tribes. From this location, territorial governor William Henry Harrison carried out his duties to negotiate treaties with tribes in order to obtain land cessions. In 1802, Harrison called a council at Vincennes to determine the ownership of land that became known as the Vincennes Tract. This portion of land was approximately thirty-six miles on both sides and about twenty-five miles north and south of Vincennes. Although no treaty agreement was drawn up Harrison nevertheless concluded that the participants had reached a consensus, and he proceeded to inform President Thomas Jefferson.

Following the secret directive of February 1803, in which President Jefferson told Harrison that "the Indians . . . in their interests and their tranquility it is best they should see only the present page of their history," Harrison called a treaty council to be held at Fort Wayne, an American military garrison located in the northeastern section of the Indiana Territory. Harrison brought along surveyor Thomas Freeman, who had been surveying the tract since 1802, a detachment of U.S. regulars under the command of Lieutenant Nathan Heald to reinforce the garrison in the event of possible unrest during the course of treating, and other territorial dignitaries. Harrison used this council to negotiate and draft a treaty giving the United States ownership of the Vincennes Tract. Citing the 1795 Greenville treaty as the only land cession treaty they intended to follow, chiefs—including Buckongahelas of the Delaware, who walked out in a fury—disagreed over giving any more land to the United States. Other chiefs showed their distrust by not showing up at all. Eventually, Harrison got his treaty on June 7, 1803, through the efforts and influence of Fort Wayne Indian agent William Wells and Wells's father-in-law, Little Turtle of the Miami. Later, in August of that year, Harrison met with leaders of the Kaskaskia Nation to receive ownership of their lands in Illinois in exchange for increasing their annuities and taking them under the protection of the U.S. government. On the same day, Harrison also set an agreement with the Eel River Miami for narrow sections of one acre on a proposed route for overland travel, as well as for the establishment of "houses of entertainment" (inns and taverns) and ferries as needed— between Vincennes and the village of Kaskaskia and from Vincennes to Clarksville along the Ohio River.

In the autumn of 1804, at Vincennes, Harrison treated with the Delaware and the Piankashaw for the purpose of obtaining more land, particularly the vast acres below the Vincennes Tract running south-east along the Ohio River towards Clarksville. Upset, the Miami insisted that Harrison should have included them; as they had allowed the Delaware to reside in lands belonging to them, therefore they ought to be involved. In addition to the Miami complaint, that winter the Delaware reversed their support of the land transaction because, according to them, Harrison had seduced them by offering instruction in farming and domestic arts as well as supplies to make them more self-sustaining and increased their annuities to induce their agreement. So, in August 1805, Harrison met again with the Delaware as well as the Miami, the Eel River Miami, the Potawatomi, and the Wea at Vincennes in particular, on the lands of his estate just north of the village. There, they all came to agreement over ceding and relinquishing forever the land south of the Vincennes Tract, which was the subject of the treaty of 1804. For this act came increases in annuities. One outcome of this agreement was the establishment in writing that the Miami, Eel River, and Wea all considered themselves members who had lands in common, not separate entities able to negotiate away the lands of the other. The treaty further stated that they as a whole were the rightful owners of lands above the Vincennes Tract and on the Wabash not ceded to the United States. For this, these tribes, plus the Potawatomi, agreed that the Delaware had the right to sell the land south of the Vincennes Tract. More treaties followed; by 1809, the tribes were essentially landlocked from the Ohio River. White settlers moved onto the newly acquired lands.

In the meantime, these treaties did not sit well with many tribes. While they fought over who owned lands, Tecumseh, the Shawnee leader, urged them to see land ownership as collective—that all tribes owned all the land, and no one chief had the right to sell it off to the United States. Tecumseh and his brother, the Prophet, were especially incensed over the Treaty of Fort Wayne in 1809, so much so that Tecumseh paid a call on Harrison at Vincennes in 1810. Tecumseh tried to provoke Harrison, but to no avail. Harrison stood firm against reversing any treaties, and more would come in the future. In the autumn of 1811, it was from Vincennes that Harrison launched and returned from his campaign up the Wabash against the Prophet's town near Tippecanoe.

Vincennes was founded in 1732 by Le Sieur de Vincennes, commander of the garrison he established. French settlement continued into the British era following the French and Indian Wars. French residents not infrequently intermarried with the Native Americans in the region, building not only family bonds but commercial ventures of the fur trade. During the American period, following the takeover of the city by George Rogers Clark, the Americans established Fort Knox. Later, with the encouragement of Harrison, Fort Knox was moved upriver about two miles from town to enable better oversight of river traffic and to relieve the town of the difficulties of soldiers on leave. When the war seemed likely, Harrison urged the garrison to return to the village.

Sally Colford Bennett

See also Battle of Tippecanoe; Harrison, William Henry; Jefferson, Thomas; Tecumseh; Treaty with the Delaware–August 18, 1804; Treaty with the Delaware, Etc.–June 7, 1803; Treaty with the Delaware, Etc.–August 21, 1805; Treaty with the Delaware, Etc.–September 30, 1809; Treaty with the Piankeshaw–August 27, 1804; Treaty with the Wyandot, Etc.–August 3, 1795; Wabash River, Indiana; Wells, William.

References and Further Reading

Esarey, Logan, ed. 1922. *Governor's Messages and Letters: Messages and Letters of William Henry Harrison*, vol. I. Indianapolis: Indiana Historical Collections.

Tanner, Helen Hornbeck, ed. 1987. *Atlas of Great Lakes Indian History.* Norman: University of Oklahoma Press.

Woehrmann, Paul. 1971. *At the Headwaters of the Maumee, a History of the Forts of Fort Wayne.* Indianapolis: Indiana Historical Society.

Wabash River, Indiana

Running west-southwest nearly five hundred miles from the middle of the state of Indiana to the south, where it empties into the Ohio River, the Wabash River gave title to treaties in 1826, 1828, 1834, 1838, and 1840 that eventually forced the removal of the Miami nation from Indiana. The Miami, who settled along the tributaries in the late seventeenth century and gave the Wabash its name, ceded land to the United States, which by 1830 had caused the Miami to retreat to a smaller reserve near Logansport. In return, the Miami received money and goods. Some Miami and mixed-blood Miami received individual land grants, giving them private ownership of smaller sections. With the Treaty of the Forks of the

Wabash in 1840, the Miami ceded the last of the tracts of their land south of the Wabash and were encouraged to migrate to the Kansas Territory.

As a water highway for centuries, the Wabash witnessed the intrusion first of French, then of British, and later of American traders. The Wabash provided a portage between its forks and the Miami village known as Kekionga, modern Fort Wayne, Indiana, where the St. Joseph and St. Mary rivers join to form the Maumee, which empties into Lake Erie. This portage allowed for nearly continuous travel from Canadian cities in the north to the Gulf of Mexico in the south. After the American Revolution, in 1787 the United States laid claim to the region and established Fort Knox at Vincennes along the banks of the Wabash. During these years, the Wabash Confederacy played an important role as white settlers came to the region. The Confederacy consisted of the Wea and the Piankashaw and also the Kickapoo, Mascouten, and Eel River tribes.

The Miami figured prominently in the Wabash region, where they had established villages on the Eel, Mississinewa, Tippecanoe, and Vermilion rivers. A powerful band of warriors, the Miami feared incursions of Americans on their land and raided American settlements in Kentucky, Ohio, and southern Indiana in the 1780s and early 1790s. Influential leaders brought prominence to the tribe in the late eighteenth century and the early decades of the nineteenth century, most notably Chief Little Turtle, who saw that the coming influx of U.S. settlers could not be stopped despite the Indians' making war on them. After the Battle of Fallen Timbers, Little Turtle and other tribal leaders capitulated, signing the Treaty of Greenville in 1795. In the following decade, as the rise of the Shawnee Prophet took hold of the younger generation of Miami, Little Turtle could not persuade them to keep peace with the Americans. He died as the War of 1812 broke out; he did not live to see its devastating effects on his people and their lands.

Much of the activity that contributed to the War of 1812 in the West occurred along the Wabash River. The land around the juncture of the Wabash and the Tippecanoe rivers was claimed by the Potawatomi under the leadership of Main Poc. It was he who offered to have the Shawnee Prophet (who was Tecumseh's brother and was also known as Tenskwatawa) and his followers settled there instead of remaining at their ever more crowded village near Greenville, Ohio. In 1808, the Shawnee Prophet established his village, known as Prophetstown, on the Wabash near the Tippecanoe River. He saw the village as a place where his followers could remain apart from the encroaching Americans, for many tribal nations—including the Potawatomi, the Shawnee, and some Miami—objected to the land acquisition treaties pushed upon them by William Henry Harrison, governor of Indiana Territory, during the first decade of the nineteenth century. Particularly aggravating to Tecumseh was the 1809 treaty at Fort Wayne. This treaty allowed large sections of land along the Wabash and north of Vincennes to come into the hands of the United States. The succession of treaties from 1803 through 1809 had essentially landlocked the tribes, cutting off access to the Ohio River and the state of Kentucky, creating a buffer between the tribes and the growing white settlement. Although many Miami sided with their own leaders, some found the message of the Shawnee brothers more promising.

Governor Harrison was concerned about the increasing concentration of warriors at Prophetstown, and his spies returned with false reports that the Prophet's influence was waning. In the summer of 1810, Harrison sent his own interpreter, Joseph Barron, to warn the Prophet of the strength of the U.S. Army and the militia. Neither deterred nor intimidated, Tecumseh came down the Wabash and arrived at Vincennes in August, accompanied by armed warriors. At first, he tried to reason with the governor by outlining his intention to form a confederation of tribes; he explained that it was essential to hold secure individual tribal lands and to have no more land cessions, that he objected to and would continue to reject the recent treaty at Fort Wayne until Harrison rescinded the treaty. During his weeklong council with Harrison, Tecumseh tried to make his point, but to no avail. Though Harrison offered to relay Tecumseh's concerns to President Madison, little more would be done.

As tensions increased in the Indiana Territory in 1811, the U.S. government sent the 4th Regiment of U.S. Infantry to shore up the defenses. In the course of Governor William Henry Harrison's autumn campaign against the Shawnee Prophet, the United States established another garrison, known as Fort Harrison, farther up the Wabash River at present-day Terre Haute, Indiana. The line of march to Prophetstown was along the Wabash. Combining U.S. regulars and militia forces from Kentucky and Indiana, the Battle of Tippecanoe took place in the early morning of November 7, 1811, not far from the Wabash. Though it began with a surprise attack by the combined native forces, the U.S. forces won the battle, going on to destroy the nearby village.

When the War of 1812 began, many tribes along the Wabash supported the British. Following the war, this disaffection with the United States contributed to the push for land cessions, then for an in-state reservation, and finally for total removal to Kansas Territory.

Sally Colford Bennett

See also Battle of Fallen Timbersm 1794; Battle of Tippecanoe; Harrison, William Henry; Tecumseh; Tippecanoe River, Indiana; Treaty with the Delaware, Etc.–September 30, 1809; Treaty with the Wyandot, Etc.–August 3, 1795; Vincennes, Indiana; Wells, William.

References and Further Readings

Edmunds, R. David. 1983. *The Shawnee Prophet*. Lincoln: University of Nebraska Press.

Edmunds, R. David. 1984. *Tecumseh and the Quest for Indian Leadership*. The Library of American Biography, ed. Oscar Handlin. Boston: Little, Brown.

Rafert, Stewart. 1996. *The Miami Indians of Indiana: A Persistent People 1654–1994*. Indianapolis: Indiana Historical Society.

Sugden, John. 1997. *Tecumseh, A Life*. New York: Henry Holt.

Tanner, Helen Hornbeck, ed. 1987. *Atlas of Great Lakes Indian History*. Norman: University of Oklahoma Press.

Primary Source Documents

Treaty with the Delawares, 1778

Sept. 17, 1778. | 7 Stat., 13.

Articles of agreement and confederation, made and entered into by Andrew and Thomas Lewis, Esquires, Commissioners for, and in Behalf of the United States of North-America of the one Part, and Capt. White Eyes, Capt. John Kill Buck, Junior, and Capt. Pipe, Deputies and Chief Men of the Delaware Nation of the other Part.

ARTICLE 1.

That all offences or acts of hostilities by one, or either of the contracting parties against the other, be mutually forgiven, and buried in the depth of oblivion, never more to be had in remembrance.

ARTICLE 2.

That a perpetual peace and friendship shall from henceforth take place, and subsist between the contracting parties aforesaid, through all succeeding generations: and if either of the parties are engaged in a just and necessary war with any other nation or nations, that then each shall assist the other in due proportion to their abilities, till their enemies are brought to reasonable terms of accommodation: and that if either of them shall discover any hostile designs forming against the other, they shall give the earliest notice thereof, that timeous measures may be taken to prevent their ill effect.

ARTICLE 3.

And whereas the United States are engaged in a just and necessary war, in defence and support of life, liberty and independence, against the King of England and his adherents, and as said King is yet possessed of several posts and forts on the lakes and other places, the reduction of which is of great importance to the peace and security of the contracting parties, and as the most practicable way for the troops of the United States to some of the posts and forts is by passing through the country of the Delaware nation, the aforesaid deputies, on behalf of themselves and their nation, do hereby stipulate and agree to give a free passage through their country to the troops aforesaid, and the same to conduct by the nearest and best ways to the posts, forts or towns of the enemies of the United States, affording to said troops such supplies of corn, meat, horses, or whatever may be in their power for the accommodation of such troops, on the commanding officer's, &c. paying, or engaging to pay, the full value of whatever they can supply

them with. And the said deputies, on the behalf of their nation, engage to join the troops of the United States aforesaid, with such a number of their best and most expert warriors as they can spare, consistent with their own safety, and act in concert with them; and for the better security of the old men, women and children of the aforesaid nation, whilst their warriors are engaged against the common enemy, it is agreed on the part of the United States, that a fort of sufficient strength and capacity be built at the expense of the said States, with such assistance as it may be in the power of the said Delaware Nation to give, in the most convenient place, and advantageous situation, as shall be agreed on by the commanding officer of the troops aforesaid, with the advice and concurrence of the deputies of the aforesaid Delaware Nation, which fort shall be garrisoned by such a number of the troops of the United States, as the commanding officer can spare for the present, and hereafter by such numbers, as the wise men of the United States in council, shall think most conducive to the common good.

ARTICLE 4.

For the better security of the peace and friendship now entered into by the contracting parties, against all infractions of the same by the citizens of either party, to the prejudice of the other, neither party shall proceed to the infliction of punishments on the citizens of the other, otherwise than by securing the offender or offenders by imprisonment, or any other competent means, till a fair and impartial trial can be had by judges or juries of both parties, as near as can be to the laws, customs and usages of the contracting parties and natural justice: The mode of such trials to be hereafter fixed by the wise men of the United States in Congress assembled, with the assistance of such deputies of the Delaware nation, as may be appointed to act in concert with them in adjusting this matter to their mutual liking. And it is further agreed between the parties aforesaid, that neither shall entertain or give countenance to the enemies of the other, or protect in their respective states, criminal fugitives, servants or slaves, but the same to apprehend, and secure and deliver to the State or States, to which such enemies, criminals, servants or slaves respectively belong.

ARTICLE 5.

Whereas the confederation entered into by the Delaware nation and the United States, renders the first dependent on the latter for all the articles of clothing, utensils and implements of war, and it is judged not only reasonable, but indispensably necessary, that the aforesaid Nation be supplied with such articles from time to time, as far as the United States may have it in their power, by a well-regulated trade, under the conduct of an intelligent, candid agent, with an adequate salary, one more influenced by the love of his country, and a constant attention to the duties of his department by promoting the common interest, than the sinister purposes of converting and binding all the duties of his office to his private emolument: Convinced of the necessity of such measures, the Commissioners of the United States, at the earnest solicitation of the deputies aforesaid, have engaged in behalf of the United States, that such a trade shall be afforded said nation, conducted on such principles of mutual interest as the wisdom of the United States in Congress assembled shall think most conducive to adopt for their mutual convenience.

ARTICLE 6.

Whereas the enemies of the United States have endeavored, by every artifice in their power, to possess the Indians in general with an opinion, that it is the design of the States aforesaid, to extirpate the Indians and take possession of their country: to obviate such false suggestion, the United States do engage to guarantee to the aforesaid nation of Delawares, and their heirs, all their territorial rights in the fullest and most ample manner, as it hath been bounded by former treaties, as long as they the said Delaware nation shall abide by, and hold fast the chain of friendship now entered into. And it is further agreed on between the contracting parties should it for the future be found conducive for the mutual interest of both parties to invite any other tribes who have been friends to the interest of the United States, to join the present confederation, and to form a state whereof the Delaware nation shall be the head, and have a representation in Congress: Provided, nothing contained in this article to be considered as conclusive until it meets with the approbation of Congress. And it is also the intent and meaning of this article, that no protection or countenance shall be afforded to any who are at present our enemies, by which they might escape the punishment they deserve.

In witness whereof, the parties have hereunto interchangeably set their hands and seals, at Fort Pitt,

September seventeenth, anno Domini one thousand seven hundred and seventy-eight.

Andrew Lewis, [L. S.],
Thomas Lewis, [L. S.],
White Eyes, his x mark, [L. S.],
The Pipe, his x mark, [L. S.],
John Kill Buck, his x mark, [L. S.].

In presence of—
Lach'n McIntosh, brigadier-general, commander the Western Department,
Daniel Brodhead, colonel Eighth Pennsylvania Regiment,
W. Crawford, colonel,
John Campbell,
John Stephenson,
John Gibson, colonel Thirteenth Virginia Regiment,
A. Graham, brigade major,
Lach. McIntosh, Jr., major brigade,
Benjamin Mills,
Joseph L. Finley, captain Eighth Pennsylvania Regiment,
John Finley, captain Eighth Pennsylvania Regiment.

Fort Stanwix Treaty, 1784

ARTICLE 1

Six hostages shall be immediately delivered to the commissioners by the said nations, to remain in possession of the United States, till all prisoners, white and black, which were taken by the said Senecas, Mohawks, Onondagas and Cayugas, or by any of them, in the late war, from among the people of the United States, shall be delivered up.

ARTICLE 2

The Oneida and Tuscarora nations shall be secured in the possession of the lands on which there are settled.

ARTICLE 3

A line shall be drawn, beginning at the mouth of a creek about four miles east of Niagara, called Oyonwayea, or Johnston's Landing-Place, upon the lake named by the Indians Oswego, and by us Ontario; from thence southerly in a direction always four miles east of the carrying-path, between Lake

Erie and Ontario, to the mouth of Tehoseroron or Buffaloe Creek on Lake Erie; then south to the north boundary of the state of Pennsylvania; thence west to the end of the said north boundary; then south along the west boundary of the said state, to the river Ohio; the said land from the mouth of the Oyonwayea to the Ohio, shall be the western boundary of the lands of the Six Nations, so that the Six Nations shall and do yield to the United States, all claims to the country west of the said boundary, and then they shall be secured in the peaceful possession of the lands they inhabit east and north of the same, reserving only six miles square round the fort of Oswego, to the United States, for the support of the same.

ARTICLE 4

The Commissioners of the United States, in consideration of the present circumstances of the Six Nations, and in executing of the humane and liberal views of the United States upon the signing of the above articles, will order goods to be delivered to the said Six Nations for their use and comfort.

Oliver Wolcott
Richard Butler
Arthur Lee

Mohawks:
Onogwendahonji, his x mark
Touighnatogon, his x mark

Onondagas:
Oheadarighton, his x mark
Kendarindgon, his x mark

Senekas:
Tayagonendagighti, his x mark
Tehonwaeaghrigagi, his x mark

Oneidas:
Otyadonenghti, his x mark
Dagaheari, his x mark

Cayuga:
Oraghgoanendagen, his x mark

Tuscaroras:
Ononghsawenghti, his x mark,
Tharondawagon, his x mark

Seneka Abeal:
Kayenthoghke, his x mark

Witness:
Sam. Jo. Atlee
James Dean
Wm. Maclay
Saml. Montgomery
Fras. Johnston
Derick Lane, captain
Pennsylvaina Commissioners
John Mercer, lieutenant
Aaron Hill
William Pennington, lieutenant
Alexander Campbell
Mahlon Hord, ensign
Saml. Kirkland, missionary
Haugh Peeles

Treaty with the Cherokee, 1785
Nov. 28, 1785. | 7 Stat., 18.

Articles concluded at Hopewell, on the Keowee, between Benjamin Hawkins, Andrew Pickens, Joseph Martin, and Lachlan M'Intosh, Commissioners Plenipotentiary of the United States of America, of the one Part, and the Head-Men and Warriors of all the Cherokees of the other.

The Commissioners Plenipotentiary of the United States, in Congress assembled, give peace to all the Cherokees, and receive them into the favor and protection of the United States of America, on the following conditions:

ARTICLE 1.

The Head-Men and Warriors of all the Cherokees shall restore all the prisoners, citizens of the United States, or subjects of their allies, to their entire liberty: They shall also restore all the Negroes, and all other property taken during the late war from the citizens, to such person, and at such time and place, as the Commissioners shall appoint.

ARTICLE 2.

The Commissioners of the United States in Congress assembled, shall restore all the prisoners taken from the Indians, during the late war, to the Head-Men and Warriors of the Cherokees, as early as is practicable.

ARTICLE 3.

The said Indians for themselves and their respective tribes and towns do acknowledge all the Cherokees to be under the protection of the United States of America, and of no other sovereign whosoever.

ARTICLE 4.

The boundary allotted to the Cherokees for their hunting grounds, between the said Indians and the citizens of the United States, within the limits of the United States of America, is, and shall be the following, viz. Beginning at the mouth of Duck river, on the Tennessee; thence running north-east to the ridge dividing the waters running into Cumberland from those running into the Tennessee; thence eastwardly along the said ridge to a north-east line to be run, which shall strike the river Cumberland forty miles above Nashville; thence along the said line to the river; thence up the said river to the ford where the Kentucky road crosses the river; thence to Campbell's line, near Cumberland gap; thence to the mouth of Claud's creek on Holstein; thence to the Chimney-top mountain; thence to Camp-creek, near the mouth of Big Limestone, on Nolichuckey; thence a southerly course six miles to a mountain; thence south to the North-Carolina line; thence to the South-Carolina Indian boundary, and along the same south-west over the top of the Oconee mountain till it shall strike Tugaloo river; thence a direct line to the top of the Currohee mountain; thence to the head of the south fork of Oconee river.

ARTICLE 5.

If any citizen of the United States, or other person not being an Indian, shall attempt to settle on any of the lands westward or southward of the said boundary which are hereby allotted to the Indians for their hunting grounds, or having already settled and will not remove from the same within six months after the ratification of this treaty, such person shall forfeit the protection of the United States, and the Indians may punish him or not as they please: Provided nevertheless, That this article shall not extend to the people settled between the fork of French Broad and Holstein rivers, whose particular situation shall be transmitted to the United States in Congress assembled for their decision thereon, which the Indians agree to abide by.

ARTICLE 6.

If any Indian or Indians, or person residing among them, or who shall take refuge in their nation, shall commit a robbery, or murder, or other capital crime, on any citizen of the United States, or person under their protection, the nation, or the tribe to which such offender or offenders may belong, shall be bound to deliver him or them up to be punished according to the ordinances of the United States; Provided, that the punishment shall not be greater than if the robbery or murder, or other capital crime had been committed by a citizen on a citizen.

ARTICLE 7.

If any citizen of the United States, or person under their protection, shall commit a robbery or murder, or other capital crime, on any Indian, such offender or offenders shall be punished in the same manner as if the murder or robbery, or other capital crime, had been committed on a citizen of the United States; and the punishment shall be in presence of some of the Cherokees, if any shall attend at the time and place, and that they may have an opportunity so to do, due notice of the time of such intended punishment shall be sent to some one of the tribes.

ARTICLE 8.

It is understood that the punishment of the innocent under the idea of retaliation, is unjust, and shall not be practiced on either side, except where there is a manifest violation of this treaty; and then it shall be preceded first by a demand of justice, and if refused, then by a declaration of hostilities.

ARTICLE 9.

For the benefit and comfort of the Indians, and for the prevention of injuries or oppressions on the part of the citizens or Indians, the United States in Congress assembled shall have the sole and exclusive right of regulating the trade with the Indians, and managing all their affairs in such manner as they think proper.

ARTICLE 10.

Until the pleasure of Congress be known, respecting the ninth article, all traders, citizens of the United States, shall have liberty to go to any of the tribes or towns of the Cherokees to trade with them, and they shall be protected in their persons and property, and kindly treated.

ARTICLE 11.

The said Indians shall give notice to the citizens of the United States, of any designs which they may know or suspect to be formed in any neighboring tribe, or by any person whosoever, against the peace, trade or interest of the United States.

ARTICLE 12.

That the Indians may have full confidence in the justice of the United States, respecting their interests, they shall have the right to send a deputy of their choice, whenever they think fit, to Congress.

ARTICLE 13.

The hatchet shall be forever buried, and the peace given by the United States, and friendship re-established between the said states on the one part, and all the Cherokees on the other, shall be universal; and the contracting parties shall use their utmost endeavors to maintain the peace given as aforesaid, and friendship re-established.

In witness of all and every thing herein determined, between the United States of America and all the Cherokees, we, their underwritten Commissioners, by virtue of our full powers, have signed this definitive treaty, and have caused our seals to be hereunto affixed. Done at Hopewell, on the Keowee, this twenty-eighth of November, in the year of our Lord one thousand seven hundred and eighty-five.

Benjamin Hawkins, [L. S.],
And'w Pickens, [L. S.],
Jos. Martin, [L. S.],
Lach'n McIntosh Koatohee, or Corn Tassel of Toquo, his x mark, [L. S.],
Scholauetta, or Hanging Man of Chota, his x mark, [L. S.],
Tuskegatahu, or Long Fellow of Chistohoe, his x mark, [L. S.],
Ooskwha, or Abraham of Chilkowa, his x mark, [L. S.],
Kolakusta, or Prince of Noth, his x mark, [L. S.],
Newota, or the Gritzs of Chicamaga, his x mark, [L. S.],
Konatota, or the Rising Fawn of Highwassay, his x mark, [L. S.],
Tuckasee, or Young Terrapin of Allajoy, his x mark, [L. S.],
Toostaka, or the Waker of Oostanawa, his x mark, [L. S.],
Untoola, or Gun Rod of Seteco, his x mark, [L. S.],
Unsuokanail, Buffalo White Calf New Cussee, his x mark, [L. S.],
Kostayeak, or Sharp Fellow Wataga, his x mark, [L. S.],
Chonosta, of Cowe, his x mark, [L. S.],

Chescoonwho, Bird in Close of Tomotlug, his x mark, [L. S.],
Tuckasee, or Terrapin of Hightowa, his x mark, [L. S.],
Chesetoa, or the Rabbit of Tlacoa, his x mark, [L. S.],
Chesecotetona, or Yellow Bird of the Pine Log, his x mark, [L. S.],
Sketaloska, Second Man of Tillico, his x mark, [L. S.],
Chokasatahe, Chickasaw Killer Tasonta, his x mark, [L. S.],
Onanoota, of Koosoate, his x mark, [L. S.],
Ookoseta, or Sower Mush of Kooloque, his x mark, [L. S.],
Umatooetha, the Water Hunter Choikamawga, his x mark, [L. S.],
Wyuka, of Lookout Mountain, his x mark, [L. S.],
Tulco, or Tom of Chatuga, his x mark, [L. S.],
Will, of Akoha, his x mark, [L. S.],
Necatee, of Sawta, his x mark, [L. S.],
Amokontakona, Kutcloa, his x mark, [L. S.],
Kowetatahee, in Frog Town, his x mark, [L. S.],
Keukuck, Talcoa, his x mark, [L. S.],
Tulatiska, of Chaway, his x mark, [L. S.],
Wooaluka, the Waylayer, Chota, his x mark, [L. S.],
Tatliusta, or Porpoise of Tilassi, his x mark, [L. S.],
John, of Little Tallico, his x mark, [L. S.],
Skeleak, his x mark, [L. S.],
Akonoluchta, the Cabin, his x mark, [L. S.],
Cheanoka, of Kawetakac, his x mark, [L. S.],
Yellow Bird, his x mark, [L. S.].

Witness:
Wm. Blount,
Sam'l Taylor, Major,
John Owen,
Jess. Walton,
Jno. Cowan, capt. comm'd't,
Thos. Gregg,
W. Hazzard,
James Madison,
Arthur Cooley,
Sworn interpreters.

Treaty with the Six Nations, 1794

Nov. 11, 1794. | 7 Stat., 44. | Proclamation, Jan. 21, 1795.

A Treaty between the United States of America, and the Tribes of Indians called the Six Nations.

The President of the United States having determined to hold a conference with the Six Nations of Indians, for the purpose of removing from their minds all causes of complaint, and establishing a firm and permanent friendship with them; and Timothy Pickering being appointed sole agent for that purpose; and the agent having met and conferred with the Sachems, Chiefs and Warriors of the Six Nations, in a general council: Now, in order to accomplish the good design of this conference, the parties have agreed on the following articles; which, when ratified by the President, with the advice and consent of the Senate of the United States, shall be binding on them and the Six Nations.

ARTICLE 1.
Peace and friendship are hereby firmly established, and shall be perpetual, between the United States and the Six Nations.

ARTICLE 2.
The United States acknowledge the lands reserved to the Oneida, Onondaga and Cayuga Nations, in their respective treaties with the state of New-York, and called their reservations, to be their property; and the United States will never claim the same, nor disturb them or either of the Six Nations, nor their Indian friends residing thereon and united with them, in the free use and enjoyment thereof: but the said reservations shall remain theirs, until they choose to sell the same to the people of the United States, who have the right to purchase.

ARTICLE 3.
The land of the Seneka nation is bounded as follows: Beginning on Lake Ontario, at the north-west corner of the land they sold to Oliver Phelps, the line runs westerly along the lake, as far as O-yong-wong-yeh Creek, at Johnson's Landing-place, about four miles eastward from the fort of Niagara; then southerly up that creek to its main fork, then straight to the main fork of Stedman's creek, which empties into the river Niagara, above fort Schlosser, and then onward, from that fork, continuing the same straight course, to that river; (this line, from the mouth of O-yong-wong-yeh Creek to the river Niagara, above fort Schlosser, being the eastern boundary of a strip of land, extending from the same line to Niagara river, which the Seneka nation ceded to the King of Great-Britain, at a treaty held about thirty years ago, with Sir William Johnson;) then the line runs along the river Niagara to Lake Erie; then along Lake Erie to the north-east corner of a triangular piece of land which the United States conveyed to the state of Pennsylvania, as by the President's patent, dated the third day of March, 1792; then due south to the northern boundary of that state; then due east to the south-west corner of the land sold by the Seneka nation to Oliver Phelps; and then north and northerly, along Phelps's line, to the place of beginning on Lake Ontario. Now, the United States acknowledge all the land within the aforementioned boundaries, to be the property of the Seneka nation; and the United States will never claim the same, nor disturb the Seneka nation, nor any of the Six Nations, or of their Indian friends residing thereon and united with them, in the free use and enjoyment thereof: but it shall remain theirs, until they choose to sell the same to the people of the United States, who have the right to purchase.

ARTICLE 4.
The United States having thus described and acknowledged what lands belong to the Oneidas, Onondagas, Cayugas and Senekas, and engaged never to claim the same, nor to disturb them, or any of the Six Nations, or their Indian friends residing thereon and united with them, in the free use and enjoyment thereof: Now, the Six Nations, and each of them, hereby engage that they will never claim any other lands within the boundaries of the United States; nor ever disturb the people of the United States in the free use and enjoyment thereof.

ARTICLE 5.
The Seneka nation, all others of the Six Nations concurring, cede to the United States the right of making a wagon road from Fort Schlosser to Lake Erie, as far south as Buffaloe Creek; and the people of the United States shall have the free and undisturbed use of this road, for the purposes of travelling and transportation. And the Six Nations, and each of them, will forever allow to the people of the United States, a free passage through their lands, and the

free use of the harbors and rivers adjoining and within their respective tracts of land, for the passing and securing of vessels and boats, and liberty to land their cargoes where necessary for their safety.

ARTICLE 6.

In consideration of the peace and friendship hereby established, and of the engagements entered into by the Six Nations; and because the United States desire, with humanity and kindness, to contribute to their comfortable support; and to render the peace and friendship hereby established, strong and perpetual; the United States now deliver to the Six Nations, and the Indians of the other nations residing among and united with them, a quantity of goods of the value of ten thousand dollars. And for the same considerations, and with a view to promote the future welfare of the Six Nations, and of their Indian friends aforesaid, the United States will add the sum of three thousand dollars to the one thousand five hundred dollars, heretofore allowed them by an article ratified by the President, on the twenty-third day of April, 1792; a making in the whole, four thousand five hundred dollars; which shall be expended yearly forever, in purchasing clothing, domestic animals, implements of husbandry, and other utensils suited to their circumstances, and in compensating useful artificers, who shall reside with or near them, and be employed for their benefit. The immediate application of the whole annual allowance now stipulated, to be made by the superintendent appointed by the President for the affairs of the Six Nations, and their Indian friends aforesaid.

ARTICLE 7.

Lest the firm peace and friendship now established should be interrupted by the misconduct of individuals, the United States and Six Nations agree, that for injuries done by individuals on either side, no private revenge or retaliation shall take place; but, instead thereof, complaint shall be made by the party injured, to the other: By the Six Nations or any of them, to the President of the United States, or the Superintendent by him appointed: and by the Superintendent, or other person appointed by the President, to the principal chiefs of the Six Nations, or of the nation to which the offender belongs: and such prudent measures shall then be pursued as shall be necessary to preserve our peace and friendship unbroken; until the legislature (or great council) of the United States shall make other equitable provision for the purpose.

NOTE. It is clearly understood by the parties to this treaty, that the annuity stipulated in the sixth article, is to be applied to the benefit of such of the Six Nations and of their Indian friends united with them as aforesaid, as do or shall reside within the boundaries of the United States: For the United States do not interfere with nations, tribes or families, of Indians elsewhere resident.

In witness whereof, the said Timothy Pickering, and the sachems and war chiefs of the said Six Nations, have hereto set their hands and seals.

Done at Konondaigua, in the State of New York, the eleventh day of November, in the year one thousand seven hundred and ninety-four.

Timothy Pickering, [L. S.],
Onoyeahnee, his x mark, [L. S.],
Konneatorteeooh, his x mark, or Handsome
    Lake, [L. S.],
Tokenhyouhau, his x mark, alias Captain
    Key, [L. S.],
Oneshauee, his x mark, [L. S.],
Hendrick Aupaumut, [L. S.],
David Neesoonhuk, his x mark, [L. S.],
Kanatsoyh, alias Nicholas Kusik, [L. S.],
Sohhonteoquent, his x mark, [L. S.],
Ooduhtsait, his x mark, [L. S.],
Konoohqung, his x mark, [L. S.],
Tossonggaulolus, his x mark, [L. S.],
John Skenendoa, his x mark, [L. S.],
Oneatorleeooh, his x mark, [L. S.],
Kussauwatau, his x mark, [L. S.],
Eyootenyootauook, his x mark, [L. S.],
Kohnyeaugong, his x mark, alias Jake Stroud,
    [L. S.],
Shaguiesa, his x mark, [L. S.],
Teeroos, his x mark, alias Captain Prantup,
    [L. S.],
Sooshaoowau, his x mark, [L. S.],
Henry Young Brant, his x mark, [L. S.],
Sonhyoowauna, his x mark, or Big Sky, [L. S.],
Onaahhah, his x mark, [L. S.],
Hotoshahenh, his x mark, [L. S.],
Kaukondanaiya, his x mark, [L. S.],
Nondiyauka, his x mark, [L. S.],
Kossishtowau, his x mark, [L. S.],
Oojaugenta, his x mark, or Fish Carrier, [L. S.],

Toheonggo, his x mark, [L. S.],
Ootaguasso, his x mark, [L. S.],
Joonondauwaonch, his x mark, [L. S.],
Kiyauhaonh, his x mark, [L. S.],
Ootaujeaugenh, his x mark, or Broken Axe,
    [L. S.],
Tauhoondos, his x mark, or Open the Way,
    [L. S.],
Twaukewasha, his x mark, [L. S.],
Sequidongquee, his x mark, alias Little
    Beard, [L. S.],
Kodjeote, his x mark, or Half Town, [L. S.],
Kenjauaugus, his x mark, or Stinking Fish,
    [L. S.],
Soonohquaukau, his x mark, [L. S.],
Twenniyana, his x mark, [L. S.],
Jishkaaga, his x mark, or Green Grasshopper,
    alias Little Billy, [L. S.],
Tuggehshotta, his x mark, [L. S.],
Tehongyagauna, his x mark, [L. S.],
Tehongyoowush, his x mark, [L. S.],
Konneyoowesot, his x mark, [L. S.],
Tioohquottakauna, his x mark, or Woods on
    Fire, [L. S.],
Taoundaudeesh, his x mark, [L. S.],
Honayawus, his x mark, alias Farmer's
    Brother, [L. S.],
Soggooyawauthau, his x mark, alias Red
    Jacket, [L. S.],
Konyootiayoo, his x mark, [L. S.],
Sauhtakaongyees, his x mark, or Two Skies of
    a length, [L. S.],
Ounnashattakau, his x mark, [L. S.],
Kaungyanehquee, his x mark, [L. S.],
Sooayoowau, his x mark, [L. S.],
Kaujeagaonh, his x mark, or Heap of Dogs,
    [L. S.],
Soonoohshoowau, his x mark, [L. S.],
Thaoowaunias, his x mark, [L. S.],
Soonongjoowau, his x mark, [L. S.],
Kiantwhauka, his x mark, alias Cornplanter,
    [L. S.]
Kaunehshonggoo, his x mark, [L. S.].

Witnesses:
Israel Chapin,
William Shepard, jr.,
James Smedley,
John Wickham,
Augustus Porter,
James K. Garnsey,
William Ewing,

Israel Chapin, jr.,
Horatio Jones,
Joseph Smith,
Jasper Parish.
Interpreters.
Henry Abeele.

Treaty with the Sauk and Foxes, 1804

Nov. 3, 1804. | 7 Stat., 84. | Ratified Jan. 25, 1805. | Proclaimed Feb. 21, 1805.
A treaty between the United States of America and the United tribes of Sac and Fox Indians.

ARTICLES of a treaty made at St. Louis in the district of Louisiana between William Henry Harrison, governor of the Indiana territory and of the district of Louisiana, superintendent of Indian affairs for the said territory and district, and commissioner plenipotentiary of the United States for concluding any treaty or treaties which may be found necessary with any of the north western tribes of Indians of the one part, and the chiefs and head men of the united Sac and Fox tribes of the other part.

ARTICLE 1.
The United States receive the united Sac and Fox tribes into their friendship and protection, and the said tribes agree to consider themselves under the protection of the United States, and of no other power whatsoever.

ARTICLE 2.
The general boundary line between the lands of the United States and of the said Indian tribes shall be as follows, to wit: Beginning at a point on the Missouri river opposite to the mouth of the Gasconade river; thence in a direct course so as to strike the river Jeffreon at the distance of thirty miles from its mouth, and down the said Jeffreon to the Mississippi, thence up the Mississippi to the mouth of the Ouisconsing river and up the same to a point which shall be thirty-six miles in a direct line from the mouth of the said river, thence by a direct line to the point where the Fox river (a branch of the Illinois) leaves the small lake called Sakaegan, thence down the Fox river to the Illinois river, and down the same

to the Mississippi. And the said tribes, for and in consideration of the friendship and protection of the United States which is now extended to them, of the goods (to the value of two thousand two hundred and thirty-four dollars and fifty cents) which are now delivered, and of the annuity hereinafter stipulated to be paid, do hereby cede and relinquish forever to the United States, all the lands included within the above-described boundary.

ARTICLE 3.

In consideration of the cession and relinquishment of land made in the preceding article, the United States will deliver to the said tribes at the town of St. Louis or some other convenient place on the Mississippi yearly and every year goods suited to the circumstances of the Indians of the value of one thousand dollars (six hundred of which are intended for the Sacs and four hundred for the Foxes) reckoning that value at the first cost of the goods in the city or place in the United States where they shall be procured. And if the said tribes shall hereafter at an annual delivery of the goods aforesaid, desire that a part of their annuity should be furnished in domestic animals, implements of husbandry and other utensils convenient for them, or in compensation to useful artificers who may reside with or near them, and be employed for their benefit, the same shall at the subsequent annual delivery be furnished accordingly.

ARTICLE 4.

The United States will never interrupt the said tribes in the possession of the lands which they rightfully claim, but will on the contrary protect them in the quiet enjoyment of the same against their own citizens and against all other white persons who may intrude upon them. And the said tribes do hereby engage that they will never sell their lands or any part thereof to any sovereign power, but the United States, nor to the citizens or subjects of any other sovereign power, nor to the citizens of the United States.

ARTICLE 5.

Lest the friendship which is now established between the United States and the said Indian tribes should be interrupted by the misconduct of individuals, it is hereby agreed that for injuries done by individuals no private revenge or retaliation shall take place, but, instead thereof, complaints shall be made by the party injured to the other—by the said tribes or either of them to the superintendent of Indian affairs or one of his deputies, and by the superintendent or other person appointed by the President, to the chiefs of the said tribes. And it shall be the duty of the said chiefs upon complaint being made as aforesaid to deliver up the person or persons against whom the complaint is made, to the end that he or they may be punished agreeably to the laws of the state or territory where the offence may have been committed; and in like manner if any robbery, violence or murder shall be committed on any Indian or Indians belonging to the said tribes or either of them, the person or persons so offending shall be tried, and if found guilty, punished in the like manner as if the injury had been done to a white man. And it is further agreed, that the chiefs of the said tribes shall, to the utmost of their power exert themselves to recover horses or other property which may be stolen from any citizen or citizens of the United States by any individual or individuals of their tribes, and the property so recovered shall be forthwith delivered to the superintendent or other person authorized to receive it, that it may be restored to the proper owner; and in cases where the exertions of the chiefs shall be ineffectual in recovering the property stolen as aforesaid, if sufficient proof can be obtained that such property was actually stolen by any Indian or Indians belonging to the said tribes or either of them, the United States may deduct from the annuity of the said tribes a sum equal to the value of the property which has been stolen. And the United States hereby guarantee to any Indian or Indians of the said tribes a full indemnification for any horses or other property which may be stolen from them by any of their citizens; provided that the property so stolen cannot be recovered and that sufficient proof is produced that it was actually stolen by a citizen of the United States.

ARTICLE 6.

If any citizen of the United States or other white person should form a settlement upon lands which are the property of the Sac and Fox tribes, upon complaint being made thereof to the superintendent or other person having charge of the affairs of the Indians, such intruder shall forthwith be removed.

ARTICLE 7.

As long as the lands which are now ceded to the United States remain their property, the Indians belonging to the said tribes, shall enjoy the privilege of living and hunting upon them.

ARTICLE 8.
As the laws of the United States regulating trade and intercourse with the Indian tribes, are already extended to the country inhabited by the Saukes and Foxes, and as it is provided by those laws that no person shall reside as a trader in the Indian country without a license under the hand [and] seal of the superintendent of Indian affairs, or other person appointed for the purpose by the President, the said tribes do promise and agree that they will not suffer any trader to reside amongst them without such license; and that they will from time to time give notice to the superintendent or to the agent for their tribes of all the traders that may be in their country.

ARTICLE 9.
In order to put a stop to the abuses and impositions which are practiced upon the said tribes by the private traders, the United States will at a convenient time establish a trading house or factory where the individuals of the said tribes can be supplied with goods at a more reasonable rate than they have been accustomed to procure them.

ARTICLE 10.
In order to evince the sincerity of their friendship and affection for the United States and a respectful deference for their advice by an act which will not only be acceptable to them but to the common Father of all the nations of the earth; the said tribes do hereby solemnly promise and agree that they will put an end to the bloody war which has heretofore raged between their tribes and those of the Great and Little Osages. And for the purpose of burying the tomahawk and renewing the friendly intercourse between themselves and the Osages, a meeting of their respective chiefs shall take place, at which under the direction of the above-named commissioner or the agent of Indian affairs residing at St. Louis, an adjustment of all their differences shall be made and peace established upon a firm and lasting basis.

ARTICLE 11.
As it is probable that the government of the United States will establish a military post at or near the mouth of the Ouisconsing river; and as the land on the lower side of the river may not be suitable for that purpose, the said tribes hereby agree that a fort may be built either on the upper side of the Ouiscon-

sing or on the right bank of the Mississippi, as the one or the other may be found most convenient; and a tract of land not exceeding two miles square shall be given for that purpose. And the said tribes do further agree, that they will at all times allow to traders and other persons travelling through their country under the authority of the United States a free and safe passage for themselves and their property of every description. And that for such passage they shall at no time and on no account whatever be subject to any toll or exaction.

ARTICLE 12.
This treaty shall take effect and be obligatory on the contracting parties as soon as the same shall have been ratified by the President by and with the advice and consent of the Senate of the United States.

In testimony whereof, the said William Henry Harrison, and the chiefs and head men of the said Sac and Fox tribes, have hereunto set their hands and affixed their seals.

Done at Saint Louis, in the district of Louisiana, on the third day of November, one thousand eight hundred and four, and of the independence of the United States the twenty-ninth.

> William Henry Harrison, [L. S.],
> Layauvois, or Lalyurva, his x mark, [L. S.],
> Pashepaho, or the giger, his x mark, [L. S.],
> Quashquame, or jumping fish, his x mark, [L. S.],
> Outchequaka, or sun fish, his x mark, [L. S.],
> Hahshequarhiqua, or the bear, his x mark, [L. S.].

In presence of (the words "a branch of the Illinois," in the third line of the second article, and the word "forever," in the fifth line of the same article, being first interlined)—

> Wm. Prince, secretary to the commissioner,
> John Griffin, one of the judges of the Indiana Territory,
> J. Bruff, major artillery, United States,
> Amos Stoddard, captain, Corps Artillerists,
> P. Chouteau,
> Vigo,
> S. Warrel, lieutenant, United States Artillery,
> D. Delamay,
> Joseph Barron,
> Hypolite Bolen, his x mark.
> Sworn interpreters.

ADDITIONAL ARTICLE.

It is agreed that nothing in this treaty contained, shall affect the claim of any individual or individuals who may have obtained grants of land from the Spanish government, and which are not included within the general boundary line laid down in this treaty, provided that such grant have at any time been made known to the said tribes and recognized by them.

Treaty with the Sioux, Etc., 1825

Aug. 19, 1825. | 7 Stat., 272. | Proclamation.
Feb. 6, 1826.

Treaty with the Sioux and Chippewa, Sacs and Fox, Menominie, Ioway, Sioux, Winnebago, and a portion of the Ottawa, Chippewa, and Potawattomie, Tribes.

THE United States of America have seen with much regret, that wars have for many years been carried on between the Sioux and the Chippewas, and more recently between the confederated tribes of Sacs and Foxes, and the Sioux; and also between the Ioways and Sioux; which, if not terminated, may extend to the other tribes, and involve the Indians upon the Missouri, the Mississippi, and the Lakes, in general hostilities. In order, therefore, to promote peace among these tribes, and to establish boundaries among them and the other tribes who live in their vicinity, and thereby to remove all causes of future difficulty, the United States have invited the Chippewa, Sac, and Fox, Menominie, Ioway, Sioux, Winnebago, and a portion of the Ottawa, Chippewa and Potawatomie Tribes of Indians living upon the Illinois, to assemble together, and in a spirit of mutual conciliation to accomplish these objects; and to aid therein, have appointed William Clark and Lewis Cass, Commissioners on their part, who have met the Chiefs, Warriors, and Representatives of the said tribes, and portion of tribes, at Prairie des Chiens, in the Territory of Michigan, and after full deliberation, the said tribes, and portions of tribes, have agreed with the United States, and with one another, upon the following articles.

ARTICLE 1.

There shall be a firm and perpetual peace between the Sioux and Chippewas; between the Sioux and the confederated tribes of Sacs and Foxes; and between the Ioways and the Sioux.

ARTICLE 2.

It is agreed between the confederated Tribes of the Sacs and Foxes, and the Sioux, that the Line between their respective countries shall be as follows: Commencing at the mouth of the Upper Ioway River, on the west bank of the Mississippi, and ascending the said Ioway river, to its left fork; thence up that fork to its source; thence crossing the fork of Red Cedar River, in a direct line to the second or upper fork of the Desmoines river; and thence in a direct line to the lower fork of the Calumet river; and down that river to its juncture with the Missouri river. But the Yancton band of the Sioux tribe, being principally interested in the establishment of the line from the Forks of the Desmoines to the Missouri, and not being sufficiently represented to render the definitive establishment of that line proper, it is expressly declared that the line from the forks of the Desmoines to the forks of the Calumet river, and down that river to the Missouri, is not to be considered as settled until the assent of the Yancton band shall be given thereto. And if the said band should refuse their assent, the arrangement of that portion of the boundary line shall be void, and the rights of the parties to the country bounded thereby, shall be the same as if no provision had been made for the extension of the line west of the forks of the Desmoines. And the Sacs and Foxes relinquish to the tribes interested therein, all their claim to land on the east side of the Mississippi river.

ARTICLE 3.

The Ioways accede to the arrangement between the Sacs and Foxes, and the Sioux; but it is agreed between the Ioways and the confederated tribes of the Sacs and Foxes, that the Ioways have a just claim to a portion of the country between the boundary line described in the next preceding article, and the Missouri and Mississippi; and that the said Ioways, and Sacs and Foxes, shall peaceably occupy the same, until some satisfactory arrangement can be made between them for a division of their respective claims to country.

ARTICLE 4.

The Ottoes not being represented at this Council, and the Commissioners for the United States being anxious that justice should be done to all parties, and having reason to believe that the Ottoes have a just claim to a portion of the country upon the Missouri, east and south of the boundary line dividing the Sacs and Foxes and the Ioways, from the Sioux, it is agreed between the parties interested therein, and the United States, that the claim of the Ottoes shall not be affected by any thing herein contained; but the same shall remain as valid as if this treaty had not been formed.

ARTICLE 5.
It is agreed between the Sioux and the Chippewas, that the line dividing their respective countries shall commence at the Chippewa River, half a day's march below the falls; and from thence it shall run to Red Cedar River, immediately below the falls; from thence to the St. Croix River, which it strikes at a place called the standing cedar, about a day's paddle in a canoe, above the Lake at the mouth of that river; thence passing between two lakes called by the Chippewas "Green Lakes," and by the Sioux "the lakes they bury the Eagles in," and from thence to the standing cedar that "the Sioux Split"; thence to Rum River, crossing it at the mouth of a small creek called Choaking creek, a long day's march from the Mississippi; thence to a point of woods that projects into the prairie, half a day's march from the Mississippi; thence in a straight line to the mouth of the first river which enters the Mississippi on its west side above the mouth of Sac river; thence ascending the said river (above the mouth of Sac river) to a small lake at its source; thence in a direct line to a lake at the head of Prairie river, which is supposed to enter the Crow Wing river on its South side; thence to Otter-tail lake Portage; thence to said Ottertail lake, and down through the middle thereof, to its outlet; thence in a direct line, so as to strike Buffalo river, half way from its source to its mouth, and down the said river to Red River; thence descending Red river to the mouth of Outard or Goose creek: The eastern boundary of the Sioux commences opposite the mouth of Ioway river, on the Mississippi, runs back two or three miles to the bluffs, follows the bluffs, crossing Bad axe river, to the mouth of Black river, and from Black river to half a day's march below the Falls of the Chippewa River.

ARTICLE 6.
It is agreed between the Chippewas and Winnebagoes, so far as they are mutually interested therein, that the southern boundary line of the Chippewa country shall commence on the Chippewa river aforesaid, half a day's march below the falls on that river, and run thence to the source of Clear Water river, a branch of the Chippewa; thence south to Black river; thence to a point where the woods pro-

ject into the meadows, and thence to the Plover Portage of the Ouisconsin.

ARTICLE 7.
It is agreed between the Winnebagoes and the Sioux, Sacs and Foxes, Chippewas and Ottawas, Chippewas and Potawatomies of the Illinois, that the Winnebago country shall be bounded as follows: south easterly by Rock River, from its source near the Winnebago lake, to the Winnebago village, about forty miles above its mouth; westerly by the east line of the tract, lying upon the Mississippi, herein secured to the Ottawa, Chippewa and Potawatomie Indians, of the Illinois; and also by the high bluff, described in the Sioux boundary, and running north to Black river: from this point the Winnebagoes claim up Black river, to a point due west from the source of the left fork of the Ouisconsin; thence to the source of the said fork, and down the same to the Ouisconsin; thence down the Ouisconsin to the portage, and across the portage to Fox river; thence down Fox river to the Winnebago lake, and to the grand Kan Kanlin, including in their claim the whole of Winnebago lake; but, for the causes stated in the next article, this line from Black river must for the present be left indeterminate.

ARTICLE 8.
The representatives of the Menominies not being sufficiently acquainted with their proper boundaries, to settle the same definitively, and some uncertainty existing in consequence of the cession made by that tribe upon Fox River and Green Bay, to the New York Indians, it is agreed between the said Menominie tribe, and the Sioux, Chippewas, Winnebagoes, Ottawa, Chippewa and Potawatomie Indians of the Illinois, that the claim of the Menominies to any portion of the land within the boundaries allotted to either of the said tribes, shall not be barred by any stipulation herein; but the same shall remain as valid as if this treaty had not been concluded. It is, however, understood that the general claim of the Menominies is bounded on the north by the Chippewa country, on the east by Green Bay and lake Michigan extending as far south as Millawaukee river, and on the West they claim to Black River.

ARTICLE 9.
The country secured to the Ottawa, Chippewa, and Potawatomie tribes of the Illinois, is bounded as follows: Beginning at the Winnebago village, on Rock river, forty miles from its mouth and running thence

down the Rock river to a line which runs from Lake Michigan to the Mississippi, and with that line to the Mississippi, opposite to Rock Island; thence up that river to the United States reservation, at the mouth of the Ouisconsin; thence with the south and east lines of the said reservation to the Ouisconsin; thence, southerly, passing the heads of the small streams emptying into the Mississippi, to the Rock river at the Winnebago village. The Illinois Indians have also a just claim to a portion of the country bounded south by the Indian boundary line aforesaid, running from the southern extreme of lake Michigan, east by lake Michigan, north by the Menominie country, and north-west by Rock river. This claim is recognized in the treaty concluded with the said Illinois tribes at St. Louis, August 24, 1816, but as the Millewakee and Manetoowalk bands are not represented at this Council, it cannot be now definitively adjusted.

ARTICLE 10.
All the tribes aforesaid acknowledge the general controlling power of the United States, and disclaim all dependence upon, and connection with, any other power. And the United States agree to, and recognize, the preceding boundaries, subject to the limitations and restrictions before provided. It being, however, well understood that the reservations at Fever River, at the Ouisconsin, and St. Peters, and the ancient settlements at Prairie des Chiens and Green Bay, and the land property thereto belonging, and the reservations made upon the Mississippi, for the use of the half breeds, in the treaty concluded with the Sacs and Foxes, August 24, 1824, are not claimed by either of the said tribes.

ARTICLE 11.
The United States agree, whenever the President may think it necessary and proper, to convene such of the tribes, either separately or together, as are interested in the lines left unsettled herein, and to recommend to them an amicable and final adjustment of their respective claims, so that the work, now happily begun, may be consummated. It is agreed, however, that a Council shall be held with the Yancton band of the Sioux, during the year 1826, to explain to them the stipulations of this treaty, and to procure their assent thereto, should they be disposed to give it, and also with the Ottoes, to settle and adjust their title to any of the country claimed by the Sacs, Foxes, and Ioways.

ARTICLE 12.
The Chippewa tribe being dispersed over a great extent of country, and the Chiefs of that tribe having requested, that such portion of them as may be thought proper, by the Government of the United States, may be assembled in 1826, upon some part of Lake Superior, that the objects and advantages of this treaty may be fully explained to them, so that the stipulations thereof may be observed by the warriors. The Commissioners of the United States assent thereto, and it is therefore agreed that a council shall accordingly be held for these purposes.

ARTICLE 13.
It is understood by all the tribes, parties hereto, that no tribe shall hunt within the acknowledged limits of any other without their assent, but it being the sole object of this arrangement to perpetuate a peace among them, and amicable relations being now restored, the Chiefs of all the tribes have expressed a determination, cheerfully to allow a reciprocal right of hunting on the lands of one another, permission being first asked and obtained, as before provided for.

ARTICLE 14.
Should any causes of difficulty hereafter unhappily arise between any of the tribes, parties hereunto, it is agreed that the other tribes shall interpose their good offices to remove such difficulties; and also that the government of the United States may take such measures as they may deem proper, to effect the same object.

ARTICLE 15.
This treaty shall be obligatory on the tribes, parties hereto, from and after the date hereof, and on the United States, from and after its ratification by the government thereof.

Done, and signed, and sealed, at Prairie des Chiens, in the territory of Michigan, this nineteenth day of August, one thousand eight hundred and twenty-five, and of the independence of the United States the fiftieth.

William Clark, [L. S.],
Lewis Cass, [L. S.].

Sioux:
Wa-ba-sha, x or the leaf, [L. S.],
Pe-tet-te x Corbeau, little crow, [L. S.],

The Little x of the Wappitong tribe, [L. S.],
Tartunka-nasiah x Sussitong, [L. S.],
Sleepy Eyes, x Sossitong, [L. S.],
Two faces x do [L. S.],
French Crow x Wappacoota, [L. S.],
Kee-jee x do [L. S.],
Tar-se-ga x do [L. S.],
Wa-ma-de-tun-ka x black dog, [L. S.],
Wan-na-ta x Yancton, or he that charges on his
    enemies, [L. S.],
Red Wing x [L. S.],
Ko-ko-ma-ko x [L. S.],
Sha-co-pe x the Sixth, [L. S.],
Pe-ni-si-on x [L. S.],
Eta-see-pa x Wabasha's band, [L. S.],
Wa-ka-u-hee, x Sioux band, rising thunder,
    [L. S.],
The Little Crow, x Sussetong, [L. S.],
Po-e-ha-pa x Me-da-we-con-tong, or eagle head,
    [L. S.],
Ta-ke-wa-pa x Wappitong, or medicine blanket,
    [L. S.],
Tench-ze-part, x his bow, [L. S.],
Masc-pu-lo-chas-tosh, x the white man, [L. S.],
Te-te-kar-munch, x the buffaloman, [L. S.],
Wa-sa-o-ta x Sussetong, or a great of hail, [L. S.],
Oeyah-ko-ca, x the crackling tract, [L. S.],
Mak-to-wah-ke-ark, x the bear, [L. S.].

Winnebagoes:
Les quatres jambes, x [L. S.],
Carimine, x the turtle that walks, [L. S.],
De-ca-ri, x [L. S.],
Wan-ca-ha-ga, x or snake's skin, [L. S.],
Sa-sa-ma-ni, x [L. S.],
Wa-non-che-qua, x the merchant, [L. S.],
Chon-que-pa, x or dog's head, [L. S.],
Cha-rat-chon, x the smoker, [L. S.],
Ca-ri-ca-si-ca, x he that kills the crow, [L. S.],
Watch-kat-o-que, x the grand canoe, [L. S.],
Ho-wa-mick-a, x the little elk, [L. S.].

Menominees:
Ma-can-me-ta, x medicine bear, [L. S.],
Chau-wee-nou-mi-tai, x medicine south wind,
    [L. S.],
Char-o-nee, x [L. S.],
Ma-wesh-a, x the little wolf, [L. S.],
A-ya-pas-mis-ai, x the thunder that turns,
    [L. S.],
Cha-ne-pau, x the riband, [L. S.],
La-me-quon, x the spoon, [L. S.],

En-im-e-tas, x the barking wolf, [L. S.],
Pape-at, x the one just arrived, [L. S.],
O-que-men-ce, x the little chief, [L. S.].

Chippewas:
Shinguaba x W'Ossin, 1st chief of the Chippewa
    nation, Saulte St. Marie, [L. S.],
Gitspee x Jiauba, 2d chief, [L. S.],
Gitspee x Waskee, or le boeuf of la pointe lake
    Superior, [L. S.],
Nain-a-boozhu, x of la pointe lake Superior,
    [L. S.],
Monga, x Zid or loon's foot of Fond du Lac,
    [L. S.],
Weescoup, x or sucre of Fond du Lac, [L. S.],
Mush-Koas, x or the elk of Fond du Lac, [L. S.],
Nau-bun x Aqeezhik, of Fond du Lac, [L. S.],
Kau-ta-waubeta, x or broken tooth of Sandy
    lake, [L. S.],
Pugisaingegen, x or broken arm of Sandy lake,
    [L. S.],
Kwee-weezaishish, x or gross guelle of Sandy
    lake, [L. S.],
Ba-ba-see-kundade, x or curling hair of Sandy
    lake, [L. S.],
Paashineep, x or man shooting at the mark of
    Sandy lake, [L. S.],
Pu-ga-a-gik, x the little beef, Leech lake, [L. S.],
Pee-see-ker, x or buffalo, St. Croix band, [L. S.],
Nau-din, x or the wind, St. Croix band, [L. S.],
Nau-quan-a-bee, x of Mille lac, [L. S.],
Tu-kau-bis-hoo, x or crouching lynx of Lac
    Courte Oreille, [L. S.],
The Red Devil, x of Lac Courte Oreille, [L. S.],
The Track, x of Lac Courte Oreille, [L. S.],
Ne-bo-na-bee, x the mermaid Lac Courte
    Oreille, [L. S.],
Pi-a-gick, x the single man St. Croix, [L. S.],
Pu-in-a-ne-gi, x, or the hole in the day, Sandy
    lake, [L. S.],
Moose-o-mon-e, x plenty of elk, St. Croix band,
    [L. S.],
Nees-o-pe-na, x or two birds of Upper Red
    Cedar lake, [L. S.],
Shaata, x the pelican of Leech lake, [L. S.],
Che-on-o-quet, x the great cloud of Leech lake,
    [L. S.],
I-au-ben-see, x the little buck of Red lake,
    [L. S.],
Kia-wa-tas, x the tarrier of Leech lake, [L. S.],
Mau-ge-ga-bo, x the leader of Leech lake,
    [L. S.],

Nan-go-tuck, x the flame of Leech lake,
   [L. S.],
Nee-si-day-sish, x the sky of Red lake,
   [L. S.],
Pee-chan-a-nim, x striped feather of Sandy lake,
   [L. S.],
White Devil, x of Leech lake, [L. S.],
Ka-ha-ka, x the sparrow, Lac,
Courte Oreille, [L. S.]
I-au-be-ence, x little buck, of Rice lake, Ca-ba-
   ma-bee, x the assembly of St. Croix, [L. S.],
Nau-gau-nosh, x the forward man lake
   Flambeau, [L. S.],
Caw-win-dow, x he that gathers berries of
   Sandy Lake, [L. S.],
On-que-ess, the mink, lake Superior, [L. S.],
Ke-we-ta-ke-pe, x all round the sky, [L. S.],
The-sees, x [L. S.].

Ottawas:
Chaboner, x or Chambly, [L. S.],
Shaw-fau-wick, x the mink, [L. S.].

Potawatomies:
Ignace, x [L. S.],
Ke-o-kuk, x [L. S.],
Che-chan-quose, x the little crane, [L. S.],
Taw-wa-na-nee, x the trader, [L. S.].

Sacs:
Na-o-tuk, x the stabbing chief, [L. S.],
Pish-ken-au-nee, x all fish, [L. S.],
Po-ko-nau-qua, x or broken arm, [L. S.],
Wau-kau-che, x eagle nose, [L. S.],
Quash-kaume, x jumping fish, [L. S.],
Ochaach, x the fisher, [L. S.],
Ke-o-kuck, x the watchful fox, [L. S.],
Skin-gwin-ee-see, the x ratler, [L. S.],
Was-ar-wis-ke-no, x the yellow bird, [L. S.],
Pau-ko-tuk, x the open sky, [L. S.],
Au-kaak-wan-e-suk, x he that vaults on the
   earth, [L. S.],
Mu-ku-taak-wan-wet, x [L. S.],
Mis-ke-bee, x the standing hair, [L. S.].

Foxes:
Wan-ba-law, x the playing fox, [L. S.],
Ti-a-mah, x the bear that makes the rocks shake,
   [L. S.],
Pee-ar-maski, x the jumping sturgeon, [L. S.],
Shagwa-na-tekwishu, x the thunder that is
   heard all over the world, [L. S.],

Mis-o-win, x moose deer horn, [L. S.],
No-ko-wot, x the down of the fur, [L. S.],
Nau-sa-wa-quot, x the bear that sleeps on the
   forks, [L. S.],
Shin-quin-is, x the ratler, [L. S.],
O-lo-pee-aau, x or Mache-paho-ta, the bear,
   [L. S.],
Keesis, x the sun, [L. S.],
No-wank, x he that gives too little, [L. S.],
Kan-ka-mote, x [L. S.],
Neek-waa, x [L. S.],
Ka-tuck-e-kan-ka, x the fox with a spotted
   breast, [L. S.],
Mock-to-back-sa-gum, x black tobacco, [L. S.],
Wes-kesa, x the bear family, [L. S.].

Ioways:
Ma-hos-ka, x the white cloud, [L. S.],
Pumpkin, x [L. S.],
Wa-ca-nee, x the painted medicine, [L. S.],
Tar-no-mun, x a great many deer, [L. S.],
Wa-hoo-ga, x the owl, [L. S.],
Ta-ca-mo-nee, x the lightning, [L. S.],
Wa-push-a, x the man killer, [L. S.],
To-nup-he-non-e, x the flea, [L. S.],
Mon-da-tonga, x [L. S.],
Cho-wa-row-a, x [L. S.].

Witnesses:
Thomas Biddle, secretary,
R. A. McCabe, Captain Fifth Infantry,
R. A. Forsyth,
N. Boilvin, United States Indian agent,
C. C. Trowbridge, sub Indian agent,
Henry R. Schoolcraft, United States Indian
   agent,
B. F. Harney, Surgeon U. S. Army,
W. B. Alexander, sub Indian agent,
Thomas Forsyth, agent Indian affairs,
Marvien Blondau,
David Bailey,
James M'Ilvaine, lieutenant U. S. Army,
Law. Taliaferro, Indian agent for Upper
   Mississippi,
John Holiday,
William Dickson,
S. Campbell, United States interpreter,
J. A. Lewis,
William Holiday,
Dunable Denejlevy,
Bela Chapman.

Treaty with the Chickasaw, 1830

Aug. 31, 1830. | Unratified. | Indian Office, box 1, Treaties, 1802–1853. | See note, ante, p. 360.

Articles of a treaty, entered into at Franklin, Tennessee, this 31st day of August, 1830, by John H. Eaton, Secretary of War, and General John Coffee, commissioners appointed by the President, on the part of the United States, and the chiefs and head men of the Chickasaw Nation of Indians, duly authorized, by the whole nation, to conclude a treaty.

ARTICLE 1.

The Chickasaw Nation hereby cede to the United States all the lands owned and possessed by them, on the East side of the Mississippi River, where they at present reside, and which lie north of the following boundary, viz: beginning at the mouth of the Oacktibbyhaw (or Tibbee) creek; thence, up the same, to a point, being a marked tree, on the old Natchez road, about one mile Southwardly from Wall's old place; thence, with the Choctaw boundary, and along it, Westwardly, through the Tunicha old fields, to a point on the Mississippi river, about twenty-eight miles, by water, below where the St. Francis river enters said stream, on the West side. All the lands North, and North-East of said boundary, to latitude thirty-five North the South boundary of the State of Tennessee, being owned by the Chickasaws, are hereby ceded to the United States.

ARTICLE 2.

In consideration of said cession, the United States agree to furnish to the Chickasaw Nation of Indians, a country, West of the territory of Arkansaw, to lie South of latitude thirty-six degrees and a half, and of equal extent with the one ceded; and in all respects as to timber, water and soil, it shall be suited to the wants and condition of said Chickasaw people. It is agreed further, that the United States will send one or more commissioners to examine and select a country of the description stated, who shall be accompanied by an interpreter and not more than twelve persons of the Chickasaws, to be chosen by the nation, to examine said country; and who, for their expenses and services, shall be allowed two dollars a day each, while so engaged. If, after proper examination, a country suitable to their wants and condition can not be found; then, it is stipulated and agreed, that this treaty, and all its provisions, shall be considered null and void. But, if a country shall be found and approved, the President of the United States shall cause a grant in fee simple to be made out, to be signed by him as other grants are usually signed, conveying the country to the Chickasaw people, and to their children, so long as they shall continue to exist as a nation, and shall reside upon the same.

ARTICLE 3.

The Chickasaws being a weak tribe, it is stipulated that the United States will, at all times, extend to them their protection and care against enemies of every description, but it is, at the same time, agreed, that they shall act peaceably, and never make war, nor resort to arms, except with the consent and approval of the President, unless in cases where they may be invaded by some hostile power or tribe.

ARTICLE 4.

As further consideration, the United States agree, that each warrior and widow having a family, and each white man, having an Indian family, shall be entitled to a half section of land, and if they have no family, to half that quantity. The delegation present, having full knowledge of the population of their country, stipulate, that the first class of cases (those with families), shall not exceed five hundred, and that the other class shall not exceed one hundred persons. The reservations secured under this article, shall be granted in fee simple, to those who choose to remain, and become subject to the laws of the whites; and who, having recorded such intention with the agent, before the time of the first removal, shall continue to reside upon, and cultivate the same, for five years; at the expiration of which time, a grant shall be issued. But should they prefer to remove, and actually remove, then the United States, in lieu of such reservations will pay for the same, at the rate of one dollar and a half per acre; the same to be paid in ten equal, annual installments, to commence after the period of the ratification of this treaty, if, at that time, they shall have removed.

ARTICLE 5.

It is agreed, that the United States, as further consideration, will pay to said Nation of Indians, fifteen thousand dollars annually, for twenty years; the first payment to be made after their removal shall take place, and they be settled at their new homes, West of the Mississippi.

ARTICLE 6.

Whereas Levi Colbert, George Clobber, Tessemingo, William McGilvery and Saml. Seeley Senr, have been long known, as faithful and steady friends of the United States, and regardless of the interest of their own people; to afford them an earnest of our good feeling, now that they are about to seek a new home; the commissioners, of their own accord, and without any thing of solicitation or request, on the part of said persons, have proposed, and do agree, that they have reservations of four sections each, to include their present improvements, as nearly as may be; or, if they have improvements at any other place than one, then, equally to divide said reservations, so that two sections may be laid off at one place of improvement, and two at another; or, the whole at one place, as the party entitled may choose. They shall be entitled to the same in fee simple, to be resided upon; or, if they prefer it, they may, with the consent of the President, sell and convey the same, in fee. And it is further agreed, that upon the same terms and conditions, a reservation of two sections, to be surveyed together, and to include the improvements of the party entitled, shall and the same is hereby declared to be, secured to Capt. James Brown, James Colbert, John McLish & Isaac Alberson.

ARTICLE 7.

The delegation having selected the following persons, as worthy their regard and confidence, to wit;— Ish to yo to pe, To pul ka, Ish te ke yo ka tubbe, Ish te ke cha, E le paum be, Pis te la tubbe, Ish tim mo lat ka, Pis ta tubbe, Im mo hoal te tubbe, Ba ka tubbe, Ish to ye tubbe, Ah to ko wa, Pak la na ya ubbe. In hie yo che tubbe, Thomas Sealy, Tum ma sheck ah, Im mo la subbe, Am le mi ya tubbe; Benjamin Love and Malcomb McGee;—it is consented that each of said persons shall be entitled to a reservation of one section of land to be located in a body, to include their present improvement, and upon which, intending to become resident citizens of the country, they may continue, and at the end of five years, shall receive a grant for the same; or, should they prefer to remove, they shall be entitled, in lieu thereof, to receive from the United States, one dollar and twenty-five cents per acre for the same, to be paid in two equal, annual installments, to commence after the ratification of this treaty, and after the nation shall have removed.

ARTICLE 8.

No person receiving a special reservation, shall be entitled to claim any further reservation, under the provisions of the fourth article of this treaty.

ARTICLE 9.

At the request of the delegation, it is agreed that Levi Colbert shall have an additional section of land, to that granted him in the 6th article, to be located where he may prefer, and subject to the conditions contained in said sixth article.

ARTICLE 10.

All the reservations made by this treaty, shall be in sections, half sections, or quarter sections, agreeably to the legal surveys made, and shall include the present houses and improvements of the reserves, as nearly as may be.

ARTICLE 11.

It is agreed that the Chickasaw people, in removing to their new homes, shall go there at the expense of the United States; and that when they shall have arrived at their new homes, the United States will furnish to each one, for the space of one year, meat and corn rations, for himself and his family; that thereby, time may be afforded to clear the ground, and prepare a crop. And the better to effect this object, it is agreed that one-half the nation shall remove in the fall of 1831, and the other half the following fall. The supplies to be furnished by the United States, are to be delivered at one or two places in the nation, which shall be as convenient to the body of the people as may be practicable; having regard to the position or places, where the supplies may be had or deposited, with the greatest convenience, and least expense to the United States.

ARTICLE 12.

The United States, at the time of the removal of each portion of the nation, at the valuation of some respectable person, to be appointed by the President, agree to purchase all the stock they may desire to part with, (except horses), and to pay them therefor, at their new homes, as early as practicable after the ratification of this treaty. Also, to receive their agricultural and farming utensils, and to furnish them, at the West, with axes, hoes and ploughs, suited to their wants respectively. Also, to furnish each family with a spinning wheel and cards, and a loom to every six families.

ARTICLE 13.

A council house, and two houses of public worship, which may be used for the purposes of schools,

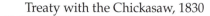

shall be built by the United States; and the sum of four thousand dollars shall be appropriated for that purpose. Also, one blacksmith, and no more, shall be employed at the expense of the government, for twenty years, for the use of the Indians; and a mill-wright for five years, to aid them in erecting their saw and grist-mills.

ARTICLE 14.
The sum of two thousand dollars a year, shall be paid for ten years, for the purpose of employing suitable teachers of the Christian religion, and superintending common schools in the nation. And it is further consented, that twenty Chickasaw boys of promise, from time to time, for the period of twenty years, shall be selected from the nation by the chiefs, to be educated within the States at the expense of the United States, under the direction of the Secretary of War.

ARTICLE 15.
A desire having been expressed by Levi Colbert, that two of his younger sons, Abijah Jackson Colbert, and Andrew Morgan Colbert, aged seven and five years, might be educated under the direction and care of the President of the United States;—and George Colbert having also expressed—a wish that his grand-son, Andrew J. Frazier, aged about twelve years, might have a similar attention: It is consented, that at a proper age, as far as they may be found to have capacity, they shall receive a liberal education, at the expense of the United States, under the direction and control of the President.

ARTICLE 16.
The United States shall have authority, after the ratification of this treaty by the Senate, to survey and prepare the country for sale; but no sale shall take place before the fall of 1832, or until they shall remove. And that every clause and article herein contained may be strictfully fulfilled;—it is stipulated and agreed, that the lands herein ceded shall be, and the same are hereby pledged, for the payment of the several sums which are secured and directed to be paid, under the several provisions of this treaty.

ARTICLE 17.
The United States, and the Chickasaw nation of Indians herein stipulate, that perpetual peace, and unaltered and lasting friendship, shall be maintained between them.

It is agreed, that the President of the United States will use his good offices, and kind mediation, and make a request of the governor and legislature of the State of Mississippi, not to extend their laws over the Chickasaws; or to suspend their operation, until they shall have time to remove, as limited in this treaty.

In witness of all and every thing herein determined, between the United States, and the delegation representing the whole Chickasaw nation, the parties heave hereunto set their hands and seals, at Franklin, Tennessee, within the United States, this thirty-first day of August, one thousand eight hundred and thirty.

Jn H Eaton, Secr. of War.
Jno. Coffee.
Levi Colbert, his x mark.
George Colbert, his x mark.
James Colbert, his x mark.
Wm. McGilvery, his x mark.
James Brown, his x mark.
Isaac Alberson, his x mark.
To pul ka, his x mark.
Ish te ke yo ka tubbe, his x mark.
Ish te ke cha, his x mark.
Im me houl te tubbe, his x mark.
In ha yo chet tubbe, his x mark.
Ish te ya tubbe, his x mark.
Ah to ko wa, his x mark.
Ook la na ya ubbe, his x mark.
Im mo la subbe, his x mark.
Hush ta ta be, his x mark.
In no wa ke che, his x mark.
Oh he cubbe, his x mark.
Kin hi che, his x mark.
J. W. Lish.

Signed in presence of us,
Preston Hay, Secretary.
Benj. Reynolds, U. S. agent.
Benjamin Love, interpreter.
R. M. Gavock.
R. P. Currin.
Lemuel Smith.
Leml. Donelson.
Jos. H. Fry.
James H. Wilson.
J. R. Davis.

Articles, supplementary to a treaty this day entered into, between John H. Eaton and John Coffee, on the part of the United States, and the Chiefs of the Chickasaw nation.

ARTICLE 1.

It is agreed that the United States will furnish the Chickasaw nation, to be distributed by the agent, under the direction of the chiefs, at or before the time of their removal West of the Mississippi river, three hundred rifles, with moulds and wipers; also, three hundred pounds of good powder, and twelve hundred pounds of lead. They will also furnish as aforesaid, three hundred copper or brass kettles, and six hundred blankets. Likewise three thousand weight of leaf tobacco.

ARTICLE 2.

Colbert's Island, in the Tennessee river, just below the mouth of Caney Creek, supposed to contain five hundred acres, has always been in the use and occupancy of George Colbert, and has been admitted by the nation, to be his individual property. It is agreed now, that he shall be recognized, as having a title to the same, and that he shall receive from the United States, in consideration of it, one thousand dollars, to be paid in one year after the Chickasaws shall remove to their new homes.

ARTICLE 3.

James Colbert has represented, that he has a claim of thirteen hundred dollars, of money due from a citizen of the United States, —that he has become insolvent, and is unable to pay it. It is further represented, that by the rule of the Chickasaw people, where an Indian cannot pay a debt due to a white man, the nation assumes it. Also, Levi Colbert shews, that some time since, he purchased of a white citizen, a horse which was stolen, and proven and taken out of his possession, as stolen property, for which he has not, and cannot, obtain remuneration. Being now about to leave their ancient homes, for a new one, too distant to attend to their business here;—it is agreed that a section of land may be located and reserved, to be bound by sectional lines; which land, with the consent of the President, they may sell.

ARTICLE 4.

The Chickasaw delegation request, that a reservation of land may be made in favor of their excellent agent, Col. Benjamin Reynolds, who, since he has been among them, has acted uprightly and faithfully, and of their sub-agent, Major John L. Allen, who also, has been of much service:—The commissioners

accordingly consent thereto; and it is stipulated that Col. Reynolds shall have a reservation of five quarter sections of land, to be bounded by sectional lines, or quarter sectional lines, and to lie together, in a body; and in further consideration, it is stipulated, with the consent of said Reynolds, that his pension of two hundred and forty dollars a year, granted to him by the United States, shall thereafter cease and determine. The application in favor of the sub-agent, Maj. Allen, is also recognized, and a reservation of a quarter section is admitted to his wife, to whom and for whose benefit a grant shall issue. But said reservations shall not be located, so as to interfere with other claims to reservations, secured under this treaty, nor shall this treaty be affected if this article is not ratified.

ARTICLE 5.

The 4th article of the treaty of 19th October 1818, which reserves a salt lick, and authorizes Levi Colbert and James Brown to lease the same for a reasonable quantity of salt, is hereby changed;—And with the consent of the commissioners present, the following agreement, made by Robert P. Currin, for himself and William B. Lewis, is entered as part of this treaty, to wit;

Whereas a lease of land, of four miles square, was secured under the fourth article of a treaty, concluded on the 19th day of October 1818, between the United States and the Chickasaw nation of Indians; and Levi Colbert and James Brown, under the same treaty, were appointed agents and trustees by the Chickasaw nation to make said lease. And whereas William B. Lewis, a citizen of the United States afterwards procured from said trustees, Colbert and Brown, a lease for the same, on condition of his paying annually, a certain amount of salt to said nation, provided he should succeed in finding salt water. And whereas the said William B. Lewis and Robert P. Currin, who subsequently became interested with him, have, as is shown, expended about the sum of three thousand dollars, in endeavoring to find salt water, but without success. And the Indians, who are about to leave their ancient country, being desirous to have this land and lease placed in such a condition, as that some benefit may result to their nation, They do hereby agree with said Robert P. Currin, a citizen of the United States, for himself, and as the agent and attorney in fact of the said William B. Lewis (John H. Eaton and John Coffee, the United States commissioners, to treat with said

Chickasaw nation being present and assenting thereto); that the lease heretofore made, be so changed, that the rent therein agreed to be paid is entirely released and discharged, from the date of said lease, together with all claim arising on account of the same.

And it is now agreed, that said lease shall remain, as heretofore made, with this alteration: that two thousand dollars shall be paid to said Colbert and Brown, trustees as aforesaid, for the Chickasaw nation: to wit: five hundred dollars now in hand; five hundred dollars on the first day of October one thousand eight hundred and thirty-one; and one thousand dollars on the first day of October one thousand eight hundred and thirty-two. And it is further agreed, in consideration of said alteration of said original contract and lease, herein made and agreed upon; and the said Robert P. Currin, for himself and the said William B. Lewis, for each and for both, he having full authority to act in the premises, will annually pay to said trustees, four bushels of salt, or the value thereof, as they and the nation may agree to and direct.

In testimony whereof, and in the presence of the commissioners, appointed to treat with the Chickasaw nation of people, on the part of the United States, the parties respectively have hereto set their hands and affixed their seals, this first day of September, one thousand eight hundred and thirty.

> Jn. H. Eaton, Secty. of War.
> Jno. Coffee.
> Levi Colbert, his x mark.
> George Colbert, his x mark.
> James Colbert, his x mark.
> Wm. McGilvery, his x mark.
> Isaac Alberson, his x mark.
> James Bown, his x mark.
> To pul ka, his x mark.
> Ish te ki yo ka tubbe, his x mark.
> Ish te he cha, his x mark.
> Im me houl te tubbe, his x mark.
> In hei yo chit tubbe, his x mark.
> Ish te ya tubbe, his x mark.
> Ah to ko wa, his x mark.
> Ook la na ya ubbe, his x mark.
> Im mo la tubbe, his x mark.
> Hush ta ta be, his x mark.
> In no wa ke che, his x mark.
> On he cubbe, his x mark.

> Kin hu che, his x mark.
> J. W. Lish.
>
> Signed in presence of us,
> Preston Hay, secretary.
> Benj. Reynolds, U. S. agent.
> Benjamin Love, as interpreter.
> R. M. Gavock.
> Leml. Donelson.
> Leml. Smith.
> R. P. Currin.
> Jos. H. Fry.
> James H. Wilson.
> J. R. Davis.

Treaty with the Choctaw, 1830
Sept. 27, 1830. | 7 Stat., 333. | Proclamation, Feb. 24, 1831.

A treaty of perpetual, friendship, cession and limits, entered into by John H. Eaton and John Coffee, for and in behalf of the Government of the United States, and the Mingoes, Chiefs, Captains and Warriors of the Choctaw Nation, begun and held at Dancing Rabbit Creek, on the fifteenth of September, in the year eighteen hundred and thirty.

WHEREAS the General Assembly of the State of Mississippi has extended the laws of said State to persons and property within the chartered limits of the same, and the President of the United States has said that he cannot protect the Choctaw people from the operation of these laws; Now therefore that the Choctaw may live under their own laws in peace with the United States and the State of Mississippi they have determined to sell their lands east of the Mississippi and have accordingly agreed to the following articles of treaty: a Perpetual peace and friendship is pledged and agreed upon by and between the United States and the Mingoes, Chiefs, and Warriors of the Choctaw Nation of Red People; and that this may be considered the Treaty existing between the parties all other Treaties heretofore existing and inconsistent with the provisions of this are hereby declared null and void.

ARTICLE 2.
The United States under a grant specially to be made by the President of the U.S. shall cause to be con-

veyed to the Choctaw Nation a tract of country west of the Mississippi River, in fee simple to them and their descendants, to inure to them while they shall exist as a nation and live on it, beginning near Fort Smith where the Arkansas boundary crosses the Arkansas River, running thence to the source of the Canadian fork; if in the limits of the United States, or to those limits; thence due south to Red River, and down Red River to the west boundary of the Territory of Arkansas; thence north along that line to the beginning. The boundary of the same to be agreeably to the Treaty made and concluded at Washington City in the year 1825. The grant to be executed so soon as the present Treaty shall be ratified.

ARTICLE 3.

In consideration of the provisions contained in the several articles of this Treaty, the Choctaw nation of Indians consent and hereby cede to the United States, the entire country they own and possess, east of the Mississippi River; and they agree to move beyond the Mississippi River, early as practicable, and will so arrange their removal, that as many as possible of their people not exceeding one half of the whole number, shall depart during the falls of 1831 and 1832; the residue to follow during the succeeding fall of 1833, a better opportunity in this manner will be afforded the Government, to extend to them the facilities and comforts which it is desirable should be extended in conveying them to their new homes.

ARTICLE 4.

The Government and people of the United States are hereby obliged to secure to the said Choctaw Nation of Red People the jurisdiction and government of all the persons and property that may be within their limits west, so that no Territory or state shall ever have a right to pass laws for the government of the Choctaw Nation of Red People and their descendants; and that no part of the land granted them shall ever be embraced in any Territory or State; but the F. S. shall forever secure said Choctaw Nation from, and against, all laws except such as from time to time may be enacted in their own National Councils, not inconsistent with the Constitution, Treaties, and Laws of the United States; and except such as may, and which have been enacted by Congress, to the extent that Congress under the Constitution are required to exercise a legislation over Indian affairs. But the Choctaws, should this treaty be ratified, express a

wish that Congress may grant to the Choctaws the right of punishing by their own laws any white man who shall come into their nation and infringe any of their national regulations.

ARTICLE 5.

The United States are obliged to protect the Choctaws from domestic strife and from foreign enemies on the same principles that the citizens of the United States are protected, so that whatever would be a legal demand upon the U.S. for defense or for wrongs committed by an enemy, on a citizen of the U.S. shall be equally binding in favor of the Choctaws, and in all cases where the Choctaws shall be called upon by a legally authorized officer of the U.S. to fight an enemy, such Choctaw shall receive the pay and other emoluments, [this paragraph was not ratified] which citizens of the U.S. receive in such cases, provided, no war shall be undertaken or prosecuted by said Choctaw Nation but by declaration made in full Council, and to be approved by the U.S. unless it be in self defense against an open rebellion or against an enemy marching into their country, in which cases they shall defend, until the U.S. are advised thereof.

ARTICLE 6.

Should a Choctaw or any party of Choctaws commit acts of violence upon the person or property of a citizen of the U.S. or join any war party against any neighbouring tribe of Indians, without the authority in the preceding article; and except to oppose an actual or threatened invasion or rebellion, such person so offending shall be delivered up to an officer of the U.S. if in the power of the Choctaw Nation, that such offender may be punished as may be provided in such cases, by the laws of the U.S.; but if such offender is not within the control of the Choctaw Nation, then said Choctaw Nation shall not be held responsible for the injury done by said offender.

ARTICLE 7.

All acts of violence committed upon persons and property of the people of the Choctaw Nation either by citizens of the U.S. or neighbouring Tribes of Red People, shall be referred to some authorized Agent by him to be referred to the President of the U.S. who shall examine into such cases and see that every possible degree of justice is done to said Indian party of the Choctaw Nation.

ARTICLE 8.

Offenders against the laws of the U.S. or any individual State shall be apprehended and delivered to any duly authorized person where such offender may be found in the Choctaw country, having fled from any part of U.S. but in all such cases application must be made to the Agent or Chiefs and the expense of his apprehension and delivery provided for and paid by the U. States.

ARTICLE 9.

Any citizen of the U.S. who may be ordered from the Nation by the Agent and constituted authorities of the Nation and refusing to obey or return into the Nation without the consent of the aforesaid persons, shall be subject to such pains and penalties as may be provided by the laws of the U.S. in such cases. Citizens of the U.S. traveling peaceably under the authority of the laws of the U.S. shall be under the care and protection of the nation.

ARTICLE 10.

No person shall expose goods or other article for sale as a trader, without a written permit from the constituted authorities of the Nation, or authority of the laws of the Congress of the U.S. under penalty of forfeiting the Articles, and the constituted authorities of the Nation shall grant no license except to such persons as reside in the Nation and are answerable to the laws of the Nation. The U.S. shall be particularly obliged to assist to prevent ardent spirits from being introduced into the Nation.

ARTICLE 11.

Navigable streams shall be free to the Choctaws who shall pay no higher toll or duty than citizens of the U.S. It is agreed further that the U.S. shall establish one or more Post Offices in said Nation, and may establish such military post roads, and posts, as they may consider necessary.

ARTICLE 12.

All intruders shall be removed from the Choctaw Nation and kept without it. Private property to be always respected and on no occasion taken for public purposes without just compensation being made therefor to the rightful owner. If an Indian unlawfully take or steal any property from a white man a citizen of the U.S. the offender shall be punished. And if a white man unlawfully take or steal any thing from an Indian, the property shall be restored and the offender punished. It is further agreed that

when a Choctaw shall be given up to be tried for any offense against the laws of the U.S. if unable to employ counsel to defend him, the U.S. will do it, that his trial may be fair and impartial.

ARTICLE 13.

It is consented that a qualified Agent shall be appointed for the Choctaws every four years, unless sooner removed by the President; and he shall be removed on petition of the constituted authorities of the Nation, the President being satisfied there is sufficient cause shown. The Agent shall fix his residence convenient to the great body of the people; and in the selection of an Agent immediately after the ratification of this Treaty, the wishes of the Choctaw Nation on the subject shall be entitled to great respect.

ARTICLE 14.

Each Choctaw head of a family being desirous to remain and become a citizen of the States, shall be permitted to do so, by signifying his intention to the Agent within six months from the ratification of this Treaty, and he or she shall thereupon be entitled to a reservation of one section of six hundred and forty acres of land, to be bounded by sectional lines of survey; in like manner shall be entitled to one half that quantity for each unmarried child which is living with him over ten years of age; and a quarter section to such child as may be under 10 years of age, to adjoin the location of the parent. If they reside upon said lands intending to become citizens of the States for five years after the ratification of this Treaty, in that case a grant in fee simple shall issue; said reservation shall include the present improvement of the head of the family, or a portion of it. Persons who claim under this article shall not lose the privilege of a Choctaw citizen, but if they ever remove are not to be entitled to any portion of the Choctaw annuity.

ARTICLE 15.

To each of the Chiefs in the Choctaw Nation (to wit) Greenwood Laflore, Nutackachie, and Mushulatubbe there is granted a reservation of four sections of land, two of which shall include and adjoin their present improvement, and the other two located where they please but on unoccupied unimproved lands, such sections shall be bounded by sectional lines, and with the consent of the President they may sell the same. Also to the three principal Chiefs and to their successors in office there shall be paid two hundred and fifty dollars annually while they shall continue in their respective offices, except to Mushulatubbe, who as he has an annuity of one hundred and fifty dollars for life under a former treaty, shall receive only the additional sum of one hundred dollars, while he shall continue in office as Chief; and if in addition to this the Nation shall think proper to elect an additional principal Chief of the whole to superintend and govern upon republican principles he shall receive annually for his services five hundred dollars, which allowance to the Chiefs and their successors in office, shall continue for twenty years. At any time when in military service, and while in service by authority of the U.S. the district Chiefs under and by selection of the President shall be entitled to the pay of Majors; the other Chief under the same circumstances shall have the pay of a Lieutenant Colonel. The Speakers of the three districts, shall receive twenty-five dollars a year for four years each; and the three secretaries one to each of the Chiefs, fifty dollars each for four years. Each Captain of the Nation, the number not to exceed ninety-nine, thirty-three from each district, shall be furnished upon removing to the West, with each a good suit of clothes and a broad sword as an outfit, and for four years commencing with the first of their removal shall each receive fifty dollars a year, for the trouble of keeping their people at order in settling; and whenever they shall be in military service by authority of the U.S. shall receive the pay of a captain.

ARTICLE 16.
In wagons; and with steam boats as may be found necessary—the U.S. agree to remove the Indians to their new homes at their expense and under the care of discreet and careful persons, who will be kind and brotherly to them. They agree to furnish them with ample corn and beef, or pork for themselves and families for twelve months after reaching their new homes. It is agreed further that the U.S. will take all their cattle, at the valuation of some discreet person to be appointed by the President, and the same shall be paid for in money after their arrival at their new homes; or other cattle such as may be desired shall be furnished them, notice being given through their Agent of their wishes upon this subject before their removal that time to supply the demand may be afforded.

ARTICLE 17.
The several annuities and sums secured under former Treaties to the Choctaw nation and people shall continue as though this Treaty had never been made.

And it is further agreed that the U.S. in addition will pay the sum of twenty thousand dollars for twenty years, commencing after their removal to the west, of which, in the first year after their removal, ten thousand dollars shall be divided and arranged to such as may not receive reservations under this Treaty.

ARTICLE 18.
The U.S. shall cause the lands hereby ceded to be surveyed; and surveyors may enter the Choctaw Country for that purpose, conducting themselves properly and disturbing or interrupting none of the Choctaw people. But no person is to be permitted to settle within the nation, or the lands to be sold before the Choctaws shall remove. And for the payment of the several amounts secured in this Treaty, the lands hereby ceded are to remain a fund pledged to that purpose, until the debt shall be provided for and arranged. And further it is agreed, that in the construction of this Treaty wherever well founded doubt shall arise, it shall be construed most favorably towards the Choctaws.

ARTICLE 19.
The following reservations of land are hereby admitted. To Colonel David Fulsom four sections of which two shall include his present improvement, and two may be located elsewhere, on unoccupied, unimproved land.

To I. Garland, Colonel Robert Cole, Tuppanahomer, John Pytchlynn, Charles Juzan, Johokebetubbe, Eaychahobia, Ofehoma, two sections, each to include their improvements, and to be bounded by sectional lines, and the same may be disposed of and sold with the consent of the President. And that others not provided for, may be provided for, there shall be reserved as follows:

First. One section to each head of a family not exceeding Forty in number, who during the present year, may have had in actual cultivation, with a dwelling house thereon fifty acres or more. Secondly, three quarter sections after the manner aforesaid to each head of a family not exceeding four hundred and sixty, as shall have cultivated thirty acres and less than fifty, to be bounded by quarter section lines of survey, and to be contiguous and adjoining. Third; One half section as aforesaid to those who shall have cultivated from twenty to thirty acres the number not to exceed four hundred. Fourth; a quarter section as aforesaid to such as shall have cultivated from twelve to twenty acres, the number not to exceed three hundred and fifty, and one half that quantity to such as shall have cultivated from two to twelve acres, the number also not to exceed three hundred and fifty persons. Each of said class of cases shall be subject to the limitations contained in the first class, and shall be so located as to include that part of the improvement which contains the dwelling house. If a greater number shall be found to be entitled to reservations under the several classes of this article, than is stipulated for under the limitation prescribed, then and in that case the Chiefs separately or together shall determine the persons who shall be excluded in the respective districts.

Fifth; Any Captain the number not exceeding ninety persons, who under the provisions of this article shall receive less than a section, he shall be entitled, to an additional quantity of half a section adjoining to his other reservation. The several reservations secured under this article, may be sold with the consent of the President of the U.S. but should any prefer it or omit to take a reservation for the quantity he may be entitled to, the U.S. will on his removing pay fifty cents an acre, after reaching their new homes, provided that before the first of January next they shall adduce to the Agent, or some other authorized person to be appointed, proof of his claim and the quantity of it. Sixth; likewise children of the Choctaw Nation residing in the Nation, who have neither father nor mother a list of which, with satisfactory proof of Parentage and orphanage being filed with Agent in six months to be forwarded to the War Department, shall be entitled to a quarter section of Land, to be located under the direction of the President, and with his consent the same may be sold and the proceeds applied to some beneficial purpose for the benefit of said orphans.

ARTICLE 20.
The U.S. agree and stipulate as follows, that for the benefit and advantage of the Choctaw people, and to improve their condition, there shall be educated under the direction of the President and at the expense of the U.S. forty Choctaw youths for twenty years. This number shall be kept at school, and as they finish their education others, to supply their places shall be received for the period stated. The U.S. agree also to erect a Council House for the nation at some convenient central point, after their people shall be settled; and a House for each Chief, also a Church for each of the three Districts, to be used also as school houses, until the Nation may conclude to build others; and for these purposes ten thousand dollars shall be appropriated; also fifty thousand dollars (viz.) twenty-five hundred dollars annually shall be given for the support of three teachers of schools for twenty years. Likewise there shall be furnished to the Nation, three Blacksmiths one for each district for sixteen years, and a qualified Mill Wright for five years; Also there shall be furnished the following articles, twenty-one hundred blankets, to each warrior who emigrates a rifle, moulds, wipers and ammunition. One thousand axes, ploughs, hoes, wheels and cards each; and four hundred looms. There shall also be furnished, one ton of iron and two hundred weight of steel annually to each District for sixteen years.

ARTICLE 21.
A few Choctaw Warriors yet survive who marched and fought in the army with General Wayne, the whole number stated not to exceed twenty. These it is agreed shall hereafter while they live, receive twenty-five dollars a year; a list of them to be early as practicable, and within six months, made out, and presented to the Agent, to be forwarded to the War Department.

ARTICLE 22.
The Chiefs of the Choctaws who have suggested that their people are in a state of rapid advancement in education and refinement, and have expressed a solicitude that they might have the privilege of a Delegate on the floor of the House of Representatives extended to them. The Commissioners do not feel that they can under a treaty stipulation accede to the request, but at their desire, present it in the Treaty, that Congress may consider of, and decide the application.

Done, and signed, and executed by the commissioners of the United States, and the chiefs, captains, and head men of the Choctaw nation, at Dancing Rabbit creek, this 27th day of September, eighteen and thirty.

    Jno. H. Eaton, [L. S.],
    Jno. Coffee, [L. S.],
    Greenwood Leflore, [L. S.],
    Musholatubbee, his x mark, [L. S.],
    Nittucachee, his x mark, [L. S.],
    Holarterhoomah, his x mark, [L. S.],

Hopiaunchabubbee, his x mark, [L. S.],
Zishomingo, his x mark, [L. S.],
Captainthalke, his x mark, [L. S.],
James Shield, his x mark, [L. S.],
Pistiyubbee, his x mark, [L. S.],
Yobalarunehabubbee, his x mark, [L. S.],
Holubbee, his x mark, [L. S.],
Robert Cole, his x mark, [L. S.],
Mokelareharhopin, his x mark, [L. S.],
Lewis Perry, his x mark, [L. S.],
Artonamarstubbe, his x mark, [L. S.],
Hopeatubbee, his x mark, [L. S.],
Hoshahoomah, his x mark, [L. S.],
Chuallahoomah, his x mark, [L. S.],
Joseph Kincaide, his x mark, [L. S.],
Eyarhocuttubbee, his x mark, [L. S.],
Iyacherhopia, his x mark, [L. S.],
Offahoomah, his x mark, [L. S.],
Archalater, his x mark, [L. S.],
Onnahubbee, his x mark, [L. S.],
Pisinhocuttubbee, his x mark, [L. S.],
Tullarhacher, his x mark, [L. S.],
Little leader, his x mark, [L. S.],
Maanhutter, his x mark, [L. S.],
Cowehoomah, his x mark, [L. S.],
Tillamoer, his x mark, [L. S.],
Imnullacha, his x mark, [L. S.],
Artopilachubbee, his x mark, [L. S.],
Shupherunchahubbee, his x mark, [L. S.],
Nitterhoomah, his x mark, [L. S.],
Oaklaryubbee, his x mark, [L. S.],
Pukumna, his x mark, [L. S.],
Arpalar, his x mark, [L. S.],
Holber, his x mark, [L. S.],
Hoparmingo, his x mark, [L. S.],
Isparhoomah, his x mark, [L. S.],
Tieberhoomah, his x mark, [L. S.],
Tishoholarter, his x mark, [L. S.],
Mahayarchubbee, his x mark, [L. S.],
Artooklubbetushpar, his x mark, [L. S.],
Metubbee, his x mark, [L. S.],
Arsarkatubbee, his x mark, [L. S.],
Issaterhoomah, his x mark, [L. S.],
Chohtahmatahah, his x mark, [L. S.],
Tunnuppashubbee, his x mark, [L. S.],
Okocharyer, his x mark, [L. S.],
Hoshhopia, his x mark, [L. S.],
Warsharshahopia, his x mark, [L. S.],
Maarshunchahubbee, his x mark, [L. S.],
Misharyubbee, his x mark, [L. S.],
Daniel McCurtain, his x mark, [L. S.],
Tushkerharcho, his x mark, [L. S.],

Hoktoontubbee, his x mark, [L. S.],
Nuknacrahookmarhee, his x mark, [L. S.],
Mingo hoomah, his x mark, [L. S.],
James Karnes, his x mark, [L. S.],
Tishohakubbee, his x mark, [L. S.],
Narlanalar, his x mark, [L. S.],
Pennasha, his x mark, [L. S.],
Inharyarker, his x mark, [L. S.],
Mottubbee, his x mark, [L. S.],
Narharyubbee, his x mark, [L. S.],
Ishmaryubbee, his x mark, [L. S.],
James McKing, [L. S.],
Lewis Wilson, his x mark, [L. S.],
Istonarkerharcho, his x mark, [L. S.],
Hohinshamartarher, his x mark , [L. S.],
Kinsulachubbee, his x mark, [L. S.],
Emarhinstubbee, his x mark, [L. S.],
Gysalndalra, bm, his x mark, [L. S.],
Thomas Wall, [L. S.],
Sam. S. Worcester, [L. S.],
Arlartar, his x mark, [L. S.],
Nittahubbee, his x mark, [L. S.],
Tishonouan, his x mark, [L. S.],
Warsharchahoomah, his x mark, [L. S.],
Isaac James, his x mark, [L. S.],
Hopiaintushker, his x mark, [L. S.],
Aryoshkermer, his x mark, [L. S.],
Shemotar, his x mark, [L. S.],
Hopiaisketina, his x mark, [L. S.],
Thomas Leflore, his x mark, [L. S.],
Arnokechatubbee, his x mark, [L. S.],
Shokoperlukna, his x mark, [L. S.],
Posherhoomah, his x mark, [L. S.],
Robert Folsom, his x mark, [L. S.],
Arharyotubbee, his x mark, [L. S.],
Kushonolarter, his x mark, [L. S.],
James Vaughan, his x mark, [L. S.],
Phiplip, his x mark, [L. S.],
Meshameye, his x mark, [L. S.],
Ishteheka, his x mark, [L. S.],
Heshohomme, his x mark, [L. S.],
John McKolbery, his x mark, [L. S.],
Benjm. James, his x mark, [L. S.],
Tikbachahambe, his x mark, [L. S.],
Aholiktube, his x mark, [L. S.],
Walking Wolf, his x mark, [L. S.],
John Waide, his x mark, [L. S.],
Big Axe, his x mark, [L. S.],
Bob, his x mark, [L. S.],
Tushkochaubbee, his x mark, [L. S.],
Ittabe, his x mark, [L. S.],
Tishowakayo, his x mark, [L. S.],

Folehommo, his x mark, [L. S.],
John Garland, his x mark, [L. S.],
Koshona, his x mark, [L. S.],
Ishleyohamobe, his x mark, [L. S.],
Jacob Folsom, [L. S.],
William Foster, [L. S.],
Ontioerharcho, his x mark, [L. S.],
Hugh A. Foster, [L. S.],
Pierre Juzan, [L. S.],
Jno. Pitchlynn, jr., [L. S.],
David Folsom, [L. S.],
Sholohommastube, his x mark, [L. S.],
Tesho, his x mark, [L. S.],
Lauwechubee, his x mark, [L. S.],
Hoshehammo, his x mark, [L. S.],
Ofenowo, his x mark, [L. S.],
Ahekoche, his x mark, [L. S.],
Kaloshoube, his x mark, [L. S.],
Atoko, his x mark, [L. S.],
Ishtemeleche, his x mark, [L. S.],
Emthtohabe, his x mark, [L. S.],
Silas D. Fisher, his x mark, [L. S.],
Isaac Folsom, his x mark, [L. S.],
Hekatube, his x mark, [L. S.],
Hakseche, his x mark, [L. S.],
Jerry Carney, his x mark, [L. S.],
John Washington, his x mark, [L. S.],
Panshastubbee, his x mark, [L. S.],
P. P. Pitchlynn, his x mark, [L. S.],
Joel H. Nail, his x mark, [L. S.],
Hopia Stonakey, his x mark, [L. S.],
Kocohomma, his x mark, [L. S.],
William Wade, his x mark, [L. S.],
Panshstickubbee, his x mark, [L. S.],
Holittankchahubbee, his x mark,
    [L. S.],
Oklanowa, his x mark, [L. S.],
Neto, his x mark, [L. S.],
James Fletcher, his x mark, [L. S.],
Silas D. Pitchlynn, [L. S.],
William Trahorn, his x mark, [L. S.],
Toshkahemmitto, his x mark, [L. S.],
Tethetayo, his x mark, [L. S.],
Emokloshahopie, his x mark, [L. S.],
Tishoimita, his x mark, [L. S.],
Thomas W. Foster, his x mark, [L. S.],
Zadoc Brashears, his x mark, [L. S.],
Levi Perkins, his x mark, [L. S.],
Isaac Perry, his x mark, [L. S.],
Ishlonocka Hoomah, his x mark, [L. S.],
Hiram King, his x mark, [L. S.],
Ogla Enlah, his x mark, [L. S.],

Nultlahtubbee, his x mark, [L. S.],
Tuska Hollattuh, his x mark, [L. S.],
Kothoantchahubbee, his x mark, [L. S.],
Eyarpulubbee, his x mark, [L. S.],
Okentahubbe, his x mark, [L. S.],
Living War Club, his x mark, [L. S.],
John Jones, his x mark, [L. S.],
Charles Jones, his x mark, [L. S.],
Isaac Jones, his x mark, [L. S.],
Hocklucha, his x mark, [L. S.],
Muscogee, his x mark., [L. S.],
Eden Nelson, his x mark, [L. S.].

In presence of—
E. Breathitt secretary to the Commission,
William Ward, agent for Choctaws,
John Pitchlyn, United States interpreter,
M. Mackey, United States interpreter,
Geo. S. Gaines, of Alabama,
R. P. Currin,
Luke Howard,
Sam. S. Worcester,
Jno. N. Byrn,
John Bell,
Jno. Bond.

SUPPLEMENTARY ARTICLES TO THE PRECEDING TREATY.
Sept. 28, 1830. | 7 Stat., 340.

Various Choctaw persons have been presented by the Chiefs of the nation, with a desire that they might be provided for. Being particularly deserving, an earnestness has been manifested that provision might be made for them. It is therefore by the undersigned commissioners here assented to, with the understanding that they are to have no interest in the reservations which are directed and provided for under the general Treaty to which this is a supplement.

As evidence of the liberal and kind feelings of the President and Government of the United States the Commissioners agree to the request as follows, (to wit) Pierre Juzan, Peter Pitchlynn, G. W. Harkins, Jack Pitchlynn, Israel Fulsom, Louis Laflore, Benjamin James, Joel H. Nail, Hopoynjahubbee, Onorkubbee, Benjamin Laflore, Michael Laflore and Allen Yates and wife shall be entitled to a reservation of two sections of land each to include their improvement where they at present reside, with the exception of the three first named persons and Benjamin Laflore, who are authorized to locate one of their sections on any other unimproved and unoccupied land, within their respective districts.

ARTICLE 2.
And to each of the following persons there is allowed a reservation of a section and a half of land, (to wit) James L. McDonald, Robert Jones, Noah Wall, James Campbell, G. Nelson, Vaughn Brashears, R. Harris, Little Leader, S. Foster, J. Vaughn, L. Durans, Samuel Long, T. Magagha, Thos. Everge, Giles Thompson, Tomas Garland, John Bond, William Laflore, and Turner Brashears, the two first named persons, may locate one section each, and one section jointly on any unimproved and unoccupied land, these not residing in the Nation; The others are to include their present residence and improvement.

Also one section is allowed to the following persons (to wit) Middleton Mackey, Wesley Train, Choclehomo, Moses Foster, D. W. Wall, Charles Scott, Molly Nail, Susan Colbert, who was formerly Susan James, Samuel Garland, Silas Fisher, D. McCurtain, Oaklahoma, and Polly Fillecuthey, to be located in entire sections to include their present residence and improvement, with the exception of Molly Nail and Susan Colbert, who are authorized to locate theirs, on any unimproved unoccupied land.

John Pitchlynn has long and faithfully served the nation in character of U. States Interpreter, he has acted as such for forty years, in consideration it is agreed, in addition to what has been done for him there shall be granted to two of his children, (to wit) Silas Pitchlynn, and Thomas Pitchlynn one section of land each, to adjoin the location of their father; likewise to James Madison and Peter sons of Mushulatubbee one section of land each to include the old house and improvement where their father formerly lived on the old military road adjoining a large Prairie.

And to Henry Groves son of the Chief Natticache there is one section of land given to adjoin his father's land.

And to each of the following persons half a section of land is granted on any unoccupied and unimproved lands in the Districts where they respectively live (to wit) Willis Harkins, James D. Hamilton, William Juzan, Tobias Laflore, Jo Doke, Jacob Fulsom, P. Hays, Samuel Worcester, George Hunter, William Train, Robert Nail and Alexander McKee.

And there is given a quarter section of land each to Delila and her five fatherless children, she being a Choctaw woman residing out of the nation; also the same quantity to Peggy Trihan, another Indian woman residing out of the nation and her two fatherless children; and to the widows of Pushmilaha, and Pucktshenubbee, who were formerly distinguished Chiefs of the nation and for their children four quarter sections of land, each in trust for themselves and their children.

All of said last mentioned reservations are to be located under and by direction of the President of the U. States.

ARTICLE 3.
The Choctaw people now that they have ceded their lands are solicitous to get to their new homes early as possible and accordingly they wish that a party may be permitted to proceed this fall to ascertain whereabouts will be most advantageous for their people to be located.

It is therefore agreed that three or four persons (from each of the three districts) under the guidance of some discreet and well qualified person or persons may proceed during this fall to the West upon an examination of the country.

For their time and expenses the U. States agree to allow the said twelve persons two dollars a day each, not to exceed one hundred days, which is deemed to be ample time to make an examination.

If necessary, pilots acquainted with the country will be furnished when they arrive in the West.

ARTICLE 4.
John Donly of Alabama who has several Choctaw grand children and who for twenty years has carried the mail through the Choctaw Nation, a desire by the Chiefs is expressed that he may have a section of land, it is accordingly granted, to be located in one entire section, on any unimproved and unoccupied land.

Allen Glover and George S. Gaines licensed Traders in the Choctaw Nation, have accounts amounting to upwards of nine thousand dollars against the Indians who are unable to pay their said debts without distressing their families; a desire is expressed by the chiefs that two sections of land be set apart to be sold and the proceeds thereof to be applied toward the payment of the aforesaid debts. It is agreed that two sections of any unimproved and unoccupied land be granted to George S. Gaines who will sell the same for the best price he can obtain and apply the proceeds thereof to the credit of the Indians on their accounts due to the before mentioned Glover and Gaines; and shall make the application to the poorest Indian first.

At the earnest and particular request of the Chief Greenwood Laflore there is granted to David Haley one half section of land to be located in a half section on any unoccupied and unimproved land as a compensation, for a journey to Washington City with dispatches to the Government and returning others to the Choctaw Nation.

The foregoing is entered into, as supplemental to the treaty concluded yesterday.

Done at Dancing Rabbit creek the 28th day of September, 1830.

> Jno. H. Eaton, [L. S.],
> Jno. Coffee, [L. S.],
> Greenwood Leflore, [L. S.],
> Nittucachee, his x mark, [L. S.],
> Mushulatubbee, his x mark, [L. S.],
> Offahoomah, his x mark, [L. S.],
> Eyarhoeuttubbee, his x mark, [L. S.],
> Iyaeherhopia, his x mark, [L. S.],
> Holubbee, his x mark, [L. S.],
> Onarhubbee, his x mark, [L. S.],
> Robert Cole, his x mark, [L. S.],
> Hopiaunchahubbee, his x mark, [L. S.],
> David Folsom, [L. S.],
> John Garland, his x mark, [L. S.],
> Hopiahoomah, his x mark, [L. S.],
> Captain Thalko, his x mark, [L. S.],
> Pierre Juzan, [L. S.],
> Immarstarher, his x mark, [L. S.],
> Hoshimhamartar, his x mark, [L. S.].

In presence of—
E. Breathitt, Secretary to Commissioners,
W. Ward, Agent for Choctaws,
M. Mackey, United States Interpreter,
John Pitchlynn, United States Interpreter,
R. P. Currin,
Jno. W. Byrn,
Geo. S. Gaines.

Treaty with the Creeks, 1832

Mar., 24, 1832. | 7 Stat., 366. | Proclamation, Apr. 4, 1832.

Articles of a treaty made at the City of Washington between Lewis Cass, thereto specially authorized by the President of the United States, and the Creek tribe of Indians.

ARTICLE 1.
The Creek tribe of Indians cede to the United States all their land, East of the Mississippi river.

ARTICLE 2.
The United States engage to survey the said land as soon as the same can be conveniently done, after the ratification of this treaty, and when the same is surveyed to allow ninety principal Chiefs of the Creek tribe to select one section each, and every other head of a Creek family to select one half section each, which tracts shall be reserved from sale for their use for the term of five years, unless sooner disposed of by them. A census of these persons shall be taken under the direction of the President and the selections shall be made so as to include the improvements of each person within his selection, if the same can be so made, and if not, then all the persons belonging to the same town, entitled to selections, and who cannot make the same, so as to include their improvements, shall take them in one body in a proper form. And twenty sections shall be selected, under the direction of the President for the orphan children of the Creeks, and divided and retained or sold for their benefit as the President may direct. Provided however that no selections or locations under this treaty shall be so made as to include the agency reserve.

ARTICLE 3.
These tracts may be conveyed by the persons selecting the same, to any other persons for a fair consideration, in such manner as the President may direct. The contract shall be certified by some person appointed for that purpose by the President but shall not be valid 'till the President approves the same. A title shall be given by the United States on the completion of the payment.

ARTICLE 4.
At the end of five years, all the Creeks entitled to these selections, and desirous of remaining, shall receive patents therefor in fee simple, from the United States.

ARTICLE 5.

All intruders upon the country hereby ceded shall be removed therefrom in the same manner as intruders may be removed by law from other public land until the country is surveyed, and the selections made; excepting however from this provision those white persons who have made their own improvements, and not expelled the Creeks from theirs. Such persons may remain 'till their crops are gathered. After the country is surveyed and the selections made, this article shall not operate upon that part of it not included in such selections. But intruders shall, in the manner before described, be removed from these selections for the term of five years from the ratification of this treaty or until the same are conveyed to white persons.

ARTICLE 6.

Twenty-nine sections in addition to the foregoing may be located, and patents for the same shall then issue to those persons, being Creeks, to whom the same may be assigned by the Creek tribe. But whenever the grantees of these tracts possess improvements, such tracts shall be so located as to include the improvements, and as near as may be in the centre. And there shall also be granted by patent to Benjamin Marshall, one section of land, to include his improvements on the Chatahoochee river, to be bounded for one mile in a direct line along the said river, and to run back for quantity. There shall also be granted to Joseph Bruner a colored man, one half section of land, for his services as an interpreter.

ARTICLE 7.

All the locations authorized by this treaty, with the exception of that of Benjamin Marshall shall be made in conformity with the lines of the surveys; and the Creeks relinquish all claim for improvements.

ARTICLE 8.

An additional annuity of twelve thousand dollars shall be paid to the Creeks for the term of five years, and thereafter the said annuity shall be reduced to ten thousand dollars, and shall be paid for the term of fifteen years. All the annuities due to the Creeks shall be paid in such manner as the tribe may direct.

ARTICLE 9.

For the purpose of paying certain debts due by the Creeks, and to relieve them in their present distressed condition, the sum of one hundred thousand dollars, shall be paid to the Creek tribe as soon as may be after the ratification hereof, to be applied to the payment of their just debts, and then to their own relief, and to be distributed as they may direct, and which shall be in full consideration of all improvements.

ARTICLE 10.

The sum of sixteen thousand dollars shall be allowed as a compensation to the delegation sent to this place, and for the payment of their expenses, and of the claims against them.

ARTICLE 11.

The following claims shall be paid by the United States.

> For ferries, bridges and causeways, three thousand dollars, provided that the same shall become the property of the United States.

> For the payment of certain judgments obtained against the chiefs eight thousand five hundred and seventy dollars.

> For losses for which they suppose the United States responsible, seven thousand seven hundred and ten dollars.

> For the payment of improvements under the treaty of 1826 one thousand dollars.

The three following annuities shall be paid for life.

> To Tuske-hew-haw-Cusetaw two hundred dollars.

> To the Blind Uchu King one hundred dollars.

> To Neah Mico one hundred dollars.

There shall be paid the sum of fifteen dollars, for each person who has emigrated without expense to the United States, but the whole sum allowed under this provision shall not exceed fourteen hundred dollars.

> There shall be divided among the persons, who suffered in consequence of being

prevented from emigrating, three thousand dollars.

The land hereby ceded shall remain as a fund from which all the foregoing payments except those in the ninth and tenth articles shall be paid.

ARTICLE 12.
The United States are desirous that the Creeks should remove to the country west of the Mississippi, and join their countrymen there; and for this purpose it is agreed, that as fast as the Creeks are prepared to emigrate, they shall be removed at the expense of the United States, and shall receive subsistence while upon the journey, and for one year after their arrival at their new homes—Provided however, that this article shall not be construed so as to compel any Creek Indian to emigrate, but they shall be free to go or stay, as they please.

ARTICLE 13.
There shall also be given to each emigrating warrior a rifle, moulds, wiper and ammunition and to each family one blanket. Three thousand dollars, to be expended as the President may direct, shall be allowed for the term of twenty years for teaching their children. As soon as half their people emigrate, one blacksmith shall be allowed them, and another when two-thirds emigrate, together with one ton of iron and two hundred weight of steel annually for each blacksmith.—These blacksmiths shall be supported for twenty years.

ARTICLE 14.
The Creek country west of the Mississippi shall be solemnly guaranteed to the Creek Indians, nor shall any State or Territory ever have a right to pass laws for the government of such Indians, but they shall be allowed to govern themselves, so far as may be compatible with the general jurisdiction which Congress may think proper to exercise over them. And the United States will also defend them from the unjust hostilities of other Indians, and will also as soon as the boundaries of the Creek country West of the Mississippi are ascertained, cause a patent or grant to be executed to the Creek tribe; agreeably to the 3d section of the act of Congress of May 2d, [28,] 1830, entitled "An act to provide for an exchange of lands with the Indians residing in any of the States, or Territories, and for their removal West of the Mississippi."

ARTICLE 15.
This treaty shall be obligatory on the contracting parties, as soon as the same shall be ratified by the United States.

In testimony whereof, the said Lewis Cass, and the undersigned chiefs of the said tribe, have hereunto set their hands at the city of Washington, this 24th day of March, A. D. 1832.

> Lewis Cass,
> Opothleholo, his x mark,
> Tuchebatcheehadgo, his x mark,
> Efiematla, his x mark,
> Tuchebatche Micco, his x mark,
> Tomack Micco, his x mark,
> William McGilvery, his x mark,
> Benjamin Marshall.
>
> In the presence of—
> Samuel Bell,
> William R. King,
> John Tipton,
> William Wilkins,
> C. C. Clay,
> J. Speight,
> Samuel W. Mardis,
> J. C. Isacks,
> John Crowell, I. A.,
> Benjamin Marshall,
> Thomas Carr,
> John H. Brodnax,
> Interpreters.

Treaty with the Seminole, 1832
May 9, 1832. | 7 Stat., 368. | Proclamation, April 12, 1834.

The Seminole Indians, regarding with just respect, the solicitude manifested by the President of the United States or the improvement of their condition, by recommending a removal to a country more suitable to their habits and wants than the one they at present occupy in the Territory of Florida, are willing that their confidential chiefs, Jumper, Fuch-a-lus-ti-had-jo, Charley Emartla, Coi-had-jo, Holati Emartla Ya-hadjo; Sam Jones, accompanied by their agent Major Phagan, and their faithful interpreter Abraham, should be sent at the expense of the United States as early as convenient to examine the country assigned to the Creeks west of the Mississippi river, and should they be satisfied with the character of that country, and of the favorable disposition of the Creeks to reunite with the Seminoles as one people; the articles of the compact and agreement, herein stipulated at Payne's landing on one Ocklewaha river, this ninth day of May, one thousand eight hundred and thirty-two, between James Gadsden, for and in behalf of the Government of the United States, and the undersigned chiefs and head-men for and in behalf of the Seminole Indians, shall be binding on the respective parties.

ARTICLE 1.
The Seminole Indians relinquish to the United States, all claim to the lands they at present occupy in the Territory of Florida, and agree to emigrate to the country assigned to the Creeks, west of the Mississippi river; it being understood that an additional extent of territory, proportioned to their numbers, will be added to the Creek country, and that the Seminoles will be received as a constituent part of the Creek nation and be re-admitted to all the privileges as members of the same.

ARTICLE 2.
For and in consideration of the relinquishment of claim in the first article of this agreement, and in full compensation for all the improvements, which may have been made on the lands thereby ceded; the United States stipulate to pay to the Seminole Indians, fifteen thousand, four hundred (15,400) dollars, to be divided among the chiefs and warriors of the several towns, in a ratio proportioned to their population, the respective proportions of each to be paid on their arrival in the country they consent to remove to; it being understood that their faithful interpreters Abraham and Cudjo shall receive two hundred dollars each of the above sum, in full remuneration for the improvements to be abandoned on the lands now cultivated by them.

ARTICLE 3.
The United States agree to distribute as they arrive at their new homes in the Creek Territory, west of the Mississippi river, a blanket and a homespun frock, to each of the warriors, women and children of the Seminole tribe of Indians.

ARTICLE 4.
The United States agree to extend the annuity for the support of a blacksmith, provided for in the sixth article of the treaty at Camp Moultrie for ten (10) years beyond the period therein stipulated, and in addition to the other annuities secured under that treaty: the United States agree to pay the sum of three thousand (3,000) dollars a year for fifteen (15) years, commencing after the removal of the whole tribe; these sums to be added to the Creek annuities, and the whole amount to be so divided, that the chiefs and warriors of the Seminole Indians may receive their equitable proportion of the same as members of the Creek confederation—

ARTICLE 5.
The United States will take the cattle belonging to the Seminoles at the valuation of some discreet person to be appointed by the President, and the same shall be paid for in money to the respective owners, after their arrival at their new homes; or other cattle such as may be desired will be furnished them, notice being given through their agent of their wishes upon this subject, before their removal, that time may be afforded to supply the demand.

ARTICLE 6.
The Seminoles being anxious to be relieved from repeated vexatious demands for slaves and other property, alleged to have been stolen and destroyed by them, so that they may remove unembarrassed to their new homes; the United States stipulate to have the same property investigated, and to liquidate such as may be satisfactorily established, provided the amount does not exceed seven thousand (7,000) dollars.—

ARTICLE 7.
The Seminole Indians will remove within three (3) years after the ratification of this agreement, and the expenses of their removal shall be defrayed by the United States, and such subsistence shall also be furnished them for a term not exceeding twelve (12) months, after their arrival at their new residence; as in the opinion of the President, their numbers and circumstances may require, the emigration to commence as early as practicable in the year eighteen hundred and thirty-three (1833), and with those Indians at present occupying the Big Swamp, and other parts of the country beyond the limits as defined in the second article of the treaty concluded at Camp Moultrie creek, so that the whole of that

proportion of the Seminoles may be removed within the year aforesaid, and the remainder of the tribe, in about equal proportions, during the subsequent years of eighteen hundred and thirty-four and five, (1834 and 1835.)—

In testimony whereof, the commissioner, James Gadsden, and the undersigned chiefs and head men of the Seminole Indians, have hereunto subscribed their names and affixed their seals. Done at camp at Payne's landing, on the Ocklawaha river in the territory of Florida, on this ninth day of May, one thousand eight hundred and thirty-two, and of the independence of the United States of America the fifty-sixth.

> James Gadsden, [L. S.],
> Holati Emartla, his x mark, [L. S.],
> Jumper, his x mark, [L. S.],
> Fuch-ta-lus-ta-Hadjo, his x mark, [L. S.],
> Charley Emartla, his x mark, [L. S.],
> Coa Hadjo, his x mark, [L. S.],
> Ar-pi-uck-i, or Sam Jones, his x mark, [L. S.],
> Ya-ha Hadjo, his x mark, [L. S.],
> Mico-Noha, his x mark, [L. S.],
> Tokose-Emartla, or Jno. Hicks. his x mark, [L. S.],
> Cat-sha-Tusta-nuck-i, his x mark, [L. S.],
> Hola-at-a-Mico, his x mark, [L. S.],
> Hitch-it-i-Mico, his x mark, [L. S.],
> E-ne-hah, his x mark, [L. S.],
> Ya- ha- emartla Chup- ko, his mark, [L. S.],
> Moke-his-she-lar-ni, his x mark, [L. S.].

Witnesses:
Douglas Vass, Secretary to Commissioner,
John Phagan, Agent,
Stephen Richards, Interpreter,
Abraham, Interpreter, his x mark,
Cudjo, Interpreter, his x mark,
Erastus Rogers,
B. Joscan.

Treaty of Chicago, 1834

Articles of a treaty made at Chicago, in the State of Illinois, on the twenty-sixth day of September, in the year of our Lord one thousand eight hundred and thirty-three, between George B. Porter, Thomas J. V. Owen and William Weatherford, Commissioners on the part of the United States of the one part, and the United Nation of Chippewa, Ottowa and Potawatamie Indians of the other part, being fully represented by the Chiefs and Head-men whose names are hereunto subscribed—which Treaty is in the following words, to wit:

ARTICLE 1.
The said United Nation of Chippewa, Ottowa, and Potawatamie Indians, cede to the United States all their land, along the western shore of Lake Michigan, and between this Lake and the land ceded to the United States by the Winnebago nation, at the treaty of Fort Armstrong made on the 15th September 1832—bounded on the north by the country lately ceded by the Menominees, and on the south by the country ceded at the treaty of Prairie du Chien made on the 29th July 1829—supposed to contain about five millions of acres.

ARTICLE 2.
In part consideration of the above cession it is hereby agreed, that the United States shall grant to the said United Nation of Indians to be held as other Indian lands are held which have lately been assigned to emigrating Indians, a tract of country west of the Mississippi river, to be assigned to them by the President of the United States—to be not less in quantity than five millions of acres, and to be located as follows: beginning at the mouth of Boyer's river on the east side of the Missouri river, thence down the said river to the mouth of Naudoway river, thence due east to the west line of the State of Missouri, thence along the said State line to the northwest corner of the State, thence east along the said State line to the point where it is intersected by the western boundary line of the Sacs and Foxes— thence north along the said line of the Sacs and Foxes, so far as that when a straight line shall be run therefrom to the mouth of Boyer's river (the place of beginning) it shall include five millions of acres. And as it is the wish of the Government of the United States that the said nation of Indians should remove to the country thus assigned to them as soon as conveniently can be done; and it is deemed advisable on the part of their Chiefs and Headmen that a deputation should visit the said country west of the Mississippi and thus be assured that full justice has been

done, it is hereby stipulated that the United States will defray the expenses of such deputation, to consist of not more than fifty persons, to be accompanied by not more than five individuals to be nominated by themselves, and the whole to be under the general direction of such officer of the United States Government as has been or shall be designated for the purpose.—And it is further agreed that as fast as the said Indians shall be prepared to emigrate, they shall be removed at the expense of the United States, and shall receive subsistence while upon the journey, and for one year after their arrival at their new homes.—It being understood, that the said Indians are to remove from all that part of the land now ceded, which is within the State of Illinois, immediately on the ratification of this treaty, but to be permitted to retain possession of the country north of the boundary line of the said State, for the term of three years, without molestation or interruption and under the protection of the laws of the United States.

ARTICLE 3.
And in further consideration of the above cession, it is agreed, that there shall be paid by the United States the sums of money hereinafter mentioned: to wit.

One hundred thousand dollars to satisfy sundry individuals, in behalf of whom reservations were asked, which the Commissioners refused to grant: and also to indemnify the Chippewa tribe who are parties to this treaty for certain lands along the shore of Lake Michigan, to which they make claim, which have been ceded to the United States by the Menominee Indians— the manner in which the same is to be paid is set forth in Schedule "A" hereunto annexed.

One hundred and fifty thousand dollars to satisfy the claims made against the said United Nation which they have here admitted to be justly due, and directed to be paid, according to Schedule "B" hereunto annexed.

One hundred thousand dollars to be paid in goods and provisions, a part to be delivered on the signing of this treaty and the residue during the ensuing year.

Two hundred and eighty thousand dollars to be paid in annuities of fourteen thousand dollars a year, for twenty years.

One hundred and fifty thousand dollars to be applied to the erection of mills, farm houses, Indian houses and blacksmith shops, to agricultural improvements, to the purchase of agricultural implements and stock, and for the support of such physicians, millers, farmers, blacksmiths and other mechanics, as the President of the United States shall think proper to appoint.

Seventy thousand dollars for purposes of education and the encouragement of the domestic arts, to be applied in such manner, as the President of the United States may direct.—[The wish of the Indians being expressed to the Commissioners as follows: The united nation of Chippewa, Ottowa and Potawatamie Indians being desirous to create a perpetual fund for the purposes of education and the encouragement of the domestic arts, wish to invest the sum of seventy thousand dollars in some safe stock, the interest of which only is to be applied as may be necessary for the above purposes. They therefore request the President of the United States, to make such investment for the nation as he may think best. If however, at any time hereafter, the said nation shall have made such advancement in civilization and have become so enlightened as in the opinion of the President and Senate of the United States they shall be capable of managing so large a fund with safety they may withdraw the whole or any part of it.]

Four hundred dollars a year to be paid to Billy Caldwell, and three hundred dollars a year, to be paid to Alexander Robinson, for life, in addition to the annuities already granted them—Two hundred dollars a year to be paid to Joseph Lafromboise and two hundred dollars a year to be paid to Shabehnay, for life.

Two thousand dollars to be paid to Wau-pon-eh-see and his band, and fifteen hundred dollars to Awn-kote and his band, as the consideration for nine sections of land, granted to them by the 3d Article of the Treaty of Prairie du Chien of the 29th of July 1829 which are hereby assigned and surrendered to the United States.

ARTICLE 4.
A just proportion of the annuity money, secured as well by former treaties as the present, shall be paid west of the Mississippi to such portion of the nation as shall have removed thither during the ensuing three years.—After which time, the whole amount of the annuities shall be paid at their location west of the Mississippi.

ARTICLE 5.
[Stricken out.]

This treaty after the same shall have been ratified by the President and Senate of the United States, shall be binding on the contracting parties.

In testimony whereof, the said George B. Porter, Thomas J. V. Owen, and William Weatherford, and the undersigned chiefs and head men of the said nation of Indians, have hereunto set their hands at Chicago, the said day and year.

G. B. Porter,
Th. J. V. Owen,
William Weatherford,
To-pen-e-bee, his x mark,
Sau-ko-noek,
Che-che-bin-quay, his x mark,
Joseph, his x mark,
Wah-mix-i-co, his x mark,
Ob-wa-qua-unk, his x mark,
N-saw-way-quet, his x mark,
Puk-quech-a-min-nee, his x mark,
Nah-che-wine, his x mark,
Ke-wase, his x mark,
Wah-bou-seh, his x mark,
Mang-e-sett, his x mark,
Caw-we-saut, his x mark,
Ah-be-te-ke-zhic, his x mark,
Pat-e-go-shuc, his x mark,
E-to-wow-cote, his x mark,
Shim-e-nah, his x mark,
O-chee-pwaise, his x mark,
Ce-nah-ge-win, his x mark,

Shaw-waw-nas-see, his x mark,
Shab-eh-nay, his x mark,
Mac-a-ta-o-shic, his x mark,
Squah-ke-zic, his x mark,
Mah-che-o-tah-way, his x mark,
Cha-ke-te-ah, his x mark,
Me-am-ese, his x mark,
Shay-tee, his x mark,
Kee-new, his x mark,
Ne-bay-noc-scum, his x mark,
Naw-bay-caw, his x mark,
O'Kee-mase, his x mark,
Saw-o-tup, his x mark,
Me-tai-way, his x mark,
Na-ma-ta-way-shuc, his x mark,
Shaw-waw-nuk-wuk, his x mark,
Nah-che-wah, his x mark,
Sho-bon-nier, his x mark,
Me-nuk-quet, his x mark,
Chis-in-ke-bah, his x mark,
Mix-e-maung, his x mark,
Nah-bwait, his x mark,
Sen-e-bau-um, his x mark,
Puk-won, his x mark,
Wa-be-no-say, his x mark,
Mon-tou-ish, his x mark,
No-nee, his x mark,
Mas-quat, his x mark,
Sho-min, his x mark,
Ah-take, his x mark,
He-me-nah-wah, his x mark,
Che-pec-co-quah, his x mark,
Mis-quab-o-no-quah, his x mark,
Wah-be-Kai, his x mark,
Ma-ca-ta-ke-shic, his x mark,
Sho-min, (2d.) his x mark,
She-mah-gah, his x mark,
O'ke-mah-wah-ba-see, his x mark,
Na-mash, his x mark,
Shab-y-a-tuk, his x mark,
Ah-cah-o-mah, his x mark,
Quah-quah, tah, his x mark,
Ah-sag-a-mish-cum, his x mark,
Pa-mob-a-mee, his x mark,
Nay-o-say, his x mark,
Ce-tah-quah, his x mark,
Ce-ku-tay, his x mark,
Sauk-ee, his x mark,
Ah-quee-wee, his x mark,
Ta-cau-ko, his x mark,
Me-shim-e-nah, his x mark,
Wah-sus-kuk, his x mark,

Pe-nay-o-cat, his x mark,
Pay-maw-suc, his x mark,
Pe-she-ka, his x mark,
Shaw-we-mon-e-tay, his x mark,
Ah-be-nab, his x mark,
Sau-sau-quas-see, his x mark.

In presence of—
Wm. Lee D. Ewing, secretary to commission,
E. A. Brush,
Luther Rice, interpreter,
James Conner, interpreter,
John T. Schermerhorn, commissioner, etc. west,
A. C. Pepper, S. A. R. P.
Gho. Kercheval, sub-agent,
Geo. Bender, major, Fifth Regiment Infantry,
D. Wilcox, captain, Fifth Regiment,
J. M. Baxley, captain, Fifth Infantry,
R. A. Forsyth, U. S. Army,
L. T. Jamison, lieutenant, U. S. Army,
E. K. Smith, lieutenant, Fifth Infantry,
P. Maxwell, assistant surgeon,
J. Allen, lieutenant, Fifth Infantry,
I. P. Simonton, lieutenant, U. S. Army,
George F. Turner, assistant surgeon, U. S. Army,
Richd. J. Hamilton,
Robert Stuart,
Jona. McCarty,
Daniel Jackson, of New York,
Jno. H. Kinzie,
Robt. A. Kinzie,
G. S. Hubbard,
J. C. Schwarz, adjutant general M. M.
Jn. B. Beaubrier,
James Kinzie,
Jacob Beeson,
Saml. Humes Porter,
Andw. Porter,
Gabriel Godfroy,
A. H. Arndt,
Laurie Marsh,
Joseph Chaunier,
John Watkins,
B. B. Kercheval,
Jas. W. Berry,
Wm. French,
Thomas Forsyth,
Pierre Menard, Fils,
Edmd. Roberts,
Geo. Hunt,
Isaac Nash.

Treaty with the Cherokee, 1835
Dec. 29, 1835. | 7 Stat., 478. | Proclamation, May 23, 1836.
Articles of a treaty, concluded at New Echota in the State of Georgia on the 29th day of Decr. 1835 by General William Carroll and John F. Schermerhorn commissioners on the part of the United States and the Chiefs Head Men and People of the Cherokee tribe of Indians.

WHEREAS the Cherokees are anxious to make some arrangements with the Government of the United States whereby the difficulties they have experienced by a residence within the settled parts of the United States under the jurisdiction and laws of the State Governments may be terminated and adjusted; and with a view to reuniting their people in one body and securing a permanent home for themselves and their posterity in the country selected by their forefathers without the territorial limits of the State sovereignties, and where they can establish and enjoy a government of their choice and perpetuate such a state of society as may be most consonant with their views, habits and condition; and as may tend to their individual comfort and their advancement in civilization.

And whereas a delegation of the Cherokee nation composed of Messrs. John Ross Richard Taylor Danl. McCoy Samuel Gunter and William Rogers with full power and authority to conclude a treaty with the United States did on the 28th day of February 1835 stipulate and agree with the Government of the United States to submit to the Senate to fix the amount which should be allowed the Cherokees for their claims and for a cession of their lands east of the Mississippi river, and did agree to abide by the award of the Senate of the United States themselves and to recommend the same to their people for their final determination.

And whereas on such submission the Senate advised "that a sum not exceeding five millions of dollars be paid to the Cherokee Indians for all their lands and possessions east of the Mississippi river."

And whereas this delegation after said award of the Senate had been made, were called upon to submit propositions as to its disposition to be arranged in a treaty which they refused to do, but insisted that the same "should be referred to their nation and there in general council to deliberate and determine on the subject in order to ensure harmony and good feeling among themselves."

And whereas a certain other delegation composed of John Ridge Elias Boudinot Archilla Smith S. W. Bell John West Wm. A. Davis and Ezekiel West, who represented that portion of the nation in favor of emigration to the Cherokee country west of the Mississippi entered into propositions for a treaty with John F. Schermerhorn commissioner on the part of the United States which were to be submitted to their nation for their final action and determination.

And whereas the Cherokee people at their last October council at Red Clay, fully authorized and empowered a delegation or committee of twenty persons of their nation to enter into and conclude a treaty with the United States commissioner then present, at that place or elsewhere and as the people had good reason to believe that a treaty would then and there be made or at a subsequent council at New Echota which the commissioners it was well known and understood, were authorized and instructed to convene for said purpose; and since the said delegation have gone on to Washington city, with a view to close negotiations there, as stated by them notwithstanding they were officially informed by the United States commissioner that they would not be received by the President of the United States; and that the Government would transact no business of this nature with them, and that if a treaty was made it must be done here in the nation, where the delegation at Washington last winter urged that it should be done for the purpose of promoting peace and harmony among the people; and since these facts have also been corroborated to us by a communication recently received by the commissioner from the Government of the United States and read and explained to the people in open council and therefore believing said delegation can effect nothing and since our difficulties are daily increasing and our situation is rendered more and more precarious uncertain and insecure in consequence of the legislation of the States; and seeing no effectual way of relief, but in accepting the liberal overtures of the United States.

And whereas Genl William Carroll and John F. Schermerhorn were appointed commissioners on the part of the United States, with full power and authority to conclude a treaty with the Cherokees

east and were directed by the President to convene the people of the nation in general council at New Echota and to submit said propositions to them with power and authority to vary the same so as to meet the views of the Cherokees in reference to its details.

And whereas the said commissioners did appoint and notify a general council of the nation to convene at New Echota on the 21st day of December 1835; and informed them that the commissioners would be prepared to make a treaty with the Cherokee people who should assemble there and those who did not come they should conclude gave their assent and sanction to whatever should be transacted at this council and the people having met in council according to said notice.

Therefore the following articles of a treaty are agreed upon and concluded between William Carroll and John F. Schermerhorn commissioners on the part of the United States and the chiefs and head men and people of the Cherokee nation in general council assembled this 29th day of Decr 1835.

ARTICLE 1.
The Cherokee nation hereby cede relinquish and convey to the United States all the lands owned claimed or possessed by them east of the Mississippi river, and hereby release all their claims upon the United States for spoliations of every kind for and in consideration of the sum of five millions of dollars to be expended paid and invested in the manner stipulated and agreed upon in the following articles. But as a question has arisen between the commissioners and the Cherokees whether the Senate in their resolution by which they advised "that a sum not exceeding five millions of dollars be paid to the Cherokee Indians for all their lands and possessions east of the Mississippi river" have included and made any allowance or consideration for claims for spoliations it is therefore agreed on the part of the United States that this question shall be again submitted to the Senate for their consideration and decision and if no allowance was made for spoliations that then an additional sum of three hundred thousand dollars be allowed for the same.

ARTICLE 2.
Whereas by the treaty of May 6th 1828 and the supplementary treaty thereto of Feb. 14th 1833 with the Cherokees west of the Mississippi the United States guarantied and secured to be conveyed by patent, to

the Cherokee nation of Indians the following tract of country "Beginning at a point on the old western territorial line of Arkansas Territory being twenty-five miles north from the point where the territorial line crosses Arkansas river, thence running from said north point south on the said territorial line where the said territorial line crosses Verdigris river; thence down said Verdigris river to the Arkansas river; thence down said Arkansas to a point where a stone is placed opposite the east or lower bank of Grand river at its junction with the Arkansas; thence running south forty-four degrees west one mile; thence in a straight line to a point four miles northerly, from the mouth of the north fork of the Canadian; thence along the said four mile line to the Canadian; thence down the Canadian to the Arkansas; thence down the Arkansas to that point on the Arkansas where the eastern Choctaw boundary strikes said river and running thence with the western line of Arkansas Territory as now defined, to the southwest corner of Missouri; thence along the western Missouri line to the land assigned the Senecas; thence on the south line of the Senecas to Grand river; thence up said Grand river as far as the south line of the Osage reservation, extended if necessary; thence up and between said south Osage line extended west if necessary, and a line drawn due west from the point of beginning to a certain distance west, at which a line running north and south from said Osage line to said due west line will make seven millions of acres within the whole described boundaries. In addition to the seven millions of acres of land thus provided for and bounded, the United States further guaranty to the Cherokee nation a perpetual outlet west, and a free and unmolested use of all the country west of the western boundary of said seven millions of acres, as far west as the sovereignty of the United States and their right of soil extend:

Provided however That if the saline or salt plain on the western prairie shall fall within said limits prescribed for said outlet, the right is reserved to the United States to permit other tribes of red men to get salt on said plain in common with the Cherokees; And letters patent shall be issued by the United States as soon as practicable for the land hereby guarantied."

And whereas it is apprehended by the Cherokees that in the above cession there is not contained a sufficient quantity of land for the accommodation of the whole nation on their removal west of the Missis-

sippi the United States in consideration of the sum of five hundred thousand dollars therefore hereby covenant and agree to convey to the said Indians, and their descendants by patent, in fee simple the following additional tract of land situated between the west line of the State of Missouri and the Osage reservation beginning at the southeast corner of the same and runs north along the east line of the Osage lands fifty miles to the northeast corner thereof; and thence east to the west line of the State of Missouri; thence with said line south fifty miles; thence west to the place of beginning; estimated to contain eight hundred thousand acres of land; but it is expressly understood that if any of the lands assigned the Quapaws shall fall within the aforesaid bounds the same shall be reserved and excepted out of the lands above granted and a pro rata reduction shall be made in the price to be allowed to the United States for the same by the Cherokees.

ARTICLE 3.
The United States also agree that the lands above ceded by the treaty of Feb. 14 1833, including the outlet, and those ceded by this treaty shall all be included in one patent executed to the Cherokee nation of Indians by the President of the United States according to the provisions of the act of May 28 1830. It is, however, agreed that the military reservation at Fort Gibson shall be held by the United States. But should the United States abandon said post and have no further use for the same it shall revert to the Cherokee nation. The United States shall always have the right to make and establish such post and military roads and forts in any part of the Cherokee country, as they may deem proper for the interest and protection of the same and the free use of as much land, timber, fuel and materials of all kinds for the construction and support of the same as may be necessary; provided that if the private rights of individuals are interfered with, a just compensation therefor shall be made.

ARTICLE 4.
The United States also stipulate and agree to extinguish for the benefit of the Cherokees the titles to the reservations within their country made in the Osage treaty of 1825 to certain half-breeds and for this purpose they hereby agree to pay to the persons to whom the same belong or have been assigned or to their agents or guardians whenever they shall execute after the ratification of this treaty a satisfactory conveyance for the same, to the United States, the

sum of fifteen thousand dollars according to a schedule accompanying this treaty of the relative value of the several reservations.

And whereas by the several treaties between the United States and the Osage Indians the Union and Harmony Missionary reservations which were established for their benefit are now situated within the country ceded by them to the United States; the former being situated in the Cherokee country and the latter in the State of Missouri. It is therefore agreed that the United States shall pay the American Board of Commissioners for Foreign Missions for the improvements on the same what they shall be appraised at by Capt. Geo. Vashon Cherokee sub-agent Abraham Redfield and A. P. Chouteau or such persons as the President of the United States shall appoint and the money allowed for the same shall be expended in schools among the Osages and improving their condition. It is understood that the United States are to pay the amount allowed for the reservations in this article and not the Cherokees.

ARTICLE 5.
The United States hereby covenant and agree that the lands ceded to the Cherokee nation in the forgoing article shall, in no future time without their consent, be included within the territorial limits or jurisdiction of any State or Territory. But they shall secure to the Cherokee nation the right by their national councils to make and carry into effect all such laws as they may deem necessary for the government and protection of the persons and property within their own country belonging to their people or such persons as have connected themselves with them: provided always that they shall not be inconsistent with the constitution of the United States and such acts of Congress as have been or may be passed regulating trade and intercourse with the Indians; and also, that they stall not be considered as extending to such citizens and army of the United States as may travel or reside in the Indian country by permission according to the laws and regulations established by the Government of the same.

ARTICLE 6.
Perpetual peace and friendship shall exist between the citizens of the United States and the Cherokee Indians. The United States agree to protect the Cherokee nation from domestic strife and foreign enemies and against intestine wars between the several tribes. The Cherokees shall endeavor to preserve and maintain the peace of the country and not make war upon their neighbors; they shall also be protected against interruption and intrusion from citizens of the United States, who may attempt to settle in the country without their consent; and all such persons shall be removed from the same by order of the President of the United States. But this is not intended to prevent the residence among them of useful farmers, mechanics and teachers for the instruction of Indians according to treaty stipulations.

ARTICLE 7.
The Cherokee nation having already made great progress in civilization and deeming it important that every proper and laudable inducement should be offered to their people to improve their condition as well as to guard and secure in the most effectual manner the rights guaranteed to them in this treaty, and with a view to illustrate the liberal and enlarged policy of the Government of the United States towards the Indians in their removal beyond the territorial limits of the States, it is stipulated that they shall be entitled to a delegate in the House of Representatives of the United States whenever Congress shall make provision for the same.

ARTICLE 8.
The United States also agree and stipulate to remove the Cherokees to their new homes and to subsist them one year after their arrival there and that a sufficient number of steamboats and baggage-wagons shall be furnished to remove them comfortably, and so as not to endanger their health, and that a physician well supplied with medicines shall accompany each detachment of emigrants removed by the Government. Such persons and families as in the opinion of the emigrating agent are capable of subsisting and removing themselves shall be permitted to do so; and they shall be allowed in full for all claims for the same twenty dollars for each member of their family; and in lieu of their one year's rations they shall be paid the sum of thirty-three dollars and thirty-three cents if they prefer it.

Such Cherokees also as reside at present out of the nation and shall remove with them in two years west of the Mississippi shall be entitled to allowance for removal and subsistence as above provided.

ARTICLE 9.

The United States agree to appoint suitable agents who shall make a just and fair valuation of all such improvements now in the possession of the Cherokees as add any value to the lands; and also of the ferries owned by them, according to their net income; and such improvements and ferries from which they have been dispossessed in a lawless manner or under any existing laws of the State where the same may be situated.

The just debts of the Indians shall be paid out of any monies due them for their improvements and claims; and they shall also be furnished at the discretion of the President of the United States with a sufficient sum to enable them to obtain the necessary means to remove themselves to their new homes, and the balance of their dues shall be paid them at the Cherokee agency west of the Mississippi. The missionary establishments shall also be valued and appraised in a like manner and the amount of them paid over by the United States to the treasurers of the respective missionary societies by whom they have been established and improved in order to enable them to erect such buildings and make such improvements among the Cherokees west of the Mississippi as they may deem necessary for their benefit. Such teachers at present among the Cherokees as this council shall select and designate shall be removed west of the Mississippi with the Cherokee nation and on the same terms allowed to them.

ARTICLE 10.

The President of the United States shall invest in some safe and most productive public stocks of the country for the benefit of the whole Cherokee nation who have removed or shall remove to the lands assigned by this treaty to the Cherokee nation west of the Mississippi the following sums as a permanent fund for the purposes hereinafter specified and pay over the net income of the same annually to such person or persons as shall be authorized or appointed by the Cherokee nation to receive the same and their receipt shall be a full discharge for the amount paid to them viz: the sum of two hundred thousand dollars in addition to the present annuities of the nation to constitute a general fund the interest of which shall be applied annually by the council of the nation to such purposes as they may deem best for the general interest of their people. The sum of fifty thousand dollars to constitute an orphans' fund the annual income of which shall be

expended towards the support and education of such orphan children as are destitute of the means of subsistence. The sum of one hundred and fifty thousand dollars in addition to the present school fund of the nation shall constitute a permanent school fund, the interest of which shall be applied annually by the council of the nation for the support of common schools and such a literary institution of a higher order as may be established in the Indian country. And in order to secure as far as possible the true and beneficial application of the orphans' and school fund the council of the Cherokee nation when required by the President of the United States shall make a report of the application of those funds and he shall at all times have the right if the funds have been misapplied to correct any abuses of them and direct the manner of their application for the purposes for which they were intended. The council of the nation may by giving two years' notice of their intention withdraw their funds by and with the consent of the President and Senate of the United States, and invest them in such manner as they may deem most proper for their interest. The United States also agree and stipulate to pay the just debts and claims against the Cherokee nation held by the citizens of the same and also the just claims of citizens of the United States for services rendered to the nation and the sum of sixty thousand dollars is appropriated for this purpose but no claims against individual persons of the nation shall be allowed and paid by the nation. The sum of three hundred thousand dollars is hereby set apart to pay and liquidate the just claims of the Cherokees upon the United States for spoliations of every kind, that have not been already satisfied under former treaties.

ARTICLE 11.

The Cherokee nation of Indians believing it will be for the interest of their people to have all their funds and annuities under their own direction and future disposition hereby agree to commute their permanent annuity of ten thousand dollars for the sum of two hundred and fourteen thousand dollars, the same to be invested by the President of the United States as a part of the general fund of the nation; and their present school fund amounting to about fifty thousand dollars shall constitute a part of the permanent school fund of the nation.

ARTICLE 12.

Those individuals and families of the Cherokee nation that are averse to a removal to the Cherokee country west of the Mississippi and are desirous to become citizens of the States where they reside and such as are qualified to take care of themselves and their property shall be entitled to receive their due portion of all the personal benefits accruing under this treaty for their claims, improvements and per capita; as soon as an appropriation is made for this treaty.

Such heads of Cherokee families as are desirous to reside within the States of No. Carolina, Tennessee, and Alabama subject to the laws of the same; and who are qualified or calculated to become useful citizens shall be entitled, on the certificate of the commissioners to a preemption right to one hundred and sixty acres of land or one quarter section at the minimum Congress price; so as to include the present buildings or improvements of those who now reside there and such as do not live there at present shall be permitted to locate within two years any lands not already occupied by persons entitled to pre-emption privilege under this treaty and if two or more families live on the same quarter section and they desire to continue their residence in these States and are qualified as above specified they shall, on receiving their pre-emption certificate be entitled to the right of pre-emption to such lands as they may select not already taken by any person entitled to them under this treaty.

It is stipulated and agreed between the United States and the Cherokee people that John Ross, James Starr, George Hicks, John Gunter, George Chambers, John Ridge, Elias Boudinot, George Sanders, John Martin , William Rogers, Roman Nose Situwake, and John Timpson shall be a committee on the part of the Cherokees to recommend such persons for the privilege of pre-emption rights as may be deemed entitled to the same under the above articles and to select the missionaries who shall be removed with the nation; and that they be hereby fully empowered and authorized to transact all business on the part of the Indians which may arise in carrying into effect the provisions of this treaty and settling the same with the United States. If any of the persons above mentioned should decline acting or be removed by death; the vacancies shall be filled by the committee themselves.

It is also understood and agreed that the sum of one hundred thousand dollars shall be expended by the commissioners in such manner as the committee deem best for the benefit of the poorer class of Cherokees as shall remove west or have removed west and are entitled to the benefits of this treaty. The same to be delivered at the Cherokee agency west as soon after the removal of the nation as possible.

ARTICLE 13.
In order to make a final settlement of all the claims of the Cherokees for reservations granted under former treaties to any individuals belonging to the nation by the United States it is therefore hereby stipulated and agreed and expressly understood by the parties to this treaty—that all the Cherokees and their heirs and descendants to whom any reservations have been made under any former treaties with the United States, and who have not sold or conveyed the same by deed or otherwise and who in the opinion of the commissioners have complied with the terms on which the reservations were granted as far as practicable in the several cases; and which reservations have since been sold by the United States shall constitute a just claim against the United States and the original reservee or their heirs or descendants shall be entitled to receive the present value thereof from the United States as unimproved lands. And all such reservations as have not been sold by the United States and where the terms on which the reservations were made in the opinion of the commissioners have been complied with as far as practicable, they or their heirs or descendants shall be entitled to the same. They are hereby granted and confirmed to them—and also all persons who were entitled to reservations under the treaty of 1817 and who as far as practicable in the opinion of the commissioners, have complied with the stipulations of said treaty, although by the treaty of 1819 such reservations were included in the unceded lands belonging to the Cherokee nation are hereby confirmed to them and they shall be entitled to receive a grant for the same. And all such reservees as were obliged by the laws of the States in which their reservations were situated, to abandon the same or purchase them from the States shall be deemed to have a just claim against the United States for the amount by them paid to the States with interest thereon for such reservations and if obliged to abandon the same, to the present value of such reservations as unimproved lands but in all cases where the reservees have sold their reservations or any part thereof and conveyed the same by deed or otherwise and have been paid for the same, they their heirs or

descendants or their assigns shall not be considered as having any claims upon the United States under this article of the treaty nor be entitled to receive any compensation for the lands thus disposed of. It is expressly understood by the parties to this treaty that the amount to be allowed for reservations under this article shall not be deducted out of the consideration money allowed to the Cherokees for their claims for spoilations and the cession of their lands; but the same is to be paid for independently by the United States as it is only a just fulfillment of former treaty stipulations.

ARTICLE 14.
It is also agreed on the part of the United States that such warriors of the Cherokee nation as were engaged on the side of the United States in the late war with Great Britain and the southern tribes of Indians, and who were wounded in such service shall be entitled to such pensions as shall be allowed them by the Congress of the United States to commence from the period of their disability.

ARTICLE 15.
It is expressly understood and agreed between the parties to this treaty that after deducting the amount which shall be actually expended for the payment for improvements, ferries, claims, for spoliations, removal subsistence and debts and claims upon the Cherokee nation and for the additional quantity of lands and goods for the poorer class of Cherokees and the several sums to be invested for the general national funds; provided for in the several articles of this treaty the balance whatever the same may be shall be equally divided between all the people belonging to the Cherokee nation east according to the census just completed; and such Cherokees as have removed west since June 1833 who are entitled by the terms of their enrollment and removal to all the benefits resulting from the final treaty between the United States and the Cherokees east they shall also be paid for their improvements according to their approved value before their removal where fraud has not already been shown in their valuation.

ARTICLE 16.
It is hereby stipulated and agreed by the Cherokees that they shall remove to their new homes within two years from the ratification of this treaty and that during such time the United States shall protect and defend them in their possessions and property and free use and occupation of the same and such per-

sons as have been dispossessed of their improvements and houses; and for which no grant has actually issued previously to the enactment of the law of the State of Georgia, of December 1835 to regulate Indian occupancy shall be again put in possession and placed in the same situation and condition, in reference to the laws of the State of Georgia, as the Indians that have not been dispossessed; and if this is not done, and the people are left unprotected, then the United States shall pay the several Cherokees for their losses and damages sustained by them in consequence thereof. And it is also stipulated and agreed that the public buildings and improvements on which they are situated at New Echota for which no grant has been actually made previous to the passage of the above recited act if not occupied by the Cherokee people shall be reserved for the public and free use of the United States and the Cherokee Indians for the purpose of settling and closing all the Indian business arising under this treaty between the commissioners of claims and the Indians.

The United States, and the several States interested in the Cherokee lands, shall immediately proceed to survey the lands ceded by this treaty; but it is expressly agreed and understood between the parties that the agency buildings and that tract of land surveyed and laid off for the use of Colonel R. J. Meigs Indian agent or heretofore enjoyed and occupied by his successors in office shall continue subject to the use and occupancy of the United States, or such agent as may be engaged specially superintending the removal of the tribe.

ARTICLE 17.
All the claims arising under or provided for in the several articles of this treaty, shall be examined and adjudicated by such commissioners as shall be appointed by the President of the United States by and with the advice and consent of the Senate of the United States for that purpose and their decision shall be final and on their certificate of the amount due the several claimants they shall be paid by the United States. All stipulations in former treaties which have not been superseded or annulled by this shall continue in full force and virtue.

ARTICLE 18.
Whereas in consequence of the unsettled affairs of the Cherokee people and the early frosts, their crops are insufficient to support their families and great distress is likely to ensue and whereas the nation

will not, until after their removal be able advantageously to expend the income of the permanent funds of the nation it is therefore agreed that the annuities of the nation which may accrue under this treaty for two years, the time fixed for their removal shall be expended in provision and clothing for the benefit of the poorer class of the nation and the United States hereby agree to advance the same for that purpose as soon after the ratification of this treaty as an appropriation for the same shall be made. It is however not intended in this article to interfere with that part of the annuities due the Cherokees west by the treaty of 1819.

ARTICLE 19.
This treaty after the same shall be ratified by the President and Senate of the United States shall be obligatory on the contracting parties.

ARTICLE 20.
[Supplemental article. Stricken out by Senate.]

In testimony whereof, the commissioners and the chiefs, head men, and people whose names are hereunto annexed, being duly authorized by the people in general council assembled, have affixed their hands and seals for themselves, and in behalf of the Cherokee nation.

I have examined the foregoing treaty, and although not present when it was made, I approve its provisions generally, and therefore sign it.

> Wm. Carroll,
> J. F. Schermerhorn,
> Major Ridge, his x mark, [L. S.],
> James Foster, his x mark, [L. S.],
> Tesa-ta-esky, his x mark, [L. S.],
> Charles Moore, his x mark, [L. S.],
> George Chambers, his x mark, [L. S.],
> Tah-yeske, his x mark, [L. S.],
> Archilla Smith, his x mark, [L. S.],
> Andrew Ross, [L. S.],
> William Lassley, [L. S.],
> Cae-te-hee, his x mark , [L. S.],
> Te-gah-e-ske, his x mark, [L. S.],
> Robert Rogers, [L. S.],
> John Gunter, [L. S.],
> John A. Bell, [L. S.],
> Charles F. Foreman, [L. S.],
> William Rogers, [L. S.],

> George W. Adair, [L. S.],
> Elias Boudinot, [L. S.],
> James Starr, his x mark, [L. S.],
> Jesse Half-breed, his x mark, [L. S.].

Signed and sealed in presence of—
Western B. Thomas, secretary,
Ben. F. Currey, special agent,
M. Wolfe Batman, first lieutenant, sixth U. S. infantry, disbursing agent,
Jon. L. Hooper, lieutenant, fourth Infantry,
C. M Hitchcock, M. D., assistant surgeon, U.S.A,
G. W. Currey,
Wm. H. Underwood,
Cornelius D. Terhune,
John W. H. Underwood.

In compliance with instructions of the council at New Echota, we sign this treaty.

> Stand Watie,
> John Ridge.

March 1, 1836.
Witnesses:
Elbert Herring,
Alexander H. Everett,
John Robb,
D. Kurtz,
Wm.Y. Hansell,
Samuel J. Potts,
Jno. Litle,
S. Rockwell.

Dec. 31, 1835 | 7 Stat., 487.

Whereas the western Cherokees have appointed a delegation to visit the eastern Cherokees to assure them of the friendly disposition of their people and their desire that the nation should again be united as one people and to urge upon them the expediency of accepting the overtures of the Government; and that, on their removal they may be assured of a hearty welcome and an equal participation with them in all the benefits and privileges of the Cherokee country west and the undersigned two of said delegation being the only delegates in the eastern nation from the west at the signing and sealing of the treaty lately concluded at New Echota between their eastern brethren and the United States; and having fully understood the provisions of the same they agree to it in behalf of the western Cherokees. But it is expressly understood that nothing in this treaty shall affect any claims of the western Cherokees on the United States. In testimony whereof, we have, this 31st day of December, 1835, hereunto set our hands and seals.

James Rogers,
John Smith,
Delegates from the western Cherokees.

Test:
Ben. F. Currey, special agent,
M. W. Batman, first lieutenant, Sixth Infantry,
Jno. L. Hooper, lieutenant, Fourth Infantry,
Elias Boudinot.

Treaty with the Chippewa (Ojibwe), 1837

Articles of a treaty made and concluded at St. Peters (the confluence of the St. Peters and Mississippi rivers) in the Territory of Wisconsin, between the United States of America, by their commissioner, Henry Dodge, Governor of said Territory, and the Chippewa nation of Indians, by their chiefs and headmen.

ARTICLE 1.
The said Chippewa nation cede to the United States all that tract of country included within the following boundaries:

Beginning at the junction of the Crow Wing and Mississippi rivers, between twenty and thirty miles above where the Mississippi is crossed by the forty-sixth parallel of north latitude, and running thence to the north point of Lake St. Croix, one of the sources of the St. Croix river; thence to and along the dividing ridge between the waters of Lake Superior and those of the Mississippi, to the sources of the Ocha-sua-sepe a tributary of the Chippewa river; thence to a point on the Chippewa river, twenty miles below the outlet of Lake De Flambeau; thence to the junction of the Wisconsin and Pelican rivers; thence on an east course twenty-five miles;

thence southerly, on a course parallel with that of the Wisconsin river, to the line dividing the territories of the Chippewas and Menomonies; thence to the Plover Portage; thence along the southern boundary of the Chippewa country, to the commencement of the boundary line dividing it from that of the Sioux, half a days march below the falls on the Chippewa river; thence with said boundary line to the mouth of Wah-tap river, at its junction with the Mississippi; and thence up the Mississippi to the place of beginning.

ARTICLE 2.
In consideration of the cession aforesaid, the United States agree to make to the Chippewa nation, annually, for the term of twenty years, from the date of the ratification of this treaty, the following payments.

1. Nine thousand five hundred dollars, to be paid in money.
2. Nineteen thousand dollars, to be delivered in goods.
3. Three thousand dollars for establishing three blacksmiths shops, supporting the blacksmiths, and furnishing them with iron and steel.
4. One thousand dollars for farmers, and for supplying them and the Indians, with implements of labor, with grain or seed; and whatever else may be necessary to enable them to carry on their agricultural pursuits.
5. Two thousand dollars in provisions.
6. Five hundred dollars in tobacco.

The provisions and tobacco to be delivered at the same time with the goods, and the money to be paid; which time or times, as well as the place or places where they are to be delivered, shall be fixed upon under the direction of the President of the United States.

The blacksmiths shops to be placed at such points in the Chippewa country as shall be designated by the Superintendent of Indian Affairs, or under his direction.

If at the expiration of one or more years the Indians should prefer to receive goods, instead of the nine thousand dollars agreed to be paid to them in money, they shall be at liberty to do so. Or, should they conclude to appropriate a portion of that annuity to the establishment and support of a school or schools among them, this shall be granted them.

ARTICLE 3.
The sum of one hundred thousand dollars shall be paid by the United States, to the half-breeds of the Chippewa nation, under the direction of the President. It is the wish of the Indians that their two sub-agents Daniel P. Bushnell, and Miles M. Vineyard, superintend the distribution of this money among their half-breed relations.

ARTICLE 4.
The sum of seventy thousand dollars shall be applied to the payment, by the United States, of certain claims against the Indians; of which amount twenty-eight thousand dollars shall, at their request, be paid to William A. Aitkin, twenty-five thousand to Lyman M. Warren, and the balance applied to the liquidation of other just demands against them—which they acknowledge to be the case with regard to that presented by Hercules L. Dousman, for the sum of five thousand dollars; and they request that it be paid.

ARTICLE 5.
The privilege of hunting, fishing, and gathering the wild rice, upon the lands, the rivers and the lakes included in the territory ceded, is guaranteed to the Indians, during the pleasure of the President of the United States.

ARTICLE 6.
This treaty shall be obligatory from and after its ratification by the President and Senate of the United States.

Done at St. Peters in the Territory of Wisconsin the twenty-ninth day of July eighteen hundred and thirty-seven.

Henry Dodge, Commissioner.

From Leech lake:
Aish-ke-bo-ge-koshe, or Flat Mouth,
R-che-o-sau-ya, or the Elder Brother,
Chiefs.
Pe-zhe-kins, the Young Buffalo,
Ma-ghe-ga-bo, or La Trappe,
O-be-gwa-dans, the Chief of the Earth,
Wa-bose, or the Rabbit,

Che-a-na-quod, or the Big Cloud,
Warriors.

From Gull lake and Swan river:
Pa-goo-na-kee-zhig, or the Hole in the Day,
Songa-ko-mig, or the Strong Ground,
Chiefs.
Wa-boo-jig, or the White Fisher,
Ma-cou-da, or the Bear's Heart,
Warriors.

From St. Croix river:
Pe-zhe-ke, or the Buffalo,
Ka-be-ma-be, or the Wet Month,
Chiefs.
Pa-ga-we-we-wetung, Coming Home
    Hollowing,
Ya-banse, or the Young Buck,
Kis-ke-ta-wak, or the Cut Ear,
Warriors.

From Lake Courteoville:
Pa-qua-a-mo, or the Wood Pecker.
Chief.

From Lac De Flambeau:
Pish-ka-ga-ghe, or the White Crow,
Na-wa-ge-wa, or the Knee,
O-ge-ma-ga, or the Dandy,
Pa-se-quam-jis, or the Commissioner,
Wa-be-ne-me, or the White Thunder,
Chiefs.

From La Pointe, (on Lake Superior):
Pe-zhe-ke, or the Buffalo,
Ta-qua-ga-na, or Two Lodges Meeting,
Cha-che-que-o,
Chiefs.

From Mille Lac:
Wa-shask-ko-kone, or Rats Liver,
Wen-ghe-ge-she-guk, or the First Day,
Chiefs.
Ada-we-ge-shik, or Both Ends of the Sky,
Ka-ka-quap, or the Sparrow,
Warriors.

From Sandy Lake:
Ka-nan-da-wa-win-zo, or Le Brocheux,
We-we-shan-shis, the Bad Boy, or Big
    Mouth,
Ke-che-wa-me-te-go, or the Big Frenchman,
Chiefs.

Na-ta-me-ga-bo, the Man that stands First,
Sa-ga-ta-gun, or Spunk,
Warriors.

From Snake river:
Naudin, or the Wind,
Sha-go-bai, or the Little Six,
Pay-ajik, or the Lone Man,
Na-qua-na-bie, or the Feather,
Chiefs.
Ha-tau-wa,
Wa-me-te-go-zhins, the Little Frenchman,
Sho-ne-a, or Silver,
Warriors.

From Fond du Lac, (on Lake Superior):
Mang-go-sit, or the Loons Foot,
Shing-go-be, or the Spruce,
Chiefs.

From Red Cedar lake:
Mont-so-mo, or the Murdering Yell.

From Red lake:
Francois Goumean (a half breed).

From Leech lake:
Sha-wa-ghe-zhig, or the Sounding Sky,
Wa-zau-ko-ni-a, or Yellow Robe.
Warriors.

Signed in presence of—
Verplanck Van Antwerp, Secretary to the
    Commissioner.
M. M. Vineyard, U. S. Sub-Indian Agent.
Daniel P. Bushnell.
Law. Taliaferro, Indian Agent at St. Peters.
Martin Scott, Captain, Fifth Regiment Infantry.
J. Emerson, Assistant Surgeon, U. S. Army.
H. H. Sibley.
H. L. Dousman.
S. C. Stambaugh.
E. Lockwood.
Lyman M. Warren. J.
N. Nicollet.
Harmen Van Antwerp.
Wm. H. Forbes.
Jean Baptiste Dubay, Interpreter.
Peter Quinn, Interpreter.
S. Campbell, U. S. Interpreter.
Stephen Bonga, Interpreter.
Wm. W Coriell.

Treaty with the Chippewa (Ojibwe), 1842

Articles of a treaty made and concluded at La Pointe of Lake Superior, in the Territory of Wisconsin, between Robert Stuart commissioner on the part of the United States, and the Chippewa Indians of the Mississippi, and Lake Superior, by their chiefs and headmen.

ARTICLE 1.

The Chippewa Indians of the Mississippi and Lake Superior, cede to the United States all the country within the following bounderies; viz: beginning at the mouth of Chocolate river of Lake Superior; thence northwardly across said lake to intersect the boundery line between the United States and the Province of Canada; thence up said Lake Superior, to the mouth of the St. Louis, or Fond du Lac river (including all the islands in said lake); thence up said river to the American Fur Company's trading post, at the southwardly bend thereof, about 22 miles from its mouth; thence south to intersect the line of the treaty of 29th July 1837, with the Chippewas of the Mississippi; thence along said line to its southeastwardly extremity, near the Plover portage on the Wisconsin river; thence northeastwardly, along the boundery line, between the Chippewas and Menomonees, to its eastern termination, (established by the treaty held with the Chippewas, Menomonees, and Winnebagoes, at Butte des Morts, August 11th 1827) on the Skonawby river of Green Bay; thence northwardly to the source of Chocolate river; thence down said river to its mouth, the place of beginning; it being the intention of the parties to this treaty, to include in this cession, all the Chippewa lands eastwardly of the aforesaid line running from the American Fur Company's trading post on the Fond du Lac river to the intersection of the line of the treaty made with the Chippewas of the Mississippi July 29th 1837.

ARTICLE 2.

The Indians stipulate for the right of hunting on the ceded territory, with the other usual privileges of occupancy, until required to remove by the President of the United States, and that the laws of the United States shall be continued in force, in respect to their trade and inter course with the whites, until otherwise ordered by Congress.

ARTICLE 3.

It is agreed by the parties to this treaty, that whenever the Indians shall be required to remove from the ceded district, all the unceded lands belonging to the Indians of Fond du Lac, Sandy Lake, and Mississippi bands, shall be the common property and home of all the Indians, party to this treaty.

ARTICLE 4.

In consideration of the foregoing cession, the United States, engage to pay to the Chippewa Indians of the Mississippi, and Lake Superior, annually, for twenty-five years, twelve thousand five hundred (12,500) dollars, in specie, ten thousand five hundred (10,500) dollars in goods, two thousand (2,000) dollars in provisions and tobacco, two thousand (2,000) dollars for the support of two blacksmiths shops, (including pay of smiths and assistants, and iron steel &c.) one thousand (1,000) dollars for pay of two farmers, twelve hundred (1,200) for pay of two carpenters, and two thousand (2,000) dollars for the support of schools for the Indians party to this treaty; and further the United States engage to pay the sum of five thousand (5,000) dollars as an agricultural fund, to be expended under the direction of the Secretary of War. And also the sum of seventy-five thousand (75,000) dollars, shall be allowed for the full satisfaction of their debts within the ceded district, which shall be examined by the commissioner to this treaty, and the amount to be allowed decided upon by him, which shall appear in a schedule hereunto annexed. The United States shall pay the amount so allowed within three years.

Whereas the Indians have expressed a strong desire to have some provision made for their half breed relatives, therefore it is agreed, that fifteen thousand (15,000) dollars shall be paid to said Indians, next year, as a present, to be disposed of, as they, together with their agent, shall determine in council.

ARTICLE 5.

Whereas the whole country between Lake Superior and the Mississippi, has always been understood as belonging in common to the Chippewas, party to this treaty; and whereas the bands bordering on Lake Superior, have not been allowed to participate in the annuity payments of the treaty made with the Chippewas of the Mississippi, at St. Peters July 29th 1837, and whereas all the unceded lands belonging to the aforesaid Indians, are hereafter to be held in common, therefore, to remove all occasion for jealousy and discontent, it is agreed that all the annuity due by the said treaty, as also the annuity due by the present treaty, shall henceforth be equally divided among the Chippewas of the Mississippi and Lake Superior, party to this treaty, so that every person shall receive an equal share.

ARTICLE 6.

The Indians residing on the Mineral district, shall be subject to removal therefrom at the pleasure of the President of the United States.

ARTICLE 7.

This treaty shall be obligatory upon the contracting parties when ratified by the President and Senate of the United States.

In testimony whereof the said Robert Stuart commissioner, on the part of the United States, and the chiefs and headmen of the Chippewa Indians of the Mississippi and Lake Superior, have hereunto set their hands, at La Pointe of Lake Superior, Wisconsin Territory this fourth day of October in the year of our Lord one thousand eight hundred and forty-two.

Robert Stuart, Commissioner.
Jno. Hulbert, Secretary.

Po go ne gi shik,
Son go com ick,
Ka non do ur uin zo,
Na tum e gaw bon,
Ua bo jig,
Pay pe si gon de bay,
Kui ui sen shis,
Ott taw wance,
Bai ie jig,
Show ne aw,
Ki uen zi,
Wi aw bis ke kut te way,
A pish ka go gi,
May tock cus e quay,
She maw gon e,
Ki ji ua be she shi,
Ke kon o tum,
Shin goob,
Na gan nab,
Mong o zet,
Gitchi waisky,
Mi zi,
Ta qua gone e,
O kon di kan,

Kis ke taw wac,
Pe na shi,
Guck we san sish,
Ka she osh e,
Medge waw gwaw wot,
Ne qua ne be,
Ua shash ko kum,
No din,
Be zhi ki,
Ka bi na be,
Ai aw bens,
Sha go bi,
Ua be she shi,
Que way zhan sis,
Ne na nang eb,
Be bo kon uen,
Ki uen zi.

In presence of—
Henry Blanchford, interpreter.
Samuel Ashmun, interpreter.
Justin Rice.
Charles H. Oakes.
William A. Aitkin.
William Brewster.
Charles M. Borup.
Z. Platt.
C. H. Beaulieau.
L. T. Jamison.
James P. Scott.
Cyrus Mendenhall.
L. M. Warren.

Copy of the Robinson Treaty, 1850

Made in the Year 1850 With the Ojibewa Indians of Lake Superior conveying Certain Lands to the Crown

THIS AGREEMENT, made and entered into on the seventh day of September, in the year of Our Lord one thousand eight hundred and fifty, at Sault Ste. Marie, in the Province of Canada, between the Honorable WILLIAM BENJAMIN ROBINSON, of the one part, on behalf of HER MAJESTY THE QUEEN, and JOSEPH PEANDECHAT, JOHN IUINWAY, MISHE-MUCKQUA, TOTOMENCIE, Chiefs, and JACOB WARPELA, AHMUTCHI-WAGABOU, MICHEL SHELAGESHICK, MANIT-SHAINSE, and CHIGINANS, principal men of the OJIBEWA Indians inhabiting the Northern Shore of Lake Superior, in the said Province of Canada, from Batchewana Bay to Pigeon River, at the western extremity of said Lake, and inland throughout that extent to the height of land which separates the territory covered by the charter of the Honorable the Hudson's Bay Company from the said tract, and also the Islands in the said Lake within the boundaries of the British possessions therein, of the other part, witnesseth:

THAT for and in consideration of the sum of two thousand pounds of good and lawful money of Upper Canada, to them in hand paid, and for the further perpetual annuity of five hundred pounds, the same to be paid and delivered to the said Chiefs and their Tribes at a convenient season of each summer, not later than the first day of August at the Honorable the Hudson's Bay Company's Posts of Michipicoton and Fort William, they the said chiefs and principal men do freely, fully and voluntarily surrender, cede, grant and convey unto Her Majesty, Her heirs and successors forever, all their right, title and interest in the whole of the territory above described, save and except the reservations set forth in the schedule hereunto annexed, which reservations shall be held and occupied by the said Chiefs and their Tribes in common, for the purpose of residence and cultivation, and should the said Chiefs and their respective Tribes at any time desire to dispose of any mineral or other valuable productions upon the said reservations, the same will be at their request sold by order of the Superintendent General of the Indian Department for the time being, for their sole use and benefit, and to the best advantage.

And the said William Benjamin Robinson of the first part, on behalf of Her Majesty and the Government of this Province, hereby promises and agrees to make the payments as before mentioned; and further to allow the said chiefs and their tribes the full and free privilege to hunt over the territory now ceded by them, and to fish in the waters thereof as they have heretofore been in the habit of doing, saving and excepting only such portions of the said territory as may from time to time be sold or leased to individuals, or companies of individuals, and occupied by them with the consent of the Provincial Government. The parties of the second part further promise and agree that they will not sell, lease, or otherwise dispose of any portion of their reservations without the consent of the Superintendent General of Indian Affairs being first had and obtained; nor will they at any time hinder or prevent persons from exploring or searching for mineral or other valuable productions in any part of the territory hereby ceded to Her Majesty as before mentioned. The parties of the second part also agree that in case the Government of this Province should before the date of this agreement have sold, or bargained to sell, any mining locations or other property on the portions of the territory hereby reserved for their use and benefit, then and in that case such sale, or promise of sale, shall be forfeited, if the parties interested desire it, by the Government, and the amount accruing therefrom shall be paid to the tribe to whom the reservation belongs. The said William Benjamin Robinson on behalf of Her Majesty, who desires to deal liberally and justly with all Her subjects, further promises and agrees that in case the territory hereby ceded by the parties of the second part shall at any future period produce an amount which will enable the Government of this Province without incurring loss to increase the annuity hereby secured to them, then, and in that case, the same shall be augmented from time to time, provided that the amount paid to each individual shall not exceed the sum of one pound provincial currency in any one year, or such further sum as Her Majesty may be graciously pleased to order; and provided further that the number of Indians entitled to the benefit of this Treaty shall amount to two thirds of their present numbers (which is twelve hundred and forty) to entitle them to claim the full benefit thereof, and should their numbers at any future period not amount to two thirds of twelve hundred and forty, the annuity shall be diminished in proportion to their actual numbers.

Schedule of Reservations made by the above named subscribing Chiefs and principal men.

FIRST—Joseph Pean-de-chat and his Tribe, the reserve to commence about two miles from Fort William (inland), on the right bank of the River Kiminitiquia thence westerly six miles, parallel to the shores of the lake; thence northerly five miles; thence easterly to the right bank of the said river, so as not to interfere with any acquired rights of the Honorable Hudson's Bay Company.

SECOND—Four miles square at Gros Cap, being a valley near the Honorable Hudson's Bay Company's post of Michipicoton, for Totominai and Tribe.

THIRD—Four miles square on Gull River, near Lake Nipigon, on both sides of said river, for the Chief Mishimuckqua and Tribe.

And should the said Chiefs and their respective Tribes at any time desire to dispose of any part of such reservations, or of any mineral or other valuable productions thereon, the same will be sold or leased at their request by the Superintendent-General of Indian Affairs for the time being, or other officer having authority so to do, for their sole benefit, and to the best advantage.

And the said William Benjamin Robinson of the first part, on behalf of Her Majesty and the Government of this Province, hereby promises and agrees to make, or cause to be made, the payments as before mentioned; and further to allow the said Chiefs and their Tribes the full and free privilege to hunt over the Territory now ceded by them, and to fish in the waters thereof, as they have heretofore been in the habit of doing; saving and excepting such portions of the said Territory as may from time to time be sold or leased to individuals or companies of individuals, and occupied by them with the consent of the Provincial Government.

The parties of the second part further promise and agree that they will not sell, lease, or otherwise dispose of any portion of their Reservations without the consent of the Superintendent-General of Indian Affairs, or other officer of like authority, being first had and obtained. Nor will they at any time hinder or prevent persons from exploring or searching for minerals, or other valuable productions, in any part of the Territory hereby ceded to Her Majesty, as before mentioned. The parties of the second part also agree, that in case the Government of this Province should before the date of this agreement have sold, or bargained to sell, any mining locations, or other property, on the portions of the Territory hereby reserved for their use; then and in that case such sale, or promise of sale, shall be perfected by the Government, if the parties claiming it shall have fulfilled all the conditions upon which such locations were made, and the amount accruing therefrom shall be paid to the Tribe to whom the Reservation belongs.

The said William Benjamin Robinson, on behalf of Her Majesty, who desires to deal liberally and justly with all her subjects, further promises and agrees, that should the Territory hereby ceded by the parties of the second part at any future period produce such an amount as will enable the Government of this Province, without incurring loss, to increase the annuity hereby secured to them, then and in that case the same shall be augmented from time to time, provided that the amount paid to each individual shall not exceed the sum of one pound Provincial Currency in any one year, or such further sum as Her Majesty may be graciously pleased to order; and provided further that the number of Indians entitled to the benefit of this treaty shall amount to two-thirds of their present number, which is fourteen hundred and twenty-two, to entitle them to claim the full benefit thereof. And should they not at any future period amount to two-thirds of fourteen hundred and twenty-two, then the said annuity shall be diminished in proportion to their actual numbers.

The said William Benjamin Robinson of the first part further agrees, on the part of Her Majesty and the Government of this Province, that in consequence of the Indians inhabiting French River and Lake Nipissing having become parties to this treaty, the further sum of one hundred and sixty pounds Provincial Currency shall be paid in addition to the two thousand pounds above mentioned.

Schedule of Reservations made by the above-named subscribing Chiefs and Principal Men.

FIRST—Pamequonaishcung and his Band, a tract of land to commence seven miles, from the mouth of the River Maganetawang, and extending six miles east and west by three miles north.

SECOND—Wagemake and his Band, a tract of land to commence at a place called Nekickshegeshing, six miles from east to west, by three miles in depth.

THIRD—Kitcheposkissegan (by Papasainse), from Point Grondine westward, six miles inland, by two miles in front, so as to include the small Lake Nessinassung a tract for themselves and their Bands.

FOURTH—Wabakekik, three miles front, near Shebawenaning, by five miles inland, for himself and Band.

FIFTH—Namassin and Naoquagabo and their Bands, a tract of land commencing near Qacloche, at the Hudson Bay Company's boundary; thence westerly to the mouth of Spanish River; then four miles up the south bank of said river, and across to the place of beginning.

SIXTH—Shawenakishick and his Band, a tract of land now occupied by them, and contained between two rivers, called Whitefish River, and Wanabitaseke, seven miles inland.

SEVENTH—Windawtegawinini and his Band, the Peninsula east of Serpent River, and formed by it, now occupied by them.

EIGHTH—Ponekeosh and his Band, the land contained between the River Mississaga and the River Penebewabecong, up to the first rapids.

NINTH—Dokis and his Band, three miles square at Wanabeyakokaun, near Lake Nipissing and the island near the Fall of Okickandawt.

TENTH—Shabokishick and his Band, from their present planting grounds on Lake Nipissing to the Hudson Bay Company's post, six miles in depth.

ELEVENTH—Tagawinini and his Band, two miles square at Wanabitibing, a place about forty miles inland, near Lake Nipissing.

TWELFTH—Keokouse and his Band, four miles front from Thessalon River eastward, by four miles inland.

THIRTEENTH—Mishequanga and his Band, two miles on the lake shore east and west of Ogawaminang, by one mile inland.

FOURTEENTH—For Shinguacouse and his Band, a tract of land extending from Maskinongé Bay, inclusive, to Partridge Point, above Garden River on the front, and inland ten miles, throughout the whole distance; and also Squirrel Island.

FIFTEENTH—For Nebenaigoching and his Band, a tract of land extending from Wanabekineyunnung west of Gros Cap to the boundary of the lands ceded by the Chiefs of Lake Superior, and inland ten miles throughout the whole distance, including Batchewanaung Bay; and also the small island at Sault Ste. Marie used by them as a fishing station.

SIXTEENTH—For Chief Mekis and his Band, residing at Wasaquesing (Sandy Island), a tract of land at a place on the main shore opposite the Island; being the place now occupied by them for residence and cultivation, four miles square.

SEVENTEENTH—For Chief Muckatamishaquet and his Band, a tract of land on the east side of the River Naishconteong, near Pointe aux Barils, three miles square; and also a small tract in Washauwenega Bay — now occupied by a part of the Band — three miles square.

Treaty of Ft. Laramie, 1851

Articles of a treaty made and concluded at Fort Laramie, in the Indian Territory, between D. D. Mitchell, superintendent of Indian affairs, and Thomas Fitzpatrick, Indian agent, commissioners specially appointed and authorized by the President of the United States, of the first part, and the chiefs, headmen, and braves of the following Indian nations, residing south of the Missouri River, east of the Rocky Mountains, and north of the lines of Texas and New Mexico, viz, the Sioux or Dahcotahs, Cheyennes, Arrapahoes, Crows. Assinaboines, Gros-Ventre Mandans, and Arrickaras, parties of the second part, on the seventeenth day of September, A. D. one thousand eight hundred and fifty-one.

ARTICLE 1.
The aforesaid nations, parties to this treaty, having assembled for the purpose of establishing and confirming peaceful relations amongst themselves, do hereby covenant and agree to abstain in future from all hostilities whatever against each other, to maintain good faith and friendship in all their mutual intercourse, and to make an effective and lasting peace.

ARTICLE 2.
The aforesaid nations do hereby recognize the right of the United States Government to establish roads, military and other posts, within their respective territories.

ARTICLE 3.
In consideration of the rights and privileges acknowledged in the preceding article, the United States bind themselves to protect the aforesaid Indian nations against the commission of all depredations by the people of the said United States, after the ratification of this treaty.

ARTICLE 4.
The aforesaid Indian nations do hereby agree and bind themselves to make restitution or satisfaction for any wrongs committed, after the ratification of this treaty, by any band or individual of their people, on the people of the United States, whilst lawfully residing in or passing through their respective territories.

ARTICLE 5.
The aforesaid Indian nations do hereby recognize and acknowledge the following tracts of country, included within the metes and boundaries hereinafter designated, as their respective territories, viz:

The territory of the Sioux or Dahcotah Nation, commencing the mouth of the White Earth River, on the Missouri River: thence in a southwesterly direction to the forks of the Platte River: thence up the north fork of the Platte River to a point known as the Red Bute, or where the road leaves the river; thence along the range of mountains known as the Black Hills, to the head-waters of Heart River; thence down Heart River to its mouth; and thence down the Missouri River to the place of beginning.

The territory of the Gros Ventre, Mandans, and Arrickaras Nations, commencing at the mouth of Heart River; thence up the Missouri River to the mouth of the Yellowstone River; thence up the Yellowstone River to the mouth of Powder River in a southeasterly direction, to the head-waters of the Little Missouri River; thence along the Black Hills to the head of Heart River, and thence down Heart River to the place of beginning.

The territory of the Assinaboin Nation, commencing at the mouth of Yellowstone River; thence up the Missouri River to the mouth of the Muscle-shell River; thence from the mouth of the Muscle-shell River in a southeasterly direction until it strikes the head-waters of Big Dry Creek; thence down that creek to where it empties into the Yellowstone River, nearly opposite the mouth of Powder River, and thence down the Yellowstone River to the place of beginning.

This treaty as signed was ratified by the Senate with an amendment changing the annuity in Article 7 from fifty to ten years, subject to acceptance by the tribes. Assent of all tribes except the Crows was procured (see Upper Platte C., 570, 1853, Indian Office) and in subsequent agreements this treaty has been recognized as in force (see post p. 776).

The territory of the Blackfoot Nation, commencing at the mouth of Muscle-shell River; thence up the Missouri River to its source; thence along the main range of the Rocky Mountains, in a southerly direction, to the head-waters of the northern source of the Yellowstone River; thence down the Yellowstone River to the mouth of Twenty-five Yard Creek; thence across to the head-waters of the Muscle-shell River, and thence down the Muscle-shell River to the place of beginning.

The territory of the Crow Nation, commencing at the mouth of Powder River on the Yellowstone; thence up Powder River to its source; thence along the main range of the Black Hills and Wind River Mountains to the head-waters of the Yellowstone River; thence down the Yellowstone River to the mouth of Twenty-five Yard Creek; thence to the head waters of the Muscle-shell River; thence down the Muscle-shell River to its mouth; thence to the head-waters of Big Dry Creek, and thence to its mouth.

The territory of the Cheyennes and Arrapahoes, commencing at the Red Bute, or the place where the road leaves the north fork of the Platte River; thence up the north fork of the Platte River to its source; thence along the main range of the Rocky Mountains to the head-waters of the Arkansas River; thence down the Arkansas River to the crossing of the Santa Fé road; thence in a northwesterly direction to the forks of the Platte River, and thence up the Platte River to the place of beginning.

It is, however, understood that, in making this recognition and acknowledgement, the aforesaid Indian nations do not hereby abandon or prejudice any rights or claims they may have to other lands; and further, that they do not surrender the privilege of hunting, fishing, or passing over any of the tracts of country heretofore described.

ARTICLE 6.
The parties to the second part of this treaty having selected principals or head-chiefs for their respective nations, through whom all national business will hereafter be conducted, do hereby bind themselves to sustain said chiefs and their successors during good behavior.

ARTICLE 7.
In consideration of the treaty stipulations, and for the damages which have or may occur by reason thereof to the Indian nations, parties hereto, and for their maintenance and the improvement of their moral and social customs, the United States bind themselves to deliver to the said Indian nations the sum of fifty thousand dollars per annum for the term of ten years, with the right to continue the same at the discretion of the President of the United States for a period not exceeding five years thereafter, in provisions, merchandise, domestic animals, and agricultural implements, in such proportions as may be deemed best adapted to their condition by the President of the United States, to be distributed in proportion to the population of the aforesaid Indian nations.

ARTICLE 8.
It is understood and agreed that should any of the Indian nations, parties to this treaty, violate any of the provisions thereof, the United States may withhold the whole or a portion of the annuities mentioned in the preceding article from the nation so offending, until, in the opinion of the President of the United States, proper satisfaction shall have been made.

In testimony whereof the said D. D. Mitchell and Thomas Fitzpatrick commissioners as aforesaid, and the chiefs, headmen, and braves, parties hereto, have set their hands and affixed their marks, on the day and at the place first above written.

D. D. Mitchell
Thomas Fitzpatrick.
Commissioners.

Sioux:
Mah-toe-wha-you-whey, his x mark.

Mah-kah-toe-zah-zah, his x mark.
Bel-o-ton-kah-tan-ga, his x mark.
Nah-ka-pah-gi-gi, his x mark.
Mak-toe-sah-bi-chis, his x mark.
Meh-wha-tah-ni-hans-kah, his x mark.

Cheyennes:
Wah-ha-nis-satta, his x mark.
Voist-ti-toe-vetz, his x mark.
Nahk-ko-me-ien, his x mark.
Koh-kah-y-wh-cum-est, his x mark.

Arrapahoes:
Bè-ah-té-a-qui-sah, his x mark.
Neb-ni-bah-seh-it, his x mark.
Beh-kah-jay-beth-sah-es, his x mark.

Crows:
Arra-tu-ri-sash, his x mark.
Doh-chepit-seh-chi-es, his x mark.

Assinaboines:
Mah-toe-wit-ko, his x mark.
Toe-tah-ki-eh-nan, his x mark.

Mandans and Gros Ventres:
Nochk-pit-shi-toe-pish, his x mark.
She-oh-mant-ho, his x mark.

Arickarees:
Koun-hei-ti-shan, his x mark.
Bi-atch-tah-wetch, his x mark.

In the presence of—
A. B. Chambers, secretary.
S. Cooper, colonel, U. S. Army.
R. H. Chilton, captain, First Drags.
Thomas Duncan, captain, Mounted Riflemen.
Thos. G. Rhett, brevet captain R. M. R.
W. L. Elliott, first lieutenant R. M. R.
C. Campbell, interpreter for Sioux.
John S. Smith, interpreter for Cheyennes.
Robert Meldrum, interpreter for the Crows.
H. Culbertson, interpreter for Assiniboines and
    Gros Ventres.
Francois L'Etalie, interpreter for Arick arees.
John Pizelle, interpreter for the Arrapahoes.
B. Gratz Brown.
Robert Campbell.
Edmond F. Chouteau.

Treaty with the Comanche, Kiowa, and Apache, 1853

July 27, 1853. | 10 Stats., 1013. | Ratified Apr. 12, 1854. | Proclaimed Feb. 12, 1855 [4].

Articles of a treaty, made and concluded at Fort Atkinson, in the Indian Territory, of the United States of America, on the 27th day of July, anno Domini eighteen hundred and fifty-three, between the United States of America, by Thomas Fitzpatrick, Indian agent, and sole commissioner, duly appointed for that purpose, and the Camanche, and Kiowa, and Apache tribes or nations of Indians, inhabiting the said territory south of the Arkansas River.

ARTICLE 1.
Peace, friendship, and amity shall hereafter exist between the United States and the Camanche and Kiowa, and Apache tribes of Indians, parties to this treaty, and the same shall be perpetual.

ARTICLE 2.
The Camanche, Kiowa, and Apache tribes of Indians do hereby jointly and severally covenant that peaceful relations shall likewise be maintained amongst themselves in future; and that they will abstain from all hostilities whatsoever against each other, and cultivate mutual good-will and friendship.

ARTICLE 3.
The aforesaid Indian tribes do also hereby fully recognize and acknowledge the right of the United States to lay off and mark out roads or highways—to make reservations of land necessary thereto—to locate depots—and to establish military and other posts within the territories inhabited by the said tribes; and also to prescribe and enforce, in such manner as the President or the Congress of the United States shall from time to time direct, rules and regulations to protect the rights of persons and property among the said Indian tribes.

ARTICLE 4.
The Camanche, Kiowa, and Apache tribes, parties as before recited, do further agree and bind themselves to make restitution or satisfaction for any injuries done by any band or any individuals of their respective tribes to the people of the United States who may be lawfully residing in or passing through their said territories; and to abstain hereafter from levying

contributions from, or molesting them in any manner; and, so far as may be in their power, to render assistance to such as need relief, and to facilitate their safe passage.

ARTICLE 5.

The Camanche, and Kiowa, and Apache tribes of Indians, parties to this treaty, do hereby solemnly covenant and agree to refrain in future from warlike incursions into the Mexican provinces, and from all depredations upon the inhabitants thereof; and they do likewise bind themselves to restore all captives that may hereafter be taken by any of the bands, war-parties, or individuals of the said several tribes, from the Mexican provinces aforesaid, and to make proper and just compensation for any wrongs that may be inflicted upon the people thereof by them, either to the United States or to the Republic of Mexico, as the President of the United States may direct and require.

ARTICLE 6.

In consideration of the foregoing agreements on the part of the Camanche, and Kiowa, and Apache tribes, parties to this treaty—of the losses which they may sustain by reason of the travel of the people of the United States through their territories—and for the better support, and the improvement of the social condition of the said tribes—the United States do bind themseles, and by these presents stipulate to deliver to the Camanche, Kiowa, and Apache tribes aforesaid, the sum of eighteen thousand dollars per annum, for and during the term of ten years next ensuing from this date, and for the additional term of five years, if, in the opinion of the President of the United States, such extension shall be advisable;—the same to be given to them in goods, merchandise, provisions, or agricultural implements, or in such shape as may be best adapted to their wants, and as the President of the United States may designate, and to be distributed amongst the said several tribes in proportion to the respective numbers of each tribe.

ARTICLE 7.

The United States do moreover bind themselves, in consideration of the covenants contained in the preceding articles of this treaty, to protect and defend the Indian tribes, parties hereto, against the committal of any depredations upon them, and in their territories, by the people of the United States, for and during the term for which this treaty shall be in force, and to compensate them for any injuries that may result therefrom.

ARTICLE 8.

It is also stipulated and provided, by and between the parties to this treaty, that should any of the Indian tribes aforesaid violate any of the conditions, provisions, or agreements herein contained, or fail to perform any of the obligations entered into on their part, then the United States may withhold the whole or a part of the annuities mentioned in the sixth article of this treaty, from the tribe so offending, until, in the opinion of the President or the Congress of the United States, proper satisfaction shall have been made, or until persons amongst the said Indians offending against the laws of the United States shall have been delivered up to justice.

ARTICLE 9.

It is also consented to and determined between the parties hereto, that the annuities to be given on the part of the United States, as provided in the sixth article of this treaty, shall be delivered to the said Indian tribes collectively, at or in the vicinity of Beaver Creek, yearly, during the month of July in each year, until some other time and place shall have been designated by the President of the United States, in which event the said Indian tribes shall have due notice thereof, and the place of distribution which may be selected shall always be some point within the territories occupied by the said tribes.

ARTICLE 10.

It is agreed between the United States and the Camanche, Kiowa, and Apache tribes of Indians, that, should it at any time hereafter be considered by the United States as a proper policy to establish farms among and for the benefit of said Indians, it shall be discretionary with the President, by and with the advice and consent of the Senate, to change the annuities herein provided for, or any part thereof, into a fund for that purpose.

In witness whereof, the said Thomas Fitzpatrick, Indian Agent, and sole commissioner on the part of the United States, and the undersigned chiefs and headmen of the Camanche and Kiowa, and Apache tribes or nations, have hereunto set their hands, at Fort Atkinson, in the Indian Territory of the United

States, this twenty-seventh day of July, A. D. eighteen hundred and fifty-three.

Thomas Fitzpatrick, Indian Agent, and
   Commissioner on behalf of the United States.
B. Gratz Brown, Secretary.
R. H. Chilton.
B. T. Moylero.
Wulea-boo, his x mark (Shaved Head) chief
   Camanche
Wa-ya-ba-tos-a, his x mark (White Eagle)
   chief of band
Hai-nick-seu, his x mark (The Crow) chief
   of band
Paro-sa-wa-no, his x mark (Ten Sticks) chief
   of band
Wa-ra-kon-alta, his x mark (Poor Cayote Wolf)
   chief of band
Ka-na-re-tah, his x mark (One that Rides the
   Clouds) chief of the southern Camanches
To-hau-sen, his x mark (Little Mountain) chief
   Kiowas
Si-tank-ki, his x mark (Sitting Bear) war chief
Tah-ka-eh-bool, his x mark (The Bad Smelling
   Saddle) headman
Che-koon-ki, his x mark (Black Horse) headman
On-ti-an-te, his x mark (The Snow Flake)
   headman
El-bo-in-ki, his x mark (Yellow Hair) headman
Si-tah-le, his x mark (Poor Wolf) chief Apache
Oh-ah-te-kah, his x mark (Poor Bear) headman
Ah-zaah, his x mark (Prairie Wolf) headman
Kootz-zah, his x mark (The Cigar) headman

Witness:
B. B. Dayton,
Geo. M. Alexander,
T. Polk,
Geo. Collier, jr.

We do hereby accept and consent to the Senate amendments to the treaty aforesaid, and agree that the same may be considered as a part thereof.

In testimony whereof we have hereunto set our hands and affixed our seals, this 21st day of July, A. D. 1854.

Camanches:
   To-che-ra-nah-boo, (Shaved Head,) his x mark.
   Wa-ya-ba-to-sa, (White Eagle,) his x mark.

Hai-nick-seu, (Crow,) his x mark.
Ty-har-re-ty, (One who runs after women,) his x
   mark.
Para-sar-a-man-no, (Ten Bears,) his x mark.

Kiowas:
To-han-seu, (Little Mountain,) his x mark.
Ti-sank-ki, (Sitting Bear,) his x mark.
Ko-a-ty-ka, (Wolf outside,) his x mark.

Executed in presence of—
Aquilla T. Ridgely, assistant surgeon, U. S.
   Army.
A. H. Plummer, brevet second lieutenant, Sixth
   Infantry.
Paul Carrey.
John Kinney, United States interpreter.
H. E. Nixon, clerk.

I certify that the foregoing amendments to the treaty of 27th day of July, 1853, was read and explained to the chiefs, and that they consented to, and signed the same on the 21st day of July, 1854.

   J. W. Whitfield, Indian Agent.

Treaty with the Chippewa, 1854
Sept. 30, 1854. | 10 Stats., 1109. | Ratified Jan. 10, 1855. | Proclaimed Jan. 29, 1855.
Articles of a treaty made and concluded at La Pointe, in the State of Wisconsin, between Henry C. Gilbert and David B. Herriman, commissioners on the part of the United States, and the Chippewa Indians of Lake Superior and the Mississippi, by their chiefs and head-men.

ARTICLE 1.
The Chippewas of Lake Superior hereby cede to the United States all the lands heretofore owned by them in common with the Chippewas of the Mississippi, lying east of the following boundary-line, to wit: Beginning at a point, where the east branch of Snake River crosses the southern boundary-line of the Chippewa country, running thence up the said branch to its source, thence nearly north, in a straight line, to the mouth of East Savannah River, thence up the St. Louis River to the mouth of East Swan River, thence up the East Swan River to its source, thence in

a straight line to the most westerly bend of Vermillion River, and thence down the Vermillion River to its mouth.

The Chippewas of the Mississippi hereby assent and agree to the foregoing cession, and consent that the whole amount of the consideration money for the country ceded above, shall be paid to the Chippewas of Lake Superior, and in consideration thereof the Chippewas of Lake Superior hereby relinquish to the Chippewas of the Mississippi, all their interest in and claim to the lands heretofore owned by them in common, lying west of the above boundry-line.

ARTICLE 2.
The United States agree to set apart and withhold from sale, for the use of the Chippewas of Lake Superior, the following-described tracts of land, viz:

1st. For the L'Anse and Vieux De Sert bands, all the unsold lands in the following townships in the State of Michigan: Township fifty-one north range thirty-three west; township fifty-one north range thirty-two west; the east half of township fifty north range thirty-three west; the west half of township fifty north range thirty-two west, and all of township fifty-one north range thirty-one west, lying west of Huron Bay.

2d. For the La Pointe band, and such other Indians as may see fit to settle with them, a tract of land bounded as follows: Beginning on the south shore of Lake Superior, a few miles west of Montreal River, at the mouth of a creek called by the Indians Ke-che-se-be-we-she, running thence south to a line drawn east and west through the centre of township forty-seven north, thence west to the west line of said township, thence south to the southeast corner of township forty-six north, range thirty-two west, thence west the width of two townships, thence north the width of two townships, thence west one mile, thence north to the lake shore, and thence along the lake shore, crossing Shag-waw-me-quon Point, to the place of beginning. Also two hundred acres on the northern extremity of Madeline Island, for a fishing ground.

3d. For the other Wisconsin bands, a tract of land lying about Lac De Flambeau, and another tract on Lac Court Orielles, each equal in extent to three townships, the boundaries of which shall be here-

after agreed upon or fixed under the direction of the President.

4th. For the Fond Du Lac bands, a tract of land bounded as follows: Beginning at an island in the St. Louis River, above Knife Portage, called by the Indians Paw-paw-sco-me-me-tig, running thence west to the boundary-line heretofore described, thence north along said boundary-line to the mouth of Savannah River, thence down the St. Louis River to the place of beginning. And if said tract shall contain less than one hundred thousand acres, a strip of land shall be added on the south side thereof, large enough to equal such deficiency.

5th. For the Grand Portage band, a tract of land bounded as follows: Beginning at a rock a little east of the eastern extremity of Grand Portage Bay, running thence along the lake shore to the mouth of a small stream called by the Indians Maw-ske-gwaw-caw-maw-se-be, or Cranberry Marsh River, thence up said stream, across the point to Pigeon River, thence down Pigeon River to a point opposite the starting-point, and thence across to the place of beginning.

6th. The Ontonagon band and that subdivision of the La Pointe band of which Buffalo is chief, may each select, on or near the lake shore, four sections of land, under the direction of the President, the boundaries of which shall be defined hereafter. And being desirous to provide for some of his connections who have rendered his people important services, it is agreed that the chief Buffalo may select one section of land, at such place in the ceded territory as he may see fit, which shall be reserved for that purpose, and conveyed by the United States to such person or persons as he may direct.

7th. Each head of a family, or single person over twenty-one years of age at the present time of the mixed bloods, belonging to the Chippewas of Lake Superior, shall be entitled to eighty acres of land, to be selected by them under the direction of the President, and which shall be secured to them by patent in the usual form.

ARTICLE 3.
The United States will define the boundaries of the reserved tracts, whenever it may be necessary, by actual survey, and the President may, from time to

time, at his discretion, cause the whole to be sur-veyed, and may assign to each head of a family or single person over twenty-one years of age, eighty acres of land for his or their separate use; and he may, at his discretion, as fast as the occupants become capable of transacting their own affairs, issue patents therefor to such occupants, with such restrictions of the power of alienation as he may see fit to impose. And he may also, at his discretion, make rules and regulations, respecting the disposi-tion of the lands in case of the death of the head of a family, or single person occupying the same, or in case of its abandonment by them. And he may also assign other lands in exchange for mineral lands, if any such are found in the tracts herein set apart. And he may also make such changes in the bound-aries of such reserved tracts or otherwise, as shall be necessary to prevent interference with any vested rights. All necessary roads, highways, and railroads, the lines of which may run through any of the reserved tracts, shall have the right of way through the same, compensation being made therefor as in other cases.

ARTICLE 4.

In consideration of and payment for the country hereby ceded, the United States agree to pay to the Chippewas of Lake Superior, annually, for the term of twenty years, the following sums, to wit: five thousand dollars in coin; eight thousand dollars in goods, household furniture and cooking utensils; three thousand dollars in agricultural implements and cattle, carpenter's and other tools and building materials, and three thousand dollars for moral and educational purposes, of which last sum, three hun-dred dollars per annum shall be paid to the Grand Portage band, to enable them to maintain a school at their village. The United States will also pay the further sum of ninety thousand dollars, as the chiefs in open council may direct, to enable them to meet their present just engagements. Also the fur-ther sum of six thousand dollars, in agricultural implements, household furniture, and cooking utensils, to be distributed at the next annuity pay-ment, among the mixed bloods of said nation. The United States will also furnish two hundred guns, one hundred rifles, five hundred beaver-traps, three hundred dollars' worth of ammunition, and one thousand dollars' worth of ready-made clothing, to be distributed among the young men of the nation, at the next annuity payment.

ARTICLE 5.

The United States will also furnish a blacksmith and assistant, with the usual amount of stock, dur-ing the continuance of the annuity payments, and as much longer as the President may think proper, at each of the points herein set apart for the residence of the Indians, the same to be in lieu of all the employees to which the Chippewas of Lake Superior may be entitled under previous existing treaties.

ARTICLE 6.

The annuities of the Indians shall not be taken to pay the debts of individuals, but satisfaction for depreda-tions committed by them shall be made by them in such manner as the President may direct.

ARTICLE 7.

No spirituous liquors shall be made, sold, or used on any of the lands herein set apart for the residence of the Indians, and the sale of the same shall be prohib-ited in the Territory hereby ceded, until otherwise ordered by the President.

ARTICLE 8.

It is agreed, between the Chippewas of Lake Supe-rior and the Chippewas of the Mississippi, that the former shall be entitled to two-thirds, and the latter to one-third, of all benefits to be derived from former treaties existing prior to the year 1847.

ARTICLE 9.

The United States agree that an examination shall be made, and all sums that may be found equitably due to the Indians, for arrearages of annuity or other thing, under the provisions of former treaties, shall be paid as the chiefs may direct.

ARTICLE 10.

All missionaries, and teachers, and other persons of full age, residing in the territory hereby ceded, or upon any of the reservations hereby made by authority of law, shall be allowed to enter the land occupied by them at the minimum price whenever the surveys shall be completed to the amount of one quarter-section each.

ARTICLE 11.

All annuity payments to the Chippewas of Lake Superior, shall hereafter be made at L'Anse, La Pointe, Grand Portage, and on the St. Louis River;

and the Indians shall not be required to remove from the homes hereby set apart for them. And such of them as reside in the territory hereby ceded, shall have the right to hunt and fish therein, until otherwise ordered by the President.

ARTICLE 12.
In consideration of the poverty of the Bois Forte Indians who are parties to this treaty, they having never received any annuity payments, and of the great extent of that part of the ceded country owned exclusively by them, the following additional stipulations are made for their benefit. The United States will pay the sum of ten thousand dollars, as their chiefs in open council may direct, to enable them to meet their present just engagements. Also the further sum of ten thousand dollars, in five equal annual payments, in blankets, cloth, nets, guns, ammunitions, and such other articles of necessity as they may require.

They shall have the right to select their reservation at any time hereafter, under the direction of the President; and the same may be equal in extent, in proportion to their numbers, to those allowed the other bands, and be subject to the same provisions.

They shall be allowed a blacksmith, and the usual smithshop supplies, and also two persons to instruct them in farming, whenever in the opinion of the President it shall be proper, and for such length of time as he shall direct.

It is understood that all Indians who are parties to this treaty, except the Chippewas of the Mississippi, shall hereafter be known as the Chippewas of Lake Superior. Provided, That the stipulation by which the Chippewas of Lake Superior relinquishing their right to land west of the boundary-line shall not apply to the Bois Forte band who are parties to this treaty.

ARTICLE 13.
This treaty shall be obligatory on the contracting parties, as soon as the same shall be ratified by the President and Senate of the United States.

In testimony whereof, the said Henry C. Gilbert, and the said David B. Herriman, commissioners as aforesaid, and the undersigned chiefs and headmen of the Chippewas of Lake Superior and the Mississippi, have hereunto set their hands and seals, at the place

aforesaid, this thirtieth day of September, one thousand eight hundred and fifty-four.

Henry C. Gilbert,
David B. Herriman, Commissioners.
Richard M. Smith, Secretary.

La Pointe Band:
Ke-che-waish-ke, or the Buffalo, 1st chief, his x mark. [L. S.],
Chay-che-que-oh, 2d chief, his x mark. [L. S.],
A-daw-we-ge-zhick, or Each Side of the Sky, 2d chief, his x mark. [L. S.],
O-ske-naw-way, or the Youth, 2d chief, his x mark. [L. S.],
Maw-caw-day-pe-nay-se, or the Black Bird, 2d chief, his x mark. [L. S.],
Naw-waw-naw-quot, headman, his x mark. [L. S.],
Ke-wain-zeence, headman, his x mark. [L. S.],
Waw-baw-ne-me-ke, or the White Thunder, 2d chief, his x mark. [L. S.],
Pay-baw-me-say, or the Soarer, 2d chief, his x mark. [L. S.],
Naw-waw-ge-waw-nose, or the Little Current, 2d chief, his x mark. [L. S.],
Maw-caw-day-waw-quot, or the Black Cloud, 2d chief, his x mark. [L. S.],
Me-she-naw-way, or the Disciple, 2d chief, his x mark. [L. S.],
Key-me-waw-naw-um, headman, his x mark. [L. S.],
She-gog headman, his x mark. [L. S.].

Ontonagon Band:
O-cun-de-cun, or the Buoy 1st chief, his x mark. [L. S.],
Waw-say-ge-zhick, or the Clear Sky, 2d chief, his x mark. [L. S.],
Keesh-ke-taw-wug, headman, his x mark. [L. S.].

L'Anse Band:
David King, 1st chief, his x mark. [L. S.],
John Southwind, headman, his x mark. [L. S.],
Peter Marksman, headman, his x mark. [L. S.],
Naw-taw-me-ge-zhick, or the First Sky, 2d chief, his x mark. [L. S.],
Aw-se-neece, headman, his x mark. [L. S.].

Vieux De Sert Band:
May-dway-aw-she, 1st chief, his x mark. [L. S.],

Posh-quay-gin, or the Leather, 2d chief, his x mark. [L. S.].

Grand Portage Band:
Shaw-gaw-naw-sheence, or the Little Englishman, 1st chief, his x mark. [L. S.],
May-mosh-caw-wosh, headman, his x mark. [L. S.],
Aw-de-konse, or the Little Reindeer, 2d chief, his x mark. [L. S.],
Way-we-ge-wam, headman, his x mark. [L. S.].

Fond Du Lac Band:
Shing-goope, or the Balsom, 1st chief, his x mark. [L. S.],
Mawn-go-sit, or the Loon's Foot, 2d chief, his x mark. [L. S.],
May-quaw-me-we-ge-zhick, headman, his x mark. [L. S.],
Keesh-kawk, headman, his x mark. [L. S.],
Caw-taw-waw-be-day, headman, his x mark. [L. S.],
O-saw-gee, headman, his x mark. [L. S.],
Ke-che-aw-ke-wain-ze, headman, his x mark. [L. S.],
Naw-gaw-nub, or the Foremost Sitter, 2d chief, his x mark. [L. S.],
Ain-ne-maw-sung, 2d chief, his x mark. [L. S.],
Naw-aw-bun-way, headman, his x mark. [L. S.],
Wain-ge-maw-tub, headman, his x mark. [L. S.],
Aw-ke-wain-zeence, headman, his x mark. [L. S.],
Shay-way-be-nay-se, headman, his x mark. [L. S.],
Paw-pe-oh, headman, his x mark. [L. S.].

Lac Court Oreille Band:
Aw-ke-wain-ze, or the Old Man, 1st chief, his x mark. [L. S.],
Key-no-zhance, or the Little Jack Fish, 1st chief, his x mark. [L. S.],
Key-che-pe-nay-se, or the Big Bird, 2d chief, his x mark. [L. S.],
Ke-che-waw-be-shay-she, or the Big Martin, 2d chief, his x mark. [L. S.],
Waw-be-shay-sheence, headman, his x mark. [L. S.],
Quay-quay-cub, headman, his x mark. [L. S.],
Shaw-waw-no-me-tay, headman, his x mark. [L. S.],
Nay-naw-ong-gay-be, or the Dressing Bird, 1st chief, his x mark. [L. S.],

O-zhaw-waw-sco-ge-zhick, or the Blue Sky, 2d chief, his x mark. [L. S.],
I-yaw-banse, or the Little Buck, 2d chief, his x mark. [L. S.],
Ke-che-e-nin-ne, headman, his x mark. [L. S.],
Haw-daw-gaw-me, headman, his x mark. [L. S.],
Way-me-te-go-she, headman, his x mark. [L. S.],
Pay-me-ge-wung, headman, his x mark. [L. S.].

Lac Du Flambeau Band:
Aw-mo-se, or the Wasp, 1st chief, his x mark. [L. S.],
Ke-nish-te-no, 2d chief, his x mark. [L. S.],
Me-gee-see, or the Eagle, 2d chief, his x mark. [L. S.],
Kay-kay-co-gwaw-nay-aw-she, headman, his x mark. [L. S.],
O-che-chog, headman, his x mark. [L. S.],
Nay-she-kay-gwaw-nay-be, headman, his x mark. [L. S.],
O-scaw-bay-wis, or the Waiter, 1st chief, his x mark. [L. S.],
Que-we-zance, or the White Fish, 2d chief, his x mark. [L. S.],
Ne-gig, or the Otter, 2d chief, his x mark. [L. S.],
Nay-waw-che-ge-ghick-may-be, headman, his x mark. [L. S.],
Quay-quay-ke-cah, headman, his x mark. [L. S.].

Bois Forte Band:
Kay-baish-caw-daw-way, or Clear Round the Prairie, 1st chief, his x mark. [L. S.],
Way-zaw-we-ge-zhick-way-sking, headman, his x mark. [L. S.],
O-saw-we-pe-nay-she, headman, his x mark. [L. S.].

The Mississippi Bands:
Que-we-san-se, or Hole in the Day, head chief, his x mark. [L. S.],
Caw-nawn-daw-waw-win-zo, or the Berry Hunter, 1st chief, his x mark. [L. S.],
Waw-bow-jieg, or the White Fisher, 2d chief, his x mark. [L. S.],
Ot-taw-waw, 2d chief, his x mark. [L. S.],
Que-we-zhan-cis, or the Bad Boy, 2d chief, his x mark. [L. S.],
Bye-a-jick, or the Lone Man, 2d chief, his x mark. [L. S.],
I-yaw-shaw-way-ge-zhick, or the Crossing Sky, 2d chief, his x mark. [L. S.],

Maw-caw-day, or the Bear's Heart, 2d chief, his x mark. [L. S.],

Ke-way-de-no-go-nay-be, or the Northern Feather, 2d chief, his x mark. [L. S.],

Me-squaw-dace, headman, his x mark. [L. S.],

Naw-gaw-ne-gaw-bo, headman, his x mark. [L. S.],

Wawm-be-de-yea, headman, his x mark. [L. S.],

Waish-key, headman, his x mark. [L. S.],

Caw-way-caw-me-ge-skung, headman, his x mark. [L. S.],

My-yaw-ge-way-we-dunk, or the One who carries the Voice, 2d chief, his x mark. [L. S.].

John F. Godfroy, Interpreters.
Geo. Johnston, Interpreters.
S. A. Marvin, Interpreters.
Louis Codot, Interpreters.
Paul H. Beaulieu, Interpreters.
Henry Blatchford, Interpreters.
Peter Floy, Interpreters.

Executed in the presence of—
Henry M. Rice,
J. W. Lynde,
G. D. Williams,
B. H. Connor,
E. W. Muldough,
Richard Godfroy,
D. S. Cash,
H. H. McCullough,
E. Smith Lee,
Wm. E. Vantassel,
L. H. Wheeler.

Treaty with the Nisqualli, Puyallup, Etc., 1854

Dec. 26, 1854. | 10 Stat., 1132. | Ratified Mar. 3, 1855. | Proclaimed Apr. 10, 1855.

Articles of agreement and convention made and concluded on the She-nah-nam, or Medicine Creek, in the Territory of Washington, this twenty-sixth day of December, in the year one thousand eight hundred and fifty-four, by Isaac I. Stevens, governor and superintendent of Indian affairs of the said Territory, on the part of the United States, and the undersigned chiefs, head-men, and delegates of the Nisqually, Puyallup, Steilacoom, Squawskin, S'Homamish, Stehchass, T' Peek-sin, Squi-aitl, and Sa-heh-wamish tribes and bands of Indians, occupying the lands lying round the head of Puget's Sound and the adjacent inlets, who, for the purpose of this treaty, are to be regarded as one nation, on behalf of said tribes and bands, and duly authorized by them.

ARTICLE 1.

The said tribes and bands of Indians hereby cede, relinquish, and convey to the United States, all their right, title, and interest in and to the lands and country occupied by them, bounded and described as follows, to wit: Commencing at the point on the eastern side of Admiralty Inlet, known as Point Pully, about midway between Commencement and Elliott Bays; thence running in a southeasterly direction, following the divide between the waters of the Puyallup and Dwamish, or White Rivers, to the summit of the Cascade Mountains; thence southerly, along the summit of said range, to a point opposite the main source of the Skookum Chuck Creek; thence to and down said creek, to the coal mine; thence northwesterly, to the summit of the Black Hills; thence northerly, to the upper forks of the Satsop River; thence northeasterly, through the portage known as Wilkes's Portage, to Point Southworth, on the western side of Admiralty Inlet; thence around the foot of Vashon's Island, easterly and southeasterly, to the place of beginning.

ARTICLE 2.

There is, however, reserved for the present use and occupation of the said tribes and bands, the following tracts of land, viz: The small island called Klahche-min, situated opposite the mouths of Hammersley's and Totten's Inlets, and separated from Hartstene Island by Peale's Passage, containing about two sections of land by estimation; a square tract containing two sections, or twelve hundred and eighty acres, on Puget's Sound, near the mouth of the She-nah-nam Creek, one mile west of the meridian line of the United States land survey, and a square tract containing two sections, or twelve hundred and eighty acres, lying on the south side of Commencement Bay; all which tracts shall be set apart, and, so far as necessary, surveyed and marked out for their exclusive use; nor shall any white man be permitted to reside upon the same without permission of the tribe and the superintendent or agent. And the said tribes and bands agree to remove to and settle upon the same within one year after the ratification of this treaty, or sooner if the means are furnished them. In the mean time, it shall be lawful for them to reside upon any ground not in the actual claim and occupation of citizens of the United States, and upon any ground claimed or occupied, if with the permission of the owner or claimant. If necessary for the public convenience, roads may be run through their reserves, and, on the other hand, the right of way with free access from the same to the nearest public highway is secured to them.

ARTICLE 3.
The right of taking fish, at all usual and accustomed grounds and stations, is further secured to said Indians in common with all citizens of the Territory, and of erecting temporary houses for the purpose of curing, together with the privilege of hunting, gathering roots and berries, and pasturing their horses on open and unclaimed lands: Provided, however, That they shall not take shellfish from any beds staked or cultivated by citizens, and that they shall alter all stallions not intended for breeding-horses, and shall keep up and confine the latter.

ARTICLE 4.
In consideration of the above session, the United States agree to pay to the said tribes and bands the sum of thirty-two thousand five hundred dollars, in the following manner, that is to say: For the first year after the ratification hereof, three thousand two hundred and fifty dollars; for the next two years, three thousand dollars each year; for the next three years, two thousand dollars each year; for the next four years fifteen hundred dollars each year; for the next five years twelve hundred dollars each year; and for the next five years one thousand dollars each year; all which said sums of money shall be applied to the use and benefit of the said Indians, under the direction of the President of the United States, who may from time to time determine, at his discretion, upon what beneficial objects to expend the same. And the superintendent of Indian affairs, or other proper officer, shall each year inform the President of the wishes of said Indians in respect thereto.

ARTICLE 5.
To enable the said Indians to remove to and settle upon their aforesaid reservations, and to clear, fence, and break up a sufficient quantity of land for cultivation, the United States further agree to pay the sum of three thousand two hundred and fifty dollars, to

be laid out and expended under the direction of the President, and in such manner as he shall approve.

ARTICLE 6.
The President may hereafter, when in his opinion the interests of the Territory may require, and the welfare of the said Indians be promoted, remove them from either or all of said reservations to such other suitable place or places within said Territory as he may deem fit, on remunerating them for their improvements and the expenses of their removal, or may consolidate them with other friendly tribes or bands. And he may further, at his discretion, cause the whole or any portion of the lands hereby reserved, or of such other land as may be selected in lieu thereof, to be surveyed into lots, and assign the same to such individuals or families as are willing to avail themselves of the privilege, and will locate on the same as a permanent home, on the same terms and subject to the same regulations as are provided in the sixth article of the treaty with the Omahas, so far as the same may be applicable. Any substantial improvements heretofore made by any Indian, and which he shall be compelled to abandon in consequence of this treaty, shall be valued under the direction of the President, and payment be made accordingly therefor.

ARTICLE 7.
The annuities of the aforesaid tribes and bands shall not be taken to pay the debts of individuals.

ARTICLE 8.
The aforesaid tribes and bands acknowledge their dependence on the Government of the United States, and promise to be friendly with all citizens thereof, and pledge themselves to commit no depredations on the property of such citizens. And should any one or more of them violate this pledge, and the fact be satisfactorily proved before the agent, the property taken shall be returned, or in default thereof, or if injured or destroyed, compensation may be made by the Government out of their annuities. Nor will they make war on any other tribe except in self-defence, but will submit all matters of difference between them and other Indians to the Government of the United States, or its agent, for decision, and abide thereby. And if any of the said Indians commit any depredations on any other Indians within the Territory, the same rule shall prevail as that prescribed in this article, in cases of depredations against citizens. And the said tribes agree not

to shelter or conceal offenders against the laws of the United States, but to deliver them up to the authorities for trial.

ARTICLE 9.

The above tribes and bands are desirous to exclude from their reservations the use of ardent spirits, and to prevent their people from drinking the same; and therefore it is provided, that any Indian belonging to said tribes, who is guilty of bringing liquor into said reservations, or who drinks liquor, may have his or her proportion of the annuities withheld from him or her for such time as the President may determine.

ARTICLE 10.

The United States further agree to establish at the general agency for the district of Puget's Sound, within one year from the ratification hereof, and to support, for a period of twenty years, an agricultural and industrial school, to be free to children of the said tribes and bands, in common with those of the other tribes of said district, and to provide the said school with a suitable instructor or instructors, and also to provide a smithy and carpenter's shop, and furnish them with the necessary tools, and employ a blacksmith, carpenter, and farmer, for the term of twenty years, to instruct the Indians in their respective occupations. And the United States further agree to employ a physician to reside at the said central agency, who shall furnish medicine and advice to their sick, and shall vaccinate them; the expenses of the said school, shops, employées, and medical attendance, to be defrayed by the United States, and not deducted from the annuities.

ARTICLE 11.

The said tribes and bands agree to free all slaves now held by them, and not to purchase or acquire others hereafter.

ARTICLE 12.

The said tribes and bands finally agree not to trade at Vancouver's Island, or elsewhere out of the dominions of the United States; nor shall foreign Indians be permitted to reside in their reservations without consent of the superintendent or agent.

ARTICLE 13.

This treaty shall be obligatory on the contracting parties as soon as the same shall be ratified by the President and Senate of the United States.

In testimony whereof, the said Isaac I. Stevens, governor and superintendent of Indian Affairs, and the undersigned chiefs, headmen, and delegates of the aforesaid tribes and bands, have hereunto set their hands and seals at the place and on the day and year hereinbefore written.

Isaac I. Stevens, [L. S.], Governor and
    Superintendent Territory of Washington.
Qui-ee-metl, his x mark. [L. S.],
Sno-ho-dumset, his x mark. [L. S.],
Lesh-high, his x mark. [L. S.],
Slip-o-elm, his x mark. [L. S.],
Kwi-ats, his x mark. [L. S.],
Stee-high, his x mark. [L. S.],
Di-a-keh, his x mark. [L. S.],
Hi-ten, his x mark. [L. S.],
Squa-ta-hun, his x mark. [L. S.],
Kahk-tse-min, his x mark. [L. S.],
Sonan-o-yutl, his x mark. [L. S.],
Kl-tehp, his x mark. [L. S.],
Sahl-ko-min, his x mark. [L. S.],
T'bet-ste-heh-bit, his x mark. [L. S.],
Tcha-hoos-tan, his x mark. [L. S.],
Ke-cha-hat, his x mark. [L. S.],
Spee-peh, his x mark. [L. S.],
Swe-yah-tum, his x mark. [L. S.],
Cha-achsh, his x mark. [L. S.],
Pich-kehd, his x mark. [L. S.],
S'Klah-o-sum, his x mark. [L. S.],
Sah-le-tatl, his x mark. [L. S.],
See-lup, his x mark. [L. S.],
E-la-kah-ka, his x mark. [L. S.],
Slug-yeh, his x mark. [L. S.],
Hi-nuk, his x mark. [L. S.],
Ma-mo-nish, his x mark. [L. S.],
Cheels, his x mark. [L. S.],
Knutcanu, his x mark. [L. S.],
Bats-ta-kobe, his x mark. [L. S.],
Win-ne-ya, his x mark. [L. S.],
Klo-out, his x mark. [L. S.],
Se-uch-ka-nam, his x mark. [L. S.],
Ske-mah-han, his x mark. [L. S.],
Wuts-un-a-pum, his x mark. [L. S.],
Quuts-a-tadm, his x mark. [L. S.],
Quut-a-heh-mtsn, his x mark. [L. S.],
Yah-leh-chn, his x mark. [L. S.],
To-lahl-kut, his x mark. [L. S.],
Yul-lout, his x mark. [L. S.],
See-ahts-oot-soot, his x mark. [L. S.],
Ye-takho, his x mark. [L. S.],
We-po-it-ee, his x mark. [L. S.],

Kah-sld, his x mark. [L. S.],
La'h-hom-kan, his x mark. [L. S.],
Pah-how-at-ish, his x mark. [L. S.],
Swe-yehm, his x mark. [L. S.],
Sah-hwill, his x mark. [L. S.],
Se-kwaht, his x mark. [L. S.],
Kah-hum-klt, his x mark. [L. S.],
Yah-kwo-bah, his x mark. [L. S.],
Wut-sah-le-wun, his x mark. [L. S.],
Sah-ba-hat, his x mark. [L. S.],
Tel-e-kish, his x mark. [L. S.],
Swe-keh-nam, his x mark. [L. S.],
Sit-oo-ah, his x mark. [L. S.],
Ko-quel-a-cut, his x mark. [L. S.]
Jack, his x mark. [L. S.],
Keh-kise-bel-lo, his x mark. [L. S.],
Go-yeh-hn, his x mark. [L. S.],
Sah-putsh, his x mark. [L. S.],
William, his x mark. [L. S.].

Executed in the presence of us—
M. T. Simmons, Indian agent,
James Doty, secretary of the commission,
C. H. Mason, secretary Washington Territory,
W. A. Slaughter, first lieutenant, Fourth Infantry,
James McAlister,
E. Giddings, jr.,
George Shazer,
Henry D. Cock,
S. S. Ford, jr.,
John W. McAlister,
Clovington Cushman,
Peter Anderson,
Samuel Klady,
W. H. Pullen,
P. O. Hough,
E. R. Tyerall,
George Gibbs,
Benj. F. Shaw, interpreter,
Hazard Stevens.

Treaty with the Yakima, 1855

June 9, 1855. | 12 Stat., 951. | Ratified Mar. 8, 1859. | Proclaimed Apr. 18, 1859.

Articles of agreement and convention made and concluded at the treaty-ground, Camp Stevens, Walla-Walla Valley, this ninth day of June, in the year one thousand eight hundred and fifty-five, by and between Isaac I. Stevens, governor and superinten-

dent of Indian affairs for the Territory of Washington, on the part of the United States, and the undersigned head chiefs, chiefs, head-men, and delegates of the Yakama, Palouse, Pisquouse, Wenatshapam, Klikatat, Klinquit, Kow-was-say-ee, Li-ay-was, Skinpah, Wish-ham. Shyiks, Ochechotes, Kah milt-pah, and Se-ap-cat, confederated tribes and bands of Indians, occupying lands hereinafter bounded and described and lying in Washington Territory, who for the purposes of this treaty are to be considered as one nation, under the name of "Yakama," with Kamaiakun as its head chief, on behalf of and acting for said tribes and bands, and being duly authorized thereto by them.

ARTICLE 1.
The aforesaid confederated tribes and bands of Indians hereby cede, relinquish, and convey to the United States all their right, title, and interest in and to the lands and country occupied and claimed by them, and bounded and described as follows, to wit:

Commencing at Mount Ranier, thence northerly along the main ridge of the Cascade Mountains to the point where the northern tributaries of Lake Che-lan and the southern tributaries of the Methow River have their rise; thence southeasterly on the divide between the waters of Lake Che-lan and the Methow River to the Columbia River; thence, crossing the Columbia on a true east course, to a point whose longitude is one hundred and nineteen degrees and ten minutes, (119° 10') which two latter lines separate the above confederated tribes and bands from the Oakinakane tribe of Indians; thence in a true south course to the forty-seventh (47°) parallel of latitude: thence east on said parallel to the main Palouse River, which two latter lines of boundary separate the above confederated tribes and bands from the Spokanes; thence down the Palouse River to its junction with the Mohhah-ne-she, or southern tributary of the same; thence in a southesterly direction, to the Snake River, at the mouth of the Tucannon River, separating the above confederated tribes from the Nez Percé tribe of Indians; thence down the Snake River to its junction with the Columbia River; thence up the Columbia River to the "White Banks" below the Priest's Rapids; thence westerly to a lake called "La Lac"; thence southerly to a point on the Yakama River called Toh-mah-luke; thence, in a southwesterly direction, to the Columbia River, at the western extremity of the "Big Island," between the mouths of the Umatilla River and Butler Creek; all which latter boundaries separate the above confederated tribes and bands from the Walla-Walla,

Cayuse, and Umatilla tribes and bands of Indians; thence down the Columbia River to midway between the mouths of White Salmon and Wind Rivers; thence along the divide between said rivers to the main ridge of the Cascade Mountains; and thence along said ridge to the place of beginning.

ARTICLE 2.

There is, however, reserved, from the lands above ceded for the use and occupation of the aforesaid confederated tribes and bands of Indians, the tract of land included within the following boundaries, to wit: Commencing on the Yakama River, at the mouth of the Attah-nam River; thence westerly along said Attah-nam River to the forks; thence along the southern tributary to the Cascade Mountains; thence southerly along the main ridge of said mountains, passing south and east of Mount Adams, to the spur whence flows the waters of the Klickatat and Pisco Rivers; thence down said spur to the divide between the waters of said rivers; thence along said divide to the divide separating the waters of the Satass River from those flowing into the Columbia River; thence along said divide to the main Yakama, eight miles below the mouth of the Satass River; and thence up the Yakama River to the place of beginning.

All which tract shall be set apart and, so far as necessary, surveyed and marked out, for the exclusive use and benefit of said confederated tribes and bands of Indians, as an Indian reservation; nor shall any white man, excepting those in the employment of the Indian Department, be permitted to reside upon the said reservation without permission of the tribe and the superintendent and agent. And the said confederated tribes and bands agree to remove to, and settle upon, the same, within one year after the ratification of this treaty. In the mean time it shall be lawful for them to reside upon any ground not in the actual claim and occupation of citizens of the United States; and upon any ground claimed or occupied, if with the permission of the owner or claimant.

Guaranteeing, however, the right to all citizens of the United States to enter upon and occupy as settlers any lands not actually occupied and cultivated by said Indians at this time, and not included in the reservation above named.

And provided, That any substantial improvements heretofore made by any Indian, such as fields enclosed and cultivated, and houses erected upon the lands hereby ceded, and which he may be compelled to abandon in consequence of this treaty, shall be valued, under the direction of the President of the United States, and payment made therefor in money; or improvements of an equal value made for said Indian upon the reservation. And no Indian will be required to abandon the improvements aforesaid, now occupied by him, until their value in money, or improvements of an equal value shall be furnished him as aforesaid.

ARTICLE 3.

And provided, That, if necessary for the public convenience, roads may be run through the said reservation; and on the other hand, the right of way, with free access from the same to the nearest public highway, is secured to them; as also the right, in common with citizens of the United States, to travel upon all public highways.

The exclusive right of taking fish in all the streams, where running through or bordering said reservation, is further secured to said confederated tribes and bands of Indians, as also the right of taking fish at all usual and accustomed places, in common with the citizens of the Territory, and of erecting temporary buildings for curing them; together with the privilege of hunting, gathering roots and berries, and pasturing their horses and cattle upon open and unclaimed land.

ARTICLE 4.

In consideration of the above cession, the United States agree to pay to the said confederated tribes and bands of Indians, in addition to the goods and provisions distributed to them at the time of signing this treaty, the sum of two hundred thousand dollars, in the following manner, that is to say: Sixty thousand dollars, to be expended under the direction of the President of the United States, the first year after the ratification of this treaty, in providing for their removal to the reservation, breaking up and fencing farms, building houses for them, supplying them with provisions and a suitable outfit, and for such other objects as he may deem necessary, and the remainder in annuities, as follows: For the first five years after the ratification of the treaty, ten thousand dollars each year, commencing September first, 1856; for the next five years, eight thousand dollars each year; for the next five years, six thousand dollars per year; and for the next five years, four thousand dollars per year.

All which sums of money shall be applied to the use and benefit of said Indians, under the direction of the President of the United States, who may from time to time determine, at his discretion, upon what beneficial objects to expend the same for them. And the superintendent of Indian affairs, or other proper officer, shall each year inform the President of the wishes of the Indians in relation thereto.

ARTICLE 5.

The United States further agree to establish at suitable points within said reservation, within one year after the ratification hereof, two schools, erecting the necessary buildings, keeping them in repair, and providing them with furniture, books, and stationery, one of which shall be an agricultural and industrial school, to be located at the agency, and to be free to the children of the said confederated tribes and bands of Indians, and to employ one superintendent of teaching and two teachers; to build two blacksmiths' shops, to one of which shall be attached a tin-shop, and to the other a gunsmith's shop; one carpenter's shop, one wagon and plough maker's shop, and to keep the same in repair and furnished with the necessary tools; to employ one superintendent of farming and two farmers, two blacksmiths, one tinner, one gunsmith, one carpenter, one wagon and plough maker, for the instruction of the Indians in trades and to assist them in the same; to erect one saw-mill and one flouring-mill, keeping the same in repair and furnished with the necessary tools and fixtures; to erect a hospital, keeping the same in repair and provided with the necessary medicines and furniture, and to employ a physician; and to erect, keep in repair, and provided with the necessary furniture, the building required for the accommodation of the said employees. The said buildings and establishments to be maintained and kept in repair as aforesaid, and the employees to be kept in service for the period of twenty years.

And in view of the fact that the head chief of the said confederated tribes and bands of Indians is expected, and will be called upon to perform many services of a public character, occupying much of his time, the United States further agree to pay to the said confederated tribes and bands of Indians five hundred dollars per year, for the term of twenty years after the ratification hereof, as a salary for such person as the said confederated tribes and bands of Indians may select to be their head chief, to build for him at a suitable point on the reservation a comfort-able house, and properly furnish the same, and to plough and fence ten acres of land. The said salary to be paid to, and the said house to be occupied by, such head chief so long as he may continue to hold that office.

And it is distinctly understood and agreed that at the time of the conclusion of this treaty Kamaiakun is the duly elected and authorized head chief of the confederated tribes and bands aforesaid, styled the Yakama Nation, and is recognized as such by them and by the commissioners on the part of the United States holding this treaty; and all the expenditures and expenses contemplated in this article of this treaty shall be defrayed by the United States, and shall not be deducted from the annuities agreed to be paid to said confederated tribes and band of Indians. Nor shall the cost of transporting the goods for the annuity payments be a charge upon the annuities, but shall be defrayed by the United States.

ARTICLE 6.

The President may, from time to time, at his discretion, cause the whole or such portions of such reservation as he may think proper, to be surveyed into lots, and assign the same to such individuals or families of the said confederated tribes and bands of Indians as are willing to avail themselves of the privilege, and will locate on the same as a permanent home, on the same terms and subject to the same regulations as are provided in the sixth article of the treaty with the Omahas, so far as the same may be applicable.

ARTICLE 7.

The annuities of the aforesaid confederated tribes and bands of Indians shall not be taken to pay the debts of individuals.

ARTICLE 8.

The aforesaid confederated tribes and bands of Indians acknowledge their dependence upon the Government of the United States, and promise to be friendly with all citizens thereof, and pledge themselves to commit no depredations upon the property of such citizens.

And should any one or more of them violate this pledge, and the fact be satisfactorily proved before the agent, the property taken shall be returned, or in default thereof, or if injured or destroyed, compensation may be made by the Government out of the annuities.

Nor will they make war upon any other tribe, except in self-defence, but will submit all matters of difference between them and other Indians to the Government of the United States or its agent for decision, and abide thereby. And if any of the said Indians commit depredations on any other Indians within the Territory of Washington or Oregon, the same rule shall prevail as that provided in this article in case of depredations against citizens. And the said confederated tribes and bands of Indians agree not to shelter or conceal offenders against the laws of the United States, but to deliver them up to the authorities for trial.

ARTICLE 9.

The said confederated tribes and bands of Indians desire to exclude from their reservation the use of ardent spirits, and to prevent their people from drinking the same, and, therefore, it is provided that any Indian belonging to said confederated tribes and bands of Indians, who is guilty of bringing liquor into said reservation, or who drinks liquor, may have his or her annuities withheld from him or her for such time as the President may determine.

ARTICLE 10.

And provided, That there is also reserved and set apart from the lands ceded by this treaty, for the use and benefit of the aforesaid confederated tribes and bands, a tract of land not exceeding in quantity one township of six miles square, situated at the forks of the Pisquouse or Wenatshapam River, and known as the "Wenatshapam Fishery," which said reservation shall be surveyed and marked out whenever the President may direct, and be subject to the same provisions and restrictions as other Indian reservations.

ARTICLE 11.

This treaty shall be obligatory upon the contracting parties as soon as the same shall be ratified by the President and Senate of the United States.

In testimony whereof, the said Isaac I. Stevens, governor and superintendent of Indian affairs for the Territory of Washington, and the undersigned head chief, chiefs, headmen, and delegates of the aforesaid confederated tribes and bands of Indians, have hereunto set their hands and seals, at the place and on the day and year hereinbefore written.

Isaac I. Stevens,
Governor and Superintendent. [L. S.],

Kamaiakun, his x mark. [L. S.],
Skloom, his x mark. [L. S.],
Owhi, his x mark. [L. S.],
Te-cole-kun, his x mark. [L. S.],
La-hoom, his x mark. [L. S.],
Me-ni-nock, his x mark. [L. S.],
Elit Palmer, his x mark. [L. S.],
Wish-och-kmpits, his x mark. [L. S.],
Koo-lat-toose, his x mark. [L. S.],
Shee-ah-cotte, his x mark. [L. S.],
Tuck-quille, his x mark. [L. S.],
Ka-loo-as, his x mark. [L. S.],
Scha-noo-a, his x mark. [L. S.],
Sla-kish, his x mark. [L. S.].

Signed and sealed in the presence of—
James Doty, secretary of treaties,
Mie. Cles. Pandosy, O. M. T.,
Wm. C. McKay,
W. H. Tappan, sub Indian agent, W. T.,
C. Chirouse, O. M. T.,
Patrick McKenzie, interpreter,
A. D. Pamburn, interpreter,
Joel Palmer, superintendent Indian affairs, O. T.,
W. D. Biglow,
A. D. Pamburn, interpreter.

Treaty with the Nez Percés, 1863

June 9, 1863. | 14 Stats., 647. | Ratified Apr. 17, 1867. | Proclaimed Apr. 20, 1867.

Articles of agreement made and concluded at the council-ground, in the valley of the Lapwai, W. T., on the ninth day of June, one thousand eight hundred and sixty-three, between the United States of America, by C. H. Hale, superintendent of Indian affairs, and Charles Hutchins and S. D. Howe, U. S. Indian agents for the Territory of Washington, acting on the part and in behalf of the United States, and the Nez Percé Indians, by the chiefs, head-men, and delegates of said tribe, such articles being supplementary and amendatory to the treaty made between the United States and said tribe on the 11th day of June, 1855.

ARTICLE 1.

The said Nez Percé tribe agree to relinquish, and do hereby relinquish, to the United States the lands heretofore reserved for the use and occupation of the said tribe, saving and excepting so much thereof as is described in Article II for a new reservation.

ARTICLE 2.

The United States agree to reserve for a home, and for the sole use and occupation of said tribe, the tract of land included within the following boundaries, to wit: Commencing at the northeast corner of Lake Wa-ha, and running thence, northerly, to a point on the north bank of the Clearwater River, three miles below the mouth of the Lapwai, thence down the north bank of the Clearwater to the mouth of the Hatwai Creek; thence, due north, to a point seven miles distant; thence, eastwardly, to a point on the north fork of the Clearwater, seven miles distant from its mouth; thence to a point on Oro Fino Creek, five miles above its mouth; thence to a point on the north fork of the south fork of the Clearwater, five miles above its mouth; thence to a point on the south fork of the Clearwater, one mile above the bridge, on the road leading to Elk City, (so as to include all the Indian farms now within the forks); thence in a straight line, westwardly, to the place of beginning.

All of which tract shall be set apart, and the above-described boundaries shall be surveyed and marked out for the exclusive use and benefit of said tribe as an Indian reservation, nor shall any white man, excepting those in the employment of the Indian Department, be permitted to reside upon the said reservation without permission of the tribe and the superintendent and agent; and the said tribe agrees that so soon after the United States shall make the necessary provision for fulfilling the stipulations of this instrument as they can conveniently arrange their affairs, and not to exceed one year from its ratification, they will vacate the country hereby relinquished, and remove to and settle upon the lands herein reserved for them (except as may be hereinafter provided.) In the meantime it shall be lawful for them to reside upon any ground now occupied or under cultivation by said Indians at this time, and not included in the reservation above named. And it is provided, that any substantial improvement heretofore made by any Indian, such as fields enclosed and cultivated, or houses erected upon the lands hereby relinquished, and which he may be compelled to abandon in consequence of this treaty, shall be valued under the direction of the President of the United States, and payment therefor shall be made in stock or in improvements of an equal value for said Indian upon the lot which may be assigned to him within the bounds of the reservation, as he may choose, and no Indian will be required to abandon the improvements aforesaid, now occupied by

him, until said payment or improvement shall have been made. And it is further provided, that if any Indian living on any of the land hereby relinquished should prefer to sell his improvements to any white man, being a loyal citizen of the United States, prior to the same being valued as aforesaid, he shall be allowed so to do, but the sale or transfer of said improvements shall be made in the presence of, and with the consent and approval of, the agent or superintendent, by whom a certificate of sale shall be issued to the party purchasing, which shall set forth the amount of the consideration in kind. Before the issue of said certificate, the agent or superintendent shall be satisfied that a valuable consideration is paid, and that the party purchasing is of undoubted loyalty to the United States Government. No settlement or claim made upon the improved lands by any Indian will be permitted, except as herein provided, prior to the time specified for their removal. Any sale or transfer thus made shall be in the stead of payment for improvements from the United States.

ARTICLE 3.

The President shall, immediately after the ratification of this treaty, cause the boundary-lines to be surveyed, and properly marked and established; after which, so much of the lands hereby reserved as may be suitable for cultivation shall be surveyed into lots of twenty acres each, and every male person of the tribe who shall have attained the age of twenty-one years, or is the head of a family, shall have the privilege of locating upon one lot as a permanent home for such person, and the lands so surveyed shall be allotted under such rules and regulations as the President shall prescribe, having such reference to their settlement as may secure adjoining each other the location of the different families pertaining to each band, so far as the same may be practicable. Such rules and regulations shall be prescribed by the President, or under his direction, as will insure to the family, in case of the death of the head thereof, the possession and enjoyment of such permanent home, and the improvements thereon. When the assignments as above shall have been completed, certificates shall be issued by the Commissioner of Indian Affairs, or under his direction, for the tracts assigned in severalty, specifying the names of the individuals to whom they have been assigned respectively, and that said tracts are set apart for the perpetual and exclusive use and benefit of such assignees and their heirs. Until otherwise provided by law, such tracts shall be exempt from levy, taxation, or sale, and shall be alienable in fee, or leased, or otherwise disposed of, only to the United States, or to persons then being members of the Nez Percé tribe, and of Indian blood, with the permission of the President, and under such regulations as the Secretary of the Interior or the Commissioner of Indian Affairs shall prescribe; and if any such person or family shall at any time neglect or refuse to occupy and till a portion of the land so assigned, and on which they have located, or shall rove from place to place, the President may cancel the assignment, and may also withhold from such person or family their proportion of the annuities or other payments due them until they shall have returned to such permanent home, and resumed the pursuits of industry; and in default of their return, the tract may be declared abandoned, and thereafter assigned to some other person or family of such tribe. The residue of the land hereby reserved shall be held in common for pasturage for the sole use and benefit of the Indians: Provided, however, That from time to time, as members of the tribe may come upon the reservation, or may become of proper age, after the expiration of the time of one year after the ratification of this treaty, as aforesaid, and claim the privileges granted under this article, lots may be assigned from the lands thus held in common, wherever the same may be suitable for cultivation. No State or territorial legislature shall remove the restriction herein provided for, without the consent of Congress, and no State or territorial law to that end shall be deemed valid until the same has been specially submitted to Congress for its approval.

ARTICLE 4.
In consideration of the relinquishment herein made the United States agree to pay to the said tribe, in addition to the annuities provided by the treaty of June 11, 1855, and the goods and provisions distributed to them at the time of signing this treaty, the sum of two hundred and sixty-two thousand and five hundred dollars, in manner following, to wit:

First. One hundred and fifty thousand dollars, to enable the Indians to remove and locate upon the reservation, to be expended in the ploughing of land, and the fencing of the several lots, which may be assigned to those individual members of the tribe who will accept the same in accordance with the provisions of the preceding article, which said sum shall be divided into four annual instalments, as follows: For the first year after the ratification of this treaty, seventy thousand dollars; for the second year, forty thousand dollars; for the third year, twenty-five thousand dollars; for the fourth year, fifteen thousand dollars.

Second. Fifty thousand dollars to be paid the first year after the ratification of this treaty in agricultural implements, to include wagons or carts, harness, and cattle, sheep, or other stock, as may be deemed most beneficial by the superintendent of Indian affairs, or agent, after ascertaining the wishes of the Indians in relation thereto.

Third. Ten thousand dollars for the erection of a saw and flouring mill, to be located at Kamia, the same to be erected within one year after the ratification hereof.

Fourth. Fifty thousand dollars for the boarding and clothing of the children who shall attend the schools, in accordance with such rules or regulations as the Commissioner of Indian Affairs may prescribe, providing the schools and boarding-houses with necessary furniture, the purchase of necessary wagons, teams, agricultural implements, tools, &c., for their use, and for the fencing of such lands as may be needed for gardening and farming purposes, for the use and benefit of the schools, to be expended as follows: The first year after the ratification of this treaty, six thousand dollars; for the next fourteen years, three thousand dollars each year; and for the succeeding year, being the sixteenth and last instalment, two thousand dollars.

Fifth. A further sum of two thousand five hundred dollars shall be paid within one year after the ratification hereof, to enable the Indians to build two churches, one of which is to be located at some suitable point on the Kamia, and the other on the Lapwai.

ARTICLE 5.
The United States further agree, that in addition to a head chief the tribe shall elect two subordinate chiefs, who shall assist him in the performance of his public services, and each subordinate chief shall have the same amount of land ploughed and fenced, with comfortable house and necessary furniture, and to whom the same salary shall be paid as is already provided for the head chief in article 5 of the treaty of June 11, 1855, the salary to be paid and the houses and land to be occupied during the same period and under like restrictions as therein mentioned.

And for the purpose of enabling the agent to erect said buildings, and to plough and fence the land, as well as to procure the necessary furniture, and to complete and furnish the house, &c., of the head chief, as heretofore provided, there shall be appropriated, to be expended within the first year after the ratification hereof, the sum of two thousand five hundred dollars.

And inasmuch as several of the provisions of said art. 5th of the treaty of June 11, 1855, pertaining to the erection of school-houses, hospital, shops, necessary buildings for employe[e]s and for the agency, as well as providing the same with necessary furniture, tools, &c., have not yet been complied with, it is hereby stipulated that there shall be appropriated, to be expended for the purposes herein specified during the first year after the ratification hereof, the following sums, to wit:

First. Ten thousand dollars for the erection of the two schools, including boarding-houses and the necessary out-buildings; said schools to be conducted on the manual-labor system as far as practicable.

Second. Twelve hundred dollars for the erection of the hospital, and providing the necessary furniture for the same.

Third. Two thousand dollars for the erection of a blacksmith's shop, to be located at Kamia, to aid in the completion of the smith's shop at the agency, and to purchase the necessary tools, iron, steel, &c.; and to keep the same in repair and properly stocked with necessary tools and materials, there shall be appropriated thereafter, for the fifteen years next succeeding, the sum of five hundred dollars each year.

Fourth. Three thousand dollars for erection of houses for employe[e]s, repairs of mills, shops, &c., and providing necessary furniture, tools, and materials. For the same purpose, and to procure from year to year the necessary articles—that is to say, sawlogs, nails, glass, hardware, &c.—there shall be appropriated thereafter, for the twelve years next succeeding, the sum of two thousand dollars each year; and for the next three years, one thousand dollars each year.

And it is further agreed that the United States shall employ, in addition to those already mentioned in art. 5th of the treaty of June 11, 1855, two matrons to take charge of the boarding-schools, two assistant teachers, one farmer, one carpenter, and two millers.

All the expenditures and expenses contemplated in this treaty, and not otherwise provided for, shall be defrayed by the United States.

ARTICLE 6.
In consideration of the past services and faithfulness of the Indian chief, Timothy, it is agreed that the United States shall appropriate the sum of six hundred dollars, to aid him in the erection of a house upon the lot of land which may be assigned to him, in accordance with the provisions of the third article of this treaty.

ARTICLE 7.
The United States further agree that the claims of certain members of the Nez Percé tribe against the Government for services rendered and for horses furnished by them to the Oregon mounted volunteers, as appears by certificate issued by W. H. Fauntleroy, A. R. Qr. M. and Com. Oregon volunteers, on the 6th of March, 1856, at Camp Cornelius, and amounting to the sum of four thousand six hundred and sixty-five dollars, shall be paid to them in full, in gold coin.

ARTICLE 8.
It is also understood that the aforesaid tribe do hereby renew their acknowledgments of dependence upon the Government of the United States, their promises of friendship, and other pledges, as set forth in the eighth article of the treaty of June 11, 1855; and further, that all the provisions of said treaty which are not abrogated or specifically changed by any article herein contained, shall remain the same to all intents and purposes as formerly,—the same obligations resting upon the United States, the same privileges continued to the Indians outside of the reservation, and the same rights secured to citizens of the U. S. as to right of way upon the streams and over the roads which may run through said reservation, as are therein set forth.

But it is further provided, that the United States is the only competent authority to declare and establish such necessary roads and highways, and that no other right is intended to be hereby granted to citizens of the United States than the right of way upon or over such roads as may thus be legally established: Provided, however, That the roads now usually travelled shall, in the mean time, be taken and deemed as within the meaning of this article, until otherwise enacted by act of Congress or by the authority of the Indian Department.

And the said tribe hereby consent, that upon the public roads which may run across the reservation there may be established, at such points as shall be necessary for public convenience, hotels, or stage-stands, of the number and necessity of which the agent or superintendent shall be the sole judge, who shall be competent to license the same, with the privilege of using such amount of land for pasturage and other purposes connected with such establishment as the agent or superintendent shall deem necessary, it being understood that such lands for pasturage are to be enclosed, and the boundaries thereof described in the license.

And it is further understood and agreed that all ferries and bridges within the reservation shall be held and managed for the benefit of said tribe.

Such rules and regulations shall be made by the Commissioner of Indian Affairs, with the approval of the Secretary of the Interior, as shall regulate the travel on the highways, the management of the ferries and bridges, the licensing of public houses, and the leasing of lands, as herein provided, so that the rents, profits, and issues thereof shall inure to the benefit of said tribe, and so that the persons thus licensed, or necessarily employed in any of the above relations, shall be subject to the control of the Indian Department, and to the provisions of the act of Congress "to regulate trade and intercourse with the Indian tribes, and to preserve peace on the frontiers."

All timber within the bounds of the reservation is exclusively the property of the tribe, excepting that the U. S. Government shall be permitted to use thereof for any purpose connected with its affairs, either in carrying out any of the provisions of this treaty, or in the maintaining of its necessary forts or garrisons.

The United States also agree to reserve all springs or fountains not adjacent to, or directly connected with, the streams or rivers within the lands hereby relinquished, and to keep back from settlement or entry so much of the surrounding land as may be necessary to prevent the said springs or fountains being enclosed; and, further, to preserve a perpetual right of way to and from the same, as watering places, for the use in common of both whites and Indians.

ARTICLE 9.

Inasmuch as the Indians in council have expressed their desire that Robert Newell should have confirmed to him a piece of land lying between Snake and Clearwater Rivers, the same having been given to him on the 9th day of June, 1861, and described in an instrument of writing bearing that date, and signed by several chiefs of the tribe, it is hereby agreed that the said Robert Newell shall receive from the United States a patent for the said tract of land.

ARTICLE 10.

This treaty shall be obligatory upon the contracting parties as soon as the same shall be ratified by the President and Senate of the United States.

In testimony whereof the said C. H. Hale, superintendent of Indian affairs, and Charles Hutchins and S. D. Howe, United States Indian agents in the Territory of Washington, and the chiefs, headmen, and delegates of the aforesaid Nez Perce tribe of Indians, have hereunto set their hands and seals at the place and on the day and year hereinbefore written.

> Calvin H. Hale, Superintendent Indian Affairs, Wash. T. [SEAL.]
> Chas. Hutchins, United States Indian agent, Wash. T. [SEAL.]
> S. D. Howe, United States Indian agent, Wash. T. [SEAL.]
> Fa-Ind-7-1803 Lawyer, Head Chief Nez Perces Nation. [SEAL.]
> Ute-sin-male-e-cum, x [SEAL.]
> Ha-harch-tuesta, x [SEAL.]
> Tip-ulania-timecca, x [SEAL.]
> Es-coatum, x [SEAL.]
> Timothy, x [SEAL.]
> Levi, x [SEAL.]
> Jason, x [SEAL.]
> Ip-she-ne-wish-kin, (Capt. John,) x [SEAL.]
> Weptas-jump-ki, x [SEAL.]
> We-as-cus, x [SEAL.]
> Pep-hoom-kan, (Noah,) x [SEAL.]
> Shin-ma-sha-ho-soot, x [SEAL.]
> Nie-ki-lil-meh-hoom, (Jacob,) x [SEAL.]
> Stoop-toop-nin, x [SEAL.]
> Su-we-cus, x [SEAL.]

Wal-la-ta-mana, x [SEAL.]
He-kaikt-il-pilp, x [SEAL.]
Whis-tas-ket, x [SEAL.]
Neus-ne-keun, x [SEAL.]
Kul-lou-o-haikt, x [SEAL.]
Wow-en-am-ash-il-pilp, x [SEAL.]
Kan-pow-e-een, x [SEAL.]
Watai-watai-wa-haikt, x [SEAL.]
Kup-kup-pellia, x [SEAL.]
Wap-tas-ta-mana, x [SEAL.]
Peo-peo-ip-se-wat, x [SEAL.]
Louis-in-ha-cush-nim, x [SEAL.]
Lam-lim-si-lilp-nim, x [SEAL.]
Tu-ki-lai-kish, x [SEAL.]
Sah-kan-tai, (Eagle,) x [SEAL.]
We-ah-se-nat, x [SEAL.]
Hin-mia-tun-pin, x [SEAL.]
Ma-hi-a-kim, x [SEAL.]
Shock-lo-turn-wa-haikt, (Jonah,) x [SEAL.]
Kunness-tak-mal, x [SEAL.]
Tu-lat-sy-wat-kin, x [SEAL.]
Tuck-e-tu-et-as, x [SEAL.]
Nic-a-las-in, x [SEAL.]
Was-atis-il-pilp, x [SEAL.]
Wow-es-en-at-im, x [SEAL.]
Hiram, x [SEAL.]
Howlish-wampum, x [SEAL.]
Wat-ska-leeks, x [SEAL.]
Wa-lai-tus, x [SEAL.]
Ky-e-wee-pus, x [SEAL.]
Ko-ko-il-pilp, x [SEAL.]
Reuben, Tip-ia-la-na-uy-kalatsekin, x [SEAL.]
Wish-la-na-ka-nin, x [SEAL.]
Me-tat-ueptas, (Three Feathers,) x [SEAL.]
Ray-kay-mass, x [SEAL.]

Signed and sealed in presence of—
George F. Whitworth, Secretary.
Justus Steinberger, Colonel U. S. Volunteers.
R. F. Malloy, Colonel Cavalry, O. V.
J. S. Rinearson, Major First Cavalry Oregon
    Volunteers.
William Kapus, First Lieutenant and Adjutant
    First W. T. Infantry U. S. Volunteers.
Harrison Olmstead.
Jno. Owen, (Bitter Root.).
James O'Neill.
J. B. Buker, M. D.
George W. Elber.
A. A. Spalding, assistant interpreter.
Perrin B. Whitman, interpreter for the council.

Treaty with the Cheyenne and Arapaho, 1865

Oct, 14, 1865. | 14 Stats., 703. | Ratified May 22, 1866. | Proclaimed Feb. 2, 1867.

Articles of a treaty made and concluded at the camp on the Little Arkansas River, in the State of Kansas, on the fourteenth day of October, in the year of our Lord one thousand eight hundred and sixty-five, by and between John B. Sanborn, William S. Harney, Thomas Murphy, Kit Carson, William W. Bent, Jesse H. Leavenworth, and James Steele, commissioners on the part of the United States, and the undersigned, chiefs and head-men of and representing the confederate tribes of Arrapahoe and Cheyenne Indians of the Upper Arkansas River, they being duly authorized by their respective tribes to act in the premises.

ARTICLE 1.

It is agreed by the parties to this treaty that hereafter perpetual peace shall be maintained between the people and Government of the United States and the Indians parties hereto, and that the Indians parties hereto, shall forever remain at peace with each other, and with all other Indians who sustain friendly relations with the Government of the United States. For the purpose of enforcing the provisions of this article it is agreed that in case hostile acts or depredations are committed by the people of the United States, or by Indians on friendly terms with the United States, against the tribe or tribes, or the individual members of the tribe or tribes, who are parties to this treaty, such hostile acts or depredations shall not be redressed by a resort to arms, but the party or parties aggrieved shall submit their complaints through their agent to the President of the United States, and thereupon an impartial arbitration shall be had, under his direction, and the award thus made shall be binding on all parties interested, and the Government of the United States will in good faith enforce the same. And the Indians, parties hereto, on their part, agree, in case crimes or other violations of law shall be committed by any person or persons, members of their tribe, such person or persons shall, upon complaint being made, in writing, to their agent, superintendent of Indian affairs, or to other proper authority, by the party injured, and verified by affidavit, be delivered to the person duly authorized to take such person or persons into custody, to the end that such person or persons may be punished according to the laws of the United States.

ARTICLE 2.

The United States hereby agree that the district of country embraced within the following limits, or such portion of the same as may hereafter be designated by the President of the United States for that purpose, viz: commencing at the mouth of the Red Creek or Red Fork of the Arkansas River; thence up said creek or fork to its source; thence westwardly to a point on the Cimarone River, opposite the mouth of Buffalo Creek; thence due north to the Arkansas River; thence down the same to the beginning, shall be, and is hereby, set apart for the absolute and undisturbed use and occupation of the tribes who are parties to this treaty, and of such other friendly tribes as they may from time to time agree to admit among them, and that no white person, except officers, agents, and employees of the Government, shall go upon or settle within the country embraced within said limits, unless formerly admitted and incorporated into some one of the tribes lawfully residing there, according to its laws and usages: Provided, however, That said Indians shall not be required to settle upon said reservation until such time as the United States shall have extinguished all claims of title thereto on the part of other Indians, so that the Indians parties hereto may live thereon at peace with all other tribes: Provided, however, That as soon as practicable, with the assent of said tribe, the President of the United States shall designate for said tribes a reservation, no part of which shall be within the State of Kansas, and cause them as soon as practicable to remove to and settle thereon, but no such reservation shall be designated upon any reserve belonging to any other Indian tribe or tribes without their consent.

The Indians parties hereto, on their part, expressly agree to remove to and accept as their permanent home the country embraced within said limits whenever directed so to do by the President of the United States, in accordance with the provisions of this treaty, and that they will not go from said country for hunting or other purposes without the consent in writing of their agent or other authorized person, such written consent in all cases specifying the purpose for which such leave is granted, and shall be borne with them upon their excursions as evidence that they are rightfully away from their reservation, and shall be respected by all officers, employees, and citizens of the United States as their sufficient safeguard and protection against injury or damage in person or property by any and all persons whomsoever.

It is further agreed by the Indians parties hereto that when absent from their reservation they will refrain from the commission of any depredations or injuries to the person or property of all persons sustaining friendly relations with the Government of the United States; that they will not, while so absent, encamp by day or night within ten miles of any of the main traveled routes or roads through the country to which they go, or of the military posts, towns, or villages therein, without the consent of the commanders of such military posts, or of the civil authorities of such towns or villages; and that henceforth they will, and do hereby, relinquish all claims or rights in and to any portion of the United States or Territories, except such as is embraced within the limits aforesaid, and more especially their claims and rights in and to the country bounded as follows, viz: beginning at the junction of the north and south forks of the Platte River; thence up the north fork to the top of the principal range of the Rocky Mountains, or to the Red Buttes; thence southwardly along the summit of the Rocky Mountains to the headwaters of the Arkansas River; thence down the Arkansas River to the Cimarone crossing of the same; thence to the place of beginning; which country they claim to have originally owned, and never to have relinquished the title thereto.

ARTICLE 3.

It is further agreed that until the Indians parties hereto have removed to the reservation provided for by the preceding article in pursuance of the stipulations thereof, said Indians shall be, and they are hereby, expressly permitted to reside upon and range at pleasure throughout the unsettled portions of that part of the country they claim as originally theirs, which lies between the Arkansas and Platte Rivers; and that they shall and will not go elsewhere, except upon the terms and conditions prescribed by the preceding article in relation to leaving the reservation thereby provided for: Provided, That the provisions of the preceding article in regard to encamping within ten miles of main travelled routes, military posts, towns, and villages shall be in full force as to occupancy of the country named and permitted by the terms of this article: Provided, further, That they, the said Indians, shall and will at all times during such occupancy, without delay, report to the commander of the nearest military post the presence in or approach to said country of any hostile bands of Indians whatsoever.

ARTICLE 4.

It is further agreed by the parties hereto that the United States may lay off and build through the reservation, provided for by Article 2 of this treaty, such roads or highways as may be deemed necessary; and may also establish such military posts within the same as may be found necessary in order to preserve peace among the Indians, and in order to enforce such laws, rules, and regulations as are now, or may from time to time be, prescribed by the President and Congress of the United States for the protection of the rights of persons and property among the Indians residing upon said reservation; and further, that in time of war such other military posts as may be considered essential to the general interests of the United States may be established: Provided, however, That upon the building of such roads, or establishment of such military posts, the amount of injury sustained by reason thereof by the Indians inhabiting said reservation shall be ascertained under direction of the President of the United States, and thereupon such compensation shall be made to said Indians as in the judgment of the Congress of the United States may be deemed just and proper.

ARTICLE 5.

At the special request of the Cheyenne and Arapahoe Indians, parties to this treaty, the United States agree to grant, by patent in fee-simple, to the following-named persons, all of whom are related to the Cheyennes or Arapahoes by blood, to each an amount of land equal to one section of six hundred and forty acres, viz: To Mrs. Margaret Wilmarth and her children, Virginia Fitzpatrick, and Andrew Jackson Fitzpatrick; to Mrs. Mary Keith and her children, William Keith, Mary J. Keith, and Francis Keith; to Mrs. Matilda Pepperdin and her child, Miss Margaret Pepperdin; to Robert Poisal and John Poisal; to Edmund Guerrier, Rosa Guerrier, and Julia Guerrier; to William W. Bent's daughter, Mary Bent Moore, and her three children, Adia Moore, William Bent Moore, and George Moore; to William W. Bent's children, George Bent, Charles Bent, and Julia Bent; to A-ma-che, the wife of John Prowers, and her children, Mary Prowers and Susan Prowers; to the children of Ote-se-ot-see, wife of John Y. Sickles, viz: Margaret, Minnie, and John; to the children of John S. Smith, inter-

preter, William Gilpin Smith, and daughter Armama; to Jenny Lind Crocker, daughter of Ne-sou-hoe, or Are-you-there, wife of Lieutenant Crocker; to—Winsor, daughter of Tow-e-nah, wife of A. T. Winsor, sutler, formerly at Fort Lyon. Said lands to be selected under the direction of the Secretary of the Interior, from the reservation established by the 1st article of their treaty of February 18, A. D. 1861: Provided, That said locations shall not be made upon any lands heretofore granted by the United States to any person, State, or corporation, for any purpose.

ARTICLE 6.

The United States being desirous to express its condemnation of, and, as far as may be, repudiate the gross and wanton out-rages perpetrated against certain bands of Cheyenne and Arrapahoe Indians, on the twenty-ninth day of November, A. D. 1864, at Sand Creek, in Colorado Territory, while the said Indians were at peace with the United States, and under its flag, whose protection they had by lawful authority been promised and induced to seek, and the Government being desirous to make some suitable reparation for the injuries then done, will grant three hundred and twenty acres of land by patent to each of the following-named chiefs of said bands, viz: Moke-ta-ve-to, or Black Kettle; Oh-tah-ha-ne-so-weel, or Seven Bulls; Alik-ke-home-ma, or Little Robe; Moke-tah-vo-ve-hoe, or Black White Man; and will in like manner grant to each other person of said bands made a widow, or who lost a parent upon that occasion, one hundred and sixty acres of land, the names of such persons to be ascertained under the direction of the Secretary of the Interior: Provided, That said grants shall be conditioned that all devises, grants, alienations, leases, and contracts relative to said lands, made or entered into during the period of fifty years from the date of such patents, shall be unlawful and void. Said lands shall be selected under the direction of the Secretary of the Interior within the limits of country hereby set apart as a reservation for the Indians parties to this treaty, and shall be free from assessment and taxation so long as they remain inalienable. The United States will also pay in United States securities, animals, goods, provisions, or such other useful articles as may, in the discretion of the Secretary of the Interior, be deemed best adapted to the respective wants and conditions of the persons named in the schedule hereto annexed, they being present and members of the bands who suffered at Sand Creek, upon the occasion aforesaid, the sums set opposite their names, respectively, as a compensation for property belonging to them, and then and there destroyed or taken from them by the United States troops aforesaid.

ARTICLE 7.

The United States agree that they will expend annually during the period of forty years, from and after the ratification of this treaty, for the benefit of the Indians who are parties hereto, and of such others as may unite with them in pursuance of the terms hereof, in such manner and for such purposes as, in the judgment of the Secretary of the Interior, for the time being, will best subserve their wants and interests as a people, the following amounts, that is to say, until such time as said Indians shall be removed to their reservation, as provided for by Article 2 of this treaty, an amount which shall be equal to twenty dollars per capita for each person entitled to participate in the beneficial provisions of this treaty, and from and after the time when such removal shall have been accomplished, an amount which shall be equal to forty dollars per capita for each person entitled as aforesaid. Such proportion of the expenditure provided for by this article as may be considered expedient to distribute in the form of annuities shall be delivered to said Indians as follows, viz: one-third thereof during the spring, and two-thirds thereof during the autumn of each year.

For the purpose of determining from time to time the aggregate amount to be expended under the provisions of this article, it is agreed that the number entitled to its beneficial provisions the coming year is two thousand eight hundred, and that an accurate census of the Indians entitled shall be taken at the time of the annuity payment in the spring of each year by their agent or other person designated for that purpose by the Secretary of the Interior, which census shall be the basis on which the amount to be expended the next ensuing year shall be determined.

ARTICLE 8.

The Indians parties to this treaty expressly covenant and agree that they will use their utmost endeavor to induce that portion of the respective tribes not now present to unite with them and acceed to the provisions of this treaty, which union and accession shall be evidenced and made binding on all parties whenever such absentees shall have participated in the beneficial provisions of this treaty.

ARTICLE 9.

Upon the ratification of this treaty all former treaties are hereby abrogated.

In testimony whereof, the said Commissioners as aforesaid, and the undersigned chiefs and headmen of the confederated tribes of the Arrapahoes and Cheyennes of the Upper Arkansas, have hereunto set their hands and seals, at the place ard on the day and year first hereinbefore written.

John B. Sanborn, [SEAL.]
Wm. S. Harney, [SEAL.]
Thos. Murphy, [SEAL.]
Kit Carson, [SEAL.]
Wm. W. Bent, [SEAL.]
J. H. Leavenworth, [SEAL.]
James Steele, [SEAL.]

Commissioners on the part of the
    United States.

Moke-ta-ve-to, or Black Kettle, head chief, his x
    mark. [SEAL.]
Oh-to-ah-ne-so-to-wheo, or Seven Bulls, chief,
    his x mark. [SEAL.]
Hark-kah-o-me, or Little Robe, chief, his x
    mark. [SEAL.]
Moke-tah-vo-ve-ho, or Black White Man, chief,
    his x mark. [SEAL.]
Mun-a-men-ek, or Eagle's Head, headman, his x
    mark. [SEAL.]
O-to-ah-nis-to, or Bull that Hears, headman, his
    x mark. [SEAL.]

On the part of the Cheyennes.

Oh-has-tee, or Little Raven, head chief, his x
    mark. [SEAL.]
Oh-hah-mah-hah, or Storm, chief, his x mark.
    [SEAL.]
Pah-uf-pah-top, or Big Mouth, chief, his x mark.
    [SEAL.]
Ah-cra-kah-tau-nah, or Spotted Wolf, chief, his
    x mark. [SEAL.]
Ah-nah-wat-tan, or Black Man, headman, his x
    mark. [SEAL.]
Nah-a-nah-cha, or Chief in Everything,
    headman, his x mark. [SEAL.]
Chi-e-nuk, or Haversack, headman, his x mark.
    [SEAL.]

On the part of the Arrapahoes.
Signed and sealed in the presence of—
John S. Smith, United States interpreter.
W. R. Irwin, secretaries.
O. T. Atwood, secretaries.
S. A. Kingman, secretaries.
D. C. McNeil.
E. W. Wynkoop.
Bon. H. Van Havre.
J. E. Badger.
W. W. Rich.

N. B.—*The Apache tribe was brought into the provisions of the above treaty by the second article of the treaty with the Apaches, Cheyennes and Arrapahoes, proclaimed May 26, 1866.*

Treaty with the Seminole, 1866

Mar. 21, 1866. | 14 Stats., 755. | Ratified, July 19, 1866. | Proclamed, Aug. 16, 1866.

Articles of a treaty made and concluded at Washington, D.C., March 21, A.D., 1866, between the United States Government, by its commissioners, D.N. Cooley, Commissioner of Indian Affairs, Elijah Sells, superintendent of Indian affairs, and Ely S. Parker, and the Seminole Indians, by their chiefs, John Chup-co, or Long John, Cho-cote-harjo, Fos-ha[r]-jo, John F. Brown.

Whereas existing, treaties between the United States and the Seminole Nation are insufficient to meet their mutual necessities; and

Whereas the Seminole Nation made a treaty with the so-called Confederate States, August 1st, 1861, whereby they threw off their allegiance to the United States, and unsettled their treaty relations with the United States, and thereby incurred the liability of forfeiture of all lands and other property held by grant or gift of the United States; and whereas a treaty of peace and amity was entered into between the United States and the Seminole and other tribes at Fort Smith, September 13 [10,] 1865, whereby the Seminoles revoked, canceled, and repudiated the said treaty with the so-called Confederate States; and whereas the United States, through its commissioners, in said treaty of peace promised to enter into treaty with the Seminole Nation to arrange and settle all questions relating to and growing out of said

treaty with the so-called Confederate States; and whereas the United States, in view of said treaty of the Seminole Nation with the enemies of the Government of the United States, and the consequent liabilities of said Seminole Nation, and in view of its urgent necessities for more lands in the Indian Territory, requires a cession by said Seminole Nation of part of its present reservation, and is willing to pay therefor a reasonable price, while at the same time providing new and adequate land for them:

Now, therefore, the United States, by its commissioners aforesaid, and the above-named delegates of the Seminole Nation, the day and year above written, mutually stipulate and agree, on behalf of the respective parties, as follows, to wit;

ARTICLE 1.

There shall be perpetual peace between the United States and the Seminole Nation, and the Seminoles agree to be and remain firm allies of the United States, and always faithfully aid the Government thereof to suppress insurrection and put down its enemies.

The Seminoles also agree to remain at peace with all other Indian tribes and with themselves. In return for these pledges of peace and friendship, the United States guarantee them quiet possession of their country, and protection against hostilities on the part of other tribes; and, in the event of such hostilities, that the tribe commencing and prosecuting the same shall make just reparation therefor. Therefore the Seminoles agree to a military occupation of their country at the option and expense of the United States.

A general amnesty of all past offences against the laws of the United States, committed by any member of the Seminole Nation, is hereby declared; and the Seminoles, anxious for the restoration of kind and friendly feelings among themselves, do hereby declare an amnesty for all past offenses against their government, and no Indian or Indians shall be proscribed or any act of forfeiture or confiscation passed against those who have remained friendly to or taken up arms against the United States, but they shall enjoy equal privileges with other members of said tribe, and all laws heretofore passed inconsistent herewith are hereby declared inoperative.

A copy of this agreement, which has never been ratified, is found in an Appendix to the Report of the Commissioner of Indian Affairs for 1865, with the report of the negotiating commissioners, which copy has been reproduced in the appendix to this compilation, post, p. 1050.

ARTICLE 2.

The Seminole Nation covenant that henceforth in said nation slavery shall not exist, nor involuntary servitude, except for and in punishment of crime, whereof the offending party shall first have been duly convicted in accordance with law, applicable to all the members of said nation. And inasmuch as there are among the Seminoles many persons of African descent and blood, who have no interest or property in the soil, and no recognized civil rights it is stipulated that hereafter these persons and their descendants, and such other of the same race as shall be permitted by said nation to settle there, shall have and enjoy all the rights of native citizens, and the laws of said nation shall be equally binding upon all persons of whatever race or color, who may be adopted as citizens or members of said tribe.

ARTICLE 3.

In compliance with the desire of the United States to locate other Indians and freedmen thereon, the Seminoles cede and convey to the United States their entire domain, being the tract of land ceded to the Seminole Indians by the Creek Nation under the provisions of article first, (1st,) treaty of the United States with the Creeks and Seminoles, made and concluded at Washington, D. C., August 7, 1856. In consideration of said grant and cession of their lands, estimated at two million one hundred and sixty-nine thousand and eighty (2,169,080) acres, the United States agree to pay said Seminole Nation the sum of three hundred and twenty-five thousand three hundred and sixty-two ($325,362) dollars, said purchase being at the rate of fifteen cents per acre. The United States having obtained by grant of the Creek Nation the westerly half of their lands, hereby grant to the Seminole Nation the portion thereof hereafter described, which shall constitute the national domain of the Seminole Indians. Said lands so granted by the United States to the Seminole Nation are bounded and described as follows, to wit: Beginning on the Canadian River where the line dividing the Creek lands according to the terms of their sale to the United States by their treaty of February 6, 1866, following said line due north to where said line crosses the north fork of the Canadian River; thence up said north fork of the Canadian River a distance sufficient to make two hundred thousand acres by running due south to the Cana-

dian River; thence down said Canadian River to the place of beginning. In consideration of said cession of two hundred thousand acres of land described above, the Seminole Nation agrees to pay therefor the price of fifty cents per acre, amounting to the sum of one hundred thousand dollars, which amount shall be deducted from the sum paid by the United States for Seminole lands under the stipulations above written. The balance due the Seminole Nation after making said deduction, amounting to one hundred thousand dollars, the United States agree to pay in the following manner, to wit: Thirty thousand dollars shall be paid to enable the Seminoles to occupy, restore, and improve their farms, and to make their nation independent and self-sustaining, and shall be distributed for that purpose under the direction of the Secretary of the Interior; twenty thousand dollars shall be paid in like manner for the purpose of purchasing agricultural implements, seeds, cows, and other stock; fifteen thousand dollars shall be paid for the erection of a mill suitable to accommodate said nation of Indians; seventy thousand dollars to remain in the United States Treasury, upon which the United States shall pay an annual interest of five per cent.; fifty thousand of said sum of seventy thousand dollars shall be a permanent school-fund, the interest of which shall be paid annually and appropriated to the support of schools; the remainder of the seventy thousand dollars, being twenty thousand dollars, shall remain a permanent fund. This refers to the Creek treaty of June 14, 1866, post, p. 931. See Annual Report of Commissioner of Indian Affairs, 1866, p. 10, interest of which shall be paid annually for the support of the Seminole government; forty thousand three hundred and sixty-two dollars shall be appropriated and expended for subsisting said Indians, discriminating in favor of the destitute; all of which amounts, excepting the seventy thousand dollars to remain in the Treasury as a permanent fund, shall be paid upon the ratification of said treaty, and disbursed in such manner as the Secretary of the Interior may direct. The balance, fifty thousand dollars, or so much thereof as may be necessary to pay the losses ascertained and awarded as hereinafter provided, shall be paid when said awards shall have been duly made and approved by the Secretary of the Interior. And in case said fifty thousand dollars shall be insufficient to pay all said awards, it shall be distributed pro rata to those whose claims are so allowed; and until said awards shall be thus paid, the United States agree to pay to said Indians, in such manner and for such purposes as the Secretary of the Interior may direct, interest at the rate of five per cent. per annum from the date of the ratification of this treaty.

ARTICLE 4.

To reimburse such members of the Seminole Nation as shall be duly adjudged to have remained loyal and faithful to their treaty relations to the United States, during the recent rebellion of the so-called Confederate States for the losses actually sustained by them thereby, after the ratification of this treaty, or so soon thereafter as the Secretary of the Interior shall direct, he shall appoint a board of commissioners, not to exceed three in number, who shall proceed to the Seminole country and investigate and determine said losses. Previous to said investigation the agent of the Seminole Nation shall prepare a census or enumeration of said tribe, and make a roll of all Seminoles who did in no manner aid or abet the enemies of the Government, but remained loyal during said rebellion; and no award shall be made by said commissioners for such losses unless the name of the claimant appear on said roll, and no compensation shall be allowed any person for such losses whose name does not appear on said roll, unless said claimant, within six months from the date of the completion of said roll, furnishes proof satisfactory to said board, or to the Commissioner of Indian Affairs, that he has at all times remained loyal to the United States, according to his treaty obligations. All evidence touching said claims shall be taken by said commissioners, or any of them, under oath, and their awards made, together with the evidence, shall be transmitted to the Commissioner of Indian Affairs, for his approval, and that of the Secretary of the Interior. Said commissioners shall be paid by the United States such compensation as the Secretary of the Interior may direct. The provisions of this article shall extend to and embrace the claims for losses sustained by loyal members of said tribe, irrespective of race or color, whether at the time of said losses the claimants shall have been in servitude or not; provided said claimants are made members of said tribe by the stipulations of this treaty.

ARTICLE 5.

The Seminole Nation hereby grant a right of way through their lands to any company which shall be duly authorized by Congress, and shall, with the express consent and approbation of the Secretary of the Interior, undertake to construct a railroad from any point on their eastern to their western or south-

ern boundary; but said railroad company, together with all its agents and employés, shall be subject to the laws of the United States relating to the intercourse with Indian tribes, and also to such rules and regulations as may be prescribed by the Secretary of the Interior for that purpose. And the Seminoles agree to sell to the United States, or any company duly authorized as aforesaid, such lands, not legally owned or occupied by a member or members of the Seminole Nation lying along the line of said contemplated railroad, not exceeding on each side thereof a belt or strip of land three miles in width, at such price per acre as may be eventually agreed upon between said Seminole Nation and the party or parties building said road—subject to the approval of the President of the United States: Provided, however, That said land thus sold shall not be reconveyed, leased, or rented to, or be occupied by, any one not a citizen of the Seminole Nation, according to its laws and recognized usages: Provided also, That officers, servants, and employés of said railroad necessary to its construction and management shall not be excluded from such necessary occupancy, they being subject to the provisions of the Indian-intercourse laws, and such rules and regulations as may be established by the Secretary of the Interior; nor shall any conveyance of said lands be made to the party building and managing said road, until its completion as a first-class railroad and its acceptance as such by the Secretary of the Interior.

ARTICLE 6.

Inasmuch as there are no agency buildings upon the new Seminole reservation, it is therefore further agreed that the United States shall cause to be constructed, at an expense not exceeding ten thousand (10,000) dollars, suitable agency buildings, the site whereof shall be selected by the agent of said tribe, under the direction of the superintendent of Indian affairs; in consideration whereof, the Seminole Nation hereby relinquish and cede forever to the United States one section of their lands upon which said agency buildings shall be directed, [erected,] which land shall revert to said nation when no longer used by the United States, upon said nation paying a fair value for said buildings at the time vacated.

ARTICLE 7.

The Seminole Nation agrees to such legislation as Congress and the President may deem necessary for the better administration of the rights of person and property within the Indian Territory: Provided, however, [That] said legislation shall not in any manner interfere with or annul their present tribal organization, rights, laws, privileges, and customs.

The Seminole Nation also agree that a general council, consisting of delegates elected by each nation, a tribe lawfully resident within the Indian Territory, may be annually convened in said Territory which council shall be organized in such manner and possess such powers as are hereinafter described:

1st. After the ratification of this treaty, and as soon as may be deemed practicable by the Secretary of the Interior, and prior to the first session of said council, a census or enumeration of each tribe lawfully resident in said Territory shall be taken, under the direction of the superintendent of Indian affairs, who, for that purpose, is hereby authorized to designate and appoint competent persons, whose compensation shall be fixed by the Secretary of the Interior and paid by the United States.

2d. The first general council shall consist of one member from each tribe, and an additional member for each one thousand Indians, or each fraction of a thousand greater than five hundred, being members of any tribe lawfully resident in said Territory, and shall be elected by said tribes, respectively, who may assent to the establishment of said general council; and if none should be thus formally selected by any nation or tribe, the said nation or tribe shall be represented in said general council by the chiefs and headmen of said tribes, to be taken in the order of their rank, in the same number and proportion as above indicated. After the said census shall have been taken and completed, the superintendent of Indian affairs shall publish and declare to each tribe the number of members of said council to which they shall be entitled under the provisions of this article; and the persons so entitled to represent said tribe shall meet at such time and place as he shall appoint; but thereafter the time and place of the sessions of said council shall be determined by its action: Provided, That no session in any one year shall exceed the term of thirty days, And provided That special sessions of said council may be called by said superintendent whenever, in his judgment, or that of the Secretary of the Interior, the interest of said tribes shall require.

3d. Said general council shall have power to legislate upon all rightful subjects and matters pertain-

ing to the intercourse and relations of the Indian tribes and nations resident in said Territory; the arrest and extradition of criminals and offenders escaping from one tribe to another; the administration of justice between members of the several tribes of said Territory, and persons other than Indians and members of said tribes or nations; the construction of works of internal improvement and the common defence and safety of the nation of said Territory. All laws enacted by said council shall take effect at such time as may therein be provided, unless suspended by direction of the Secretary of the Interior or the President of the United States. No law shall be enacted inconsistent with the Constitution of the United States, or the laws of Congress, or existing treaty stipulations with the United States; nor shall said council legislate upon matters pertaining to the organization, laws, or customs of the several tribes except as herein provided for.

4th. Said council shall be presided over by the superintendent of Indian affairs, or, in case of his absence for any cause, the duties of said superintendent enumerated in this article shall be performed by such person as the Secretary of the Interior may direct.

5th. The Secretary of the Interior shall appoint a secretary of said council, whose duty it shall be to keep an accurate record of all the proceedings of said council, and who shall transmit a true copy of all such proceedings, duly certified by the superintendent of Indian affairs, to the Secretary of the Interior immediately after the session of said council. He shall be paid out of the Treasury of the United States an annual salary of five hundred dollars.

6th. The members of said council shall be paid by the United States the sum of four dollars per diem during the time actually in attendance upon the sessions of said council, and at the rate of four dollars for every twenty miles necessarily traveled by them in going to said council and returning to their homes, respectively, to be certified by the secretary of the said council and the sup[erintenden]t of Indian affairs.

7th. The Seminoles also agree that a court or courts may be established in said Territory, with such jurisdiction and organized in such manner as Congress may by law provide.

ARTICLE 8.

The stipulations of this treaty are to be a full settlement of all claims of said Seminole Nation for damages and losses of every kind growing out of the late rebellion, and all expenditures by the United States of annuities in clothing and feeding refugee and destitute Indians since the diversion of annuities for that purpose, consequent upon the late war with the so-called Confederate States. And the Seminoles hereby ratify and confirm all such diversions of annuities heretofore made from the funds of the Seminole Nation by the United States. And the United States agree that no annuities shall be diverted from the object for which they were originally devoted by treaty stipulations, with the Seminoles, to the use of refugee and destitute Indians, other than the Seminoles or members of the Seminole Nation, after the close of the present fiscal year, June thirtieth, eighteen hundred and sixty-six.

ARTICLE 9.

The United States re-affirms and reassumes all obligations of treaty stipulations entered into before the treaty of said Seminole Nation with the so-called Confederate States, August first, eighteen hundred and sixty-one, not inconsistent herewith; and further agree to renew all payments of annuities accruing by force of said treaty stipulations, from and after the close of the present fiscal year, June thirtieth, in the year of our Lord one thousand eight hundred and sixty-six, except as is provided in article eight, (viii.).

ARTICLE 10.

A quantity of land not exceeding six hundred and forty acres, to be selected according to legal subdivisions, in one body, and which shall include their improvements, is hereby granted to every religious society or denomination which has erected, or which, with the consent of the Indians, may hereafter erect, buildings within the Seminole country for missionary or educational purposes; but no land thus granted, nor the buildings which have been or may be erected thereon, shall ever be sold or otherwise disposed of except with the consent and approval of the Secretary of the Interior. And whenever any such land or buildings shall be so sold or disposed of, the proceeds thereof shall be applied, under the direction of the Secretary of the Interior, to the support and maintenance of other similar establishments for the benefit of the Seminoles and such other persons as may be, or may hereafter become, members of the tribe according to its laws, customs, and usages.

ARTICLE 11.

It is further agreed that all treaties heretofore entered into between the United States and the Seminole Nation which are inconsistent with any of the articles or provisions of this treaty shall be, and are hereby, rescinded and annulled.

In testimony whereof, the said Dennis N. Cooley, Commissioner of Indian affairs, Elijah Sells, superintendent of Indian affairs, and Col. Ely S. Parker, as aforesaid, and the undersigned, persons representing the Seminole nation, have hereunto set their hands and seals the day and year first above written.

Dennis N. Cooley, [SEAL.]
Commissioner of Indian Affairs.

Elijah Sells, [SEAL.]
Superintendent Indian Affairs.

Col. Ely S. Parker, [SEAL.]
Special commissioner.

John Chup-co, his x mark, [SEAL.]
King or head chief.

Cho-cote-harjo, his x mark, [SEAL.]
Counselor.

Fos-harjo, his x mark, chief. [SEAL.]
John F. Brown, [SEAL.]
Special delegate for Southern Seminoles.

In presence of—
Robert Johnson, his x mark.
United States interpreter for Seminole
    Indians.
Geo. A. Reynolds, United States Indian agent
    for Seminoles.
Ok-tus-sus-har-jo, his x mark, or Sands.
Cow-e-to-me-ko, his x mark.
Che-chu-chee, his x mark.
Harry Island, his x mark.
United States interpreter for Creek Indians.
J. W. Dunn, United States Indian agent for the
    Creek Nation.
Perry Fuller.

Signed by John F. Brown, special delegate for the Southern Seminoles, in presence of, this June thirtieth, eighteen hundred and sixty-six—

W.R. Irwin.
J. M. Tebbetts.
Geo. A. Reynolds, United States Indian agent.
Robert Johnson, his x mark, United States
    interpreter.

Treaty with the Choctaw and Chickasaw, 1866

Apr. 28, 1866. | 14 Stats., 769. | Ratified June 28, 1866. | Proclaimed July 10, 1866.

Articles of agreement and convention between the United States and the Choctaw and Chickasaw Nations of Indians, made and concluded at the City of Washington the twenty-eighth day of April, in the year eighteen hundred and sixty-six, by Dennis N. Cooley, Elijah Sells, and E. S. Parker, special commissioners on the part of the United States, and Alfred Wade, Allen Wright, James Riley, and John Page, commissioners on the part of the Choctaws, and Winchester Colbert, Edmund Pickens, Holmes Colbert, Colbert Carter, and Robert H. Love, commissioners on the part of the Chickasaws.

ARTICLE 1.

Permanent peace and friendship are hereby established between the United States and said nations; and the Choctaws and Chickasaws do hereby bind themselves respectively to use their influence and to make every exertion to induce Indians of the plains to maintain peaceful relations with each other, with other Indians, and with the United States.

ARTICLE 2.

The Choctaws and Chickasaws hereby covenant and agree that henceforth neither slavery nor involuntary servitude, otherwise than in punishment of crime whereof the parties shall have been duly convicted, in accordance with laws applicable to all members of the particular nation, shall ever exist in said nations.

ARTICLE 3.

The Choctaws and Chickasaws, in consideration of the sum of three hundred thousand dollars, hereby cede to the United States the territory west of the 98° west longitude, known as the leased district, provided that the said sum shall be invested and held by the United States, at an interest not less than five per cent., in trust for the said nations, until the legislatures of the Choctaw and Chickasaw Nations respectively shall have made such laws, rules, and regulations as may be necessary to give all persons of African descent, resident in the said nation at the date of the treaty of Fort Smith, and their descendants, heretofore held in slavery among said nations, all the rights, privileges, and immunities, including the right of suffrage, of citizens of said nations, except in the annuities, moneys, and public domain claimed by, or belonging to, said nations respectively; and also to give to such persons who were residents as aforesaid, and their descendants, forty acres each of the land of said nations on the same terms as the Choctaws and Chickasaws, to be selected on the survey of said land, after the Choctaws and Chickasaws and Kansas Indians have made their selections as herein provided; and immediately on the enactment of such laws, rules, and regulations, the said sum of three hundred thousand dollars shall be paid to the said Choctaw and Chickasaw Nations in the proportion of three-fourths to the former and one-fourth to the latter, less such sum, at the rate of one hundred dollars per capita, as shall be sufficient to pay such persons of African descent before referred to as within ninety days after the passage of such laws, rules, and regulations shall elect to remove and actually remove from the said nations respectively. And should the said laws, rules, and regulations not be made by the legislatures of the said nations respectively, within two years from the ratification of this treaty, then the said sum of three hundred thousand dollars shall cease to be held in trust for the said Choctaw and Chickasaw Nations, and be held for the use and benefit of such of said persons of African descent as the United States shall remove from the said Territory in such manner as the United States shall deem proper,—the United States agreeing, within ninety days from the expiration of the said two years, to remove from said nations all such persons of African descent as may be willing to remove; those remaining or returning after having been removed from said nations to have no benefit of said sum of three hundred thousand dollars, or any part thereof, but shall be upon the same footing as other citizens of the United States in the said nations.

ARTICLE 4.

The said nations further agree that all negroes, not otherwise disqualified or disabled, shall be competent witnesses in all civil and criminal suits and proceedings in the Choctaw and Chickasaw courts, any law to the contrary notwithstanding; and they fully recognize the right of the freedmen to a fair remuneration on reasonable and equitable contracts for their labor, which the law should aid them to enforce. And they agree, on the part of their respective nations, that all laws shall be equal in their operation upon Choctaws, Chickasaws, and negroes, and that no distinction affecting the latter shall at any time be made, and that they shall be treated with kindness and be protected against injury; and they further agree, that while the said freedmen, now in the Choctaw and Chickasaw Nations, remain in said nations, respectively, they shall be entitled to as much land as they may cultivate for the support of themselves and families, in cases where they do not support themselves and families by hiring, not interfering with existing improvements without the consent of the occupant, it being understood that in the event of the making of the laws, rules, and regulations aforesaid, the forty acres aforesaid shall stand in place of the land cultivated as last aforesaid.

ARTICLE 5.

A general amnesty of all past offences against the laws of the United States, committed before the signing of this treaty by any member of the Choctaw or Chickasaw Nations, is hereby declared; and the United States will especially request the States of Missouri, Kansas, Arkansas, and Texas to grant the like amnesty as to all offences committed by any member of the Choctaw or Chickasaw Nation. And the Choctaws and Chickasaws, anxious for the restoration of kind and friendly feelings among themselves, do hereby declare an amnesty for all past offences against their respective governments, and no Indian or Indians shall be proscribed, or any act of forfeiture or confiscation passed against those who may have remained friendly to the United States, but they shall enjoy equal privileges with other members of said tribes, and all laws heretofore passed inconsistent herewith are hereby declared inoperative. The people of the Choctaw and Chickasaw Nations stipulate and agree to deliver up to any duly authorized agent of the United States all public property in their possession which belong to the late "so-called Confederate States of America," or the United States, without any reservation whatever; particularly ordnance, ordnance-stores, and arms of all kinds.

ARTICLE 6.

The Choctaws and Chickasaws hereby grant a right of way through their lands to any company or companies which shall be duly authorized by Congress, or by the legislatures of said nations, respectively, and which shall, with the express consent and approbation of the Secretary of the Interior, undertake to construct a railroad through the Choctaw and Chickasaw Nations from the north to the south thereof, and from the east to the west side thereof, in accordance with the provisions of the 18th article of the treaty of June twenty-second, one thousand eight hundred and fifty-five, which provides that for any property taken or destroyed in the construction thereof full compensation shall be made to the party or parties injured, to be ascertained and determined in such manner as the President of the United States shall direct. But such railroad company or companies, with all its or their agents and employés shall be subject to the laws of the United States relating to intercourse with Indian tribes, and also to such rules and regulations as may be prescribed by the Secretary of the Interior for that purpose. And it is also stipulated and agreed that the nation through which the road or roads aforesaid shall pass may subscribe to the stock of the particular company or companies such amount or amounts as they may be able to pay for in alternate sections of unoccupied lands for a space of six miles on each side of said road or roads, at a price per acre to be agreed upon between said Choctaw and Chickasaw Nations and the said company or companies, subject to the approval of the President of the United States: Provided, however, That said land, thus subscribed, shall not be sold, or demised, or occupied by any one not a citizen of the Choctaw or Chickasaw Nations, according to their laws and recognized usages: Provided, That the officers, servants, and employés of such companies necessary to the construction and management of said road or roads shall not be excluded from such occupancy as their respective functions may require, they being subject to the provisions of the Indian intercourse law and such rules and regulations as may be established by the Secretary of the Interior: And provided also, That the stock thus subscribed by either of said nations shall have the force and effect of a first-mortgage bond on all that part of said road, appurtenances, and equipments situated and used within said nations respectively, and shall be a perpetual lien on the same, and the said nations shall have the right, from year to year, to elect to receive their equitable proportion of declared dividends of profits on their said stock, or interest on the par value at the rate of six per cent. per annum.

2. And it is further declared, in this connection, that as fast as sections of twenty miles in length are completed, with the rails laid ready for use, with all water and other stations necessary to the use thereof, as a first-class road, the said company or companies shall become entitled to patents for the alternate sections aforesaid, and may proceed to dispose thereof in the manner herein provided for, subject to the approval of the Secretary of the Interior.

3. And it is further declared, also, in case of one or more of said alternate sections being occupied by any member or members of said nations respectively, so that the same cannot be transferred to the said company or companies, that the said nation or nations, respectively, may select any unoccupied section or sections, as near as circumstances will permit, to the said width of six miles on each side of said road or roads, and convey the same as an equivalent for the section or sections so occupied as aforesaid.

ARTICLE 7.

The Choctaws and Chickasaws agree to such legislation as Congress and the President of the United States may deem necessary for the better administration of justice and the protection of the rights of person and property within the Indian Territory: Provided, however, Such legislation shall not in anywise interfere with or annul their present tribal organization, or their respective legislatures or judiciaries, or the rights, laws, privileges, or customs of the Choctaw and Chickasaw Nations respectively.

ARTICLE 8.

The Choctaws and Chickasaws also agree that a council, consisting of delegates elected by each nation or tribe lawfully resident within the Indian Territory, may be annually convened in said Territory, to be organized as follows:

1. After the ratification of this treaty, and as soon as may be deemed practicable by the Secretary of the Interior, and prior to the first session of said assembly, a census of each tribe, lawfully resident in said Territory, shall be taken, under the direction of the Superintendent of Indian Affairs, by competent persons, to be appointed by him, whose compensation shall be fixed by the Secretary of the Interior and paid by the United States.

2. The council shall consist of one member from each tribe or nation whose population shall exceed five hundred, and an additional member for each one thousand Indians, native or adopted, or each fraction of a thousand greater than five hundred being members of any tribe lawfully resident in said Territory, and shall be selected by the tribes or nations respectively who may assent to the establishment of said general assembly; and if none should be thus formally selected by any nation or tribe, it shall be represented in said general assembly by the chief or chiefs and head-men of said tribes, to be taken in the order of their rank as recognized in tribal usage in the number and proportions above indicated.

3. After the said census shall have been taken and completed, the superintendent of Indian affairs shall publish and declare to each tribe the number of members of said council to which they shall be entitled under the provisions of this article; and the persons so to represent the said tribes shall meet at such time and place as he shall designate, but thereafter the time and place of the sessions of the general assembly shall be determined by itself: Provided, That no session in any one year shall exceed the term of thirty days, and provided that the special sessions may be called whenever, in the judgment of the Secretary of the Interior, the interests of said tribes shall require it.

4. The general assembly shall have power to legislate upon all subjects and matters pertaining to the intercourse and relations of the Indian tribes and nations resident in the said Territory, the arrest and extradition of criminals escaping from one tribe to another, the administration of justice between members of the several tribes of the said Territory, and persons other than Indians and members of said tribes or nations, the construction of works of internal improvement, and the common

defence and safety of the nations of the said Territory. All laws enacted by said council shall take effect at the times therein provided, unless suspended by the Secretary of the Interior or the President of the United States. No law shall be enacted inconsistent with the Constitution of the United States or the laws of Congress, or existing treaty stipulations with the United States; nor shall said council legislate upon matters pertaining to the legislative, judicial, or other organization, laws, or customs of the several tribes or nations, except as herein provided for.

5. Said council shall be presided over by the superintendent of Indian affairs, or, in case of his absence from any cause, the duties of the superintendent enumerated in this article shall be performed by such person as the Secretary of the Interior shall indicate.

6. The Secretary of the Interior shall appoint a secretary of said council, whose duty it shall be to keep an accurate record of all the proceedings of said council, and to transmit a true copy thereof, duly certified by the superintendent of Indian affairs, to the Secretary of the Interior immediately after the sessions of said council shall terminate. He shall be paid five hundred dollars, as an annual salary, by the United States.

7. The members of the said council shall be paid by the United States four dollars per diem while in actual attendance thereon, and four dollars mileage for every twenty miles going and returning therefrom by the most direct route, to be certified by the secretary of said council and the presiding officer.

8. The Choctaws and Chickasaws also agree that a court or courts may be established in said Territory with such jurisdiction and organization as Congress may prescribe: Provided, That the same shall not interfere with the local judiciary of either of said nations.

9. Whenever Congress shall authorize the appointment of a Delegate from said Territory, it shall be the province of said council to elect one from among the nations represented in said council.

10. And it is further agreed that the superintendent of Indian affairs shall be the executive of the said Territory, with the title of "governor of the Territory of Oklahoma," and that there shall be a secretary of the said Territory, to be appointed by the said superintendent; that the duty of the said governor, in addition to those already imposed on the superintendent of Indian affairs, shall be such as properly belong to an executive officer charged with the execution of the laws, which the said council is authorized to enact under the provisions of this treaty; and that for this purpose he shall have authority to appoint a marshal of said Territory and an interpreter; the said marshal to appoint such deputies, to be paid by fees, as may be required to aid him in the execution of his proper functions, and be the marshal of the principal court of said Territory that may be established under the provisions of this treaty.

11. And the said marshal and the said secretary shall each be entitled to a salary of five hundred dollars per annum, to be paid by the United States, and such fees in addition thereto as shall be established by said governor, with the approbation of the Secretary of the Interior, it being understood that the said fee-lists may at any time be corrected and altered by the Secretary of the Interior, as the experience of the system proposed herein to be established shall show to be necessary, and shall in no case exceed the fees paid to marshals of the United States for similar services.

    The salary of the interpreter shall be five hundred dollars, to be paid in like manner by the United States.

12. And the United States agree that in the appointment of marshals and deputies, preference, qualifications being equal, shall be given to competent members of the said nations, the object being to create a laudable ambition to acquire the experience necessary for political offices of importance in the respective nations.

13. And whereas it is desired by the said Choctaw and Chickasaw Nations that the said council should consist of an upper and lower house, it is hereby agreed that whenever a majority of the tribes or nations represented in said council shall desire the same, or the Congress of the United States shall so prescribe, there shall be, in addition to the council now provided for, and which

shall then constitute the lower house, an upper house, consisting of one member from each tribe entitled to representation in the council now provided for—the relations of the two houses to each other being such as prevail in the States of the United States; each house being authorized to choose its presiding officer and clerk to perform the duties appropriate to such offices; and it being the duty, in addition, of the clerks of each house to make out and transmit to the territorial secretary fair copies of the proceedings of the respective houses immediately after their respective sessions, which copies shall be dealt with by said secretary as is now provided in the case of copies of the proceedings of the council mentioned in this act, and the said clerks shall each be entitled to the same per diem as members of the respective houses, and the presiding officers to doube that sum.

ARTICLE 9.

Such sums of money as have, by virtue of treaties existing in the year eighteen hundred and sixty-one, been invested for the purposes of education, shall remain so invested, and the interest thereof shall be applied for the same purposes, in such manner as shall be designated by the legislative authorities of the Choctaw and Chickasaw Nations, respectively.

ARTICLE 10.

The United States re-affirms all obligations arising out of treaty stipulations or acts of legislation with regard to the Choctaw and Chickasaw Nations, entered into prior to the late rebellion, and in force at that time, not inconsistent herewith; and further agrees to renew the payment of all annuities and others moneys accruing under such treaty stipulations and acts of legislation, from and after the close of the fiscal year ending on the thirtieth of June, in the year eighteen hundred and sixty-six.

ARTICLE 11.

Whereas the land occupied by the Choctaw and Chickasaw Nations, and described in the treaty between the United States and said nations, of June twenty-second, eighteen hundred and fifty-five, is now held by the members of said nations in common, under the provisions of the said treaty; and whereas it is believed that the holding of said land in severalty will promote the general civilization of said nations, and tend to advance their permanent welfare and the best interests of their individual members, it is hereby agreed that, should the Choctaw and the Chickasaw people, through their respective legislative councils, agree to the survey and dividing their land on the system of the United States, the land aforesaid east of the ninety-eighth degree of west longitude shall be, in view of the arrangements herein-after mentioned, surveyed and laid off in ranges, townships, sections, and parts of sections; and that for the purpose of facilitating such surveys and for the settlement and distribution of said land as hereinafter provided, there shall be established at Boggy Depot, in the Choctaw Territory, a land-office; and that, in making the said surveys and conducting the business of the said office, including the appointment of all necessary agents and surveyors, the same system shall be pursued which has heretofore governed in respect to the public lands of the United States, it being understood that the said surveys shall be made at the cost of the United States and by their agents and surveyors, as in the case of their own public lands, and that the officers and employés shall receive the same compensation as is paid to officers and employés in the land-offices of the United States in Kansas.

ARTICLE 12.

The maps of said surveys shall exhibit, as far as practicable, the outlines of the actual occupancy of members of the said nations, respectively; and when they are completed, shall be returned to the said land-office at Boggy Depot for inspection by all parties interested, when notice for ninety days shall be given of such return, in such manner as the legislative authorities of the said nations, respectively, shall prescribe, or, in the event of said authorities failing to give such notice in a reasonable time, in such manner as the register of said land-office shall prescribe, calling upon all parties interested to examine said maps to the end that errors, if any, in the location of such occupancies, may be corrected.

ARTICLE 13.

The notice required in the above article shall be given, not only in the Choctaw and Chicksaw Nations, but by publication in newspapers printed in the States of Mississippi and Tennessee, Louisiana, Texas, Arkansas, and Alabama, to the end that such Choctaws and Chickasaws as yet remain outside of the Choctaw and Chickasaw

Nations, may be informed and have opportunity to exercise the rights hereby given to resident Choctaws and Chickasaws: Provided, That before any such absent Choctaw or Chickasaw shall be permitted to select for him or herself, or others, as hereinafter provided, he or she shall satisfy the register of the land-office of his or her intention, or the intention of the party for whom the selection is to be made, to become bona-fide resident in the said nation within five years from the time of selection; and should the said absentee fail to remove into said nation, and occupy and commence an improvement on the land selected within the time aforesaid, the said selection shall be cancelled, and the land shall thereafter be discharged from all claim on account thereof.

ARTICLE 14.

At the expiration of the ninety days aforesaid the legislative authorities of the said nations, respectively, shall have the right to select one quarter-section of land in each of the counties of said nations respectively, in trust for the establishment of seats of justice therein, and also as many quarter-sections as the said legislative councils may deem proper for the permanent endowment of schools, seminaries, and colleges in said nation, provided such selection shall not embrace or interfere with any improvement in the actual occupation of any member of the particular nation without his consent; and provided the proceeds of sale of the quarter-sections selected for seats of justice shall be appropriated for the erection or improvement of public buildings in the county in which it is located.

ARTICLE 15.

At the expiration of the ninety days' notice aforesaid, the selection which is to change the tenure of the land in the Choctaw and Chickasaw Nations from a holding in common to a holding in severalty shall take place, when every Choctaw and Chickasaw shall have the right to one quarter-section of land, whether male or female, adult or minor, and if in actual possession or occupancy of land improved or cultivated by him or her, shall have a prior right to the quarter-section in which his or her improvement lies; and every infant shall have selected for him or her a quarter-section of land in such location as the father of such infant, if there be a father living, and if no father living, then the mother or guardian, and should there be neither father, mother, nor guardian,

then as the probate judge of the county, acting for the best interest of such infant, shall select.

ARTICLE 16.

Should an actual occupant of land desire, at any time prior to the commencement of the surveys aforesaid, to abandon his improvement, and select and improve other land, so as to obtain the prior right of selection thereof, he or she shall be at liberty to do so; in which event the improvement so abandoned shall be open to selection by other parties: Provided, That nothing herein contained shall authorize the multiplication of improvements so as to increase the quantity of land beyond what a party would be entitled to at the date of this treaty.

ARTICLE 17.

No selection to be made under this treaty shall be permitted to deprive or interfere with the continued occupation, by the missionaries established in the respective nations, of their several missionary establishments; it being the wish of the parties hereto to promote and foster an influence so largely conducive to civilization and refinement. Should any missionary who has been engaged in missionary labor for five consecutive years before the date of this treaty in the said nations, or either of them, or three consecutive years prior to the late rebellion, and who, if absent from the said nations, may desire to return, wish to select a quarter-section of land with a view to a permanent home for himself and family, he shall have the privilege of doing so, provided no selection shall include any public buildings, schools or seminary; and a quantity of land not exceeding six hundred and forty acres, to be selected according to legal subdivisions in one body, and to include their improvements, is hereby granted to every religious society or denomination which has erected, or which, with the consent of the Indians, may hereafter erect buildings within the Choctaw and Chickasaw country for missionary or educational purposes; but no land thus granted, nor the buildings which have been or may be erected thereon, shall ever be sold or otherwise disposed of, except with the consent of the legislatures of said nations respectively and approval of the Secretary of the Interior; and whenever such lands or buildings shall be sold or disposed of, the proceeds thereof shall be applied, under the direction of the Secretary of the Interior, to the support and maintenance of other similar establishments for the benefit of the Choctaws and Chickasaws, and such other persons as may hereafter become members of their nations, according to their laws, customs, and usages.

ARTICLE 18.
In making a selection for children the parent shall have a prior right to select land adjacent to his own improvements or selection, provided such selection shall be made within thirty days from the time at which selections under this treaty commence.

ARTICLE 19.
The manner of selecting as aforesaid shall be by an entry with the register of the land-office, and all selections shall be made to conform to the legal subdivisions of the said lands as shown by the surveys aforesaid on the maps aforesaid; it being understood that nothing herein contained is to be construed to confine a party selecting to one section, but he may take contiguous parts of sections by legal subdivisions in different sections, not exceeding together a quarter-section.

ARTICLE 20.
Prior to any entries being made under the foregoing provisions, proof of improvements, or actual cultivation, as well as the number of persons for whom a parent or guardian, or probate judge of the county proposes to select, and of their right to select, and of his or her authority to select, for them, shall be made to the register and receiver of the land-office, under regulations to be prescribed by the Secretary of the Interior.

ARTICLE 21.
In every township the sections of land numbered sixteen and thirty-six shall be reserved for the support of schools in said township: Provided, That if the same has been already occupied by a party or parties having the right to select it, or it shall be so sterile as to be unavailable, the legislative authorities of the particular nations shall have the right to select such other unoccupied sections as they may think proper.

ARTICLE 22.
The right of selection hereby given shall not authorize the selection of any land required by the United States as a military post, or Indian agency, not exceeding one mile square, which, when abandoned, shall revert to the nation in which the land lies.

ARTICLE 23.
The register of the land-office shall inscribe in a suitable book or books, in alphabetical order, the name of every individual for whom a selection shall be made, his or her age, and a description of the land selected.

ARTICLE 24.
Whereas it may be difficult to give to each occupant of an improvement a quarter-section of land, or even a smaller subdivision, which shall include such improvement, in consequence of such improvements lying in towns, villages, or hamlets, the legislative authorities of the respective nations shall have power, where, in their discretion, they think it expedient, to lay off into town lots any section or part of a section so occupied, to which lots the actual occupants, being citizens of the respective nations, shall have pre-emptive right, and, upon paying into the treasury of the particular nation the price of the land, as fixed by the respective legislatures, exclusive of the value of said improvement, shall receive a conveyance thereof. Such occupant shall not be prejudiced thereby in his right to his selection elsewhere. The town lots which may be unoccupied shall be disposed of for the benefit of the particular nation, as the legislative authorities may direct from time to time. When the number of occupants of the same quarter-section shall not be such as to authorize the legislative authorities to lay out the same, or any part thereof, into town lots, they may make such regulations for the disposition thereof as they may deem proper, either by subdivision of the same, so as to accommodate the actual occupants, or by giving the right of prior choice to the first occupant in point of time, upon paying the others for their improvements, to be valued in such way as the legislative authorities shall prescribe, or otherwise. All occupants retaining their lots under this section, and desiring, in addition, to make a selection, must pay for the lots so retained, as in the case of town lots. And any Choctaw or Chickasaw who may desire to select a sectional division other than that on which his homestead is, without abandoning the latter, shall have the right to purchase the homestead sectional division at such price as the respective legislatures may prescribe.

ARTICLE 25.
During ninety days from the expiration of the ninety days' notice aforesaid, the Choctaws and Chickasaws shall have the exclusive right to make selec-

tions, as aforesaid, and at the end of that time the several parties shall be entitled to patents for their respective selections, to be issued by the President of the United States, and countersigned by the chief executive officer of the nation in which the land lies, and recorded in the records of the executive office of the particular nation; and copies of the said patents, under seal, shall be evidence in any court of law or equity.

ARTICLE 26.
The right here given to the Choctaws and Chickasaws, respectively, shall extend to all persons who have become citizens by adoption or intermarriage of either of said nations, or who may here-after become such.

ARTICLE 27.
In the event of disputes arising in regard to the rights of parties to select particular quarter-sections or other divisions of said land, or in regard to the adjustment of boundaries, so as to make them conform to legal divisions and subdivisions such disputes shall be settled by the register of the land-office and the chief executive officer of the nation in which the land lies, in a summary way, after hearing the parties; and if said register and chief officer cannot agree, the two to call in a third party, who shall constitute a third referee, the decision of any two of whom shall be final, without appeal.

ARTICLE 28.
Nothing contained in any law of either of the said nations shall prevent parties entitled to make selections contiguous to each other; and the Choctaw and Chickasaw Nations hereby agree to repeal all laws inconsistent with this provision.

ARTICLE 29.
Selections made under this treaty shall, to the extent of one quarter-section, including the homestead or dwelling, be inalienable for the period of twenty-one years from the date of such selection, and upon the death of the party in possession shall descend according to the laws of the nation where the land lies; and in the event of his or her death without heirs, the said quarter-section shall escheat to and become the property of the nation.

ARTICLE 30.
The Choctaw and Chickasaw Nations will receive into their respective districts east of the ninety-eighth degree of west longitude, in the proportion of one-fourth in the Chickasaw and three-fourths in the Choctaw Nation, civilized Indians from the tribes known by the general name of the Kansas Indians, being Indians to the north of the Indian Territory, not exceeding ten thousand in number, who shall have in the Choctaw and Chickasaw Nations, respectively, the same rights as the Choctaws and Chickasaws, of whom they shall be the fellow-citizens, governed by the same laws, and enjoying the same privileges, with the exception of the right to participate in the Choctaw and Chickasaw annuities and other moneys, and in the public domain, should the same, or the proceeds thereof, be divided per capita among the Choctaws and Chickasaws, and among others the right to select land as herein provided for Choctaws and Chickasaws, after the expiration of the ninety days during which the selections of land are to be made, as aforesaid, by said Choctaws and Chickasaws; and the Choctaw and Chickasaw Nations pledge themselves to treat the said Kansas Indians in all respects with kindness and forbearance, aiding them in good faith to establish themselves in their new homes, and to respect all their customs and usages not inconsistent with the constitution and laws of the Choctaw and Chickasaw Nations respectively. In making selections after the advent of the Indians and the actual occupancy of land in said nation, such occupancy shall have the same effect in their behalf as the occupancies of Choctaws and Chickasaws; and after the said Choctaws and Chickasaws have made their selections as aforesaid, the said persons of African descent mentioned in the third article of the treaty, shall make their selections as therein provided, in the event of the making of the laws, rules, and regulations aforesaid, after the expiration of ninety days from the date at which the Kansas Indians are to make their selections as therein provided, and the actual occupancy of such persons of African descent shall have the same effect in their behalf as the occupancies of the Choctaws and Chickasaws.

ARTICLE 31.
And whereas some time must necessarily elapse before the surveys, maps, and selections herein provided for can be completed so as to permit the said Kansas Indians to make their selections in their order, during which time the United States may desire to remove the said Indians from their present abiding places, it is hereby agreed that the

said Indians may at once come into the Choctaw and Chickasaw Nations, settling themselves temporarily as citizens of the said nations, respectively, upon such land as suits them and is not already occupied.

ARTICLE 32.
At the expiration of two years, or sooner, if the President of the United States shall so direct, from the completion of the surveys and maps aforesaid, the officers of the land-offices aforesaid shall deliver to the executive departments of the Choctaw and Chickasaw Nations, respectively, all such documents as may be necessary to elucidate the land-title as settled according to this treaty, and forward copies thereof, with the field-notes, records, and other papers pertaining to said titles, to the Commissioner of the General Land Office; and thereafter grants of land and patents therefor shall be issued in such manner as the legislative authorities of said nations may provide for all the unselected portions of the Choctaw and Chickasaw districts as defined by the treaty of June twenty-second, eighteen hundred and fifty-five.

ARTICLE 33.
All lands selected as herein provided shall thereafter be held in severalty by the respective parties, and the unselected land shall be the common property of the Choctaw and Chickasaw Nations, in their corporate capacities, subject to the joint control of their legislative authorities.

ARTICLE 34.
Should any Choctaw or Chickasaw be prevented from selecting for him or herself during the ninety days aforesaid, the failure to do so shall not authorize another to select the quarter-section containing his improvement, but he may at any time make his selection thereof, subject to having his boundaries made to conform to legal divisions as aforesaid.

ARTICLE 35.
Should the selections aforesaid not be made before the transfer of the land records to the executive authorities of said nations, respectively, they shall be made according to such regulations as the legislative authorities of the two nations, respectively, may prescribe, to the end that full justice and equity may be done to the citizens of the respective territories.

ARTICLE 36.
Should any land that has been selected under the provisions of this treaty be abandoned and left uncultivated for the space of seven years by the party selecting the same, or his heirs, except in the case of infants under the age of twenty-one years, or married women, or persons non compos mentis, the legislative authorities of the nation where such land lies may either rent the same for the benefit of those interested, or dispose of the same otherwise for their benefit, and may pass all laws necessary to give effect to this provision.

ARTICLE 37.
In consideration of the right of selection hereinbefore accorded to certain Indians other than the Choctaws and Chickasaws, the United States agree to pay to the Choctaw and Chickasaw Nations, out of the funds of Indians removing into said nations respectively, under the provisions of this treaty, such sum as may be fixed by the legislatures of said nations, not exceeding one dollar per acre, to be divided between the said nations in the proportion of one-fourth to the Chickasaw Nation and three-fourths to the Choctaw Nation, with the understanding that at the expiration of twelve months the actual number of said immigrating Indians shall be ascertained, and the amount paid that may be actually due at the rate aforesaid; and should still further immigrations take place from among said Kansas Indians, still further payments shall be made accordingly from time to time.

ARTICLE 38.
Every white person who, having married a Choctaw or Chickasaw, resides in the said Choctaw or Chickasaw Nation, or who has been adopted by the legislative authorities, is to be deemed a member of said nation, and shall be subject to the laws of the Choctaw and Chickasaw Nations according to his domicile, and to prosecution and trial before their tribunals, and to punishment according to their laws in all respects as though he was a native Choctaw or Chickasaw.

ARTICLE 39.
No person shall expose goods or other articles for sale as a trader without a permit of the legislative authorities of the nation he may propose to trade in; but no license shall be required to authorize any member of the Choctaw or Chickasaw Nations to trade in the Choctaw or Chickasaw country who is

authorized by the proper authority of the nation, nor to authorize Choctaws or Chickasaws to sell flour, meal, meat, fruit, and other provisions, stock, wagons, agricultural implements, or tools brought from the United States into the said country.

ARTICLE 40.

All restrictions contained in any treaty heretofore made, or in any regulation of the United States upon the sale or other disposition of personal chattel property by Choctaws or Chickasaws are hereby removed.

ARTICLE 41.

All persons who are members of the Choctaw or Chickasaw Nations, and are not otherwise disqualified or disabled, shall hereafter be competent witnesses in all civil and criminal suits and proceedings in any courts of the United States, any law to the contrary notwithstanding.

ARTICLE 42.

The Choctaw and Chickasaw Nations shall deliver up persons accused of crimes against the United States who may be found within their respective limits on the requisition of the governor of any State for a crime committed against the laws of said State, and upon the requisition of the judge of the district court of the United States for the district within which the crime was committed.

ARTICLE 43.

The United States promise and agree that no white person, except officers, agents, and employés of the Government, and of any internal improvement company, or persons travelling through, or temporarily sojourning in, the said nations, or either of them, shall be permitted to go into said Territory, unless formally incorporated and naturalized by the joint action of the authorities of both nations into one of the said nations of Choctaws and Chickasaws, according to their laws, customs, or usages; but this article is not to be construed to affect parties heretofore adopted, or to prevent the employment temporarily of white persons who are teachers, mechanics, or skilled in agriculture, or to prevent the legislative authorities of the respective nations from authorizing such works of internal improvement as they may deem essential to the welfare and prosperity of the community, or be taken to interfere with or invalidate any action which has heretofore been had in this connection by either of the said nations.

ARTICLE 44.

Post-offices shall be established and maintained by the United States at convenient places in the Choctaw and Chickasaw Nations, to and from which the mails shall be carried at reasonable intervals, at the rates of postage prevailing in the United States.

ARTICLE 45.

All the rights, privileges, and immunities heretofore possessed by said nations or individuals thereof, or to which they were entitled under the treaties and legislation heretofore made and had in connection with them, shall be, and are hereby declared to be, in full force, so far as they are consistent with the provisions of this treaty.

ARTICLE 46.

Of the moneys stipulated to be paid to the Choctaws and Chickasaws under this treaty for the cession of the leased district, and the admission of the Kansas Indians among them, the sum of one hundred and fifty thousand dollars shall be advanced and paid to the Choctaws, and fifty thousand dollars to the Chickasaws, through their respective treasurers, as soon as practicable after the ratification of this treaty, to be repaid out of said moneys or any other moneys of said nations in the hands of the United States; the residue, not affected by any provisions of this treaty, to remain in the Treasury of the United States at an annual interest of five per cent., no part of which shall be paid out as annuity, but shall be annually paid to the treasurer of said nations, respectively, to be regularly and judiciously applied, under the direction of their respective legislative councils, to the support of their government, the purposes of education, and such other objects as may be best calculated to promote and advance the welfare and happiness of said nations and their people respectively. As soon as practicable after the lands shall have been surveyed and assigned to the Choctaws and Chickasaws in severalty as herein provided, upon application of their respective legislative councils, and with the assent of the President of the United States, all the annuities and funds invested and held in trust by the United States for the benefit of said nations respectively shall be capitalized or converted into money, as the case may be; and the aggregate amounts thereof belonging to each nation shall be equally divided and paid per capita to the individuals thereof respectively, to aid and assist them in improving their homesteads and increasing or acquiring flocks and herds, and thus encourage them to make proper efforts to maintain successfully the new relations which the holding of their lands in severalty will involve: Provided, nevertheless, That there shall be retained by the United States such sum as the President shall deem sufficient of the said moneys to be invested, that the interest thereon may be sufficient to defray the expenses of the government of said nations respectively, together with a judicious system of education, until these objects can be provided for by a proper system of taxation; and whenever this shall be done to the satisfaction of the President of the United States, the moneys so retained shall be divided in the manner and for the purpose above mentioned.

ARTICLE 48.

Immediately after the ratification of this treaty there shall be paid, out of the funds of the Choctaws and Chickasaws in the hands of the United States, twenty-five thousand dollars to the Choctaw and twenty-five thousand dollars to the Chickasaw commissioners, to enable them to discharge obligations incurred by them for various incidental and other expenses to which they have been subjected, and for which they are now indebted.

ARTICLE 49.

And it is further agreed that a commission, to consist of a person or persons to be appointed by the President of the United States, not exceeding three, shall be appointed immediately on the ratification of this treaty, who shall take into consideration and determine the claim of such Choctaws and Chickasaws as allege that they have been driven during the late rebellion from their homes in the Choctaw [and Chickasaw] Nations on account of their adhesion to the United States, for damages, with power to make such award as may be consistent with equity and good conscience, taking into view all circumstances, whose report, when ratified by the Secretary of the Interior, shall be final, and authorize the payment of the amount from any moneys of said nations in the hands of the United States as the said commission may award.

ARTICLE 50.

Whereas Joseph G. Heald and Reuben Wright, of Massachusetts, were licensed traders in the Choctaw country at the commencement of the rebellion, and claim to have sustained large losses on account of said rebellion, by the use of their property by said nation, and that large sums of money are due them for goods and property taken, or sold to the members of said nation, and money advanced to said nation; and whereas other loyal citizens of the United States may have just claims of the same character: It is hereby agreed and stipulated that the commission provided for in the preceding article shall investigate said claims, and fully examine the same; and such sum or sums of money as shall by the report of said commission, approved by the Secretary of the Interior, be found due to such persons, not exceeding ninety thousand dollars, shall be paid by the United States to the persons entitled thereto, out of any money belonging to said nation in the possession of the United States: Provided, That no claim for goods or property of any kind shall be allowed or paid, in whole or part, which shall have been used by said nation or any member thereof in aid of the rebellion, with the consent of said claimants: Provided also, That if the aggregate of said claims thus allowed and approved shall exceed said sum of ninety thousand dollars, then that sum shall be applied pro rata in payment of the claims so allowed.

ARTICLE 51.

It is further agreed that all treaties and parts of treaties inconsistent herewith be, and the same are hereby, declared null and void.

In testimony whereof, the said Dennis N. Cooley, Elijah Sells, and E. S. Parker, commissioners in behalf of the United States, and the said commissioners on behalf of the Choctaw and Chickasaw nations, have hereunto set their hands and seals the day and year first above written.

D. N. Cooley, Commissioner of Indian Affairs, [SEAL.]
Elijah Sells, superintendent of Indian affairs, [SEAL.]
E. S. Parker, special commissioner, [SEAL.]

Commissioners for United States.
Alfred Wade, [SEAL.]
Allen Wright, [SEAL.]
James Riley, [SEAL.]
John Page, [SEAL.]

Choctaw commissioners.
Winchester Colbert, [SEAL.]
Edmund (his x mark) Pickens, [SEAL.]

Holmes Colbert, [SEAL.]
Colbert Carter, [SEAL.]
Robert H. Love, [SEAL.]

Chickasaw commissioners.
Campbell Leflore, Secretary of Choctaw delegation.
E. S. Mitchell, Secretary of Chickasaw delegation.

In presence of—
Jno. H. B. Latrobe,
P. P. Pitchlynn, Principal chief Choctaws.

Douglas H. Cooper.
J. Harlan.
Charles E. Mix.

Treaty with the Creeks, 1866

June 14, 1866. | 14 Stats., 785. | Ratified July 19, 1866. | Proclaimed Aug. 11, 1866.

Treaty of cession and indemnity concluded at the city of Washington on the fourteenth day of June, in the year of our Lord one thousand eight hundred and sixty-six, by and between the United States, represented by Dennis N. Cooley, Commissioner of Indian Affairs, Elija Sells, superintendent of Indian affairs for the southern superintendency, and Col. Ely S. Parker, special commissioner, and the Creek Nation of Indians, represented by Ok-tars-sars-harjo, or Sands; Cow-e-to-me-co and Che-chu-chee, delegates at large, and D. N. McIntosh and James Smith, special delegates of the Southern Creeks.

PREAMBLE.
Whereas existing treaties between the United States and the Creek Nation have become insufficient to meet their mutual necessities; and whereas the Creeks made a treaty with the so-called Confederate States, on the tenth of July, one thousand eight hundred and sixty-one, whereby they ignored their allegiance to the United States, and unsettled the treaty relations existing between the Creeks and the United States, and did so render themselves liable to forfeit to the United States all benefits and advantages enjoyed by them in lands, annuities, protection, and immunities, including their lands and other property held by grant or gift from the United States; and whereas in view of said liabilities the United States require of the Creeks a portion of their land whereon to settle other Indians; and whereas a treaty of peace and amity was entered into between the United States and the Creeks and other tribes at Fort Smith, September thirteenth [tenth,] eighteen hundred and sixty-five, whereby the Creeks revoked, cancelled, and repudiated the aforesaid treaty made with the so-called Confederate States; and whereas the United States, through its commissioners, in said treaty of peace and amity, promised to enter into treaty with the Creeks to arrange and settle all questions relating to and growing out of said treaty with the so-called Confederate States: Now, therefore, the United States, by its commissioners, and the above-named delegates of the Creek Nation, the day and year above mentioned, mutually stipulate and agree, on behalf of the respective parties, as follows, to wit:

ARTICLE 1.
There shall be perpetual peace and friendship between the parties to this treaty, and the Creeks bind themselves to remain firm allies and friends of the United States, and never to take up arms against the United States, but always faithfully to aid in putting down its enemies. They also agree to remain at peace with all other Indian tribes; and, in return, the United States guarantees them quiet possession of their country, and protection against hostilities on the part of other tribes. In the event of hostilites, the United States agree that the tribe commencing and prosecuting the same shall, as far as may be practicable, make just reparation therefor. To insure this protection, the Creeks agree to a military occupation of their country, at any time, by the United States, and the United States agree to station and continue in said country from time to time, at its own expense, such force as may be necessary for that purpose. A general amnesty of all past offenses against the laws of the United States, committed by any member of the Creek Nation, is hereby declared. And the Creeks, anxious for the restoration of kind and friendly feelings among themselves, do hereby declare an amnesty for all past offenses against their government, and no Indian or Indians shall be proscribed, or any act of forfeiture or confiscation passed against those who have remained friendly to, or taken up arms against, the United States, but they shall enjoy equal privileges with other members of said tribe, and all laws heretofore passed inconsistent herewith are hereby declared inoperative.

ARTICLE 2.

The Creeks hereby covenant and agree that henceforth neither slavery nor involuntary servitude, otherwise than in the punishment of crimes, whereof the parties shall have been duly convicted in accordance with laws applicable to all members of said tribe, shall ever exist in said nation; and inasmuch as there are among the Creeks many persons of African descent, who have no interest in the soil, it is stipulated that hereafter these persons lawfully residing in said Creek country under their laws and usages, or who have been thus residing in said country, and may return within one year from the ratification of this treaty, and their descendants and such others of the same race as may be permitted by the laws of the said nation to settle within the limits of the jurisdiction of the Creek Nation as citizens [thereof,] shall have and enjoy all the rights and privileges of native citizens, including an equal interest in the soil and national funds, and the laws of the said nation shall be equally binding upon and give equal protection to all such persons, and all others. This agreement, a copy of which has been obtained from the report of the negotiating commissioners, found accompanying the Report of the Commissioner of Indian Affairs for 1865, is set forth in the Appendix to this Compilation, post, p. 1050. soever race or color, who may be adopted as citizens or members of said tribe.

ARTICLE 3.

In compliance with the desire of the United States to locate other Indians and freedmen thereon, the Creeks hereby cede and convey to the United States, to be sold to and used as homes for such other civilized Indians as the United States may choose to settle thereon, the west half of their entire domain, to be divided by a line running north and south; the eastern half of said Creek lands, being retained by them, shall, except as herein otherwise stipulated, be forever set apart as a home for said Creek Nation; and in consideration of said cession of the west half of their lands, estimated to contain three millions two hundred and fifty thousand five hundred and sixty acres, the United States agree to pay the sum of thirty (30) cents per acre, amounting to nine hundred and seventy-five thousand one hundred and sixty-eight dollars, in the manner hereinafter provided, to wit: two hundred thousand dollars shall be paid per capita in money, unless otherwise directed by the President of the United States, upon the ratification of this treaty, to enable the Creeks to

occupy, restore, and improve their farms, and to make their nation independent and self-sustaining, and to pay the damages sustained by the mission schools on the North Fork and the Arkansas Rivers, not to exceed two thousand dollars, and to pay the delegates such per diem as the agent and Creek council may agree upon, as a just and fair compensation, all of which shall be distributed for that purpose by the agent, with the advice of the Creek council, under the direction of the Secretary of the Interior. One hundred thousand dollars shall be paid in money and divided to soldiers that enlisted in the Federal Army and the loyal refugee Indians and freedmen who were driven from their homes by the rebel forces, to reimburse them in proportion to their respective losses; four hundred thousand dollars be paid in money and divided per capita to said Creek Nation, unless otherwise directed by the President of the United States, under the direction of the Secretary of the Interior, as the same may accrue from the sale of land to other Indians. The United States agree to pay to said Indians, in such manner and for such purposes as the Secretary of the Interior may direct, interest at the rate of five per cent. per annum from the date of the ratification of this treaty, on the amount hereinbefore agreed upon for said ceded lands, after deducting the said two hundred thousand dollars; the residue, two hundred and seventy-five thousand one hundred and sixty-eight dollars, shall remain in the Treasury of the United States, and the interest thereon, at the rate of five per centum per annum, be annually paid to said Creeks as above stipulated.

ARTICLE 4.

Immediately after the ratification of this treaty the United States agree to ascertain the amount due the respective soldiers who enlisted in the Federal Army, loyal refugee Indians and freedmen, in proportion to their several losses, and to pay the amount awarded each, in the following manner, to wit: A census of the Creeks shall be taken by the agent of the United States for said nation, under the direction of the Secretary of the Interior, and a roll of the names of all soldiers that enlisted in the Federal Army, loyal refugee Indians, and freedmen, be made by him. The superintendent of Indian affairs for the Southern superintendency and the agent of the United States for the Creek Nation shall proceed to investigate and determine from said roll the amounts due the respective refugee Indians, and shall transmit to the Commissioner of Indian affairs for his approval, and that of the Secretary of the Interior, their awards, together with the reasons therefor. In case the awards so made shall be duly approved, said awards shall be paid from the proceeds of the sale of said lands within one year from the ratification of this treaty, or so soon as said amount of one hundred thousand ($100,000) dollars can be raised from the sale of said land to other Indians.

ARTICLE 5.

The Creek Nation hereby grant a right of way through their lands, to the Choctaw and Chickasaw country, to any company which shall be duly authorized by Congress, and shall, with the express consent and approbation of the Secretary of the Interior, undertake to construct a railroad from any point north of to any point in or south of the Creek country, and likewise from any point on their eastern to their western or southern boundary, but said railroad company, together with all its agents and employés, shall be subject to the laws of the United States relating to intercourse with Indian tribes, and also to such rules and regulations as may be prescribed by the Secretary of the Interior for that purpose, and the Creeks agree to sell to the United States, or any company duly authorized as aforesaid, such lands not legally owned or occupied by a member or members of the Creek Nation, lying along the line of said contemplated railroad, not exceeding on each side thereof a belt or strip of land three miles in width, at such price per acre as may be eventually agreed upon between said Creek Nation and the party or parties building said road, subject to the approval of the President of the United States: Provided, however, That said land thus sold shall not be reconveyed, leased, or rented to, or be occupied by any one not a citizen of the Creek Nation, according to its laws and recognized usages: Provided, also, That officers, servants, and employés of said railroad necessary to its construction and management, shall not be excluded from such necessary occupancy, they being subject to the provisions of the Indian intercourse law and such rules and regulations as may be established by the Secretary of the Interior, nor shall any conveyance of any of said lands be made to the party building and managing said road until its completion as a first-class railroad, and its acceptance as such by the Secretary of the Interior.

ARTICLE 6.
[Stricken out.]

ARTICLE 7.
The Creeks hereby agree that the Seminole tribe of Indians may sell and convey to the United States all or any portion of the Seminole lands, upon such terms as may be mutually agreed upon by and between the Seminoles and the United States.

ARTICLE 8.
It is agreed that the Secretary of the Interior forthwith cause the line dividing the Creek country, as provided for by the terms of the sale of Creek lands to the United States in article third of this treaty, to be accurately surveyed under the direction of the Commissioner of Indian Affairs, the expenses of which survey shall be paid by the United States.

ARTICLE 9.
Inasmuch as the agency buildings of the Creek tribe have been destroyed during the late war, it is further agreed that the United States shall at their own expense, not exceeding ten thousand dollars, cause to be erected suitable agency buildings, the sites whereof shall be selected by the agent of said tribe, in the reduced Creek reservation, under the direction of the superintendent of Indian affairs.

In consideration whereof, the Creeks hereby cede and relinquish to the United States one section of their lands, to be designated and selected by their agent, under the direction of the superintendent of Indian affairs, upon which said agency buildings shall be erected, which section of land shall revert to the Creek nation when said agency buildings are no longer used by the United States, upon said nation paying a fair and reasonable value for said buildings at the time vacated.

ARTICLE 10.
The Creeks agree to such legislation as Congress and the President of the United States may deem necessary for the better administration of justice and the protection of the rights of person and property within the Indian territory: Provided, however, [That] said legislation shall not in any manner interfere with or annul their present tribal organization, rights, laws, privileges, and customs. The Creeks also agree that a general council, consisting of delegates elected by each nation or tribe lawfully resident within the Indian territory, may be annually convened in said territory, which council shall be organized in such manner and possess such powers as are hereinafter described.

First. After the ratification of this treaty, and as soon as may be deemed practicable by the Secretary of the Interior, and prior to the first session of said council, a census, or enumeration of each tribe lawfully resident in said territory, shall be taken under the direction of the superintendent of Indian affairs, who for that purpose is hereby authorized to designate and appoint competent persons, whose compensation shall be fixed by the Secretary of the Interior, and paid by the United States.

Second. The first general council shall consist of one member from each tribe, and an additional member from each one thousand Indians, or each fraction of a thousand greater than five hundred, being members of any tribe lawfully resident in said territory, and shall be selected by said tribes respectively, who may assent to the establishment of said general council, and if none should be thus formerly selected by any nation or tribe, the said nation or tribe shall be represented in said general council by the chief or chiefs and head men of said tribe, to be taken in the order of their rank as recognized in tribal usage, in the same number and proportion as above indicated. After the said census shall have been taken and completed, the superintendent of Indian affairs shall publish and declare to each tribe the number of members of said council to which they shall be entitled under the provisions of this article, and the persons entitled to so represent said tribes shall meet at such time and place as he shall appoint, but thereafter the time and place of the sessions of said council shall be determined by its action: Provided, That no session in any one year shall exceed the term of thirty days, and provided that special sessions of said council may be called whenever, in the judgment of the Secretary of the Interior, the interest of said tribe shall require.

Third. Said general council shall have power to legislate upon all rightful subjects and matters pertaining to the intercourse and relations of the Indian tribes and nations resident in said territory, the arrest and extradition of criminals and offenders escaping from one tribe to another, the administration of justice between members of the several tribes of said territory, and persons other than Indians and members of said tribes or nations, the construction of works of internal improvement, and the common defence and safety of the nations of said territory. All laws enacted by said general council shall take effect at such time as may therein be provided, unless suspended by direction of the Secretary of the Interior or the President of the United States. No law shall be enacted inconsistent with the Constitution of the United States, or the laws of Congress, or existing treaty stipulations with the United States, nor shall said council legislate upon matters pertaining to the organization, laws, or customs of the several tribes, except as herein provided for.

Fourth. Said council shall be presided over by the superintendent of Indian affairs, or, in case of his absence from any cause, the duties of said superintendent enumerated in this article shall be performed by such person as the Secretary of the Interior may direct.

Fifth. The Secretary of the Interior shall appoint a secretary of said council, whose duty it shall be to keep an accurate record of all the proceedings of said council, and who shall transmit a true copy of all such proceedings, duly certified by the superintendent of Indian affairs, to the Secretary of the Interior immediately after the sessions of said council shall terminate. He shall be paid out of the Treasury of the United States an annual salary of five hundred dollars.

Sixth. The members of said council shall be paid by the United States the sum of four dollars per diem during the time actually in attendance on the sessions of said council, and at the rate of four dollars for every twenty miles necessary[il]ly traveled by them in going to and returning to their homes respectively, from said council, to be certified by the secretary of said council and the superintendent of Indian affairs.

Seventh. The Creeks also agree that a court or courts may be established in said territory, with such jurisdiction and organized in such manner as Congress may by law provide.

ARTICLE 11.
The stipulations of this treaty are to be a full settlement of all claims of said Creek Nation for damages and losses of every kind growing out of the late rebellion and all expenditures by the United States of annuities in clothing and feeding refugee and destitute Indians since the diversion of annuities for that purpose consequent upon the late war with the so-called Confederate States; and the Creeks hereby rat-

ify and confirm all such diversions of annuities heretofore made from the funds of the Creek Nation by the United States, and the United States agree that no annuities shall be diverted from the objects for which they were originally devoted by treaty stipulations with the Creeks, to the use of refugee and destitute Indians other than the Creeks or members of the Creek Nation after the close of the present fiscal year, June thirtieth, eighteen hundred and sixty-six.

ARTICLE 12.

The United States re-affirms and re-assumes all obligations of treaty stipulations with the Creek Nation entered into before the treaty of said Creek Nation with the so-called Confederate States, July tenth, eighteen hundred and sixty-one, not inconsistent herewith; and further agrees to renew all payments accruing by force of said treaty stipulations from and after the close of the present fiscal year, June thirtieth, eighteen hundred and sixty-six, except as is provided in article eleventh.

ARTICLE 13.

A quantity of one hundred and sixty acres, to be selected according to legal subdivision, in one body, and to include their improvements, is hereby granted to every religious society or denomination, which has erected, or which, with the consent of the Indians, may hereafter erect, buildings within the Creek country for missionary or educational purposes; but no land thus granted, nor the buildings which have been or may be erected thereon, shall ever be sold or otherwise disposed of, except with the consent and approval of the Secretary of the Interior; and whenever any such lands or buildings shall be so sold or disposed of, the proceeds thereof shall be applied, under the direction of the Secretary of the Interior, to the support and maintenance of other similar establishments for the benefit of the Creeks and such other persons as may be or may hereafter become members of the tribe according to its laws, customs, and usages; and if at any time said improvements shall be abandoned for one year for missionary or educational purposes, all the rights herein granted for missionary and educational purposes shall revert to the said Creek Nation.

ARTICLE 14.

It is further agreed that all treaties heretofore entered into between the United States and the Creek Nation which are inconsistent with any of the articles or provisions of this treaty shall be, and are hereby, rescinded and annulled; and it is further agreed that ten thousand dollars shall be paid by the United States, or so much thereof as may be necessary, to pay the expenses incurred in negotiating the foregoing treaty.

In testimony whereof, we, the commissioners representing the United States and the delegates representing the Creek nation, have hereunto set our hands and seals at the place and on the day and year above written.

D. N. Cooley, Commissioner Indian Affairs.
   [SEAL.]
Elijah Sells, Superintendent Indian Affairs.
   [SEAL.]
Ok-ta-has Harjo, his x mark. [SEAL.]
Cow Mikko, his x mark. [SEAL.]
Cotch-cho-chee, his x mark. [SEAL.]
D. N. McIntosh. [SEAL.]
James M. C. Smith. [SEAL.]

In the presence of—
J. W. Dunn, United States Indian agent.
J. Harlan, United States Indian agent.
Charles E. Mix.
J. M. Tebbetts.
Geo. A. Reynolds, United States Indian agent.
John B. Sanborn.
John F. Brown, Seminole delegate.
John Chupco, his x mark.
Fos-har-jo, his x mark.
Cho-cote-huga, his x mark.
R. Fields, Cherokee delegate.
Douglas H. Cooper.
Wm. Penn Adair.
Harry Island, his x mark, United States interpreter, Creek Nation.
Suludin Watie.

Treaty with the Cherokee, 1866

July 19, 1866. | 14 Stats., 799. | Ratified July 27, 1866. | Proclaimed Aug. 11, 1866.

Articles of agreement and convention at the city of Washington on the nineteenth day of July, in the year of our Lord one thousand eight hundred and sixty-six, between the United States, represented by Dennis N. Cooley, Commissioner of Indian Affairs, [and]

Elijah Sells, superintendent of Indian affairs for the southern superintendency, and the Cherokee Nation of Indians, represented by its delegates, James McDaniel, Smith Christie, White Catcher, S. H. Benge, J. B. Jones, and Daniel H. Ross—John Ross, principal chief of the Cherokees, being too unwell to join in these negotiations.

PREAMBLE.
Whereas existing treaties between the United States and the Cherokee Nation are deemed to be insufficient, the said contracting parties agree as follows, viz:

ARTICLE 1.
The pretended treaty made with the so-called Confederate States by the Cherokee Nation on the seventh day of October, eighteen hundred and sixty-one, and repudiated by the national council of the Cherokee Nation on the eighteenth day of February, eighteen hundred and sixty-three, is hereby declared to be void.

ARTICLE 2.
Amnesty is hereby declared by the United States and the Cherokee Nation for all crimes and misdemeanors committed by one Cherokee on the person or property of another Cherokee, or of a citizen of the United States, prior to the fourth day of July, eighteen hundred and sixty-six; and no right of action arising out of wrongs committed in aid or in the suppression of the rebellion shall be prosecuted or maintained in the courts of the United States or in the courts of the Cherokee Nation.

But the Cherokee Nation stipulate and agree to deliver up to the United States, or their duly authorized agent, any or all public property, particularly ordnance, ordnance stores, arms of all kinds, and quartermaster's stores, in their possession or control, which belonged to the United States or the so-called Confederate States, without any reservation.

ARTICLE 3.
The confiscation laws of the Cherokee Nation shall be repealed, and the same, and all sales of farms, and improvements on real estate, made or pretended to be made in pursuance thereof, are hereby agreed and declared to be null and void, and the former owners of such property so sold, their heirs or assigns, shall have the right peaceably to re-occupy their homes, and the purchaser under the confiscation laws, or his heirs or assigns, shall be repaid by the treasurer of the Cherokee Nation from the national funds, the money paid for said property and the cost of permanent improvements on such real estate, made thereon since the confiscation sale; the cost of such improvements to be fixed by a commission, to be composed of one person designated by the Secretary of the Interior and one by the principal chief of the nation, which two may appoint a third in cases of disagreement, which cost so fixed shall be refunded to the national treasurer by the returning Cherokees within three years from the ratification hereof.

ARTICLE 4.
All the Cherokees and freed persons who were formerly slaves to any Cherokee, and all free negroes not having been such slaves, who resided in the Cherokee Nation prior to June first, eighteen hundred and sixty-one, who may within two years elect not to reside northeast of the Arkansas River and southeast of Grand River, shall have the right to settle in and occupy the Canadian district southwest of the Arkansas River, and also all that tract of country lying northwest of Grand River, and bounded on the southeast by Grand River and west by the Creek reservation to the northeast corner thereof; from thence west on the north line of the Creek reservation to the ninety-sixth degree of west longitude; and thence north on said line of longitude so far that a line due east to Grand River will include a quantity of land equal to one hundred and sixty acres for each person who may so elect to reside in the territory above-described in this article: Provided, That that part of said district north of the Arkansas River shall not be set apart until it shall be found that the Canadian district is not sufficiently large to allow one hundred and sixty acres to each person desiring to obtain settlement under the provisions of this article.

ARTICLE 5.
The inhabitants electing to reside in the district described in the preceding article shall have the right to elect all their local officers and judges, and the number of delegates to which by their numbers they may be entitled in any general council to be established in the Indian Territory under the provisions of this treaty, as stated in Article XII, and to control all their local affairs, and to establish all necessary police regulations and rules for the administration of justice in said district, not inconsistent with the constitution of the Cherokee Nation or the laws of the United States; Provided, The Cherokees residing in

said district shall enjoy all the rights and privileges of other Cherokees who may elect to settle in said district as hereinbefore provided, and shall hold the same rights and privileges and be subject to the same liabilities as those who elect to settle in said district under the provisions of this treaty; Provided also, That if any such police regulations or rules be adopted which, in the opinion of the President, bear oppressively on any citizen of the nation, he may suspend the same. And all rules or regulations in said district, or in any other district of the nation, discriminating against the citizens of other districts, are prohibited, and shall be void.

ARTICLE 6.
The inhabitants of the said district hereinbefore described shall be entitled to representation according to numbers in the national council, and all laws of the Cherokee Nation shall be uniform throughout said nation. And should any such law, either in its provisions or in the manner of its enforcement, in the opinion of the President of the United States, operate unjustly or injuriously in said district, he is hereby authorized and empowered to correct such evil, and to adopt the means necessary to secure the impartial administration of justice, as well as a fair and equitable application and expenditure of the national funds as between the people of this and of every other district in said nation.

ARTICLE 7.
The United States court to be created in the Indian Territory; and until such court is created therein, the United States district court, the nearest to the Cherokee Nation, shall have exclusive original jurisdiction of all causes, civil and criminal, wherein an inhabitant of the district hereinbefore described shall be a party, and where an inhabitant outside of said district, in the Cherokee Nation, shall be the other party, as plaintiff or defendant in a civil cause, or shall be defendant or prosecutor in a criminal case, and all process issued in said district by any officer of the Cherokee Nation, to be executed on an inhabitant residing outside of said district, and all process issued by any officer of the Cherokee Nation outside of said district, to be executed on an inhabitant residing in said district, shall be to all intents and purposes null and void, unless indorsed by the district judge for the district where such process is to be served, and said person, so arrested, shall be held in custody by the officer so arresting him, until he shall

be delivered over to the United States marshal, or consent to be tried by the Cherokee court: Provided, That any or all the provisions of this treaty, which make any distinction in rights and remedies between the citizens of any district and the citizens of the rest of the nation, shall be abrogated whenever the President shall have ascertained, by an election duly ordered by him, that a majority of the voters of such district desire them to be abrogated, and he shall have declared such abrogation: And provided further, That no law or regulation, to be hereafter enacted within said Cherokee Nation or any district thereof, prescribing a penalty for its violation, shall take effect or be enforced until after ninety days from the date of its promulgation, either by publication in one or more newspapers of general circulation in said Cherokee Nation, or by posting up copies thereof in the Cherokee and English languages in each district where the same is to take effect, at the usual place of holding district courts.

ARTICLE 8.
No license to trade in goods, wares, or merchandise merchandise shall be granted by the United States to trade in the Cherokee Nation, unless approved by the Cherokee national council, except in the Canadian district, and such other district north of Arkansas River and west of Grand River occupied by the so-called southern Cherokees, as provided in Article 4 of this treaty.

ARTICLE 9.
The Cherokee Nation having, voluntarily, in February, eighteen hundred and sixty-three, by an act of the national council, forever abolished slavery, hereby covenant and agree that never hereafter shall either slavery or involuntary servitude exist in their nation otherwise than in the punishment of crime, whereof the party shall have been duly convicted, in accordance with laws applicable to all the members of said tribe alike. They further agree that all freedmen who have been liberated by voluntary act of their former owners or by law, as well as all free colored persons who were in the country at the commencement of the rebellion, and are now residents therein, or who may return within six months, and their descendants, shall have all the rights of native Cherokees: Provided, That owners of slaves so emancipated in the Cherokee Nation shall never receive any compensation or pay for the slaves so emancipated.

ARTICLE 10.

Every Cherokee and freed person resident in the Cherokee Nation shall have the right to sell any products of his farm, including his or her live stock, or any merchandise or manufactured products, and to ship and drive the same to market without restraint, paying any tax thereon which is now or may be levied by the United States on the quantity sold outside of the Indian Territory.

ARTICLE 11.

The Cherokee Nation hereby grant a right of way not exceeding two hundred feet wide, except at stations, switches, waterstations, or crossing of rivers, where more may be indispensable to the full enjoyment of the franchise herein granted, and then only two hundred additional feet shall be taken, and only for such length as may be absolutely necessary, through all their lands, to any company or corporation which shall be duly authorized by Congress to construct a railroad from any point north to any point south, and from any point east to any point west of, and which may pass through, the Cherokee Nation. Said company or corporation, and their employés and laborers, while constructing and repairing the same, and in operating said road or roads, including all necessary agents on the line, at stations, switches, water tanks, and all others necessary to the successful operation of a railroad, shall be protected in the discharge of their duties, and at all times subject to the Indian intercourse laws, now or which may hereafter be enacted and be in force in the Cherokee Nation.

ARTICLE 12.

The Cherokees agree that a general council, consisting of delegates elected by each nation or tribe lawfully residing within the Indian Territory, may be annually convened in said Territory, which council shall be organized in such manner and possess such powers as hereinafter prescribed.

First. After the ratification of this treaty, and as soon as may be deemed practicable by the Secretary of the Interior, and prior to the first session of said council, a census or enumeration of each tribe lawfully resident in said Territory shall be taken under the direction of the Commissioner of Indian Affairs, who for that purpose is hereby authorized to designate and appoint competent persons, whose compensation shall be fixed by the Secretary of the Interior, and paid by the United States.

Second. The first general council shall consist of one member from each tribe, and an additional member for each one thousand Indians, or each fraction of a thousand greater than five hundred, being members of any tribe lawfully resident in said Territory, and shall be selected by said tribes respectively, who may assent to the establishment of said general council; and if none should be thus formally selected by any nation or tribe so assenting, the said nation or tribe shall be represented in said general council by the chief or chiefs and headmen of said tribes, to be taken in the order of their rank as recognized in tribal usage, in the same number and proportion as above indicated. After the said census shall have been taken and completed, the superintendent of Indian affairs shall publish and declare to each tribe assenting to the establishment of such council the number of members of such council to which they shall be entitled under the provisions of this article, and the persons entitled to represent said tribes shall meet at such time and place as he shall approve; but thereafter the time and place of the sessions of said council shall be determined by its action: Provided, That no session in any one year shall exceed the term of thirty days: And provided, That special sessions of said council may be called by the Secretary of the Interior whenever in his judgment the interest of said tribes shall require such special session.

Third. Said general council shall have power to legislate upon matters pertaining to the intercourse and relations of the Indian tribes and nations and colonies of freedmen resident in said Territory; the arrest and extradition of criminals and offenders escaping from one tribe to another, or into any community of freedmen; the administration of justice between members of different tribes of said Territory and persons other than Indians and members of said tribes or nations; and the common defence and safety of the nations of said Territory.

All laws enacted by such council shall take effect at such time as may therein be provided, unless suspended by direction of the President of the United States. No law shall be enacted inconsistent with the Constitution of the United States, or laws of Congress, or existing treaty stipulations with the United States. Nor shall said council legislate upon matters other than those above indicated: Provided, however, That the legislative power of such general council may be enlarged by the consent of the national council of each nation or tribe assenting to its establishment, with the approval of the President of the United States.

Fourth. Said council shall be presided over by such person as may be designated by the Secretary of the Interior.

Fifth. The council shall elect a secretary, whose duty it shall be to keep an accurate record of all the proceedings of said council, and who shall transmit a true copy of all such proceedings, duly certified by the presiding officer of such council, to the Secretary of the Interior, and to each tribe or nation represented in said council, immediately after the sessions of said council shall terminate. He shall be paid out of the Treasury of the United States an annual salary of five hundred dollars.

Sixth. The members of said council shall be paid by the United States the sum of four dollars per diem during the term actually in attendance on the sessions of said council, and at the rate of four dollars for every twenty miles necessarily traveled by them in going from and returning to their homes, respectively, from said council, to be certified by the secretary and president of the said council.

ARTICLE 13.
The Cherokees also agree that a court or courts may be established by the United States in said Territory, with such jurisdiction and organized in such manner as may be prescribed by law: Provided, That the judicial tribunals of the nation shall be allowed to retain exclusive jurisdiction in all civil and criminal cases arising within their country in which members of the nation, by nativity or adoption, shall be the only parties, or where the cause of action shall arise in the Cherokee Nation, except as otherwise provided in this treaty.

ARTICLE 14.
The right to the use and occupancy of a quantity of land not exceeding one hundred and sixty acres, to be selected according to legal subdivisions in one body, and to include their improvements, and not including the improvements of any member of the Cherokee Nation, is hereby granted to every society or denomination which has erected, or which with the consent of the national council may hereafter

erect, buildings within the Cherokee country for missionary or educational purposes. But no land thus granted, nor buildings which have been or may be erected thereon, shall ever be sold or [o]therwise disposed of except with the consent and approval of the Cherokee national council and the Secretary of the Interior. And whenever any such lands or buildings shall be sold or disposed of, the proceeds thereof shall be applied by said society or societies for like purposes within said nation, subject to the approval of the Secretary of the Interior.

ARTICLE 15.
The United States may settle any civilized Indians, friendly with the Cherokees and adjacent tribes, within the Cherokee country, on unoccupied lands east of 96°, on such terms as may be agreed upon by any such tribe and the Cherokees, subject to the approval of the President of the United States, which shall be consistent with the following provisions, viz: Should any such tribe or band of Indians settling in said country abandon their tribal organization, there being first paid into the Cherokee national fund a sum of money which shall sustain the same proportion to the then existing national fund that the number of Indians sustain to the whole number of Cherokees then residing in the Cherokee country, they shall be incorporated into and ever after remain a part of the Cherokee Nation, on equal terms in every respect with native citizens. And should any such tribe, thus settling in said country, decide to preserve their tribal organizations, and to maintain their tribal laws, customs, and usages, not inconsistent with the constitution and laws of the Cherokee Nation, they shall have a district of country set off for their use by metes and bounds equal to one hundred and sixty acres, if they should so decide, for each man, woman, and child of said tribe, and shall pay for the same into the national fund such price as may be agreed on by them and the Cherokee Nation, subject to the approval of the President of the United States, and in cases of disagreement the price to be fixed by the President.

And the said tribe thus settled shall also pay into the national fund a sum of money, to be agreed on by the respective parties, not greater in proportion to the whole existing national fund and the probable proceeds of the lands herein ceded or authorized to be ceded or sold than their numbers bear to the whole number of Cherokees then residing in said country, and thence afterwards they shall enjoy all the rights of native Cherokees. But no Indians who have no tribal organizations, or who shall determine to abandon their tribal organizations, shall be permitted to settle east of the 96° of longitude without the consent of the Cherokee national council, or of a delegation duly appointed by it, being first obtained. And no Indians who have and determine to preserve the tribal organizations shall be permitted to settle, as herein provided, east of the 96° of longitude without such consent being first obtained, unless the President of the United States, after a full hearing of the objections offered by said council or delegation to such settlement, shall determine that the objections are insufficient, in which case he may authorize the settlement of such tribe east of the 96° of longitude.

ARTICLE 16.

The United States may settle friendly Indians in any part of the Cherokee country west of 96°, to be taken in a compact form in quantity not exceeding one hundred and sixty acres for each member of each of said tribes thus to be settled; the boundaries of each of said districts to be distinctly marked, and the land conveyed in fee-simple to each of said tribes to be held in common or by their members in severalty as the United States may decide.

Said lands thus disposed of to be paid for to the Cherokee Nation at such price as may be agreed on between the said parties in interest, subject to the approval of the President; and if they should not agree, then the price to be fixed by the President.

The Cherokee Nation to retain the right of possession of and jurisdiction over all of said country west of 96° of longitude until thus sold and occupied, after which their jurisdiction and right of possession to terminate forever as to each of said districts thus sold and occupied.

ARTICLE 17.

The Cherokee Nation hereby cedes, in trust to the United States, the tract of land in the State of Kansas which was sold to the Cherokees by the United States, under the provisions of the second article of the treaty of 1835; and also that strip of the land ceded to the nation by the fourth article of said treaty which is included in the State of Kansas, and the Cherokees consent that said lands may be

included in the limits and jurisdiction of the said State.

The lands herein ceded shall be surveyed as the public lands of the United States are surveyed, under the direction of the Commissioner of the General Land-Office, and shall be appraised by two disinterested persons, one to be designated by the Cherokee national council and one by the Secretary of the Interior, and, in case of disagreement, by a third person, to be mutually selected by the aforesaid appraisers. The appraisement to be not less than an average of one dollar and a quarter per acre, exclusive of improvements.

And the Secretary of the Interior shall, from time to time, as such surveys and appraisements are approved by him, after due advertisements for sealed bids, sell such lands to the highest bidders for cash, in parcels not exceeding one hundred and sixty acres, and at not less than the appraised value: Provided, That whenever there are improvements of the value of fifty dollars made on the lands not being mineral, and owned and personally occupied by any person for agricultural purposes at the date of the signing hereof, such person so owning, and in person residing on such improvements, shall, after due proof, made under such regulations as the Secretary of the Interior may prescribe, be entitled to buy, at the appraised value, the smallest quantity of land in legal subdivisions which will include his improvements, not exceeding in the aggregate one hundred and sixty acres; the expenses of survey and appraisement to be paid by the Secretary out of the proceeds of sale of said land: Provided, That nothing in this article shall prevent the Secretary of the Interior from selling the whole of said lands not occupied by actual settlers at the date of the ratification of this treaty, not exceeding one hundred and sixty acres to each person entitled to pre-emption under the pre-emption laws of the United States, in a body, to any responsible party, for cash, for a sum not less than one dollar per acre.

ARTICLE 18.

That any lands owned by the Cherokees in the State of Arkansas and in States east of the Mississippi may be sold by the Cherokee Nation in such manner as their national council may prescribe, all such sales being first approved by the Secretary of the Interior.

ARTICLE 19.
All Cherokees being heads of families residing at the date of the ratification of this treaty on any of the lands herein ceded, or authorized to be sold, and desiring to remove to the reserved country, shall be paid by the purchasers of said lands the value of such improvements, to be ascertained and appraised by the commissioners who appraise the lands, subject to the approval of the Secretary of the Interior; and if he shall elect to remain on the land now occupied by him, shall be entitled to receive a patent from the United States in fee-simple for three hundred and twenty acres of land to include his improvements, and thereupon he and his family shall cease to be members of the nation.

And the Secretary of the Interior shall also be authorized to pay the reasonable costs and expenses of the delegates of the southern Cherokees.

The moneys to be paid under this article shall be paid out of the proceeds of the sales of the national lands in Kansas.

ARTICLE 20.
Whenever the Cherokee national council shall request it, the Secretary of the Interior shall cause the country reserved for the Cherokees to be surveyed and allotted among them, at the expense of the United States.

ARTICLE 21.
It being difficult to learn the precise boundary line between the Cherokee country and the States of Arkansas, Missouri, and Kansas, it is agreed that the United States shall, at its own expense, cause the same to be run as far west as the Arkansas, and marked by permanent and conspicuous monuments, by two commissioners, one of whom shall be designated by the Cherokee national council.

ARTICLE 22.
The Cherokee national council, or any duly appointed delegation thereof, shall have the privilege to appoint an agent to examine the accounts of the nation with the Government of the United States at such time as they may see proper, and to continue or discharge such agent, and to appoint another, as may be thought best by such council or delegation; and such agent shall have free access to all accounts and books in the executive departments relating to the business of said Cherokee Nation, and an opportunity to examine the same in the presence of the officer having such books and papers in charge.

ARTICLE 23.
All funds now due the nation, or that may hereafter accrue from the sale of their lands by the United States, as hereinbefore provided for, shall be invested in the United States registered stocks at their current value, and the interest on all said funds shall be paid semi-annually on the order of the Cherokee Nation, and shall be applied to the following purposes, to wit: Thirty-five per cent. shall be applied for the support of the common-schools of the nation and educational purposes; fifteen per cent. for the orphan fund, and fifty per cent. for general purposes, including reasonable salaries of district officers; and the Secretary of the Interior, with the approval of the President of the United States, may pay out of the funds due the nation, on the order of the national council or a delegation duly authorized by it, such amount as he may deem necessary to meet outstanding obligations of the Cherokee Nation, caused by the suspension of the payment of their annuities, not to exceed the sum of one hundred and fifty thousand dollars.

ARTICLE 24.
As a slight testimony for the useful and arduous services of the Rev. Evan Jones, for forty years a missionary in the Cherokee Nation, now a cripple, old and poor, it is agreed that the sum of three thousand dollars be paid to him, under the direction of the Secretary of the Interior, out of any Cherokee fund in or to come into his hands not otherwise appropriated.

ARTICLE 25.
A large number of the Cherokees who served in the Army of the United States having died, leaving no heirs entitled to receive bounties and arrears of pay on account of such service, it is agreed that all bounties and arrears for service in the regiments of Indian United States volunteers which shall remain unclaimed by any person legally entitled to receive the same for two years from the ratification of this treaty, shall be paid as the national council may direct, to be applied to the foundation and support of an asylum for the education of orphan children, which asylum shall be under the control of the national council, or of such benevolent society as

said council may designate, subject to the approval of the Secretary of the Interior.

ARTICLE 26.
The United States guarantee to the people of the Cherokee Nation the quiet and peaceable possession of their country and protection against domestic feuds and insurrections, and against hostilities of other tribes. They shall also be protected against inter[r]uptions or intrusion from all unauthorized citizens of the United States who may attempt to settle on their lands or reside in their territory. In case of hostilities among the Indian tribes, the United States agree that the party or parties commencing the same shall, so far as practicable, make reparation for the damages done.

ARTICLE 27.
The United States shall have the right to establish one or more military posts or stations in the Cherokee Nation, as may be deemed necessary for the proper protection of the citizens of the United States lawfully residing therein and the Cherokee and other citizens of the Indian country. But no sutler or other person connected therewith, either in or out of the military organization, shall be permitted to introduce any spirit[u]ous, vinous, or malt liquors into the Cherokee Nation, except the medical department proper, and by them only for strictly medical purposes. And all persons not in the military service of the United States, not citizens of the Cherokee Nation, are to be prohibited from coming into the Cherokee Nation, or remaining in the same, except as herein otherwise provided; and it is the duty of the United States Indian agent for the Cherokees to have such persons, not lawfully residing or sojourning therein, removed from the nation, as they now are, or hereafter may be, required by the Indian intercourse laws of the United States.

ARTICLE 28.
The United States hereby agree to pay for provisions and clothing furnished the army under Appotholehala in the winter of 1861 and 1862, not to exceed the sum of ten thousand dollars, the accounts to be ascertained and settled by the Secretary of the Interior.

ARTICLE 29.
The sum of ten thousand dollars or so much thereof as may be necessary to pay the expenses of the delegates and representatives of the Cherokees invited by the Government to visit Washington for the purposes of making this treaty, shall be paid by the United States on the ratification of this treaty.

ARTICLE 30.
The United States agree to pay to the proper claimants all losses of property by missionaries or missionary societies, resulting from their being ordered or driven from the country by United States agents, and from their property being taken and occupied or destroyed by by United States troops, not exceeding in the aggregate twenty thousand dollars, to be ascertained by the Secretary of the Interior.

ARTICLE 31.
All provisions of treaties heretofore ratified and in force, and not inconsistent with the provisions of this treaty, are hereby re-affirmed and declared to be in full force; and nothin herein shall be construed as an acknowledgment by the United States, or as a relinquishment by the Cherokee Nation of any claims or demands under the guarantees of former treaties, except as herein expressly provided.

In testimony whereof, the said commissioners on the part of the United States, and the said delegation on the part of the Cherokee Nation, have hereunto set their hands and seals at the city of Washington, this ninth [nineteenth] day of July, A. D. one thousand eight hundred and sixty-six.

D. N. Cooley, Commissioner of Indian Affairs.
Elijah Sells, Superintendent of Indian Affairs.
Smith Christie,
White Catcher,
James McDaniel,
S. H. Benge,
Danl. H. Ross,
J. B. Jones.

Delegates of the Cherokee Nation, appointed by Resolution of the National Council.
    In presence of—
W. H. Watson,
J. W. Wright.

Signatures witnessed by the following-named persons, the following interlineations being made before signing: On page 1st the word "the" interlined, on page 11 the word "the" struck out, and to said page 11 sheet attached requiring publication of laws; and on page 34th the word "ceded" struck out and the words "neutral lands" inserted. Page 471/2 added relating to expenses of treaty.

Thomas Ewing, jr.
Wm. A. Phillips,
J. W. Wright.

Treaty with the Kiowa, Comanche, and Apache, 1867

Oct. 21, 1867. | 15 Stats., 589. | Ratified, July 25, 1868. | Proclaimed Aug. 25, 1868.

Articles of a treaty concluded at the Council Camp on Medicine Lodge Creek, seventy miles south of Fort Larned, in the State of Kansas, on the twenty-first day of October, eighteen hundred and sixty-seven, by and between the United States of America, represented by its commissioners duly appointed thereto to-wit: Nathaniel G. Taylor, William S. Harney, C. C. Augur, Alfred S. [H.] Terry, John B. Sanborn, Samuel F. Tappan, and J. B. Henderson, of the one part, and the Kiowa, Comanche, and Apache Indians, represented by their chiefs and headmen duly authorized and empowered to act for the body of the people of said tribes (the names of said chiefs and headmen being hereto subscribed) of the other part, witness:

Whereas, on the twenty-first day of October, eighteen hundred and sixty-seven, a treaty of peace was made and entered into at the Council Camp, on Medicine Lodge Creek, seventy miles south of Fort Larned, in the State of Kansas, by and between the United States of America, by its commissioners Nathaniel G. Taylor, William S. Harney, C. C. Augur, Alfred H. Terry, John B. Sanborn, Samuel F. Tappan, and J. B. Henderson, of the one part, and the Kiowa and Comanche tribes of Indians, of the Upper Arkansas, by and through their chiefs and headmen whose names are subscribed thereto, of the other part, reference being had to said treaty; and whereas, since the making and signing of said treaty, at a council held at said camp on this day, the chiefs and headmen of the Apache nation or tribe of Indians express to the commissioners on the part of the United States, as aforesaid, a wish to be confederated with the said Kiowa and Comanche tribes, and to be placed, in every respect, upon an equal footing with said tribes; and whereas, at a council held at the same place and on

the same day, with the chiefs and headmen of the said Kiowa and Comanche Tribes, they consent to the confederation of the said Apache tribe, as desired by it, upon the terms and conditions hereinafter set forth in this supplementary treaty: Now, therefore, it is hereby stipulated and agreed by and between the aforesaid commissioners, on the part of the United States, and the chiefs and headmen of the Kiowa and Comanche tribes, and, also, the chiefs and headmen of the said Apache tribe, as follows, to-wit:

ARTICLE 1.

The said Apache tribe of Indians agree to confederate and become incorporated with the said Kiowa and Comanche Indians, and to accept as their permanent home the reservation described in the aforesaid treaty with said Kiowa and Comanche tribes, concluded as aforesaid at this place, and they pledge themselves to make no permanent settlement at any place, nor on any lands, outside of said reservation.

ARTICLE 2.

The Kiowa and Comanche tribes, on their part, agree that all the benefits and advantages arising from the employment of physicians, teachers, carpenters, millers, engineers, farmers, and blacksmiths, agreed to be furnished under the provisions of their said treaty, together with all the advantages to be derived from the construction of agency buildings, warehouses, mills, and other structures, and also from the establishment of schools upon their said reservation, shall be jointly and equally shared and enjoyed by the said Apache Indians, as though they had been originally a part of said tribes; and they further agree that all other benefits arising from said treaty shall be jointly and equally shared as aforesaid.

ARTICLE 3.

The United States, on its part, agrees that clothing and other articles named in Article X. of said original treaty, together with all money or other annuities agreed to be furnished under any of the provisions of said treaty, to the Kiowa and Comanches, shall be shared equally by the Apaches. In all cases where specific articles of clothing are agreed to be furnished to the Kiowas and Comanches, similar articles shall be furnished to the Apaches, and a separate census of the Apaches shall be annually taken and returned by the agent, as provided for the other tribes. And the United States further agrees, in consideration of the incorporation of said Apaches, to increase the annual appropriation of money, as provided for in

Article X. of said treaty, from twenty-five thousand to thirty thousand dollars; and the latter amount shall be annually appropriated, for the period therein named, for the use and benefit of said three tribes, confederated as herein declared; and the clothing and other annuities, which may from time to time be furnished to the Apaches, shall be based upon the census of the three tribes, annually to be taken by the agent, and shall be separately marked, forwarded, and delivered to them at the agency house, to be built under the provisions of said original treaty.

ARTICLE 4.

In consideration of the advantages conferred by this supplementary treaty upon the the Apache tribe of Indians, they agree to observe and faithfully comply with all the stipulations and agreements entered into by the Kiowas and Comanches in said original treaty. They agree, in the same manner, to keep the peace toward the whites and all other persons under the jurisdiction of the United States, and to do and perform all other things enjoined upon said tribes by the provisions of said treaty; and they hereby give up and forever relinquish to the United States all rights, privileges, and grants now vested in them, or intended to be transferred to them, by the treaty between the United States and the Cheyenne and Arapahoe tribes of Indians, concluded at the camp on the Little Arkansas River, in the State of Kansas, on the fourteenth day of October, one thousand eight hundred and sixty-five, and also by the supplementary treaty, concluded at the same place on the seventeenth day of the same month, between the United States, of the one part, and the Cheyenne, Arapahoe, and Apache tribes, of the other part. In testimony of all which, the said parties have hereunto set their hands and seals at the place and on the day hereinbefore stated.

N. G. Taylor, [SEAL.]
President of Indian Commission.

Wm. S. Harney, [SEAL.]
Brevet Major-General, Commissioner, &c.

C. C. Augur, [SEAL.]
Brevet Major-General.

Alfred H. Terry, [SEAL.]
Brevet Major-General and Brigadier-General.
John B. Sanborn, [SEAL.]
Samuel F. Tappan, [SEAL.]

J. B. Henderson, [SEAL.]
On the part of the Kiowas:
Satanka, or Sitting bear, his x mark, [SEAL.]
Sa-tan-ta, or White Bear, his x mark, [SEAL.]
Wah-toh-konk, or Black Eagle, his x mark, [SEAL.]
Ton-a-en-ko, or Kicking Eagle, his x mark, [SEAL.]
Fish-e-more, or Stinking Saddle, his x mark, [SEAL.]
Ma-ye-tin, or Woman's Heart, his x mark, [SEAL.]
Sa-tim-gear, or Stumbling Bear, his x mark, [SEAL.]
Sa-pa-ga, or One Bear, his x mark, [SEAL.]
Cor-beau, or The Crow, his x mark, [SEAL.]
Sa-ta-more, or Bear Lying Down, his x mark, [SEAL.]

On the part of the Comanches:
Parry-wah-say-men, or Ten Bears, his x mark, [SEAL.]
Tep-pe-navon, or Painted Lips, his x mark, [SEAL.]
To-she-wi, or Silver Brooch, his x mark, [SEAL.]
Cear-chi-neka, or Standing Feather, his x mark, [SEAL.]
Ho-we-ar, or Gap in the Woods, his x mark, [SEAL.]
Tir-ha-yah-gua-hip, or Horse's Back, his x mark, [SEAL.]
Es-a-man-a-ca, or Wolf's Name, his x mark, [SEAL.]
Ah-te-es-ta, or Little Horn, his x mark, [SEAL.]
Pooh-yah-to-yeh-be, or Iron Mountain, his x mark, [SEAL.]
Sad-dy-yo, or Dog Fat, his x mark, [SEAL.]

On the part of the Apaches:
Mah-vip-pah, Wolf's Sleeve, his x mark, [SEAL.]
Kon-zhon-ta-co, Poor Bear, his x mark, [SEAL.]
Cho-se-ta, or Bad Back, his x mark, [SEAL.]
Nah-tan, or Brave Man, his x mark, [SEAL.]
Ba-zhe-ech, Iron Shirt, his x mark, [SEAL.]
Til-la-ka, or White Horn, his x mark, [SEAL.]

Attest:
Ashton S. H. White, secretary.
Geo. B. Willis, reporter.
Philip McCusker, interpreter.
John D. Howland, clerk Indian Commission.

Sam'l S. Smoot, United States surveyor.
A. A. Taylor.
J. H. Leavenworth, United States Indian agent.
Thos. Murphy, superintendent Indian affairs.
Joel H. Elliott, major, Seventh U.S. Cavalry.

Treaty with the Navajo, 1868

June 1, 1868. | 15 Stats., p. 667. | Ratified July 25, 1868. | Proclaimed Aug. 12, 1868.

Articles of a treaty and agreement made and entered into at Fort Sumner, New Mexico, on the first day of June, one thousand eight hundred and sixty-eight, by and between the United States, represented by its commissioners, Lieutenant-General W. T. Sherman and Colonel Samuel F. Tappan, of the one part, and the Navajo Nation or tribe of Indians, represented by their chiefs and head-men, duly authorized and empowered to act for the whole people of said nation or tribe, (the names of said chiefs and head-men being hereto subscribed,) of the other part, witness:

ARTICLE 1.

From this day forward all war between the parties to this agreement shall forever cease. The Government of the United States desires peace, and its honor is hereby pledged to keep it. The Indians desire peace, and they now pledge their honor to keep it.

If bad men among the whites, or among other people subject to the authority of the United States, shall commit any wrong upon the person or property of the Indians, the United States will, upon proof made to the agent and forwarded to the Commissioner of Indian Affairs at Washington City, proceed at once to cause the offender to be arrested and punished according to the laws of the United States, and also to reimburse the injured persons for the loss sustained.

If the bad men among the Indians shall commit a wrong or depredation upon the person or property of any one, white, black, or Indian, subject to the authority of the United States and at peace therewith, the Navajo tribe agree that they will, on proof made to their agent, and on notice by him, deliver up the wrongdoer to the United States, to be tried and punished according to its laws; and in case they wilfully refuse so to do, the person injured shall be reimbursed for his loss from the annuities or other moneys due or to become due to them under this treaty, or any others that may be made with the United States. And the President may prescribe such rules and regulations for ascertaining damages under this article as in his judgment may be proper; but no such damage shall be adjusted and paid until examined and passed upon by the Commissioner of Indian Affairs, and no one sustaining loss whilst violating, or because of his violating, the provisions of this treaty or the laws of the United States, shall be reimbursed therefor.

ARTICLE 2.

The United States agrees that the following district of country, to wit: bounded on the north by the 37th degree of north latitude, south by an east and west line passing through the site of old Fort Defiance, in Cañon Bonito, east by the parallel of longitude which, if prolonged south, would pass through old Fort Lyon, or the Ojo-de-oso, Bear Spring, and west by a parallel of longitude about 109° 30° west of Greenwich, provided it embraces the outlet of the Cañon-de-Chilly, which cañon is to be all included in this reservation, shall be, and the same is hereby, set apart for the use and occupation of the Navajo tribe of Indians, and for such other friendly tribes or individual Indians as from time to time they may be willing, with the consent of the United States, to admit among them; and the United States agrees that no persons except those herein so authorized to do, and except such officers, soldiers, agents, and employées of the Government, or of the Indians, as may be authorized to enter upon Indian reservations in discharge of duties imposed by law, or the orders of the President, shall ever be permitted to pass over, settle upon, or reside in, the territory described in this article.

ARTICLE 3.

The United States agrees to cause to be built, at some point within said reservation, where timber and water may be convenient, the following buildings: a warehouse, to cost not exceeding twenty-five hundred dollars; an agency building for the residence of the agent, not to cost exceeding three thousand dollars; a carpenter-shop and blacksmith-shop, not to cost exceeding one thousand dollars each; and a schoolhouse and chapel, so soon as a sufficient number of children can be induced to attend school, which shall not cost to exceed five thousand dollars.

ARTICLE 4.

The United States agrees that the agent for the Navajos shall make his home at the agency building; that he shall reside among them, and shall keep an office open at all times for the purpose of prompt and diligent inquiry into such matters of complaint by or against the Indians as may be presented for investigation, as also for the faithful discharge of other duties enjoined by law. In all cases of depredation on person or property he shall cause the evidence to be taken in writing and forwarded, together with his finding, to the Commissioner of Indian Affairs, whose decision shall be binding on the parties to this treaty.

ARTICLE 5.

If any individual belonging to said tribe, or legally incorporated with it, being the head of a family, shall desire to commence farming, he shall have the privilege to select, in the presence and with the assistance of the agent then in charge, a tract of land within said reservation, not exceeding one hundred and sixty acres in extent, which tract, when so selected, certified, and recorded in the "land-book" as herein described, shall cease to be held in common, but the same may be occupied and held in the exclusive possession of the person selecting it, and of his family, so long as he or they may continue to cultivate it.

Any person over eighteen years of age, not being the head of a family, may in like manner select, and cause to be certified to him or her for purposes of cultivation, a quantity of land, not exceeding eighty acres in extent, and thereupon be entitled to the exclusive possession of the same as above directed.

For each tract of land so selected a certificate containing a description thereof, and the name of the person selecting it, with a certificate endorsed thereon, that the same has been recorded, shall be delivered to the party entitled to it by the agent, after the same shall have been recorded by him in a book to be kept in his office, subject to inspection, which said book shall be known as the "Navajo land-book."

The President may at any time order a survey of the reservation, and when so surveyed, Congress shall provide for protecting the rights of said settlers in their improvements, and may fix the character of the title held by each.

The United States may pass such laws on the subject of alienation and descent of property between the Indians and their descendants as may be thought proper.

ARTICLE 6.

In order to insure the civilization of the Indians entering into this treaty, the necessity of education is admitted, especially of such of them as may be settled on said agricultural parts of this reservation, and they therefore pledge themselves to compel their children, male and female, between the ages of six and sixteen years, to attend school; and it is hereby made the duty of the agent for said Indians to see that this stipulation is strictly complied with; and the United States agrees that, for every thirty children between said ages who can be induced or compelled to attend school, a house shall be provided, and a teacher competent to teach the elementary branches of an English education shall be furnished, who will reside among said Indians, and faithfully discharge his or her duties as a teacher.

The provisions of this article to continue for not less than ten years.

ARTICLE 7.

When the head of a family shall have selected lands and received his certificate as above directed, and the agent shall be satisfied that he intends in good faith to commence cultivating the soil for a living, he shall be entitled to receive seeds and agricultural implements for the first year, not exceeding in value one hundred dollars, and for each succeeding year he shall continue to farm, for a period of two years, he shall be entitled to receive seeds and implements to the value of twenty-five dollars.

ARTICLE 8.

In lieu of all sums of money or other annuities provided to be paid to the Indians herein named under any treaty or treaties heretofore made, the United States agrees to deliver at the agency-house on the reservation herein named, on the first day of September of each year for ten years, the following articles, to wit:

Such articles of clothing, goods, or raw materials in lieu thereof, as the agent may make his estimate for, not exceeding in value five dollars per Indian—each Indian being encouraged to manufacture their own clothing, blankets, &c.; to be furnished with no article which they can manufacture themselves. And, in order that the Commissioner of Indian Affairs may be able to estimate properly for the articles herein named, it shall be the duty of the agent each year to forward to him a full and exact census of the Indians, on which the estimate from year to year can be based.

And in addition to the articles herein named, the sum of ten dollars for each person entitled to the beneficial effects of this treaty shall be annually appropriated for a period of ten years, for each person who engages in farming or mechanical pursuits, to be used by the Commissioner of Indian Affairs in the purchase of such articles as from time to time the condition and necessities of the Indians may indicate to be proper; and if within the ten years at any time it shall appear that the amount of money needed for clothing, under the article, can be appropriated to better uses for the Indians named herein, the Commissioner of Indian Affairs may change the appropriation to other purposes, but in no event shall the amount of this appropriation be withdrawn or discontinued for the period named, provided they remain at peace. And the President shall annually detail an officer of the Army to be present and attest the delivery of all the goods herein named to the Indians, and he shall inspect and report on the quantity and quality of the goods and the manner of their delivery.

ARTICLE 9.
In consideration of the advantages and benefits conferred by this treaty, and the many pledges of friendship by the United States, the tribes who are parties to this agreement hereby stipulate that they will relinquish all right to occupy any territory outside their reservation, as herein defined, but retain the right to hunt on any unoccupied lands contiguous to their reservation, so long as the large game may range thereon in such numbers as to justify the chase; and they, the said Indians, further expressly agree:

1st. That they will make no opposition to the construction of railroads now being built or hereafter to be built across the continent.

2d. That they will not interfere with the peaceful construction of any railroad not passing over their reservation as herein defined.

3d. That they will not attack any persons at home or travelling, nor molest or disturb any wagon-

trains, coaches, mules, or cattle belonging to the people of the United States, or to persons friendly therewith.

4th. That they will never capture or carry off from the settlements women or children.

5th. They will never kill or scalp white men, nor attempt to do them harm.

6th. They will not in future oppose the construction of railroads, wagon-roads, mail stations, or other works of utility or necessity which may be ordered or permitted by the laws of the United States; but should such roads or other works be constructed on the lands of their reservation, the Government will pay the tribe whatever amount of damage may be assessed by three disinterested commissioners to be appointed by the President for that purpose, one of said commissioners to be a chief or head-men of the tribe.

7th. They will make no opposition to the military posts or roads now established, or that may be established, not in violation of treaties heretofore made or hereafter to be made with any of the Indian tribes.

ARTICLE 10.
No future treaty for the cession of any portion or part of the reservation herein described, which may be held in common, shall be of any validity or force against said Indians unless agreed to and executed by at least three-fourths of all the adult male Indians occupying or interested in the same; and no cession by the tribe shall be understood or construed in such manner as to deprive, without his consent, any individual member of the tribe of his rights to any tract of land selected by him as provided in article [5] of this treaty.

ARTICLE 11.
The Navajos also hereby agree that at any time after the signing of these presents they will proceed in such manner as may be required of them by the agent, or by the officer charged with their removal, to the reservation herein provided for, the United States paying for their subsistence en route, and providing a reasonable amount of transportation for the sick and feeble.

ARTICLE 12.
It is further agreed by and between the parties to this agreement that the sum of one hundred and

fifty thousand dollars appropriated or to be appropriated shall be disbursed as follows, subject to any condition provided in the law, to wit:

1st. The actual cost of the removal of the tribe from the Bosque Redondo reservation to the reservation, say fifty thousand dollars.

2d. The purchase of fifteen thousand sheep and goats, at a cost not to exceed thirty thousand dollars.

3d. The purchase of five hundred beef cattle and a million pounds of corn, to be collected and held at the military post nearest the reservation, subject to the orders of the agent, for the relief of the needy during the coming winter.

4th. The balance, if any, of the appropriation to be invested for the maintenance of the Indians pending their removal, in such manner as the agent who is with them may determine.

5th. The removal of this tribe to be made under the supreme control and direction of the military commander of the Territory of New Mexico, and when completed, the management of the tribe to revert to the proper agent.

ARTICLE 13.
The tribe herein named, by their representatives, parties to this treaty, agree to make the reservation herein described their permanent home, and they will not as a tribe make any permanent settlement elsewhere, reserving the right to hunt on the lands adjoining the said reservation formerly called theirs, subject to the modifications named in this treaty and the orders of the commander of the department in which said reservation may be for the time being; and it is further agreed and understood by the parties to this treaty, that if any Navajo Indian or Indians shall leave the reservation herein described to settle elsewhere, he or they shall forfeit all the rights, privileges, and annuities conferred by the terms of this treaty; and it is further agreed by the parties to this treaty, that they will do all they can to induce Indians now away from reservations set apart for the exclusive use and occupation of the Indians, leading a nomadic life, or engaged in war against the people of the United States, to abandon such a life and settle permanently in one of the territorial reservations set apart for the exclusive use and occupation of the Indians.

In testimony of all which the said parties have hereunto, on this the first day of June, one thousand eight hundred and sixty-eight, at Fort Sumner, in the Territory of New Mexico, set their hands and seals.

W. T. Sherman, Lieutenant-General, Indian
    Peace Commissioner.
S. F. Tappan, Indian Peace Commissioner.

Barboncito, chief, his x mark,
Armijo, his x mark,
Delgado, his mark,
Manuelito, his x mark,
Largo, his x mark,
Herrero, his x mark,
Chiqueto, his x mark,
Muerto de Hombre, his x mark,
Hombro, his x mark,
Narbono, his x mark,
Narbono Segundo, his x mark,
Gañado Mucho, his x mark

Council:
Riquo, his x mark,
Juan Martin, his x mark,
Serginto, his x mark,
Grande, his x mark,
Inoetenito, his x mark,
Muchachos Mucho, his x mark,
Chiqueto Segundo, his x mark,
Cabello Amarillo, his x mark,
Francisco, his x mark,
Torivio, his x mark,
Desdendado, his x mark,
Juan, his x mark,
Guero, his x mark,
Gugadore, his x mark,
Cabason, his x mark,
Barbon Segundo, his x mark,
Cabares Colorados, his x mark

Attest:
Geo. W. G. Getty, colonel Thirty-seventh
    Infantry, brevet major-general U. S. Army,
B. S. Roberts, brevet brigadier-general U. S.
    Army, lieutenant-colonel Third Cavalry,
J. Cooper McKee, brevet lieutenant-colonel,
    surgeon U. S. Army,
Theo. H. Dodd, United States Indian agent for
    Navajos,

Chas. McClure, brevet major and commissary of subsistence, U. S. Army,

James F. Weeds, brevet major and assistant surgeon, U. S. Army,

J. C. Sutherland, interpreter,

William Vaux, chaplain U. S. Army

Treaty with the Eastern Band Shoshoni and Bannock, 1868

July 3, 1968

Articles of a treaty made and concluded at Fort Bridger, Utah Territory, on the third day of July, in the year of our Lord one thousand eight hundred and sixty-eight, by and between the undersigned commissioners on the part of the United States, and the undersigned chiefs and head-men of and representing the Shoshonee (eastern band)and Bannack tribes of Indians, they being duly authorized to act in the premises:

ARTICLE 1.

From this day forward peace between the parties to this treaty shall forever continue. The Government of the United States desires peace, and its honor is hereby pledged to keep it. The Indians desire peace, and they hereby pledge their honor to maintain it.

If bad men among the whites, or among other people subject to the authority of the United States, shall commit any wrong upon the person or property of the Indians, the United States will, upon proof made to the agent and forwarded to the Commissioner of Indian Affairs, at Washington City, proceed at once to cause the offender to be arrested and punished according to the laws of the United States, and also re-imburse the injured person for the loss sustained.

If bad men among the Indians shall commit a wrong or depredation upon the person or property of any one, white, black, or Indian, subject to the authority of the United States, and at peace therewith, the Indians herein named solemnly agree that they will, on proof made to their agent and notice by him, deliver up the wrong-doer to the United States, to be tried and punished according to the laws; and in case they wilfully refuse so to do, the person injured

shall be re-imbursed for his loss from the annuities or other moneys due or to become due to them under this or other treaties made with the United States. And the President, on advising with the Commissioner of Indian Affairs, shall prescribe such rules and regulations for ascertaining damages under the provisions of this article as in his judgment may be proper. But no such damages shall be adjusted and paid until thoroughly examined and passed upon by the Commissioner of Indian Affairs, and no one sustaining loss while violating or because of his violating the provisions of this treaty or the laws of the United States, shall be reimbursed therefor.

ARTICLE 2.

It is agreed that whenever the Bannacks desire a reservation to be set apart for their use, or whenever the President of the United States shall deem it advisable for them to be put upon a reservation, he shall cause a suitable one to be selected for them in their present country, which shall embrace reasonable portions of the "PortNeuf" and "Kansas Prairie" countries, and that, when this reservation is declared, the United States will secure to the Bannacks the same rights and privileges therein, and make the same and like expenditures therein for their benefit, except the agency-house and residence of agent, in proportion to their numbers, as herein provided for the Shoshonee reservation. The United States further agrees that the following district of country, to wit: Commencing at the mouth of Owl Creek and running due south to the crest of the divide between the Sweet-water and Papo Agie Rivers; thence along the crest of said divide and the summit of Wind River Mountains to the longitude of North Fork of Wind River; thence due north to mouth of said North Fork and up its channel to a point twenty miles above its mouth; thence in a straight line to head-waters of Owl Creek and along middle of channel of Owl Creek to place of beginning, shall be and the same is set apart for the absolute and undisturbed use and occupation of the Shoshonee Indians herein named, and for such other friendly tribes or individual Indians as from time to time they may be willing, with the consent of the United States, to admit amongst them; and the United States now solemnly agrees that no persons except those herein designated and authorized so to do, and except such officers, agents, and employés of the Government as may be authorized to enter upon Indian reservations in discharge of duties enjoined by law, shall ever be permitted to pass over, settle upon, or reside in the territory described in this article for the use of said Indians, and henceforth they will and do hereby relinquish all title, claims, or rights in and to any portion of the territory of the United States, except such as is embraced within the limits aforesaid.

ARTICLE 3.
The United States agrees, at its own proper expense, to construct at a suitable point of the Shoshonee reservation a warehouse or store-room for the use of the agent in storing goods belonging to the Indians, to cost not exceeding two thousand dollars; an agency building for the residence of the agent, to cost not exceeding three thousand; a residence for the physician, to cost not more than two thousand dollars; and five other buildings, for a carpenter, farmer, blacksmith, miller, and engineer, each to cost not exceeding two thousand dollars; also a school-house or mission building so soon as a sufficient number of children can be induced by the agent to attend school, which shall not cost exceeding twenty-five hundred dollars.

The United States agrees further to cause to be erected on said Shoshonee reservation, near the other buildings herein authorized, a good steam circular-saw mill, with a grist-mill and shingle-machine attached, the same to cost not more than eight thousand dollars.

ARTICLE 4.
The Indians herein named agree, when the agency house and other buildings shall be constructed on their reservations named, they will make said reservations their permanent home, and they will make no permanent settlement elsewhere; but they shall have the right to hunt on the unoccupied lands of the United States so long as game may be found thereon, and so long as peace subsists among the whites and Indians on the borders of the hunting districts.

ARTICLE 5.
The United States agrees that the agent for said Indians shall in the future make his home at the agency building on the Shoshonee reservation, but shall direct and supervise affairs on the Bannack reservation; and shall keep an office open at all times for the purpose of prompt and diligent inquiry into such

matters of complaint by and against the Indians as may be presented for investigation under the provisions of their treaty stipulations, as also for the faithful discharge of other duties enjoined by law. In all cases of depredation on person or property he shall cause the evidence to be taken in writing and forwarded, together with his finding, to the Commissioner of Indian Affairs, whose decision shall be binding on the parties to this treaty.

ARTICLE 6.
If any individual belonging to said tribes of Indians, or legally incorporated with them, being the head of a family, shall desire to commence farming, he shall have the privilege to select, in the presence and with the assistance of the agent then in charge, a tract of land within the reservation of his tribe, not exceeding three hundred and twenty acres in extent, which tract so selected, certified, and recorded in the "land-book," as herein directed, shall cease to be held in common, but the same may be occupied and held in the exclusive possession of the person selecting it, and of his family, so long as he or they may continue to cultivate it.

Any person over eighteen years of age, not being the head of a family, may in like manner select and cause to be certified to him or her, for purposes of cultivation, a quantity of land not exceeding eighty acres in extent, and thereupon be entitled to the exclusive possession of the same as above described. For each tract of land so selected a certificate, containing a description thereof, and the name of the person selecting it, with a certificate indorsed thereon that the same has been recorded, shall be delivered to the party entitled to it by the agent, after the same shall have been recorded by him in a book to be kept in his office subject to inspection, which said book shall be known as the "Shoshone (eastern band) and Bannack land-book."

The President may at any time order a survey of these reservations, and when so surveyed Congress shall provide for protecting the rights of the Indian settlers in these improvements, and may fix the character of the title held by each. The United States may pass such laws on the subject of alienation and descent of property as between Indians, and on all subjects connected with the government of the Indians on said reservations, and the internal police thereof, as may be thought proper.

ARTICLE 7.

In order to insure the civilization of the tribes entering into this treaty, the necessity of education is admitted, especially of such of them as are or may be settled on said agricultural reservations, and they therefore pledge themselves to compel their children, male and female, between the ages of six and sixteen years, to attend school; and it is hereby made the duty of the agent for said Indians to see that this stipulation is strictly complied with; and the United States agrees that for every thirty children between said ages who can be induced or compelled to attend school, a house shall be provided and a teacher competent to teach the elementary branches of an English education shall be furnished, who will reside among said Indians and faithfully discharge his or her duties as a teacher. The provisions as this article to continue for twenty years.

ARTICLE 8.

When the head of a family or lodge shall have selected lands and received his certificate as above directed, and the agent shall be satisfied that he intends in good faith to commence cultivating the soil for a living, he shall be entitled to receive seeds and agricultural implements for the first year, in value one hundred dollars, and for each succeeding year he shall continue to farm, for a period of three years more, he shall be entitled to receive seeds and implements as aforesaid in value twenty-five dollars per annum.

And it is further stipulated that such persons as commence farming shall receive instructions from the farmers herein provided for, and whenever more than one hundred persons on either reservation shall enter upon the cultivation of the soil, a second blacksmith shall be provided, with such iron, steel, and other material as may be required.

ARTICLE 9.

In lieu of all sums of money or other annuities provided to be paid to the Indians herein named, under any and all treaties heretofore made with them, the United States agrees to deliver at the agency-house on the reservation here in provided for, on the first day of September of each year, for thirty years, the following articles, to wit:

For each male person over fourteen years of age, a suit of good substantial woollen clothing, consisting of coat, hat, pantaloons, flannel shirt, and a pair of woollen socks; for each female over twelve years of age, a flannel skirt, or the goods necessary to make it, a pair of woollen hose, twelve yards of calico; and twelve yards of cotton domestics.

For the boys and girls under the ages named, such flannel and cotton goods as may be needed to make each a suit as aforesaid, together with a pair of woollen hose for each.

And in order that the Commissioner of Indian Affairs may be able to estimate properly for the articles herein named, it shall be the duty of the agent each year to forward to him a full and exact census of the Indians, on which the estimate from year to year can be based; and in addition to the clothing herein named, the sum of ten dollars shall be annually appropriated for each Indian roaming and twenty dollars for each Indian engaged in agriculture, for a period of ten years, to be used by the Secretary of the Interior in the purchase of such articles as from time to time the condition and necessities of the Indians may indicate to be proper. And if at any time within the ten years it shall appear that the amount of money needed for clothing under this article can be appropriated to better uses for the tribes herein named, Congress may by law change the appropriation to other purposes; but in no event shall the amount of this appropriation be withdrawn or discontinued for the period named. And the President shall annually detail an officer of the Army to be present and attest the delivery of all the goods herein named to the Indians, and he shall inspect and report on the quantity and quality of the goods and the manner of their delivery.

ARTICLE 10.

The United States hereby agrees to furnish annually to the Indians the physician, teachers, carpenter, miller, engineer, farmer, and blacksmith, as herein contemplated, and that such appropriations shall be made from time to time, on the estimates of the Secretary of the Interior, as will be sufficient to employ such persons.

ARTICLE 11.

No treaty for the cession of any portion of the reservations herein described which may be held in common shall be of any force or validity as against the said Indians, unless executed and signed by at least a majority of all the adult male Indians occupying or interested in the same; and no cession by the tribe shall be understood or construed in such manner as to deprive without his consent, any individual member of the tribe of his right to any tract of land selected by him, as provided in Article 6 of this treaty.

ARTICLE 12.

It is agreed that the sum of five hundred dollars annually, for three years from the date when they commence to cultivate a farm, shall be expended in presents to the ten persons of said tribe who, in the judgment of the agent, may grow the most valuable crops for the respective year.

ARTICLE 13.

It is further agreed that until such time as the agency-buildings are established on the Shoshonee reservation, their agent shall reside at Fort Bridger, U. T., and their annuities shall be delivered to them at the same place in June of each year.

    N. G. Taylor, [SEAL.],
    W. T. Sherman, [SEAL.] Lieutenant-
      General.Wm. S. Harney, [SEAL.],
    John B. Sanborn, [SEAL.],
    S. F. Tappan, [SEAL.],
    C. C. Augur, [SEAL.],
    Brevet Major-General, U. S. Army,
      Commissioners.,
    Alfred H. Terry, [SEAL.],
    Brigadier-General and Brevet Major-General,
      U. S. Army

Attest:
A. S. H. White, Secretary

Shoshones:
Wash-a-kie, his x mark,
Wau-ny-pitz, his x mark,
Toop-se-po-wot, his x mark,
Nar-kok, his x mark,
Taboonshe-ya, his x mark,
Bazeel, his x mark,
Pan-to-she-ga, his x mark,
Ninny-Bitse, his x mark.

Bannacks:
Taggee, his x mark.
Tay-to-ba, his x mark.
We-rat-ze-won-a-gen, his x mark.
Coo-sha-gan, his x mark.

Pan-sook-a-motse, his x mark.
A-wite-etse, his x mark.

Witnesses:
Henry A. Morrow,
Lieutenant-Colonel Thirty-sixth Infantry and,
Brevet Colonel U. S. Army. Commanding Fort
    Bridger,
Luther Manpa, United States Indian agent,
W. A. Carter,
J. Van Allen Carter, interpreter.

Treaties 1 and 2, 1871
Treaty No. 1, Aug 3, 1871
Treaty No. 2. Aug. 21, 1871
Between Her Majesty the Queen and the Chippewa and Cree Indians of Manitoba and Country Adjacent with Adhesions
Treaty No. 1

ARTICLES OF A TREATY made and concluded this third day of August in the year of Our Lord one thousand eight hundred and seventy-one, between Her Most Gracious Majesty the Queen of Great Britain and Ireland by Her Commissioner, Wemyss M. Simpson, Esquire, of the one part, and the Chippewa and Swampy Cree Tribes of Indians, inhabitants of the country within the limits hereinafter defined and described, by their Chiefs chosen and named as hereinafter mentioned, of the other part.

Whereas all the Indians inhabiting the said country have pursuant to an appointment made by the said Commissioner, been convened at a meeting at the Stone Fort, otherwise called Lower Fort Garry, to deliberate upon certain matters of interest to Her Most Gracious Majesty, of the one part, and to the said Indians of the other, and whereas the said Indians have been notified and informed by Her Majesty's said Commissioner that it is the desire of Her Majesty to open up to settlement and immigration a tract of country bounded and described as hereinafter mentioned, and to obtain the consent thereto of her Indian subjects inhabiting the said tract, and to make a treaty and arrangements with them so that there may be peace and good will between them and Her Majesty, and that they may know and be assured of what allowance they are to count upon and receive year by year from Her ajesty's bounty and benevolence.

And whereas the Indians of the said tract, duly convened in council as aforesaid, and being requested by Her Majesty's said Commissioner to name certain Chiefs and Headmen who should be authorized on their behalf to conduct such negotiations and sign any treaty to be founded thereon, and to become responsible to Her Majesty for the faithful performance by their respective bands of such obligations as should be assumed by them, the said Indians have thereupon named the following persons for that purpose, that is to say:

Mis-koo-kenew or Red Eagle (Henry Prince), Ka-ke-ka-penais, or Bird for ever, Na-sha-ke-penais, or Flying down bird, Na-na-wa-nanaw, or Centre of Bird's Tail, Ke-we-tayash, or Flying round, Wa-ko-wush, or Whip-poor-will, Oo-za-we-kwun, or Yellow Quill,— and thereupon in open council the different bands have presented their respective Chiefs to His Excellency the Lieutenant Governor of the Province of Manitoba and of the North-West Territory being present at such council, and to the said Commissioner, as the Chiefs and Headman for the purposes aforesaid of the respective bands of Indians inhabiting the said district hereinafter described; and whereas the said Lieutenant Governor and the said Commissioner then and there received and acknowledged the persons so presented as Chiefs and Headmen for the purpose aforesaid; and whereas the said Commissioner has proceeded to negotiate a treaty with the said Indians, and the same has finally been agreed upon and concluded as follows, that is to say:

The Chippewa and Swampy Cree Tribes of Indians and all other the Indians inhabiting the district hereinafter described and defined do hereby cede, release, surrender and yield up to Her Majesty the Queen and successors forever all the lands included within the following limits, that is to say: Beginning at the international boundary line near its junction with the Lake of the Woods, at a point due north from the centre of Roseau Lake; thence to run due north to the centre of Roseau Lake; thence northward to the centre of White Mouth Lake, otherwise called White Mud Lake; thence by the middle of the lake and the middle of the river issuing therefrom to the mouth thereof in Winnipeg River; thence by the Winnipeg River to its mouth; thence westwardly, including all the islands near the south end of the lake, across the lake to the mouth of Drunken River; thence westwardly to a point on Lake Manitoba half

way between Oak Point and the mouth of Swan Creek; thence across Lake Manitoba in a line due west to its western shore; thence in a straight line to the crossing of the rapids on the Assiniboine; thence due south to the international boundary line; and thence eastwardly by the said line to the place of beginning. To have and to hold the same to Her said Majesty the Queen and Her successors for ever; and Her Majesty the Queen hereby agrees and undertakes to lay aside and reserve for the sole and exclusive use of the Indians the following tracts of land, that is to say: For the use of the Indians belonging to the band of which Henry Prince, otherwise called Mis-koo-ke-new is the Chief, so much of land on both sides of the Red River, beginning at the south line of St. Peter's Parish, as will furnish one hundred and sixty acres for each family of five, or in that proportion for larger or smaller families; and for the use of the Indians of whom Na-sha-ke-penais, Na-na-wa-nanaw, Ke-we-tayash and Wa-ko-wush are the Chiefs, so much land on the Roseau River as will furnish one hundred and sixty acres for each family of five, or in that proportion for larger or smaller families, beginning from the mouth of the river; and for the use of the Indians of which Ka-ke-ka-penais is the Chief, so much land on the Winnipeg River above Fort Alexander as will furnish one hundred and sixty acres for each family of five, or in that proportion for larger or smaller families, beginning at a distance of a mile or thereabout above the Fort; and for the use of the Indians of whom Oo-za-we-kwun is Chief, so much land on the south and east side of the Assiniboine, about twenty miles above the Portage, as will furnish one hundred and sixty acres for each family of five, or in that proportion for larger or smaller families, reserving also a further tract enclosing said reserve to comprise an equivalent to twenty-five square miles of equal breadth, to be laid out round the reserve, it being understood, however, that if, at the date of the execution of this treaty, there are any settlers within the bounds of any lands reserved by any band, Her Majesty reserves the right to deal with such settlers as She shall deem just, so as not to diminish the extent of land allotted to the Indians.

And with a view to show the satisfaction of Her Majesty with the behaviour and good conduct of Her Indians parties to this treaty, She hereby, through Her Commissioner, makes them a present of three dollars for each Indian man, woman and child belonging to the bands here represented.

And further, Her Majesty agrees to maintain a school on each reserve hereby made whenever the Indians of the reserve should desire it.

Within the boundary of Indian reserves, until otherwise enacted by the proper legislative authority, no intoxicating liquor shall be allowed to be introduced or sold, and all laws now in force or hereafter to be enacted to preserve Her Majesty's Indian subjects inhabiting the reserves or living elsewhere from the evil influence of the use of intoxicating liquors shall be strictly enforced.

Her Majesty's Commissioner shall, as soon as possible after the execution of this treaty, cause to be taken an accurate census of all the Indians inhabiting the district above described, distributing them in families, and shall in every year ensuing the date hereof, at some period during the month of July in each year, to be duly notified to the Indians and at or near their respective reserves, pay to each Indian family of five persons the sum of fifteen dollars Canadian currency, or in like proportion for a larger or smaller family, such payment to be made in such articles as the Indians shall require of blankets, clothing, prints (assorted colours), twine or traps, at the current cost price in Montreal, or otherwise, if Her Majesty shall deem the same desirable in the interests of Her Indian people, in cash.

And the undersigned Chiefs do hereby bind and pledge themselves and their people strictly to observe this treaty and to maintain perpetual peace between themselves and Her Majesty's white subjects, and not to interfere with the property or in any way molest the persons of Her Majesty's white or other subjects.

IN WITNESS WHEREOF, Her Majesty's said Commissioner and the said Indian Chiefs have hereunto subscribed and set their hand and seal at Lower Fort Garry, this day and year herein first above named.
Signed, sealed and delivered in the presence of, the same having been first read and explained:

ADAMS G. ARCHIBALD,
Lieut.-Gov. of Man. and N.W. Territories.
JAMES McKAY, P.L.C.
A. G. IRVINE, Major,
ABRAHAM COWLEY,
DONALD GUNN, M.L.C.,

THOMAS HOWARD, P.S.,
HENRY COCHRANE,
JAMES McARRISTER,
HUGH McARRISTER,
E. ALICE ARCHIBALD,
HENRI BOUTHILLIER,
WEMYSS M. SIMPSON. [L.S.], Indian Commissioner,
MIS-KOO-KEE-NEW, or RED EAGLE, (HENRY PRINCE), his x mark,
KA-KE-KA-PENAIS (or BIRD FOR EVER), WILLIAM PENNEFATHER, his x mark,
NA-SHA-KE-PENNAIS, or FLYING DOWN BIRD, his x mark,
NA-HA-WA-NANAN, or CENTRE OF BIRD'S TAIL, his x mark,
KE-WE-TAY-ASH, or FLYINGROUND, his x mark,
WA-KO-WUSH, or WHIP-POOR-WILL, his x mark,
OO-ZA-WE-KWUN, or YELLOW QUILL, his x mark

Memorandum of things outside of the Treaty which were promised at the Treaty at the Lower Fort, signed the third day of August, A.D. 1871.

- For each Chief who signed the treaty, a dress distinguishing him as Chief.
- For braves and for councillors of each Chief a dress; it being supposed that the braves and councillors will be two for each Chief.
- For each Chief, except Yellow Quill, a buggy.
- For the braves and councillors of each Chief, except Yellow Quill, a buggy.
- In lieu of a yoke of oxen for each reserve, a bull for each, and a cow for each Chief; a boar for each reserve and a sow for each Chief, and a male and female of each kind of animal raised by farmers, these when the Indians are prepared to receive them.
- A plough and a harrow for each settler cultivating the ground.
- These animals and their issue to be Government property, but to be allowed for the use of the Indians, under the superintendence and control of the Indian Commissioner.
- The buggies to be the property of the Indians to whom they are given.
- The above contains an inventory of the terms concluded with the Indians.

WEMYSS M. SIMPSON,
MOLYNEUX St. JOHN,
A. G. ARCHIBALD,
JAS. McKAY.

COPY of a Report of a Committee of the Honourable the Privy Council, approved by His Excellency the Governor General in Council on the 30th April, 1875.

On a memorandum dated 27th April, 1875, from the Honourable the Minister of the Interior, bringing under consideration the very unsatisfactory state of affairs arising out of the so-called "outside promises" in connection with the Indian Treaties Nos. 1 and 2, Manitoba and North-west Territories, concluded, the former on the 3rd August, 1871, and the latter on 21st of the same month, and recommending for the reasons stated:

1st. That the written memorandum attached to Treaty No. 1 be considered as part of that Treaty and of Treaty No. 2, and that the Indian Commissioner be instructed to carry out the promises therein contained, in so far as they have not yet been carried out, and that the Commissioner be advised to inform the Indians that he has been authorized so to do.

2nd. That the Indian Commissioner be instructed to inform the Indians, parties to Treaties Nos. 1 and 2, that, while the Government cannot admit their claim to any thing which is not set forth in the treaty, and in the memorandum attached thereto, which treaty is binding alike upon the Government and upon the Indians, yet, as there seems to have been some misunderstanding between the Indian Commissioner and the Indians in the matter of Treaties Nos. 1 and 2, the Government, out of good feeling to the Indians and as a matter of benevolence, is willing to raise the annual payment to each Indian under Treaties Nos. 1 and 2, from $3 to $5 per annum, and make payment over and above such sum of $5, of $20 each and every year to each Chief, and a suit of clothing every three years to each Chief and each Headman, allowing two Headmen to each band, on the express understanding, however, that each Chief or other Indian who shall receive such increased annuity or annual payment shall be held to abandon all claim whatever against the Government in connection with the so-called "outside promises," other than those contained in the memorandum attached to the treaty.

The Committee submit the foregoing recommendation for Your Excellency's approval:

W. A. HIMSWORTH,
Clerk Privy Council.

Certified,
W. A. HIMSWORTH,
Clerk Privy Council.

We, the undersigned Chiefs and Headmen of Indian bands, representing bands of Indians who were parties to the Treaties Nos. 1 and 2, mentioned in the report of the Committee of the Queen's Privy Council of Canada, above printed, having had communication thereof, and fully understanding the same assent thereto and accept the increase of annuities therein mentioned, on the condition therein stated, and with the assent and approval of their several bands, it being agreed, however, with the Queen's Commissioners, that the number of braves and councillors for each Chief shall be four, as at present, instead of two, as printed 1875.

In the presence of the following:

ALEX. MORRIS, L.G. [S.L.].
JAMES McKAY.
ISAAC COWIE.
FRANCIS FIELD.
JOHN A. DAVIDSON.
CHARLES WOOD.

Representing East-Manitoba or Elm Point:
SON-SONSE, chief, his x mark,
NA-KA-NA-WA-TANG, his x mark,
PA-PA-WE-GUN-WA-TAK, his x mark,

Councillors.
Representing Fairford Prairie:
MA-SAH-KEE-YASH, chief, his x mark,
DAVID MARSDEN, Councillor, his x mark,
JOSEPH SUMNER, Councillor, his x mark,

Representing Fairford Prairie:
RICHARD WOODHOUSE, chief,
JOHN ANDERSON, Councillor,
JOHN THOMPSON, Councillor, his x mark

Formerly Crane River and now Ebb and Flow Lake:
    PENAISE, chief, his x mark (son of deceased Broken Finger.),
    BAPTISTE, Councillor, his x mark,
    KAH-NEE-QUA-NASH, Councillor, his x mark,

Representing Water Hen Band:
    KA-TAH-KAK-WA-NA-YAAS, chief, his x mark,
    WA-WAH-KOW-WEK-AH-POW, Councillor, his x mark,

Représentants de la rivière de la Tortue et de la rivière de la Vallée ainsi que de Riding Mountain:
    KEE-SICK-KOO-WE-NIN, chief, his x mark (in place of Mekis, dead.),
    KEE-SAY-KEE-SICK, Councillor, his x mark,
    NOS-QUASH, brave, his x mark,
    BAPTISTE, brave, his x mark,

Representing the St. Peter's Band:
    MIS-KOO-KE-NEW, (or Red Eagle), his x mark,
    MA-TWA-KA-KEE-TOOT, his x mark,
    I-AND-WAY-WAY, his x mark,
    MA-KO-ME-WE-KUN, his x mark,
    AS-SHO-AH-MEY, his x mark.

No. 124
We, the undersigned Chiefs and Headmen of Indian bands representing bands of Indians who were parties to the Treaties Nos. 1 and 2, mentioned in the report of a Committee of the Queen's Privy Council of Canada, "as printed on the other side of this parchment," having had communication thereof and fully understanding the same, assent thereto and accept the increase of annuities therein mentioned on the condition therein stated, and with the assent and approval of their several bands, it being agreed, however, with the Queen's Commissioners, that the number of braves and councillors for each Chief shall be four, as at present, instead of two, as printed 1875.

Signed near Fort Alexander, on the Indian Reserve, the twenty-third day of August in the year of Our Lord one thousand eight hundred and seventy-five.

Witnesses:
J. A. N. PROVENCHER, Indian Commissioner.
J. DUBUC,
A. DUBUC,
JOSEPH MONKMAN, Interpreter.

WM. LOUNT,
H. L. REYNOLDS.
KAKEKEPENAIS, or (WILLIAM PENNEFATHER), his x mark,
JOSEPH KENT, his x mark,
PETANAQUAGE, or (HENRY VANE), his x mark,
PETER HENDERSON, his x mark,
KAY-PAYAHSINISK, his x mark.

Signed at Broken Head River, the twenty-eighth day of August, in the year of our Lord one thousand eight hundred and seventy-five.

Witnesses:
J. A. N. PROVENCHER, Indian Commissioner.
J. DUBUC,
H. L. REYNOLDS,
DANIEL DEVLIN,
HENRY COOK.
NASHAKEPENAIS, his x mark
AHKEESEEKWASKEMG, his x mark
NAYWAHEHEEKEEGIK, his x mark
MAYJAHKEEGEEQUAN, his x mark
PAYSAUGA, his x mark

124
We the undersigned Chiefs and Headmen of Indian bands representing bands of Indians who were parties to the Treaties Nos. 1 and 2 mentioned in the report of a Committee of the Queen's Privy Council of Canada, as printed on the other side of this sheet, having had communication thereof and full understanding of the same, assent thereto and accept the increase of annuities therein mentioned, on the condition therein stated, and with the assent and approval of their several bands, it being agreed, however, with the Queen's Commissioners, that the number of braves and councillors for each Chief shall be four, as at present, instead of two, as printed.

Signed on the reserve at Rosseau River, 8th day of September, 1875.

J. A. N. PROVENCHER,
Indian Commissioner.

Witness:
JAS. F. GRAHAM.
MA-NA-WA-NANAN, (or CENTRE OF BIRD'S TAIL) Chief, his x mark,

KE-WE-SAY-ASH, (or FLYING ROUND), Chief,
 his x mark,
WA-KOO-WUSH, (or WHIPPOORWILL) Chief,
 his x mark,
OSAH-WEE-KA-KAY, Councillor, his x mark,
OSAYS-KOO-KOON, Councillor, his x mark,
SHAY-WAY-ASH, Councillor, his x mark,
SHE-SHE-PENSE, Councillor, his x mark,
MA-MAH-TAK-CUM-E-CUP, Councillor, his x
 mark,
PAH-TE-CU-WEE-NINN, Councillor, his x
 mark,
PAH-TE-CU-WEE-NINN, Councillor, his x
 mark,
AK-KA-QUIN-IASH, Brave, his x mark,
ANA-WAY-WEE-TIN, Brave, his x mark,
TIBIS-QUO-GE-SICK, Brave, his x mark,
NE-SHO-TA, Brave, his x mark,
NAT-TEE-KEE-GET, Brave, his x mark

Treaty No. 2

ARTICLES OF TREATY made and concluded this twenty-first day of August, in the year of Our Lord one thousand eight hundred and seventy-one, between Her Most Gracious Majesty the Queen of Great Britain and Ireland, by Her Commissioner Wemyss M. Simpson, Esquire, of the one part, and the Chippewa Tribe of Indians, inhabitants of the country within the limits hereinafter defined and described, by their Chiefs chosen and named as hereinafter mentioned, of the other part.

Whereas, all the Indians inhabiting the said country have, pursuant to an appointment made by the said Commissioner, been convened at a meeting at Manitoba Post to deliberate upon certain matters of interest to Her Most Gracious Majesty, of the one part, and to the said Indians of the other; and whereas the said Indians have been notified and informed by Her Majesty's said Commissioner that it is the desire of Her Majesty to open up to settlement and immigration a tract of country bounded and described as hereinafter mentioned and to obtain the consent thereto of her Indian subjects inhabiting the said tract, and to make a treaty and arrangement with them, so that there may be peace and good will between them and Her Majesty and that they may know and be assured of what allowance they are to count upon and receive from Her Majesty's bounty and benevolence.

And whereas the Indians of the said tract, duly convened in council as aforesaid, and being requested by Her Majesty's said Commissioner to name certain Chiefs and Headmen who should be authorized on their behalf to conduct such negotiations and sign any treaty to be founded thereon, and to become responsible to Her Majesty for the faithful performance by their respective bands of such obligations as shall be assumed by them, the said Indians have thereupon named the following persons for that purpose, that is to say:

For the Swan Creek and Lake Manitoba Indians, Sou-sonse or Little Long Ears; for the Indians of Fairford and the neighboring localities, Ma-sah-kee-yash or "He who flies to the bottom," and Richard Woodhouse, whose Indian name is Ke-wee-tah-quun-na-yash or "He who flies round the feathers"; for the Indians of Waterhen River and Crane River and the neighboring localities, Francois, or Broken Fingers; and for the Indians of Riding Mountains and Dauphin Lake and the remainder of the territory hereby ceded, Mekis (the Eagle), or Giroux.

And, thereupon, in open council the different bands have presented their respective Chiefs to His Excellency the Lieutenant Governor of Manitoba and of the North-west Territory being present at such council and to the said Commissioner, as the Chiefs and Headmen, for the purposes aforesaid, of the respective bands of Indians inhabiting the said district hereinafter described; and whereas the said Lieutenant Governor and the said Commissioner then and there received and acknowledged the persons so presented as Chiefs and Headmen for the purposes aforesaid of the respective bands of Indians inhabiting the said district hereinafter described; and whereas the said Commissioner has proceeded to negotiate a treaty with the said Indians, and the same has finally been agreed upon and concluded, as follows, that is to say:

The Chippewa Tribe of Indians and all other the Indians inhabiting the district hereinafter described and defined do hereby cede, release, surrender and yield up to Her Majesty the Queen, and Her successors forever, all the lands included within the following limits, that is to say:

All that tract of country lying partly to the north and partly to the west of a tract of land ceded to Her

Majesty the Queen by the Indians inhabiting the Province of Manitoba, and certain adjacent localities, under the terms of a treaty made at Lower Fort Garry on the third day of August last past, the land now intended to be ceded and surrendered being particularly described as follows, that is to say: Beginning at the mouth of Winnipeg River, on the north line of the lands ceded by said treaty; thence running along the eastern shore of Lake Winnipeg northwardly as far as the mouth of Beren's River; thence across said lake to its western shore, at the north bank of the mouth of the Little Saskatchewan or Dauphin River; thence up said stream and along the northern and western shores thereof, and of St. Martin's Lake, and along the north bank of the stream flowing into St. Martin's Lake from Lake Manitoba by the general course of such stream to such last-mentioned lake; thence by the eastern and northern shores of Lake Manitoba to the mouth of the Waterhen River; thence by the eastern and northern shores of said river up stream to the northernmost extremity of a small lake known as Waterhen Lake; thence in a line due west to and across lake Winnepegosis; thence in a straight line to the most northerly waters forming the source of the Shell River; thence to a point west of the same two miles distant from the river, measuring at right angles thereto; thence by a line parallel with the Shell River to its mouth, and thence crossing the Assiniboine River and running parallel thereto and two miles distant therefrom, and to the westward thereof, to a point opposite Fort Ellice; thence in a south-westwardly course to the north-western point of the Moose Mountains; thence by a line due south to the United States frontier; thence by the frontier eastwardly to the westward line of said tract ceded by treaty as aforesaid; thence bounded thereby by the west, northwest and north lines of said tract, to the place of beginning, at the mouth of Winnipeg River. To have and to hold the same to Her Majesty the Queen and Her successors forever; and Her Majesty the Queen hereby agrees and undertakes to lay aside and reserve for the sole and exclusive use of the Indians inhabiting the said tract the following lots of land, that is to say:

For the use of the Indians belonging to the band of which Mekis is Chief, so much land between Turtle River and Valley River, on the south side of Lake Dauphin, as will make one hundred and sixty acres for each family of five persons, or in the same proportion for a greater or smaller number of persons.

And for the use of the Indians belonging to the band of which François, or Broken Fingers, is Chief, so much land on Crane River, running into Lake Manitoba, as will make one hundred and sixty acres for each family of five persons, or in the same proportion for a greater or smaller number of persons. And for the use of the band of Indians belonging to the bands of which Ma-sah-kee-yash and Richard Woodhouse are Chiefs, so much land on the river between Lake Manitoba and St. Martin's Lake, known as "Fairford River," and including the present Indian mission grounds, as will make one hundred and sixty acres for each family of five persons, or in the same proportion for a greater or smaller number of persons.

And for the use of the Indians of whom Sou-sonce is Chief, so much land on the east side of Lake Manitoba, to be laid off north of the creek near which a fallen elm tree now lies, and about half way between Oak Point and Manitoba Post, so much land as will make one hundred and sixty acres for each family of five persons, or in the same proportion for a greater or smaller number of persons. Saving, nevertheless, the rights of any white or other settler now in occupation of any lands within the lines of any such reserve.

And with a view to show the satisfaction of Her Majesty with the behaviour and good conduct of Her Indians, parties to this treaty, She hereby, through Her Commissioner, makes them a present of three dollars for each Indian man, woman and child belonging to the band here represented.

And further, Her Majesty agrees to maintain a school in each reserve hereby made, whenever the Indians of the reserve shall desire it.

Her Majesty further agrees with Her said Indians that within the boundary of Indian reserves, until otherwise enacted by the proper legislative authority, no intoxicating liquor shall be allowed to be introduced or sold, and all laws now in force or hereafter to be enacted to preserve Her Indian subjects inhabiting the reserves or living elsewhere within Her North-West Territories, from the evil influence of the use of intoxicating liquors, shall be strictly enforced.

And further, that Her Majesty's Commissioner shall, as soon as possible after the execution of this treaty, cause to be taken an accurate census of all the

Indians inhabiting the tract above described, distributing them in families, and shall in every year ensuing the date hereof, at some period during the month of August in each year to be duly notified to the Indians, and at or near their respective reserves, pay to each Indian family of five persons the sum of fifteen dollars, Canadian currency, or in like proportion for a larger or smaller family, such payment to be made in such articles as the Indians shall require of blankets, clothing, prints (assorted colours), twine or traps, at the current cash price in Montreal, or otherwise, if Her Majesty shall deem the same desirable in the interest of Her Indian people, in cash.

And the undersigned Chiefs, on their own behalf and on behalf of all other Indians inhabiting the tract within ceded, do hereby solemnly promise and engage to strictly observe this treaty, and also to conduct and behave themselves as good and loyal subjects of Her Majesty the Queen. They promise and engage that they will in all respects obey and abide by the law; that they will maintain peace and good order between each other, and also between themselves and other tribes of Indians, and between themselves and others of Her Majesty's subjects, whether Indians or whites, now inhabiting or hereafter to inhabit any part of the said ceded tract, and that they will not molest the person or property of any inhabitants of such ceded tract, or the property of Her Majesty the Queen, or interfere with or trouble any person passing or travelling through the said tract, or any part thereof, and that they will aid and assist the officers of Her Majesty in bringing to justice and punishment any Indian offending against the stipulations of this treaty, or infringing the laws in force in the country so ceded.

IN WITNESS WHEREOF, Her Majesty's said Commissioner and the said Indian Chiefs have hereunto subscribed and set their hands at Manitoba Post this day and year herein first above named.

Signed by the Chiefs within named, in presence of the following witnesses, the same having been first read and explained:

ADAMS G. ARCHIBALD,
Lieut. Gov. of Manitoba and the N.-W.
    Territories,

JAMES McKAY, P.L.C.,
MOLYNEUX St. JOHN,

E. A. ARCHIBALD,
LILY ARCHIBALD,
HENRI BOUTHILLIER,
PAUL DE LARONDE,
DONALD McDONALD,
ELIZA McDONALD,
ALEXANDER MUIR, Sr.,
WEMYSS M. SIMPSON, [L.S.] Indian
    Commissioner,
MEKIS, his x mark,
SOU-SONCE, his x mark,
MA-SAH-KEE-YASH, his x mark,
FRANÇOIS, his x mark,
RICHARD WOODHOUSE.

Treaty 3, 1871

Oct. 3, 1873
Between Her Majesty the Queen and the Saulteaux Tribe of the Ojibbeway Indians at the Northwest Angle on the Lake of the Woods with Adhesions

ORDER IN COUNCIL SETTING UP COMMISSION FOR TREATY 3

The Committee have had under consideration the memorandum dated 19th April, 1871, from the Hon. the Secretary of State for the provinces submitting with reference to his report of the 17th of the same month that the Indians mentioned in the last paragraph of that report and with whom it will be necessary first to deal occupy the country from the water shed of Lake Superior to the north west angle of the Lake of the Woods and from the American border to the height of land from which the streams flow towards Hudson's Bay.

That they are composed of Saulteaux and Lac Seul Indians of the Ojibbeway Nation, and number about twenty-five hundred men, women and children, and, retaining what they desire in reserves at certain localities where they fish for sturgeon, would, it is thought be willing to surrender for a certain annual payment their lands to the Crown. That the American Indians to the south of them surrendered their lands to the Government of the United States for an annual payment which has been stated to him (but not on authority) to amount to ten dollars per head for each man, woman and child of which six dollars is paid in goods and four in money. That to treat with these Indians with advantage he recommends that Mr. Simon J. Dawson of the Department of Public Works and Mr. Robert Pither of the Hudson's Bay Company's service be associated with Mr. Wemyss M. Simpson—and further that the presents which were promised the Indians last year and a similar quantity for the present year should be collected at Fort Francis not later than the middle of June also that four additional suits of Chiefs' clothes and flags should be added to those now in store at Fort Francis—and further that a small house and store for provisions should be constructed at Rainy River at the site and of the dimensions which Mr. Simpson may deem best—that the assistance of the Department of Public Works will be necessary should his report be adopted in carrying into effect the recommendations therein made as to provisions, clothes and construction of buildings.

He likewise submits that it will be necessary that the sum of Six Thousand dollars in silver should be at Fort Francis subject to the Order of the above named Commissioners on the fifteenth day of June next—And further recommends that in the instructions to be given to them they should be directed to make the best arrangements in their power but authorized if need be to give as much as twelve dollars a family for each family not exceeding five—with such small Sum in addition where the family exceeds five as the Commissioners may find necessary—Such Subsidy to be made partly in goods and provisions and partly in money or wholly in goods and provisions should the Commissioners so decide for the surrender of the lands described in the earlier part of this report.

The Committee concur in the foregoing recommendations and submit the same for Your Excellency's approval.

Signed: Charles Tupper
25 April/71

TREATY No. 3
ARTICLES OF A TREATY made and concluded this third day of October, in the year of Our Lord one thousand eight hundred and seventy-three, between Her Most Gracious Majesty the Queen of Great Britain and Ireland, by Her Commissioners, the Honourable Alexander Morris, Lieutenant-Governor of the Province of Manitoba and the North-west Territories; Joseph Alfred Norbert Provencher and Simon James Dawson, of the one part, and the Saulteaux Tribe of the Ojibway Indians, inhabitants of

the country within the limits hereinafter defined and described, by their Chiefs chosen and named as hereinafter mentioned, of the other part.

Whereas the Indians inhabiting the said country have, pursuant to an appointment made by the said Commissioners, been convened at a meeting at the north-west angle of the Lake of the Woods to deliberate upon certain matters of interest to Her Most Gracious Majesty, of the one part, and the said Indians of the other.

And whereas the said Indians have been notified and informed by Her Majesty's said Commissioners that it is the desire of Her Majesty to open up for settlement, immigration and such other purpose as to Her Majesty may seem meet, a tract of country bounded and described as hereinafter mentioned, and to obtain the consent thereto of Her Indian subjects inhabiting the said tract, and to make a treaty and arrange with them so that there may be peace and good will between them and Her Majesty and that they may know and be assured of what allowance they are to count upon and receive from Her Majesty's bounty and benevolence.

And whereas the Indians of the said tract, duly convened in council as aforesaid, and being requested by Her Majesty's said Commissioners to name certain Chiefs and Headmen, who should be authorized on their behalf to conduct such negotiations and sign any treaty to be founded thereon, and to become responsible to Her Majesty for their faithful performance by their respective bands of such obligations as shall be assumed by them, the said Indians have thereupon named the following persons for that purpose, that is to say:—

KEK-TA-PAY-PI-NAIS (Rainy River.),
KITCHI-GAY-KAKE (Rainy River.),
NOTE-NA-QUA-HUNG (North-West Angle.),
NAWE-DO-PE-NESS (Rainy River.),
POW-WA-SANG (North-West Angle.),
CANDA-COM-IGO-WE-NINIE (North-West Angle.),
PAPA-SKO-GIN (Rainy River.),
MAY-NO-WAH-TAW-WAYS-KIONG (North-West Angle.),
KITCHI-NE-KA-LE-HAN (Rainy River.),
SAH-KATCH-EWAY (Lake Seul.),
MUPA-DAY-WAH-SIN (Kettle Falls.),
ME-PIE-SIES (Rainy Lake, Fort Frances.),

OOS-CON-NA-GEITH (Rainy Lake.),
WAH-SHIS-KOUCE (Eagle Lake.),
KAH-KEE-Y-ASH (Flower Lake.),
GO-BAY (Rainy Lake.),
KA-MO-TI-ASH (White Fish Lake.),
NEE-SHO-TAL (Rainy River.),
KEE-JE-GO-KAY (Rainy River.),
SHA-SHA-GANCE (Shoal Lake.),
SHAH-WIN-NA-BI-NAIS (Shoal Lake.),
AY-ASH-A-WATH (Buffalo Point.),
PAY-AH-BEE-WASH (White Fish Bay.),
KAH-TAY-TAY-PA-E-CUTCH (Lake of the
    Woods.)

And thereupon, in open council, the different bands having presented their Chiefs to the said Commissioners as the Chiefs and Headmen for the purposes aforesaid of the respective bands of Indians inhabiting the said district hereinafter described:

And whereas the said Commissioners then and there received and acknowledged the persons so presented as Chiefs and Headmen for the purpose aforesaid of the respective bands of Indians inhabiting the said district hereinafter described;

And whereas the said Commissioners have proceeded to negotiate a treaty with the said Indians, and the same has been finally agreed upon and concluded, as follows, that is to say:—

The Saulteaux Tribe of the Ojibbeway Indians and all other the Indians inhabiting the district hereinafter described and defined, do hereby cede, release, surrender and yield up to the Government of the Dominion of Canada for Her Majesty the Queen and Her successors forever, all their rights, titles and privileges whatsoever, to the lands included within the following limits, that is to say:—

Commencing at a point on the Pigeon River route where the international boundary line between the Territories of Great Britain and the United States intersects the height of land separating the waters running to Lake Superior from those flowing to Lake Winnipeg; thence northerly, westerly and easterly along the height of land aforesaid, following its sinuosities, whatever their course may be, to the point at which the said height of land meets the summit of the watershed from which the streams flow to Lake Nepigon; thence northerly and westerly, or whatever may be its course, along the ridge separating the waters of the Nepigon and the Winnipeg to the height of land dividing the waters of the Albany and the Winnipeg; thence westerly and north-westerly along the height of land dividing the waters flowing to Hudson's Bay by the Albany or other rivers from those running to English River and the Winnipeg to a point on the said height of land bearing north forty-five degrees east from Fort Alexander, at the mouth of the Winnipeg; thence south forty-five degrees west to Fort Alexander, at the mouth of the Winnipeg; thence southerly along the eastern bank of the Winnipeg to the mouth of White Mouth River; thence southerly by the line described as in that part forming the eastern boundary of the tract surrendered by the Chippewa and Swampy Cree tribes of Indians to Her Majesty on the third of August, one thousand eight hundred and seventy-one, namely, by White Mouth River to White Mouth Lake, and thence on a line having the general bearing of White Mouth River to the forty-ninth parallel of north latitude; thence by the forty-ninth parallel of north latitude to the Lake of the Woods, and from thence by the international boundary line to the place beginning.

The tract comprised within the lines above described, embracing an area of fifty-five thousand square miles, be the same more or less. To have and to hold the same to Her Majesty the Queen, and Her successors forever.

And Her Majesty the Queen hereby agrees and undertakes to lay aside reserves for farming lands, due respect being had to lands at present cultivated by the said Indians, and also to lay aside and reserve for the benefit of the said Indians, to be administered and dealt with for them by Her Majesty's Government of the Dominion of Canada, in such a manner as shall seem best, other reserves of land in the said territory hereby ceded, which said reserves shall be selected and set aside where it shall be deemed most convenient and advantageous for each band or bands of Indians, by the officers of the said Government appointed for that purpose, and such selection shall be so made after conference with the Indians; provided, however, that such reserves, whether for farming or other purposes, shall in no wise exceed in all one square mile for each family of five, or in that proportion for larger or smaller families; and such selections shall be made if possible during the course of next summer, or as soon thereafter as may be found practicable, it being understood, however, that if at the time of any such selection of any reserve, as aforesaid, there are any settlers within the bounds of the lands reserved by any band, Her Majesty reserves the right to deal with such settlers as She shall deem just so as not to diminish the extent of land allotted to Indians; and provided also that the aforesaid reserves of lands, or any interest or right therein or appurtenant thereto, may be sold, leased or otherwise disposed of by the said Government for the use and benefit of the said Indians, with the consent of the Indians entitled thereto first had and obtained.

And with a view to show the satisfaction of Her Majesty with the behaviour and good conduct of Her Indians She hereby, through Her Commissioners, makes them a present of twelve dollars for each man, woman and child belonging to the bands here represented, in extinguishment of all claims heretofore preferred.

And further, Her Majesty agrees to maintain schools for instruction in such reserves hereby made as to Her Government of Her Dominion of Canada may seem advisable whenever the Indians of the reserve shall desire it.

Her Majesty further agrees with Her said Indians that within the boundary of Indian reserves, until otherwise determined by Her Government of the Dominion of Canada, no intoxicating liquor shall be allowed to be introduced or sold, and all laws now in force or hereafter to be enacted to preserve Her Indian subjects inhabiting the reserves or living elsewhere within Her North-west Territories, from the evil influences of the use of intoxicating liquors, shall be strictly enforced.

Her Majesty further agrees with Her said Indians that they, the said Indians, shall have right to pursue their avocations of hunting and fishing throughout the tract surrendered as hereinbefore described, subject to such regulations as may from time to time be made by Her Government of Her Dominion of Canada, and saving and excepting such tracts as may, from time to time, be required or taken up for settlement, mining, lumbering or other purposes by Her said Government of the Dominion of Canada, or by any of the subjects thereof duly authorized therefor by the said Government.

It is further agreed between Her Majesty and Her said Indians that such sections of the reserves above indicated as may at any time be required for Public Works or buildings of what nature soever may be appropriated for that purpose by Her Majesty's Government of the Dominion of Canada, due compensation being made for the value of any improvements thereon.

And further, that Her Majesty's Commissioners shall, as soon as possible after the execution of this treaty, cause to be taken an accurate census of all the Indians inhabiting the tract above described, distributing them in families, and shall in every year ensuing the date hereof, at some period in each year to be duly notified to the Indians, and at a place or places to be appointed for that purpose within the territory ceded, pay to each Indian person the sum of five dollars per head yearly.

It is further agreed between Her Majesty and the said Indians that the sum of fifteen hundred dollars per annum shall be yearly and every year expended by Her Majesty in the purchase of ammunition and twine for nets for the use of the said Indians.

It is further agreed between Her Majesty and the said Indians that the following articles shall be supplied to any band of the said Indians who are now actually cultivating the soil or who shall hereafter commence to cultivate the land, that is to say: two hoes for every family actually cultivating, also one spade per family as aforesaid, one plough for every ten families as aforesaid, five harrows for every twenty families as aforesaid, one scythe for every family as aforesaid, and also one axe and one cross-cut saw, one hand-saw, one pit-saw, the necessary files, one grind-stone, one auger for each band, and also for each Chief for the use of his band one chest of ordinary carpenter's tools; also for each band enough of wheat, barley, potatoes and oats to plant the land actually broken up for cultivation by such band; also for each band one yoke of oxen, one bull and four cows; all the aforesaid articles to be given once for all for the encouragement of the practice of agriculture among the Indians.

It is further agreed between Her Majesty and the said Indians that each Chief duly recognized as such shall receive an annual salary of twenty-five dollars per annum, and each subordinate officer, not exceeding three for each band, shall receive fifteen dollars per annum; and each such Chief and subordinate officer as aforesaid shall also receive once in every three years a suitable suit of clothing; and each Chief shall receive, in recognition of the closing of the treaty, a suitable flag and medal.

And the undersigned Chiefs, on their own behalf and on behalf of all other Indians inhabiting the tract within ceded, do hereby solemnly promise and engage to strictly observe this treaty, and also to conduct and behave themselves as good and loyal subjects of Her Majesty the Queen. They promise and engage that they will in all respects obey and abide by the law, that they will maintain peace and good order between each other, and also between themselves and other tribes of Indians, and between themselves and others of Her Majesty's subjects, whether Indians or whites, now inhabiting or hereafter to inhabit any part of the said ceded tract, and that they will not molest the person or property of any inhabitants of such ceded tract, or the property of Her Majesty the Queen, or interfere with or trouble any person passing or travelling through the said tract, or any part thereof; and that they will aid and assist the officers of Her Majesty in bringing to justice and punishment any Indian offending against the stipulations of this treaty, or infringing the laws in force in the country so ceded.

IN WITNESS WHEREOF, Her Majesty's said Commissioners and the said Indian Chiefs have hereunto subscribed and set their hands at the North-West Angle of the Lake of the Woods this day and year herein first above named.

Signed by the Chiefs within named, in presence of the following witnesses, the same having been first read and explained by the Honorable James McKay:

JAMES McKAY,
MOLYNEUX St. JOHN,
ROBERT PITHER,
CHRISTINE V. K. MORRIS,
CHARLES NOLIN,
A. McDONALD, Capt., Comg. Escort to Lieut.
   Governor,
JAS. F. GRAHAM,
JOSEPH NOLIN,
A. McLEOD,
GEORGE McPHERSON, Sr.,
SEDLEY BLANCHARD,
W. FRED. BUCHANAN,

FRANK G. BECHER,
ALFRED CODD, M.D.,
G. S. CORBAULT,
PIERRE LEVIELLER,
NICHOLAS CHATELAINE,
ALEX. MORRIS L.G.,
J. A. N. PROVENCHER, Ind. Comr.,
S. J. DAWSON,
KEE-TA-KAY-PI-NAIS, his x mark,
KITCHI-GAY-KAKE, his x mark,
NO-TE-NA-QUA-HUNG, his x mark,
MAWE-DO-PE-NAIS, his x mark,
POW-WA-SANG, his x mark,
CANDA-COM-IGO-WI-NINE, his x mark,
MAY-NO-WAH-TAW-WAYS-KUNG, his x
   mark,
KITCHI-NE-KA-BE-HAN, his x mark,
SAH-KATCH-EWAY, his x mark,
MUKA-DAY-WAH-SIN, his x mark,
ME-KIE-SIES, his x mark,
OOS-CON-NA-GEISH, his x mark,
WAH-SHIS-KOUCE, his x mark,
KAH-KEE-Y-ASH, his x mark,
GO-BAY, his x mark,
KA-ME-TI-ASH, his x mark,
NEE-SHO-TAL, his x mark,
KEE-JEE-GO-KAY, his x mark,
SHA-SHA-GAUCE, his x mark,
SHAW-WIN-NA-BI-NAIS, his x mark,
AY-ASH-A-WASH, his x mark,
PAY-AH-BEE-WASH, his x mark,
KAH-TAY-TAY-PA-O-CUTCH, his x mark

We, having had communication of the treaty, a certified copy whereof is hereto annexed, but not having been present at the councils held at the North-West Angle of the Lake of the Woods between Her Majesty's Commissioners, and the several Indian Chiefs and others therein named, at which the articles of the said treaty were agreed upon, hereby for ourselves and the several bands of Indians which we represent, in consideration of the provisions of the said treaty being extended to us and the said bands which we represent, transfer, surrender and relinquish to Her Majesty the Queen, Her heirs and successors, to and for the use of Her Government of Her Dominion of Canada, all our right, title and privilege whatsoever, which we, the said Chiefs and the said bands which we represent have, hold or enjoy, of, in and to the territory described and fully set out in the said articles of treaty, and every part thereof. To have and to hold the same unto and to

the use of Her said Majesty the Queen, Her heirs and successors forever.

And we hereby agree to accept the several provisions, payments and reserves of the said treaty, as therein stated, and solemnly promise and engage to abide by, carry out and fulfil all the stipulations, obligations and conditions therein contained, on the part of the said Chiefs and Indians therein named, to be observed and performed; and in all things to conform to the articles of the said treaty as if we ourselves and the bands which we represent had been originally contracting parties thereto, and had been present and attached our signatures to the said treaty.

IN WITNESS WHEREOF, Her Majesty's said Commissioners and the said Indian Chiefs have hereunto subscribed and set their hands, this thirteenth day of October, in the year of Our Lord one thousand eight hundred and seventy-three.

Signed by S. J. Dawson, Esquire, one of Her Majesty's said Commissioners, for and on behalf and with the authority and consent of the Honorable Alexander Morris, Lieutenant Governor of Manitoba and the North-West Territories, and J. A. N. Provencher, Esq., the remaining two Commissioners, and himself and by the Chiefs within named, on behalf of themselves and the several bands which they represent, the same and the annexed certified copy of articles of treaty having been first read and explained in presence of the following witnesses:

THOS. A. P. TOWERS,
JOHN AITKEN,
A. J. McDONALD,
UNZZAKI,
JAS. LOGANOSH, his x mark,
PINLLSISE

For and on behalf of the Commissioners, the Honorable Alexander Morris, Lieut. Governor of Manitoba and the NorthWest Territories, Joseph Albert Norbert Provencher, Esquire, and the undersigned

S. J. DAWSON, Commissioner,
PAY-BA-MA-CHAS, his x mark,
RE-BA-QUIN, his x mark,
ME-TAS-SO-QUE-NE-SKANK, his x mark

To S. J. Dawson, Esquire, Indian Commissioner, &c., &c., &c.

SIR, —We hereby authorize you to treat with the various bands belonging to the Salteaux Tribe of the Ojibbeway Indians inhabiting the North-West Territories of the Dominion of Canada not included in the foregoing certified copy of articles of treaty, upon the same conditions and stipulations as are therein agreed upon, and to sign and execute for us and in our name and on our behalf the foregoing agreement annexed to the foregoing treaty.

NORTH-WEST ANGLE, LAKE OF THE WOODS, October 4th, A.D. 1873.

ALEX. MORRIS,
Lieutenant-Governor.
J. A. N. PROVENCHER,
Indian Commissioner.

ADHESION BY HALFBREEDS OF RAINY RIVER AND LAKE (A.)
This Memorandum of Agreement made and entered into this twelfth day of September one thousand eight hundred and seventy-five, between Nicholas Chatelaine, Indian interpreter at Fort Francis and the Rainy River and acting herein solely in the latter capacity for and as representing the said Halfbreeds, on the one part, and John Stoughton Dennis, Surveyor General of Dominion Lands, as representing Her Majesty the Queen through the Government of the Dominion, of the other part, Witnesseth as follows:—

Whereas the Half-breeds above described, by virtue of their Indian blood, claim a certain interest or title in the lands or territories in the vicinity of Rainy Lake and the Rainy River, for the commutation or surrender of which claims they ask compensation from the Government.

And whereas, having fully and deliberately discussed and considered the matter, the said Halfbreeds have elected to join in the treaty made between the Indians and Her Majesty, at the North-West Angle of the Lake of the Woods, on the third day of October, 1873, and have expressed a desire thereto, and to become subject to the terms and conditions thereof in all respects saving as hereinafter set forth.

It is now hereby agreed upon by and between the said parties hereto (this agreement, however, to be subject in all respects to approval and confirmation by the Government, without which the same shall be considered as void and of no effect), as follows, that is to say: The Half-breeds, through Nicholas Chatelaine, their Chief above named, as representing them herein, agree as follows, that is to say:-

That they hereby fully and voluntarily surrender to Her Majesty the Queen to be held by Her Majesty and Her successors for ever, any and all claim, right, title or interest which they, by virtue of their Indian blood, have or possess in the lands or territories above described, and solemnly promise to observe all the terms and conditions of the said treaty (a copy whereof, duly certified by the Honourable the Secretary of State of the Dominion has been this day placed in the hands of the said Nicholas Chatelaine).

In consideration of which Her Majesty agrees as follows, that is to say:

That the said Half-breeds, keeping and observing on their part the terms and conditions of the said treaty shall receive compensation in the way of reserves of land, payments, annuities and presents, in manner similar to that set forth in the several respects for the Indians in the said treaty; it being understood, however, that any sum expended annually by Her Majesty in the purchase of ammunition and twine for nets for the use of the said Half-breeds shall not be taken out of the fifteen hundred dollars set apart by the treaty for the purchase annually of those articles for the Indians, but shall be in addition thereto, and shall be a pro rata amount in the proportion of the number of Half-breeds parties hereto to the number of Indians embraced in the treaty; and it being further understood that the said Half-breeds shall be entitled to all the benefits of the said treaty as from the date thereof, as regards payments and annuities, in the same manner as if they had been present and had become parties to the same at the time of the making thereof.

And whereas the said Half-breeds desire the land set forth as tracts marked (A) and (B) on the rough diagram attached hereto, and marked with the initials of the parties aforementioned to this agreement, as their reserves (in all eighteen square miles), to which they would be entitled under the provisions of the treaty, the same is hereby agreed to on the part of the Government.

Should this agreement be approved by the Government, the reserves as above to be surveyed in due course.

Signed at Fort Francis, the day and date above mentioned, in presence of us as witnesses:

A. R. TILLIE,
CHAS. S. CROWE,
W. B. RICHARDSON,
L. KITTSON,
J. S. DENNIS, [L.S.],
NICHOLAS CHATELAINE. [L.S.], his x mark

ADHESION OF LAC SEUL INDIANS TO TREATY No. 3
LAC SEUL, 9th June, 1874.
We, the Chiefs and Councillors of Lac Seul, Seul, Trout and Sturgeon Lakes, subscribe and set our marks, that we and our followers will abide by the articles of the Treaty made and concluded with the Indians at the North-West Angle of the Lake of the Woods, on the third day of October, in the year of Our Lord one thousand eight hundred and seventy-three, between Her Most Gracious Majesty the Queen of Great Britain and Ireland, by Her Commissioners, Hon. Alexander Morris, Lieutenant Governor of Manitoba and the North-West Territories, Joseph Albert N. Provencher, and Simon J. Dawson, of the one part, and the Saulteaux tribes of Ojibewas Indians, inhabitants of the country as defined by the Treaty aforesaid.

IN WITNESS WHEREOF, Her Majesty's Indian Agent and the Chiefs and Councillors have hereto set their hands at Lac Seul, on the 9th day of June, 1874.

(Signed) ACKEMENCE, Councillors. his x mark
    MAINEETAINEQUIRE, his x mark
    NAH-KEE-JECKWAHE, his x mark

The whole Treaty explained by R. J. N. PITHER.
Witnesses:
    (Signed) JAMES McKENZIE,
    OUIS KITTSON,
    NICHOLAS CHATELAINE, his x mark,
    R. J. N. PITHER, Indian Agent,
    JOHN CROMARTY, Chief. his x mark

Treaty 4, 1874

Sept. 15, 1874

Between Her Majesty the Queen and the Cree and Saulteaux Tribes of Indians at the Qu'Appelle and Fort Ellice

ORDER IN COUNCIL SETTING UP COMMISSION FOR TREATY No. 4

On a Memorandum, dated 20th July 1874, from the Honorable the Minister of the Interior, stating that he has had before him a Minute of the Council of the North West of the 14th March last, recommending that Treaties should this year be concluded with the Tribes of Indians inhabiting the Territory therein indicated, lying West of the Boundary of Treaty No. 2, and between the International Boundary Line and the Saskatchewan.

That he has also had before him several Despatches from the Lieutenant Governor of later date urging the necessity of these Treaties.

That looking to these representations and to the fact that the Mounted Police Force is now moving into the Territory in question with a view of taking up their winter quarters at Fort Pelly, and considering the operations of the Boundary Commission which are continually moving westward into the Indian Country, and also the steps which are being taken in connection with the proposed Telegraph Line from Fort Garry westward, all which proceedings are calculated to further unsettle and excite the Indian mind, already in a disturbed condition; he recommends that three Commissioners be appointed by His Excellency the Governor General for the purpose of making Treaties during the current year with such of the Indians Bands as they may find it expedient to deal with, inhabiting the portion of the North-West Territories which may be approximately described as lying between the Westerly Boundary of Treaty No. 2 and the 110th degree of West Longitude, and bounded on the South by the International Boundary Line, and on the North by Lake Winnipeg, and by the Saskatchewan River, including a strip of country ten miles north of that River to the Forks and thence following the South branch of the said River until it meets the 110th degree of West Longitude.

The Minister further recommends that the Commissioners to be appointed for this purpose be instructed to confer with the Lieutenant Governor of the North

West Territories on the subject of the Treaties, and that, in the event of permanent annuities being granted to the Tribes with whom Treaties may be made, such annuities should not be fixed at a higher rate than those sanctioned by the Treaties already concluded with the Indians of the North West.

The Committee submit the above recommendation for Your Excellency's approval.

(sgd.) L. S. HUNTINGDON.
    Approved
    23 July, 1874
    Dufferin

APPROVAL OF TREATY No. 4

On a Memorandum dated 29th October, 1874 from the Hon. Mr. Mackenzie submitting for the consideration of Your Excellency in Council Copies of a Treaty and supplementary Treaty with the Cree, Saulteaux and other Indians inhabiting the Territory affected by such Treaty, the former concluded on the 15th September last, and the latter on the 21st September last, by His Honor the Lieutenant Governor of the North West Territories, the Hon. the Minister of the Interior, and W. J. Christie, Esquire, of Brockville, Ont., the Commissioners specially appointed for that purpose, under Orders in Council dated 23rd July and 26th August respectively.

Mr. Mackenzie states that the Territory covered by the Treaties may be approximately described as lying between the Western boundary of Treaty No.2 and the 1101/2 degree of West Longitude, and bounded on the South by the International Boundary, and on the North by the Red Deer River, and its Lakes, Red Deer and Etoimami, to the source of its Western Branch thence in a straight line to the source of the Northern Branch of the Qu'Appelle, thence along and including said stream to the Forks near Long Lake; thence along and including the Valley of the West Branch of the Qu'Appelle to the South Saskatchewan, thence along and including said River to the mouth of Maple Creek, thence along said Creek, to a point opposite the Cypress Hills, thence due South to the Boundary Line, and that the Area of the Territory above described comprises about 50,000 Square Miles.

That the terms of the Treaties are nearly identical with those of the Treaty concluded last year at the North-West Angle of the Lake of the Woods.

That the principal conditions of the Treaties may be briefly stated as follows:

- 1st A Money present to each Chief of $25; to each Headman not exceeding four in each Band $15 and to every other Indian, man, woman and Child in the Band $12.
- 2nd An Annual payment in perpetuity, of the same sums to the Chiefs and Headmen (not exceeding four in each Band) and $5 to every other man, woman and Child in the Band.
- 3rd Certain trifling presents of clothing every third year, to the Chiefs and Headmen.
- 4th A supply of Ammunition and twine every year to the value of $750.
- 5th Presents of Agricultural implements, Cattle, grain, Carpenter's tools, etc., proportioned to the number of families in the Band actually engaged in farming.
- 6th Reserves to be selected of the same extent in proportion to the numbers of the Bands, and on the same conditions as in the previous Treaty.
- 7th Schools to be established on each Reserve as soon as the Indians settle thereon.
- 8th Intoxicating liquors to be excluded from the Reserve.
- Mr. Mackenzie states that the Treaties appear to him to be satisfactory and he therefore recommends that they be approved by Your Excellency in Council.

He further submits that he is of opinion that the satisfactory conclusion of the Treaties is mainly due to patience, firmness, tact and ability displayed by the Commissioners in the conduct of the negotiations.

The Committee concur in the foregoing Report and recommend and advise that the Treaties be approved and accepted and be enrolled in the usual manner.

signed by: A. Mackenzie.
    Approved
    4th November 1876
    Dufferin.

TREATY No. 4
ARTICLES OF A TREATY made and concluded this fifteenth day of September, in the year of Our Lord one thousand eight hundred and seventy-four, between Her Most Gracious Majesty the Queen of Great Britain and Ireland, by Her Commissioners, the Honourable Alexander Morris, Lieutenant Governor of the Province of Manitoba and the North-West Territories; the Honourable David Laird, Minister of the Interior, and William Joseph Christie, Esquire, of Brockville, Ontario, of the one part; and the Cree, Saulteaux and other Indians, inhabitants of the territory within the limits hereinafter defined and described by their Chiefs and Headmen, chosen and named as hereinafter mentioned, of the other part.

Whereas the Indians inhabiting the said territory have, pursuant to an appointment made by the said Commissioners, been convened at a meeting at the Qu'Appelle Lakes, to deliberate upon certain matters of interest to Her Most Gracious Majesty, of the one part, and the said Indians of the other.

And whereas the said Indians have been notified and informed by Her Majesty's said Commissioners that it is the desire of Her Majesty to open up for settlement, immigration, trade and such other purposes as to Her Majesty may seem meet, a tract of country bounded and described as hereinafter mentioned, and to obtain the consent thereto of Her Indian subjects inhabiting the said tract, and to make a treaty and arrange with them, so that there may be peace and good will between them and Her Majesty and between them and Her Majesty's other subjects, and that Her Indian people may know and be assured of what allowance they are to count upon and receive from Her Majesty's bounty and benevolence.

And whereas the Indians of the said tract, duly convened in Council as aforesaid, and being requested by Her Majesty's said Commissioners to name certain Chiefs and Headmen, who should be authorized on their behalf to conduct such negotiations and sign any treaty to be founded thereon, and to become responsible to Her Majesty for their faithful performance by their respective bands of such obligations as shall be assumed by them the said Indians, have thereupon named the following persons for that purpose, that is to say: Ka-ki-shi-way, or "Loud Voice," (Qu'Appelle River); Pis-qua, or "The Plain" (Leech Lake); Ka-wey-ance, or "The Little Boy" (Leech Lake); Ka-kee-na-wup, or "One that sits like an Eagle" (Upper Qu'Appelle Lakes); Kus-kee-tew-mus-coo-mus-qua, or "Little Black Bear" (Cypress Hills); Ka-ne-on-us-ka-tew, or "One that walks on four claws" (Little Touchwood Hills); Cau-ah-ha-cha-pew, or "Making ready the Bow" (South side of the South Branch of the Saskatchewan); Kii-

si-caw-ah-chuck, or "Day-Star" (South side of the South Branch of the Saskatchewan); Ka-na-ca-toose, "The Poor Man" (Touchwood Hills and Qu'Appelle Lakes); Ka-kii-wis-ta-haw, or "Him that flies around" (towards the Cypress Hills); Cha-ca-chas (Qu'Appelle River); Wah-pii-moose-too-siis, or "The White Calf" (or Pus-coos) (Qu'Appelle River); Gabriel Cote, or Mee-may, or "The Pigeon" (Fort Pelly).

And thereupon in open council the different bands, having presented the men of their choice to the said Commissioners as the Chiefs and Headmen, for the purpose aforesaid, of the respective bands of Indians inhabiting the said district hereinafter described.

And whereas the said Commissioners have proceeded to negotiate a treaty with the said Indians, and the same has been finally agreed upon and concluded as follows, that is to say:—

The Cree and Saulteaux Tribes of Indians, and all other the Indians inhabiting the district hereinafter described and defined, do hereby cede, release, surrender and yield up to the Government of the Dominion of Canada, for Her Majesty the Queen, and Her successors forever, all their rights, titles and privileges whatsoever, to the lands included within the following limits, that is to say:—

Commencing at a point on the United States frontier due south of the northwestern point of the Moose Mountains; thence due north to said point of said mountains: thence in a north-easterly course to a point two miles due west of Fort Ellice; thence in a line parallel with and two miles westward from the Assiniboine River to the mouth of the Shell River; thence parallel to the said river and two miles distant therefrom to its source; thence in a straight line to a point on the western shore of Lake Winnipegosis, due west from the most northern extremity of Waterhen Lake; thence east to the centre of Lake Winnipegosis; thence northwardly, through the middle of the said lake (including Birch Island), to the mouth of Red Deer River; thence westwardly and southwestwardly along and including the said Red Deer River and its lakes, Red Deer and Etoimaini, to the source of its western branch; thence in a straight line to the source of the northern branch of the Qu'Appelle; thence along and including said stream to the forks near Long Lake; thence along and including the valley of the west branch of the Qu'Appelle to the South Saskatchewan; thence along and including said river to the mouth of Maple Creek; thence southwardly along said creek to a point opposite the western extremity of the Cypress Hills; thence due south to the international boundary; thence east along the said boundary to the place of commencement. Also all their rights, titles and privileges whatsoever to all other lands wheresoever situated within Her Majesty's North-West Territories, or any of them. To have and to hold the same to Her Majesty the Queen and Her successors for ever.

And Her Majesty the Queen hereby agrees, through the said Commissioners, to assign reserves for said Indians, such reserves to be selected by officers of Her Majesty's Government of the Dominion of Canada appointed for that purpose, after conference with each band of the Indians, and to be of sufficient area to allow one square mile for each family of five, or in that proportion for larger or smaller families; provided, however, that it be understood that, if at the time of the selection of any reserves, as aforesaid, there are any settlers within the bounds of the lands reserved for any band, Her Majesty retains the right to deal with such settlers as She shall deem just, so as not to diminish the extent of land allotted to the Indians; and provided, further, that the aforesaid reserves of land, or any part thereof, or any interest or right therein, or appurtenant thereto, may be sold, leased or otherwise disposed of by the said Government for the use and benefit of the said Indians, with the consent of the Indians entitled thereto first had and obtained, but in no wise shall the said Indians, or any of them, be entitled to sell or otherwise alienate any of the lands allotted to them as reserves.

In view of the satisfaction with which the Queen views the ready response which Her Majesty's Indian subjects have accorded to the invitation of Her said Commissioners to meet them on this occasion, and also in token of their general good conduct and behaviour, She hereby, through Her Commissioners, makes the Indians of the bands here represented a present, for each Chief of twenty-five dollars in cash, a coat and a Queen's silver medal; for each Headman, not exceeding four in each band, fifteen dollars in cash and a coat; and for every other man, woman and child twelve dollars in cash; and for those here assembled some powder, shot, blankets, calicoes, strouds and other articles.

As soon as possible after the execution of this treaty Her Majesty shall cause a census to be taken of all the Indians inhabiting the tract hereinbefore described, and shall, next year, and annually afterwards for ever, cause to be paid in cash at some suitable season to be duly notified to the Indians, and at a place or places to be appointed for that purpose, within the territory ceded, each Chief twenty-five dollars; each Headman not exceeding four to a band, fifteen dollars; and to every other Indian man, woman and child, five dollars per head; such payment to be made to the heads of families for those belonging thereto, unless for some special reason it be found objectionable.

Her Majesty also agrees that each Chief and each Headman, not to exceed four in each band, once in every three years during the term of their offices shall receive a suitable suit of clothing, and that yearly and every year She will cause to be distributed among the different bands included in the limits of this treaty powder, shot, ball and twine, in all to the value of seven hundred and fifty dollars; and each Chief shall receive hereafter, in recognition of the closing of the treaty, a suitable flag.

It is further agreed between Her Majesty and the said Indians that the following articles shall be supplied to any band thereof who are now actually cultivating the soil, or who shall hereafter settle on their reserves and commence to break up the land, that is to say: two hoes, one spade, one scythe and one axe for every family so actually cultivating, and enough seed wheat, barley, oats and potatoes to plant such land as they have broken up; also one plough and two harrows for every ten families so cultivating as aforesaid, and also to each Chief for the use of his band as aforesaid, one yoke of oxen, one bull, four cows, a chest of ordinary carpenter's tools, five hand saws, five augers, one cross-cut saw, one pit-saw, the necessary files and one grindstone, all the aforesaid articles to be given, once for all, for the encouragement of the practice of agriculture among the Indians.

Further, Her Majesty agrees to maintain a school in the reserve allotted to each band as soon as they settle on said reserve and are prepared for a teacher.

Further, Her Majesty agrees that within the boundary of the Indian reserves, until otherwise determined by the Government of the Dominion of Canada, no intoxicating liquor shall be allowed to be introduced or sold, and all laws now in force, or hereafter to be enacted, to preserve Her Indian subjects, inhabiting the reserves, or living elsewhere within the North-West Territories, from the evil effects of intoxicating liquor, shall be strictly enforced.

And further, Her Majesty agrees that Her said Indians shall have right to pursue their avocations of hunting, trapping and fishing throughout the tract surrendered, subject to such regulations as may from time to time be made by the Government of the country, acting under the authority of Her Majesty, and saving and excepting such tracts as may be required or taken up from time to time for settlement, mining or other purposes, under grant or other right given by Her Majesty's said Government.

It is further agreed between Her Majesty and Her said Indian subjects that such sections of the reserves above indicated as may at any time be required for public works or building of whatsoever nature may be appropriated for that purpose by Her Majesty's Government of the Dominion of Canada, due compensation being made to the Indians for the value of any improvements thereon, and an equivalent in land or money for the area of the reserve so appropriated.

And the undersigned Chiefs and Headmen, on their own behalf and on behalf of all other Indians inhabiting the tract within ceded, do hereby solemnly promise and engage to strictly observe this treaty, and also to conduct and behave themselves as good and loyal subjects of Her Majesty the Queen. They promise and engage that they will, in all respects, obey and abide by the law, that they will maintain peace and good order between each other, and between themselves and other tribes of Indians and between themselves and others of Her Majesty's subjects, whether Indians, Half-breeds, or whites, now inhabiting or hereafter to inhabit any part of the said ceded tract; and that they will not molest the person or property of any inhabitant of such ceded tract, or the property of Her Majesty the Queen, or interfere with or trouble any person passing or travelling through the said tract, or any part thereof, and that they will assist the officers of Her Majesty in bringing to justice and punishment any Indian offending against the stipulations of this treaty, or infringing the laws in force in the country so ceded.

IN WITNESS WHEREOF Her Majesty's said Commissioners, and the said Indian Chiefs and Headmen, have hereunto subscribed and set their hands, at Qu'Appelle, this day and year herein first above written.

Signed by the Chiefs and Headmen within named in presence of the following witnesses, the same having been first read and explained by Charles Pratt:

W. OSBORNE SMITH, C.M.G.,
Lt.-Col. D.A.G. Commg,
Dominion Forces in North-West.,
PASCAL BRELAND,
EDWARD MCKAY,
CHARLES PRATT,
PIERRE POITRAS,
BAPTIST DAVIS, his x mark,
PIERRE DENOMME, his x mark,
JOSEPH McKAY,
DONALD McDONALD,
A. McDONALD,
Capt. Provl. Battn. Infantry,
GEO. W. STREET,
Ens. Provl. Battn. Infantry,
ALFRED CODD, M.D.,
Surgeon Provl. Battn. Infantry,
W. M. HERCHMER, Captain,
C. DE COUYES, Ensign,
JOS. POITRON, x,
M. G. DICKIESON,
Private Secy. Min. of Interior,
PETER LAPIERRE,
HELEN M. McLEAN,
FLORA GARRIOGH,
JOHN COTTON, Lt. Canadian Artillery,
JOHN ALLAN, Lt. Provl. Battn. Infantry,
ALEXANDER MORRIS, Lt.-Gov. North-West
    Territories,
DAVID LAIRD, Indian Commissioner,
WILLIAM J. CHRISTIE, his x mark,
KA-KII-SHI-WAY, his x mark,
PIS-QUA, his x mark,
KA-WEZAUCE, his x mark,
KA-KEE-NA-WUP, his x mark,
KUS-KEE-TEW-MUS-COO-MUS-QUA, his x
    mark,
KA-NE-ON-US-KA-TEW, his x mark,
CAN-AH-HA-CHA-PEU, his x mark,
KII-SI-CAW-AH-CHUCK, his x mark,
KA-WA-CA-TOOSE, his x mark,
KA-KU-WIS-TA-HAW, his x mark,

CHA-CA-CHAS, his x mark,
WA-PII-MOOSE-TOO-SUS, his x mark,
GABRIEL COTÉ OR MEE-MAY, his x mark

We, members of the Saulteaux Tribe of Indians, having had communication of the treaty hereto annexed, made on the 15th day of September instant, between Her Majesty the Queen and the Cree and Saulteaux Indians, and other Indians at Qu'Appelle lakes, but not having been present at the councils held at Qu'Appelle lakes between Her Majesty's Commissioners and the several Indian Chiefs, and other therein named, at which the articles of the said treaty were agreed upon, hereby for ourselves and the band which we represent, in consideration of the provisions of the said treaty being extended to us and the said band which we represent, transfer, surrender and relinquish to Her Majesty the Queen, Her heirs and successors, to and for the use of Her Government of Her Dominion of Canada, all our right, title and privileges whatsoever which we and the said band which we represent, have held or enjoy, of, in and to the territory described and fully set out in the said articles of treaty and every part thereof also all our right, title and privilege whatsoever, to all other lands, wherever situated, whether within the limits of any treaty formerly made or hereafter to be made with the Saulteaux Tribe or any other tribe of Indians inhabiting Her Majesty's North-West Territories, or any of them. To have and to hold the same unto and to use of Her said Majesty the Queen, Her heirs and successors forever.

And we hereby agree to accept the several provisions, payments and reserves of the said treaty, signed at the Qu'Appelle lakes, as therein stated, and solemnly promise and engage to abide by, carry out and fulfil all the stipulations, obligations and conditions therein contained on the part of said Chiefs and Indians therein named to be observed and performed, and in all things to conform to the articles of the said treaty, as if we ourselves, and the band which we represent, had been originally contracting parties thereto and had been present and attached our signatures to the said treaty.

IN WITNESS WHEREOF Her Majesty's said Commissioners and the said Indian Chief and Headman have hereunto subscribed and set their hands at Fort Ellice, this twenty-first day of September, in the year of Our Lord one thousand eight hundred and seventy-four.

Signed by the parties hereto, in the presence of the undersigned witnesses, the same having been first explained to the Indians by Joseph Robillard:

ARCH. McDONALD,
GEORGE FLETT,
A. MAXWELL,
DAVID ARMIT,
HENRY McKAY,
ELLEN McDONALD,
MARY ARMIT,
ALEXANDER MORRIS, Lt.-Gov. North-West
    Territories,
DAVID LAIRD, Indian Commissioner,
W. J. CHRISTIE, Indian Commissioner,
WAY-WA-SE-CA-POW, or the MAN PROUD
    OF STANDING UPRIGHT, his x mark,
OTA-MA-KOO-EWIN, or SHA-POUS-E-
    TUNG'S-FIRST SON, THE MAN WHO
    STANDS ON THE EARTH, his x mark

We, members of the Cree, Saulteaux and Stonie Tribes of Indians, having had communication of the treaty hereto annexed, made on the 15th day of September last between Her Majesty the Queen and the Cree and Saulteaux Indians, and other Indians at Qu'Appelle Lakes, but not having been present at the councils held at the Qu'Appelle Lakes between Her Majesty's Commissioners and several Indian Chiefs and others therein contained, at which the articles of the said treaty were agreed upon, hereby, for ourselves and the bands which we represent, in consideration of the provisions of the said treaty having extended to us and the said bands which we represent, transfer, surrender and relinquish to Her Majesty the Queen, Her heirs and successors, to and for the use of Her Government of Her Dominion of Canada, all our right, title and privileges whatsoever which we and the said bands which we represent have held or enjoy, of, in and to the territory described and fully set out in the said articles of treaty and every part thereof; also, all our right, title and privileges whatsoever to all other lands wherever situated, whether within the limit of any treaty formerly made or hereafter to be made with the Saulteaux Tribe or any other tribe of Indians inhabiting Her Majesty's North-West Territories, or any of them. To have and to hold the same unto and to the use of Her said Majesty the Queen, Her heirs and successors forever.

And we hereby agree to accept the several provisions, payments and reserves of the said treaty, signed at the Qu'Appelle Lakes, as therein stated, and solemnly promise and engage to abide by, carry out and fulfill all the stipulations, obligations and conditions therein contained on the part of said Chiefs and Indians therein named to be observed and performed, and in all things to conform to the articles of the said treaty as if we, ourselves, and the bands which we represent, had been originally contracting parties thereto, and had been present and attached our signatures to the said treaty.

IN WITNESS WHEREOF, Her Majesty's Commissioners and the said Indian Chiefs have hereunto subscribed and set their hands at Qu'Appelle Lakes this eighth day of September, in the year or Our Lord one thousand eight hundred and seventy-five.

Signed by the parties hereto in the presence of the undersigned witnesses, the same having been first explained to the Indians by William the second McKay.

WILLIAM S. McKAY,
ARCH. McDONALD,
PASCAL BRELAND,
WILLIAM WAGNER,
W. J. CHRISTIE, Indian Commissioner,
M. G. DICKIESON, Acting Ind'n Com'r.,
W. F. WRIGHT,
CHEE x CUK, his x mark

We, members of the Cree, Saulteaux and Stonie Tribes of Indians, having had communication of the treaty hereto annexed, made on the 15th day of September last between Her Majesty the Queen and the Cree and Saulteaux Indians and other Indians at the Qu'Appelle Lakes, but not having been present at the councils held at the Qu'Appelle Lakes, between Her Majesty's Commissioners and the several Indian Chiefs and others therein named, at which the articles of the said treaty were agreed upon, hereby for ourselves and the bands which we represent, in consideration of the provisions of the said treaty having extended to us, and the said bands which we represent, transfer, surrender and relinquish to Her Majesty the Queen, Her heirs and successors, to and for the use of Her Government of Her Dominion of Canada, all our right, title and privileges whatsoever which we and the said bands which we represent have held or enjoy, of, in and to the territory described and fully set out in the said articles of treaty, and every part thereof; also, all our right, title, and privileges whatsoever to all other lands wherever situated, whether within the limit of any treaty formerly made, of hereafter to be made with the Saulteaux Tribe or any other tribe of Indians inhabiting Her Majesty's North-West Territories, or any of them. To have and to hold the same unto and to the use of Her said Majesty the Queen, Her heirs and successors forever.

And we hereby agree to accept the several provisions, payments and reserves of the said treaty signed at the Qu'Appelle Lakes, as therein stated, and solemnly promise and engage to abide by, carry out and fulfil all the stipulations, obligations and conditions therein contained on the part of said Chiefs and Indians therein named to be observed and performed, and in all things to conform to the articles of the said treaty as if we ourselves and the bands which we represent had been originally contracting parties thereto and had been present and attached our signatures to the said treaty.

IN WITNESS WHEREOF, Her Majesty's Commissioners and the said Indian Chiefs have hereunto subscribed and set their hands at Qu'Appelle Lakes this ninth day of September, in the year of Our Lord one thousand eight hundred and seventy-five.

Signed by the parties hereto, in the presence of the undersigned witnesses, the same having been first explained to the Indians by Charles Pratt.

    Witness CHARLES PRATT,
    Witness ARCH. McDONALD,
    Witness JOSEPH READER,
    PASCAL BRELAND,
    W. J. CHRISTIE, Ind. Comr.,
    M. G. DICKIESON, Ind. Comr.,
    W. F. WRIGHT,
    WAH-PEE-MAKWA, his x mark,
    THE WHITE BEAR, his x mark,
    OKANES, his x mark,
    PAYEPOT, his x mark,
    LE CROUP DE PHEASANT, his x mark,
    KITCHI-KAH-ME-WIN, his x mark

We, members of the Cree and Saulteaux Tribes of Indians, having had communication of the treaty made on the 15th day of September, 1874, between Her Majesty the Queen and the Cree and Saulteaux Indians and other Indians at Qu'Appelle Lakes, but not having been present at the councils held at Qu'Appelle Lakes between Her Majesty's Commissioners and the several Indian Chiefs and others therein named, at which the articles of the said treaty were agreed upon, hereby for ourselves and the band which we represent, in consideration of the provisions of the said treaty having extended to us and the said band which we represent, transfer, surrender and relinquish to Her Majesty the Queen, Her heirs and successors, to and for the use of Her Government of Her Dominion of Canada, all our right, title and privileges whatsoever which we and the said band which we represent have held or enjoy, of, in and to the territory described and fully set out in the said articles of treaty and every part thereof; also our right, title and privileges whatsoever to all other lands wherever situated, whether within the limits of any treaty formerly made or hereafter to be made with the Saulteaux Tribe or any other tribe of Indians inhabiting Her Majesty's North-West Territories, or any of them. To have and to hold the same unto and to the use of Her said Majesty the Queen, Her heirs and successors for ever.

And we hereby agree to accept the several provisions, payment and reserves of the said treaty signed at the Qu'Appelle Lakes as therein stated, and solemnly promise and engage to abide by, carry out and fulfil all the stipulations, obligations and conditions therein contained, on the part of said Chiefs and Indians therein named to be observed and performed, and in all things to conform to the articles of the said treaty as if we ourselves and the band which we represent had been originally contracting parties thereto, and had been present and attached our signatures to the said treaty.

IN WITNESS WHEREOF, Her Majesty's Commissioners and the Indian Chiefs have hereunto subscribed and set their hands at Swan Lake, this twenty-fourth day of September, in the year of Our Lord one thousand eight hundred and seventy-five.

Signed by the parties hereto, in the presence of the undersigned witnesses, the same having been first explained to the Indians by George Brass.

    ARCH. McDONALD, Witness,
    DONALD McDONALD, Witness,
    GEORGE BRASS, Witness, his x mark,
    W. J. CHRISTIE, Indian Comr.,

M. G. DICKIESON, Acting Indian Comr.,
OW-TAH-PEE-KA-KAW, his x mark,
KII-SHI-KOUSE, his x mark

We, members of the Saulteaux Tribe of Indians, having had communication of the treaty hereto annexed, made on the 15th day of September, A.D. 1874, between Her Majesty the Queen and the Cree and Saulteaux Indians and other Indians at Qu'Appelle Lakes, but not having been present at the councils held at the Qu'Appelle Lakes between Her Majesty's Commissioners and the several Indian Chiefs and others therein named, at which the articles of the said treaty were agreed upon, hereby for ourselves and the band which we represent, in consideration of the provisions of the said treaty having extended to us and the said band which we represent, transfer, surrender and relinquish to Her Majesty the Queen, Her heirs and successors, to and for the use of Her Government of Her Dominion of Canada, all our right, title and privileges whatsoever which we and the said band which we represent have held or enjoy, of, in and to the territory described and fully set out in the said articles of treaty and every part thereof; also, all our right, title and privileges whatsoever to all other lands wherever situated, whether within the limit of any treaty formerly made or hereafter to be made with the Saulteaux Tribe or any other tribe of Indians inhabiting Her Majesty's North-West Territories, or any of them. To have and to hold the same unto and to use of Her said Majesty the Queen, Her heirs and successors forever.

And we hereby agree to accept the several provisions, payments and reserves of the said treaty signed at the Qu'Appelle Lakes as therein stated, and solemnly promise and engage to abide by, carry out and fulfill all the stipulations, obligations and conditions therein contained on the part of the said Chiefs and Indians therein named to be observed and performed, and in all things to conform to the articles of the said treaty as if we ourselves and the band which we represent had been originally contracting parties thereto, and had been present and attached our signatures to the said treaty.

IN WITNESS WHEREOF, Her Majesty's Commissioners and the said Indian Chief and Headmen have hereunto subscribed and set their hands at Fort Pelly, this twenty-fourth day of August, in the year of Our Lord one thousand eight hundred and seventy-six.

Signed by the parties hereto in the presence of the undersigned witnesses, the same having been first read and explained by A. McKAY:

AND. McDONALD,
ALEX. LORD RUSSELL,
GEORGE FLETT,
HUGH McBEATH,
A. McKAY,
W. H. NAGLE,
OO-ZA-WASK-OO-QUIN-APE, (or YELLOW
    QUILL), his x mark,
KENISTIN (or CREE), his x mark,
NE-PIN-AWA (or SUMMER FUR), his x mark

We, members of the Assiniboine Tribe of Indians, having had communication of the treaty hereto annexed, made on the 15th day of September, one thousand eight hundred and seventy-four, between Her Majesty the Queen and the Cree Saulteaux Indians, and other Indians at Qu'Appelle Lakes, but not having been present at the councils held at Qu'Appelle Lakes between Her Majesty's Commissioners and the several Indian Chiefs and others therein named, at which the articles of the said treaty were agreed upon, hereby for ourselves, and the band which we represent, in consideration of the provisions of the treaty being extended to us and the said band which we represent, transfer, surrender and relinquish to Her Majesty the Queen, Her heirs and successors, to and for the use of Her Government of Her Dominion of Canada, all our right, title and privileges whatsoever which we and the bands which we represent have held or enjoy, of, in and to the territory described and fully set out in the said articles of treaty and every part thereof; also our right, title and privileges whatsoever to all other lands wherever situated, whether within the limit of any treaty formerly made or hereafter to be made with the Assiniboine Tribe or any other tribe of Indians inhabiting Her Majesty's North-West Territories, or any of them. To have and to hold the same unto and to the use of Her said Majesty the Queen, Her Heirs and successors forever.

And we hereby agree to accept the several provisions and the payment in the following manner, viz.: That those who have not already received payment receive this year the sums of twelve dollars for the year 1876, which shall be considered their first year of payment, and five dollars for the year 1877, making together the sum of seventeen dollars apiece to those who have never been paid, and five dollars per annum for every subsequent year, and also the reserves of the said treaty signed at Qu'Appelle Lakes, as therein stated, and solemnly promise and agree to abide by, carry out and fulfil all the stipulations, obligations and conditions therein contained on the part of the said Chiefs and Indians therein named to be observed and performed, and in all things to conform to the articles of the said treaty as if we ourselves and the band which we represent had been originally contracting parties thereto and had been present and attached our signatures to the said treaty.

IN WITNESS WHEREOF, Major James M. Walsh, Inspector of North-West Mounted Police, in command at Forth Walsh, and the said Indian Chiefs and Headmen, have hereunto set their hands at Fort Walsh, this twenty-fifth day of September, in the year of Our Lord one thousand eight hundred and seventy-seven.

Signed by the parties hereto in the presence of the undersigned witnesses, the same having been first explained by Constant Provost to the Indians.

    J. H. McILLREE, Sub-Inspector,
    PERCY REGINALD NEALE, Sub-Inspector,
      N.W.M.P,
    J. M. WALSH,
    LONG LODGE TEPEE HOSKA, his x mark,
    THE ONE THAT FETCHED THE COAT, his x
      mark,
    WICH-A-WOS-TAKA, his x mark,
    THE POOR MAN, his x mark

Treaty 5, 1875

Sept. 24, 1875
Between Her Majesty the Queen and the Saulteaux and Swampy Cree Tribes of Indians at Beren's River and Norway House with Adhesions

ARTICLES OF A TREATY made and concluded at Beren's River the 20th day of September, and at Norway House the 24th day of September, in the year of Our Lord one thousand eight hundred and seventy-five, between "Her Most Gracious Majesty the Queen" of Great Britain and Ireland, by Her Commissioners the Honourable Alexander Morris, Lieutenant-Governor of the Province of Manitoba and the North-west Territories, and the Honourable James McKay, of the one part, and the Saulteaux and Swampy Cree tribes of Indians, inhabitants of the country within the limits hereinafter defined and described, by their Chiefs, chosen and named as hereinafter mentioned, of the other part.

WHEREAS, the Indians inhabiting the said country have, pursuant to an appointment made by the said Commissioners, been convened at meetings at Beren's River and Norway House to deliberate upon certain matters of interest to Her Most Gracious Majesty, of the one part, and the said Indians of the other.

AND WHEREAS the said Indians have been notified and informed by Her Majesty's said Commissioners that it is the desire of Her Majesty to open up for settlement, immigration and such other purposes as to Her Majesty may seem meet, a tract of country bounded and described as hereinafter mentioned, and to obtain the consent thereto of Her Indian subjects inhabiting the said tract, and to make a treaty and arrange with them, so that there may be peace and good will between them and Her Majesty, and that they may know and be assured of what allowance they are to count upon and receive from Her Majesty's bounty and benevolence.

AND WHEREAS the Indians of said tract, duly convened in council as aforesaid, and being requested by Her Majesty's said Commissioners to name certain Chiefs and Headmen who should be authorized on their behalf to conduct such negotiations and sign any treaty to be founded thereon, and to become responsible to Her Majesty for the faithful performance by their respective bands of such obligations as shall be assumed by them the said Indians, have thereupon named the following persons for that purpose, that is to say:

For the Indians within the Beren's River region and their several bands: Nah-wee-kee-sick-quah-yash, Chief; Kah-nah-wah-kee-wee-nin and Nah-kee-quan-nay-yash, Councillors, and Pee-wah-roo-wee-nin, of Poplar River; Councillors for the Indians within the Norway House region and their several bands: David Rundle, Chief, James Cochrane, Harry Constatag and Charles Pisequinip, Councillors; and Ta-pas-ta-num, or Donald William Sinclair Ross, Chief, James Garrioch and Proud McKay, Councillors.

AND THEREUPON, in open council, the different bands having presented their Chiefs to the said Commissioners as the Chiefs and Headmen for the purposes aforesaid of the respective Bands of Indians inhabiting the said district hereinafter described. AND WHEREAS the said Commissioners then and there received and acknowledged the persons so presented as Chiefs and Headmen, for the purposes aforesaid, of the respective Bands of Indians inhabiting the said district hereinafter described.

AND WHEREAS the said Commissioners have proceeded to negotiate a treaty with the said Indians, and the same has been finally agreed upon and concluded as follows, that is to say:

The Saulteaux and Swampy Cree Tribes of Indians and all other the Indians inhabiting the district hereinafter described and defined, do hereby cede, release, surrender and yield up to the Government of the Dominion of Canada, for Her Majesty the Queen and Her successors for ever, all their rights, titles and privileges whatsoever to the lands included within the following limits, that is to say:

Commencing at the north corner or junction of Treaties Nos. 1 and 3; then easterly along the boundary of Treaty No. 3 to the "Height of Land," at the northeast corner of the said treaty limits, a point dividing the waters of the Albany and Winnipeg Rivers; thence due north along the said "Height of Land " to a point intersected by the 53° of north latitude; and thence north-westerly to "Favourable Lake"; thence following the east shore of said lake to its northern limit; thence north-westerly to the north end of Lake Winnipegoosis; then westerly to the "Height of Land" called "Robinson's Portage"; thence north-westerly to the east end of "Cross Lake"; thence north-westerly crossing "Foxes Lake"; thence north-westerly to the north end of "Split Lake"; thence south-westerly to "Pipestone Lake," on "Burntwood River "; thence south-westerly to the western point of "John Scott's Lake"; thence south-westerly to the north shore of "Beaver Lake"; thence south-westerly to the west end of "Cumberland Lake"; thence due south to the "Saskatchewan River"; thence due south to the north-west corner of the northern limits of Treaty No. 4, including all territory within the said limits, and all islands on all lakes within the said limits, as above described; and it being also understood that in all cases where lakes form the treaty limits, ten miles from the shore of the lake should be included in the treaty.

And also all their rights, titles and privileges whatsoever to all other lands wherever situated in the North-west Territories or in any other Province or portion of Her Majesty's dominions situated and being within the Dominion of Canada;

The tract comprised within the lines above described, embracing an area of one hundred thousand square miles, be the same more or less;

To have and to hold the same to Her Majesty the Queen, and Her successors forever;

And Her Majesty the Queen hereby agrees and undertakes to lay aside reserves for farming lands, due respect being had to lands at present cultivated by the said Indians, and other reserves for the benefit of the said Indians, to be administered and dealt with for them by Her Majesty's Government of the Dominion of Canada, provided all such reserves shall not exceed in all one hundred and sixty acres for each family of five, or in that proportion for larger or smaller families-in manner following, that is to say: For the Band of "Saulteaux, in the Beren's River" region, now settled or who may within two years settle therein, a reserve commencing at the outlet of Beren's River into Lake Winnipeg, and extending along the shores of said lake, and up said river and into the interior behind said lake and river, so as to comprehend one hundred and sixty acres for each family of five, a reasonable addition being, however, to be made by Her Majesty to the extent of the said reserve for the inclusion in the tract so reserved of swamp, but reserving the free navigation of the said lake and river, and free access to the shores and waters thereof, for Her Majesty and all Her subjects, and expecting thereout such land as may have been granted to or stipulated to be held by the "Hudson Bay Company," and also such land as Her Majesty or Her successors, may in Her good pleasure, see fit to grant to the Mission established at or near Beren's River by the Methodist Church of Canada, for a church, school-house, parsonage, burial ground and farm, or other mission purposes; and to the Indians residing at Poplar River, falling into Lake Winnipeg north of Beren's River, a reserve not exceeding one hundred and sixty acres to each family of five, respecting, as much as possible, their present improvements:

And inasmuch as a number of the Indians now residing in and about Norway House of the band of whom David Rundle is Chief are desirous of removing to a locality where they can cultivate the soil, Her Majesty the Queen hereby agrees to lay aside a reserve on the west side of Lake Winnipeg, in the vicinity of Fisher River, so as to give one hundred acres to each family of five, or in that proportion for larger or smaller families, who shall remove to the said locality within "three years," it being estimated that ninety families or thereabout will remove within the said period, and that a reserve will be laid aside sufficient for that or the actual number; and it is further agreed that those of the band who remain in the vicinity of "Norway House" shall retain for their own use their present gardens, buildings and improvements, until the same be departed with by the Queen's Government, with their consent first had and obtained, for their individual benefit, if any value can be realized therefore:

And with regard to the Band of Wood Indians, of whom Ta-pas-ta-num, or Donald William Sinclair Ross, is Chief, a reserve at Otter Island, on the west side of Cross Lake, of one hundred and sixty acres for each family of five or in that proportion for smaller families-reserving, however, to Her Majesty, Her successors and Her subjects the free navigation of all lakes and rivers and free access to the shores thereof; Provided, however, that Her Majesty reserves the right to deal with any settlers within the bounds of any lands reserved for any band as She shall deem fit, and also that the aforesaid reserves of land or any interest therein may be sold or otherwise disposed of by Her Majesty's Government for the use and benefit of the said Indians entitled thereto, with their consent first had and obtained.

And with a view to show the satisfaction of Her Majesty with the behaviour and good conduct of Her Indians, She hereby, through Her Commissioners, makes them a present of five dollars for each man, woman and child belonging to the bands here represented, in extinguishment of all claims heretofore preferred.

And further, Her Majesty agrees to maintain schools for instruction in such reserves hereby made as to Her Government of the Dominion of Canada may seem advisable, whenever the Indians of the reserve shall desire it.

Her Majesty further agrees with Her said Indians, that within the boundary of Indian reserves, until otherwise determined by Her Government of the Dominion of Canada, no intoxicating liquor shall be allowed to be introduced or sold, and all laws now in force, or hereafter to be enacted, to preserve Her Indian subjects inhabiting the reserves, or living elsewhere within Her North-west Territories, from the evil influence of the use of intoxicating liquors, shall be strictly enforced.

Her Majesty further agrees with Her said Indians, that they, the said Indians, shall have right to pursue their avocations of hunting and fishing throughout the tract surrendered as hereinbefore described, subject to such regulations as may from time to time be made by Her Government of Her Dominion of Canada, and saving and excepting such tracts as may from time to time be required or taken up for settlement, mining, lumbering or other purposes, by Her said Government of the Dominion of Canada, or by any of the subjects thereof duly authorized therefor by the said Government.

It is further agreed between Her Majesty and Her said Indians that such sections of the reserves above indicated as may at any time be required for public works or buildings, of what nature soever, may be appropriated for that purpose by Her Majesty's Government of the Dominion of Canada, due compensation being made for the value of any improvements thereon.

And further, that Her Majesty's Commissioners shall, as soon as possible after the execution of this treaty, cause to be taken an accurate census of all the Indians inhabiting the tract above described, distributing them in families, and shall in every year ensuing the date hereof, at some period in each year to be duly notified to the Indians, and at a place or places to be appointed for that purpose within the territory ceded, pay to each Indian person the sum of five dollars per head yearly.

It is further agreed between Her Majesty and the said Indians that the sum of five hundred dollars per annum shall be yearly and every year expended by Her Majesty in the purchase of ammunition, and twine for nets, for the use of the said Indians, in manner following, that is to say: in the reasonable discretion as regards the distribution thereof among the Indians inhabiting the several reserves or otherwise included therein of Her Majesty's Indian Agent have the supervision of this treaty.

It is further agreed between Her Majesty and the said Indians that the following articles shall be supplied to any band of the said Indians who are now cultivating the soil, or who shall hereafter commence to cultivate the land, that is to say: Two hoes for every family actually cultivating; also one spade per family as aforesaid; one plough for every ten families as aforesaid; five harrows for every twenty families as aforesaid; one scythe for every family as aforesaid, and also one axe; and also one cross-cut saw, one hand-saw, one pit-saw, the necessary files, one grindstone, and one auger for each band; and also for each Chief, for the use of his band, one chest of ordinary carpenter's tools; also for each band enough of wheat, barley, potatoes and oats to plant the land actually broken up for cultivation by such band; also for each band one yoke of oxen, one bull and four cows all the aforesaid articles to be given once for all for the encouragement of the practice of agriculture among the Indians.

It is further agreed between Her Majesty and the said Indians that each Chief duly recognized as such shall receive an annual salary of twenty-five dollars per annum, and each subordinate officer, not exceeding three for each band, shall receive fifteen dollars per annum; and each such Chief and subordinate officer as aforesaid shall also receive, once every three years, a suitable suit of clothing; and each Chief shall receive, in recognition of the closing of the treaty, a suitable flag and medal.

And the undersigned Chiefs, on their own behalf and on behalf of all other Indians inhabiting the tract within ceded, do hereby solemnly promise and engage to strictly observe this treaty, and also to conduct and behave themselves as good and loyal subjects of Her Majesty the Queen. They promise and engage that they will, in all respects, obey and abide by the law, and they will maintain peace and good order between each other, and also between themselves and other Tribes of Indians, and between themselves and others of Her Majesty's subjects, whether Indians or whites, now inhabiting or hereafter to inhabit any part of the said ceded tracts, and that they will not molest the person or property of any inhabitant of such ceded tracts, or the property of Her Majesty the Queen, or interfere with or trouble any person passing or travelling through the said

tracts, or any part thereof; and that they will aid and assist the officers of Her Majesty in bringing to justice and punishment any Indian offending against the stipulations of this treaty, or infringing the laws in force in the country so ceded.

IN WITNESS WHEREOF, Her Majesty's said Commissioners and the said Indian Chiefs have hereunto subscribed and set their hands at "Beren's River" this twentieth day of September, A.D. 1875, and at Norway House on the twenty-fourth day of the month and year herein first above named.

Signed by the Chiefs within named in presence of the following witnesses, the same having been first read and explained by the Honourable James McKay:

THOS. HOWARD,
A. G. JACKES, M.D.,
CHRISTINE MORRIS,
E. C. MORRIS,
ELIZABETH YOUNG,
WILLIAM McKAY,
JOHN Mc KAY,
EGERTON RYERSON YOUNG,
ALEX. MORRIS, L.G. [L.S.],
JAMES McKAY, [L.S.],
NAH-WEE-KEE-SICK-QUAH-YASH, otherwise, JACOB BERENS, Chief, his x mark,
KAH-NAH-WAH-KEE-WEE-NIN, otherwise, ANTOINE GOUIN, his x mark,
NAH-KEE-QUAN-NAY-YASH, his x mark,
PEE-WAH-ROO-WEE-NIN, his x mark,
Councillors.

Signed at Norway House by the Chiefs and Councillors hereunto his subscribing in the presence of the undersigned witnesses, the same having been first read and explained by the Honourable James McKay:

RODK. ROSS,
JOHN H. RUTTAN, Methodist Minister,
O. GRINDER, Methodist Min.,
D. C. McTAVISH,
ALEX. SINCLAIR,
L. C. McTAVISH,
CHRISTINE V. K. MORRIS,
E. C. MORRIS,
A. G. JACKES, M.D.,
THOS. HOWARD.,

ALEX. MORRIS, L.G., [L.S.],
JAMES McKAY, [L.S.],
DAVID RUNDLE, Chief. his x mark,
JAMES COCHRANE, his x mark,
HARRY CONSTATAG, his x mark,
CHARLES PISEQUINIP, Councillors, his x
   mark,
TA-PAS-TA-NUM, or, DONALD WILLIAM, his
   x mark,
SINCLAIR ROSS, Chief, his x mark,
GEORGE GARRIOCK, his x mark,
PROUD McKAY,Councillors. his x mark.

We, the Band of the Saulteaux Tribe of Indians residing at the mouth of the Saskatchewan River, on both sides thereof, having had communication of the foregoing treaty, hereby, and in consideration of the provisions of the said treaty being extended to us, transfer, surrender and relinquish to Her Majesty the Queen, Her heirs and successors, to and for the use of the Government of Canada, all our right, title and privileges whatsoever, which we have or enjoy in the territory described in the said treaty, and every part thereof, to have and to hold to the use of Her Majesty the Queen and Her heirs and successors for ever. And Her Majesty agrees, through the said Commissioners, to assign a reserve of sufficient area to allow one hundred and sixty acres to each family of five, or in that proportion for larger or smaller families-such reserve to be laid off and surveyed next year on the south side of the River Saskatchewan.

And having regard to the importance of the land where the said Indians are now settled in respect of the purposes of the navigation of the said river and transport in connection therewith, and otherwise, and in view of the fact that many of the said Indians have now houses and gardens on the other side of the river and elsewhere which they will abandon, Her Majesty agrees, through Her said Commissioners, to grant a sum of five hundred dollars to the said Band to be paid in equitable proportions to such of them as have houses, to assist them in removing their houses to the said reserve or building others.

And the said Indians, represented herein by their Chiefs and Councillors, presented as such by the Band, do hereby agree to accept the several provisions, payments and other benefits as stated in the said treaty, and solemnly promise and engage to abide by, carry out and fulfil all the stipulations, obligations and conditions therein contained, on the part of the said Chiefs and Indians therein named, to be observed and performed, and in all things to conform to the articles of the said treaty as if we ourselves had been originally contracting parties thereto.

IN WITNESS WHEREOF, Her Majesty's said Commissioners and the said Indian Chief and Councillors have hereunto subscribed and set their hands, at the Grand Rapids, this twenty-seventh day of September, in the year of Our Lord one thousand eight hundred and seventy-five.

Signed by the parties in the presence of the undersigned witnesses, the same having been first explained to the Indians by the Honourable James McKay.

   THOS. HOWARD,
   RODK. ROSS,
   E. C. MORRIS,
   A. G. JACKES, M.D.,
   ALEX. MATHESON,
   JOSEPH HOUSTON,
   CHRISTINE V. K. MORRIS,
   ALEX. MORRIS, L.G. [L.S.],
   JAMES McKAY, [L.S.],
   PETER BEARDY, Chief, his x mark,
   JOSEPH ATKINSON, his x mark,
   ROBERT S. ANDERSON, Councillors. his x
      mark.

ADHESION BY SAULTEAUX OR CHIPPEWA INDIANS
MEMORANDUM.
The Queen's Indian Commissioners having met Thick-foot and a portion of the Island Band of Indians at Wa-pang or Dog-head Island on the 28th day of September, A.D. 1875, request him to notify the Island Indians and those of Jack-head Point to meet at Wa-pang an Indian Agent next summer to receive payments under the treaty which they have made with the Indians of Norway House, Beren's River, Grand Rapids and Lake Winnipeg, and in which they are included, at a time of which they will be notified, and to be prepared then to designate their Chief and two Councillors. The Commissioners have agreed to give some of the "Norway House" Indians a reserve at Fisher Creek, and they will give land to the Island Indians at the same place.

Given at Wa-pang this 28th day of September, A.D. 1875, under our hands.

ALEX. MORRIS, L.G.,
JAMES McKAY

I accept payments under the treaty for myself and those who may adhere to me, and accept the same and all its provisions as a Principal Indian, and agree to notify the Indians as above written.

THICK-FOOT, his x mark

WA-PANG, September 28th, 1875.
Witness:
THOS. HOWARD,
RODK. ROSS

ADHESION BY SAULTEAUX OR CHIPPEWA INDIANS

We, the Band of Saulteaux Tribe of Indians residing at the mouth of Black River, on the east shore of Lake Winnipeg, having had communication of the treaty made and concluded at Beren's River the 20th day of September, 1875, between Her Most Gracious Majesty the Queen, by Her Commissioners the Honourable Alexander Morris, Lieutenant-Governor of the Province of Manitoba and the Northwest Territories, and the Honourable James McKay, and the different tribes of Indians and inhabitants of the country within the limits mentioned in the said treaty, hereby, and in consideration of the provisions of the said treaty being extended to us, transfer, surrender and relinquish to Her Majesty the Queen, Her heirs and successors, to and for the use of the Government of Canada, all our rights, titles and privileges whatsoever which we may have or enjoy in the territory descript in the said treaty, and every part thereof-and to hold to the use of Her Majesty the Queen, and heirs and successors forever. And Her Majesty agrees through the Acting Indian Superintendent, to assign the reserve of sufficient area to allow one hundred and sixty acres to each family of five, or in that proportion for smaller or larger families, on the banks of the said Black River.

IN WITNESS WHEREOF, the said Acting Indian Superintendent and the said Indians, represented by their Chief and Councillors, have hereunto subscript and set their hands at Winnipeg, the seventh day of September, in the year of Our Lord one thousand eight hundred seventy-six.

Witness:
J. A. N. PROVENCHER,
JAS. F. GRAHAM,
H. MARTINEAU,
J. P. WRIGHT,
JAMES BIRD, his x mark,
JOSEPH SAYER, his x mark,
JOHN SAYER. his x mark

ADHESION BY SAULTEAUX OR CHIPPEWA AND CREE INDIANS

ARTICLE OF AGREEMENT AND ADHESION TO A TREATY made and concluded at Beren's River on the 20th day of September and at Norway House the 24th day of September, in the year of Our Lord one thousand eight hundred and seventy-five, between Her Most Gracious Majesty the Queen of Great Britain and Ireland, by Her Commissioners, the Honourable Alexander Morris, Lieutenant-Governor of the Province of Manitoba and the North-west Territories, and the Honourable James McKay, of the one part, and the Saulteaux and Swampy Cree Tribes of Indians, inhabitants of the country within the limits hereinafter defined and described, by their Chiefs, chosen and named as hereinafter mentioned, of the other part:

We, the Band of Saulteaux and Swampy Cree Indians, residing at the "Pas," on the Saskatchewan River, Birch River, the Pas Mountain and File Lake, and known as "The Pas Band"; and at Cumberland Island, Sturgeon River, Angling River, Pine Bluff, Beaver Lake and the Ratty Country, and known as "The Cumberland Band"; and at Moose Lake and Cedar Lake, and known as "The Moose Lake Band," having had communication of the aforesaid treaty, of which a true copy is hereunto annexed, hereby, and in consideration of the provisions of the said treaty being extended to us, transfer, surrender and relinquish to Her Majesty the Queen, Her heirs and successors, to and for the use of the Government of Canada, all our rights, title and privileges whatsoever, which we have or enjoy in the territory described in the said treaty and every part thereof, to have and to hold to the use of Her Majesty the Queen and Her heirs and successors forever.

And Her Majesty agrees, through Her representative as hereinafter named, to assign a reserve of sufficient area to allow one hundred and sixty acres to each family of five, or in that proportion for larger or smaller families, such reserves to be subject to the approval of Her Majesty's Government of the Dominion of Canada, and to be laid off and surveyed as soon as may be found practicable, in manner following, that is to say: For the "Pas" Band, a reserve on both sides of the Saskatchewan River at the "Pas"; but as the area of land fit for cultivation in that vicinity is very limited, and insufficient to allow of a reserve being laid off to meet the requirements of the Band, that the balance of such reserve shall be at "Birch River" and the "Pas Mountain"; for the "Cumberland Band" a reserve at "Cumberland Island," and as the land fit for cultivation there is also limited and insufficient to meet their requirements, that the balance of that reserve shall be at a point between the "Pine Bluff" and "Lime Stone Rock," on "Cumberland Lake"; and for the "Moose Lake Band" a reserve at the north end of "Moose Lake," called Little Narrows-reserving, however, to Her Majesty, Her heirs, successors, and Her subjects, the free navigation of all lakes and rivers, and free access to the shores thereof, and excepting thereout such land as may have been granted to or stipulated to be held by the Hudson's Bay Company at the Pas and Cumberland Island, and also such land as Her Majesty or Her successors may in their good pleasure see fit to grant to the missions established at the "Pas" and Cumberland Island by the Church Missionary Society, and the mission established at Cumberland Island by the Roman Catholic Church; and provided Her Majesty, Her heirs and successors, reserve the right to deal with any settlers within the bounds of any lands reserved for any Band as She shall deem fit.

And the said Indians, represented herein by their Chiefs and Councillors, presented as such by the Bands, do hereby agree to accept the several provisions, payments, and other benefits, as stated in the said treaty, and solemnly promise and engage to abide by, carry out and fulfil all stipulations, obligations and conditions therein contained, on the part of the said Chiefs and Indians therein named, to be observed and performed, and in all things to conform to the articles of the said treaty, as if we ourselves had been originally contracting parties thereto.

IN WITNESS WHEREOF, the Honourable Thomas Howard, acting herein for Her Majesty under special authority of the Honourable Alexander Morris, Lieutenant-Governor of Manitoba and of the Northwest Territories, and Chief Superintendent of Indian Affairs for the Manitoba Superintendency, and the said Chiefs and Councillors, have hereunto subscribed and set their hands at the "Pas," on the Saskatchewan River, this seventh day of September, in the year of Our Lord one thousand eight hundred and seventy-six.

Signed by the Chiefs and Councillors within named, in the presence of the following witnesses, the treaty and this adhesion, having been first read and explained by the Rev. Henry Cochrane:

H. BELLANGER,
HENRY COCHRANE, Missionary,
CHARLES D. RICKARDS,
CHARLES ADAMS, C. Clk., H.B. Co.,
WALTER R. NURSEY,
JOHN CLEMONS,
THOMAS NIXON, Jr.,
ROBERT BALLENDINE,
A. M. MUCKLE, J.P.,
THOS. HOWARD, [L.S.],

"Pas" Band
JOHN CONSTANT, Chief, his x mark,
JAMES COOK, Sr., his x mark,
JOHN BELL, Jr., his x mark,
PETER BELL, his x mark,
DONALD COOK, Sr., his x mark,
Councillors

"Cumberland" Band
JOHN COCHRANE, Chief, his x mark,
PETER CHAPMAN, his x mark,
ALBERT FLETT, his x mark,
Councillors

"Moose Lake" Band
O-TIN-IK-IM-AW, Chief, his x mark,
MA-IK-WUH-E-HA-POW, his x mark,
WA-ME-KWUW-UH-OP, his x mark,
KA-CHA-CHUCK-OOS, his x mark,
Councillors

ADHESION BY SAULTEAUX OR CHIPPEWA INDIANS
ARTICLES OF AGREEMENT AND ADHESION TO A TREATY made and concluded at Beren's River the 20th day of September, and at Norway House the

24th day of September, in the year of Our Lord one thousand eight hundred and seventy-five between Her Most Gracious Majesty the Queen of Great Britain and Ireland, by Her Commissioners, the Honourable Alexander Morris, Lieutenant-Governor of the Province of Manitoba and the North-west Territories, and the Honourable James McKay, of the one part, and the Saulteaux and Swampy Cree Tribes of Indians, inhabitants of the country within the limits hereinafter defined and described, by their Chiefs, chosen and named as hereinafter mentioned, of the other part.

We, the Band of Saulteaux Indians residing in the vicinity of the Grand Rapids of the Beren's River, having had communication of the aforesaid treaty, of which a true copy is hereunto annexed, hereby and in consideration of the provisions of the said treaty being extended to us, transfer, surrender and relinquish to Her Majesty the Queen, Her heirs and successors, to and for the use of the Government of Canada, all our rights, titles and privileges whatsoever, which we have or enjoy in the territory described in the said treaty, and every part thereof, to have and to hold to the use of Her Majesty the Queen, and Her heirs and successors forever.

And Her Majesty agrees, through Her representatives as hereinafter named to assign a reserve of sufficient area to allow one hundred and sixty acres to each family of five, or in that proportion for larger or smaller families, such reserve to be laid off and surveyed as soon as may be found practicable, at or near the Sandy Narrows of the Beren's River, on both sides of the said river, reserving the free navigation of the said river, and free access to the shores thereof, to all Her Majesty's subjects.

And the said Indians, represented herein by their Chief and Councillor, presented as such by the Band, do hereby agree to accept the several provisions, payments and other benefits, as stated in the said treaty, and solemnly promise and engage to abide by, carry out and fulfil all the stipulations, obligations and conditions therein contained, on the part of the said Chief and Indians therein named, to be observed and performed, and in all things to conform to the articles of the said treaty, as if we ourselves had been originally contracting parties thereto.

IN WITNESS WHEREOF, the Honourable Thomas Howard, and John Lestock Reid, Esquire, acting herein for Her Majesty, under special authority of the Honourable Alexander Morris, Lieutenant-Governor of Manitoba and the North-west Territories, and Chief Superintendent of Indian Affairs for the Manitoba Superintendency, and the said Chief and Councillor, have hereunto subscribed and set their hands at the Beren's River, this fourth day of August, A.D. 1876.

Signed by the Chief and Councillor within named in the presence of the following witnesses, the treaty and this adhesion having been first read and explained by the Rev. H. Cochrane

> HENRY COCHRANE, Missionary,
> JAMES FLETT,
> OWEN HUGHES,
> ALEXANDER BEGG,
> A. M. MUCKLE, J.P.,
> GEO. COLDEE,
> THOMAS PRATT,
> WILLIAM McKAY,
> THOMAS NIXON, Jr.,
> THOS. HOWARD, [L.S.],
> J. LESTOCK REID, [L.S.],
> NAH-WEE-KEE-SICK-QUAH-YASH,
> (Or JACOB BERENS, of Beren's River), his x mark,
> Chief, NUN-AK-OW-AH-NUK-WAPE, his x mark,
> Councillor

ADHESION BY SAULTEAUX AND CHIPPEWA INDIANS
ARTICLES OF AGREEMENT AND ADHESION TO A TREATY made and concluded at Beren's River the 20th day of September, and at Norway House the 24th day of September, in the year of Our Lord one thousand eight hundred and seventy five, between Her Most Gracious Majesty the Queen of Great Britain and Ireland, by Her Commissioners, the Honourable Alexander Morris, Lieutenant-Governor of the Province of Manitoba and the North-west Territories, and the Honourable James McKay, of the one part, and the Saulteaux and Swampy Cree Tribes of Indians, inhabitants of the country within the limits hereinafter defined and described, by their Chiefs, chosen and named as hereinafter mentioned, of the other part:

We, the Band of Saulteaux Indians residing at or near the Big Island and the other islands in Lake Winnipeg, and also on the shores thereof, having had communication of the aforesaid treaty, of which a true copy is hereunto annexed, hereby, and in consideration of the provisions of the said treaty being extended to us, transfer, surrender, and relinquish to Her Majesty the Queen, Her heirs and successors, to and for the use of the Government of Canada, all our right, title and privileges whatsoever, which we have or enjoy in the territory described in the said treaty, and every part thereof, to have and to hold to the use of Her Majesty the Queen, and Her heirs and successors forever.

And Her Majesty agrees, through Her representatives as hereinafter named, to assign reserves of sufficient area to allow one hundred and sixty acres to each family of five, or in that proportion for larger or smaller families, such reserves to be selected for said Indians by a Dominion Land Surveyor, or other officer named for that purpose, with the approval of the said Indians, as soon as practicable.

And the said Indians, represented herein by their Chief and Councillors, presented as such by the Band, do hereby agree to accept the several provisions, payments and other benefits as stated in the said treaty, and solemnly promise and engage to abide by, carry out and fulfil all the stipulations, obligations and conditions therein contained, on the part of the said Chief and Indians therein named, to be observed and performed, and in all things to conform to the articles of the said treaty, as if we ourselves had been originally contracting parties thereto.

IN WITNESS WHEREOF, the Honourable Thomas Howard, and John Lestock Reid, Esquire, acting herein for Her Majesty, under special authority of the Honourable Alexander Morris, Lieutenant-Governor of Manitoba and of the North-west Territories, and Chief Superintendent of Indian Affairs for the Manitoba Superintendency, and the said Chief and Councillors, have hereunto subscribed and set their hands, at Wapang, or Dog Head, Lake Winnipeg, this twenty-six day of July, A.D. 1876.

Signed by the Chief and Councillors within named in the presence of the following witnesses, treaty and this adhesion having been first read and explained by the Rev. Henry Cochrane:

W. W. KIRBY, Archdeacon of York,
HENRY COCHRANE, Missionary,

ALEXANDER BEGG,
WILLIAM LEACK,
THOMAS NIXON, Jr.,
A. M. MUCKLE, J.P.,
THOS. HOWARD, [L.S.],
J. LESTOCK REID, [L.S.],
SA-KA-CHE-WAYAS, Chief, (Blood Vein River.), his x mark,
KA-TUK-E-PIN-AIS or HARDISTY, (Big Island.), his x mark,
THICKFOOT, (Dog Head.), his x mark,
SANG-GWA-WA- KA-POW, or JAMES SINCLAIR, (Jack Head), his x mark,
Councillors

I, the Honourable Alexander Morris, Lieutenant-Governor of Manitoba and the North-west Territories, do hereby certify that the foregoing is a true copy of the treaty of which it purports to be a copy.

Given under my hand and seal at Fort Garry, this nineteenth day of July, A.D. 1876.

ALEXANDER MORRIS, L.G. [L.S.]

ADHESION TO TREATY 5 BY SPLIT LAKE AND NELSON HOUSE.

We, the undersigned Chiefs and Headmen, on behalf of ourselves and the other members of the Split Lake and Nelson House Bands of Indians, having had communication of the Treaty with certain Bands of Saulteaux and Swampy Cree Indians, known as Treaty No. 5, hereby in consideration of the provisions of the said Treaty being extended to us, it being understood and agreed that the said provisions shall not be retroactive, transfer, surrender, and relinquish to His Majesty the King, his heirs and successors, to and for the use of the Government of Canada, all our right, title and privileges whatsoever, which we have or enjoy in the territory described in the said Treaty, and every part thereof, to have and to hold to the use of His Majesty the King, and his heirs and successors forever.

And we also hereby transfer, surrender and relinquish to His Majesty the King, His heirs and successors, to and for the use of the Government of the Dominion of Canada, all our right, title and interest whatsoever which we and the said Bands which we represent hold and enjoy, or have held and enjoyed, of, in and to the territory within the following limits: All that portion of the North West Territories of Canada comprised within the following limits, that is to say; commencing where the sixtieth parallel of latitude intersects the water's edge of the West shore of Hudson Bay, thence West along the said parallel to the North East corner of the Province of Saskatchewan, thence south along the East boundary of the said Province, to the Northerly limit of the Indian treaty number Five, thence North Easterly, then South Easterly, then South Westerly and again South Easterly following the northerly limit of the said Treaty number Five to the intersection of a line drawn from the North East corner of the Province of Manitoba, North Fifty-five degrees East; thence on the said line produced fifty miles; thence North twenty-five degrees East one hundred and eighty miles more or less to a point situated due South of Cape Tatnam, thence due North ninety-eight miles more or less to the said Cape Tatnam; thence South Westerly and then Northerly following the water's edge of the West shore of Hudson Bay to the point of commencement, together with all the foreshores, and Islands adjacent to the said described tract of land, and containing approximately an area of one hundred and thirty-three thousand four hundred (133,400) square miles.

And also, all our right, title and interest whatsoever to all other lands wherever situated, whether within the limits of any other treaty heretofore made, or hereafter to be made with the Indians, and whether the said lands are situated in the North West Territories or elsewhere in His Majesty's Dominions, to have and to hold the same unto and for the use of His Majesty, the King, His heirs and successors forever.

And we hereby agree to accept the several benefits, payments and reserves promised to and accepted by the Indians adhering to the said Treaty No. 5. And we solemnly engage to abide by, carry out and fulfil all the stipulations, obligations and conditions therein contained on the part of the Chiefs and Indians therein named to be observed and performed, and we agree in all things to conform to the articles of the said treaty, as if we ourselves and the Bands which we represent had been originally contracting parties thereto and had attached our signatures to the said treaty.

And his Majesty hereby agrees to set apart Reserves of land of a like proportionate area to those mentioned in the original Treaty No. 5.

And his Majesty further hereby agrees to provide a grant proportionate to that mentioned in the original treaty to be yearly and every year expended by His Majesty in the purchase of ammunition and twine for nets for the use of the said Indians; and to further increase this annual grant in lieu of other supplies provided by the said treaty when this action is shown to be in the interests of the Indians.

And his Majesty further agrees to pay to each Indian a gratuity of Five Dollars in cash, once for all, in addition to the Five Dollars annuity promised by the Treaty in order to show the satisfaction of His Majesty with the behaviour and good conduct of his Indians and in extinguishment of all their past claims.

IN WITNESS WHEREOF, His Majesty's Special Commissioner and the Chiefs and Councillors of the Bands hereby giving their adhesion to the said treaty have hereunto subscribed and set their hands at Split Lake this Twenty-sixth day of June in the year of our Lord one thousand nine hundred and eight.

Signed by the parties hereto in the presence of the undersigned witnesses, the same having been first explained to the Indians by JOHN SEMMENS, Commissioner.

W. J. GRANT, M.D., Medical Officer,
R. J. SPENCER, Clerk,
H. McKAY, Commissioner,
G. J. WARDNER, Constable,
H. C. McLEOD, H. B. COY,
J. M. THOMAS, C.F,
[Name in Cree characters],
WM. KECHE-KESIK, his x mark,
[Name in Cree characters],
CHARLES MORRIS, his x mark,
[Name in Cree characters],
ALBERT SPENCE, his x mark

IN WITNESS WHEREOF, His Majesty's Special Commissioner and the Chiefs and Councillors of the Bands hereby giving their adhesion to the said treaty have hereunto subscribed and set their hands at Nelson House this thirtieth day of July in the year of our Lord one thousand nine hundred and eight.

Signed by the parties hereto in the presence of the undersigned witnesses, the same having been first explained to the Indians by JOHN SEMMENS, Commissioner.

W. J. GRANT, M.D., Medical Officer,
R. J. SPENCER, Clerk,
H. McKAY, Commissioner,
G. J. WARDNER, Constable,
FRED. A. SEMMENS,
G. D. BUTLER, S/Sergt. R.N.W.M. Police,
CHARLES GEORGE FOX, Missionary-
    Anglican,
GEO THOS. VINCENT,
ALEXANDER FLETT,
WILLIAM ISBESTER,
F. A. SEMMENS,
[Name in Cree characters],
PETER MOOSE, Chief, his x mark,
[Name in Cree characters),
MURDOCH HART, Councillor, his x mark,
[Name in Cree characters],
JAMES SPENCE, Councillor, his x mark

ADHESION TO TREATY No. 5
1908 —NORWAY HOUSE, CROSS LAKE, and FISHER RIVER.
Dated respectively: 8th July 1908; 15th July 1908; 24th August 1908.
WE, the undersigned principal men of the non-treaty Indians resident at the places hereinafter mentioned at which this adhesion has been signed having had communication of the Treaty with certain Bands of Saulteaux and Swampy Cree Indians, known as Treaty No. 5, hereby, in consideration of the provisions of the said Treaty being extended to us, it being understood and agreed that the said provisions shall not be retroactive, transfer, surrender and relinquish to His Majesty the King, his heirs and successors, to and for the use of the Government of Canada, all our right, title, and privileges whatsoever, which we have or enjoy in the territory described in the said treaty, and every part thereof, to have and to hold to the use of His Majesty the King, and his heirs and successors forever.

And also, all our right, title and interest whatsoever to all other lands wherever situated, whether within the limits of any other treaty heretofore made, or hereafter to be made with the Indians, and whether the said lands are situated in the North West Territories or elsewhere in His Majesty's Dominions, to have and to hold the same unto and for the use of His Majesty the King, His heirs and successors forever.

And His Majesty hereby agrees to set apart Reserves of land of a like proportionate area to those mentioned in the original Treaty No. 5, or if thought advisable, to add to Reserves already set aside proportionate areas for the Indians now by this Instrument giving their adhesion to the said Treaty.

And His Majesty further hereby agrees to provide a grant proportionate to that mentioned in the original Treaty to be yearly and every year expended by His Majesty in the purchase of ammunition and twine for nets for the use of the said Indians.

AND we hereby agree to accept the several benefits, payments and reserves promised to the Indians adhering to the said Treaty No. 5, it being understood and agreed by us that the said benefits and payments shall not be retroactive. And we solemnly engage to abide by, carry out and fulfil all the stipulations, obligations and conditions therein contained on the part of the Chiefs and Indians therein named to be observed and performed, and we agree in all things to conform to the articles of the said treaty, as if we ourselves and the Bands which we represent had been originally contracting parties thereto and had attached our signatures to the said treaty.

IN WITNESS WHEREOF His Majesty's Special Commissioner and the Chiefs and Councillors of the Bands hereby giving their adhesion to the said treaty have hereunto subscribed and set their hands at Norway House this eighth day of July and at Cross Lake this fifteenth day of July and at Fisher River this twenty-fourth day of August in the year of our Lord one thousand nine hundred and eight.

Signed by the parties hereto in the resence of the undersigned witnesses, the same having been first mark explained to the Indians by

JOHN SEMMENS, Commissioner,
SANDY SANDERS, his x mark,
PETER x MAHAM, his x mark,
THOMAS x GRIEVE, his x mark,
and 224 others at Norway House.
DANIEL MESWAKUN, his x mark,
DAVID MONEAS, his x mark,
SIMON MONEAS, his x mark,

and 70 others at Cross Lake.
PETER MURDO, his x mark,
JAMES KIRKNESS, his x mark,
and 17 others at Fisher River.

Witnessed by
R. J. SPENCER,
Clerk.

ADHESION TO TREATY No. 5
OXFORD HOUSE, GOD'S LAKE, and ISLAND LAKE BANDS.

Dated 29th day of July 1909

We, the undersigned Chiefs and Headmen, on behalf of ourselves and the other members of the Oxford House, God's Lake and Island Lake Band of Indians, having had communication of the Treaty with certain Bands of Saulteaux and Swampy Cree Indians, known as Treaty No. 5, hereby in consideration of the provisions of the said Treaty being extended to us, it being understood and agreed that the said provisions shall not be retroactive, transfer, surrender and relinquish to His Majesty the King, his heirs and successors, to and for the use of the Government of Canada, all our right, title and privileges whatsoever, which we have or enjoy in the territory described in the said Treaty, and every part thereof, to have and to hold to the use of His Majesty the King, and his heirs and successors forever.

And we also hereby transfer, surrender and relinquish to His Majesty the King, His heirs and successors, to and for the use of the Government of the Dominion of Canada, all our right, title and interest whatsoever which we and the said Bands which we represent hold and enjoy, or have held and enjoyed, of, in and to the territory within the following limits:—All that portion of the North West Territories of Canada comprised within the following limits, that is to say; commencing where the sixtieth parallel of latitude intersects the water's edge of the West shore of Hudson Bay, thence West along the said parallel to the North East corner of the Province of Saskatchewan, thence south along the East boundary of the said Province to the Northerly limit of the Indian treaty number Five, thence North Easterly, then South Easterly, then South Westerly and again South Easterly following the northerly limit of the said Treaty number Five to the intersection of a line drawn from the North East corner of the Province of Manitoba, North Fifty-five degrees East; thence

on the said line produced fifty miles; thence North twenty-five degrees East one hundred and eighty miles more or less to a point situated due South of Cape Tatnam, thence due North ninety-eight miles more or less to the said Cape Tatnam; thence South Westerly and then Northerly following the water's edge of the West shore of Hudson Bay to the point of commencement, together with all the foreshores, and Islands adjacent to the said described tract of land, and containing approximately an area of one hundred and thirty-three thousand four hundred (133,400) square miles.

And also, all our right, title and interest whatsoever to all other lands wherever situated, whether within the limits of any other treaty heretofore made, of hereafter to be made with the Indians, and whether the said lands are situated in the North West Territories or elsewhere in His Majesty's Dominions, to have and to hold the same unto and for the use of His Majesty, the King, His heirs and successors forever.

And we hereby agree to accept the several benefits, payments and reserves promised to and accepted by the Indians adhering to the said Treaty No. 5. And we solemnly engage to abide by, carry out and fulfil all the stipulations, obligations and conditions therein contained on the part of the Chiefs and Indians therein named to be observed and performed, and we agree in all things to conform to the articles of the said treaty, as if we ourselves and the Bands which we represent had been originally contracting parties thereto and had attached our signatures to the said treaty.

And His Majesty hereby agrees to set apart Reserves of land of a like proportionate area to those mentioned in the original Treaty No. 5.

And His Majesty further hereby agrees to provide a grant proportionate to that mentioned in the original Treaty to be yearly and every year expended by His Majesty in the purchase of ammunition and twine for nets for the use of the said Indians; and to further increase this annual grant in lieu of other supplies provided by the said treaty when this action is shown to be in the interests of the Indians.

And His Majesty further agrees to pay to each Indian a gratuity of Five Dollars in cash, once for all, in addition to the Five Dollars annuity promised by the Treaty in order to show the satisfaction of His Majesty with the behaviour and good conduct of his Indians and in extinguishment of all their past claims.

IN WITNESS WHEREOF, His Majesty's Special Commissioner and the Chiefs and Councillors of the Bands hereby giving their adhesion to the said treaty have hereunto subscribed and set their hands at Oxford House this Twenty Ninth day of July in the year of Our Lord one thousand nine hundred and nine.

Signed by the parties hereto in the presence of the undersigned witnesses, the same having been first explained to the Indians by

> JOHN SEMMENS, Commissioner,
> H. S. STEAD, Secretary,
> WALTER ROSS, M.D.C.M.,
> CHRISTY THOMPSON,
> H. A. McIVER,
> A. E. KEMP,
> BERTHA STEAD,
> BARBARA ROSS,
> JEREMIAS CHUBB Chief, his x mark,
> ROBERT CHUBB, H.S.S., Councillor., his x mark,
> JAMES NATAWAYO, Councillor, H.S.S., his x mark,

And at God's Lake this 6th day of August in the year of Our Lord one thousand nine hundred and nine.

Signed by the parties hereto in the presence of the undersigned witnesses, the same having been first explained to the Indians by

> H.S. STEAD, Secretary,
> A. B. MASSIL,
> E. T. BEVINGTON,
> A. SWAIN,
> C. THOMPSON,
> WALTER ROSS, M.D.C.M.,
> WM. M. McEWEN, Commissary,
> BARBARA ROSS,
> BERTHA STEAD,
> JOHN SEMMENS, Commissioner,
> [Name in Cree characters],
> (PETER WATT), Chief, his x mark,
> [Name in Cree characters],
> (BIG SIMON), Councillor., his x mark,
> PETER CHUBB, Councillor H.S.S., his x mark

And at Island Lake this 13th day of August in the year of Our Lord one thousand nine hundred and nine.

Signed by the parties hereto in the presence of the undersigned witnesses, the same having been first explained to the Indians by

> H. S. STEAD, Secretary,
> BERTHA STEAD,
> BARBARA ROSS,
> CHARLES B. ISBESTER,
> C. CUNNUNGHAM,
> WM. M. McEWEN, Commissary,
> WALTER ROSS, M.D.C.M.,
> ALEX H. CUNNINGHAM,
> JOHN SEMMENS, Commissioner,
> GEORGE NOTT, Chief, H.S.S., his x mark
> JOSEPH LINKLATER, Councillor H.S.S., his x mark
> JOHN MASON Councillor, H.S.S., his x mark

WE, the undersigned Chiefs and Headmen, on behalf of ourselves and the other members of the Deer Lake, Fort York and Fort Churchill Bands of Indians, having had communication of the Treaty with certain Bands of Saulteaux and Swampy Cree Indians, known as Treaty No. 5, hereby in consideration of the provisions of the said Treaty being extended to us, it being understood and agreed that the said provisions shall not be retroactive, transfer, surrender and relinquish to His Majesty the King, his heirs and successors, to and for the use of the Government of Canada, all our right, title and privileges whatsoever, which we have or enjoy in the territory described in the said Treaty, and every part thereof, to have and to hold to the use of His Majesty the King, and his heirs and successors forever.

And we also hereby transfer, surrender and relinquish to His Majesty the King, His heirs and successors, to and for the use of the Government of the Dominion of Canada, all our right, title and interest whatsoever which we and the said Bands which we represent hold and enjoy, or have held and enjoyed, of, in and to the territory within the following limits; All that portion of the North West Territories of Canada comprised within the following limits, that is to say; commencing where the sixtieth parallel of latitude intersects the water's edge of the West shore of Hudson Bay, thence West along the said parallel to the North East corner of the Province of Saskatchewan, thence south along the East boundary of the said Province to the Northerly limit of the Indian treaty number Five, thence North Easterly, then South Easterly, then South Westerly and again south Easterly following the northerly limit of the said Treaty Number Five to the intersection of a line drawn from the North East corner of the Province of Manitoba, North Fifty-five degrees East; thence on the said line produced fifty miles; thence North twenty-five degrees East one hundred and eighty miles more or less to a point situated due South of Cape Tatnam, thence due North ninety-eight miles more or less to the said Cape Tatnam; thence South Westerly and then Northerly following the water's edge of the West shore of Hudson Bay to the point of commencement, together with all the foreshores, and Islands adjacent to the said described tract of land, and containing approximately an area of one hundred and thirty-three thousand four hundred (133,400) square miles.

And also, all our right, title and interest whatsoever to all other lands wherever situated, whether within the limits of any other treaty heretofore made, or hereafter to be made with the Indians, and whether the said lands are situated in the North West Territories or elsewhere in His Majesty's Dominions, to have and to hold the same unto and for the use of His Majesty the King, His heirs and successors forever.

And we hereby agree to accept the several benefits, payments and reserves promised to and accepted by the Indians adhering to the said Treaty No. 5. And we solemnly engage to abide by, carry out and fulfil all the stipulations, obligations and conditions therein contained on the part of the Chiefs and Indians therein named to be observed and performed, and we agree in all things to conform to the articles of the said Treaty, as if we ourselves and the Bands which we represent had been originally contracting parties thereto and had attached our signatures to the said Treaty.

And His Majesty hereby agrees to set apart Reserves of land of a like proportionate area to those mentioned in the original Treaty No. 5.

And His Majesty further hereby agrees to provide a grant proportionate to that mentioned in the original Treaty to be yearly and every year expended by His Majesty in the purchase of ammunition and twine for nets for the use of the said Indians; and to further increase this annual grant in lieu of other supplies

provided by the said Treaty when this action is shown to be in the interests of the Indians.

And His Majesty further agrees to pay to each Indian a gratuity of Five Dollars in cash, once for all, in addition to the Five Dollars annuity promised by the Treaty in order to show the satisfaction of His Majesty with the behaviour and good conduct of his Indians and in extinguishment of all their past claims.

IN WITNESS WHEREOF, His Majesty's Special Commissioner and the Chiefs and Councillors of the Bands hereby giving their adhesion to the said Treaty have hereunto subscribed and set their hands at Deer's Lake East this ninth day of June in the year of our Lord one thousand nine hundred and ten.

Signed by the parties hereto in the presence of the undersigned witnesses, the same having been first explained to the Indians by

[L.S.] ROBERT FIDDLER, Chief of Deer's Lake East., his x mark
    A. VERNON THOMAS, secretary to
      Commissioner,
    HARVEY J. HASSARD, Physician,
    WM. M. McEWEN, Commissary

Signed at Fort Churchill, August 1st, 1910, by

    JOHN SEMMENS, [L.S.], Commissioner,
    FRENCH JOHN, Chief. [L.S.], his x mark,
    SAM CHINASHAGUN, Councillor [L.S.], his x
      mark,
    THOMAS CRAZY, Councillor [L.S.], his x mark

Witnessed by:

C. N. C. HAYTER, Sgt. R.N.W.M.P.,
ASHTON ASHTON
F. C. SEVIER, Missionary in Charge,
A. VERNON THOMAS, Clerk,
HARVEY. J. HASSARD, Physician,
JAMES MELVILLE, MACOUN,
THOMAS N. MARCELLUS,
WM. M. McEWEN, Commissary,
JOHN SEMMENS [L.S.], Commissioner

Signed at York Factory, August 10th, 1910.

[Name in Indian characters] [L.S.],

CHARLES WASTASEKOOT, Chief., his x mark,
[Name in Indian characters] [L.S.],
ROBERT BEARDY, Councillor, his x mark
[Name in Indian characters] [L.S.],
SANDY BEARDY, his x mark

Witnessed by:
HARVEY J. HANSARD, Physician,
LESLIE LAING,
THOS. TURNBULL,
RICHARD FARIES, clk. in H.O,
R. L. BAYLIS,
A. VERNON THOMAS, Clerk,
JOHN SEMMENS [L.S.], Commissioner

Treaty 6, 1876
Aug. 28, Sept. 9, 1876
Between Her Majesty the Queen and the Plain and Wood Cree Indians and Other Tribes of Indians at Fort Carlton, Fort Pitt and Battle River with Adhesions

ARTICLES OF A TREATY made and concluded near Carlton on the 23rd day of August and on the 28th day of said month, respectively, and near Fort Pitt on the 9th day of September, in the year of Our Lord one thousand eight hundred and seventy-six, between Her Most Gracious Majesty the Queen of Great Britain and Ireland, by Her Commissioners, the Honourable Alexander Morris, Lieutenant-Governor of the Province of Manitoba and the North-west Territories, and the Honourable James McKay, and the Honourable William Joseph Christie, of the one part, and the Plain and Wood Cree and the other Tribes of Indians, inhabitants of the country within the limits hereinafter defined and described by their Chiefs, chosen and named as hereinafter mentioned, of the other part.

Whereas the Indians inhabiting the said country have, pursuant to an appointment made by the said Commissioners, been convened at meetings at Fort Carlton, Fort Pitt and Battle River, to deliberate upon certain matters of interest to Her Most Gracious Majesty, of the one part, and the said Indians of the other.

And whereas the said Indians have been notified and informed by Her Majesty's said Commissioners

that it is the desire of Her Majesty to open up for settlement, immigration and such other purposes as to Her Majesty may seem meet, a tract of country bounded and described as hereinafter mentioned, and to obtain the consent thereto of Her Indian subjects inhabiting the said tract, and to make a treaty and arrange with them, so that there may be peace and good will between them and Her Majesty, and that they may know and be assured of what allowance they are to count upon and receive from Her Majesty's bounty and benevolence.

And whereas the Indians of the said tract, duly convened in council, as aforesaid, and being requested by Her Majesty's said Commissioners to name certain Chiefs and Headmen, who should be authorized on their behalf to conduct such negotiations and sign any treaty to be founded thereon, and to become responsible to Her Majesty for their faithful performance by their respective Bands of such obligations as shall be assumed by them, the said Indians have thereupon named for that purpose, that is to say, representing the Indians who make the treaty at Carlton, the several Chiefs and Councillors who have subscribed hereto, and representing the Indians who make the treaty at Fort Pitt, the several Chiefs and Councillors who have subscribed hereto.

And thereupon, in open council, the different Bands having presented their Chiefs to the said Commissioners as the Chiefs and Headmen, for the purposes aforesaid, of the respective Bands of Indians inhabiting the said district hereinafter described.

And whereas, the said Commissioners then and there received and acknowledged the persons so presented as Chiefs and Headmen, for the purposes aforesaid, of the respective Bands of Indians inhabiting the said district hereinafter described.

And whereas, the said Commissioners have proceeded to negotiate a treaty with the said Indians, and the same has been finally agreed upon and concluded, as follows, that is to say:

The Plain and Wood Cree Tribes of Indians, and all other the Indians inhabiting the district hereinafter described and defined, do hereby cede, release, surrender and yield up to the Government of the Dominion of Canada, for Her Majesty the Queen and Her successors forever, all their rights, titles and privileges, whatsoever, to the lands included within the following limits, that is to say:

Commencing at the mouth of the river emptying into the north-west angle of Cumberland Lake; thence westerly up the said river to its source; thence on a straight line in a westerly direction to the head of Green Lake; thence northerly to the elbow in the Beaver River; thence down the said river northerly to a point twenty miles from the said elbow; thence in a westerly direction, keeping on a line generally parallel with the said Beaver River (above the elbow), and about twenty miles distant therefrom, to the source of the said river; thence northerly to the north-easterly point of the south shore of Red Deer Lake, continuing westerly along the said shore to the western limit thereof; and thence due west to the Athabasca River; thence up the said river, against the stream, to the Jaspar House, in the Rocky Mountains; thence on a course south-easterly, following the easterly range of the mountains, to the source of the main branch of the Red Deer River; thence down the said river, with the stream, to the junction therewith of the outlet of the river, being the outlet of the Buffalo Lake; thence due east twenty miles; thence on a straight line south-eastwardly to the mouth of the said Red Deer River on the south branch of the Saskatchewan River; thence eastwardly and northwardly, following on the boundaries of the tracts conceded by the several treaties numbered four and five to the place of beginning.

And also, all their rights, titles and privileges whatsoever to all other lands wherever situated in the North-west Territories, or in any other Province or portion of Her Majesty's Dominions, situated and being within the Dominion of Canada.

The tract comprised within the lines above described embracing an area of 121,000 square miles, be the same more or less.

To have and to hold the same to Her Majesty the Queen and Her successors forever.

And Her Majesty the Queen hereby agrees and undertakes to lay aside reserves for farming lands, due respect being had to lands at present cultivated by the said Indians, and other reserves for the benefit of the said Indians, to be administered and dealt with for them by Her Majesty's Govern-

ment of the Dominion of Canada; provided, all such reserves shall not exceed in all one square mile for each family of five, or in that proportion for larger or smaller families, in manner following, that is to say: that the Chief Superintendent of Indian Affairs shall depute and send a suitable person to determine and set apart the reserves for each band, after consulting with the Indians thereof as to the locality which may be found to be most suitable for them.

Provided, however, that Her Majesty reserves the right to deal with any settlers within the bounds of any lands reserved for any Band as She shall deem fit, and also that the aforesaid reserves of land, or any interest therein, may be sold or otherwise disposed of by Her Majesty's Government for the use and benefit of the said Indians entitled thereto, with their consent first had and obtained; and with a view to show the satisfaction of Her Majesty with the behaviour and good conduct of Her Indians, She hereby, through Her Commissioners, makes them a present of twelve dollars for each man, woman and child belonging to the Bands here represented, in extinguishment of all claims heretofore preferred.

And further, Her Majesty agrees to maintain schools for instruction in such reserves hereby made as to Her Government of the Dominion of Canada may seem advisable, whenever the Indians of the reserve shall desire it.

Her Majesty further agrees with Her said Indians that within the boundary of Indian reserves, until otherwise determined by Her Government of the Dominion of Canada, no intoxicating liquor shall be allowed to be introduced or sold, and all laws now in force, or hereafter to be enacted, to preserve Her Indian subjects inhabiting the reserves or living elsewhere within Her North-west Territories from the evil influence of the use of intoxicating liquors, shall be strictly enforced.

Her Majesty further agrees with Her said Indians that they, the said Indians, shall have right to pursue their avocations of hunting and fishing throughout the tract surrendered as hereinbefore described, subject to such regulations as may from time to time be made by Her Government of Her Dominion of Canada, and saving and excepting such tracts as may from time to time be required or taken up for settlement, mining, lumbering or other purposes by Her said Government of the Dominion of Canada, or by any of the subjects thereof duly authorized therefor by the said Government.

It is further agreed between Her Majesty and Her said Indians, that such sections of the reserves above indicated as may at any time be required for public works or buildings, of what nature soever, may be appropriated for that purpose by Her Majesty's Government of the Dominion of Canada, due compensation being made for the value of any improvements thereon.

And further, that Her Majesty's Commissioners shall, as soon as possible after the execution of this treaty, cause to be taken an accurate census of all the Indians inhabiting the tract above described, distributing them in families, and shall, in every year ensuing the date hereof, at some period in each year, to be duly notified to the Indians, and at a place or places to be appointed for that purpose within the territory ceded, pay to each Indian person the sum of $5 per head yearly.

It is further agreed between Her Majesty and the said Indians, that the sum of $1,500.00 per annum shall be yearly and every year expended by Her Majesty in the purchase of ammunition, and twine for nets, for the use of the said Indians, in manner following, that is to say: In the reasonable discretion, as regards the distribution thereof among the Indians inhabiting the several reserves, or otherwise, included herein, of Her Majesty's Indian Agent having the supervision of this treaty.

It is further agreed between Her Majesty and the said Indians, that the following articles shall be supplied to any Band of the said Indians who are now cultivating the soil, or who shall hereafter commence to cultivate the land, that is to say: Four hoes for every family actually cultivating; also, two spades per family as aforesaid: one plough for every three families, as aforesaid; one harrow for every three families, as aforesaid; two scythes and one whetstone, and two hay forks and two reaping hooks, for every family as aforesaid, and also two axes; and also one cross-cut saw, one hand-saw, one pit-saw, the necessary files, one grindstone and one auger for each Band; and also for each Chief for the use of his Band, one chest of ordinary car-

penter's tools; also, for each Band, enough of wheat, barley, potatoes and oats to plant the land actually broken up for cultivation by such Band; also for each Band four oxen, one bull and six cows; also, one boar and two sows, and one hand-mill when any Band shall raise sufficient grain therefor. All the aforesaid articles to be given once and for all for the encouragement of the practice of agriculture among the Indians.

It is further agreed between Her Majesty and the said Indians, that each Chief, duly recognized as such, shall receive an annual salary of twenty-five dollars per annum; and each subordinate officer, not exceeding four for each Band, shall receive fifteen dollars per annum; and each such Chief and subordinate officer, as aforesaid, shall also receive once every year, a suitable suit of clothing, and each Chief shall receive, in recognition of the closing of the treaty, a suitable flag and medal, and also as soon as convenient, one horse, harness and wagon.

That in the event hereafter of the Indians comprised within this treaty being overtaken by any pestilence, or by a general famine, the Queen, on being satisfied and certified thereof by Her Indian Agent or Agents, will grant to the Indians assistance of such character and to such extent as Her Chief Superintendent of Indian Affairs shall deem necessary and sufficient to relieve the Indians from the calamity that shall have befallen them.

That during the next three years, after two or more of the reserves hereby agreed to be set apart to the Indians shall have been agreed upon and surveyed, there shall be granted to the Indians included under the Chiefs adhering to the treaty at Carlton, each spring, the sum of one thousand dollars, to be expended for them by Her Majesty's Indian Agents, in the purchase of provisions for the use of such of the Band as are actually settled on the reserves and are engaged in cultivating the soil, to assist them in such cultivation.

That a medicine chest shall be kept at the house of each Indian Agent for the use and benefit of the Indians at the direction of such agent.

That with regard to the Indians included under the Chiefs adhering to the treaty at Fort Pitt, and to those under Chiefs within the treaty limits who may hereafter give their adhesion thereto (exclusively, however, of the Indians of the Carlton region), there shall, during three years, after two or more reserves shall have been agreed upon and surveyed be distributed each spring among the Bands cultivating the soil on such reserves, by Her Majesty's Chief Indian Agent for this treaty, in his discretion, a sum not exceeding one thousand dollars, in the purchase of provisions for the use of such members of the Band as are actually settled on the reserves and engaged in the cultivation of the soil, to assist and encourage them in such cultivation.

That in lieu of waggons, if they desire it and declare their option to that effect, there shall be given to each of the Chiefs adhering hereto at Fort Pitt or elsewhere hereafter (exclusively of those in the Carlton district), in recognition of this treaty, as soon as the same can be conveniently transported, two carts with iron bushings and tires.

And the undersigned Chiefs on their own behalf and on behalf of all other Indians inhabiting the tract within ceded, do hereby solemnly promise and engage to strictly observe this treaty, and also to conduct and behave themselves as good and loyal subjects of Her Majesty the Queen.

They promise and engage that they will in all respects obey and abide by the law, and they will maintain peace and good order between each other, and also between themselves and other tribes of Indians, and between themselves and others of Her Majesty's subjects, whether Indians or whites, now inhabiting or hereafter to inhabit any part of the said ceded tracts, and that they will not molest the person or property of any inhabitant of such ceded tracts, or the property of Her Majesty the Queen, or interfere with or trouble any person passing or travelling through the said tracts, or any part thereof, and that they will aid and assist the officers of Her Majesty in bringing to justice and punishment any Indian offending against the stipulations of this treaty, or infringing the laws in force in the country so ceded.

IN WITNESS WHEREOF, Her Majesty's said Commissioners and the said Indian Chiefs have hereunto subscribed and set their hands at or near Fort Carlton, on the days and year aforesaid, and near Fort Pitt on the day above aforesaid.

Treaty 7, 1877

Sept. 22, Dec. 4, 1877
Treaty and Supplementary Treaty No. 7 made 22nd Sept., and 4th Dec., 1877, between her Majesty the Queen and the Blackfeet and other Indian Tribes, at the Blackfoot Crossing of Bow River and Fort MacLeod.

ORDER IN COUNCIL SETTING UP COMMISSION FOR TREATY No. 7

On a Report dated 28th June 1877 from the Honourable the Minister of the Interior stating that it having been decided that a Treaty should be made this year with the Blackfeet and other Indians occupying the unceded territory North of the Boundary Line, East of the Rocky Mountains, and West and South of Treaties Nos. 4 and 6, His Honor Lieut. Governor Laird was in the early part of the year instructed to notify the Indians that Commissioners would be sent in the Fall to negotiate a Treaty with them at such time and place as His Honor might appoint for that purpose.

That His Honor has advised the Department that he has accordingly notified the Indians to assemble at Fort MacLeod on the 13th September next to meet the Commissioners to be appointed to negotiate a Treaty with them. That the necessary funds to meet the expense of the Treaty have been duly provided in the Estimates for the coming year.

That the Territory to be included in the proposed Treaty is occupied by the Blackfeet, Crees, Sarcees and Peigans and may be estimated approximately at about 35,000 Square Miles in area.

The Minister recommends that His Honor the Lieutenant Governor of the North West Territories and Lieut. Colonel James F. Macleod, C.M.G., Commissioner of the Mounted Police, be appointed Commissioners for the purpose of negotiating the proposed Treaty.

The Committee submit the foregoing recommendations for approval.

Signed: A. Mackenzie

Approved

12 July 1877
Signed: Mr. B. Richards
Deputy Governor

ARTICLES OF A TREATY

Made and concluded this twenty-second day of September, in the year of Our Lord, one thousand eight hundred and seventy-seven, between Her Most Gracious Majesty the Queen of Great Britain and Ireland, by Her Commissioners, the Honorable David Laird, Lieutenant-Governor and Indian Superintendent of the North-West Territories, and James Farquharson MacLeod, C.M.G., Commissioner of the North-West Mounted Police, of the one part, and the Blackfeet, Blood, Piegan, Sarcee, Stony and other Indians, inhabitants of the Territory north of the United States Boundary Line, east of the central range of the Rocky Mountains, and south and west of Treaties numbers six and four, by their Head Chiefs and Minor Chiefs or Councillors, chosen as hereinafter mentioned, of the other part.

WHEREAS the Indians inhabiting the said Territory, have, pursuant to an appointment made by the said Commissioners, been convened at a meeting at the "Blackfoot Crossing" of the Bow River, to deliberate upon certain matters of interest to Her Most Gracious Majesty, of the one part, and the said Indians of the other;

And whereas the said Indians have been informed by Her Majesty's Commissioners that it is the desire of Her Majesty to open up for settlement, and such other purposes as to Her Majesty may seem meet, a tract of country, bounded and described as hereinafter mentioned, and to obtain the consent thereto of Her Indian subjects inhabiting the said tract, and to make a Treaty, and arrange with them, so that there may be peace and good will between them and Her Majesty, and between them and Her Majesty's other subjects; and that Her Indian people may know and feel assured of what allowance they are to count upon and receive from Her Majesty's bounty and benevolence;

And whereas the Indians of the said tract, duly convened in Council, and being requested by Her Majesty's Commissioners to present their Head Chiefs and Minor Chiefs, or Councillors, who shall be authorized, on their behalf, to conduct such negotiations and sign any Treaty to be founded thereon, and to become responsible to Her Majesty for the faithful performance, by their respective Bands of such obligations as should be assumed by them, the said Blackfeet, Blood, Piegan and Sarcee Indians have therefore acknowledged for that purpose, the several Head and Minor Chiefs, and the said Stony Indians, the Chiefs and Councillors who have subscribed hereto, that thereupon in open Council the said Commissioners received and acknowledged the Head and Minor Chiefs and the Chiefs and Councillors presented for the purpose aforesaid;

And whereas the said Commissioners have proceeded to negotiate a Treaty with the said Indians; and the same has been finally agreed upon and concluded as follows, that is to say: the Blackfeet, Blood, Piegan, Sarcee, Stony and other Indians inhabiting the district hereinafter more fully described and defined, do hereby cede, release, surrender, and yield up to the Government of Canada for Her Majesty the Queen and her successors for ever, all their rights, titles, and privileges whatsoever to the lands included within the following limits, that is to say:

Commencing at a point on the International Boundary due south of the western extremity of the Cypress Hills, thence west along the said boundary to the central range of the Rocky Mountains, or to the boundary of the Province of British Columbia, thence north-westerly along the said boundary to a point due west of the source of the main branch of the Red Deer River, thence south-westerly and southerly following on the boundaries of the Tracts ceded by the Treaties numbered six and four to the place of commencement;

And also all their rights, titles and privileges whatsoever, to all other lands wherever situated in the North-West Territories, or in any other portion of the Dominion of Canada:

To have and to hold the same to Her Majesty the Queen and her successors for ever:

And Her Majesty the Queen hereby agrees with her said Indians, that they shall have right to pursue their vocations of hunting throughout the Tract surrendered as heretofore described, subject to such regulations as may, from time to time, be made by the Government of the country, acting under the authority of Her Majesty and saving and excepting such Tracts as may be required or taken up from time to time for settlement, mining, trading or other purposes by Her Government of Canada; or by any of Her Majesty's subjects duly authorized therefor by the said Government.

It is also agreed between Her Majesty and Her said Indians that Reserves shall be assigned them of sufficient area to allow one square mile for each family of five persons, or in that proportion for larger and smaller families, and that said Reserves shall be located as follows, that is to say:

First. —The Reserves of the Blackfeet, Blood and Sarcee Bands of Indians, shall consist of a belt of land on the north side of the Bow and South Saskatchewan Rivers, of an average width of four miles along said rivers, down stream, commencing at a point on the Bow River twenty miles north-westerly of the Blackfoot Crossing thereof, and extending to the Red Deer River at its junction with the South Saskatchewan; also for the term of ten years, and no longer, from the date of the concluding of this Treaty, when it shall cease to be a portion of said Indian Reserves, as fully to all intents and purposes as if it had not at any time been included therein, and without any compensation to individual Indians for improvements, of a similar belt of land on the south side of the Bow and Saskatchewan Rivers of an average width of one mile along said rivers, down stream; commencing at the aforesaid point on the Bow River, and extending to a point one mile west of the coal seam on said river, about five miles below the said Blackfoot Crossing; beginning again one mile east of the said coal seam and extending to the mouth of Maple Creek at its junction with the South Saskatchewan; and beginning again at the junction of the Bow River with the latter river, and extending on both sides of the South Saskatchewan in an average width on each side thereof of one mile, along said river against the stream, to the junction of the Little Bow River with the latter river, reserving to Her Majesty, as may now or hereafter be required by Her for the use of Her Indian and other subjects, from all the Reserves hereinbefore described, the right to navigate the above mentioned rivers, to land and receive fuel cargoes on the shores and banks thereof, to build bridges and establish ferries thereon, to use the fords thereof and all the trails leading thereto, and to open such other roads through the said Reserves as may appear to Her Majesty's Government of Canada, necessary for the ordinary travel of her Indian and other subjects, due compensation being paid to individual Indians for improvements, when the same may be in any manner encroached upon by such roads.

Secondly —That the Reserve of the Piegan Band of Indians shall be on the Old Man's River, near the foot of the Porcupine Hills, at a place called "Crow's Creek."

And, Thirdly —The Reserve of the Stony Band of Indians shall be in the vicinity of Morleyville.

In view of the satisfaction of Her Majesty with the recent general good conduct of her said Indians, and in extinguishment of all their past claims, she hereby, through her Commissioners, agrees to make them a present payment of twelve dollars each in cash to each man, woman, and child of the families here represented.

Her Majesty also agrees that next year, and annually afterwards forever, she will cause to be paid to the said Indians, in cash, at suitable places and dates, of which the said Indians shall be duly notified, to each Chief, twenty-five dollars, each minor Chief or Councillor (not exceeding fifteen minor Chiefs to the Blackfeet and Blood Indians, and four to the Piegan and Sarcee Bands, and five Councillors to the Stony Indian Bands), fifteen dollars, and to every other Indian of whatever age, five dollars; the same, unless there be some exceptional reason, to be paid to the heads of families for those belonging thereto.

Further, Her Majesty agrees that the sum of two thousand dollars shall hereafter every year be expended in the purchase of ammunition for distribution among the said Indians; Provided that if at any future time ammunition become comparatively unnecessary for said Indians, Her Government, with the consent of said Indians, or any of the Bands thereof, may expend the proportion due to such Band otherwise for their benefit.

Further, Her Majesty agrees that each Head Chief and Minor Chief, and each Chief and Councillor duly recognized as such, shall, once in every three years, during the term of their office, receive a suitable suit of clothing, and each Head Chief and Stony Chief, in recognition of the closing of the Treaty, a suitable medal and flag, and next year, or as soon as convenient, each Head Chief, and Minor Chief, and Stony Chief shall receive a Winchester rifle.

Further, Her Majesty agrees to pay the salary of such teachers to instruct the children of said Indians as to Her Government of Canada may seem advisable,

when said Indians are settled on their Reserves and shall desire teachers.

Further, Her Majesty agrees to supply each Head and Minor Chief, and each Stony Chief, for the use of their Bands, ten axes, five handsaws, five augers, one grindstone, and the necessary files and whetstones.

And further, Her Majesty agrees that the said Indians shall be supplied as soon as convenient, after any Band shall make due application therefor, with the following cattle for raising stock, that is to say: for every family of five persons, and under, two cows; for every family of more than five persons, and less than ten persons, three cows, for every family of over ten persons, four cows; and every Head and Minor Chief, and every Stony Chief, for the use of their Bands, one bull; but if any Band desire to cultivate the soil as well as raise stock, each family of such Band shall receive one cow less than the above mentioned number, and in lieu thereof, when settled on their Reserves and prepared to break up the soil, two hoes, one spade, one scythe, and two hay forks, and for every three families, one plough and one harrow, and for each Band, enough potatoes, barley, oats, and wheat (if such seeds be suited for the locality of their Reserves) to plant the land actually broken up. All the aforesaid articles to be given, once for all, for the encouragement of the practice of agriculture among the Indians.

And the undersigned Blackfeet, Blood, Piegan and Sarcee Head Chiefs and Minor Chiefs, and Stony Chiefs and Councillors on their own behalf and on behalf of all other Indians inhabiting the Tract within ceded do hereby solemnly promise and engage to strictly observe this Treaty, and also to conduct and behave themselves as good and loyal subjects of Her Majesty the Queen. They promise and engage that they will, in all respects, obey and abide by the Law, that they will maintain peace and good order between each other and between themselves and other tribes of Indians, and between themselves and others of Her Majesty's subjects, whether Indians, Half Breeds or Whites, now inhabiting, or hereafter to inhabit, any part of the said ceded tract; and that they will not molest the person or property of any inhabitant of such ceded tract, or the property of Her Majesty the Queen, or interfere with or trouble any person, passing or travelling through the said tract or any part thereof, and that they will assist the officers of Her Majesty in bringing to justice and punishment any Indian offending against the stipula-

tions of this Treaty, or infringing the laws in force in the country so ceded.

IN WITNESS WHEREOF HER MAJESTY'S said Commissioners, and the said Indian Head and Minor Chiefs, and Stony Chiefs and Councillors, have hereunto subscribed and set their hands, at the "Blackfoot Crossing" of the Bow River, the day and year herein first above written.

Signed by the Chiefs and Councillors within named in presence of the following witnesses, the same having been first explained by James Bird, Interpreter.

> DAVID LAIRD, Lieutenant-Governor of North-West Territories, and Special Indian Commissioner,
> A. G. IRVINE, Ass't. Com., N.W.M.P.,
> J. McDOUGALL, Missionary,
> JEAN L'HEUREUX,
> W. WINDER, Inspector,
> T. N. F. CROZIER, Inspector,
> E. DALRYMPLE CLARK, Lieut & Adjutant N.W.M.P.,
> A. SHURTLIFF, Sub Inspector,
> C. E. DENING, Sub Inspector,
> W. D. AUTROBUS, Sub Inspector,
> FRANK NORMAN, Staff Constable,
> MARY J. MACLEOD,
> JULIA WINDER,
> JULIA SHURTLIFF,
> E. HARDISTY,
> A. McDOUGALL,
> E. A. BARRETT,
> JAMES F. MACLEOD, Lieut.-Colonel,
> Com. N.W.M.P., and Special Indian Commissioner,
> CHAPO-MEXICO, or Crowfoot, Head Chief of the South Blackfeet,
> MATOSE-APIW, or Old Sun, Head Chief of the North Blackfeet,
> STAMISCOTOCAR, or Bull Head, Head Chief of the Sarcees,
> MEKASTO, or Red Crow, Head Chief of the South Bloods
> CONSTANTINE SCOLLEN, Priest, witness to signatures of Stonixosak and those following.
>
> CHARLES E. CONRAD,
> THOS J. BOGG,
> NATOSE-ONISTORS, or Medicine Calf,

POKAPIW-OTOIAN, or Bad Head,

SOTENAH, or Rainy Chief, Head Chief of the
North Bloods,

TAKOYE-STAMIX, or Fiend Bull,

AKKA-KITCIPIMIW-OTAS, or Many Spotted
Horse,

ATTISTAH-MACAN, or Running Rabbit,

PITAH-PEKIS, or Eagle Rib,

SAKOYE-AOTAN, or Heavy Shield, Head
Chief of the Middle Blackfeet,

ZOATZE-TAPITAPIW, or Setting on an Eagle
Tail, Head Chief of the North Piegans,

AKKA-MAKKOYE, or Many Swans,

APENAKO-SAPOP, or Morning Plume, his x
mark,

MAS-GWA-AH-SID, or Bear's Paw,

CHE-NE-KA, or John,

KI-CHI-PWOT, or Jacob,

STAMIX-OSOK, or Bull Backfat,

EMITAH-APISKINNE,or White Striped Dog,

MATAPI-KOMOTZIW, or the Captive or Stolen
Person,

APAWAWAKOSOW, or White Antelope,

MAKOYE-KIN, or Wolf Collar,

AYE-STIPIS-SIMAT, or Heavily Whipped,

KISSOUM, or Day Light,

PITAH-OTOCAN, or Eagle Head,

APAW-STAMIX, or Weasel Bull,

ONISTAH -POKAH, or White Calf,

NETAH-KITEI-PI-MEW or Only Spot,

AKAK-OTOS, or Many Horses,

STOKIMATIS, or The Drum,

PITAH-ANNES, or Eagle Robe,

PITAH-OTISKIN, or Eagle Shoe,

STAMIXO-TA-KA-PIW, or Bull Turn Round,

MASTE-PITAH, or Crow Eagle,

JAMES DIXON,

ABRAHAM KECHEPWOT,

PATRICK KECHEPWOT,

GEORGE MOY-ANY-MEN,

GEORGE CRAWLOR,

EKAS-KINE, or Low Horn,

KAYO-OKOSIS, or Bear Shield,

PONOKAH-STAMIX, or Bull Elk,

OMAKSI SAPOP, or Big Plume,

ONISTAH, or Calf Robe,

PITAH-SIKSINUM, or White Eagle,

APAW-ONISTAW, or Weasel Calf,

ATTISTA-HAES, or Rabbit Carrier,

PITAH, or Eagle,

PITAH-ONISTAH, or Eagle White Calf,

KAYE-TAPO, or Going to Bear

We the members of the Blackfoot tribe of Indians having had explained to us the terms of the Treaty made and concluded at the Blackfoot Crossing of the Bow River, on the twenty-second day of September, in the year of our Lord one thousand eight hundred and seventy-seven;

Between Her Majesty the Queen, by Her Commissioners duly appointed to negotiate the said Treaty and the Blackfeet, Blood, Piegan, Sarcee, Stony and other Indian inhabitants of the country within the limits defined in the said Treaty, but not having been present at the Councils at which the articles of the said Treaty were agreed upon, do now hereby, for ourselves and the Bands which we represent, in consideration of the provisions of the said Treaty being extended to us and the Bands which we represent, transfer, surrender and relinquish to Her Majesty the Queen, Her heirs and successors, to and for the use of Her Government of the Dominion of Canada, all our right, title, and interest whatsoever which we and the said Bands which we represent have held or enjoyed of in and to the territory described and fully set out in the said Treaty; also, all our right, title, and interest whatsoever to all other lands wherever situated, whether within the limits of any other Treaty heretofore made or hereafter to be made with Indians, or elsewhere in Her Majesty's territories, to have and to hold the same unto and for the use of Her Majesty the Queen, Her heirs and successors forever;

And we hereby agree to accept the several benefits, payments, and Reserves promised to the Indians under the Chiefs adhering to the said Treaty at the Blackfoot Crossing of the Bow River, and we solemnly engage to abide by, carry out and fulfil all the stipulations, obligations and conditions therein contained on the part of the Chiefs and Indians therein named, to be observed and performed and in all things to conform to the articles of the said Treaty, as if we ourselves and the Bands which we represent had been originally contracting parties thereto and had been present at the Councils held at the Blackfoot Crossing of the Bow River, and had there attached our signatures to the said Treaty.

IN WITNESS WHEREOF, James Farquharson MacLeod, C.M.G., one of Her Majesty's Commissioners appointed to negotiate the said Treaty, and the Chief of the Band, hereby giving their adhesion to the said Treaty, have hereunto subscribed and set

their hands at Fort MacLeod, this fourth day of December, in the year of our Lord one thousand and eight hundred and seventy-seven.

Signed by the parties hereto in the presence of the undersigned witnesses, the same having been explained to the Indians by the said James Farquharson MacLeod, one of the Commissioners appointed to negotiate the said Treaty, through theinterpreter, Jerry Potts, in thepresence of

A. G. IRVINE,
Assistant Commissioner.
E. DALRMYMLE CLARK,
Lieutenant and Adjutant N.W.M.P.
CHARLES E. CONRAD,
W. WINDER,
Inspector.

Treaty 8, 1899

June 21, 1899
Treaty No. 8 MADE JUNE 21, 1899 AND ADHESIONS, REPORTS, ETC.

ARTICLES OF A TREATY made and concluded at the several dates mentioned therein, in the year of Our Lord one thousand eight hundred and ninety-nine, between Her most Gracious Majesty the Queen of Great Britain and Ireland, by Her Commissioners the Honourable David Laird, of Winnipeg, Manitoba, Indian Commissioner for the said Province and the Northwest Territories; James Andrew Joseph McKenna, of Ottawa, Ontario, Esquire, and the Honourable James Hamilton Ross, of Regina, in the Northwest Territories, of the one part; and the Cree, Beaver, Chipewyan and other Indians, inhabitants of the territory within the limits hereinafter defined and described, by their Chiefs and Headmen, hereunto subscribed, of the other part:

WHEREAS, the Indians inhabiting the territory hereinafter defined have, pursuant to notice given by the Honourable Superintendent General of Indian Affairs in the year 1898, been convened to meet a Commission representing Her Majesty's Government of the Dominion of Canada at certain places in the said territory in this present year 1899, to deliberate upon certain matters of interest of Her Most Gracious Majesty, of the one part, and the said Indians of the other.

AND WHEREAS, the said Indians have been notified and informed by Her Majesty's said Commission that it is Her desire to open for settlement, immigration, trade, travel, mining, lumbering and such other purposes as to Her Majesty may seem meet, a tract of country bounded and described as hereinafter mentioned, and to obtain the consent thereto of Her Indian subjects inhabiting the said tract, and to make a treaty, and arrange with them, so that there may be peace and good will between them and Her Majesty's other subjects, and that Her Indian people may know and be assured of what allowances they are to count upon and receive from Her Majesty's bounty and benevolence.

AND WHEREAS, the Indians of the said tract, duly convened in council at the respective points named hereunder, and being requested by Her Majesty's Commissioners to name certain Chiefs and Headmen who should be authorized on their behalf to conduct such negotiations and sign any treaty to be founded thereon, and to become responsible to Her Majesty for the faithful performance by their respective bands of such obligations as shall be assumed by them, the said Indians have therefore acknowledged for that purpose the several Chiefs and Headmen who have subscribed hereto.

AND WHEREAS, the said Commissioners have proceeded to negotiate a treaty with the Cree, Beaver, Chipewyan and other Indians, inhabiting the district hereinafter defined and described, and the same has been agreed upon and concluded by the respective bands at the dates mentioned hereunder, the said Indians DO HEREBY CEDE, RELEASE, SURRENDER AND YIELD UP to the Government of the Dominion of Canada, for Her Majesty the Queen and Her successors for ever, all their rights, titles and privileges whatsoever, to the lands included within the following limits, that is to say:

Commencing at the source of the main branch of the Red Deer River in Alberta, thence due west to the central range of the Rocky Mountains, thence northwesterly along the said range to the point where it intersects the 60th parallel of north latitude, thence east along said parallel to the point where it intersects Hay River, thence northeasterly down said river to the south shore of Great Slave Lake, thence along the said shore northeasterly (and including such rights to the islands in said lakes as the Indians mentioned in the treaty may possess), and thence easterly and northeasterly along the south shores of Christie's Bay and McLeod's Bay to old Fort Reliance near the mouth of Lockhart's River, thence southeasterly in a straight line to and including Black Lake, thence southwesterly up the stream from Cree Lake, thence including said lake southwesterly along the height of land between the Athabasca and Churchill Rivers to where it intersects the northern boundary of Treaty Six, and along the said boundary easterly, northerly and southwesterly, to the place of commencement.

AND ALSO the said Indian rights, titles and privileges whatsoever to all other lands wherever situated in the Northwest Territories, British Columbia, or in any other portion of the Dominion of Canada.

TO HAVE AND TO HOLD the same to Her Majesty the Queen and Her successors for ever.

And Her Majesty the Queen HEREBY AGREES with the said Indians that they shall have right to pursue their usual vocations of hunting, trapping and fishing throughout the tract surrendered as heretofore described, subject to such regulations as may from time to time be made by the Government of the country, acting under the authority of Her Majesty, and saving and excepting such tracts as may be required or taken up from time to time for settlement, mining, lumbering, trading or other purposes.

And Her Majesty the Queen hereby agrees and undertakes to lay aside reserves for such bands as desire reserves, the same not to exceed in all one square mile for each family of five for such number of families as may elect to reside on reserves, or in that proportion for larger or smaller families; and for such families or individual Indians as may prefer to live apart from band reserves, Her Majesty undertakes to provide land in severalty to the extent of 160 acres to each Indian, the land to be conveyed with a proviso as to non-alienation without the consent of the Governor General in Council of Canada, the selection of such reserves, and lands in severalty, to be made in the manner following, namely, the Superintendent General of Indian Affairs shall depute and send a suitable person to determine and set apart such reserves and lands, after consulting with the Indians concerned as to the locality which may be found suitable and open for selection.

Provided, however, that Her Majesty reserves the right to deal with any settlers within the bounds of any lands reserved for any band as She may see fit; and also that the aforesaid reserves of land, or any interest therein, may be sold or otherwise disposed of by Her Majesty's Government for the use and benefit of the said Indians entitled thereto, with their consent first had and obtained.

It is further agreed between Her Majesty and Her said Indian subjects that such portions of the reserves and lands above indicated as may at any time be required for public works, buildings, railways, or roads of whatsoever nature may be appropriated for that purpose by Her Majesty's Government of the Dominion of Canada, due compensation being made to the Indians for the value of any improvements thereon, and an equivalent in land, money or other consideration for the area of the reserve so appropriated.

And with a view to show the satisfaction of Her Majesty with the behaviour and good conduct of Her Indians, and in extinguishment of all their past claims, She hereby, through Her Commissioners, agrees to make each Chief a present of thirty-two dollars in cash, to each Headman twenty-two dollars, and to every other Indian of whatever age, of the families represented at the time and place of payment, twelve dollars.

Her Majesty also agrees that next year, and annually afterwards for ever, She will cause to be paid to the said Indians in cash, at suitable places and dates, of which the said Indians shall be duly notified, to each Chief twenty-five dollars, each Headman, not to exceed four to a large Band and two to a small Band, fifteen dollars, and to every other Indian, of whatever age, five dollars, the same, unless there be some exceptional reason, to be paid only to heads of families for those belonging thereto.

FURTHER, Her Majesty agrees that each Chief, after signing the treaty, shall receive a silver medal and a suitable flag, and next year, and every third year thereafter, each Chief and Headman shall receive a suitable suit of clothing.

FURTHER, Her Majesty agrees to pay the salaries of such teachers to instruct the children of said Indians as to Her Majesty's Government of Canada may seem advisable.

FURTHER, Her Majesty agrees to supply each Chief of a Band that selects a reserve, for the use of that Band, ten axes, five hand-saws, five augers, one grindstone, and the necessary files and whetstones.

FURTHER, Her Majesty agrees that each Band that elects to take a reserve and cultivate the soil, shall, as soon as convenient after such reserve is set aside and settled upon, and the Band has signified its choice and is prepared to break up the soil, receive two hoes, one spade, one scythe and two hay forks for every family so settled, and for every three families one plough and one harrow, and to the Chief, for the use of his Band, two horses or a yoke of oxen, and for each Band potatoes, barley, oats and wheat (if such seed be suited to the locality of the reserve), to plant the land actually broken up, and provisions for one month in the spring for several years while planting such seeds; and to every family one cow, and every Chief one bull, and one mowing-machine and one reaper for the use of his Band when it is ready for them; for such families as prefer to raise stock instead of cultivating the soil, every family of five persons, two cows, and every Chief two bulls and two mowing-machines when ready for their use, and a like proportion for smaller or larger families. The aforesaid articles, machines and cattle to be given one for all for the encouragement of agriculture and stock raising; and for such Bands as prefer to continue hunting and fishing, as much ammunition and twine for making nets annually as will amount in value to one dollar per head of the families so engaged in hunting and fishing.

And the undersigned Cree, Beaver, Chipewyan and other Indian Chiefs and Headmen, on their own behalf and on behalf of all the Indians whom they represent, DO HEREBY SOLEMNLY PROMISE and engage to strictly observe this Treaty, and also to conduct and behave themselves as good and loyal subjects of Her Majesty the Queen.

THEY PROMISE AND ENGAGE that they will, in all respects, obey and abide by the law; that they will maintain peace between each other, and between themselves and other tribes of Indians, and between themselves and others of Her Majesty's subjects, whether Indians, half-breeds or whites, this year inhabiting and hereafter to inhabit any part of the said ceded territory; and that they will not molest the person or property of any inhabitant of such ceded tract, or of any other district or country, or interfere with or trouble any person passing or travelling through the said tract or any part thereof, and that they will assist the officers of Her Majesty in bringing to justice and punishment any Indian offending against the stipulations of this Treaty or infringing the law in force in the country so ceded.

IN WITNESS WHEREOF Her Majesty's said Commissioners and the Cree Chief and Headmen of Lesser Slave Lake and the adjacent territory, HAVE HEREUNTO SET THEIR HANDS at Lesser Slave Lake on the twenty-first day of June, in the year herein first above written.

Signed by the parties hereto, in the presence of the undersigned witnesses, the same having been first explained to the Indians by Albert Tate and Samuel Cunningham, Interpreters.

Father A. LACOMBE,
GEO. HOLMES,
E. GROUARD, O.M.I.,
W. G. WHITE,
JAMES WALKER,
J. ARTHUR COTÉ,
A. E. SNYDER, Insp. N.W.M.P.,
H. B. ROUND,
HARRISON S. YOUNG,
J. F. PRUD'HOMME,
J. W. MARTIN,
C. MAIR,
H. A. CONROY,
PIERRE DESCHAMBEAULT,
J. H. PICARD,
RICHARD SECORD,
M. MCCAULEY,
DAVID LAIRD, Treaty Commissioner,
J.A.J. McKENNA, Treaty Commissioner,
J. H. ROSS, Treaty Commissioner,
KEE NOO SHAY OO Chief,
MOOSTOOS Headman,
FELIX GIROUX Headman,
WEE CHEE WAY SIS Headman,
CHARLES NEE SUE TA SIS Headman,
CAPTAIN Headman, from Sturgeon Lake

In witness whereof the Chairman of Her Majesty's Commissioners and the Headman of the Indians of Peace River Landing and the adjacent territory, in behalf of himself and the Indians whom he represents, have hereunto set their hands at the said Peace River Landing on the first day of July in the year of Our Lord one thousand eight hundred and ninety-nine.

Signed by the parties hereto, in the presence of the undersigned witnesses, the same having been first explained to the Indians by Father A. Lacombe and John Boucher, Interpreters.

Father A. LACOMBE,
E. GROUARD, O.M.I., Ev. d'Ibora,
GEO. HOLMES,
HENRY MCCORRISTER,
K. F. ANDERSON, SGT., N.W.M.P.,
PIERRE DESCHAMBEAULT,
H. A. CONROY,
T.A. BRICK,
HARRISON S. YOUNG,
J. W. MARTIN,
DAVID CURRY,
DAVID LAIRD, *Chairman of Indian Treaty Commissioners,*
DUNCAN TASTAOOSTS, *Headman of Crees*

In witness whereof the Chairman of Her Majesty's Commissioners and the Chief and Headmen of the Beaver and Headman of the Crees and other Indians of Vermilion and the adjacent territory, in behalf of themselves and the Indians whom they represent, have hereunto set their hands at Vermilion on the eighth day of July, in the year of our Lord one thousand eight hundred and ninety-nine.

Signed by the parties hereto, in the presence of the undersigned witnesses, the same having been first explained to the Indians by Father A. Lacombe and John Boucher, Interpreters.

Father A. LACOMBE,
E. GROUARD, O.M.I., Ev. d'Ibora,
MALCOLM SCOTT,
F.D. WILSON, H.B. Co.,
H. A. CONROY,
PIERRE DESCHAMBEAULT,
HARRISON S. YOUNG,
J. W. MARTIN,
K. F. ANDERSON, SGT., N.W.M.P.,
A.P. CLARKE,
CHAS. H. STUART WADE,
K. F. ANDERSON, SGT., N.W.M.P.,
DAVID LAIRD, *Chairman of Indian Treaty Coms.,*

AMBROSE TETE NOIRE, *Chief Beaver Indians,*
PIERROT FOURNIER, *Headman Beaver Indians*

In witness whereof the Chairman of Her Majesty's Treaty Commissioners and the Chief and Headman of the Chipewyan Indians of Fond du Lac (Lake Athabasca) and the adjacent territory, in behalf of themselves and the Indians whom they represent, have hereunto set their hands at the said Fond du Lac on the twenty-fifth and twenty-seventh days of July, in the year of Our Lord one thousand eight hundred and ninety-nine.

The Beaver Indians of Dunvegan having met on this sixth day of July, in this present year 1899, Her Majesty's Commissioners, the Honourable James Hamilton Ross and James Andrew Joseph McKenna, Esquire, and having had explained to then the terms of the Treaty unto which the Chief and Headmen of the Indians of Lesser Slave Lake and adjacent country set their hands on the twenty-first day of June, in the year herein first above written, do join in the cession made by the said Treaty, and agree to adhere to the terms thereof in consideration of the undertakings made therein.

In witness whereof Her Majesty's said Commissioners and the Headman of the said Beaver Indians have hereunto set their hands at Dunvegan on this sixth day of July, in the year herein first above written.

The Chipewyan Indians of Athabasca River, Birch River, Peace River, Slave River and Gull River, and the Cree Indians of Gull River and Deep Lake, having met at Fort Chipewyan on this thirteenth day of July, in this present year 1899, Her Majesty's Commissioners, the Honourable James Hamilton Ross and James Andrew Joseph McKenna, Esquire, and having had explained to them the terms of the Treaty unto which the Chief and Headmen of the Indians of Lesser Slave Lake and adjacent country set their hands on the twenty-first day of June, in the year herein first above written, do join in the cession made by the said Treaty, and agree to adhere to the terms thereof in consideration of the undertakings made therein.

In witness whereof Her Majesty's said Commissioners and the Chiefs and Headmen of the said Chipewyan and Cree Indians have hereunto set their hands at Fort Chipewyan on this thirteenth day of July, in the year herein first above written.

The Chipewyan Indians of Slave River and the country thereabouts having met at Smith's Landing on this seventeenth day of July, in this present year 1899, Her Majesty's Commissioners, the Honourable James Hamilton Ross and James Andrew Joseph McKenna, Esquire, and having had explained to them the terms of the Treaty unto which the Chief and Headmen of the Indians of Lesser Slave Lake and adjacent country, set their hands on the twenty-first day of June, in the year herein first above written, do join in the cession made by the said Treaty, and agree to adhere to the terms thereof in consideration of the undertakings made therein.

In witness whereof Her Majesty's said Commissioners and the Chief and Headmen of the said Chipewyan Indians have hereunto set their hands at Smith's Landing, on this seventeenth day of July, in the year herein first above written.

The Chipewyan and Cree Indians of Fort McMurray and the country thereabouts, having met at Fort McMurray, on this fourth day of August, in this present year 1899, Her Majesty's Commissioner, James Andrew Joseph McKenna, Esquire, and having had explained to them the terms of the Treaty unto which the Chief and Headmen of the Indians of Lesser Slave Lake and adjacent country set their hands on the twenty-first day of June, in the year herein first above written, do join in the cession made by the said Treaty and agree to adhere to the terms thereof in consideration of the undertakings made therein.

In witness whereof Her Majesty's said Commissioner and the Headmen of the said Chipewyan and Cree Indians have hereunto set their hands at Fort McMurray, on this fourth day of August, in the year herein first above written.

The Indians of Wapiscow and the country thereabouts having met at Wapiscow Lake on this fourteenth day of August, in this present year 1899, Her Majesty's Commissioner, the Honourable James Hamilton Ross, and having had explained to them the terms of the Treaty unto which the Chief and Headmen of the Indians of Lesser Slave Lake and adjacent country set their hands on the twenty-first day of June in the year herein first above written, do join in the cession made by the said Treaty and agree to adhere to the terms thereof in consideration of the undertakings made therein.

In witness whereof Her Majesty's said Commissioner and the Chief and Headmen of the Indians have hereunto set their hands at Wapiscow Lake, on this fourteenth day of August, in the year herein first above written.

Treaty 9, 1905

Nov. 6, 1905; Oct. 5, 1906
THE JAMES BAY TREATY (TREATY No. 9) (MADE IN 1905 AND 1906) AND ADHESIONS MADE IN 1929 AND 1930

ARTICLES OF A TREATY made and concluded at the several dates mentioned therein, in the year of Our Lord one thousand and nine hundred and five, between His Most Gracious Majesty the King of Great Britain and Ireland, by His Commissioners, Duncan Campbell Scott, of Ottawa, Ontario, Esquire, and Samuel Stewart, of Ottawa, Ontario, Esquire; and Daniel George MacMartin, of Perth, Ontario, Esquire, representing the province of Ontario, of the one part; and the Ojibeway, Cree and other Indians, inhabitants of the territory within the limits hereinafter defined and described, by their chiefs, and headmen hereunto subscribed, of the other part: —

Whereas, the Indians inhabiting the territory hereinafter defined have been convened to meet a commission representing His Majesty's government of the Dominion of Canada at certain places in the said territory in this present year of 1905, to deliberate upon certain matters of interest to His Most Gracious Majesty, of the one part, and the said Indians of the other.

And, whereas, the said Indians have been notified and informed by His Majesty's said commission that it is His desire to open for settlement, immigration, trade, travel, mining, lumbering, and such other purposes as to His Majesty may seem meet, a tract of country, bounded and described as hereinafter mentioned, and to obtain the consent thereto of His Indian subjects inhabiting the said tract, and to make a treaty and arrange with them, so that there may be peace and good-will between them and His Majesty's other subjects, and that His Indian people may know and be assured of what allowances they are to count upon and receive from His Majesty's bounty and benevolence.

And whereas, the Indians of the said tract, duly convened in council at the respective points named hereunder, and being requested by His Majesty's commissioners to name certain chiefs and headmen who should be authorized on their behalf to conduct such negotiations and sign any treaty to be found thereon, and to become responsible to His Majesty for the faithful performance by their respective bands of such obligations as shall be assumed by them, the said Indians have therefore acknowledged for that purpose the several chiefs and headmen who have subscribed hereto.

And whereas, the said commissioners have proceeded to negotiate a treaty with the Ojibeway, Cree and other Indians, inhabiting the district hereinafter defined and described, and the same has been agreed upon, and concluded by the respective bands at the dates mentioned hereunder, the said Indians do hereby cede, release, surrender and yield up to the government of the Dominion of Canada, for His Majesty the King and His successors for ever, all their rights titles and privileges whatsoever, to the lands included within the following limits, that is to say: That portion or tract of land lying and being in the province of Ontario, bounded on the south by the height of land and the northern boundaries of the territory ceded by the Robinson-Superior Treaty of 1850, and the Robinson-Huron Treaty of 1850, and bounded on the east and north by the boundaries of the said province of Ontario as defined by law, and on the west by a part of the eastern boundary of the territory ceded by the North-west Angle Treaty No. 3; the said land containing an area of ninety thousand square miles, more or less.

And also, the said Indian rights, titles and privileges whatsoever to all other lands wherever situated in Ontario, Quebec, Manitoba, the District of Keewatin, or in any other portion of the Dominion of Canada.

To have and to hold the same to His Majesty the King and His successors for ever.

And His Majesty the King hereby agrees with the said Indians that they shall have the right to pursue their usual vocations of hunting, trapping and fishing throughout the tract surrendered as heretofore described, subject to such regulations as may from time to time be made by the government of the country, acting under the authority of His Majesty,

and saving and excepting such tracts as may be required or taken up from time to time for settlement, mining, lumbering, trading or other purposes.

And His Majesty the King hereby agrees and undertakes to lay aside reserves for each band, the same not to exceed in all one square mile for each family of five, or in that proportion for larger and smaller families; and the location of the said reserves having been arranged between His Majesty's commissioners and the chiefs and headmen, as described in the schedule of reserves hereto attached, the boundaries thereof to be hereafter surveyed and defined, the said reserves when confirmed shall be held and administered by His Majesty for the benefit of the Indians free of all claims, liens, or trusts by Ontario.

Provided, however, that His Majesty reserves the right to deal with any settlers within the bounds of any lands reserved for any band as He may see fit; and also that the aforesaid reserves of land, or any interest therein, may be sold or otherwise disposed of by His Majesty's government for the use and benefit of the said Indians entitled thereto, with their consent first had and obtained; but in no wise shall the said Indians, or any of them, be entitled to sell or otherwise alienate any of the lands allotted to them as reserves.

It is further agreed between His said Majesty and His Indian subjects that such portions of the reserves and lands above indicated as may at any time be required for public works, buildings, railways, or roads of whatsoever nature may be appropriated for that purpose by His Majesty's government of the Dominion of Canada, due compensation being made to the Indians for the value of improvements thereon, and an equivalent in land, money or other consideration for the area of the reserve so appropriated.

And with a view to show the satisfaction of His Majesty with the behaviour and good conduct of His Indians, and in extinguishment of all their past claims, He hereby, through His commissioners, agrees to make each Indian a present of eight dollars in cash.

His Majesty also agrees that next year, and annually afterwards for ever, He will cause to be paid to the said Indians in cash, at suitable places and dates, of which the said Indians shall be duly notified, four dollars, the same, unless there be some exceptional

reason, to be paid only to the heads of families for those belonging thereto.

Further, His Majesty agrees that each chief, after signing the treaty, shall receive a suitable flag and a copy of this treaty to be for the use of his band.

Further, His Majesty agrees to pay such salaries of teachers to instruct the children of said Indians, and also to provide such school buildings and educational equipment as may seem advisable to His Majesty's government of Canada.

And the undersigned Ojibeway, Cree and other chiefs and headmen, on their own behalf and on behalf of all the Indians whom they represent, do hereby solemnly promise and engage to strictly observe this treaty, and also to conduct and behave themselves as good and loyal subjects of His Majesty the King.

They promise and engage that they will, in all respects, obey and abide by the law; that they will maintain peace between each other and between themselves and other tribes of Indians, and between themselves and others of His Majesty's subjects, whether Indians, half-breeds or whites, this year inhabiting and hereafter to inhabit any part of the said ceded territory; and that they will not molest the person or property of any inhabitant of such ceded tract, or of any other district or country, or interfere with or trouble any person passing or travelling through the said tract, or any part thereof, and that they will assist the officers of His Majesty in bringing to justice and punishment any Indian offending against the stipulations of this treaty, or infringing the law in force in the country so ceded.

And it is further understood that this treaty is made and entered into subject to an agreement dated the third day of July, nineteen hundred and five, between the Dominion of Canada and Province of Ontario, which is hereto attached.

In witness whereof, His Majesty's said commissioners and the said chiefs and headmen have hereunto set their hands at the places and times set forth in the year herein first above written.

Signed at Osnaburg on the twelfth day of July, 1905, by His Majesty's commissioners and the chiefs and

headmen in the presence of the undersigned witnesses, after having been first interpreted and explained.

Witnesses:

THOMAS CLOUSTON RAE, C.T., Hudsons Bay Co.,
ALEX. GEORGE MEINDL, M.D.,
JABEZ WILLIAMS, Commis, H. B. Co.,
DUNCAN CAMPBELL SCOTT,
SAMUEL STEWART,
DANIEL GEORGE MACMARTIN,
MISSABAY, his x mark,
THOMAS MISSABAY, his x mark,
GEORGE WAHWAASHKUNG, his x mark,
KWIASH, his x mark,
NAHOKEESIC, his x mark,
OOMBASH, his x mark,
DAVID SKUNK, his x mark,
JOHN SKUNK, his x mark,
THOMAS PANACHEESE his x mark

Signed at Fort Hope on the nineteenth day of July, 1905, by His Majesty's commissioners and the chiefs and headmen in the presence of the undersigned witnesses, after having been first interpreted and explained.

Witnesses:

F.X. FARARD, O.M.I.,
THOMAS CLOUSTON RAE,
ALEX. GEORGE MEINDL. M.D.,
CHAS. H.M. GORDON,H. B. Co.,
YESNO, his x mark,
DANIEL GEORGE MACMARTIN,
SAMUEL STEWART,
DUNCAN CAMPBELL SCOTT,
GEORGE his x mark NAMAY,
WENANGASIE his x mark DRAKE,
GEORGE his x mark QUISEES,
KATCHANG, his x mark,
MOONIAS, his x mark,
JOE GOODWIN, his x mark,
ABRAHAM ATLOOKAN, his x mark,
HARRY OOSKINEEGISH, his x mark,
NOAH rk NESHINAPAIS, his x mark,
JOHN A. ASHPANAQUESHKUN, his x mark,
JACOB RABBIT, his x mark

Signed at Marten Falls on the twenty-fifth day of July, 1905, by His Majesty's commissioners and the chief and headmen in the presence of the undersigned witnesses, after having been first interpreted and explained.

Witnesses:

THOMAS CLOUSTON RAE, C.T., H. B. Co.,
ALEX GEORGE MEINDL, M.D.,
SAMUEL ISERHOFF,
DUNCAN CAMPBELL SCOTT,
SAMUEL STEWART,
DANIEL GEORGE MACMARTIN,
WILLIAM WHITEHEAD, his x mark,
WILLIAM COASTER, his x mark,
DAVID KNAPAYSWET, his x mark,
OSTAMAS LONG TOM, his x mark,
WILLIAM WEENJACK, his x mark

Signed at Fort Albany on the third day of August, 1905, by His Majesty's commissioners and the chiefs and headmen in the presence of the undersigned witnesses, after having been first interpreted and explained.

Witnesses:

THOMAS CLOUSTON RAE, C.T. H. B. Co.,
G.W. COCKRAM,
A.W. PATTERSON,
ALEX. GEORGE MEINDL, M.D.,
JOSEPH PATTERSON,
MINNIE COCKRAM,
DUNCAN CAMPBELL SCOTT,
SAMUEL STEWART,
DANIEL GEORGE MACMARTIN,
CHARLIE STEPHEN, his x mark,
PATRICK STEPHEN, his x mark,
DAVID GEO. WYNNE, his x mark,
ANDREW WESLEY, his x mark,
JACOB TAHTAIL, his x mark,
JOHN WESLEY, his x mark,
XAVIER BIRD, his x mark,
PETER SACKANEY, his x mark,
WM. GOODWIN, his x mark,
SAML. SCOTT, his x mark

Signed at Moose Factory on the ninth day of August, 1905, by His Majesty's commissioners and the chiefs and headmen in the presence of the undersigned

witnesses, after having been first interpreted and explained.

Witnesses:
GEORGE MOOSONEE,
THOMAS CLOUSTON RAE, C.T.,
JOHN GEORGE MOWAT, H. B. Co.,
THOMAS BIRD HOLLAND, B.A.,
JAMES PARKINSON,
DUNCAN CAMPBELL SCOTT,
SAMUEL STEWART,
DANIEL GEORGE MACMARTIN,
SIMON his x mark SMALLBOY,
GEORGE his x mark TAPPAISE,
HENRY SAILOR, Signed in Cree syllabic,
JOHN NAKOGEE, Signed in Cree syllabic,
JOHN DICK, Signed in Cree syllabic,
SIMON QUATCHEWAN, Signed in Cree
    syllabic,
JOHN JEFFRIES, Signed in Cree syllabic,
FRED MARK, Signed in Cree syllabic,
HENRY UTAPPE, his x mark,
SIMON CHEENA, his x mark

Signed at New Post on the twenty-first day of August, 1905, by His Majesty's commissioners and the chiefs and headmen in the presence of the undersigned witnesses, after having been first interpreted and explained.

Witnesses:

THOMAS CLOUSTON RAE, C.T., H. B. Co.,
SYDNEY BLENKARNE BARRETT, H. B. Co.,
JOSEPH LOUIS VANASSE,
DUNCAN CAMPBELL SCOTT,
SAMUEL STEWART,
DANIEL GEORGE MACMARTIN.ANGUS
    WEENUSK, his x mark,
JOHN LUKE his x mark,
WILLIAM GULL, his x mark.

Signed at Abitibi on the seventh day of June, 1906, by His Majesty's commissioners and the chiefs and headmen in the presence of the undersigned witnesses, after having been first interpreted and explained.

Witnesses:

GEORGE DREVER,
ALEX. GEORGE MEINDL, M.D.,

PELHAM EDGAR,
DUNCAN CAMPBELL SCOTT,
SAMUEL STEWART,
LOUIS MCDOUGALL, his x mark
ANDREW MCDOUGALL, his x mark
OLD CHEESE, his x mark
MICHEL PENATOUCHE, his x mark
LOUI MACDOUGALL,
ANTOINE PENATOUCHE.

Signed at Matachewan on the twentieth day of June, 1906, by His Majesty's commissioners and the chiefs and headmen in the presence of the undersigned witnesses, after having been first interpreted and explained.

Witnesses:

PELHAM EDGAR,
GEORGE NOMTEITH,
ALEX. GEORGE MEINDL, M.D.,
DUNCAN CAMPBELL SCOTT,
SAMUEL STEWART,
DANIEL GEORGE MACMARTIN,
MICHEL BATISE, his x mark,
ROUND EYES, his x mark,
THOMAS FOX, his x mark,
JIMMY PIERCE, his x mark.

Signed at Mattagami on the seventh day of July, 1906, by His Majesty's commissioners and the chiefs and headmen in the presence of the undersigned witnesses, after having been first interpreted and explained.

Witnesses:

JOS. MILLER,
PELHAM EDGAR,
A.M.C. BANTING,
KENNETH ROSS,
DUNCAN CAMPBELL SCOTT,
SAMUEL STEWART,
DANIEL GEORGE MACMARTIN,
ANDREW his x markLUKE,
JOSEPH SHEMEKET, Signed in syllabic
    characters,
THOMAS CHICKEN, Signed in syllabic
    characters,
JAMES NEVUE, Signed in syllabic
    characters

Signed at Flying Post on the sixteenth day of July, 1906, by His Majesty's commissioners and the chiefs and headmen in the presence of the undersigned witnesses, after having been first interpreted and explained.

Witnesses:

A.J. MCLEOD,
PELHAM EDGAR,
ALEX. GEORGE MEINDL, M.D,
JOSEPH LOUIS VANASSE,
DUNCAN CAMPBELL SCOTT,
SAMUEL STEWART,
DANIEL GEORGE MACMARTIN,
ALBERT BLACK ICE, Signed in syllabic
    character,
JOHN ISSAC, Signed in syllabic characters,
WILLIAM FROG, Signed in syllabic characters,
THOMAS FROG, Signed in syllabic characters

Signed at New Brunswick House on the twenty-fifth day of July, 1906, by His Majesty's commissioners and the chiefs and headmen in the presence of the undersigned witnesses, after having been first interpreted and explained.

Witnesses:

GEORGE MONSONEE,
JAMES G. CHRISTIE,
GRACE MCTAVISH,
CLAUDE D. OWENS,
PELHAM EDGAR,
EDMUND MORRIS,
DUNCAN CAMPBELL SCOTT,
SAMUEL STEWART,
DANIEL GEORGE MACMARTIN,
ALEX. PEEKETAY Signed in syllabic characters.
POOTOOSH, his x mark,
PETER MITIGONABIE, his x mark,
TOM NESHWABUN, Signed in syllabic
    characters,
JACOB WINDABAIE, Signed in syllabic
    characters

Signed at Long Lake on the ninth day of August, 1906, by His Majesty's commissioners and the chiefs and headmen in the presence of the undersigned witnesses, after having been first interpreted and explained.

Witnesses:

H.A. TREMAYNE,
ISABELLA TREMAYNE,
P. GODCHERE,
PELHAM EDGAR,
DUNCAN CAMPBELL SCOTT,
SAMUEL STEWART,
DANIEL GEORGE MACMARTIN,
KWAKIGIGICKWEANG, Signed in syllabic
    characters,
KENESWABE, Signed in syllabic characters,
MATAWAGAN, Signed insyllabic characters,
ODAGAMEA, Signed in syllabic characters

Treaty 10, 1906

Sept. 19, 1906; Aug. 19, 1907
Treaty No. 10 and reports of Commissioners

On a Report dated 12th July 1906, from the Superintendent General of Indian Affairs, stating that the aboriginal title has not been extinguished in the greater portion of that part of the Province of Saskatchewan which lies north of the 54th parallel of latitude and in a small adjoining area in Alberta; that the Indians and Half-breeds of that territory are similarly situated to those whose country lies immediately to the south and west, whose claims have already been extinguished by, in the case of those who are Indians, a payment of a gratuity and annuity and the setting aside of lands as reserves, and in the case of those who are Half-breeds, by the issue of scrip; and they have from time to time pressed their claims for settlement on similar lines; that it is in the public interest that the whole of the territory included within the boundaries of the Provinces of Saskatchewan and Alberta should be relieved of the claims of the aborigines; and that $12,000.00 has been included in the estimates for expenses in the making of a treaty with Indians and in settling the claims of the Half-breeds and for paying the usual gratuities to the Indians.

The Minister recommends as follows:

That a Treaty be made with the Indians of the aforesaid territory, which is situated partly in the Province of Saskatchewan and partly in the Province of Alberta, and lying to the east of Treaty 8, and to the north of Treaties 5 and 6, and the addition to Treaty 6, which territory contains, approximately, an area of 85,000 square miles; and that the Treaty provide:

for the setting aside of reserves of an area not to exceed one square mile for each family of five for such number of families as may elect to reside on reserves, or in that proportion for larger or smaller families, and for such Indian families or individual Indians as prefer to live apart from band reserves, the setting aside of lands in severalty to the extent of 160 acres for each Indian with a proviso as to non-alienation without the consent of the Governor in Council;

for the payment at the time of the making of the Treaty of $32.00 in cash to each Chief, and $22.00 to each headman, and $12.00 to every other Indian of whatever age, and the payment every year thereafter of $25.00 to each Chief, $15.00 to each headman and $5.00 to every other Indian of whatever age;

for the making of such provision as may from time to time be deemed advisable for the education of the Indian children; and

for the affording of such assistance as may be found necessary or desirable to advance the Indians in farming or stock-raising or other work.

That the Half-breeds of the territory aforesaid be granted scrip redeemable to the amount of $240.00 in payment for Dominion Land or locatable for 240 acres of Dominion Land in the form and according to the rules followed in the issue of scrip to the Half-breeds in the territory covered by Treaty 8, which are as follows:

Every Half-breed resident in the territory to be covered by the proposed Treaty at the time of the making thereof whose claim has not been extinguished either by the issue of scrip to himself or his parents or otherwise to be granted scrip as aforesaid for land or money as he, or his parent or guardian, if he be under eighteen years of age, may elect;

The extinguishment of the claim of one parent shall not be held to debar from scrip any Half-breed who is a resident of the said territory at the time of the making of the Treaty;

In case of Half-breeds whose claims were previously extinguished and who may be residents of the said territory those of their children born in the territory or in any ceded portion of the North West outside the old boundaries of Manitoba between the 15th of July, 1870, and the end of the year 1885 are, if they have not previously received scrip, to be recognized as entitled to scrip, as they would have been recognized had their claims been presented to the Commission appointed to dispose of such claims;

The certificates for scrip issued in favour of Half-breeds under eighteen years of age shall be delivered to the father, if he be alive, and if not to the mother or guardian.

The Minister further recommends that James Andrew Joseph McKenna, of the City of Winnipeg, in the Province of Manitoba, be appointed Commissioner, to make the proposed Treaty with the Indians of the territory described herein, and to hear and determine the claims of the Half-breeds therein and issue scrip as aforesaid to those of them whom he may find to be entitled; Mr. McKenna to be allowed in addition to his regular salary extra remuneration at the rate of $5.00 per diem.

The Committee submit the same for approval.

WILFRID LAURIER

RATIFICATION OF TREATY No. 10 P.C. No. 2490
On a Memorandum dated 7th November, 1907, the Superintendent General of Indian Affairs, submitting herewith for Your Excellency's consideration Treaty No. 10 made in 1906 by the Commissioner, James Andrew Joseph McKenna, Esquire, who was appointed to negotiate the same with the Chipewyan, Cree and other Indian inhabitants of the territory situated partly in the Province of Saskatchewan and partly in the Province of Alberta and lying to the east of Treaty No. 8 and to the north of Treaties Nos. 5 and 6 and the addition to Treaty No. 6 described in the said Treaty.

The Minister also submits adhesions to the said Treaty, taken by Thomas Alexander Borthwick, Esquire, who was appointed a Commissioner to take the same during the summer of 1907 from such of the Indians of the Tribes above referred to as were not met with by Commissioner McKenna.

The Minister recommends that the said Treaty, and the adhesions thereto, be approved by Your Excellency in Council; the original Treaty and adhesions to be returned to the Department of Indian Affairs

and the copy thereof to be Kept of record in the Privy Council Office.

The Committee submit the same for approval accordingly.

WILFRID LAURIER
REPORT OF FIRST COMMISSIONER FOR
TREATY No. 10.
OTTAWA, January 18, 1907.
The Hon. Frank Oliver,
Superintendent General of Indian Affairs,
Ottawa.

SIR, —I have the honour to transmit herewith the treaty which, under the commission issued to me July 20, 1906, I made with the Chipewyan Indians of English River and Clear Lake and the Crees of Canoe Lake, in the northern part of Saskatchewan.

The arrangements which I made for meeting the Indians, of which they were advised, provided that the first meeting was to be at Portage la Loche on September 3, but unfavourable weather and the action of the Indians themselves made it impossible to carry out my programme.

On reaching Isle à la Crosse on August 26, en route to Portage la Loche, I found that all the Chipewyans from English River and some ten families from Clear Lake were gathered there, waiting for the commission, which was announced to be at that point on September 13. These Indians urged strongly that they be treated with at once, on the ground that they had been gathered there for several days, that their supplies were getting low, that it was necessary that they should return to their hunting grounds without further delay, that they had come long distances, and that they would have to travel far before reaching their winter quarters.

I decided to accede to their request, and met them on August 28, 1906.

It appeared for a time as if there would be some considerable difficulty in effecting a settlement on the lines of the treaty, for it was evident from the trend of the talk of the leaders among the Indians that there had been at work an influence which tended to make them regard the treaty as a means of enslaving them. I was able to disabuse their minds of this absurd notion and to make it clear that the government's object was simply to do for them what had been done for neighbouring Indians when the progress of trade or settlement began to interfere with the untrammelled exercise of their aboriginal privileges as hunters.

By the end of the day, the treaty was signed and the annuity and gratuity moneys paid.

The number of Indians paid at this point was:

The chief of the Clear Lake band, who was empowered to speak for his people, requested that the remainder of the band be paid at Buffalo Narrows, where they would gather to meet me on the return journey from Portage la Loche.

After treating with these Indians, I left Isle à la Crosse on August 30 for Portage la Loche, at which point I was due on September 3; but for the reasons given above, I did not reach there until the 5th.

The people at this point were all half-breeds and were dealt with as such.

On the 8th of the same month, I left for la Loche mission, across la Loche lake, a distance of nine miles, where more half-breeds had to be met and dealt with. There were at this point three aged Chipewyan women who desired to be attached to the Clear Lake band, and I entered them as members and paid them treaty.

Having completed my work at la Loche mission on the 11th, I started on my return journey to Isle à la Crosse, reaching Buffalo Narrows on the evening of the 16th. The chief of the Clear Lake band and those of his people who had not yet been paid treaty were gathered here. I met them the following day; found them satisfied with the action of their chief in becoming a party to the treaty, and paid the gratuity and annuity.

The number of Indians paid at this point, including three members of the band at Bull's House, was: — 110 Indians at $12, $1,320.

At the request of the chief, the appointment of headmen was deferred until next treaty payments, as the Indians were not then prepared to make their selections.

After completing the work at Buffalo Narrows, I pushed on to Isle à la Crosse, a distance of fifty-five miles, arriving there the same night. I met the Cree Indians of Canoe Lake the next day and explained to them all the stipulations contained in the treaty. I secured their adhesion on September 19.

The number of this band is eighty-two, consisting of one chief, two headmen and seventy-nine other Indians; the amount paid was $1,024.

The next point of destination was Stanley, where I was scheduled to meet the Indians on October 8; but between my leaving and returning to Isle à la Crosse a report came to the Hudson's Bay Company to the effect that the streams were very shallow and that travel would, therefore, be so very difficult and slow that in all probability our party would be frozen in and would have to remain at Stanley until dog trains could be procured. This report was quite confirmed by the information which Messrs. Revillon Freres had from that part of the country, and of which their manager, Monsieur Benard, very kindly apprised me. From the report it also appeared that, even if we made the trip, it would be impossible for the Indians from the northeastern portion of the country to be gathered there, and that there were at Stanley and in its immediate vicinity only a few half-breed families who had had their claims settled before they migrated to that region. I therefore decided to cancel the appointment, and sent notice to that effect to the people, assuring them at the same time that they would be visited at a future date, of which they would be duly notified.

As the discussions which took place with the bands treated with were much on the same lines, I shall confine myself to a general statement of their import.

There was a marked absence of the old Indian style of oratory, the Indians confining themselves to asking questions and making brief arguments. They all demanded even more liberal terms than were granted to Indians treated with in past years, the chief of the English River band going so far as to claim payment of 'arrears' from the year when the first treaty was made; some expected to be entirely fed by the government, after the making of the treaty; all asked for assistance in seasons of distress; and it was strongly urged that the old and indigent who were no longer able to hunt and trap and were consequently often in destitute circumstances, should be cared for by the government.

There was a general expression of fear that the making of the treaty would be followed by the curtailment of their hunting and fishing privileges, and the necessity of not allowing the lakes and the rivers to be monopolized or depleted by commercial fishing was emphasized.

There was evidenced a marked desire to secure educational privileges for their children. In this connection and speaking for the Indians generally, the chief of the English River band insisted that in the carrying out of the government's Indian educational policy among them there should be no interference with the system of religious schools now conducted by the mission, but that public aid should be given for improvement and extension along the lines already followed.

The chief of the Canoe Lake band stated that there were about twenty-five children of school age in his band, and asked that a day school be established at Canoe Lake for their benefit and that it be put under the management of a woman teacher.

There was also a demand made for a few head of cattle to be given to those of the Indians who wished to go into the industry of stock-raising.

The Indians all agreed to have one place of payment in the future; but made it a condition that the payments should be held about the middle of June of each year, as that is the only time at which the gathering for annuity payments would not interfere with their avocations to an extent that the payment would be no adequate compensation for. They selected Isle à la Crosse as the place of payment.

They further requested that medicines be furnished, and made an earnest appeal for the appointment of a resident medical man.

In my reply I convinced them that such a claim as they put forward for what they called 'arrears' had never before been heard of, and that I could not for a moment recognize any obligation on the government's part except such as would be put upon it in virtue of the execution of the treaty. I pointed out to them that the government could not undertake to maintain Indians in idleness; that the same means of

earning a livelihood would continue after the treaty was made as existed before it; and that Indians would be expected to make as good use of them in the future as in the past. I stated that the government was always ready to assist Indians in actual destitution; that in times of distress they would, without any special stipulation in the treaty, receive such assistance as it was usual to give in order to prevent starvation among them, and that the attention of the government would be called to the necessity of some special provision being made for assisting the old and indigent who were unable to work and dependent on charity for subsistence.

I guaranteed that the treaty would not lead to any forced interference with their mode of life. I explained to them that, whether treaty was made or not, they were subject to the law, bound to obey it and liable to punishment for any infringement thereof; that it was designed for the protection of all and must be respected by all the inhabitants of the country, irrespective of colour or origin; and that, in requiring them to abide by it, they were only being required to do the duty imposed upon all the people throughout the Dominion of Canada. I dwelt upon the importance, in their own interest, of the observance of the laws respecting the protection of fish and game.

As to education, the Indians were assured that there was no need for special stipulation over and above the general provision in the treaty, as it was the policy of the government to provide in every part of the country as far as circumstances would permit, for the education of the Indian children, and that the law provided for schools for Indians maintained and assisted by the government being conducted as to religious auspices in accordance with the wishes of the Indians.

It was explained that the assistance in farming and ranching mentioned in the treaty, is only to be given when the Indians are actually prepared to go into those industries. It is not likely that for many years to come, there will be a call for any but a small expenditure under these heads. It is not probable that the Indians will, while present conditions continue, engage in farming further than the raising of roots in a small way. As to cattle, I stated that the agent who will be sent to make the next treaty payments, would be asked to discuss the matter with them, but that those only who are considered able and willing to take good care of cattle would receive assistance in that form.

I promised that medicines would be placed at different points in the charge of persons to be selected by the government, and would be distributed to those of the Indians who might require them. I showed them that it would be practically impossible for the government to arrange for a resident doctor owing to the Indians being so widely scattered over such an extensive territory; but I assured them that the government would always be ready to avail itself of any opportunity of affording medical service just as it provided that the physician attached to the commission should give free attendance to all Indians whom he might find in need of treatment.

In the main, the demand will be for ammunition and twine, as the great majority of the Indians will continue to hunt and fish for a livelihood. It does not appear likely that the conditions of that part of Saskatchewan covered by the treaty will be for many years so changed as to affect hunting and trapping, and it is expected, therefore, that the great majority of the Indians will continue in these pursuits as a means of subsistence.

The Indians were given the option of taking reserves or land in severalty, when they felt the need of having land set apart for them. I made it clear that the government had no desire to interfere with their mode of life or to restrict them to reserves and that it undertook to have land in the proportions stated in the treaty set apart for them, when conditions interfered with their mode of living and it became necessary to secure them possession of land.

The Indians dealt with are in character, habit, manner of dress and mode of living similar to the Chipewyans and Crees of the Athabaska country. It is difficult to draw a line of demarcation between those who classed themselves as Indians and those who elected to be treated with as half-breeds. Both dress alike and follow the same mode of life. It struck me that the one group was, on the whole, as well able to provide for self-support as the other.

After leaving Green Lake, our route was by rivers and lakes and afforded not much opportunity for forming an opinion of the country ceded and of its resources. From our point of view, the country appeared flat. There were extensive stretches of hay-lands along the rivers and wooded heights about the lakes. The waters abound in fish, which form the chief article of food.

The Isle à la Crosse mission was founded about sixty-two years ago by Father Lafleche, who afterwards was a prominent figure in the Quebec hierarchy, and Brother Taché, who afterwards filled the See of St. Boniface. The church built by them was destroyed by fire and has been replaced by another. The building next in importance is the school conducted by the sisters. It shows marked evidence of age externally, but is cosy within, and the children whom I had the pleasure of meeting there, evidenced the kindly care and careful training of the devoted women who have gone out from the comforts of civilization to work for the betterment of the natives of the north. The priest's house is a small one. Its only door opens into a large room which occupies the greater part of the building and which is the common gathering place of the Indians and half-breeds, who sit and smoke with an ease that seemed born of long habit of free intercourse with those who have undertaken the cure of their souls.

The mission is about opposite the company's post. It is close to the shore. The site is rather flat and for miles on three sides stretches a bald prairie, though we were told that the mission when founded was on the fringe of the forest. Whatever it may have been, it is no longer a desirable situation for a boarding school, and a new one has been erected at Rivière la Plonge, some thirty miles south of the mission. The building is one hundred feet by sixty-two feet, and is two and a half storeys high. It was finished when I visited it. The site is a delightful one on a rising ground from the river, which here breaks into a cataract that the Oblate brothers have harnessed for power purposes. They cut the logs, and, with the harnessed river, sawed them into lumber, with which they built the school, a splendid monument to their mechanical skill, industry and devotion. When I was leaving Isle à la Crosse, the moving of the children from the old to the new institution had begun.

Our trip was rather a difficult one. Our transport had to be organized on short notice. The water in the rivers was pretty low, and we encountered storms on the lakes; but there was no ground for the report of shipwreck and loss which unfortunately obtained currency.

I had the pleasure of the company, on most of the inward trip, of His Lordship Bishop Pascal; and I desire to repeat here the acknowledgment I made and the gratitude I expressed to his lordship personally for the assistance of his influence on my first meeting the natives of the country, which is filled with reverence for his name because of his devoted labours.

I desire to express, also, my appreciation of the help ever readily rendered by Major Begin, of the Royal Northwest Mounted Police, who was in command of the escort; by Dr. J. J. A. Lebrecque, the medical officer; by Mr. Charles Fisher, of Duck Lake, and Mr. Charles Mair, of Ottawa, secretaries to the commission, by the Hudson's Bay Company's chief factor, and by Mr. Angus McKay, the officer of the company who was especially charged with the carrying out of the transportation contract. To the men of the country on whose labour we had so much to depend I acknowledge my obligation. They worked long hours at paddling and rowing and poling, and endured great hardships in tracking and walking our canoes and flat boats over the rapids and shoals, so that I might keep my appointments. Camp was made late and broken early. Yet there was never a complaint, but always a zestful interest and cheerfulness as pleasant as the campfires that brightened the night.

A detailed statement of the Indians treated with and of the money paid is appended.

I have the honour to be, sir
    Your obedient servant,
    J.A.J. McKenna,
    Commissioner.

Certified correct,
    J.A.J. MCKENNA,
    Commissioner, Treaty No. 10

TREATY No. 10
Articles of a treaty made and concluded at the several dates mentioned therein, in the year of our Lord one thousand nine hundred and six between His Most Gracious Majesty the King of Great Britain and Ireland by His commissioner, James Andrew Joseph McKenna, of the city of Winnipeg, in the province of Manitoba, Esquire, of the one part, and the Chipewyan, Cree and Other Indian inhabitants of the territory within the limits hereinafter defined and described by their chiefs and headmen hereunto subscribed of the other part.

Whereas the Indians inhabiting the territory hereinafter defined have, pursuant to notice given by His Majesty's said commissioner in the year 1906, been convened to meet His Majesty's said commissioner representing His Majesty's government of the Dominion of Canada at certain places in the said territory in this present year 1906 to deliberate upon certain matters of interest to His Most Gracious Majesty on the one part and the said Indians of the other.

And whereas the said Indians have been notified and informed by His Majesty's said commissioner that it is His Majesty's desire to open for settlement, immigration, trade, travel, mining, lumbering and such other purposes as to His Majesty may seem meet, a tract of country bounded and described as hereinafter mentioned and to obtain the consent thereto of his Indian subjects inhabiting the said tract and to make a treaty and arrange with them so that there may be peace and good will between them and His Majesty's other subjects, and that His Indian people may know and be assured of what allowances they are to count upon and receive from His Majesty's bounty and benevolence.

And whereas the Indians of the said tract, duly convened in council at the respective points named hereunder and being requested by His Majesty's said commissioner to name certain chiefs and headmen who should be authorized on their behalf to conduct such negotiations and sign any treaty to be founded thereon and to become responsible to His Majesty for the faithful performance by their respective bands of such obligations as shall be assumed by them, the said Indians have therefore acknowledged for that purpose the several chiefs and headmen who have subscribed hereto.

And whereas the said commissioner has proceeded to negotiate a treaty with the Chipewyan, Cree and other Indians inhabiting the said territory hereinafter defined and described and the same has been agreed upon and concluded by the respective bands at the dates mentioned hereunder;

Now therefore the said Indians do hereby cede, release, surrender and yield up to the government of the Dominion of Canada for His Majesty the King and His successors for ever all their rights, titles and privileges whatsoever to the lands included within the following limits, that is to say:

All that territory situated partly in the province of Saskatchewan and partly in the province of Alberta, and lying to the east of Treaty Eight and to the north of Treaties Five, Six and the addition to Treaty Six, containing approximately an area of eighty-five thousand eight hundred (85,800) square miles and which may be described as follows:

Commencing at the point where the northern boundary of Treaty Five intersects the eastern boundary of the province of Saskatchewan; thence northerly along the said eastern boundary four hundred and ten miles, more or less, to the sixtieth parallel of latitude and northern boundary of the said province of Saskatchewan; thence west along the said parallel one hundred and thirty miles, more or less, to the eastern boundary of Treaty Eight; thence southerly and westerly following the said eastern boundary of Treaty Eight to its intersection with the northern boundary of Treaty Six; thence easterly along the said northern boundary of Treaty Six to its intersection with the western boundary of the addition to Treaty Six; thence northerly along the said western boundary to the northern boundary of the said addition; thence easterly along the said northern boundary to the eastern boundary of the said addition; thence southerly along the said eastern boundary to its intersection with the northern boundary of Treaty Six; thence easterly along the said northern boundary and the northern boundary of Treaty Five to the point of commencement.

And also all their rights, titles and privileges whatsoever as Indians to all and any other lands wherever situated in the provinces of Saskatchewan and Alberta and the Northwest Territories or any other portion of the Dominion of Canada.

To have and to hold the same to His Majesty the King and His successors for ever.

And His Majesty the King hereby agrees with the said Indians that they shall have the right to pursue their usual vocations of hunting, trapping and fishing throughout the territory surrendered as heretofore described, subject to such regulations as may from time to time be made by the government of the country acting under the authority of His Majesty and

saving and excepting such tracts as may be required or as may be taken up from time to time for settlement, mining, lumbering, trading or other purposes.

And His Majesty the King hereby agrees and undertakes to set aside reserves of land for such bands as desire the same, such reserves not to exceed in all one square mile for each family of five for such number of families as may elect to reside upon reserves or in that proportion for larger or smaller families; and for such Indian families or individual Indians as prefer to live apart from band reserves His Majesty undertakes to provide land in severalty to the extent of one hundred and sixty (160) acres for each Indian, the land not to be alienable by the Indian for whom it is set aside in severalty without the consent of the Governor General in Council of Canada, the selection of such reserves and land in severalty to be made in the manner following, namely, the Superintendent General of Indian Affairs shall depute and send a suitable person to determine and set apart such reserves and lands, after consulting with the Indians concerned as to the locality which may be found suitable and open for selection.

Provided, however, that His Majesty reserves the right to deal with any settlers within the bounds of any lands reserved for any band or bands as He may see fit; and also that the aforesaid reserves of land, or any interest therein, may be sold or otherwise disposed of by His Majesty's government of Canada for the use and benefit of the Indians entitled thereto, with their consent first had and obtained.

It is further agreed between His Majesty and His said Indian subjects that such portions of the reserves and lands above mentioned as may at any time be required for public works, buildings, railways or roads of whatsoever nature may be appropriated for such purposes by His Majesty's government of Canada due compensation being made to the Indians for the value of any improvements thereon, and an equivalent in land, money or other consideration for the area so appropriated.

And with a view to showing the satisfaction of His Majesty with the behaviour and good conduct of His Indians and in extinguishment of all their past claims, He hereby through His commissioner agrees to make each chief a present of thirty-two (32) dollars in cash, to each headman twenty-two (22) dollars and to every other Indian of whatever age of the families represented at the time and place of payment twelve (12) dollars.

His Majesty also agrees that next year and annually thereafter for ever He will cause to be paid to the Indians in cash, at suitable places and dates of which the said Indians shall be duly notified, to each chief twenty-five (25) dollars, each headman fifteen (15) dollars and to every other Indian of whatever age five (5) dollars.

Further His Majesty agrees that each chief, after signing the treaty, shall receive a silver medal and a suitable flag, and next year and every third year thereafter each chief shall receive a suitable suit of clothing, and that after signing the treaty each headman shall receive a bronze medal and next year and every third year thereafter a suitable suit of clothing.

Further His Majesty agrees to make such provision as may from time to time be deemed advisable for the education of the Indian children.

Further His Majesty agrees to furnish such assistance as may be found necessary or advisable to aid and assist the Indians in agriculture or stock-raising or other work and to make such a distribution of twine and ammunition to them annually as is usually made to Indians similarly situated.

And the undersigned Chipewyan, Cree and other Indian chiefs and headmen on their own behalf and on behalf of all the Indians whom they represent do hereby solemnly promise and engage to strictly observe this treaty in all and every respect and to behave and conduct themselves as good and loyal subjects of His Majesty the King.

They promise and engage that they will in all respects obey and abide by the law; that they will maintain peace between each other and between their tribes and other tribes of Indians and between themselves and other of His Majesty's subjects whether whites, Indians, half-breeds or others now inhabiting or who may hereafter inhabit any part of the territory hereby ceded and herein described, and that they will not molest the person or trespass upon the property or interfere with the rights of any inhabitant of such ceded tract or of any other district or country or interfere with or trouble any person passing or travelling through the said tract or any part thereof and that they will assist the officers of

His Majesty in bringing to justice and punishment any Indian offending against the stipulations of this treaty or infringing the law in force in the country so ceded.

In witness whereof His Majesty's said commissioner and the chiefs and headmen have hereunto set their hands at Isle à la Crosse this twenty-eighth day of August in the year herein first above written.

Articles of a treaty made and concluded at the several dates mentioned therein, in the year of our Lord one thousand nine hundred and seven, between His Most Gracious Majesty the King of Great Britain and Ireland by His Commissioner Thomas Alexander Borthwick, of Mistawasis, in the province of Saskatchewan, Esquire, of the one part, and the Chipewyan, Cree and other Indian inhabitants of the territory within the limits hereinafter defined and described by their chiefs and headmen hereunto subscribed of the other part.

In witness whereof His Majesty's said commissioner and the chiefs and headmen have hereunto set their hands at Lac du Brochet this 19th day of August, in the year first above written.

In witness whereof His Majesty's said commissioner and the chiefs and headmen have hereunto set their hands at Lac du Brochet this 22nd day of August in the year first above written.

REPORT OF SECOND COMMISSION FOR TREATY NO. 10
    Mistawasis, Carlton Agency, October 14, 1907.
    Frank Pedley, Esq.
    Deputy Supt. General of Indian Affairs,
    Ottawa.

SIR, —have the honour to submit my report upon the payments of their annuities to those of the Indians of Treaty No. 10 who were treated with last year, and also transmit herewith the treaty, which, under the authority that devolved upon me by the commission issued to me on the 6th day of April, 1907, I concluded with the Chipewyan Indians living in the region of Lac du Brochet and Lac la Hache, and in the part of the district of Keewatin adjoining the northeast corner of the province of Saskatchewan.

With the view of keeping appointments for the payments of their annuities to the Indians who were treated with last year at Isle à la Crosse, I proceeded from here on June 11, and after travelling over some very bad road, I arrived at Green Lake on the afternoon of the 15th, and got to Isle à la Crosse at noon of Saturday, June 22, one day behind the date that was fixed for my arrival there. Very unfavourable weather was the cause of delay. Only the Canoe Lake band of Indians had so far assembled there to meet me; and I at once had an interview with the chief and headmen of that band, and it being Saturday, they asked that the paying of their annuities be postponed until Monday, the 24th. To that request I conceded, and accordingly they were paid on that and the following day. The Indians of English River and Clear Lake bands not having then arrived, I began taking evidence in connection with claims for scrip preferred by a number of half-breeds from Souris River who did not have a chance of meeting the commissioner of last year at Isle à la Crosse. The evidence adduced by these applicants for scrip was continued up to the 29th, when the English River and Clear Lake bands having fully arrived, were paid their annuities. The 1st of July, being Dominion Day, was, at the request of the half-breeds and Indians, observed as a holiday, and they celebrated it with great enthusiasm; the members of the commission and other gentlemen present heartily joining them and making their sports pecuniarily interesting for them.

Further dealings with the Indians and half-breeds occupied the time of the commission up to July 3, when, upon being informed that a considerable number of half-breeds and Indians were assembled at the Roman Catholic mission near Portage la Loche and expecting me there, I proceeded to that place, and after a very trying trip with rains and stormy weather, I reached there late on the evening of July 9, and owing to the number of half-breeds who had to be dealt with here, and the very inclement weather prevailing, it took up to the 14th to get through with the work. In addition to the half-breeds assembled here, I found a number of families of Indians from Whitefish Lake, who asked very earnestly that I should pay them their annuities. I explained to them that I could not do that, as it was inconsistent with the rules of the department to pay Indians of a certain treaty by the agent of another treaty. They pointed out that it was a great hardship for them to be compelled to travel over a hundred miles through a difficult section of the country going to Fort McMurray, which took them five or six days to get

there and the same number of days returning to their homes. Before leaving the mission, they handed me a petition praying that they be paid next year at Buffalo River on Buffalo Lake, to which point they can come in less than two days from Whitefish Lake.

On Monday morning, July 15, I left the mission on the return trip to Isle à la Crosse, and after an unusually favourable trip I arrived there on the 17th. Here I was detained for five days to procure tripmen to go on to Stanley, for which place I started on the morning of July 23 and arrived there on the evening of August 1. Here I met some fifty heads of families of the Lac la Ronge Indians, headed by their chief, Amos Charles, and two of their headmen, who asked that they be paid their annuities there, as many of them spent the summer and autumn on the Churchill river, and in compliance with their request they were paid on the 2nd and 3rd; the 5th and 6th were occupied taking evidence of applicants for scrip and procuring tripmen for the Lac du Brochet trip. On the morning of August 7 I left Stanley for the Hudson's Bay Company's post on the north end of Lac du Brochet, and after a successful trip reached that place on the 17th idem.

Owing to the amount of work which devolved upon the commission that was not anticipated, it was made impossible for me to reach this place, which was the stated point of rendezvous with the Indians, on the date that they were notified I was to be there to meet them; and consequently they were detained for ten days awaiting my arrival, and which led to their running out of provisions, they being all assembled with their families, and finding that they were reduced to such a state, I felt that it was proper for me to relieve their immediate necessities, and accordingly I supplied them with a limited quantity of provisions, for which they appeared to feel very thankful. I consider it proper that I should mention here that considerable help was afforded these Indians whilst waiting my arrival by Mr. A. McDermot, the Hudson's Bay Company's agent at this place, by giving them some light work to do and paying them for it in provisions, and likewise by the agent of the Revillon Bros.

On the morning of August 19 I held council with the combined Indians of the Barren Land and the Indians of Lac la Hache, the Rev. Father Turquetil acting as interpreter, which he did on all subsequent occasions during my transactions with the Indians here,

the Chipewyan language being spoken. I explained to them why I was sent to meet them, and after various thoughtful questions put by the Indians bearing upon the treaty and answered by me to their satisfaction, they asked for a short recess to discuss the terms of the treaty more fully among themselves; which was granted them. At 2 p.m. they reassembled and the Barren Land band announced that they had elected their chief and two headmen, and were prepared to accept the terms of the treaty. The Lac la Hache band intimated that some of their people were away, but would be back in a day or so, and that they would like to have their concurrence in the matter of selecting their chief and councillors; I consented to their waiting a day or so, if necessary, in order to obtain the full consent of their band to their transactions. The chief and headmen of the Barren Land band then formally signed the treaty, and without further undue delay the payments of their gratuities and annuities were begun to them, and were got through with at noon on the 21st. The number of Indians treated with in this band was 232, including:

The Lac la Hache band assembled on the 22nd, and after the terms of the treaty were read over to them for the second time and thoroughly explained in their own language, they presented their elected chief and two headmen, who then in due form signed the treaty, and the members of the band were paid in accordance with the terms of the treaty. The number of Indians paid in this band was 97, including:

This practically finished the Indian work at this point, and after a number of half-breeds' applications for scrip were received, I left this place on August 24 for Lac la Ronge, via Stanley, and on September 3, after a very unusually expeditious trip, I arrived at the paying ground at Lac la Ronge; and on the 4th and 5th paid the rest of the James Roberts band some 60 odd heads of families who were not paid at Stanley.

After taking the evidence of a number of half-breed applicants for scrip at this place, and holding council meetings with the Indians in connection with the surrender of their reserve, No. 106A, &c., I left on the 11th for Montreal Lake, and arrived there on the 16th, and the following day paid their annuities to the Indians of this place, the William Charles' band.

On the 18th I held meetings with the chief and headmen of the James Roberts' band, who accompanied me to this place, and with that of the Wm. Charles' band combined, bearing upon the surrender of their reserve, No. 106A, when after due deliberation, they unanimously agreed to relinquish the reserve to the government upon the terms set forth in an agreement signed by them on the 18th day of September, 1907; which agreement was transmitted to the Deputy Minister of Indian Affairs on the 8th instant.

On the afternoon of the 18th of September, the commission party left Montreal lake with canoes for the landing on Red Deer lake, where they arrived on the 21st, after being detained one day en route with stress of weather. At the landing teams were taken to this place (Mistawasis) where we arrived on the evening of September 24, ultimo; this completing an arduous trip of over 2,000 miles by water, in canoes, and 300 miles by land, which I have pleasure to say was performed successfully and without accident.

Concerning my staff, I am pleased to state that I was excellently equipped, and that, in general, a fine spirit existed amongst its members; of some of them I cannot speak too highly. Dr. H. A. Stewart proved himself ideally fitted for his post. Full of the kindest sympathy for the sick, he was untiring in his labours on their behalf; a skilful physician, he was most successful in his efforts to relieve their suffering, and won golden opinions from all who required his services. W. J. McLean, the senior secretary, displayed special ability in the performance of the onerous duties of his position, his previous experience in treaty payments standing him in good stead; while his knowledge of the French language, his long residence as a chief factor of the Hudson's Bay Company, in the part of the country traversed, and his personal acquaintance with many of the applicants, materially contributed to the success of my commission.

Of the rest it would be invidious to make personal mention, suffice to say that each performed his duties with energy and intelligence, sacrificing rest and comfort, and facing danger in the effort to cover distances with the least possible loss of time.

I have the honour to be, sir
Your obedient servant,
THOS. A. BORTHWICK,
Commissioner, Treaty No. 10

Treaty 11, 1922

June 27 to Aug. 30, 1921
Treaty No. 11 (June 27, 1921) and Adhesion
(July 17, 1922) with Reports, Etc.
REPORT OF THE COMMISSIONER FOR TREATY
No. 11

OTTAWA, October 12, 1921.
D. C. Scott, Esq.,
Deputy Superintendent General,
Department of Indian Affairs,
Ottawa.

SIR, —I have the honour to submit herewith the report on treaty made by me on authority granted by Order in Council, dated March 14, last, as Commissioner to negotiate a treaty with the Indians occupying the territory north of the 60th parallel and along the Mackenzie river and the Arctic ocean.

I left Edmonton on June 8, 1921, accompanied by Inspector W. B. Bruce, Constable Wood and Constable Campbell, of the Royal Canadian Mounted Police. Constable Campbell acted as my clerk for the summer.

Arriving at Fort McMurray on June 11, we left there on the 14th in a houseboat, the property of the Hudson's Bay Company, which company had made all arrangements for the transportation of the treaty party during the summer in the North.

We arrived at Fort Fitzgerald on June 18, crossed the portage to Fort Smith, and boarded the ss. *Mackenzie River* on June 20 for Fort Providence, at which place the first adhesion to Treaty 11 was to be taken. July 5 was the date set for the meeting of the Indians and myself to take place at Fort Providence, and, in order to arrive in good time, I thought it better for me and my party to proceed there by the ss. *Mackenzie River*, and let the houseboat take us up again at this point. The transportation of the houseboat across the portage at Fort Smith took several days.

On our arrival at Fort Providence, on June 20, I found the Indians were not at the post, as we were there before the date set for the meeting, so word was sent of my arrival, and the majority of the Providence Indians living at Willow Lake arrived on June 25, those at Trout Lake not till July 2. I had several meetings with them, and explained the terms of treaty. They were very apt in asking questions, and here, as in all the other posts where the treaty was signed, the questions asked and the difficulties encountered were much the same. The Indians seemed afraid, for one thing, that their liberty to hunt, trap and fish would be taken away or curtailed, but were assured by me that this would not be the case, and the Government will expect them to support themselves in their own way, and, in fact, that more twine for nets and more ammunition were given under the terms of this treaty than under any of the preceding ones; this went a long way to calm their fears. I also pointed out that any game laws made were to their advantage, and, whether they took treaty or not, they were subject to the laws of the Dominion. They also seemed afraid that they would be liable for military service if the treaty was signed, that they would be confined on the reserves, but, when told that they were exempt from military service, and that the reserves mentioned in the treaty would be of their own choosing, for their own use, and not for the white people, and that they would be free to come and go as they pleased, they were satisfied.

Practically all the bands dealt with wanted more provision for medical attendance at each post, schools for their children, and supplies for their old and destitute.

I pointed out that they were still able to make their own living, and that Dr. A. L. McDonald, of the Indian Department, was then with me, and that they could see him, and that he would attend them free if they wished, but that it was impossible for the Government to furnish regular medical attention, when they were occupying such a vast tract of territory. Schools were already established, and their children receiving free education, and supplies were left at each point for the sick and destitute.

The treaty was signed at Fort Providence on June 27, and the following were paid:—

1 Chief,
2 Headmen, and
255 others.

Our houseboat arrived on July 5, and we left Providence for Fort Simpson on the 7th, securing adhesion to the treaty there on July 11.

1 Chief,
2 Headmen, and

344 other Indians were paid.

Adhesions to the treaty were obtained at Fort Wrigley on July 13.

1 Headman, and
77 others were paid.

At Fort Norman on July 15,—

1 Chief,
2 Headmen, and
205 others were paid.

At Good Hope, July 21,—

1 Chief,
1 Headman, and
208 others were paid.

At Arctic Red River on July 26,—

1 Chief,
1 Headman, and
169 others were paid.

At Fort McPherson on July 28,—

1 Chief,
1 Headman, and
217 others were paid.

At Fort Rae on August 22,—

1 Chief
2 Headmen, and
440 others were paid.

Practically all the Indians were dealt with at Fort Providence, Simpson, Wrigley, Arctic Red River and McPherson, and about 65 per cent at Fort Norman, Fort Good Hope and Rae, the remainder of these Indians having been at these posts in the spring and left word that they were willing to take treaty, but had to return to their hunting grounds for their summer's work.

At Fort Rae is the largest band of Indians, about 800, and this is the most inaccessible, being on the arm of Great Slave Lake, difficulty in crossing this lake being experienced, more especially in the late summer and fall on account of storms, our party being stormbound at Hay River for five days prior to crossing. These Indians hunt in every direction from the fort, some as far as 200 miles, and only come to the post in spring to trade their furs, so that, in future, I would suggest that this be the first post visited when making payments.

We crossed the lake from Hay River to Rae in the Hudson Bay schooner *Fort Rae,* leaving our houseboat to take us up at Resolution, from which place we went on August 25, arriving at Fort Smith on August 30, Fort McMurray and Edmonton in September.

I much regret that I was unable, owing to the lack of time, to visit Fort Liard, and secure adhesion to the treaty by the Indians at that point, although they had sent word to Fort Simpson of their willingness to accept the same. I considered it advisable to proceed to Great Slave Lake, and cross to Fort Rae at the first opportunity, as the season was getting late.

Dr. A. L. McDonald joined the party at Fort Providence, and accompanied it to Good Hope, at that place having to return to Fort Resolution on account of smallpox having been reported, which report, fortunately, proved untrue. He joined the party again at Hay River, and remained with it until arrival at his headquarters at Fort Smith.

I was very glad to be accompanied by His Lordship Bishop Breynat, O.M.I., who has considerable influence with the Indians in the North, and would like here to express my appreciation of the help and hospitality accorded to me and my party in his missions, and I desire also to express my appreciation of the services rendered by Inspector Bruce, of the Royal Canadian Mounted Police, and by his party. Constables Woods and Campbell performed their duties in the most creditable manner.

H. A. CONROY,
Commissioner, Treaty No. 11.

TREATY NUMBER ELEVEN
ARTICLES OF A TREATY made and concluded on the several dates mentioned therein in the year of Our Lord One thousand Nine hundred and Twenty-One, between His Most Gracious Majesty George V, King of Great Britain and Ireland and of the British Dominions beyond the Seas, by His Commissioner, Henry Anthony Conroy, Esquire, of the City of Ottawa, of the One Part, and the Slave, Dogrib,

Loucheux, Hare and other Indians, inhabitants of the territory within the limits hereinafter defined and described, by their Chiefs and Headmen, hereunto subscribed, of the other part:—

WHEREAS, the Indians inhabiting the territory hereinafter defined have been convened to meet a commissioner representing His Majesty's Government of the Dominion of Canada at certain places in the said territory in this present year of 1921, to deliberate upon certain matters of interest to His Most Gracious Majesty, of the one part, and the said Indians of the other.

AND WHEREAS, the said Indians have been notified and informed by His Majesty's said commissioner that it is His desire to open for settlement, immigration, trade, travel, mining, lumbering and such other purposes as to His Majesty may seem meet, a tract of country bounded and described as hereinafter set forth, and to obtain the consent thereto of His Indian subjects inhabiting the said tract, and to make a treaty, so that there may be peace and good-will between them and His Majesty's other subjects, and that His Indian people may know and be assured of what allowances they are to expect and receive from His Majesty's bounty and benevolence.

AND WHEREAS, the Indians of the said tract, duly convened in council at the respective points named hereunder, and being requested by His Majesty's Commissioner, to name certain Chiefs and Headmen, who should be authorized on their behalf to conduct such negotiations and sign any treaty to be founded thereon, and to become responsible to His Majesty for the faithful performance by their respective bands of such obligations as shall be assumed by them, the said Indians have therefore acknowledged for that purpose the several chiefs and Headmen who have subscribed thereto.

AND WHEREAS the said Commissioner has proceeded to negotiate a treaty with the Slave, Dogrib, Loucheux, Hare and other Indians inhabiting the district hereinafter defined and described, which has been agreed upon and concluded by the respective bands at the dates mentioned hereunder, the said Indians do hereby cede, release, surrender and yield up to the Government of the Dominion of Canada, for His Majesty the King and His Successors forever, all their rights, titles, and privileges whatsoever to

the lands included within the following limits, that is to say:

Commencing at the northwesterly corner of the territory ceded under the provisions of Treaty Number Eight; thence northeasterly along the height-of-land to the point where it intersects the boundary between the Yukon Territory and the Northwest Territories; thence northwesterly along the said boundary to the shore of the Arctic ocean; thence easterly along the said shore to the mouth of the Coppermine river; thence southerly and southeasterly along the left bank of said river to Lake Gras by way of Point lake; thence along the southern shore of Lake Gras to a point situated northwest of the most western extremity of Aylmer lake; thence along the southern shore of Aylmer lake and following the right bank of the Lockhart river to Artillery lake; thence along the western shore of Artillery lake and following the right bank of the Lockhart river to the site of Old Fort Reliance where the said river enters Great Slave lake, this being the northeastern corner of the territory ceded under the provisions of Treaty Number Eight; thence westerly along the northern boundary of the said territory so ceded to the point of commencement; comprising an area of approximately three hundred and seventy-two thousand square miles.

AND ALSO, the said Indian rights, titles and privileges whatsoever to all other lands wherever situated in the Yukon Territory, the Northwest Territories or in any other portion of the Dominion of Canada.

To have and to hold the same to His Majesty the King and His Successors forever.

AND His Majesty the King hereby agrees with the said Indians that they shall have the right to pursue their usual vocations of hunting, trapping and fishing throughout the tract surrendered as heretofore described, subject to such regulations as may from time to time be made by the Government of the Country acting under the authority of His Majesty, and saving and excepting such tracts as may be required or taken up from time to time for settlement, mining, lumbering, trading or other purposes.

AND His Majesty the King hereby agrees and undertakes to lay aside reserves for each band, the same not to exceed in all one square mile for each family of five, or in that proportion for larger or smaller families;

PROVIDED, however, that His Majesty reserves the right to deal with any settlers within the boundaries of any lands reserved for any band as He may see fit; and also that the aforesaid reserves of land, or any interest therein, may be sold or otherwise disposed of by His Majesty's Government for the use and benefit of the said Indians entitled thereto, with their consent first had and obtained; but in no wise shall the said Indians, or any of them, be entitled to sell or otherwise alienate any of the lands allotted to them as reserves.

It is further agreed between His Majesty and His Indian subjects that such portions of the reserves and lands above indicated as may at any time be required for public works, buildings, railways, or roads of whatsoever nature may be appropriated for that purpose by His Majesty's Government of the Dominion of Canada, due compensation being made to the Indians for the value of any improvements thereon, and an equivalent in land, money or other consideration for the area of the reserve so appropriated.

And in order to show the satisfaction of His Majesty with the behaviour and good conduct of His Indian subjects, and in extinguishment of all their past claims hereinabove mentioned, He hereby, through his Commissioner, agrees to give to each Chief a present of thirty-two dollars in cash, to each Headman, twenty-two dollars, and to every other Indian of whatever age of the families represented, at the time and place of payment, twelve dollars.

HIS MAJESTY, also agrees that during the coming year, and annually thereafter, He will cause to be paid to the said Indians in cash, at suitable places and dates, of which the said Indians shall be duly notified, to each Chief twenty-five dollars, to each Headman fifteen dollars, and to every other Indian of whatever age five dollars, to be paid only to heads of families for the members thereof, it being provided for the purposes of this Treaty that each band having at least thirty members may have a Chief, and that in addition to a Chief, each band may have Councillors or Headmen in the proportion of two to each two hundred members of the band.

FURTHER, His Majesty agrees that each Chief shall receive once and for all a silver medal, a suitable flag and a copy of this Treaty for the use of his band; and during the coming year, and every third year thereafter, each Chief and Headman shall receive a suitable suit of clothing.

FURTHER, His Majesty agrees to pay the salaries of teachers to instruct the children of said Indians in such manner as His Majesty's Government may deem advisable.

FURTHER, His Majesty agrees to supply once and for all to each Chief of a band that selects a reserve, ten axes, five hand-saws, five augers, one grindstone, and the necessary files and whetstones for the use of the band.

FURTHER, His Majesty agrees that, each band shall receive once and for all equipment for hunting, fishing and trapping to the value of fifty dollars for each family of such band, and that there shall be distributed annually among the Indians equipment, such as twine for nets, ammunition and trapping to the value of three dollars per head for each Indian who continues to follow the vocation of hunting, fishing and trapping.

FURTHER, His Majesty agrees that, in the event of any of the Indians aforesaid being desirous of following agricultural pursuits, such Indians shall receive such assistance as is deemed necessary for that purpose.

AND the undersigned Slave, Dogrib, Loucheux, Hare and other Chiefs and Headmen, on their own behalf and on behalf of all the Indians whom they represent, do hereby solemnly promise and engage to strictly observe this Treaty, and also to conduct and behave themselves as good loyal subjects of His Majesty the King.

THEY promise and engage that they will, in all respects, obey and abide by the law; that they will maintain peace between themselves and others of His Majesty's subjects, whether Indians, half-breeds or whites, now inhabiting and hereafter to inhabit any part of the said ceded territory; that they will not molest the person or property of any inhabitant of such ceded tract, or of any other district or country, or interfere with, or trouble any person passing or travelling through the said tract or any part thereof, and that they will assist the officers of His Majesty in bringing to justice and punishment any Indian offending against the stipulations of this Treaty, or infringing the law in force in the country so ceded.

IN WITNESS WHEREOF, His Majesty's said Commissioner and the said Chiefs and Headmen have hereunto set their hands at the places and times set forth in the year herein first above written.

SIGNED AT PROVIDENCE on the twenty-seventh day of June, 1921, by His Majesty's Commissioner and the Chiefs and Headmen in the presence of the undersigned witnesses, after having been first interpreted and explained.

SIGNED at Simpson on the eleventh day of July, 1921, by His Majesty's Commissioner and the Chiefs and Headmen in the presence of the undersigned witnesses, after having been first interpreted and explained.

SIGNED at Wrigley on the thirteenth day of July, 1921, by His Majesty's Commissioner and the Chiefs and Headmen in presence of the undersigned witnesses, after having been first interpreted and explained.

SIGNED at Norman on the fifteenth day of July, 1921, by His Majesty's Commissioner and the Chiefs and Headmen in the presence of the undersigned witnesses, after having been first interpreted and explained.

SIGNED at Good Hope on the twenty-first day of July, 1921, by His Majesty's Commissioner and the Chiefs and Headmen in the presence of the undersigned witnesses, after having been first interpreted and explained.

SIGNED at Arctic Red River on the twenty-sixth day of July, 1921, by His Majesty's Commissioner and the Chiefs and Headmen in the presence of the undersigned witnesses, after having been first interpreted and explained.

SIGNED at McPherson on the twenty-eighth day of July, 1921, by His Majesty's Commissioner and the Chiefs and Headmen in the presence of the undersigned witnesses, after having been first interpreted and explained.

SIGNED at Liard on the day of, 1921, by His Majesty's Commissioners and the Chiefs and Head-men in the presence of the undersigned witnesses, after having been first interpreted and explained.

Witnesses:
    SIGNED at Rae on the twenty-second day of August, 1921, by His Majesty's Commissioner and the Chiefs and Headmen in the presence of undersigned witnesses, after having been first interpreted and explained.

ORDER IN COUNCIL RATIFYING TREATY No. 11
    P.C. 3985
    PRIVY COUNCIL CANADA
    AT THE GOVERNMENT HOUSE AT
OTTAWA,
    SATURDAY,
    the 22nd day of October, 1921.
    PRESENT:
    HIS EXCELLENCY
    THE GOVERNOR GENERAL IN COUNCIL

WHEREAS the Superintendent General of Indian Affairs submits herewith Treaty Number Eleven made, in accordance with the terms of Order in Council of 14th March, 1921 (P.C. 686), by Henry Anthony Conroy, Esquire, who was appointed a Commissioner by the said Order in Council, to negotiate with the Slave, Dogrib, Loucheux, Hare and other Indians for the cession by the said Indians to the Crown of all their rights, titles and privileges whatsoever in the territory north of the sixtieth parallel and along the Mackenzie river and the Arctic ocean in the Dominion of Canada.

THEREFORE His Excellency the Governor General in Council, on the recommendation of the Superintendent General of Indian Affairs, is pleased to ratify the said Treaty Number Eleven, made and negotiated as hereinbefore recited, and the same is hereby ratified and confirmed accordingly.

RODOLPHE BOUDREAU,
    Clerk of the Privy Council.
    The Honourable
    The Superintendent General of Indian Affairs.

Owing to the death of Commissioner Conroy on April 27, 1922, and to the fact that he had not had an opportunity during the summer of 1921 of obtaining the adhesion to the Treaty by the Slave Indians of the Liard district, it was necessary to make other arrangements. Accordingly the authority of His

Excellency the Governor General in Council was obtained for the appointment of T. W. Harris, Indian agent at Fort Simpson, N.W.T., as Commissioner to secure this adhesion.

Following is a copy of the Order in Council:—
    P.C. 993

CERTIFIED COPY of a *Report of the Committee of the Privy Council approved by His Excellency the Governor General on the 9th May, 1922*

The Committee of the Privy Council have had before them a Report, dated 2nd May, 1922, from the Superintendent General of Indian Affairs, submitting, with reference to Order in Council of the 14th March, 1921, under which Mr. H. A. Conroy, Inspector for Treaty No. 8, was authorized to act as Commissioner to negotiate a Treaty (known as Treaty No. 11) with the Indians occupying the territory north of the 60th parallel and along the Mackenzie river to the Arctic coast, that owing to lack of time Mr. Conroy was unable to visit the Fort Liard Indians last year with a view to securing their adhesion to the treaty.

The Minister states that owing to Mr. Conroy's death, which occurred on the 27th April, 1922, it is essential that someone should be deputed to complete the treaty negotiations.

The Minister, therefore, recommends that Mr. T. W. Harris, Indian agent at Fort Simpson, N.W.T., be authorized to complete the work entrusted to the late Mr. Conroy in connection with the treaty above mentioned.

The Committe concur in the foregoing recommendation and submit the same for approval.

RODOLPHE BOUDREAU,
    Clerk of the Privy Council.
    The Honourable
    The Superintendent General of Indian Affairs.

Accordingly Commissioner Harris, accompanied by His Lordship Bishop Breynat and Reverend Father Moisan, visited Fort Liard on July 17th. The terms of the treaty having been explained by the Commissioner, the Chief and Headmen, who had previously been elected, signed the treaty on behalf of the Indians as indicated in the following Indenture:—

SIGNED at Liard on the seventeenth day of July, 1922, by His Majesty's Commissioner and the Chiefs and Headmen in the presence of the undersigned witnesses, after having been first interpreted and explained.

ORDER IN COUNCIL RATIFYING ADHESION TO TREATY No. 11
March 29, 1923.
The Committee of the Privy Council, on the recommendation of the Superintendent General of Indian Affairs, submit herewith for ratification and confirmation by Your Excellency in Council, an instrument, in duplicate, containing the adhesion to Treaty No. 11 of the Indians of Fort Liard taken the seventeenth day of July, 1922, by Mr. T. W. Harris, who was appointed by an Order of Your Excellency in Council of 9th May, 1922 (P.C. No. 993), as His Majesty's Commissioner to take the said adhesion; one copy of the instrument to be returned to the Department of Indian Affairs and the other to be kept on record in the Privy Council Office.

(Sgd.) RODOLPHE BOUDREAU,
    Clerk of the Privy Council.
    The Honourable
    The Superintendent General of Indian Affairs.

Williams Treaties, 1923

Oct. 31, 1923
INDIAN TREATY
ARTICLES OF A TREATY made and concluded on the thirty-first day of October, in the year of Our Lord One thousand nine hundred and twenty-three, between His Most Gracious Majesty, George the Fifth, of the United Kingdom of Great Britain and Ireland, King, Defender of the Faith, Emperor of India, by His Commissioners: Angus Seymour Williams, of the City of Ottawa, in the Province of Ontario, Esquire, Barrister-at-law, and Departmental Solicitor of the Department of Indian Affairs; Robert Victor Sinclair, of the said City of Ottawa, Esquire, One of His Majesty's Counsel, learned in the law, and Uriah McFadden, of the City of Sault Sainte Marie, in the said Province, Esquire, one of His Majesty's Counsel learned in the law; the said Angus Seymour Williams, Chairman of the said Commission, representing the Dominion of Canada, and the said Robert Victor Sinclair and Uriah McFadden,

representing the Province of Ontario, of the One Part; and the Members of the Chippewa Tribe, inhabiting, as members of Bands thereof, reserves at Christian Island, Georgina Island and Rama, all in the Province of Ontario, by their Chiefs and Headmen, of the Other Part.

WHEREAS, the Chippewa Tribe above described, having claimed to be entitled to certain interests in the lands in the Province of Ontario, hereinafter described, such interests being the Indian title of the said tribe to fishing, hunting and trapping rights over the said lands, of which said rights His Majesty through His said Commissioners, is desirous of obtaining a surrender, and for such purpose has appointed the said Commissioners, with power on behalf of His said Majesty, to enquire into the validity of the claims of the said tribe, and, in the event of the said Commissioners determining in favour of the validity thereof, to negotiate a treaty with the said tribe for the surrender of the said rights upon the payment of such compensation therefor as may seem to the said Commissioners to be just and proper:

AND WHEREAS the said Commissioners, having duly made the said enquiry, have determined in favour of the validity of the said rights.

AND WHEREAS the Indians belonging to the said tribe, having been duly convened in council, at the respective places named hereunder, and having been requested by the said Commissioners to name certain chiefs and headmen to be authorized on their behalf to conduct negotiations with the said Commissioners for a surrender of the said rights and to sign a treaty in respect thereof and to become responsible to His Majesty for the faithful performance by the said tribe and by the respective bands thereof inhabiting the said reserves, of such obligations as shall be assumed by them under such treaty, the said Indians have therefore appointed for the purpose aforesaid the several chiefs and headmen who have subscribed to this treaty:

AND WHEREAS the said Commissioners, acting under the powers in them reposed as aforesaid, have negotiated the present treaty with the said tribe:

NOW THEREFORE THIS TREATY WITNESSETH that the said tribe and the Indians composing the same, occupying as members of bands the said

reserves, by their chiefs and headmen, duly authorized thereunto, as aforesaid, do hereby cede, release, surrender and yield up to the government of the Dominion of Canada for His Majesty the King and His Successors forever, all their right, title, interest, claim, demand and privileges whatsoever, in, to, upon, or in respect of the lands and premises described as follows, that is to say:

FIRSTLY: All that parcel of land situate in the Province of Ontario and described as commencing on the northeasterly shore of Georgian Bay at that mouth of the French River which forms the boundary between the District of Parry Sound and the District of Sudbury; thence southerly and easterly along the shores of Georgian Bay to that point on Matchedash Bay where the land included in the surrender of the eighteenth day of November, 1815, of record in Book of Surrenders, Volume I, is reached, and including all the islands in the Georgian Bay waters in which the Indians making this treaty have any interest; thence along the easterly limit of the said lands purchased in 1815 to the Narrows between Lake Couchiching and Lake Simcoe; thence due east across the said Narrows; thence southerly and easterly following the east side of the Narrows and the north shore of Lake Simcoe to the foot of McPhee Bay off the northerly part of Lake Simcoe; thence by a straight line easterly to a point thirty-three miles north of the northwest corner of the Township of Rawdon measured along the division line between the Counties of Hastings and Peterborough, which point is the most western northwest corner of the parcel surrendered on the twenty-eight day of November, 1822 (noted in Volume I of the Book of Surrenders as number twenty-seven and one-quarter, 27 1/4); thence following the north and west boundaries of the last mentioned parcel to the Ottawa River; thence westerly along the interprovincial boundary to the mouth of the Mattawa River; thence westerly by the waters of Mattawa River, Talon Chute and Talon Lake, Turtle Lake, and Trout Lake to the westerly point of Trout Lake; thence to the shore of Lake Nipissing at North Bay; thence by the north shore of Lake Nipissing to the French River; thence by those waters along the division line between the Districts of Parry Sound and Sudbury to the place of commencement: Excepting thereout and therefrom those lands which have already been set aside as Indian Reserves. The parcel hereby surrendered contains seventeen thousand, six hundred square miles, more or less.

SECONDLY: All that parcel of land situate in the Province of Ontario and described as parts of the Counties of Northumberland, Durham, Ontario and York, commencing at the point where the easterly limit of that portion of the lands said to have been ceded in 1787, which was confirmed on the first day of August, 1805, of record as number thirteen in Volume I of the Book of Surrenders, intersects the northerly shore of Lake Ontario; thence northerly along the said easterly and northerly limits of the confirmed tract to the Holland River; thence northerly along the Holland River and along the westerly shore of Lake Simcoe and Kempenfelt Bay to the Narrows between Lake Couchiching and Lake Simcoe; thence southeasterly along the shores of Lake Simcoe to the Talbot River; thence easterly along the Talbot River to the boundary between the Townships of Victoria and Ontario; thence southerly along that boundary to the northwest angle of the Township of Darlington; thence along the northerly boundary line of the Townships of Darlington, Clarke, Hope and Hamilton to Rice Lake; thence along the southern shore of said lake to River Trent along the River Trent to the Bay of Quinte; thence westerly and southerly along the shore of the Bay of Quinte to the road leading to Carrying Place and Wellers Bay; thence westerly along the northern shore of Lake Ontario to the place of beginning; excepting thereout and therefrom those lands which have already been set aside as Indian reserves. The land hereby conveyed contains two thousand, five hundred square miles more or less.

AND ALSO all the right, title, interest, claim, demand and privileges whatsoever of the said Indians, in, to, upon or in respect of all other lands, situate in the Province of Ontario to which they ever had, now have, or now claim to have any right, title, interest, claim, demand or privileges, except such reserves as have heretofore been set apart for them by His Majesty the King.

TO HAVE AND TO HOLD the same to His Majesty the King and His Successors forever:

AND THIS TREATY FURTHER WITNESSETH that in consideration of the aforesaid surrender, His Majesty, through His said Commissioners, hereby agrees, upon the execution of a treaty similar to this treaty by the Mississauga tribe inhabiting as members of bands, reserves at Rice Lake, Mud Lake, Scugog Lake and Alderville, in the Province of Ontario, to pay to each member of the said Chippewa tribe, being also a member of one of the said bands, the sum of twenty-five dollars, to be paid through the Indian agents for the respective bands, within a reasonable time after the execution of the said treaties, and a further sum of —233,375.00 dollars — to be administered for the said tribe by His Majesty's Department of Indian Affairs under and pursuant to the provisions of the Indian Act, Revised Statutes of Canada, 1906, Chapter 43 and its amendments: Making together the sum of two hundred and fifty thousand dollars.

AND THE UNDERSIGNED chiefs and headmen, on their own behalf and on behalf of all the Indians whom they represent, do hereby solemnly covenant, promise and agree to strictly observe this treaty in all respects and that they will not, nor will any of them, nor will any of the Indians whom they represent, molest or interfere with the person or property of anyone who now inhabits or shall hereafter inhabit any portion of the lands covered by this treaty, or interfere with, trouble, or molest any person passing or travelling through the said lands or any part thereof, and that they will assist the officers of His Majesty in bringing to justice and punishment any Indian, party to this treaty, who may hereafter offend against the stipulations hereof or infringe the laws in force in the lands covered hereby:

AND IT IS FURTHER UNDERSTOOD that this treaty is subject to an agreement dated the day of April, A.D. 1923, made between the Dominion of Canada and the Province of Ontario, a copy of which is hereto attached.

IN WITNESS WHEREOF, His Majesty's said Commissioners and the said chiefs and headmen have hereunto set their hands and seals at the places and times hereinafter set forth, in the year herein first above written.

SIGNED AND SEALED at Georgina Island on the thirty-first day of October, A.D. 1923, by His Majesty's Commissioners and the undersigned chiefs and headmen in the presence of the undersigned witnesses, after first having been interpreted and explained.

[signatures]

SIGNED AND SEALED at Christian Island on the third day of November, A.D. 1923, by His Majesty's Commissioners and the undersigned chiefs and headmen in the presence of the undersigned witnesses, after first having been interpreted and explained.

[signatures]

SIGNED AND SEALED at Rama on the seventh day of November, A.D. 1923, by His Majesty's Commissioners and the undersigned chiefs and headmen in the presence of the undersigned witnesses, after first having been interpreted and explained.

[signatures]

MEMORANDUM OF AGREEMENT made this — of April, 1923,
    BETWEEN:
    The Government of the Dominion of Canada, acting herein by the Honourable Charles Stewart, Superintendent General of Indian Affairs,
    of the first part,
    AND
    The Government of the Province of Ontario, acting herein by the Honourable Beniah Bowman, Minister of Lands and Forests for the said Province,
    of the other part

WHEREAS certain Indians of the Chippewa and Mississauga tribes claim that the said tribes were and are entitled to a certain interest in lands in the Province of Ontario to which the Indian title has never been extinguished by surrender or otherwise, the said lands being described as parts of the counties of Renfrew, Hastings, Haliburton, Muskoka, Parry Sound and Nipissing, and being bounded on the south and east by the lands included in the surrenders of the Indian title made on the 18th of November, 1815, the 5th of November, 1818, and November, 1822; on the north by the Ottawa and Mattawa Rivers and Lake Nipissing, and on the west by the lands included in the surrender of the Indian title made in 1850, known as the Robinson-Huron surrender, and by the Georgian Bay, the area in question including about 10,719 square miles.

AND WHEREAS a departmental enquiry made by the Department of Indian Affairs indicates that the said claim has such probable validity as to justify and require further investigation, and if found valid to be satisfied on such just and fair terms as may be settled by a treaty of surrender.

NOW THEREFORE THIS AGREEMENT made in pursuance of certian statutes of Canada and of the Province of Ontario, both intituled "an Act for the settlement of certain questions between the Governments of Canada and Ontario respecting Indian Lands," the Statute of Canada having been passed in the 54th and 55th years of the reign of Her Majesty Queen Victoria and chaptered 5, and the statute of Ontario in the 54th year of Her Majesty's said reign and chaptered 3.

WITNESSETH THAT the Governments of Canada and of the Province of Ontario have agreed as follows:

1. The Government of Canada will, pursuant to Part I of the Enquiries Act, R.S.C., 1906, c. 104, and amendments, appoint three persons as commissioners to enquire into the validity of the claim of the Chippewa and Mississauga Indians aforesaid, and will empower the said commissioners, in the event of their determining in favour of the validity of the said claim, to negotiate a treaty with the said Indians for the surrender of the said lands upon payment of such compensation as may be fixed by such treaty.

2. Of the three commissioners so named, one shall be selected by the Government of Canada, who shall be Chairman of the Commission, and the remaining two shall be selected by the Minister of Lands and Forests for the Province of Ontario and notified to the Superintendent General of Indian Affairs.

3. The question of the validity of said claim may be determined by any two of the said Commissioners and it shall be necessary that at least two of them of whom the chairman shall be one shall concur in any treaty which may be negotiated.

4. The expenses of the said commission, including the remuneration and expenses of the commissioners and any expenses

incurred for securing the attendance of witnesses or otherwise, shall be payable by the Government of Canada, but the rates of remuneration of each of the commissioners selected by the Minister of Lands and Forests for the Province of Ontario shall be agreed upon between him and the Superintendent General of Indian Affairs before the Constitution of the Commission.

5. In the event of the commissioners negotiating a treaty with the Indians the compensation to be paid to such Indians shall be payable to the Dominion of Canada by the Province of Ontario from time to time in accordance with the terms of the treaty of surrender, and shall be applied by the Dominion of Canada in accordance with the said terms.

6. In the event of provision being made by such treaty of surrender for the setting apart of reserves for the Indians, the Dominion of Canada will bear the expense to be incurred in the location and survey thereof, and the Province of Ontario will concur in the setting apart of such reserves.

7. All such reserves shall be administered by the Dominion of Canada for the benefit of the band or bands of Indians to which each may be allotted; portions thereof may, upon their surrender for the purpose by the said band or bands, be sold, leased or otherwise disposed of by letters patent under the Great Seal of Canada, and the proceeds of such sale, lease or other disposition applied for the benefit of such band or bands, provided, however, that in the event of the band or bands to which any such reserve has been allotted becoming extinct, or if for any other reason such reserve or such portion thereof as remains undisposed of is declared by the Superintendent General of Indian Affairs to be no longer required for the benefit of the said band or bands, the same shall thereafter be administered by and for the benefit of the Province of Ontario, and any balance of the proceeds of the sale or other disposition of any portion thereof then remaining under the control of the Dominion of Canada shall,

so far as the same is not still required to be applied for the benefit of the said band or bands
of Indians, be paid to the Province of Ontario, together with accrued unexpended simple interest thereon.

IN WITNESS WHEREOF these presents have been signed by the parties thereto.
Copy Of The Treaty Made November 15, 1923
Between
His Majesty The King
And
The Mississauga Indians
Of Rice Lake, Mud Lake, Scugog Lake And Alderville

INDIAN TREATY
Nov. 15, 1923

ARTICLES OF A TREATY made and concluded on the fifteenth day of November in the year of Our Lord One thousand nine hundred and twenty-three, between His Most Gracious Majesty, George the Fifth, of the United Kingdom of Great Britain and Ireland, King, Defender of the Faith, Emperor of India, by His Commissioners, Angus Seymour Williams, of the City of Ottawa, in the Province of Ontario, Esquire, Barrister-at-law, and Departmental Solicitor of the Department of Indian Affairs: Robert Victor Sinclair, of the said City of Ottawa, Esquire, one of His Majesty's Counsel, learned in the law, and Uriah McFadden, of the City of Sault Sainte Marie, in the said Province, Esquire, one of His Majesty's Counsel learned in the law, the said Angus Seymour Williams, Chairman of the said Commission, representing the Dominion of Canada, and the said Robert Victor Sinclair and Uriah McFadden, representing the Province of Ontario, of the One Part, and the members of the Mississauga Tribe, inhabiting, as members of bands thereof, reserves at Rice Lake, Mud Lake, Scugog Lake and Alderville, all in the Province of Ontario, by their chiefs and headmen, of the Other Part.

WHEREAS, the Mississauga Tribe above described, having claimed to be entitled to certain interests in the lands in the Province of Ontario, hereinafter described, such interests being the Indian title of the said tribe to fishing, hunting and trapping rights over the said lands, of which said rights, His Majesty, through His said Commissioners, is desirous of obtaining a surrender, and for such purpose has appointed the said Commissioners, with power on behalf of His said Majesty, to enquire into the validity of the claims of the said tribe, and, in the event of the said Commissioners determining in favour of the validity thereof, to negotiate a treaty with the said tribe for the surrender of the said rights upon the payment of such compensation therefor as may seem to the said Commissioners to be just and proper:

AND WHEREAS the said Commissioners, having duly made the said enquiry, have determined in favour of the validity of the said rights.

AND WHEREAS the Indians belonging to the said tribe, having been duly convened in Council, at the respective places named hereunder, and having been requested by the said Commissioners to name certain chiefs and headmen to be authorized on their behalf to conduct negotiations with the said Commissioners for a surrender of the said rights and to sign a treaty in respect thereof and to become responsible to His Majesty for the faithful performance by the said tribe and by the respective bands thereof inhabiting the said reserves, of such obligations as shall be assumed by them under such treaty, the said Indians have therefore appointed for the purposes aforesaid the several chiefs and headmen who have subscribed to this treaty:

AND WHEREAS the said Commissioners, acting under the powers in them reposed as aforesaid, have negotiated the present treaty with the said tribe:

NOW THEREFORE THIS TREATY WITNESSETH that the said tribe and the Indians composing the same, occupying as members of bands the said reserves, by their chiefs and headmen, duly authorized thereunto as aforesaid, do hereby cede, release, surrender and yield up to the Government of the Dominion of Canada for His Majesty the King and His Successors forever, all their right, title, interest, claim, demand and privileges whatsoever, in, to, upon, or in respect of the lands and premises described as follows, that is to say:

FIRSTLY: All that parcel of land situate in the Province of Ontario and described as commencing on the northeasterly shore of Georgian Bay at that mouth of the French River which forms the boundary between the District of Parry Sound and the District of Sudbury; thence southerly and easterly along the shores of Georgian Bay to that point on Matchedash Bay where the land included in the surrender of the eighteenth day of November, 1815, of record in Book of Surrenders, Volume One, is reached, and including all the islands in the Georgian Bay waters in which the Indians making this treaty have any interest; thence along the easterly limit of the said lands purchased in 1815 to the Narrows between Lake Couchiching and Lake Simcoe; thence due east across the said Narrows; thence southerly and easterly following the east side of the Narrows and the north shore of Simcoe to the foot of McPhee Bay off the northerly part of Lake Simcoe; thence by a straight line easterly to a point thirty-three miles north of the northwest corner of the Township of Rawdon measured along the division line between the Counties of Hastings and Peterborough, which point is the most western northwest corner of the parcel surrendered on the twenty-eighth day of November, 1822 (noted in Volume One of the Book of Surrenders as number twenty-seven and one-quarter, 27 1/4); thence following the north and west boundaries of the last mentioned parcel to the Ottawa River; thence westerly along the interprovincial boundary to the mouth of the Mattawa River; thence westerly along the interprovincial boundary to the mouth of the Mattawa River, Talon Chute and Talon Lake, Turtle Lake, and Trout Lake to the westerly point of Trout Lake; thence to the shore of Lake Nipissing at North Bay; thence by the north shore of Lake Nipissing to the French River; thence by those waters along the division line between the Districts of Parry Sound and Sudbury to the place of commencement: Excepting thereout and therefrom those lands which have already been set aside as Indian reserves. The parcel hereby surrendered contains seventeen thousand, six hundred square miles, more or less.

SECONDLY: All that parcel of land situate in the Province of Ontario and described as parts of the Counties of Northumberland, Durham, Ontario and York, commencing at the point where the easterly limit of that portion of the lands said to have been ceded in 1787, which was confirmed on the first of August, 1805, of record as number thirteen in Volume One, of the Book of Surrenders, intersects the northerly shore of Lake Ontario; thence northerly along the said easterly and northerly limits of the confirmed tract to the Holland River; thence northerly along the Holland

River and along the westerly shore of Lake Simcoe and Kempenfelt Bay to the Narrows between Lake Couchiching and Lake Simcoe; thence southeasterly along the shores of Lake Simcoe to the Talbot River; thence easterly along the Talbot River to the boundary between the Counties of Victoria and Ontario; thence southerly along that boundary to the northwest angle of the Township of Darlington; thence along the northerly boundary line of the Townships of Darlington, Clarke, Hope and Hamilton to Rice Lake; thence along the southern shore of said lake to River Trent along the River Trent to the Bay of Quinte; thence westerly and southerly along the shore of the Bay of Quinte to the road leading to Carrying Place and Weller's Bay; thence westerly along the northern shore of Lake Ontario to the place of beginning: Excepting thereout and therefrom those lands which have already been set aside as Indian Reserves. The land hereby conveyed contains two thousand, five hundred square miles more or less.

AND ALSO all the right, title, interest, claim, demand and privileges whatsoever of the said Indians, in, to, upon or in respect of all other lands situate in the Province of Ontario to which they ever had, now have, or now claim to have any right, title, interest, claim, demand or privileges, except such reserves as have heretofore been set apart for them by His Majesty the King.

TO HAVE AND TO HOLD the same to His Majesty the King and His Successors forever:

AND THIS TREATY FURTHER WITNESSETH that in consideration of the aforesaid surrender, His Majesty, through His said Commissioners, hereby agrees, upon the execution of a treaty similar to this treaty by the Chippewa Tribe inhabiting as members of bands, reserves at Christian Island, Georgina Island and Rama, in the Province of Ontario, to pay to each member of the said Mississauga Tribe, being also a member of one of the said bands, the sum of twenty-five dollars, to be paid through the Indian agents for the respective bands, with a reasonable time after the execution of the said treaties, and a further sum of —233,425.00 dollars— to be administered for the said tribe by His Majesty's Department of Indian Affairs under and pursuant to the provisions of the Indian Act, Revised Statutes of Canada, 1906, Chapter Forty-

three and its amendments; making together the sum of 250,000.00 dollars.

AND THE UNDERSIGNED chiefs and headmen, on their own behalf and on behalf of all the Indians whom they represent, do hereby solemnly covenant, promise and agree to strictly observe this treaty in all respects and that they will not, nor will any of them, nor will any of the Indians whom they represent, molest or interfere with the person or property of anyone who now inhabits or shall hereafter inhabit any portion of the lands covered by this treaty, or interfere with, trouble, or molest any person passing or travelling through the said lands or any part thereof, and that they will assist the officers of His Majesty in bringing to justice and punishment any Indian, party to this treaty, who may hereafter offend against the stipulations hereof or infringe the laws in force in the lands covered hereby:

AND IT IS FURTHER UNDERSTOOD that this treaty is subject to an agreement dated the day of April, A.D. 1923, made between the Dominion of Canada and the Province of Ontario, a copy of which is hereto attached.

IN WITNESS WHEREOF, His Majesty's said Commissioners and the said chiefs and headmen have hereunto set their hands and seals at the places and times hereinafter set forth, in the year herein first above written.

SIGNED AND SEALED at Alderville on the nineteenth day of November, A.D. 1923, by His Majesty's Commissioners and the undersigned chiefs and headmen in the presence of the undersigned witnesses, after first having been interpreted and explained.

[signatures]

SIGNED AND SEALED at Mud Lake on the fifteenth day of November, A.D. 1923, by His Majesty's Commissioners and the undersigned chiefs and headmen in the presence of the undersigned witnesses, after first having been interpreted and explained.

[signatures]

SIGNED AND SEALED at Rice Lake on the sixteenth day of November, A.D. 1923, by His Majesty's

Commissioners and the undersigned chiefs and headmen in the presence of the undersigned witnesses, after first having been interpreted and explained.

[signatures]

SIGNED AND SEALED at Scugog Lake on the twenty-first day of November, A.D. 1923, by His Majesty's Commissioners and the undersigned chiefs and headmen in the presence of the undersigned witnesses, after first having been interpreted and explained.

[signatures]

MEMORANDUM OF AGREEMENT made this of April, 1923,

    BETWEEN:

The Government of the Dominion of Canada, acting herein by the Honourable Charles Stewart, Superintendent General of Indian Affairs, of the first part,

    AND

The Government of the Province of Ontario, acting herein by the Honourable Beniah Bowman, Minister of Lands and Forests for the said Province,

    of the other part

WHEREAS certain Indians of the Chippewa and Mississauga tribes claim that the said tribes were and are entitled to a certain interest in lands in the Province of Ontario to which the Indian title has never been extinguished by surrender or otherwise, the said lands being described as parts of the counties of Renfrew, Hastings, Haliburton, Muskoka, Parry Sound and Nipissing, and being bounded on the south and east by the lands included in the surrenders of the Indian title made on the 18th of November, 1815, the 5th of November, 1818, and November, 1822; on the north by the Ottawa and Mattawa Rivers and Lake Nipissing, and on the west by the lands included in the surrender of the Indian title made in 1850, known as the Robinson-Huron surrender, and by the Georgian Bay, the area in question including about 10,719 square miles.

AND WHEREAS a departmental enquiry made by the Department of Indian Affairs indicates that the said claim has such probable validity as to justify and require further investigation, and if found valid to be satisfied on such just and fair terms as may be settled by a treaty of surrender.

NOW THEREFORE THIS AGREEMENT made in pursuance of certian statutes of Canada and of the Province of Ontario, both intituled "an Act for the settlement of certain questions between the Governments of Canada and Ontario respecting Indian Lands," the Statute of Canada having been passed in the 54th and 55th years of the reign of Her Majesty Queen Victoria and chaptered 5, and the statute of Ontario in the 54th year of Her Majesty's said reign and chaptered 3.

WITNESSETH THAT the Governments of Canada and of the Province of Ontario have agreed as follows: —

1. The Government of Canada will, pursuant to Part I of the Enquiries Act, R.S.C., 1906, c. 104, and amendments, appoint three persons as commissioners to enquire into the validity of the claim of the Chippewa and Mississauga Indians aforesaid, and will empower the said commissioners, in the event of their determining in favour of the validity of the said claim, to negotiate a treaty with the said Indians for the surrender of the said lands upon payment of such compensation as may be fixed by such treaty.

2. Of the three commissioners so named, one shall be selected by the Government of Canada, who shall be Chairman of the Commission, and the remaining two shall be selected by the Minister of Lands and Forests for the Province of Ontario and notified to the Superintendent General of Indian Affairs.

3. The question of the validity of said claim may be determined by any two of the said Commissioners and it shall be necessary that at least two of them of whom the chairman shall be one shall concur in any treaty which may be negotiated.

4. The expenses of the said commission, including the remuneration and expenses of the commissioners and any expenses incurred for securing the attendance of witnesses or otherwise, shall be payable by the Government of Canada, but the rates of remuneration of each of the commissioners selected by the Minister of Lands and Forests for the Province of Ontario shall be agreed upon between him and the Superintendent General of Indian Affairs before the Constitution of the Commission.

5. In the event of the commissioners negotiating a treaty with the Indians the compensation to be paid to such Indians shall be payable to the Dominion of Canada by the Province of Ontario from time to time in accordance with the terms of the treaty of surrender, and shall be applied by the Dominion of Canada in accordance with the said terms.

6. In the event of provision being made by such treaty of surrender for the setting apart of reserves for the Indians, the Dominion of Canada will bear the expense to be incurred in the location and survey thereof, and the Province of Ontario will concur in the setting apart of such reserves.

7. All such reserves shall be administered by the Dominion of Canada for the benefit of the band or bands of Indians to which each may be allotted; portions thereof may, upon their surrender for the purpose by the said band or bands, be sold, leased or otherwise disposed of by letters patent under the Great Seal of Canada, and the proceeds of such sale, lease or other disposition applied for the benefit of such band or bands, provided, however, that in the event of the band or bands to which any such reserve has been allotted becoming extinct, or if for any other reason such reserve or such portion thereof as remains undis-

posed of is declared by the Superintendent General of Indian Affairs to be no longer required for the benefit of the said band or bands, the same shall thereafter be administered by and for the benefit of the Province of Ontario, and any balance of the proceeds of the sale or other disposition of any portion thereof then remaining under the control of the Dominion of Canada shall, so far as the same is not still required to be applied for the benefit of the said band or bands of Indians, be paid to the Province of Ontario, together with accrued unexpended simple interest thereon.

IN WITNESS WHEREOF these presents have been signed by the parties thereto.

Sources:

All United States treaty texts from *Indian Affairs: Laws and Treaties, Volume. II (Treaties),* compiled and edited by Charles J. Kappler. Washington, DC: Government Printing Office, 1904.

Text used with the permission of the Oklahoma State University Library Electronic Publishing Center. http://digital.library.okstate.edu/kappler /index.htm

All Canadian treaty texts from Indian and Northern Affairs Canada. http://www.ainc-inac .gc.ca

Resources

Alternate Tribal Names and Spellings

Tribal Name	Alternate Tribal Name(s)
Abenaki (western)	Alnonba, Abnaki
Absaroke	Crow
Adai	Nateo
Adamstown	Upper Mattaponi
Alabama	Alibamu
Aleut	Alutiiq, Unangan
Anadarko	Nadaco
Anishinabe	Chippewa, Ojibwa
Apache	N de, Tinneh, Dine, Tinde, Unde, Shis Inde, Aravaipa, Bedonkohe, Chihene, Chiricahua, Chokonen, Cibecue, Jicarilla, Kiowa, Lipan, Mescalero, Mimbres, Nednhi, Tonto, Yuma
Apache Mohave	Yavapai
Appomattoc	Apamatuks
Arapahoe	Inunaina, Atsina
Arikara	Northern Pawnee, Ricara, Ree
Assiniboine	Hohe
Athapaskan	Dene
Atsina	Haaninin
Aztec	Nahua, Nahuatl
Bannock	Panaiti
Bear River Indians	Niekeni
Bellabella	Heiltsuqu, Heiltsuk
Bellacoola	Nuxalk
Beothuk	Beathunk, Betoukuag, Macquajeet, Red Indians, Skraelling, Ulno
Blackfeet/Blackfoot	Niitsitapi, Nitsi-tapi, Piegan, Ahpikuni, Pikuni (northern); Siksika, Sisaka (southern), Sihasapa, Ahkainah
Blood	Kainai, Ahkainah
Boothroyd	Chomok
Brule Sioux	Si can gu
Caddo	Adai, Eyeish, Hasinai, Hainai, Kadohodacho, Kadohadacho Confederacy, Natchitoches
Cahuilla	Agua Caliente, Cabazon, Kawasic, Morongo, Los Coyotes, Painakic, Wanikik
Calusa	Caloosa, Calos, Calosa, Carlos, Muspa
Campo	Kumeyaay
Carrier	Dakelh, Wet'suwet'en
Catawba	Esaw, Iswa, Iyeye, Nieye, Ushery
Cayuga	Kweniogwen, Iroquois
Cayuse	Wailetpu, Te-taw-ken
Chakchiuma	Shaktci Homma
Chehalis	Copalis, Humptulips, Qwaya, Satsop, Sts'Ailes, Wynoochee
Chemainus	Tsa-mee-nis

Alternate Tribal Names and Spellings (cont.)

Tribal Name	Alternate Tribal Name(s)
Chemehuevi	Nuwu, Tantawats
Chetco	Tolowa
Cherokee	Tsa-la-gi, Ani-yun-wiya, Anikituhwagi, Keetowah
Cheyenne	Dzi tsi stas, Sowonia (southern), O mi sis (northern), Tse-tsehese-staestse
Chilcotin	Esdilagh, Tl'esqox, Tl'etinqox, Xeni Gwet'in
Chimakum	Aqokdlo
Chippewa	Anishinabe, Ojibwa
Chitimacha	Chawasha, Pantch-pinunkansh, Washa, Yagenechito
Choctaw	Chakchiuma, Chatot, Cha'ta
Chumash	Santa Barbara Indians
Clackamas	Guithlakimas
Clallam	S'klallam, Nusklaim, Tlalem
Cocopah	Xawitt Kunyavaei
Coeur d'Alene	Skitswish, Schee chu'umsch, Schitsu'umsh
Comanche	Detsanayuka, Kotsoteka, Nermernuh, Noconi, Nokoni, Numunuu, Padouca (Sioux word), Penateka, Pennande, Quahadi, Yamparika
Comox	Catloltx
Copane	Kopano, Quevenes
Cora	Nayarit
Coree	Coranine
Coushatta	Koasati, Acoste
Cree	Kenistenoag, Iyiniwok, Nehiawak or Nay-hee-uh-wuk (Plains Cree), Sah-cow-ee-noo-wuk (bush Cree)
Creek	Muscogee, Abihika, Abeika, Hitchiti, Homashko
Crow	Absaroke, Apsaalooke
Cupenos	Kuupangaxwichem
Cuthead	Pabaksa
Dakelh	Carrier
Delaware	Lenni Lenape, Lenape, Abnaki, Alnanbai, Wampanoag, Munsee, Unami, Unalachitgo, Powhatan-Renápe
Dieguenos	Comeya, Tipai, Ipai, Kumeyaay
Ditidaht	Nitinaht
Eskimo	Inuit, Inupiat, Inuvialuit, Yupik, Alutiiq
Equimalt	Is-Whoy-Malth
Fox	Mesquaki, Meskwaki, Mshkwa'kiitha
Gabrieleno	Tongva
Ganawese	Conoys, Piscataways
Gitanyow	Kitwancool
Gitxsan	Tsimshian
Goshute	Kusiutta
Gros Ventre	Atsina (prairie), Hidatsa (Missouri), A'ani', Ah-ah-nee-nin, Minnetaree
Gwich'in	Loucheux
Hainai	Ioni
Havasupai	Suppai
Heiltsuk	Hailhazakv
Hidatsa	Gros Venture
Hohokam	Hoo-hoogam
Hopi	Hopitu, Hopitu Shinumu, Moqui, Hapeka
Hualapai	Hwal'bay, Walapai
Huichol	Wirrarika, Wixalika

Alternate Tribal Names and Spellings (cont.)

Tribal Name	Alternate Tribal Name(s)
Hupa	Natinnohhoi
Huron	Wendat, Wyandot
Ingalik Athapaskans	Deg Het'an
Iowa	Pahodja
Iroquois	Haudenosaunee, Hodenosaunee, Ongwanosionni, Hotinonshonni
Jemez	Tuwa
Jicarilla Apache	Tinde
Kalispel	Pend d'Oreilles
Kamia	Tipai
Kansa	Hutanga, Kansas, Kanza, Kaw,
Kato	Tlokeang
Keres	Pueblo, Acoma, Cochiti, Isleta, Laguna, San Felipe, Santa Ana, Santo Domingo, Zia
Kickapoo	Kiwigapawa
Kiowa	Kwuda, Tepda, Tepkinago, Gaigwu, Kompabianta, Kauigu
Kiowa Apache	Nadiisha Dena
Klamath	Eukshikni Maklaks, Auksni
Klickitat	Qwulhhwaipum
Kootenai	Kuronoqa, Kutenai, Kootenay, Yaqan nukiy, Akun'kunik', Ktunaxa
Koso	Panamint
Karok	Karuk, Arra-arra
Ktunaxa	Kootenay
Kumeyaay	Diegueño, Barona, Sycuan, Viejas, Campo, Cuyapaipe, Ewiiaapaayp
Kutchin	Gwich'in
Kutenai	Asanka
Lancandon	Maya, Hach Winik
Lemhi Shoshone	Agaidika, Salmon Eaters, Tukudika, Sheep Eater
Loucheux	Gwich'in
Lillooet	Lil'wat, St'át'imc, T'it'kit
Lipan	Naizhan
Lower Sioux	Mdewakanton, Wahpekute
Luiseño	Ataxum, La Jolla, Pechanga, Soboba, Quechnajuichom
Lumbee	Cheraw
Maicopa	Xalychidom Piipaash, Pipatsji
Makah	Kwenetchechat, Kwi-dai-da'ch
Mandan	Metutahanke or Mawatani (after 1837), Numakaki (before 1837)
Manhattan	Rechgawawank
Manso	Maise, Mansa, Manse, Manxo, Gorreta, Gorrite, Tanpachoa
Maricopa	Xalychidom Piipaash, Xalchidom Pii-pash, Pipatsje, Pee-posh
Miami	Twightwis, Twa-h-twa-h, Oumameg, Pkiiwileni
Micmac	Mi'kmaq
Miniconjou	Mnikawozu, Mnikowoju, Minnicoujou
Mi'kmaq	Lnu'k, L'nu'k
Missouri	Niutachi
Mixtec	Ñusabi, Nusabi
Moapa	Moapariats
Modoc	Moatokni, Okkowish
Mohave	Mojave, Tzinamaa, Ahamakav, Hamakhava
Mohawk	Kanienkahaka, Kaniengehage, Abenaki, Iroquois, Akwesasne
Mohican	Muh-he-con-neok, Mahikan, Mahican
Molala	Latiwe

Alternate Tribal Names and Spellings (cont.)

Tribal Name	Alternate Tribal Name(s)
Mono	Monache
Moratoc	Nottoway
Mosopelea	Ofom
Munsee	Minasinink, Homenethiki
Muscogee	Creek, Homashko
Nanticoke	Unalachtgo, Onehtikoki
Navajo	Diné, Dineh, Tenuai, Navaho
Nez Perce	Nee-me-poo, Nimipu, Kamuinu, Tsutpeli, Sahaptin, Chopunnish
Nisga'a	Tsimshian
Nootka	Nuu-chah-nulth
Northern Ojibwa	Saulteaux, Sauteux
Nuu-chah-nulth	Nootka
Nuxalk	Kimsquit, Kwalhnmc, South Bentick Sutslmc, Taliyumc
Ogallala	Okandanda
Ojibwa	Chippewa, Anishinabe, Missisauga, Odjbway, Saginaw
Okanagon	Isonkuaili
Omaha	UmonHon
Oneida	Iroquois
Onondaga	Iroquois
Oohenupa	Two Kettle, Oohenonpa
Osage	Wa-Shah-She, Wakon, Wazhazhe
Ottawa	Adawe, Otawaki
Otto	Chewaerae
Oulaouaes	Necariages
Oweekeno	Kwakiutl, Oweehena
Pacheenaht	Nootka
Paiute	Numa, Nuwuvi, Kuyuiticutta
Papagos	Tohono O'odham, Ak-chin, Yohono Au'autam
Parianuc	White River Utes
Passamaquoddy	Peskedemakddi
Patchogue	Unkechaug
Pawnee	Pariki, Panyi, Chahiksichahiks, Ckirihki Kuruuriki
Pechanga	Luiseño
Pecos	Pueblos from Jemez
Pend d'Oreilles	Kalispel
Penobscot	Pannawanbskek, Penaubsket
Petun	Khionontateronon, Tionontati
Piegan	Blood, Kainai, Pikuni, Pigunni, Ahpikuni
Pima	Onk Akimel Au-authm, Akimel O'odham, A-atam, Akimul Au'autam, Tohono O'odham (incorrectly)
Piro	Tortuga
Pit River	Achomawi, Atsugewi
Poosepatuck	Unkechaug
Popolucas	Chochos
Pyramid Lake Paiute	Kuyuidokado
Quapaw	Quapah, Akansea, Ouaguapas, Ugakhpa
Quechan	Yuma
Quileute	Quil-leh-ute
Quinault	Qui-nai-elts
Sac and Fox	Sauk, Asakiwaki, Meshkwakihug, Fox
Sahwnee	Shawadasay

Alternate Tribal Names and Spellings (cont.)

Tribal Name	Alternate Tribal Name(s)
Salish	Okinagan, Slathead
Saanich	Pauquachin, Tsawout, Tsartlip, Tseycum, Malahat
Sans Arc	Itazipco
Santee	Sisseton
Saponi	Monasukapanough
Sauk	Hothaaki, Sac, Sack, Sock, Thakiki
Scioto	(Five Nations of the Scioto Plains) Shawnee, Wyandot, Delaware, Munsee, Seneca
Seminole	Ikaniuksalgi, Alachua, Mikasuki
Seneca	Iroquois
Serrano	Cowangachem, Mohineyam, Qawishwallanavetum, Yuhavitam
Shawnee	Savannah, Chillicothe, Hathawekela, Mequachake, Piqua
Shoshone	Shoshoni, Snake, Nimi, Tukudeka, Agaidika
Sioux	Brule, Dakota, Hunkpapa, Isanyati, Itazipco, Lakota, Mnikawozu, Mnikowoju, Nakota, Ocheti Shakowin, Oglala, Oohenunpa, Sicangu, Sihasapa, Sisseton, Sisitonwan, Teton, Titunwan
Sissipahaw	Haw
Skagit	Humaluh
Skoskomish	Twana
Squinamish	Swinomish
Slotas	Red River Metis
Songish	Lkungen
Southern Paiute	Numa
St. Francis	Abenaki
St. Mary's Indian Band	A'qam, Ktunaxa
St. Regis Mohawk	Akwesasne, Kaniengehage
Stockbridge	Mahican
Snuneymuxw	Nanaimo
Susquehanna	Susquehannock, Conestoga, Minqua, Andaste
Taidnapam	Upper Cowlitz
Tarahumara	Raramuri
Taviwac	Uncompahgre Ute
Tejas	Hasinai, Cenis
Tenino	Melilema
Tequistlatecos	Chontales of Oaxaca
Teton	Brule, Hunkpapa, Itazipco, Mnikowoju, Oglala, Oohenunpa, Sicangu, Sihasapa, Titunwan
Tewa	Pueblo, Nambe, Pojoaque, San Ildefonso, San Juan, Santa Clara, Tesuque
Thompson	Nlaka'pamux
Tigua	Pueblo, Tiwa, Tortuga
Tillamook	Killamuck
Timucua	Utina, Acuera
T'it'kit	Lillooet
Tiwa	Pueblo, Tortuga
Tlaoquiaht	Clayoquot
Tlatlasikwala	Nuwitti
Tobacco	Khionontateronon, Tionontati
Toltec	Chiaimeca Mochanecatoca
Tonkawa	Titskan Watitch, Titskanwatitch, Tonkaweya
Tubatulabal	Bahkanapul, Kern River

Alternate Tribal Names and Spellings (cont.)

Tribal Name	Alternate Tribal Name(s)
Tunica	Yoron
Tuscarora	Skarure, Iroquois, Coree
Tututni	Tolowa
Twana	Tuadhu
Two Kettle	Oohenonpa, Oohenupa
Umpqua	Etnemitane
Uncompahgre Ute	Taviwac
Upper Chehalis	Kwaiailk
Upper Sioux	Sisseton, Wahpeton
Ute	Noochi, Notch, Nuciu, Yamparka, Parianuc, Taviwac, Wiminuc, Kapota, Muwac, Cumumba, Tumpanuwac, Uinta-ats, Pahvant, San Pitch, and Sheberetch
Viejas	Quimi
Wampanoag	Pokanoket
Wappo	Ashochimi
Warm Springs	Tilkuni
Wasco	Galasquo
Watlala	Katlagakya
Wea	Eel River, Gros, Kilataks, Mangakekis, Pepicokia, Peticotias, Piankeshaw, Wawiyatanwa
Whilkut	Redwood Indians
Winnebago	Winipig
Wichita	Kitikiti'sh, Wia Chitch (Choctaw word)
Winik	Maya
Wishram	Ilaxluit, Tlakluit
Wyandot	Huron, Talamatans
Yakama	Waptailmin, Pakiutlema, Yakima
Yaqui	Yoeme, Surem, Hiakim
Yazoo	Chakchiuma
Yoncalla	Tchayankeld
Yuchi	Chisa
Yuma	Quechan, Euqchan
Zapotec	Binigulaza
Zuni	Ashiwi, Taa Ashiwani

Source: Phil Konstantin

Tribal Name Meanings

Tribal Name	Meaning
A'ani'	white clay people
Abnaki	those living at the sunrise (easterners)
Achomawi	river, people that live at the river
Acolapissa	those who listen and see
Agaidika	salmon eaters
Ahousaht	facing opposite from the ocean, people living with their backs to the land and mountains
Ahtena	ice people
Aitchelitz	bottom
Akun'kunik'	people of the place of the flying head
Akwesasne	land where the partridge drums
Alabama	I clear the thicket
Apache	enemy (Zuni word)
Apalachicola	people of the other side
Apalachee	people of the other side
A'qam	people of the dense forest or brush
Arikara	horns or elk people, or corn eaters
Assiniboine	ones who cook using stones (Ojibwa word)
Atakapa	man eater
Atsina	white clay people
Atsugewi	hat creek indians
Avoyel	people of the rocks
Bayogoula	people of the bayou
Bedonkohe (Apache)	in front at the end people
Bidai	brushwood (Caddo word)
Binigulaza	people of the clouds
Brule	burned thighs
Caddo	true chiefs
Cahuilla	leader, master, powerful nation (all questionable)
Calusa	fierce people
Canim	canoe, broken rock
Catawba	river people
Cayuga	place where boats were taken out, place locusts were taken out, people at the mucky land
Cayuse	people of the stones or rocks (French-Canadian word)
Chakchiuma	red crawfish people
Cheam	wild strawberry place, the place to always get strawberries
Chehalis	sand, beating heart
Chemehuevi	those that play with fish (Mojave word)
Cherokee	cave people (Choctaw word), people of different speech (Creek word)
Cheslatta	top of a small mountain, small rock mountain at the east side
Chetco	close to the mouth of the stream
Cheyenne	red talkers (Dakota word), little Cree (Lakota word)
Chickahominy	hominy people
Chihene (Apache)	red paint people
Chilcotin	young man river
Chipewyan	pointed skins (Cree word)
Chitimacha	men altogether red, they have cooking vessels
Chokonen (Apache)	rising sun people
Chontal	stranger (Nahuatl word)
Choula	fox

Tribal Name Meanings (cont.)

Tribal Name	Meaning
Chowanoc	people at the south
Chumash	people who make the shell bead money
Clallam	strong people
Clatsop	dried salmon
Clayoquot	people of other tribes
Cocopah	river people
Coeur d'Alene	those who are found here or heart of an awl (French words)
Comanche	anyone who wants to fight me all the time (Ute word)
Comox	place of abundance
Cowichan	warm country, land warmed by the sun
Crow	crow, sparrowhawk, bird people, people of the large-beaked bird
Dakelh	people who travel by water
Dakota	allie
Ehdiitat Gwich'in	people who live among timber or spruce
Erie	long tail or cat people (Iroquois word)
Eskimo	eaters of raw meat (Algonquin or Cree word)
Esquimalt	the place of gradually shoaling water
Fox	red earth people
Gingolx	the place of the skulls
Gitanmaax	people who fish with burning torches
Gitwangak	place of rabbits
Gwich'in	people who live at a certain place
Gros Ventre	big bellies, one who cooks with a stone, he cooks by roasting (see Atsina)
Hach winik	true people
Hagwilget	gentle or quiet people
Han	those who live along the river
Haudenosaunee	people of the long house, people of the extended lodge
Havasupai	people of the blue green water
Heiltsuk	to speak or act correctly
Hesquiaht	people of the sound made by eating herring eggs off eel grass
Hidatsa	willow (speculation)
Hiute	bowmen
Hohokam	those who have gone
Honniasont	wearing something around the neck
Hopi	peaceful ones, people who live in a peaceful way
Houma	red
Hualapai	people of the tall pines
Huchnom	mountain people
Huichol	healers
Hul'qumi'num	those who speak the same language
Hunkpapa	campers at the opening of the circle
Hupa	trinity river
Huron	ruffian (French word)
Hwal'bay (Hualapai)	people of the tall pines
Ihanktonwan	dwellers at the end
Ihanktonwana	little dwellers at the end
Iowa	sleepy ones (Dakota word)
Iroquois	real adders (Algonquian word) or we of the extended lodge
Jatibonicu	people of the great sacred high waters
Jatibonuco	great people of the sacred high waters

Tribal Name Meanings (cont.)

Tribal Name	Meaning
Jicaque	ancient person (Nahuatl word)
Jicarilla	little basket weaver (Spanish word)
Kainai	many chiefs
Kamloops	the meeting of the waters
Kan-hatki	white earth
Kanienkahaka	people of the place of flint
Kanza	people of the south wind
Karok	upstream
Kaskaskia	he scrapes it off by means of a tool
Kato	lake
Kawchottine	people of the great hares
Ketsei	going in wet sand
Kickapoo	he stands about
Kiowa	principal people, pulling out, coming out, people of the large tent flaps
Kispiox	people of the hiding place
Kitamaat	people of the falling snow
Kitkatla	people of the salt, village by the sea
Kitselas	people of the canyon
Kitsumkalum	people of the plateau
Klallam	strong people
Klamath	people of the lake
Klickitat	beyond (Chinook word)
Kluskus	place of small whitefish
Kotsoteka	buffalo eaters
Kutcha-kutchin	those who live on the flats
Kuupangaxwichem	people who slept here
Kuyuidokado	cui-ui eaters
Kwalhioqua	lonely place in the woods (Chinook word)
Kwayhquitlum	stinking fish slime
Kwuda	people coming out
Lakota	friend or ally (same with Dakota and Nakota)
Latgawa	those living in the uplands
Lenni Lenape	genuine men
Lheidli T'enneh	people of the confluence of the two rivers
Lillooet	wild onion
Loucheux	people with slanted or crossed eyes
Machapunga	bad dust
Mahican	wolf (incorrect translation per the Mohican Nation, Stockbridge-Munsee Band)
Makah	cape people
Malahat	infested with caterpillars, place where one gets bait
Maliseet	broken talkers
Maricopa	people who live toward the water
Massachuset	at the hills
Matsqui	easy portage, easy travelling
Mdewankantonwan	dwellers of the spirit lake
Menominee	wild rice men
Metlakatla	a passage connecting two bodies of salt water
Miami	people on the peninsula, cry of the crane
Michigamea	great water
Mimbres (Apache)	willow (Spanish word)

Tribal Name Meanings (cont.)

Tribal Name	Meaning
Miniconjou	planters by water
Minnetaree	they crossed the water
Minqua	stealthy
Missouri	great muddy, people with wooden canoes
Moapa	mosquito creek people
Moatokni	southerners
Modoc	southerners
Mohave	three mountains, people of the water/river
Mohawk	the possessors of the flint, coward or man eater (Abenaki words)
Mohegan	wolf
Mohican	the people of the waters that are never still
Moneton	big water people
Munsee	at the place where the stones are gathered together
Musqueam	place always to get iris plant root
Nahane	people of the west
Nak'azdli	when arrows were flying
Narragansett	people of the small point
Nanticoke	people of the tidewaters
Nanoose	to push forward
Natsit-kutchin	those who live off the flats
Navajo	cultivated field in an arroyo (Tewa word)
Nehalem	where the people live
Nicomen	level part
Nihtat Gwich'in	people living together as a mixture
Nipmuck	freshwater fishing place
Nokoni	those who turn back
Nooksack	mountain men
Nootka	along the coast
Nusabi	people of the clouds
Oglala	scatters their own
Ojibwa	to roast till puckered up
Okanagan	head, top of head
Okelousa	blackwater
Okmulgee	where water boils up
Omaha	upstream people or people going against the current
Oneida	a boulder standing up, people of the standing stone
Onondaga	people on top of the hills
Opata	hostile people (Pima word)
Ottawa	to trade
Otto	lechers
Oweekeno	those who carry on the back, people talking right
Pahodja	dusty nones
Pakiutlema	people of the gap
Pamunkey	rising upland
Pantch-pinunkansh	men altogether red
Papagos	desert people, bean people
Pascagoula	bread people
Passamaquoddy	plenty of pollock
Paugusset	where the narrows open out
Pawnee	horn people, men of men, look like wolves
Pechanga	place where the water drips

Tribal Name Meanings (cont.)

Tribal Name	Meaning
Penateka	honey eaters
Penelakut	something buried
Pennacook	down hill
Penobscot	it forks on the white rocks or the descending ledge place, at the stone place
Pensacola	hair people
Penticton	permanent place, always place
People of the lakes	tribes near the great lakes
Peoria	carrying a pack on his back
Pequot	fox people or destroyers
Piegan	scabby robes
Piikani	poor robe
Pilthlako	big swamp
Pima	river people
Pojoaque	drinking place
Potawatomi	people of the place of the fire, keepers of the fire (fire nation, fire people)
Powhatan	falls in a current of water
Pshwanwapam	stony ground
Puyallup	shadow
Qawishwallanavetum	people that live among the rocks
Quahadi	antelope
Qualicum	where the dog salmon run
Quapaw	downstream people
Quatsino	downstream people
Qwulhhwaipum	prairie people
Raramuri	foot runner
Sac (Sauk)	people of the yellow earth or people of the outlet
Salish	flatheads
Sans Arc	without bows
Schaghticoke	at the river forks
Schitsu'umsh	the ones that were found here
Sekani	dwellers on the rocks
Semiahmoo	half moon
Seminole	separatist or breakaway, peninsula people
Seneca	place of stone, people of the standing rock, great hill people
Shawnee	south or southerners
Sicangu	burned thighs
Sihasapa Sioux	blackfeet
Siksika	blackfeet
Sioux	snake (French version of other tribe's name)
Sisitonwan	dwellers of the fish ground
Siska	uncle, lots of cracks in the rocks
Skidegate	red paint stone
Skokomish	river people
Skookumchuck	strong water
Snuneymuxw	people of many names
Spallumcheen	flat along edge
Spokane	sun people or children of the sun (generally accepted)
Spuzzum	little flat
Sts'Ailes	the beating heart

Tribal Name Meanings (cont.)

Tribal Name	Meaning
Sumas	big flat opening
Tahltan	something heavy in the water
Taino	we the good people
Takelma	those living along the river
Tamarois	out tail
Tanima	liver eaters
Tangipahoa	corn gatherers
Tantawats	southern men
Tarahumara	foot runner
Tatsanottine	people of the copper water
Tawakoni	river bend among red hills
Teetl'it Gwich'in	people who live at the head of the waters
Tejas	friendly
Tenawa	down stream
Tennuth-ketchin	middle people
Teton	dwellers of the prairie
Tewa	moccasins
Thlingchadinne	dog-flank people
Titonwan	dwellers of the plains
Tl'azt'en	people by the edge of the bay
Toltec	master builders (Nahuatl word)
Tonawanda	confluent stream
Tonkawa	they all stay together or most human of people
Toquaht	people of the narrow place in front, people of the narrow channel
Tsa-mee-nis	bitten breast
Tsattine	lives among the beavers
Tsawout	houses raised up
Tsawwassen	beach at the mouth, facing the sea
Tsay Keh Dene	people of the mountains
Tsetsaut	people of the interior (Niska word)
Tseycum	clay people
Tsleil-Waututh	people of the inlet
Tubatulabal	pinenut eaters (Shoshone word)
Tukudika	sheep eater
Tuscarora	hemp gatherers, the shirt wearing people
Two Kettle	two boilings
Uchuckledaht	there inside the bay
Ulkatcho	good feeding place where animals get fat
Unalachtgo	tidewater people
Viniintaii Gwich'in	people who live on or by the caribou trail
Vuntut Gwitch'in	dwellers among the lakes
Vvunta-ketchin	those who live among the lakes
Wahpekute	shooters among the leaves
Wahpetonwan	dwellers amoung the leaves
Wailaki	north language (Wintun word)
Wakokai	blue heron breeding place
Walapai	pine tree people
Wallawalla	little river
Wampanoag	eastern people
Wappo	brave
Waptailmin	people of the narrow river

Tribal Name Meanings (cont.)

Tribal Name	Meaning
Wasco	cup, those who have the cup
Wea	the forest people, light-skinned ones, people who live near the river eddy
Whel mux	people of spirit, people of breath
Wichita	big arbor (Choctaw word)
Winnebago	filthy water people
Wiwohka	roaring water
Wyandot	people of the peninsula, islanders
Yakama	runaway
Yamparika	rooteaters or yapeaters
Yaqan nukiy	the people where the rock is standing
Yavapai	people of the sun, crooked mouth people
Yoncalla	those living at ayankeld
Yuchi	situated yonder
Yuhavitam	people of the pines
Yuki	stranger (Wintun word)
Yurok	downstream (Karok word)

Source: Phil Konstantin

Treaties by Tribe

Tribe	Treaty Name
Aionai	Treaty with the Comanche, Aionai, Anadarko, Caddo, Etc., 1846
Anadarko	Treaty with the Comanche, Aionai, Anadarko, Caddo, Etc., 1846
Apache	Treaty with the Apache, 1852 Treaty with the Apache, Cheyenne, and Arapaho, 1865 Treaty with the Cheyenne and Arapaho, 1865 Treaty with the Comanche, Kiowa, and Apache, 1853 Treaty with the Kiowa, Comanche, and Apache, 1867
Appalachicola	Treaty with the Appalachicola Band, 1832 Treaty with the Appalachicola Band, 1833
Arapaho	Treaty with the Apache, Cheyenne, and Arapaho, 1865 Treaty with the Arapaho and Cheyenne, 1861 Treaty with the Cheyenne and Arapaho, 1865 Treaty with the Cheyenne and Arapaho, 1867 Treaty with the Northern Cheyenne and Northern Arapaho, 1868 Treaty of Fort Laramie with Sioux, Etc., 1851 Treaty with the Sioux—Brulé, Oglala, Miniconjou, Yanktonai, Hunkpapa, Blackfeet, Cuthead, Two Kettle, Sans Arcs, and Santee—and Arapaho
Arikara	Treaty with the Arikara Tribe, 1825 Agreement at Fort Berthold, 1866 Treaty of Fort Laramie with Sioux, Etc., 1851
Assinaboine	Treaty of Fort Laramie with Sioux, Etc., 1851
Bannock	Treaty with the Eastern Band Shoshoni and Bannock, 1868
Belantse-Etoa or Minitaree	Treaty with the Belantse-Etoa or Minitaree Tribe, 1825
Blackfeet	Treaty with the Blackfeet, 1855 Treaty with the Blackfeet Sioux, 1865
Blood	Treaty with the Blackfeet, 1855
Brothertown	Treaty with the New York Indians, 1838
Caddo	Treaty with the Caddo, 1835 Treaty with the Comanche, Aionai, Anadarko, Caddo, Etc., 1846
Cahokia	Treaty with the Peoria, Etc., 1818

Treaties by Tribe (cont.)

Tribe	Treaty Name
Cayuga	Agreement with the Five Nations of Indians, 1792
	Treaty with the Six Nations, 1784
	Treaty with the New York Indians, 1838
	Treaty with the Six Nations, 1789
	Treaty with the Six Nations, 1794
Cayuse	Treaty with the Walla-Walla, Cayuse, Etc., 1855
Chasta	Treaty with the Chasta, Etc., 1854
Cherokee	Treaty with the Cherokee, 1785
	Treaty with the Cherokee, 1791
	Treaty with the Cherokee, 1794
	Treaty with the Cherokee, 1798
	Treaty with the Cherokee, 1804
	Treaty with the Cherokee, 1805
	Treaty with the Cherokee, 1805
	Treaty with the Cherokee, 1806
	Treaty with the Cherokee, 1816
	Treaty with the Cherokee, 1816
	Treaty with the Cherokee, 1816
	Treaty with the Cherokee, 1817
	Treaty with the Cherokee, 1819
	Treaty with the Western Cherokee, 1828
	Treaty with the Western Cherokee, 1833
	Treaty with the Cherokee, 1835
	Treaty with the Cherokee, 1846 [Western Cherokee]
	Treaty with the Cherokee, 1866
	Treaty with the Cherokee, 1868
	Agreement with the Cherokee, 1835 (Unratified)
	Agreement with the Cherokee and Other Tribes in the Indian Territory, 1865
	Treaty with the Comanche, Etc., 1835
Cheyenne	Treaty with the Apache, Cheyenne, and Arapaho, 1865
	Treaty with the Arapaho and Cheyenne, 1861
	Treaty with the Cheyenne Tribe, 1825
	Treaty with the Cheyenne and Arapaho, 1865
	Treaty with the Cheyenne and Arapaho, 1867
	Treaty with the Northern Cheyenne and Northern Arapaho, 1868
	Treaty of Fort Laramie with Sioux, Etc., 1851
Chickasaw	Agreement with the Cherokee and Other Tribes in the Indian Territory, 1865
	Treaty with the Chickasaw, 1786
	Treaty with the Chickasaw, 1801
	Treaty with the Chickasaw, 1805
	Treaty with the Chickasaw, 1816
	Treaty with the Chickasaw, 1818

Treaties by Tribe (cont.)

Tribe	Treaty Name
Chickasaw (cont.)	Treaty with the Chickasaw, 1832
	Treaty with the Chickasaw, 1832
	Treaty with the Chickasaw, 1834
	Treaty with the Chickasaw, 1830
	Treaty with the Choctaw and Chickasaw, 1837
	Treaty with the Chickasaw, 1852
	Treaty with the Choctaw and Chickasaw, 1854
	Treaty with the Choctaw and Chickasaw, 1855
	Treaty with the Choctaw and Chickasaw, 1866
Chippewa	Treaty with the Chippewa, Etc., 1808
	Treaty with the Chippewa, 1819
	Treaty with the Chippewa, 1820
	Treaty with the Ottawa and Chippewa, 1820
	Treaty with the Chippewa, 1826
	Treaty with the Chippewa, Etc., 1827
	Treaty with the Chippewa, Etc., 1829
	Treaty with the Chippewa, Etc., 1833
	Treaty with the Chippewa, 1836
	Treaty with the Chippewa, 1837
	Treaty with the Chippewa, 1837
	Treaty with the Chippewa, 1837
	Treaty with the Chippewa, 1838
	Treaty with the Chippewa, 1839
	Treaty with the Chippewa, 1842
	Treaty with the Chippewa of the Mississippi and Lake Superior, 1847
	Treaty with the Chippewa, 1854
	Treaty with the Chippewa, 1855
	Treaty with the Chippewa of Saginaw, Etc., 1855
	Treaty with the Chippewa, Etc., 1859
	Treaty with the Chippewa of the Mississippi and the Pillager and Lake Winnibigoshish Bands, 1863
	Treaty with the Chippewa—Red Lake and Pembina Bands, 1863
	Treaty with the Chippewa—Red Lake and Pembina Bands, 1864
	Treaty with the Chippewa, Mississippi, and Pillager and Lake Winnibigoshish Bands, 1864
	Treaty with the Chippewa of Saginaw, Swan Creek, and Black River, 1864
	Treaty with the Chippewa—Bois Forte Band, 1866
	Treaty with the Chippewa of the Mississippi, 1867
	Treaty with the Ottawa, Etc., 1807
	Treaty with the Ottawa, Etc., 1816
	Treaty with the Ottawa, Etc., 1821
	Treaty with the Ottawa, Etc., 1836
	Treaty with the Ottawa and Chippewa, 1855
	Treaty with the Pillager Band of Chippewa Indians, 1847
	Treaty with the Potawatomi Nation, 1846
	Treaty with the Chippewa of Sault Ste. Marie, 1855
	Treaty with the Sioux, Etc., 1825
	Treaty with the Winnebago, Etc., 1828

Treaties by Tribe (cont.)

Tribe	Treaty Name
Chippewa (cont.)	Treaty with the Wyandot, Etc., 1785
	Treaty with the Wyandot, Etc., 1789
	Treaty with the Wyandot, Etc., 1795
	Treaty with the Wyandot, Etc., 1805
	Treaty with the Wyandot, Etc., 1815
	Treaty with the Wyandot, Etc., 1817
	Treaty with the Wyandot, Etc., 1818
Choctaw	Agreement with the Cherokee and Other Tribes in the Indian Territory, 1865
	Treaty with the Choctaw and Chickasaw, 1837
	Treaty with the Choctaw, 1786
	Treaty with the Choctaw, 1801
	Treaty with the Choctaw, 1802
	Treaty with the Choctaw, 1803
	Treaty with the Choctaw, 1805
	Treaty with the Choctaw, 1816
	Treaty with the Choctaw, 1820
	Treaty with the Choctaw, 1825
	Treaty with the Choctaw, 1830
	Treaty with the Choctaw and Chickasaw, 1854
	Treaty with the Choctaw and Chickasaw, 1855
	Treaty with the Choctaw and Chickasaw, 1866
	Treaty with the Comanche, Etc., 1835
	Treaty with the Comanche and Kiowa, 1865
Clack-A-Mas	Treaty with the Kalapuya, Etc., 1855
Columbia	Agreement with the Columbia and Colville, 1883
Colville	Agreement with the Columbia and Colville, 1883
Comanche	Treaty with the Comanche, Etc., 1835
	Treaty with the Comanche, Aionai, Anadarko, Caddo, Etc., 1846
	Treaty with the Comanche, Kiowa, and Apache, 1853
	Treaty with the Kiowa and Comanche, 1867
	Treaty with the Kiowa, Comanche, and Apache, 1867
Creeks	Agreement with the Cherokee and Other Tribes in the Indian Territory, 1865
	Treaty with the Comanche, Etc., 1835
	Treaty with the Creeks, 1790
	Treaty with the Creeks, 1796
	Treaty with the Creeks, 1802
	Treaty with the Creeks, 1805
	Treaty with the Creeks, 1814
	Treaty with the Creeks, 1818
	Treaty with the Creeks, 1821
	Treaty with the Creeks, 1821
	Treaty with the Creeks, 1825
	Treaty with the Creeks, 1826

Treaties by Tribe (cont.)

Tribe	Treaty Name
Creeks (cont.)	Treaty with the Creeks, 1827
	Treaty with the Creeks, 1832
	Treaty with the Creeks, 1833
	Treaty with the Creeks, 1838
	Treaty with the Creeks and Seminole, 1845
	Treaty with the Creeks, 1854
	Treaty with the Creeks, Etc., 1856
	Treaty with the Creeks, 1866
	Agreement with the Creeks, 1825 (Unratified)
Crow	Treaty with the Crow Tribe, 1825
	Treaty with the Crows, 1868
	Agreement with the Crows, 1880 (Unratified)
	Treaty of Fort Laramie with Sioux, Etc., 1851
Dakota	Treaty with the Blackfeet Sioux, 1865
	Treaty of Fort Laramie with Sioux, Etc., 1851
De Chutes	Treaty with the Middle Oregon Tribes, 1865
	Treaty with the Tribes of Middle Oregon, 1855
Delaware	Treaty with the Delawares, 1778
	Treaty with the Delawares, Etc., 1803
	Treaty with the Delawares, 1804
	Treaty with the Delawares, Etc., 1805
	Treaty with the Delawares, Etc., 1809
	Treaty with the Delawares, 1818
	Treaty with the Delawares, 1829
	Treaty with the Delawares, 1829
	Treaty with the Delawares, 1854
	Treaty with the Delawares, 1860
	Treaty with the Delawares, 1861
	Treaty with the Delawares, 1866
	Agreement with the Delawares and Wyandot, 1843
	Supplementary Treaty with the Miami, Etc., 1809
	Treaty with the Shawnee, Etc., 1832
	Treaty with the Wyandot, Etc., 1785
	Treaty with the Wyandot, Etc., 1789
	Treaty with the Wyandot, Etc., 1795
	Treaty with the Wyandot, Etc., 1805
	Treaty with the Wyandot, Etc., 1814
	Treaty with the Wyandot, Etc., 1815
	Treaty with the Wyandot, Etc., 1817
	Treaty with the Wyandot, Etc., 1818
Dwamish	Treaty with the Dwamish, Suquamish, Etc., 1855
Eel River	Treaty with the Delawares, Etc., 1803
	Treaty with the Delawares, Etc., 1805
	Treaty with the Delawares, Etc., 1809
	Treaty with the Eel River, Etc., 1803

Treaties by Tribe (cont.)

Tribe	Treaty Name
Eel River (cont.)	Supplementary Treaty with the Miami, Etc., 1809
	Treaty with the Miami, 1828
	Treaty with the Wyandot, Etc., 1795
Five Nations	Agreement with the Five Nations of Indians, 1792
Flathead	Treaty with the Blackfeet, 1855
	Treaty with the Flatheads, Etc., 1855
Fox	Treaty with the Foxes, 1815
Gros Ventres	Treaty with the Blackfeet, 1855
	Agreement at Fort Berthold, 1866
	Treaty of Fort Laramie with Sioux, Etc., 1851
Illinois	Treaty with the Kaskaskia, Etc., 1832
	Treaty with the Peoria, Etc., 1818
Iowa	Treaty with the Iowa, 1815
	Treaty with the Iowa, 1824.
	Treaty with the Iowa, Etc., 1836.
	Treaty with the Iowa, 1837
	Treaty with the Iowa, 1838
	Treaty with the Iowa, 1854
	Treaty with the Sauk and Fox, Etc., 1830
	Treaty with the Sauk and Fox, Etc., 1861
	Treaty with the Sioux, Etc., 1825
Kalapuya	Treaty with the Kalapuya, Etc., 1855
	Treaty with the Umpqua and Kalapuya, 1854
Kansa	Treaty with the Kansa, 1815
	Treaty with the Kansa, 1825
	Treaty with the Kansa, 1825
	Treaty with Kansa Tribe, 1846
	Treaty with the Kansa Tribe, 1859
	Treaty with the Kansa Indians, 1862
Kaskaskia	Treaty with the Delawares, Etc., 1803
	Treaty with the Eel River, Etc., 1803
	Treaty with the Kaskaskia, 1803
	Treaty with the Kaskaskia, Etc., 1832
	Treaty with the Kaskaskia, Peoria, Etc., 1854
	Treaty with the Peoria, Etc., 1818
	Treaty with the Seneca, Mixed Seneca and Shawnee, Quapaw, Etc., 1867
	Treaty with the Wyandot, Etc., 1795
Ka-Ta-Ka	Treaty with the Kiowa, Etc., 1837
Keechy	Treaty with the Comanche, Aionai, Anadarko, Caddo, Etc., 1846

Treaties by Tribe (cont.)

Tribe	Treaty Name
Kickapoo	Treaty with the Delawares, Etc., 1803
	Treaty with the Eel River, Etc., 1803
	Treaty with the Kickapoo, 1809
	Treaty with the Kickapoo, 1815
	Treaty with the Wea and Kickapoo, 1816
	Treaty with the Kickapoo, 1819
	Treaty with the Kickapoo, 1819
	Treaty with the Kickapoo, 1820
	Treaty with the Kickapoo of the Vermilion 1820
	Treaty with the Kickapoo, 1832
	Treaty with the Kickapoo, 1854
	Treaty with the Kickapoo, 1862
	Treaty with the Wyandot, Etc., 1795
Kik-Ial-Lus	Treaty with the Dwamish, Suquamish, Etc., 1855
Kiowa	Treaty with the Comanche, Kiowa, and Apache, 1853
	Treaty with the Comanche and Kiowa, 1865
	Treaty with the Kiowa, Etc., 1837
	Treaty with the Kiowa and Comanche, 1867
	Treaty with the Kiowa, Comanche, and Apache, 1867
Klamath	Treaty with the Klamath, Etc., 1864
Kootenay	Treaty with the Blackfeet, 1855
	Treaty with the Flatheads, Etc., 1855
Lepan	Treaty with the Comanche, Aionai, Anadarko, Caddo, Etc., 1846
Long-Wha	Treaty with the Comanche, Aionai, Anadarko, Caddo, Etc., 1846
Lummi	Treaty with the Dwamish, Suquamish, Etc., 1855
Makah	Treaty with the Makah, 1815
	Treaty with the Makah Tribe, 1825
	Treaty with the Makah, 1855
Mandan	Agreement at Fort Berthold, 1866
	Treaty with the Mandan Tribe, 1825
	Treaty of Fort Laramie with Sioux, Etc., 1851
Me-Sek-Wi-Guilse	Treaty with the Dwamish, Suquamish, Etc., 1855
Menominee	Treaty with the Chippewa, Etc., 1827
	Treaty with the Menominee, 1817
	Treaty with the Menominee, 1831
	Treaty with the Menominee, 1831
	Treaty with the Menominee, 1832
	Treaty with the Menominee, 1836
	Treaty with the Menominee, 1848
	Treaty with the Menominee, 1854

Treaties by Tribe (cont.)

Tribe	Treaty Name
Menominee (cont.)	Treaty with the Menominee, 1856
	Treaty with the Sioux, Etc., 1825
Miami	Treaty with the Delawares, Etc., 1803
	Treaty with the Delawares, Etc., 1805
	Treaty with the Delawares, Etc., 1809
	Supplementary Treaty with the Miami, Etc., 1809
	Treaty with the Miami, 1818
	Treaty with the Miami, 1826
	Treaty with the Miami, 1828
	Treaty with the Miami, 1834
	Treaty with the Miami, 1838
	Treaty with the Miami, 1840
	Treaty with the Miami, 1854
	Treaty with the Seneca, Mixed Seneca and Shawnee, Quapaw, Etc., 1867
	Treaty with the Wyandot, Etc., 1795
	Treaty with the Wyandot, Etc., 1814
	Treaty with the Wyandot, Etc., 1815
Middle Oregon Tribes	Treaty with the Middle Oregon Tribes, 1865
	Treaty with the Tribes of Middle Oregon, 1855
Minitaree or Belantse-Etoa	Treaty with the Belantse-Etoa or Minitaree Tribe, 1825
Mitchigamia	Treaty with the Peoria, Etc., 1818
Modoc	Treaty with the Klamath, Etc., 1864
Mohawk	Treaty with the Mohawk, 1797
	Treaty with the Six Nations, 1784
	Treaty with the Six Nations, 1789
	Treaty with the Six Nations, 1794
Molala	Treaty with the Kalapuya, Etc., 1855
	Treaty with the Molala, 1855
Muscogee	Treaty with the Comanche, Etc., 1835
Munsee	Treaty with the Chippewa, Etc., 1859
	Treaty with the New York Indians, 1838
	Treaty with the Stockbridge and Munsee, 1839
	Treaty with the Stockbridge and Munsee, 1856
	Treaty with the Wyandot, Etc., 1805
Navajo	Treaty with the Navaho, 1849
	Treaty with the Navaho, 1868
New York Indians	Treaty with the New York Indians, 1838
Nez Percé	Treaty with the Blackfeet, 1855

Treaties by Tribe (cont.)

Tribe	Treaty Name
Nex Percé (cont.)	Treaty with the Nez Percé, 1855
	Treaty with the Nez Percé, 1863
	Treaty with the Nez Percé, 1868
Nisqually	Treaty with the Nisqualli, Puyallup, Etc., 1854
Noo-Wha-Ha	Treaty with the Dwamish, Suquamish, Etc., 1855
Omaha	Treaty with the Omaha, 1854
	Treaty with the Omaha, 1865
	Treaty with the Oto, Etc., 1836
	Treaty with the Sauk and Fox, Etc., 1830
Oneida	Agreement with the Five Nations of Indians, 1792
	Treaty with the Six Nations, 1784
	Treaty with the New York Indians, 1838
	Treaty with the Oneida, Etc., 1794
	Treaty with the Oneida, 1838
	Treaty with the Six Nations, 1789
	Treaty with the Six Nations, 1794
Onondaga	Agreement with the Five Nations of Indians, 1792
	Treaty with the Six Nations, 1784
	Treaty with the New York Indians, 1838
	Treaty with the Six Nations, 1789
	Treaty with the Six Nations, 1794
Osage	Agreement with the Cherokee and Other Tribes in the Indian Territory, 1865
	Treaty with the Comanche, Etc., 1835
	Treaty with the Osage, 1808
	Treaty with the Osage, 1815
	Treaty with the Osage, 1818
	Treaty with the Osage, 1822
	Treaty with the Osage, 1825
	Treaty with the Great and Little Osage, 1825
	Treaty with the Osage, 1839
	Treaty with the Osage, 1865
Oto	Treaty with the Oto, 1817
Oto & Missouri	Treaty with the Confederated Oto and Missouri, 1854
	Treaty with the Oto and Missouri Tribe, 1825
	Treaty with the Oto and Missouri, 1833
	Treaty with the Oto, Etc., 1836
	Treaty with the Oto and Missouri, 1854
	Treaty with the Sauk and Fox, Etc., 1830
Ottawa	Treaty with the Chippewa, Etc., 1808
	Treaty with the Ottawa and Chippewa, 1820
	Treaty with the Chippewa, Etc., 1829

Treaties by Tribe (cont.)

Tribe	Treaty Name
Ottawa (cont.)	Treaty with the Chippewa, Etc., 1833
	Treaty with the Ottawa, Etc., 1807
	Treaty with the Ottawa, Etc., 1816
	Treaty with the Ottawa, Etc., 1821
	Treaty with the Ottawa, 1831
	Treaty with the Ottawa, 1833
	Treaty with the Ottawa, Etc., 1836
	Treaty with the Ottawa and Chippewa, 1855
	Treaty with the Ottawa of Blanchard's Fork and Roche De Bœuf, 1862
	Treaty with the Potawatomi Nation, 1846
	Treaty with the Seneca, Mixed Seneca and Shawnee, Quapaw, Etc., 1867
	Treaty with the Sioux, Etc., 1825
	Treaty with the Winnebago, Etc, 1828
	Treaty with the Wyandot, Etc., 1785
	Treaty with the Wyandot, Etc., 1789
	Treaty with the Wyandot, Etc., 1795
	Treaty with the Wyandot, Etc., 1805
	Treaty with the Wyandot, Etc., 1815
	Treaty with the Wyandot, Etc., 1817
	Treaty with the Wyandot, Etc., 1818
Pawnee	Treaty with the Grand Pawnee, 1818
	Treaty with the Noisy Pawnee, 1818
	Treaty with the Pawnee Republic, 1818
	Treaty with the Pawnee Marhar, 1818
	Treaty with the Pawnee Tribe, 1825
	Treaty with the Pawnee, 1833
	Treaty with the Pawnee—Grand, Loups, Republicans, Etc., 1848
	Treaty with the Pawnee, 1857
Peoria	Treaty with the Kaskaskia, Etc., 1832
	Treaty with the Kaskaskia, Peoria, Etc., 1854
	Treaty with the Peoria, Etc., 1818
	Treaty with the Seneca, Mixed Seneca and Shawnee, Quapaw, Etc., 1867
Piankeshaw	Treaty with the Delawares, Etc., 1803
	Treaty with the Eel River, Etc., 1803
	Treaty with the Kaskaskia, Peoria, Etc., 1854
	Treaty with the Piankeshaw, 1804
	Treaty with the Piankashaw, 1805
	Treaty with the Piankashaw, 1815
	Treaty with the Piankashaw and Wea, 1832
	Agreement with the Piankeshaw, 1818 (Unratified)
	Treaty with the Seneca, Mixed Seneca and Shawnee, Quapaw, Etc., 1867
	Treaty with the Wyandot, Etc., 1795
Piegan	Treaty with the Blackfeet, 1855

Treaties by Tribe (cont.)

Tribe	Treaty Name
Ponca	Treaty with the Ponca, 1817
	Treaty with the Ponca, 1825
	Treaty with the Ponca, 1858
	Treaty with the Ponca, 1865
Potawatomi	Treaty with the Chippewa, Etc., 1808
	Treaty with the Chippewa, Etc., 1829
	Treaty with the Chippewa, Etc., 1833
	Treaty with the Delawares, Etc., 1803
	Treaty with the Delawares, Etc., 1805
	Treaty with the Delawares, Etc., 1809
	Supplementary Treaty with the Miami, Etc., 1809
	Treaty with the Ottawa, Etc., 1807
	Treaty with the Ottawa, Etc., 1816
	Treaty with the Ottawa, Etc., 1821
	Treaty with the Potawatomi, 1815
	Treaty with the Potawatomi, 1818
	Treaty with the Potawatomi, 1826
	Treaty with the Potawatomi, 1827
	Treaty with the Potawatomi, 1828
	Treaty with the Potawatomi, 1832
	Treaty with the Potawatomi, 1832
	Treaty with the Potawatomi, 1832
	Treaty with the Potawatomi, 1834
	Treaty with the Potawatomi, 1834
	Treaty with the Potawatomi, 1834
	Treaty with the Potawatomi, 1834
	Treaty with the Potawatomi, 1836
	Treaty with the Potawatomi, 1836
	Treaty with the Potawatomi, 1836
	Treaty with the Potawatomi, 1836
	Treaty with the Potawatomi, 1836
	Treaty with the Potawatomi, 1836
	Treaty with the Potawatomi, 1836
	Treaty with the Potawatomi, 1836
	Treaty with the Potawatomi, 1836
	Treaty with the Potawatomi, 1837
	Treaty with the Potawatomi Nation, 1846
	Treaty with the Potawatomi, 1861
	Treaty with the Potawatomi, 1866
	Treaty with the Potawatomi, 1867
	Treaty with the Sioux, Etc., 1825
	Treaty with the Winnebago, Etc, 1828
	Treaty with the Wyandot, Etc., 1789
	Treaty with the Wyandot, Etc., 1795
	Treaty with the Wyandot, Etc., 1805
	Treaty with the Wyandot, Etc., 1815
	Treaty with the Wyandot, Etc., 1817
	Treaty with the Wyandot, Etc., 1818

Treaties by Tribe (cont.)

Tribe	Treaty Name
Puyallup	Treaty with the Nisqualli, Puyallup, Etc., 1854
Quapaw	Agreement with the Cherokee and Other Tribes in the Indian Territory, 1865 Treaty with the Comanche, Etc., 1835 Treaty with the Quapaw,1818 Treaty with the Quapaw, 1824 Treaty with the Quapaw, 1833 Treaty with the Seneca, Mixed Seneca and Shawnee, Quapaw, Etc., 1867
Qui-Nai-Elt	Treaty with the Quinaielt, Etc., 1855
Quil-Leh-Ute	Treaty with the Quinaielt, Etc., 1855
Ricara	Treaty with the Arikara Tribe, 1825 Agreement at Fort Berthold, 1866 Treaty of Fort Laramie with Sioux, Etc., 1851
Rogue River	Treaty with the Rogue River, 1853 Treaty with the Rogue River, 1854 Agreement with the Rogue River, 1853 (Unratified)
Sac & Fox	Treaty with the Fox, 1815 Treaty with the Iowa, Etc., 1836. Treaty with the Sauk and Fox, 1804 Treaty with the Sauk, 1815 Treaty with the Sauk, 1816 Treaty with the Sauk and Fox, 1822 Treaty with the Sauk and Fox, 1824 Treaty with the Sauk and Fox, Etc., 1830 Treaty with the Sauk and Fox, 1832 Treaty with the Sauk and Fox Tribe, 1836 Treaty with the Sauk and Fox, 1836 Treaty with the Sauk and Fox, 1836 Treaty with the Sauk and Fox, 1837 Treaty with the Sauk and Fox, 1837 Treaty with the Sauk and Fox, 1842 Treaty with the Sauk and Fox of Missouri, 1854 Treaty with the Sauk and Fox, 1859 Treaty with the Sauk and Fox, Etc., 1861 Treaty with the Sauk and Fox, 1867 Treaty with the Sioux, Etc., 1825 Treaty with the Wyandot, Etc., 1789
Sa-Heh-Wamish	Treaty with the Nisqualli, Puyallup, Etc., 1854
Sah-Ku-Meh-Hu	Treaty with the Dwamish, Suquamish, Etc., 1855
Scotons	Treaty with the Chasta, Etc., 1854

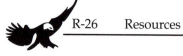

Treaties by Tribe (cont.)

Tribe	Treaty Name
Seminole	Agreement with the Cherokee and Other Tribes in the Indian Territory, 1865
	Treaty with the Creeks and Seminole, 1845
	Treaty with the Creeks, Etc., 1856
	Treaty with the Florida Tribes of Indians, 1823
	Treaty with the Seminole, 1832
	Treaty with the Seminole, 1833
	Treaty with the Seminole, 1866
Seneca	Agreement with the Cherokee and Other Tribes in the Indian Territory, 1865
	Treaty with the Comanche, Etc., 1835
	Agreement with the Five Nations of Indians, 1792
	Treaty with the Six Nations, 1784
	Treaty with the New York Indians, 1838
	Treaty with the Seneca, 1802
	Treaty with the Seneca, 1802
	Treaty with the Seneca, 1831
	Treaty with the Seneca, Etc., 1831
	Treaty with the Seneca and Shawnee, 1832
	Treaty with the Seneca, 1842
	Treaty with the Seneca, Tonawanda Band, 1857.
	Treaty with the Seneca, Mixed Seneca and Shawnee, Quapaw, Etc., 1867
	Agreement with the Seneca, 1797
	Agreement with the Seneca, 1823 (Unratified)
	Treaty with the Six Nations, 1789
	Treaty with the Six Nations, 1794
	Treaty with the Wyandot, Etc., 1814
	Treaty with the Wyandot, Etc., 1815
	Treaty with the Wyandot, Etc., 1817
	Treaty with the Wyandot, Etc., 1818
Seven Nations of Canada	Treaty with the Seven Nations of Canada, 1796
Shawnee	Agreement with the Cherokee and Other Tribes in the Indian Territory, 1865
	Treaty with the Chippewa, Etc., 1808
	Treaty with the Delawares, Etc., 1803
	Treaty with the Seneca, Etc., 1831
	Treaty with the Seneca and Shawnee, 1832
	Treaty with the Seneca, Mixed Seneca and Shawnee, Quapaw, Etc., 1867
	Treaty with the Shawnee, 1786
	Treaty with the Shawnee, 1825
	Treaty with the Shawnee, 1831
	Treaty with the Shawnee, Etc., 1832
	Treaty with the Shawnee, 1854
	Treaty with the Wyandot, Etc., 1795
	Treaty with the Wyandot, Etc., 1805
	Treaty with the Wyandot, Etc., 1814

Treaties by Tribe (cont.)

Tribe	Treaty Name
Shawnee (cont.)	Treaty with the Wyandot, Etc., 1815
	Treaty with the Wyandot, Etc., 1817
	Treaty with the Wyandot, Etc., 1818
S'homamish	Treaty with the Nisqualli, Puyallup, Etc., 1854
Shoshoni	Treaty with the Eastern Shoshoni, 1863
	Treaty with the Shoshoni—Northwestern Bands, 1863
	Treaty with the Western Shoshoni, 1863
	Treaty with the Eastern Band Shoshoni and Bannock, 1868
Shoshoni-Goship	Treaty with the Shoshoni-Goship, 1863
Sioux	Treaty with the Blackfeet Sioux, 1865
	Treaty with the Hunkpapa Band of the Sioux Tribe, 1825
	Treaty with the Sioune and Oglala Tribes, 1825 (Also Ogallala)
	Treaty with the Oto, Etc., 1836 — Yankton and Santee Bands
	Treaty with the Sauk and Fox, Etc., 1830 — Medawah-Kanton, Wahpacoota, Wahpeton, Sissetong [Sisseton], Yanckton [Yancton] and Santie Bands
	Treaty with the Sioux of the Lakes, 1815
	Treaty with the Sioux of St. Peter's River, 1815
	Treaty with the Sioux, 1816
	Treaty with the Teton, Etc., Sioux, 1825 — Teton, Yancton and Yanctonies Bands
	Treaty with the Sioux, Etc., 1825
	Treaty with the Sioux, 1836
	Treaty with the Sioux, 1836
	Treaty with the Sioux, 1837
	Treaty with the Sioux—Sisseton and Wahpeton Bands, 1851
	Treaty with the Sioux—Mdewakanton and Wahpakoota Bands, 1851 (Also Med-ay-wa-kan-toan and Wah-pay-koo-tay)
	Treaty of Fort Laramie with Sioux, Etc., 1851
	Treaty with the Sioux, 1858 — Mendawakanton and Wahpahoota Bands
	Treaty with the Sioux, 1858 — Sisseeton and Wahpaton Bands
	Treaty with the Sioux—Miniconjou Band, 1865 (Also Minneconjon)
	Treaty with the Sioux—Lower Brulé Band, 1865
	Treaty with the Sioux—Two-Kettle Band, 1865
	Treaty with the Sioux—Sans Arcs Band, 1865
	Treaty with the Sioux—Hunkpapa Band, 1865 (Also Onkpahpah)
	Treaty with the Sioux—Yanktonai Band, 1865
	Treaty with the Sioux—Upper Yanktonai Band, 1865
	Treaty with the Sioux—Oglala Band, 1865 (Also Ogallala; O'Galla)
	Treaty with the Sioux—Sisseton and Wahpeton Bands, 1867 (Also Sissiton)
	Treaty with the Sioux—Brulé, Oglala, Miniconjou, Yanktonai, Hunkpapa, Blackfeet, Cuthead, Two Kettle, Sans Arcs, and Santee—and Arapaho,
	Treaty with the Sioux, 1805

Treaties by Tribe (cont.)

Tribe	Treaty Name
Sioux (cont.)	Agreement with the Sisseton and Wahpeton Bands of Sioux Indians, 1872 (Unratified)
	Amended Agreement with Certain Sioux Indians, 1873 — Sisseton and Wahpeton Bands
	Agreement with the Sioux of Various Tribes, 1882–83 (Unratified) — Pine Ridge, Rosebud, Standing Rock, Cheyenne River, and Lower Brulé Agencies
	Treaty with the Yankton Sioux, 1815
	Treaty with the Yankton Sioux, 1837
	Treaty with the Yankton Sioux, 1858
Six Nations	Treaty with the Six Nations, 1784
	Treaty with the Six Nations, 1789
	Treaty with the Six Nations, 1794
Skai-Wha-Mish	Treaty with the Dwamish, Suquamish, Etc., 1855
Skagit	Treaty with the Dwamish, Suquamish, Etc., 1855
S'klallam	Treaty with the S'Klallam, 1855
Sk-Tah-Le-Jum	Treaty with the Dwamish, Suquamish, Etc., 1855
Snake	Treaty with the Klamath, Etc., 1864
	Treaty with the Snake, 1865
Snohomish	Treaty with the Dwamish, Suquamish, Etc., 1855
Snoqualmoo	Treaty with the Dwamish, Suquamish, Etc., 1855
Squawskin	Treaty with the Nisqualli, Puyallup, Etc., 1854
Squi-Aitl	Treaty with the Nisqualli, Puyallup, Etc., 1854
Squin-Ah-Nush	Treaty with the Dwamish, Suquamish, Etc., 1855
St. Regis	Treaty with the New York Indians, 1838
	Treaty with the Seven Nations of Canada, 1796
Stehchass	Treaty with the Nisqualli, Puyallup, Etc., 1854
Steilacoom	Treaty with the Nisqualli, Puyallup, Etc., 1854
Stockbridge	Agreement with the Five Nations of Indians, 1792
	Treaty with the New York Indians, 1838
	Treaty with the Oneida, Etc., 1794
	Treaty with the Stockbridge and Munsee, 1839
	Treaty with the Stockbridge Tribe, 1848
	Treaty with the Stockbridge and Munsee, 1856
Suquamish	Treaty with the Dwamish, Suquamish, Etc., 1855

Treaties by Tribe (cont.)

Tribe	Treaty Name
Swinamish	Treaty with the Dwamish, Suquamish, Etc., 1855
Tah-Wa-Carro	Treaty with the Comanche, Aionai, Anadarko, Caddo, Etc., 1846 Treaty with the Kiowa, Etc., 1837
Tamarois	Treaty with the Peoria, Etc., 1818
Tenino	Treaty with the Middle Oregon Tribes, 1865 Treaty with the Tribes of Middle Oregon, 1855
Teton	Treaty with the Teton, 1815
Tonkawa	Treaty with the Comanche, Aionai, Anadarko, Caddo, Etc., 1846
T'peek-Sin	Treaty with the Nisqualli, Puyallup, Etc., 1854
Tum-Waters	Treaty with the Kalapuya, Etc., 1855
Tuscarora	Agreement with the Five Nations of Indians, 1792 Treaty with the Six Nations, 1784 Treaty with the New York Indians, 1838 Treaty with the Oneida, Etc., 1794 Treaty with the Six Nations, 1789 Treaty with the Six Nations, 1794
Umatilla	Treaty with the Walla-Walla, Cayuse, Etc., 1855
Umpqua	Treaty with the Chasta, Etc., 1854 Treaty with the Umpqua—Cow Creek Band, 1853 Treaty with the Umpqua and Kalapuya, 1854
Upper Pend D'oreille	Treaty with the Blackfeet, 1855 Treaty with the Flatheads, Etc., 1855
Utah	Treaty with the Utah, 1849 Treaty with the Utah—Tabeguache Band, 1863
Ute	Treaty with the Ute, 1868
Waco	Treaty with the Comanche, Aionai, Anadarko, Caddo, Etc., 1846
Walla-Walla	Treaty with the Middle Oregon Tribes, 1865 Treaty with the Tribes of Middle Oregon, 1855 Treaty with the Walla-Walla, Cayuse, Etc., 1855
Wasco	Treaty with the Middle Oregon Tribes, 1865 Treaty with the Tribes of Middle Oregon, 1855
Wea	Treaty with the Delawares, Etc., 1803 Treaty with the Delawares, Etc., 1805 Treaty with the Kaskaskia, Peoria, Etc., 1854

Treaties by Tribe (cont.)

Tribe	Treaty Name
Wea (cont.)	Treaty with the Wea and Kickapoo, 1816
	Supplementary Treaty with the Miami, Etc., 1809
	Treaty with the Piankashaw and Wea, 1832
	Treaty with the Seneca, Mixed Seneca and Shawnee, Quapaw, Etc., 1867
	Treaty with the Wea, 1809
	Treaty with the Wea, 1818
	Treaty with the Wea, 1820
	Treaty with the Wyandot, Etc., 1795
Winnebago	Treaty with the Chippewa, Etc., 1827
	Treaty with the Sioux, Etc., 1825
	Treaty with the Winnebago, 1816
	Treaty with the Winnebago, Etc, 1828
	Treaty with the Winnebago, 1829
	Treaty with the Winnebago, 1832
	Treaty with the Winnebago, 1837
	Treaty with the Winnebago, 1846
	Treaty with the Winnebago, 1855
	Treaty with the Winnebago, 1859
	Treaty with the Winnebago, 1865
Witchetaw	Treaty with the Comanche, Etc., 1835
	Treaty with the Comanche, Aionai, Anadarko, Caddo, Etc., 1846
Wyandot	Treaty with the Chippewa, Etc., 1808
	Agreement with the Delawares and Wyandot, 1843
	Treaty with the Eel River, Etc., 1803
	Treaty with the Ottawa, Etc., 1807
	Treaty with the Seneca, Mixed Seneca and Shawnee, Quapaw, Etc., 1867
	Treaty with the Wyandot, Etc., 1785
	Treaty with the Wyandot, Etc., 1789
	Treaty with the Wyandot, Etc., 1795
	Treaty with the Wyandot, Etc., 1805
	Treaty with the Wyandot, Etc., 1814
	Treaty with the Wyandot, Etc., 1815
	Treaty with the Wyandot, Etc., 1817
	Treaty with the Wyandot, Etc., 1818
	Treaty with the Wyandot, 1818
	Treaty with the Wyandot, 1832
	Treaty with the Wyandot, 1836
	Treaty with the Wyandot, 1842
	Treaty with the Wyandot, 1850
	Treaty with the Wyandot, 1855
Yakima	Treaty with the Yakima, 1855

Source: Charles J. Kappler, *Indian Affairs: Laws and Treaties* (Washington DC: Government Printing Office, 1904). Digital copy courtesy of the Oklahoma State University Library Electronic Publishing Center

Common Treaty Names

Common Name	Full Treaty Name
Albany, Treaty of	Treaty of Albany with the Five Nations–July 31, 1684
Canandaigua Treaty	Treaty with the Six Nations–November 11, 1794
Chicago, Treaty of	Treaty with the Chippewa, Etc.–September 26, 1833
Dancing Rabbit Creek, Treaty of	Treaty with the Choctaw–September 27, 1830
Doak's Stand, Treaty of	Treaty with the Choctaw–October 18, 1820
Doaksville, Treaty of	Treaty with the Choctaw and Chickasaw–January 17, 1837
Fort Bridger, Treaty of	Treaty with the Eastern Band Shoshone and Bannock–July 3, 1868
Fort Harmar, Treaty of	Treaty with the Wyandot, Etc.–January 9, 1789
	Treaty with the Six Nations–January 9, 1789
	(Addendum) Treaty with the Cherokee–June 26, 1794
Fort Laramie, Treaty of	Treaty of Fort Laramie with the Sioux, Etc.–September 17, 1851
Fort McIntosh, Treaty of	Treaty with the Wyandot, Etc.–January 21, 1785
Fort Stanwix, Treaty of	Treaty Conference with the Six Nations at Fort Stanwix–November 5, 1768
	Treaty with the Six Nations–October 22, 1784
Greenville, Treaty of	Treaty with the Wyandot, Etc.–August 3, 1795
Holston, Treaty of	Treaty with the Cherokee–July 2, 1791
Hopewell, Treaty of	Treaty with the Cherokee–November 28, 1785
Medicine Creek, Treaty of	Treaty with the Nisqually, Puyallup, Etc.–December 26, 1854
Medicine Lodge Creek, Treaty of	Treaty with the Cheyenne and Arapaho––October 28, 1867
New Echota, Treaty of	Treaty with the Cherokee–December 29, 1835
Northwest Angle Treaty	Canadian Indian Treaty 3–October 3, 1873
Prairie du Chien, Treaty of	Treaty with the Sioux, Etc.–August 19, 1825
Qu'Appelle Treaty	Canadian Indian Treaty 4–September 15, 1874
St. Louis, Treaty of	Treaty with the Sauk and Fox–November 3, 1804

Selected Bibliography

Abele, Charles A. 1969. "The Grand Indian Council and Treaty of Prairie du Chien, 1825," Ph.D. dissertation, Loyola University of Chicago.

Anderson, George E., W. H. Ellison, and Robert F. Heizer. 1978. *Treaty Making and Treaty Rejection by the Federal Government in California, 1850–1852.* Socorro, NM: Ballena Press.

Anderson, George E., and Robert F. Heizer. 1978. "Treaty-making by the Federal Government in California 1851–1852." In *Treaty Making and Treaty Rejection by the Federal Government in California, 1850–1852,* eds. George E. Anderson, W. H. Ellison, and Robert F. Heizer, 1–36. Socorro, NM: Ballena Press.

Anderson, Harry. 1956. "The Controversial Sioux Amendment to the Fort Laramie Treaty of 1851." *Nebraska History* 37 (September): 201–220.

Asch, Michael, ed. 1998. *Aboriginal and Treaty Rights in Canada.* Vancouver: University of British Columbia Press.

Balman, Gail. 1970. "The Creek Treaty of 1866." *Chronicles of Oklahoma* 48 (Summer): 184–196.

Barce, Elmore. 1915. "Governor Harrison and the Treaty of Fort Wayne, 1809." *Indiana Magazine of History* 11 (December): 352–367.

Barnes, Lela. 1936. "Isaac McCoy and the Treaty of 1821." *Kansas Historical Quarterly* 5 (May): 122–142.

Bell, Catherine, and Karin Buss. 2000. "The Promise of Marshall on the Prairies: A Framework for Analyzing Unfulfilled Treaty Promises." *Saskatchewan Law Review* 63(2): 667.

Bigart, Robert, and Clarence Woodcock, eds. 1996. *In the Name of the Salish and Kootenai Nation: The 1885 Hell Gate Treaty and the Origin of the Flathead Indian Reservation.* Pablo, MT: Salish Kootenai College Press/University of Washington Press.

Bird, John, Lorraine Land, and Murray MacAdam, eds. 2002. *Nation to Nation: Aboriginal Sovereignty and the Future of Canada,* 2nd ed. Toronto: Irwin.

Bischoff, William N., and Charles M. Gates, eds. 1943. "The Jesuits and the Coeur D'Alene Treaty of 1858." *Pacific Northwest Quarterly* 34 (April): 169–181.

Borrows, John. 1992. "Negotiating Treaties and Land Claims: The Impact of Diversity within First Nations Property Interests." *Windsor Yearbook of Access to Justice* 12: 179.

Borrows, John. 2005. "Creating an Indigenous Legal Community." *McGill Law Journal* 50: 153.

Boxberger, Daniel L. 1979. *Handbook of Western Washington Indian Treaties.* Lummi Island, WA: Lummi Indian School of Aquaculture and Fisheries.

Boxberger, Daniel L., and Herbert C. Taylor. 1991. "Treaty or Non-Treaty Status." *Columbia,* 5(3): 40–45.

Boyd, Mark F. 1958. "Horatio S. Dexter and Events Leading to the Treaty of Moultrie Creek with the Seminole Indians." *Florida Anthropologist,* 11 (September): 65–95.

Brooks, Drex, and Patricia Nelson Limerick. 1995. *Sweet Medicine: Sites of Indian Massacres, Battlefields, and Treaties.* Albuquerque: University of New Mexico Press.

Brown, George, and Ron Maguire. 1979. *Indian Treaties in Historical Perspective.* Ottawa: Research Branch, Indian and Northern Affairs Canada.

Bugge, David, and J. Lee Corell. 1971. *The Story of the Navajo Treaties.* Window Rock, AZ: Research Section, Navajo Parks and Recreation Department, Navajo Tribe.

Burns, Robert Ignatius, ed. 1952. "A Jesuit at the Hell Gate Treaty of 1855." *Mid-American* 34 (April): 87–114. Report of Adrian Hoechen.

Bushnell, David I., Jr. 1916. "The Virginia Frontier in History–1778." Part 5, "The Treaty of Fort Pitt." *Virginia Magazine of History and Biography* 24 (April): 168–179.

Campisi, Jack. 1988. "From Stanwix to Canandaigua: National Policy, States' Rights, and Indian Land." In *Iroquois Land Claims,* eds. Christopher Vecsey and William A. Starna, 49–65. Syracuse, NY: Syracuse University Press.

Campisi, Jack. 1988. "The Oneida Treaty Period, 1783–1838." In *The Oneida Indian Experience: Two Perspectives*, eds. Jack Campisi and Laurence M. Hauptman, 48–64. Syracuse, NY: Syracuse University Press.

Canada. 1905. *Indian Treaties and Surrenders from 1680–1890*. Ottawa: S. E. Dawson. Repr., Saskatoon: Fifth House, 1992.

Canada. 1971. *Indian Treaties and Surrenders from 1680 to 1890*. 3 vols. Ottawa: Queen's Printer.

Clark, Blue. 1994. *Lone Wolf v. Hitchcock: Treaty Rights and Indian Law at the End of the Nineteenth Century*. Lincoln: University of Nebraska Press.

Clifton, James A. 1980. "Chicago, September 14, 1833: The Last Great Indian Treaty in the Old Northwest." *Chicago History* 9 (Summer): 86–97.

Cohen, Fay G. 1986. *Treaties on Trial: The Continuing Controversy over Northwest Indian Fishing Rights*. With contributions by Joan La France and Vivian L. Bowden. Seattle: University of Washington Press.

Cohen, Felix S. 1942. "Indian Treaties." In Cohen, *Handbook of Federal-Indian Law*, ed. Felix Cohen. Washington, DC: U.S. Government Printing Office.

Cohen, Felix S. 2005. *Handbook of Federal Indian Law*. Newark, NJ: LexisNexis.

Colby, Bonnie G., John E. Thorson, and Sarah Britton. 2005. *Negotiating Tribal Water Rights: Fulfilling Promises in the Arid West*. Tucson: University of Arizona Press.

Commissioner of Indian Affairs. 1975. *Article Six, Treaties between the United States and the Several Indian Tribes from 1778 to 1837*. Millwood, NY: Kraus Reprint.

Costo, Rupert, and Jeannette Henry. 1977. *Indian Treaties: Two Centuries of Dishonor*. San Francisco: Indian Historian Press.

Danziger, Edmund J., Jr. 1973. "They Would Not Be Moved: The Chippewa Treaty of 1854." *Minnesota History* 43 (Spring): 174–185.

Daugherty, W. E. 1981. *Maritime Indian Treaties in Historical Perspective*. Ottawa: Indian and Northern Affairs Canada.

Decker, Craig A. 1977. "The Construction of Indian Treaties, Agreements, and Statutes." *American Indian Law Review* 5(2): 299–311.

Deloria, Vine, Jr. 1974. *Behind the Trail of Broken Treaties: An Indian Declaration of Independence*. New York: Delacorte Press.

Deloria, Vine, Jr. 1996. "Reserving to Themselves: Treaties and the Powers of Indian Tribes." *Arizona Law Review* 38(3): 963–980.

Deloria, Vine, Jr., and David E. Wilkins. 1999. *Tribes, Treaties, and Constitutional Tribulations*. Austin: University of Texas Press.

DeMallie, Raymond J. 1977. "American Indian Treaty Making: Motives and Meanings." *American Indian Journal* 3 (January): 2–10.

DeMallie, Raymond J. 1980. "Touching the Pen: Plains Indian Treaty Councils in Ethnohistorical Perspective." In *Ethnicity in the Great Plains*, ed. Frederick C. Luebke, 38–51. Lincoln: University of Nebraska Press.

DePuy, H. 1917. *A Bibliography of the English Colonial Treaties with the American Indians: Including a Synopsis of Each Treaty*. New York: Lennox Club.

Downes, Randolph C. 1977. *Council Fires on the Upper Ohio: A Narrative of Indian Affairs in the Upper Ohio Valley until 1795*. Pittsburgh, PA: University of Pittsburgh Press.

Duff, Wilson. 1969. "The Fort Victoria Treaties." *BC Studies* 3 (Fall), 3–57.

Dustin, Fred. 1920. "The Treaty of Saginaw, 1819." *Michigan History Magazine* 4 (January): 243–278.

Edmunds, R. David. 1978. "'Nothing Has Been Effected': The Vincennes Treaty of 1792." *Indiana Magazine of History* 74 (March): 23–35.

Ellison, William H. 1978. "Rejection of California Indian Treaties: A Study in Local Influence on National Policy." In *Treaty Making and Treaty Rejection by the Federal Government in California, 1850–1852*, eds. George E. Anderson, W. H. Ellison, and Robert F. Heizer, 50–70. Socorro, NM: Ballena Press.

Fay, George Emory. 1971. *Treaties Between the Potawatomi Tribe of Indians and the United States of America, 1789–1867*. Greeley, CO: Museum of Anthropology: University of Northern Colorado.

Fay, George Emory. 1972. *Treaties and Land Cessions Between the Bands of the Sioux and the United States of America, 1805–1906*. Greeley, CO: Museum of Anthropology: University of Northern Colorado.

Fay, George Emory. 1977. *Treaties Between the Tribes of the Great Plains and the United States of America: Cheyenne and Arapaho, 1825–1900 Etc.* Greeley, CO: Museum of Anthropology: University of Northern Colorado.

Fay, George Emory. 1982. *Treaties Between the Tribes of the Great Plains and the United States of America: Comanche and Kiowa, Arikara, Gros Ventre, and Mandan, 1835–1891*. Greeley, CO: Museum of Anthropology, University of Northern Colorado.

Ferguson, Clyde R. 1979. "Confrontation at Coleraine: Creeks, Georgians and Federalist Indian Policy." *South Atlantic Quarterly* 78 (Spring): 224–243.

Ferguson, Robert B. 1985. "Treaties between the United States and the Choctaw Nation." In *The Choctaw before Removal*, ed. Carolyn Keller Reeves, 214–230. Jackson: University Press of Mississippi.

Fielder, Betty. 1955. "The Black Hawk Treaty." *Annals of Iowa* 32 (January): 535–540.

Fisher, Andrew H. 1999. "This I Know from the Old People: Yakama Indian Treaty Rights as Oral Tradition." *Montana, The Magazine of Western History* 49 (Spring): 2–17.

Fisher, Andrew H. 2004. "Tangled Nets: Treaty Rights and Tribal Identities at Celilo Falls." *Oregon Historical Quarterly* 105 (Summer): 178–211.

Fisher, Robert L. 1933. "The Treaties of Portage des Sioux." *Mississippi Valley Historical Review* 19 (March): 495–508.

Fixico, Donald L. 1984. "As Long as the Grass Grows . . . The Cultural Conflicts and Political Strategies of United States-Indian Treaties." In *Ethnicity and War*, ed. Winston A. Van Horne, 128–149. Milwaukee: University of Wisconsin System, American Ethnic Studies Committee/Urban Corridor Consortium.

Foreman, Carolyn Thomas. 1955. "The Lost Cherokee Treaty." *Chronicles of Oklahoma* 33 (Summer): 238–245.

Foreman, Grant, ed. 1936. "The Journal of the Proceedings of Our First Treaty with the Wild Indians, 1835." *Chronicles of Oklahoma* 14 (December): 394–418.

Foreman, Grant. 1948. "The Texas Comanche Treaty of 1846." *Southwestern Historical Quarterly* 51 (April): 313–332.

Franks, Kenny A. 1972–1973. "An Analysis of the Confederate Treaties with the Five Civilized Tribes." *Chronicles of Oklahoma* 50 (Winter): 458–473.

Franks, Kenny A. 1973. "The Impeachment of the Confederate Treaties with the Five Civilized Tribes." *Chronicles of Oklahoma* 51 (Spring): 21–33.

Gates, Charles M., ed. 1955. "The Indian Treaty of Point No Point." *Pacific Northwest Quarterly* 46 (April): 52–58.

Gerwing, Anselm J. 1964. "The Chicago Indian Treaty of 1838." *Journal of the Illinois State Historical Society* 57 (Summer): 117–142.

Getches, David H., and Charles F. Wilkinson. 1998. *Federal Indian Law: Cases and Materials*, 4th ed. St. Paul: West.

Gibson, Ronald V. 1977. *Jefferson Davis and the Confederacy and Treaties Concluded by the Confederate States with Indian Tribes*. Dobbs Ferry, NY: Oceana Publications.

Gold, Susan Dudley. 1997. *Indian Treaties*. New York: Twenty-First Century Books.

Goodman, Edmund Clay. 2002. "Indian Reserved Rights." In *Nontimber Forest Products in the United States*, eds. Eric T. Jones, Rebecca J. McLain, and James Weigand, 273–281. Lawrence: University Press of Kansas.

Hagan, William T. 1956. "The Sauk and Fox Treaty of 1804." *Missouri Historical Review* 51 (October): 1–7.

Haines, Francis. 1964. "The Nez Perce Tribe versus the United States." *Idaho Yesterdays* 8 (Spring): 18–25.

Halbert, Henry S. 1902. "The Story of the Treaty of Dancing Rabbit Creek." *Publications of the Mississippi Historical Society* 6: 373–402.

Harmon, George D. 1929. "The North Carolina Cherokees and the New Echota Treaty of 1835." *North Carolina Historical Review* 6 (July): 237–253.

Harring, Sidney L. 1994. *Crow Dog's Case: American Indian Sovereignty, Tribal Law, and United States Law in the Nineteenth Century*. New York: Cambridge University Press.

Hawkinson, Ella. 1934. "The Old Crossing Chippewa Treaty and Its Sequel." *Minnesota History* 15 (September): 282–300.

Hawley, Donna Lea. 1990. *The Annotated 1990 Indian Act: Including Related Treaties, Statutes, and Regulations*. Toronto: Carswell.

Hayden, Ralston. 1920. *The Senate and Treaties, 1789–1817: The Development of the Treaty-Making Functions of the United States Senate during Their Formative Period*. New York: Macmillan.

Heilbron, Bertha L. 1941. "Frank B. Mayer and the Treaties of 1851." *Minnesota History* 22 (June): 133–156.

Heizer, Robert F. 1978. "Treaties." In *Handbook of North American Indians,* vol. 8, *California,* ed. Robert F. Heizer, 701–704. Washington, DC: Smithsonian Institution.

Henderson, Archibald. 1931. "The Treaty of Long Island of Holston, July, 1777." *North Carolina Historical Review* 8 (January): 55–116.

Henderson, James [Sakej] Youngblood. 1997. "Interpreting Sui Generis Treaties." *Alberta Law Review* 36(1): 46.

Henderson, James [Sakej] Youngblood. 2000. "Constitutional Powers and Treaty Rights." *Saskatchewan Law Review* 63(2): 719.

Henslick, Harry. 1970. "The Seminole Treaty of 1866." *Chronicles of Oklahoma* 48 (Autumn): 280–294.

Hill, Burton S. 1966. "The Great Indian Treaty Council of 1851." *Nebraska History* 47 (March): 85–110.

Holmes, Jack. 1969. "Spanish Treaties with West Florida Indians, 1784–1802." *Florida Historical Society,* 48 (140–154).

Hoover, Herbert T. 1989. "The Sioux Agreement of 1889 and Its Aftermath." *South Dakota History* 19 (Spring): 56–94.

Horsman, Reginald. 1961. "The British Indian Department and the Abortive Treaty of Lower Sandusky, 1793." *Ohio Historical Quarterly* 70 (July): 189–213.

Hosen, Fredrick E. 1985. *Rifle, Blanket, and Kettle: Selected Indian Treaties and Laws.* Jefferson, NC: McFarland.

Hough, Franklin B., ed. 1861. *Proceedings of the Commissioners of Indian Affairs, Appointed by Law for the Extinguishment of Indian Titles in the State of New York.* 2 vols. Albany, NY: Joel Munsell.

Hryniewicki, Richard J. 1964. "The Creek Treaty of Washington, 1826." *Georgia Historical Quarterly* 48 (December): 425–441.

Hryniewicki, Richard J. 1968. "The Creek Treaty of November 15, 1827." *Georgia Historical Quarterly* 52 (March): 1–15.

Humphreys, A. Glen. 1971. "The Crow Indian Treaties of 1868: An Example of Power Struggle and Confusion in United States Indian Policy." *Annals of Wyoming* 43 (Spring): 73–90.

Ibbotson, Joseph D. 1938. "Samuel Kirkland, the Treaty of 1792, and the Indian Barrier State." *New York History* 19 (October): 374–391.

Imai, Shin. 1999. *Aboriginal Law Handbook.* 2nd ed. Scarborough, ON: Carswell.

Isaac, Thomas. 2001. *Aboriginal and Treaty Rights in the Maritimes: The Marshall Decision and Beyond.* Saskatoon: Purich.

Jaenen, Cornelius J. 2001. "Aboriginal Rights and Treaties in Canada." In *The Native North American Almanac,* ed. Duane Champagne, 1–6. Los Angeles: University of California Press.

Jennings, Francis, ed. 1985. *The History and Culture of Iroquois Diplomacy: An Interdisciplinary Guide to the Treaties of the Six Nations and Their League.* Syracuse, NY: Syracuse University Press.

Jones, Dorothy V. 1982. *License for Empire: By Treaty in Early America.* Chicago: University of Chicago Press.

Jones, Douglas C. 1966. *The Treaty of Medicine Lodge: The Story of the Great Treaty Council as Told by Eyewitnesses.* Norman: University of Oklahoma Press.

Jones, Douglas C. 1969. "Medicine Lodge Revisited." *Kansas Historical Quarterly* 35 (Summer): 130–142.

Josephy, Alvin M., Jr. 1965. "A Most Satisfactory Council." *American Heritage* 16 (October): 26–31, 70–76.

Kane, Lucile M. 1951. "The Sioux Treaties and the Traders." *Minnesota History* 32 (June): 65–80.

Keller, Robert H. 1971. "On Teaching Indian History: Legal Jurisdiction in Chippewa Treaties." *Ethnohistory* 19 (Summer): 209–218.

Keller, Robert H. 1978. "An Economic History of Indian Treaties in the Great Lakes Region." *American Indian Journal* 4 (February): 2–20.

Keller, Robert H. 1989. "America's Native Sweet: Chippewa Treaties and the Right to Harvest Maple Sugar." *American Indian Quarterly* 13 (Spring): 117–135.

Kellogg, Louise Phelps. 1931. "The Menominee Treaty at the Cedars, 1836." *Transactions of the Wisconsin Academy of Sciences, Arts and Letters* 26: 127–135.

Kelsey, Harry. 1973. "The California Indian Treaty Myth." *Southern California Quarterly* 55 (Fall): 225–238.

Kessell, John L. 1981. "General Sherman and the Navajo Treaty of 1868: A Basic and Expedient Misunderstanding." *Western Historical Quarterly* 12 (July): 251–272.

Kickingbird, Kirke, Lynn Kickingbird, Alexander Tallchief Skibine, and Charles Chibitty. 1980. *Indian Treaties*. Washington, DC: Institute for the Development of Indian Law.

Kickingbird, Lynn, and Curtis Berkey. 1975. "American Indian Treaties—Their Importance Today." *American Indian Journal* 1 (October): 3–7.

Kinnaird, Lucia Burk. 1932. "The Rock Landing Conference of 1789." *North Carolina Historical Review* 9 (October): 349–365.

Kvasnicka, Robert M. 1988. "United States Indian Treaties and Agreements." In *Handbook of North American Indians*, vol. 4, *History of Indian–White Relations*, ed. Wilcomb E. Washburn, 195–201. Washington, DC: Smithsonian Institution.

Lambert, Paul F. 1973. "The Cherokee Reconstruction Treaty of 1866." *Journal of the West* 12 (July): 471–489.

Lanchart, David. 1985. "Regaining Dinetah: The Navajo and the Indian Peace Commission at Fort Sumner." In *Working in the Range: Essays on the History of Western Land Management and the Environment*, ed. John R. Wunder, 25–38. Westport, CT: Greenwood Press.

Landau, Jack L. 1980. "Empty Victories: Indian Treaty Fishing Rights in the Pacific Northwest." *Environmental Law* 10: 413–456.

Lane, Barbara. 1977. "Background of Treaty Making in Western Washington." *American Indian Journal* 3 (April): 2–11.

Larson, Gustive O. 1974. "Uintah Dream: The Ute Treaty—Spanish Fork, 1865." *Brigham Young University Studies* 14 (Spring): 361–381.

Laurence, Robert. 1991. "The Abrogation of Indian Treaties by Federal Statutes Protective of the Environment." *Natural Resources Journal*, 31 (Fall): 859–886.

Lehman, J. David. 1990. "The End of the Iroquois Mystique: The Oneida Land Cession Treaties of the 1790s." *William and Mary Quarterly*, 47(4): 523–547.

Leonard, Stephen J. 1990. "John Nicolay in Colorado: A Summer Sojourn and the 1863 Ute Treaty." *Essays and Monographs in Colorado History* 11, 25–54.

Lindquist, G. E. E. 1948–1949. "Indian Treaty Making." *Chronicles of Oklahoma* 26 (Winter): 416–448.

Litton, Gaston L., ed. 1939. "The Negotiations Leading to the Chickasaw-Choctaw Agreement, January 17, 1837." *Chronicles of Oklahoma* 17 (December): 417–427.

Madill, Dennis. 1981. *British Columbia Indian Treaties in Historical Perspective*. Ottawa: Indian and Northern Affairs Canada.

Mahan, Bruce E. 1925. "The Great Council of 1825." *Palimpsest* 6 (September): 305–318.

Mahan, Bruce E. 1929. "Making the Treaty of 1842." *Palimpsest* 10 (May): 174–180.

Mahon, John K. 1962. "The Treaty of Moultrie Creek, 1823." *Florida Historical Quarterly* 40 (April): 350–372.

Mahon, John K. 1962. "Two Seminole Treaties: Payne's Landing, 1882, and Ft. Gibson, 1833." *Florida Historical Quarterly* 41 (July): 1–21.

Mainville, Robert. 2001. *An Overview of Aboriginal and Treaty Rights and Compensation for Their Breach*. Saskatoon: Purich.

Manley, Henry S. 1838. "Buying Buffalo from the Indians." *New York History* 28 (July 1947): 313–329, Buffalo Creek Treaty.

Manley, Henry S. 1932. *The Treaty of Fort Stanwix, 1784*. Rome, NY: Rome Sentinel.

Martin, John Henry. 1975. *List of Documents Concerning the Negotiation of Ratified Indian Treaties, 1801–1869*. Millwood, NY: Kraus Reprint.

McCool, Daniel. 2002. *Native Waters: Contemporary Indian Water Settlements and the Second Treaty Era*. Tucson: University of Arizona Press.

McCullar, Marion Ray. 1973. "The Choctaw-Chickasaw Reconstruction Treaty of 1866." *Journal of the West* 12 (July): 462–470.

McKenney, Thomas L. 1827. *Sketches of a Tour to the Lakes, of the Character and Customs of the Chippeway Indians, and of Incidents Connected with the Treaty of Fond du Lac*. Baltimore: Fielding Lucas, Jr.

McNeil, Kinneth. 1964–65. "Confederate Treaties with the Tribes of Indian Territory." *Chronicles of Oklahoma* 42 (Winter): 408–420.

Morris, Alexander. 1880. *The Treaties of Canada with the Indians of Manitoba and the North-West Territories*. Repr., Toronto: Coles, 1971.

Morse, Bradford. 2004. "Aboriginal and Treaty Rights in Canada." In *Canadian Charter of Rights and Freedoms/Charte Canadienne des droits et Libertés*, 4th ed., eds. Gérald-A. Beaudoin and Errol Mendes, 1171–1257. Markham, ON: LexisNexis Butterworths.

Nesper, Larry. 2002. *The Walleye War: The Struggle for Ojibwe Treaty and Spearfishing Rights*. Lincoln: University of Nebraska Press.

Parker, Arthur C. 1924. "The Pickering Treaty." *Rochester Historical Society Publication Fund Series* 3: 79–91.

Partoll, Albert J., ed. 1937. "The Blackfoot Indian Peace Council." *Frontier and Midland: A Magazine of the West* 17 (Spring): 199–207.

Partoll, Albert J. 1938. "The Flathead Indian Treaty Council of 1855." *Pacific Northwest Quarterly* 29 (July): 283–314.

Perdue, Theda, and Michael D. Green, eds. 1995. *The Cherokee Removal: A Brief History with Documents.* Boston: Bedford Books of St. Martin's Press.

Phillips, Charles, and Alan Axelrod. 2000. *Encyclopedia of Historical Treaties and Alliances.* New York: Facts on File.

Phillips, Edward Hake. 1966. "Timothy Pickering at His Best: Indian Commissioner, 1790–1794." *Essex Institute Historical Collections* 102 (July): 185–192.

Pittman, Philip M., and George M. Covington. 1992. *Don't Blame the Treaties: Native American Rights and the Michigan Indian Treaties.* West Bloomfield, MI: Altwerger and Mandel.

Powless, Irving, and G. Peter Jemison. 2000. *Treaty of Canandaigua 1794: 200 Years of Treaty Relations Between the Iroquois Confederacy and the United States.* Santa Fe, NM: Clear Light.

Price, Monroe E., and Robert N. Clinton. 1983. *Law and the American Indian: Readings, Notes and Cases.* Charlottesville, VA: Michie.

Price, Richard, ed. 1979. *The Spirit of the Alberta Indian Treaties.* Montreal: Institute for Research on Public Policy. Repr., Edmonton: University of Alberta Press, 1999.

Prucha, Francis Paul, ed. 1975. *Documents of United States Indian Policy.* Lincoln and London: University of Nebraska Press.

Prucha, Francis Paul. 1994. *American Indian Treaties: The History of a Political Anomaly.* Berkeley, Los Angeles, and London: University of California Press.

Quaife, Milo M., ed. 1918. "The Chicago Treaty of 1833." *Wisconsin Magazine of History* 1 (March): 287–303.

Quinn, William W., Jr. 1990. "Federal Acknowledgment of American Indian Tribes: The Historical Development of a Legal Concept," *American Journal of Legal History* 34 (October): 331–364.

Rakove, Jack N. 1984. "Solving a Constitutional Puzzle: The Treatymaking Clause as a Case Study." *Perspectives in American History,* s.n., 1: 233–281.

Roberts, Gary L. 1975. "The Chief of State and the Chief." *American Heritage* 26 (October): 28–33, 86–89. Creek Treaty of New York, 1790.

Royal Commission on Aboriginal Peoples. 1995. *Treaty Making in the Spirit of Co-Existence: An Alternative to Extinguishment.* Ottawa: Canada Communication Group.

Royal Commission on Aboriginal Peoples. 1996. *Report of the Royal Commission on Aboriginal Peoples.* Ottawa: Canada Communication Group.

Royce, Charles C. 1899. *Indian Land Cessions in the United States.* Washington, DC: U.S. Government Printing Office.

Rutland, Robert A. 1949–1950. "Political Background of the Cherokee Treaty of New Echota." *Chronicles of Oklahoma* 27 (Winter): 389–406.

Satz, Ronald N. 1991. "Chippewa Treaty Rights: The Reserve Rights of Wisconsin's Chippewa Indians in Historical Perspective." *Transactions of the Wisconsin Academy of Sciences, Arts and Letters,* 79(1). Madison: Wisconsin Academy of Sciences, Arts and Letters.

Schwartzman, Grace M., and Susan K. Barnard. 1991. "A Trail of Broken Promises: Georgians and the Muscogee/Creek Treaties, 1796–1826." *Georgia Historical Quarterly* 75 (Winter): 697–718.

Silliman, Sue I. 1922. "The Chicago Indian Treaty of 1821." *Michigan History Magazine* 6(1): 194–197.

Slattery, Brian. 2000. "Making Sense of Aboriginal and Treaty Rights." *Canadian Bar Review* 79: 196.

Smith, Dwight L. 1954. "Wayne and the Treaty of Greene Ville." *Ohio State Archaeological and Historical Quarterly* 63 (January): 1–7.

Smith, Dwight L. 1978. "The Land Cession Theory: A Valid Instrument of Transfer of Indian Title." In *This Land Is Ours: The Acquisition of the Public Domain,* 87–102. Indianapolis: Indiana Historical Society.

St. Germain, Jill. 2001. *Indian Treaty-Making Policy in the United States and Canada, 1867–1877.* Lincoln and London: University of Nebraska Press.

Stanley, Henry M. 1967. "A British Journalist Reports the Medicine Lodge Peace Council of 1867." *Kansas Historical Quarterly* 33 (Autumn): 249–320.

Stern, Theodore. 1956. "The Klamath Indians and the Treaty of 1864." *Oregon Historical Quarterly* 57 (September): 229–273.

Sullivan, Julie E. 2004. "Legal Analysis of the Treaty Violations That Resulted in the Nez Perce War of 1877," 40 *Idaho Law Review* 657.

Surtees, Robert J. 1988. "Canadian Indian Treaties." In *History of Indian White Relations*, ed. Wilcomb E. Washburn, 202–210. Washington, DC: Smithsonian Institution.

Taylor, Alfred A. 1924. "Medicine Lodge Peace Council." *Chronicles of Oklahoma* 2 (June): 98–117.

Townsend, Michael. 1989. "Congressional Abrogation of Indian Treaties: Reevaluation and Reform." *Yale Law Journal*, 98 (February): 793–812.

Trafzer, Clifford E., ed. 1986. *Indians, Superintendents, and Councils: Northwestern Indian Policy, 1850–1855.* Lanham, MD: University Press of America.

Treaty 7 Elders and Tribal Council with Walter Hildebrandt, Sarah Carter, and Dorothy First Rider. 1996. *The True Spirit and Original Intent of Treaty 7.* Montreal: McGill-Queen's University Press.

Van Doren, Carl, and Julian P. Boyd. 1938. *Indian Treaties Printed by Benjamin Franklin, 1736–1762.* Philadelphia: Historical Society of Pennsylvania.

Vaugeois, Denis. 2002. *The Last French and Indian War: An Inquiry into a Safe-Conduct Issued in 1760 That Acquired the Value of a Treaty in 1990.* Montreal: McGill-Queens University Press/Septentrion.

Vaughan, Alden T. 1979. *Early American Indian Documents: Treaties and Laws, 1607– 1789.* Washington, DC: University Publications of America.

Vipperman, Carl J. 1989. "The Bungled Treaty of New Echota: The Failure of Cherokee Removal, 1836–38." *Georgia Historical Quarterly* 73 (Fall): 540–558.

Watts, Charles W. 1959. "Colbert's Reserve and the Chickasaw Treaty of 1818." *Alabama Review* 12 (October): 272–280.

Watts, Tim J. 1991. *American Indian Treaty Rights: A Bibliography.* Monticello, IL: Vance Bibliographies.

Wells, Samuel J. 1983–1984. "Rum, Skins, and Powder: A Choctaw Interpreter and the Treaty of Mount Dexter." *Chronicles of Oklahoma* 61 (Winter): 422–428.

Wells, Samuel J. 1986. "International Causes of the Treaty of Mount Dexter, 1805." *Journal of Mississippi History* 48 (August): 177–185.

Wicken, William C. 2002. *Mi'kmaq Treaties on Trial: History, Land and Donald Marshall Junior.* Toronto: University of Toronto Press.

Wilkins, David E. 1996. "Indian Treaty Rights: Sacred Entitlements or 'Temporary Privileges?'" *American Indian Culture and Research Journal* 20(1): 87–129.

Wilkins, David E., and K. Tsianina Lomawaima. 2001. *Indian Sovereignty and Federal Law.* Norman: University of Oklahoma Press.

Wilkinson, Charles F. 1991. "To Feel the Summer in the Spring: The Treaty Fishing Rights of the Wisconsin Chippewa." *Wisconsin Law Review* (May–June): 375– 414.

Wilkinson, Charles F. 2000. *Messages from Frank's Landing: A Story of Salmon, Treaties, and the Indian Way.* Seattle: University of Washington Press.

Wilkinson, Charles F., and John M. Volkman. 1975. "Judicial Review of Indian Treaty Abrogation: 'As Long as Water Flows, or Grass Grows upon the Earth'—How Long a Time Is That?" *California Law Review* 63 (May): 601–661.

Williams, C. Herb, and Walt Neubrech. 1976. *Indian Treaties: American Nightmare.* Seattle: Outdoor Empire.

Wright, J. Leitch, Jr. 1967. "Creek-American Treaty of 1790: Alexander McGillivray and the Diplomacy of the Old Southwest." *Georgia Historical Quarterly* 51 (December): 379–400.

Wrone, David R. 1986–1987. "Indian Treaties and the Democratic Idea." *Wisconsin Magazine of History* 70 (Winter): 83–106.

Wunder, John R. 1985. "No More Treaties: The Resolution of 1871 and the Alteration of Indian Rights to Their Homelands." In *Working the Range: Essays on the History of Western Land Management and the Environment*, ed. John R. Wunder, 39–56. Westport, CT: Greenwood Press.

Index

Note: Page locators in **boldface** type indicate the location of a main encyclopedia entry.

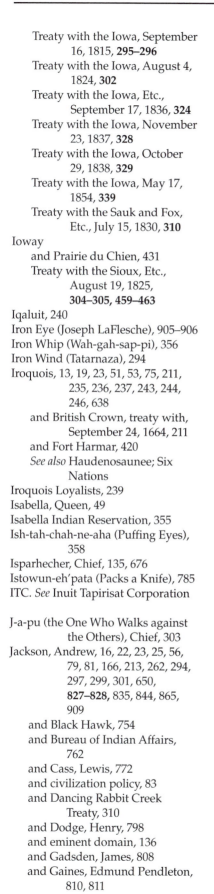